Understanding Criminal Procedure

VOLUME 1: INVESTIGATION

Carolina Academic Press Understanding Series

Understanding The First Amendment,
Sixth Edition
Russell L. Weaver

Understanding Immigration Law,
Second Edition
Kevin R. Johnson, Raquel Aldana, Ong Hing,
Leticia Saucedo, and Enid Trucios-Haynes

Understanding Insurance Law, Fifth Edition
Robert H. Jerry, II and Douglas Richmond

Understanding Intellectual Property Law,
Third Edition
Donald Chisum, Tyler T. Ochoa, Shubha
Ghosh, and Mary LaFrance

Understanding International Business and
Financial Transactions, Fourth Edition
Jerold Friedland

Understanding International Criminal Law,
Third Edition
Ellen S. Podgor and Roger S. Clark

Understanding International Law,
Second Edition
Stephen McCaffrey

Understanding Jewish Law
Steven Resnicoff

Understanding Juvenile Law, Fourth Edition
Martin Gardner

Understanding Labor Law, Fourth Edition
Douglas E. Ray, Calvin William Sharpe,
and Robert N. Strassfeld

Understanding Local Government,
Second Edition
Sandra Stevenson

Understanding the Law of Terrorism,
Second Edition
Erik Luna and Wayne McCormack

Understanding the Law of Zoning and
Land Use Controls, Third Edition
Barlow Burke

Understanding Lawyers' Ethics, Fifth Edition
Monroe H. Freedman and Abbe Smith

Understanding Modern Real Estate
Transactions, Third Edition
Alex M. Johnson, Jr.

Understanding Negotiable Instruments and
Payment Systems
William H. Lawrence

Understanding Nonprofit and Tax Exempt
Organizations, Second Edition
Nicholas Cafardi and Jaclyn Cherry

Understanding Partnership and
LLC Taxation, Fourth Edition
Jerold Friedland

Understanding Patent Law, Second Edition
Amy Landers

Understanding Products Liability Law,
Second Edition
Bruce L. Ottley, Rogelio Lasso, and
Terrence F. Kiely

Understanding Property Law, Fourth Edition
John Sprankling

Understanding Remedies, Third Edition
James Fischer

Understanding Sales and Leases of Goods,
Third Edition
William H. Henning, William H. Lawrence,
and Henry Deeb Gabriel

Understanding Secured Transactions,
Fifth Edition
William H. Lawrence, William H. Henning,
and R. Wilson Freyermuth

Understanding Securities Law, Sixth Edition
Marc I. Steinberg

Understanding Taxation of Business Entities
Walter Schwidetzky and Fred B. Brown

Understanding Torts, Fifth Edition
John Diamond, Lawrence C. Levine,
and Anita Bernstein

Understanding Trademark Law, Third Edition
Mary LaFrance

Understanding Trusts and Estates,
Fifth Edition
Roger W. Andersen

Understanding White Collar Crime,
Fourth Edition
J. Kelly Strader

Understanding Criminal Procedure

VOLUME 1: INVESTIGATION

SEVENTH EDITION

Joshua Dressler

FRANK R. STRONG CHAIR IN LAW
MICHAEL E. MORITZ COLLEGE OF LAW
THE OHIO STATE UNIVERSITY

Alan C. Michaels

DEAN AND EDWIN M. COOPERMAN PROFESSOR OF LAW
MICHAEL E. MORITZ COLLEGE OF LAW
THE OHIO STATE UNIVERSITY

Ric Simmons

CHIEF JUSTICE THOMAS J. MOYER PROFESSOR
FOR THE ADMINISTRATION OF JUSTICE AND RULE OF LAW
MICHAEL E. MORITZ COLLEGE OF LAW
THE OHIO STATE UNIVERSITY

CAROLINA ACADEMIC PRESS
Durham, North Carolina

ISBN: 978-1-61163-936-0
eISBN: 978-1-61163-992-6

Library of Congress Cataloging-in-Publication Data

Names: Dressler, Joshua, author. | Michaels, Alan C., author. | Simmons, Ric, author.
Title: Understanding criminal procedure. Volume 1, Investigation / Joshua Dressler, Alan C. Michaels, and Ric Simmons.
Description: Seventh edition. | Durham, North Carolina : Carolina Academic Press, [2017] | Includes bibliographical references and index.
Identifiers: LCCN 2017016782 | ISBN 9781611639360 (alk. paper)
Subjects: LCSH: Criminal procedure--United States.
Classification: LCC KF9619 .D74 2017 | DDC 345.73/05--dc23
LC record available at https://lccn.loc.gov/2017016782

Carolina Academic Press, LLC
700 Kent Street
Durham, North Carolina 27701
Telephone (919) 489-7486
Fax (919) 493-5668
www.cap-press.com

Printed in the United States of America

Contents

Preface

This text is intended for use in law schools, although we can report with pleasure that legal scholars, practicing attorneys, and judges have found it of value in their work.

This volume is intended for use in criminal procedure courses focusing primarily or exclusively on police investigatory process. Such courses are variously titled: *Criminal Procedure I; Criminal Procedure: Investigation; Criminal Procedure: Police Practices; Constitutional Criminal Procedure;* etc. Because some such courses also cover the defendant's right to counsel at trial and on appeal, this text includes a chapter on this non-police-practice issue. This seventh edition incorporates the many significant changes in the law that have occurred since publication of the last edition.

Because UNDERSTANDING CRIMINAL PROCEDURE is primarily designed for law students, it is written so that students can use it with confidence that it will assist them in course preparation. Indeed, frequently professors recommend or assign this text to their students to improve classroom dialogue. Based on the experience of prior editions, as well, we are confident that this sixth edition will continue to prove useful to scholars, practicing lawyers, and courts.

The text covers the most important United States Supreme Court cases in the field. Where pertinent, the Federal Rules of Criminal Procedure, federal statutes, and lower federal and state court cases are considered. The broad overarching policy issues of criminal procedure are laid out; and some of the hottest debates in the field are considered in depth and, we think, objectively.

Readers should find the text user-friendly. Students who want a thorough grasp of a topic can and should read the relevant chapter in its entirety. However, each chapter is divided into subsections, so that readers with more refined research needs can find answers to their questions efficiently. We also include citations to important scholarship, both classic and recent, into which readers may delve more deeply regarding specific topics. And because so many of the topics interrelate, cross-referencing footnotes are included so that readers can easily move from one part of the book to another, if necessary.

Gender policy of the Text. Obviously, women as well as men fill all the roles in the criminal justice system: lawyer, judge, police officer, legislator, criminal suspect, and victim. Accordingly, in even-numbered chapters, we use the male pronoun to describe hypothetical and generic parties in the criminal justice system; in odd-numbered chapters, women get equal time. Based on comments we have received about this policy, most readers like the approach or, at worst, find it only temporarily distracting.

Acknowledgments. Many persons helped make these volumes possible. We can name only a few here. Professors Lee Lamborn and the late Joseph Grano read and commented on every page of every chapter of the manuscript for the first edition. Professor George Thomas did the same with the second edition. Various people have commented on drafts of chapters of later editions. The text is much better because of their generous assistance. Mistakes and omissions are the result of our stubborn refusal to listen to advice.

   We thank our families for their love and support.

Joshua Dressler
Alan C. Michaels
Ric Simmons
January 2017

Understanding
Criminal Procedure

VOLUME 1: INVESTIGATION

Chapter 1

Introduction to Criminal Procedure

§ 1.01 The Relationship of "Criminal Law" to "Criminal Procedure"

At one level, the relationship of criminal procedure to criminal law is straightforward. Criminal procedural law ("criminal procedure," for short) is composed of the rules that regulate the inquiry into whether a violation of a criminal law ("substantive" criminal law, to distinguish it from "procedural" criminal law) has occurred, and whether the person accused of the crime committed it.

Logically, substance is anterior to procedure.[1] The substantive criminal code defines the conduct that society wishes to deter and to punish. Procedural law functions as the means by which society implements its substantive goals. For example, assume the criminal law makes it a crime to possess cocaine. Criminal procedure sets the rules for discovering and adjudicating violations of that criminal statute — for example, police may not subject suspects to unreasonable searches and seizures, or coerce confessions. If the police violate these or other procedural rules, various procedural consequences may arise, such as exclusion of evidence at trial or dismissal of the charge.

Yet, the interrelationship of procedure and substance is more complicated than the simple description in the preceding paragraph suggests. First, procedural rules can frustrate the implementation of a community's substantive goals. For example, if the rules are unduly lax, the police may mistreat suspects, and prosecutors may be able to introduce unreliable evidence against the accused, enhancing the likelihood of unjust convictions and punishment. On the other hand, if the rules unduly hinder the police and prosecutors in their pursuit of law violators, some persons who deserve to be punished are apt to avoid criminal sanction, and the deterrent value of the criminal law is likely to be undermined.

Second, the existence of some procedural rules sometimes affects legislative decisions about the substantive criminal law. In particular, to the extent that criminal procedure rules make it more difficult for the government to investigate and prosecute crime, the legislature may enact more criminal statutes or greater penalties to offset the effect of the procedural rules.[2] For example, Supreme Court rulings mandating a jury role in certain sentencing systems (a change in the criminal procedure law) led to legislative proposals to raise the minimum sentence for certain crimes (a change in the substantive criminal law). Such "spillover" effects may also be seen in procedural rules governing criminal investigations, as when the existence of minor crimes such as traffic offenses

---

1. Herbert L. Packer, *Two Models of the Criminal Process*, 113 U. Pa. L. Rev. 1, 3 (1964).
2. *See* William J. Stuntz, *The Uneasy Relationship Between Criminal Procedure and Criminal Justice*, 107 Yale L.J. 1, 4 (1997).

or certain possession offenses may be used to expand police authority to investigate more serious crimes that procedural requirements of probable cause and reasonable suspicion otherwise restrict.[3]

Third, some legal doctrines involve a mixture of procedure and substance. Consider the constitutional rule that the government must prove beyond a reasonable doubt "every fact necessary to constitute the crime . . . charged."[4] This is a procedural rule, but it cannot properly be enforced unless the term "crime," a substantive criminal law concept, is defined. For example, does the "crime" of murder include as an ingredient the "absence of a legitimate claim of self-defense"—that is, is "murder" a killing that occurs in the absence of self-defense—or is self-defense an affirmative defense to the "crime" of murder? In short, the answer to the procedural question—"Who has the burden of proof regarding the matter of self-defense?"—depends on the definition of murder, a substantive criminal law concept.

§ 1.02 Sources of Procedural Law

[A] Formal Sources

Various layers of laws and regulations govern the conduct of the participants in the criminal justice system. First, starting at the highest level, various provisions of the United States Constitution, in particular those found in the Fourth, Fifth, Sixth, Eighth, and Fourteenth Amendments, restrict the power of law enforcement officers in their relations to persons suspected of criminal activity and also govern the adjudication of criminal cases. The United States Supreme Court and lower federal and state courts frequently are called upon to interpret these federal constitutional provisions. As a result of substantial constitutional litigation, the study of some aspects of criminal procedure—in particular, police practices—is principally a study of constitutional law.

Second, at the state level, state constitutions are a potentially important source of procedural law. Beginning with force in the 1970s and gaining momentum in the 1980s, as the United States Supreme Court and lower federal courts became less sympathetic to the *federal* constitutional claims of individual petitioners, a body of *state* constitutional jurisprudence developed, in which some state courts, interpreting their own constitutions, granted relief to their residents that was unavailable under the federal Constitution.[5] This

---

3. *See* §§ 8.02[F] and 17.03[B][5], *infra*.

4. In re Winship, 397 U.S. 358, 364 (1970).

5. *See* Stephen E. Henderson, *Learning from All Fifty States: How to Apply the Fourth Amendment and Its State Analogs to Protect Third Party Information from Unreasonable Search*, 55 Cath. U. L. Rev. 373, 395–412 (2005) (counting only 18 states out of 50 as having never diverged from U.S. Supreme Court decisions on the scope of Fourth Amendment protections); Barry Latzer, *The Hidden Conservatism of the State Court "Revolution,"* 74 Judicature 190 (1991) (providing a list, by state, of the number of cases in which each state's highest court has rejected or adopted United States Supreme Court's criminal procedure decisions, from the late 1960s through 1989); Ronald K.L. Collins & David M. Skover, *The Future of Liberal Legal Scholarship*, 87 Mich. L. Rev. 189, 217 (1988) (reporting that, in their research, state courts in at least 450 cases recognized rights not available under the federal constitution); Robert F. Williams, *In the Glare of the Supreme Court: Continuing Methodology and Legitimacy Problems in Independent State Constitutional Rights Adjudication*, 72 Notre Dame L. Rev. 1015 (1997). This treatise provides non-exhaustive citations to state constitutional law decisions. Not all state courts have the authority to interpret

trend is significant because a state supreme court is the final arbiter of the meaning of its own constitution.[6]

Third, legislatures have enacted statutes and courts have adopted written rules of criminal procedure governing many aspects of the state and federal criminal justice systems. For example, at the federal level, Congress has enacted laws governing such matters as electronic surveillance of private conversations,[7] pretrial detention of dangerous persons,[8] and the qualifications for jury service.[9] Also, Congress has granted authority to the Supreme Court to promulgate written rules to govern proceedings in the federal courts, which the Court has done in the form of the Federal Rules of Criminal Procedure. In turn, Federal Rule 57 authorizes District Courts (trial courts) to make rules governing local practice.

Fourth, some law enforcement agencies promulgate written regulations that their employees are required to follow. For example, police departments frequently have rules governing, among other matters, the use of deadly force to effectuate arrests, the techniques to be followed in conducting lineups, and the procedures to be used in inspecting the contents of automobiles taken into police custody. Prosecutors' offices, in turn, often have internal guidelines governing such matters as charging decisions and plea

---

their constitutions differently from the United States Constitution. *E.g.*, Calif. Const. art. I, § 24 (in which the state constitution was amended by the initiative process to provide that in criminal cases various enumerated constitutional rights of the defendant "shall be construed by the courts of this state in a manner consistent with the Constitution of the United States"); Fla. Const. art. I, § 12 (in which the state charter was amended by initiative to provide that it "shall be construed in conformity with the 4th amendment to the United States Constitution, as interpreted by the United States Supreme Court"). Moreover, some state courts presume that their state constitutional provisions, if identical or nearly identical to federal provisions, should be interpreted in "lockstep" with the federal provision. *See, e.g.*, People v. Caballes, 851 N.E.2d 26, 31–46 (Ill. 2006) (applying the Supreme Court's interpretation of Fourth Amendment law in interpreting a state constitutional search and seizure provision under a "limited lockstep" doctrine). It should be noted that a state court may interpret its own constitutional charter *less* protectively than its federal constitutional counterpart, but if it does so, then the state court "must go on to decide the claim under federal law, assuming it has been raised." Hans A. Linde, *E Pluribus — Constitutional Theory and State Courts*, 18 Ga. L. Rev. 165, 179 (1984). If a state court interprets state law *more* protectively to the individual, however, it need not turn to federal law—the state petitioner wins her claim.

6. For thoughtful discussion of so-called "judicial federalism" generally, or of its application in criminal cases, see generally Barry Latzer, State Constitutional Criminal Law (1995); Barry Latzer, State Constitutions and Criminal Justice (1991); Shirley S. Abrahamson, *Criminal Law and State Constitutions: The Emergence of State Constitutional Law*, 63 Tex. L. Rev. 1141 (1985); Catherine Greene Burnett & Neil Colman McCabe, *A Compass in the Swamp: A Guide to Tactics in State Constitutional Law Challenges*, 25 Tex. Tech. L. Rev. 75 (1993); William J. Brennan, Jr., *The Bill of Rights and the States: The Revival of State Constitutions as Guardians of Individual Rights*, 61 N.Y.U. L. Rev. 535 (1986); William J. Brennan, Jr., *State Constitutions and the Protection of Individual Rights*, 90 Harv. L. Rev. 489 (1977); James A. Gardner, *State Constitutions as Resistance to National Power: Toward a Functional Theory of State Constitutions*, 91 Geo. L.J. 1003 (2003); James A. Gardner, *The Failed Discourse of State Constitutionalism*, 90 Mich. L. Rev. 761 (1992); Barry Latzer, *Towards the Decentralization of Criminal Procedure: State Constitutional Law and Selective Disincorporation*, 87 J. Crim. L. & Crimin. 63 (1996); Paul Marcus, *State Constitutional Protection for Defendants in Criminal Prosecutions*, 20 Ariz. St. L.J. 151 (1988); Jim Rossi, *The Puzzle of State Constitutions*, 54 Buff. L. Rev. 211 (2006); Special Project, *State Constitutions and Criminal Procedure: A Primer for the 21st Century*, 67 Or. L. Rev. 689 (Ken Gormley ed., 1988).

7. 18 U.S.C. §§ 2510–2522 (2012).

8. 18 U.S.C. §§ 3141–3156 (2012).

9. 28 U.S.C. § 1865 (2012).

bargains.[10] Although these regulations do not have the force of law, their violation may result in internal sanctions.

Fifth, on rare occasion the Supreme Court invokes its so-called "supervisory authority" over the administration of criminal justice in the federal courts to announce rules that apply throughout the federal judicial system. Similarly, some federal circuit courts have developed rules that apply to the district courts within their jurisdiction. These rules, based on federal supervisory authority, which do not apply in the state courts, are subject to revision by Congress. State courts also develop common-law rules governing some procedures in state prosecutions.

[B] Informal Sources: A Taste of Reality

Although criminal procedure rules are primarily promulgated "from on high" — by the United States Supreme Court, state supreme courts, and federal and state legislatures—the law that is enforced daily on the streets often looks considerably different. As Professor Anthony Amsterdam once observed about United States Supreme Court case law: "[o]nce uttered, these pronouncements will be interpreted by arrays of lower appellate courts, trial judges, magistrates, commissioners and police officials. *Their* interpretation . . . , for all practical purposes, will become the word of god."[11] Put more bluntly, the law at the end of a billy club or police firearm may look very different from the law handed down by nine justices of the United States Supreme Court or by a legislative body.[12]

This dichotomy between formal and informal law is inevitable. The United States Supreme Court, and each state's highest court, lack daily supervisory control over the actions of the police. Judicial authority is limited to litigated cases, and most of what occurs on the street between police officers and the citizenry is legally invisible. Even if a police officer breaches a constitutional or statutory rule, the victim of the breach may not bring the matter to the attention of a judicial body. Even among cases that enter the criminal justice system, their vast number — nearly 14 million arrests in 2009[13] — restricts the ability of high courts, with their limited dockets (the U.S. Supreme Court decided only 65 cases, mostly civil, in the 2011–2012 Court term),[14] to govern the day-to-day world of criminal proceedings.

---

10. *See, e.g.,* Kate Stith, *The Arc of the Pendulum: Judges, Prosecutors and the Exercise of Discretion,* 117 Yale L.J. 1420, 1440–43 (2008) (discussing federal prosecutorial charging and bargaining policies issued by Attorneys General Thornburgh, Reno, and Ashcroft).

11. Anthony G. Amsterdam, *The Supreme Court and the Rights of Suspects in Criminal Cases,* 45 N.Y.U. L. Rev. 785, 786 (1970).

12. Gregory Howard Williams, *Police Discretion: The Institutional Dilemma—Who Is In Charge?,* 68 Iowa L. Rev. 431, 437 (1983) ("There is little assurance that policy established by the Supreme Court will be implemented by patrol officers.").

13. U.S. Department of Justice, *Arrest in the United States, 1980–2009* (Bureau of Justice Statistics; Sept. 2011, NCJ 234319), Table 1, p. 2.

14. See <http://www.scotusblog.com/statistics> (accessed August 20, 2012).

§ 1.03 Stages of a Criminal Prosecution

[A] In General

Analytically and in law school curricula, "criminal procedure" is often divided into two parts, the investigatory and the adjudicatory stages. In the investigatory phase, the primary actors in the "drama" are police officers and those whom they suspect of criminal activity. This is the "cops and (alleged) robbers" stage of the process.

The adjudicatory phase begins when the government commits itself to bringing a suspect to trial for her alleged criminal conduct. In this stage, the focus of attention turns to the legal profession — the prosecutors, defense lawyers, and judges — who participate in the adversarial judicial system. This is the "bail to (maybe) jail" phase of the process.

In studying criminal procedure, it is important to understand the context in which the legal rules apply. What follows, therefore, is a very brief overview of the stages of a typical criminal prosecution. Because adjudicatory procedures differ by state and depend on whether the defendant is charged with a felony or a misdemeanor, primary emphasis here is on *felony* prosecutions in the *federal* system.

[B] Investigatory Stage

A criminal investigation commonly begins when a police officer, on the basis of her own observations and/or those of an informant, comes to believe that criminal activity may be afoot or has already occurred. Because there are no formal stages of a criminal investigation, most Criminal Procedure courses survey the constitutional law pertaining to the most common police investigative practices.

[1] Search and Seizure

Police officers usually search and seize persons and property during the investigatory stage. Searches and seizures occur in an almost infinite variety of ways: for example, by stopping ("seizing") a suspect on the street and frisking her ("searching") for weapons or evidence; by entering a house in order to look for a suspect or evidence of a crime; by opening containers found in an automobile stopped on the highway; and by wiretapping in order to monitor the conversations of suspects.

The Fourth Amendment to the United States Constitution prohibits unreasonable searches and seizures. At one time, most especially in the late 1950s through the mid-1970s, this proscription was interpreted to mean that, except in limited circumstances, police officers were not allowed to search or seize property without a search warrant, supported by probable cause, issued by a judge (or "magistrate"). This warrant requirement (or, at least, warrant presumption) came to be honored primarily in the breach and is of limited value today in determining the lawfulness of police conduct. Not only do police officers today rarely seek a warrant, but many searches and seizures can be conducted on less than probable cause.[15]

---

15. *See generally* chapters 17–18, *infra.*

[2] Interrogation

The police also interrogate suspects and witnesses during criminal investigations. Some interrogations occur in a police-dominated atmosphere, such as in a police station. In other circumstances, questioning occurs in a less coercive environment, such as in a person's home, automobile, or on the street, sometimes in the presence of family or friends. An interrogation may trigger various constitutional questions, including: (1) Is the suspect entitled to be represented by counsel during the questioning?; and (2) Was any ensuing confession obtained voluntarily? In particular, the Fifth Amendment privilege against compulsory self-incrimination, the Due Process Clauses of the Fifth and Fourteenth Amendments, and the Sixth Amendment guarantee of assistance of counsel during criminal prosecutions, are potentially implicated during police interrogations.[16]

[3] Identification Procedures

The police also conduct lineups, show witnesses photographs of potential suspects, take handwriting and voice exemplars, and conduct other identification procedures. The police may conduct many of these activities without prior judicial approval, and without intervention by defense counsel. Nonetheless, in some cases the Sixth Amendment right-to-counsel provision applies and, in all cases, the procedures must be conducted in a constitutionally reliable manner.[17]

[4] Arrest

Assuming that a criminal investigation results in a police determination that there is probable cause to believe that the suspect committed a crime, she may be arrested. When a routine arrest occurs in a private home, the police must ordinarily be armed with a warrant to take the suspect into custody. Arrests in public places usually can be made without an arrest warrant.[18]

Upon arrest, the suspect is usually searched and taken to the police station or to a jail, where she is "booked" (i.e., her name is logged in an arrest book or on a computer), photographed, fingerprinted, and more fully searched. Typically, any personal belongings found in her possession at the station or jail are inventoried and placed in custody for safekeeping.

[C] Adjudicatory Stage[19]

[1] Issuance of a Complaint

After a suspect is arrested and booked, a complaint is prepared by the police or a prosecutor and is filed with the court. A "complaint" is "a written statement of the essential facts constituting the offense charged."[20] It serves as the official charging

---

16. *See generally* chapters 21–25, *infra.*
17. *See generally* chapter 26, *infra.*
18. *See generally* chapter 9, *infra.*
19. Of course, the adjudicatory portion of criminal procedure constitutes a course of study unto itself, and those rules are covered thoroughly in the second volume of this text.
20. Fed. R. Crim. P. 3.

document until either an "information" or an "indictment," each of which is discussed below,[21] is issued.

[2] Probable Cause (*Gerstein*) Hearing

The police may not constitutionally arrest a person unless they have probable cause to believe that a crime has occurred and that the suspect committed it. In order to implement the Fourth Amendment bar on unreasonable seizures of persons, the Supreme Court has held that, whenever practicable, a probable cause determination should be made by a neutral and detached magistrate, rather than by a police officer.[22]

If the police apply for an arrest warrant, the requisite judicial oversight occurs. However, when the police arrest a suspect without an arrest warrant—the vast majority of cases—a prior judicial determination of probable cause is lacking. Therefore, the Supreme Court ruled in *Gerstein v. Pugh*[23] that, following a *warrantless* arrest, the Fourth Amendment requires that a prompt judicial determination of probable cause be made as a precondition to any extended restraint of the arrestee's liberty.[24]

Because a so-called "*Gerstein* hearing" serves as a post-arrest equivalent of a pre-arrest warrant-application hearing,[25] the proceeding may be conducted in the same manner as a warrant hearing: in the defendant's absence, with the probable cause determination based on hearsay testimony. If the arrestee is permitted to be present during the hearing, she is not constitutionally entitled to representation by counsel or to the full panoply of adversarial safeguards available at trial. In many jurisdictions, the probable cause hearing is conducted at the suspect's first appearance before a judicial officer, a proceeding that is discussed immediately below.

[3] First Appearance Before the Magistrate

An arrested person must be taken "without unnecessary delay,"[26] usually within 24 hours except on weekends, before a judicial officer, for a hearing variously called the "initial arraignment," "arraignment on a warrant," "arraignment on a complaint," or, simply the "first" or "initial" "appearance."

At the hearing, the arrestee receives formal notice of the charges against her, her constitutional rights in the impending prosecution are explained to her, and a date is set for a preliminary hearing. If the suspect is indigent and not presently represented by counsel, a lawyer may be appointed for her at this time. If the suspect was arrested without a warrant, a probable cause determination (a *Gerstein* hearing) is usually made at the first

---

21. *See* § 1.03[C][4], *infra*.

22. *See* Johnson v. United States, 333 U.S. 10 (1948).

23. 420 U.S. 103 (1975).

24. How promptly must the *Gerstein* hearing be held? In *County of Riverside v. McLaughlin*, 500 U.S. 44 (1991), the Supreme Court stated that the Constitution "permits a reasonable postponement of a probable cause determination while the police cope with the everyday problems of processing suspects through an overly burdened criminal justice system." Therefore, if a state wishes to combine the probable cause hearing with other pretrial proceedings, such as the first appearance before the magistrate, it may do so as long as the hearing occurs, as a general matter, within 48 hours from the time of arrest. However, a delay "for delay's sake," out of ill-will toward the suspect, or in order to secure evidence that will justify the arrest, is constitutionally unreasonable, even if it falls within the presumptive 48-hour period.

25. *See* § 10.02, *infra*.

26. Fed. R. Crim. P. 5(a)(1)(A).

appearance. Finally, and perhaps most significantly, the magistrate determines at this time whether the arrestee should be set free on her own recognizance, released on bail, or detained pending further proceedings.[27]

[4] Preliminary Hearings and Grand Jury Proceedings[28]

In most jurisdictions, a preliminary hearing (or "preliminary examination") is held within two weeks after the arrestee's initial appearance before the magistrate, unless the defendant waives the hearing.[29] The primary purpose of a preliminary hearing is to determine whether there is probable cause to believe that a criminal offense has occurred and that the arrestee committed it.[30]

The significance of the preliminary hearing in the criminal process depends on whether the state is an "information jurisdiction" (i.e., a state in which an indictment by a grand jury is not required) or an "indictment jurisdiction" (i.e., a state in which the defendant ordinarily cannot be brought to trial unless she is indicted by a grand jury).

In *information* jurisdictions, once the magistrate determines that there is sufficient evidence to "bind over" the defendant for trial, the prosecutor files an "information" with the trial court. The "information" is a document stating the charges against the defendant and the essential facts relating to them. The information replaces the complaint as the formal charging document. In the alternative, if the magistrate in an information jurisdiction does *not* find sufficient evidence to bind over the defendant, the complaint is dismissed and the defendant is discharged.

In indictment jurisdictions, by contrast, the preliminary hearing has diminished importance because the magistrate's probable cause determination may be superseded by the actions of the grand jury, i.e., if the grand jury does not indict the defendant, she must be released, even if the preliminary hearing magistrate previously determined that there was probable cause to believe that the arrestee committed an offense. Indeed, in many indictment jurisdictions, including the federal system, the preliminary examination is not held if the defendant is indicted before the date set for the preliminary hearing.[31]

In indictment jurisdictions, a person may not be brought to trial for a serious offense unless she is indicted by a grand jury or waives her right to a grand jury hearing. The Fifth Amendment to the United States Constitution provides that in federal prosecutions, "[n]o person shall be held to answer for a capital, or otherwise infamous crime, unless on a[n] . . . indictment of a Grand Jury . . ." The constitutional term "infamous crime" encompasses all felony prosecutions. This provision does not apply to the states,[32] however, so that the prevalence of grand jury proceedings varies across jurisdictions.

In a grand jury proceeding, the prosecutor makes an *ex parte* presentation to the grand jurors, who then formally decide whether sufficient evidence was introduced.[33]

---

27. *See generally* 2 Joshua Dressler & Alan C. Michaels, Understanding Criminal Procedure § 5.01 (4th ed. 2006)

28. *See generally id.* at chapter 6.

29. In the federal system, the hearing must be held no later than 14 days following the initial appearance, if the arrestee is in custody, or within 21 days if she is not. Fed. R. Crim. P. 5.1(c).

30. *See* Fed. R. Crim. P. 5.1(e).

31. *See, e.g.,* Fed. R. Crim. P. 5.1(a).

32. Hurtado v. California, 110 U.S. 516 (1884).

33. Most jurisdictions, including the federal courts (*see* United States v. Calandra, 414 U.S. 338, 343 (1974)), apply a probable cause standard, similar to that employed in preliminary hearings.

If the grand jury so finds, the jury (through the prosecutor) issues an "indictment," a document that states the charges and the relevant facts relating to them. If the jury does not vote to indict the defendant, the complaint issued against the defendant is dismissed, and she is discharged.

[5] Arraignment

If an indictment or information is filed, the defendant is arraigned in open court. At the arraignment, at which the Sixth Amendment right to counsel attaches,[34] the accused is provided with a copy of the indictment or information, after which she enters a plea to the offenses charged in it. She may plead "not guilty," "guilty," "*nolo contendere*,"[35] or (in some states) "not guilty by reason of insanity."

[6] Pretrial Motions

After arraignment, the defendant may make various pretrial motions. Among the defenses, objections, and requests that often are raised prior to trial are: (1) that the indictment or information is defective, in that it fails to allege an essential element of the crime charged, or that it fails to give the defendant sufficient notice of the facts relating to the charge against her;[36] (2) that the venue of the prosecution is improper or inconvenient;[37] (3) that the indictment or information joins offenses or parties in an improper or prejudicial manner;[38] (4) that evidence in the possession of one of the parties should be disclosed to the opposing party;[39] (5) that evidence should be suppressed because it was obtained in an unconstitutional manner; and (6) that the prosecution is constitutionally barred, such as by the Double Jeopardy and/or Speedy Trial Clauses of the Constitution.[40]

In some circumstances, if a defendant's pretrial motions are successful, the judge will dismiss the charges on her own or on the prosecutor's motion.[41] For example, if the prosecution is barred by the Double Jeopardy Clause, dismissal is obligatory. Or, if the judge grants the defendant's motion to suppress key evidence, the prosecutor might determine that continuation of the proceedings would be futile and, therefore, request dismissal of the charges.

[7] Trial

If a defendant does not plead guilty and the charges are not dismissed, a trial is held. The Sixth Amendment entitles a defendant to trial by jury in the prosecution of any serious, i.e., non-petty, offense.[42] In other cases, and sometimes even in serious cases

---

34. *See* Rothgery v. Gillespie County, 554 U.S. 191 (2008).
35. Literally, the plea means "I will not contest it [the charge]." For most purposes in a criminal proceeding, the plea is treated the same as a guilty plea.
36. *See, e.g.*, Fed. R. Crim. P. 12(b)(3).
37. *See, e.g.*, Fed. R. Crim. P. 18, 21(a).
38. *See, e.g.*, Fed. R. Crim. P. 8, 14.
39. *See, e.g.*, Fed. R. Crim. P. 16.
40. U.S. Const. amend. V (". . . nor shall any person be subject for the same offence to be twice put in jeopardy of life or limb . . ."); U.S. Const. amend. VI ("In all criminal prosecutions, the accused shall enjoy the right to a speedy. . . trial. . . .").
41. *See, e.g.*, Fed. R. Crim. P. 48.
42. *See generally* 2 Dressler & Michaels, Note 27, *supra*, at chapter 12.

when the defendant waives her jury right, the trial may be to a judge, rather than a jury—a "bench trial."

Whether the trial is to judge or jury, the defendant has a number of significant rights at trial. First, the defendant is constitutionally entitled to employ counsel at trial, and an indigent is entitled to the appointment of counsel in all felony prosecutions, as well as at any misdemeanor trial in which she will be incarcerated if convicted.[43] The defendant may also call witnesses on her own behalf, and confront and cross-examine the witnesses who testify against her.[44] The defendant is not required to testify and she "must pay no court-imposed price for the exercise of [her Fifth Amendment] constitutional privilege not to testify."[45]

[8] Sentencing and Post-Trial Proceedings

[a] Sentencing[46]

If the defendant is convicted after a trial, or if the defendant pleads guilty, the judge or jury must impose a sentence. In most jurisdictions, particularly for serious crimes, there will be an additional proceeding beyond the trial to provide the sentencer with further information that might be relevant to sentencing. At the sentencing proceeding the defendant has some, but not all, of the constitutional protections she enjoys at trial.[47]

[b] Appeal[48]

If the defendant is acquitted by the jury or by the judge in a bench trial, the government is barred by the Double Jeopardy Clause from appealing the acquittal.[49] If the defendant is convicted, she has no constitutional right to appeal her conviction.[50] However, all jurisdictions by statute permit a convicted defendant (now the "appellant") to appeal a conviction after trial. In state court systems, she may appeal to an appellate court below the state supreme court or, if there is none, directly to the state supreme court. In the federal courts, a defendant may appeal her conviction to the United States Court of Appeals for the circuit with jurisdiction over the case.

If the appellant is unsuccessful in her statutory appeal of right, she may be entitled to discretionary appeals to a higher court. For example, in a state in which an appeal of right is brought to an intermediate appellate court, the state supreme court is permitted, but usually is not required, except in capital cases, to hear the appellant's second appeal. She may also petition the United States Supreme Court to consider her case. If her appeal is ultimately successful, she ordinarily may be reprosecuted.

---

43. Gideon v. Wainwright, 372 U.S. 335 (1963) (felony cases); Argersinger v. Hamlin, 407 U.S. 25 (1972) (misdemeanor cases). *See generally* chapter 28, *infra*.

44. U.S. Const. amend. VI ("In all criminal prosecutions, the accused shall the enjoy the right . . . to be confronted with the witnesses against him; [and] to have compulsory process for obtaining witnesses in his favor. . . ."). *See generally* 2 Dressler & Michaels, Note 27, *supra*, at chapter 13.

45. Carter v. Kentucky, 450 U.S. 288, 301 (1981); *see also* Griffin v. California, 380 U.S. 609 (1965). *See generally* 2 Dressler & Michaels, Note 27, *supra*, at chapter 14.

46. *See generally* 2 Dressler & Michaels, Note 27, *supra*, at chapter 15.

47. *See generally* Alan C. Michaels, *Trial Rights at Sentencing*, 81 N.C. L. Rev. 1771 (2003).

48. *See generally*, 2 Dressler & Michaels, Note 27, *supra*, at chapter 16.

49. *See id.* at chapter 14.

50. *See* McKane v. Durston, 153 U.S. 684, 687 (1894) (dictum); Jones v. Barnes, 463 U.S. 745 (1983) (dictum).

[c] Collateral Attack of a Conviction: Habeas Corpus[51]

"The historic use of habeas corpus . . . [was] to protect those detained by the Executive without previous judicial involvement."[52] That crucial purpose, for which the writ of habeas corpus was given constitutional status from the outset,[53] has received renewed attention since the attacks of September 11, 2001, as a result of detentions by the executive branch in its efforts to combat perceived terrorism. For most of the past half-century or longer, however, the primary use of habeas corpus has been to challenge state convictions in federal courts on constitutional grounds.

After a defendant's appeals are exhausted—i.e., once her conviction is final—she may file a petition for a writ of habeas corpus in a federal district court if she believes that her continued incarceration is in violation of the United States Constitution or of a federal law.[54] A post-conviction habeas corpus proceeding is not part of the criminal appeal process itself. It is a civil action designed to overturn a presumptively valid criminal judgment. As such, it is considered a collateral attack on a criminal conviction, as distinguished from a direct criminal appeal. In this context, the purpose of a habeas petition is to convince the district (trial) court that it should compel the warden of the jail or prison holding the petitioner to bring her before the court so that it can determine whether she is being held in custody against the law.

Federal habeas corpus jurisprudence involves exceedingly intricate rules, and Supreme Court decisions, and new legislation in the 1980s and 1990s, have made it increasingly difficult for state prisoners to obtain a hearing on the merits of their federal claims. However, if the proper allegations are made, the district court may grant the petition and conduct an evidentiary hearing into the federal claim.

Because a habeas corpus petition constitutes a collateral attack on a judgment that is already final, and because federal courts are hesitant to intrude on state proceedings, the standards that a petitioner must satisfy to obtain ultimate relief in habeas are generally stricter than those that apply on direct appeals. For example, a state court conviction may only be disturbed on federal habeas review if it "involved an unreasonable application of[] clearly established Federal law, as determined by the Supreme Court . . . [or if it] was based on an unreasonable determination of the facts" in light of the evidence presented in the state proceeding.[55] Moreover, with regard to factual determinations, the prisoner seeking habeas relief must prove the unreasonableness by clear and convincing evidence.[56] In addition, certain "procedural bars," such as the prisoner's failure to raise the claim in state court first, may also lead the federal court to deny relief.

---

51. *See generally* Graham Hughes, *The Decline of Habeas Corpus (Occasional Papers from the Center for Research in Crime and Justice*, N.Y.U. School of Law, No. VIII, 1990); Richard H. Fallon, Jr. & Daniel Meltzer, *Habeas Corpus Jurisdiction, Substantive Rights, and the War on Terror*, 120 Harv. L. Rev. 2029 (2007); Joseph L. Hoffman & William J. Stuntz, *Habeas After the Revolution*, 1993 Sup. Ct. Rev. 65 (1994); Nancy J. King et al., *Habeas Litigation in U.S. District Courts* (2007); Larry W. Yackle, *A Primer on the New Habeas Corpus Statute*, 44 Buff. L. Rev. 381 (1996).

52. Fallon & Meltzer, Note 51, *supra*, at 2037.

53. U.S. Const., art. I, sec. 9.

54. 28 U.S.C. §§ 2241–2244, 2253–2255, 2261–2266 (2012). Many states have their own habeas corpus procedures, which must be exhausted before a convicted person seeks *federal* habeas relief.

55. 28 U.S.C. § 2254(d) (2012). For a discussion of the meaning of an "unreasonable"—as opposed to mistaken—application of federal law (a state court can be mistaken without being unreasonable), see Todd E. Pettys, *Federal Habeas Relief and the New Tolerance for "Reasonably Erroneous" Applications of Federal Law*, 63 Ohio St. L.J. 731 (2002).

56. 28 U.S.C. § 2254(e)(1) (2012).

However, if the prisoner overcomes these hurdles and the district court determines under these heightened standards that the petitioner is being held in custody in violation of federal law or the Constitution, it may vacate the conviction. The ruling of the district court—whether to grant or deny the petition—is potentially subject to appeal by the losing party, although in many circumstances the prisoner must make a "substantial showing of the denial of a constitutional right" to the appellate court before the court can agree to hear the appeal.

§ 1.04 Studying Constitutional Law Cases

The study of many aspects of criminal procedure, particularly the law relating to police practices, is largely the study of constitutional law, especially the decisions of the United States Supreme Court. Consequently, the following suggestions are offered to students inexperienced in analysis of constitutional cases.

[A] Read Concurring and Dissenting Opinions

To the extent that your casebook permits, pay attention to concurring and dissenting opinions, if any, in the assigned cases. Various reasons support this recommendation. First, the ideas expressed in the concurring or dissenting opinions of today sometimes become the majority views of tomorrow.

Second, sometimes a concurring or dissenting opinion explains the views of the majority better than the latter's own opinion, calls attention to unresolved issues, or suggests where the logic of the majority opinion may lead. Indeed, on occasion a concurring opinion takes on a life of its own, and is cited or applied in subsequent opinions in preference to the majority opinion.[57]

Third, as discussed in subsection [C], it is often necessary to analyze these opinions in order to determine the long-term significance of a constitutional holding.

[B] Learn Case Names

Pay attention to the names of Supreme Court cases. Unlike cases applying common law doctrine, which often are fungible, a United States Supreme Court constitutional decision represents the final official[58] word on the issue in question.[59] These opinions have the "power to shake the assembled faithful with awful tremors of exultation and loathing."[60] Consequently, lawyers tend to talk about constitutional issues in a shorthand (e.g., "Was the suspect Mirandized[61]?"). It is helpful to understand and speak this language.

---

57. *E.g.*, Justice Harlan's concurring opinion in Katz v. United States, 389 U.S. 347 (1967). *See generally* § 6.03[C], *infra*.

58. *But see* § 1.02[B], *supra*, for a "taste of reality."

59. Of course, the Supreme Court can overrule itself, or the Constitution can be amended to override an unpopular decision.

60. Amsterdam, Note 11, *supra*, at 786.

61. Miranda v. Arizona, 384 U.S. 436 (1966).

[C] Count Votes

If the casebook permits, take note of the vote breakdown in important cases. For various reasons, vote counting can prove insightful and sometimes is essential. First, the long-term importance of a decision may depend on the size of the majority. A 5–4 decision is not equivalent to a 9–0 ruling. A unanimous opinion often carries greater legitimacy and force—sometimes even moral force—with the public and within the legal community than one decided by the slimmest of margins. Moreover, a 5–4 precedent is a prime target for overruling (or, at least, narrowing) when a justice in the majority leaves the Court.

Second, vote counting is essential in ascertaining the precedential value of some cases. For example, suppose that *D* appeals her conviction on two independent grounds: (1) that police officers conducted an unconstitutional search of her house (issue A); and (2) that the officers coerced a confession from her (issue B). Assume that if either of these claims is successful *D*'s conviction must be overturned.

Assume the following scenario: four judges agree with *D* on issue A, but express no opinion regarding issue B. One judge concurs in the judgment; she rules against *D* on issue A, but in *D*'s favor on issue B. Four dissenters reject both of *D*'s claims. Thus, *D* gets what she wants: she wins her appeal, as five judges believe that she is entitled to a new trial, albeit for different reasons.

However, a good lawyer with a client who wishes to raise issue A on similar facts would observe that her chances of success with the same court are not good: four members of the court are likely to favor her client's claim regarding issue A, while five (the dissenters and the concurring judge) will probably oppose her. Likewise, another attorney, but one who seeks to raise issue B, can expect that at least four judges will oppose, and only one will favor, her client. The case would depend on the views of the four court members who expressed no opinion on issue B.

[D] Learn the Views of Individual Justices[62]

Suppose that a lawyer is considering the wisdom of appealing a criminal conviction in a case in which the law is fuzzy, i.e., there is no rule or precedent on point. In order to

---

62. For discussion of the jurisprudence of some sitting justices, *see generally* Heather K. Gerken, *Justice Kennedy and the Domains of Equal Protection*, 121 Harv. L. Rev. 104 (2007); Lisa K. Parshall, *Embracing the Living Constitution: Justice Anthony M. Kennedy's Move Away from a Conservative Methodology of Constitutional Interpretation*, 30 N.C. Central L. Rev. 25 (2007); Stephanos Bibas, *Originalism and Formalism in Criminal Procedure: The Triumph of Justice Scalia, the Unlikely Friend of Criminal Defendants?*, 94 Geo. L.J. 183 (2005); Stephen G. Calabresi & Gary Lawson, *The Unitary Executive, Jurisdiction Stripping, and the* Hamdan *Opinions: A Textualist Response to Justice Scalia*, 107 Colum. L. Rev. 1002 (2007); Christopher E. Smith & Madahvi McCall, *Justice Scalia's Influence on Criminal Justice*, 34 U. Tol. L. Rev. 535 (2003); David A. Strauss, *On the Origin of Rules (with Apologies to Darwin): A Comment on Antonin Scalia's The Rule of Law as a Law of Rules*, 75 U. Chi. L. Rev. 997 (2008); Stephen J. Wermiel, *Clarence Thomas After 10 Years: Some Reflections*, Am. U. J. Gender Soc. Pol. & L. 315 (2002); *Symposium: The Jurisprudence of Justice Ruth Bader Ginsburg: A Discussion of Fifteen Years on the U.S. Supreme Court*, 70 Ohio St. L.J. 797-1126 (2009); Paul Gewirtz, *The Pragmatic Passion of Stephen Breyer*, 115 Yale L.J. 1675 (2006); Richard A. Posner, *Justice Breyer Throws Down the Gauntlet*, 115 Yale L.J. 1699 (2006); Laura Krugman Ray, *The Style of a Skeptic: The Opinions of Chief Justice Roberts*, 83 Ind. L.J. 997 (2008); Diane S. Sykes, *"Of a Judiciary Nature": Observations on Chief Justice Roberts's First Opinions*, 34 Pepp. L. Rev. 1027 (2007);

determine whether to recommend an appeal and, if so, what arguments are most apt to be persuasive, the attorney needs to "get into the head" of the judges on the court that will hear the case. One aspect of this is to identify each judge's judicial and legal philosophy, as well as her overall belief system.[63]

It is usually too simplistic (although not always[64]) to treat a judge as a "liberal" or a "conservative" (or as an "activist" or a "non-activist"), whatever these terms may mean to the user. Some judges are "liberal," for example, in matters relating to freedom of speech but are "conservative" on questions of criminal justice. Even in the latter area, a particular judge might believe that the police should not generally be required to obtain warrants before they conduct searches (a pro-police position), but that they should usually be required to have probable cause before they conduct the searches (a pro-defense position).

In the field of Criminal Procedure, where the focus is primarily on the Supreme Court, lawyers *and law students* need to pay attention to the voting patterns of individual members of the Court. Over time, an observer can develop a sense of a justice's philosophy and can more accurately predict her vote on specific issues.

[E] Be Sensitive to Supreme Court History[65]

Just as individual justices have specific philosophical perspectives, the Supreme Court as a body—or, more correctly, a majority of it—may possess, at any given time, an

---

Russell L. Jones, *Supreme Court Nominee Samuel A. Alito, Jr.: An Analysis of the Impact He Will Have on the Fourth Amendment*, 33 S.U. L. Rev. 453 (2006). For analysis of some Justices who recently left the Court, see generally Christopher E. Smith, *The Roles of Justice John Paul Stevens in Criminal Justice Cases*, 39 Suffolk U. L. Rev. 719 (2006); Symposium, *The Jurisprudence of Justice Stevens*, 74 Fordham L. Rev. 1557, 1569–1757 (2006) (four articles on criminal justice); Scott P. Johnson, *The Judicial Behavior of Justice Souter in Criminal Cases and the Denial of a Conservative Counterrevolution*, 7 Pierce L. Rev. 1 (2008); Erwin Chemerinsky, *Assessing Chief Justice William Rehnquist*, 154 U. Pa. L. Rev. 1331 (2006); Madhavi M. McCall & Michael A. McCall, *Chief Justice William Rehnquist: His Law-and-Order Legacy and Impact on Criminal Justice*, 39 Akron L. Rev. 323 (2006); Charles D. Kelso & R. Randall Kelso, *Sandra Day O'Connor: A Justice Who Has Made a Difference in Constitutional Law*, 32 McGeorge L. Rev. 915 (2001).

63. The focus here is on the appellate court level, but lawyers must especially be sensitive to the belief-system of *trial* judges, where the vast majority of cases are ultimately resolved.

64. As just one example, Justice William Douglas took the "civil libertarian" position in 90 percent of the cases in which he cast a vote between 1953 and 1975. In contrast, Justice William Rehnquist took a civil libertarian position in only 19.6% of the cases decided between 1972, when he joined the Court, and 1985. Jefferey A. Segal & Harold J. Spaeth, *Decisional Trends on the Warren and Burger Courts: Results from the Supreme Court Data Base Project*, 73 Judicature 103, 105–06 (1989).

65. For a look at the current Roberts Court, see generally Tracey Maclin & Jennifer Rader, *No More Chipping Away: The Roberts Court Uses an Axe to Take Out the Fourth Amendment*, 81 Miss. L.J. 1183 (2012); Erwin Chemerinsky, *The Roberts Court and Criminal Procedure at Age Five*, 43 Tex. Tech. L. Rev. 13 (2010); Christopher E. Smith et al., *The Roberts Court and Criminal Justice at the Dawn of the 2008 Term*, 3 Charleston L. Rev. 26 (2009); Jonathan Witmer-Rich, *Interrogation and the Roberts Court*, 63 Fla. L. Rev. 1189 (2011). Regarding the Rehnquist Court, see generally Tinsley E. Yarbrough, The Rehnquist Court and the Constitution (2000); Craig M. Bradley, *Criminal Procedure in the Rehnquist Court: Has the Rehnquisition Begun?*, 62 Ind. L.J. 273 (1987); Robert H. Smith, *Uncoupling the "Centrist Bloc"—An Empirical Analysis of the Thesis of a Dominant, Moderate Bloc on the United States Supreme Court*, 62 Tenn. L. Rev. 1 (1994); Thomas W. Merrill, *The Making of the Second Rehnquist Court: A Preliminary Analysis*, 47 St. Louis U. L.J. 569 (2003); Stephen F. Smith, *The Rehnquist Court and Criminal Procedure*, 73 U. Colo. L. Rev. 1337 (2002); Carol

institutional philosophy or attitude regarding constitutional adjudication or, in the case of criminal procedure, criminal law jurisprudence. Moreover, certain small-group dynamics develop among the sitting justices, which can affect interpersonal relations and, ultimately, shape the work product. It is worthwhile, therefore, to be sensitive to the place of a Supreme Court opinion in the larger historical constitutional and institutional picture.

Lawyers tend to talk in general terms about the philosophical views of the "Warren Court," the "Burger Court," the "Rehnquist Court," and now the "Roberts Court," the shorthand titles for the Supreme Court, and the opinions decided by it, under the four most recent Chief Justices, Earl Warren (1953–1969), Warren Burger (1969–1986), William Rehnquist (1986–2005), and John Roberts (2005–Present).

As the footnote at the beginning of this subsection may suggest, countless books and articles have been written about the philosophies of the various Courts. As a generalization, the Warren Court used its judicial power to develop rules favorable to individuals, including those suspected of crime, *vis-à-vis* the government. In the context of criminal procedure, the Warren Court was responsible for most of the constitutional decisions that expanded the rights of persons suspected or accused of crime. Indeed, the "criminal justice revolution" — as it has often been called — was largely led by the Warren Court (or, more accurately, a majority of its members).[66] In contrast, more recent Courts — the Rehnquist and Roberts Courts, and somewhat less so, the Burger Court — favored the "crime control" model of criminal procedure,[67] which would grant legislatures and prosecutorial agencies considerable discretion in defining, investigating, and prosecuting crime.

S. Steiker, *Counter-Revolution in Constitutional Criminal Procedure? Two Audiences, Two Answers,* 94 Mich. L. Rev. 2466 (1996); Symposium: *Just Right?: Assessing the Rehnquist Court's Parting Words on Criminal Justice,* 94 Geo. L.J. 1319–1634 (2006); *A Symposium on the Legacy of the Rehnquist Court,* 74 Geo. Wash. L. Rev. 869, 956–1089 (2006) (four articles on criminal justice); Mark Tushnet, *Assessing Chief Justice William Rehnquist's Court,* 155 U. Pa. L. Rev. PENNumbra 1 (2007); Ronald F. Wright, *How the Supreme Court Delivers Fire and Ice to State Criminal Justice,* 59 Wash. & Lee L. Rev. 1429 (2002) (comparing Warren and Rehnquist courts). Regarding the Burger Court and a comparison of it to the Warren Court, see generally The Burger Years: Rights and Wrongs in the Supreme Court, 1969–1986 (Herman Schwartz ed., 1987); Albert W. Alschuler, *Failed Pragmatism: Reflections on the Burger Court,* 100 Harv. L. Rev. 1436 (1987); Peter Arenella, *Rethinking the Functions of Criminal Procedure: The Warren and Burger Courts' Competing Ideologies,* 72 Geo. L.J. 185 (1983); Jerold H. Israel, *Criminal Procedure, the Burger Court, and the Legacy of the Warren Court,* 75 Mich. L. Rev. 1319 (1977); Stephen A. Saltzburg, *The Flow and Ebb of Constitutional Criminal Procedure in the Warren and Burger Courts,* 69 Geo. L.J. 151 (1980); Louis Michael Seidman, *Factual Guilt and the Burger Court: An Examination of Continuity and Change in Criminal Procedure,* 80 Colum. L. Rev. 436 (1980); Robert Weisberg, *Criminal Procedure Doctrine: Some Versions of the Skeptical,* 76 J. Crim. L. & Criminology 832 (1985). For discussion of the Warren Court, see generally Francis A. Allen, *The Judicial Quest for Penal Justice: The Warren Court and the Criminal Cases,* 1975 U. Ill. L.F. 518; A. Kenneth Pye, *The Warren Court and Criminal Procedure,* 67 Mich. L. Rev. 249 (1968); Yale Kamisar, *The Warren Court and Criminal Justice: A Quarter-Century Retrospective,* 31 Tulsa L.J. 1 (1995); Symposium, *The Warren Court Criminal Justice Revolution: Reflections a Generation Later,* 3 Ohio St. J. Crim. L. 1–199 (2005). For statistical analyses of each Supreme Court term, including figures on voting alignments, see the annual study of the Supreme Court term, published in the first issue of each volume of the *Harvard Law Review* and the Statpack available at the Scotusblog, http://www.scotusblog.com/wp/?s=statpack.

66. For a summary of the "revolution" (or, failed revolution, according to the author), see Craig M. Bradley, The Failure of the Criminal Procedure Revolution 6–36 (1993).

67. *See* § 2.02[B], *infra.*

Some criminal procedure casebooks include a chart showing the dates on which individual Justices joined the Court. If your book has such a chart, look at it on occasion to see where specific cases fit in. If your book does not have such a chart, the following brief review may be helpful.

In theory, the Warren Court began in 1953 when President Dwight Eisenhower appointed Earl Warren as Chief Justice. However, the civil libertarian thrust of the Court took effect gradually as new appointments were made. Already on the Court in 1953, and sympathetic to the Chief Justice's views as they developed, was William Douglas, who was appointed in 1939 by President Franklin D. Roosevelt. After the Chief Justice was appointed, William Brennan (1956) and Potter Stewart (1958) joined the Court. Brennan was a major participant in the Warren Court decisions, and Stewart sometimes provided a crucial fifth vote.

The Warren Court reached its civil libertarian peak in the mid-1960s, after Presidents John F. Kennedy and Lyndon B. Johnson replaced outgoing members of the Court with: Arthur Goldberg (1962, by J.F.K.), who was himself replaced by Abe Fortas (1965, by L.B.J.); Byron White (1962, by J.F.K.); and Thurgood Marshall (1967, by L.B.J.). Of the replacements, only Justice White was often critical of Warren Court values.

The shift away from the Warren Court pro-libertarian philosophy was as gradual as its ascendancy. It began in 1969 with the election of Richard Nixon, who campaigned for office in part on the promise to nominate "law and order" justices.[68] President Nixon almost immediately filled two Court vacancies: Warren Burger (1969) and Harry Blackmun (1970), who replaced Chief Justice Warren and Justice Fortas respectively. He subsequently appointed two more Justices: William Rehnquist (1972) and Lewis Powell (1972), who replaced, respectively, frequent Warren Court dissenter John Harlan and (sometimes) civil liberties advocate Hugo Black. President Gerald Ford appointed John Stevens (1975) to replace Justice Douglas. In the context of criminal procedure, each of these changes in personnel resulted in a high court more disposed to crime control outcomes. However, over time, Justice Stevens became the Court's most consistent advocate of the displaced Warren Court values.

It was not until the 1980s that the shift away from Warren Court values became clearly evident. During this decade, Sandra Day O'Connor (1981), Antonin Scalia (1985), and Anthony Kennedy (1988) were appointed by President Ronald Reagan, replacing Justice Stewart, Chief Justice Burger,[69] and Justice Powell, respectively. With the appointment of Justice Kennedy, the balance of power definitively tipped in favor of the crime control model of criminal justice, and the Court increasingly cut back on the holdings of the Warren Court era.

The first-half of the 1990s saw the departure of the remaining members of the Warren Court. Justices Brennan (1990) and Marshall (1991), strong believers in Warren Court values, retired. President George H.W. Bush replaced them with David Souter and Clarence Thomas, respectively. In 1993, the last member of the Warren Court, Byron White, retired. President Bill Clinton appointed Ruth Bader Ginsburg as his replacement. Then, in 1994, Stephen Breyer replaced retiring Justice Blackmun. Speaking in generalizations, as there are many nuances to the justices' views that affect their votes differently across

---

68. Liva Baker, Miranda: Crime, Law and Politics 221–324 (1983).

69. Technically, Chief Justice Burger was replaced by Justice Rehnquist, who was elevated to Chief Justice. Justice Scalia filled Justice Rehnquist's old spot.

the expansive field of criminal procedure, the criminal justice opinions of Justice Souter (since retired), and Justices Ginsburg, and Breyer have frequently run counter to the pro-government positions that often prevailed in the Rehnquist Court;[70] in contrast, Justice Thomas has been a consistent advocate for crime control values. These changes in Court personnel in the early 1990s narrowed the spectrum of views on the Court (certainly so with regard to the civil libertarian side) while maintaining a narrow but sometimes decisive majority of justices on the "crime control" side of the line.

The Rehnquist Court era came to an end when the Chief Justice passed away following the end of the 2004–05 Supreme Court term. Justice O'Connor also announced her intention to retire that same summer. The 11 years between Justice Blackmun's retirement and the end of the Rehnquist Court marked the longest period in nearly two hundred years that the Court had not added a new justice. President George Bush thereafter appointed John Roberts as the new Chief Justice and, in due course, selected Samuel A. Alito Jr. to replace Justice O'Connor. And so, with the Court's 2005 term, the Roberts Court era began.

Given that Chief Justice Roberts can reasonably be expected to serve for at least twenty-five years, the "Roberts Court" will almost certainly, looking back thirty years from now, have taken twists and turns rather than being subject to a single monolithic description. In their first few terms, however, both Chief Justice Roberts and Justice Alito have shown a strong affinity for "crime control" values, resulting in even fewer victories for the defendant in criminal procedure cases than might have been expected had Justice O'Connor remained on the Court. Furthermore, Justice Roberts and Alito have followed their predecessors (Rehnquist and O'Connor) in not showing a proclivity to join the "originalist" arguments of Justices Scalia and Thomas that have sometimes led to majorities for the defendant's position in such areas as sentencing and the Confrontation Clause.

Justice Souter retired at the end of the 2008 term, allowing President Barack Obama his first opportunity to affect the Supreme Court's membership. Obama named Sonya Sotomayor, whose resume includes service as an Assistant District Attorney in New York City, as Souter's replacement. Then, at the end of the 2009 term, Justice Stevens retired, and President Obama named Solicitor General Elena Kagan to replace him. With her confirmation, for the first time in history, there are three female justices sitting on the Court simultaneously. Justice Sotomayor's and, to a somewhat lesser extent, Justice Kagan's views place them on the pro-civil-libertarian side of the spectrum.

In February of 2016, Justice Scalia suddenly passed away in the middle of the 2015 term. Political gridlock between President Obama and the Republicans who controlled Congress meant that no new justice was appointed until after President Donald Trump took office in 2017. In April of 2017, the Senate voted to confirm Neil Gorsuch, a former Tenth Circuit judge, to fill Justice Scalia's seat. Like the Justice that he replaced, Justice Gorsuch has an originalist judicial philosophy. Thus, although he is considered to be a "conservative" Justice, his originalist philosphy often leads him to a pro-civil-libertarian stance on some criminal procedure issues.

---

70. *See generally* Karen O'Connor & Barbara Palmer, *The Clinton Clones: Ginsburg, Breyer, and the Clinton Legacy*, 84 Judicature 262 (2001).

Chapter 2

Overarching Policy Issues in Criminal Procedure

The law does not develop in a philosophical or policy vacuum. Lawyers, students, and scholars must be sensitive to various overarching controversies affecting the field if they are to appreciate—and sensibly critique—the law of criminal procedure. At times, lawmakers expressly consider the issues discussed in this chapter in formulating criminal procedure doctrine; more often, however, these subjects silently animate lawmaking.

§ 2.01 Norms of the Criminal Process

The legitimacy of the United States system of criminal procedure depends on at least four sometimes overlapping, sometimes inconsistent, norms: (1) the accuracy of verdicts; (2) the fairness of the process itself; (3) the degree to which the justice system limits governmental power in relation to citizens ensnared in the criminal process; and (4) the efficiency of the process. These norms are considered in greater detail in this chapter, particularly in Sections 2.02 through 2.04.

Regarding accuracy, a perfectly accurate criminal process would result in no arrests of innocent persons or, somewhat less perfectly, innocent persons would be released prior to trial or, still less perfectly, as the result of acquittal at trial. Similarly, in an entirely accurate system, all guilty persons would be arrested and convicted. Any system that processes and evaluates information, of course, makes errors in evaluation. However, in light of what is at stake in the criminal law if errors are made—innocent persons are wrongly stigmatized by the community and lose their liberty or life as the result of unjust conviction and punishment, and guilty persons are freed, possibly to commit more crimes—a system that does not value accuracy cannot easily be characterized as legitimate.

A second way to measure the legitimacy of a criminal justice system is by determining how fairly it treats persons suspected of, or prosecuted for, alleged criminal activity. Although the "accuracy" and "fairness" norms sometimes overlap, they represent different and sometimes conflicting concerns, in part because the concept of fairness suggests that even guilty persons should be treated with care for their rights and human dignity. Of course, "fairness" and "human dignity" are imprecise concepts, so controversies abound in this realm. For example, does "fairness" require that defense lawyers be permitted to be present during police questioning, to assist their clients? Does it violate human dignity to use harsh methods (even torture) to gather information from persons accused of past, or suspected of future, acts of criminal terrorism? Is it unfair to deny a defendant the opportunity personally to confront and cross-examine his accuser when the accuser is a young child who claims the defendant sexually abused him?

A third goal of the American criminal justice system is to place sensible limits on the power of the government in its encounter with persons accused of crime. Sometimes this norm overlaps the earlier ones. For example, use of torture to secure a confession can result in inaccuracy (a false confession); and, at least until the attacks of September 11, 2001 and the Iraq War, it seemed a truism that torture is a blatant violation of the fairness norm.[1] But, the desire to promote limited government is sometimes an independent value. For example, a rule requiring the exclusion of evidence obtained by the police without a search warrant from a suspect's bedroom may result in a *less* accurate outcome (because the excluded evidence is reliable). One can also plausibly argue that it is unfair that "[t]he criminal is to go free because the constable has blundered."[2] Something more is involved, however, in enforcing a rule prohibiting the police from entering a bedroom without a warrant: it is the principle that explains the ratification of most of the provisions of the Bill of Rights, namely, that we are a political system that values individual rights and favors limited governmental power to interfere in the lives of its citizens. Therefore, according to this norm, the police should ordinarily obtain judicial approval (a search warrant) before they enter the private confines of a home.

Efficiency is a fourth norm. An inefficient system is wasteful of human and institutional resources. A system that is slow to reach an outcome can also undermine social protection by delaying the confinement and punishment of the guilty. It can also render more agonizing the experience of the innocent accused. Moreover, the provision of many procedural protections — e.g., counsel for indigents, trial by jury — are not inexpensive. On the other hand, the same grease that permits the wheels of justice to turn smoothly can sometimes undermine accuracy (e.g., if the system encourages the innocent to plead guilty) or occur at the arguable cost of fairness to the accused (e.g., by denying defendants the right to have a jury decide upon their guilt).

Readers would do well to consider whether the rules of criminal procedure, considered in this Text, further one or more of the preceding norms.

§ 2.02 Alternative Models of Criminal Justice[3]

[A] Overview

As is evident from the preceding chapter section, criminal procedural law is shaped by various overlapping, but sometimes conflicting, norms. Although society surely desires a reliable criminal justice system — one that accurately sorts out the innocent from the guilty — the criminal process is intended to vindicate other goals as well, such as

---

1. The authors *still* consider this to be so, but recent events demonstrate the point made above, namely, that "fairness" and "human dignity" — as well as what may be considered "sensible" limits on government — are not self-defining terms.

2. People v. Defore, 150 N.E. 585, 587 (N.Y. 1926) (opinion of Cardozo, J.)

3. *See generally* Herbert L. Packer, The Limits of the Criminal Sanction 149–246 (1968); Peter Arenella, *Rethinking the Functions of Criminal Procedure: The Warren and Burger Courts' Competing Ideologies*, 72 Geo. L.J. 185 (1983); Douglas Evan Beloof, *The Third Model of Criminal Process: The Victim Participation Model*, 1999 Utah L. Rev. 289; John Griffiths, *Ideology in Criminal Procedure or A Third "Model" of the Criminal Process*, 79 Yale L. J. 359 (1970); Kent Roach, *Four Models of the Criminal Process*, 89 J. Crim. L. & Criminology 671 (1999).

fair treatment of criminal suspects and racial, sexual, and economic equality in the justice system.[4] Vindication of the latter goals, however, may impair the efficiency of the criminal system, still another norm, so the matter of criminal justice goals comes down to setting priorities.

How have we — and should we — set priorities? Various scholars have sought to answer these questions by constructing models of an adversarial system of criminal justice that can account for the procedural rules that have developed and/or to suggest how a more sensible system might be formulated.

Professor Herbert Packer once identified two models of criminal procedure "that compete for priority in the operation of the criminal process."[5] He termed them the "Crime Control" (hereafter, CC) and "Due Process" (hereafter, DP) models of criminal justice. Packer's analysis has been criticized,[6] and alternative models of criminal justice have been suggested by other commentators.[7] Nonetheless, his articulation of the models has influenced thought in the field.

The models are summarized below. Although they are usually discussed as if they represent mutually exclusive visions, some commentators believe that with slight modifications of the goals, most of the differences disappear.[8] Nonetheless, the reader may find it useful to evaluate procedural law, as set out in the Text, in light of these models.

[B] Crime Control Model of Criminal Justice

The CC Model is founded on the principle that repression of crime is the most important domestic goal of government. The criminal sanction is "a positive guarantor of social freedom" and essential to the maintenance of "public order."[9] In light of the paramount significance of crime prevention, CC advocates place a premium on efficiency in the investigation and prosecution of alleged law violators.

How do we make the process efficient? First, informality is desirable. To the extent feasible, nonjudicial processes are preferable to formal, judicial ones. Great faith is placed in the expertise of police and prosecutors. "Most fact-finding in the crime control model is conducted by the police in the streets and station-houses, not by lawyers and judges

---

4. Susan R. Klein, *Enduring Principles and Current Crises in Constitutional Criminal Procedure*, 24 Law & Social Inquiry 533, 536 (1999).

5. Packer, Note 3, *supra*, at 153.

6. *E.g.*, Arenella, Note 3, *supra*, at 209–28; John Griffiths, *The Limits of Criminal Law Scholarship*, 79 Yale L.J. 1388 (1970).

7. *E.g.*, Arenella, Note 3, *supra*, at 213–28 (re-conceptualizing Packer's models); Beloof, Note 3, *supra* (advocating a "victim participation model"); Griffiths, Note 3, *supra* (advocating a "family" model of criminal justice premised on the view that rehabilitation and reintegration of an offender into society is desirable); Roach, Note 3, *supra* "describing punitive and non-punitive victims" rights models). For consideration of procedural systems in other countries, and discussion of what the United States might learn from these systems, *see* Mirjan Damaska, *Evidentiary Barriers to Conviction and Two Models of Criminal Procedure: A Comparative Study*, 121 U. Pa. L. Rev. 506 (1973); Daniel H. Foote, *The Benevolent Paternalism of Japanese Criminal Justice*, 80 Cal. L. Rev. 317 (1992); Richard S. Frase, *Comparative Criminal Justice as a Guide to American Law Reform: How Do the French Do It, How Can We Find Out, and Why Should We Care?*, 78 Cal. L. Rev. 542 (1990).

8. *See generally* Donald A. Dripps, *Beyond the Warren Court and Its Conservative Critics: Toward a Unified Theory of Constitutional Criminal Procedure*, 23 U. Mich. J.L. Ref. 591 (1990).

9. Packer, Note 3, *supra*, at 158.

in the courts."[10] Police officers are permitted substantial opportunity to function free of legal impediments (so-called "ceremonious rituals"[11]) — such as lawyers — as they investigate criminal activity, screen out the innocent, and "as expeditiously as possible, [secure] the conviction of the rest, with a minimum of occasions for challenge...."[12] Trials, with their formality, rigid rules of evidence, and adversarial conditions, are to be avoided whenever possible through guilty pleas.[13]

A second way to further efficiency is through uniformity. That is, if large numbers of cases are to be handled efficiently, "routine, stereotyped procedures are essential." According to Packer, the CC Model should look like "an assembly-line conveyor belt down which moves an endless stream of cases, never stopping."[14] Cases should not be taken off the belt unless informal procedures indicate that the suspect did not commit the offense.

Third, the CC Model functions on the premise that most suspects are factually guilty of the offense for which they are being prosecuted.[15] By assuming the factual guilt of a suspect, the CC advocate expresses confidence in the criminal justice system; and the presumption reinforces society's desire to promote efficiency without provoking accuracy concerns.

[C] Due Process Model of Criminal Justice

The values of the DP Model may be understood by contrasting them to the CC Model. First, DP advocates, while of course not discounting the desirability of preventing and punishing crime, believe in the liberal view of "the primacy of the individual and the complementary concept of limitation on official power."[16] Therefore, the DP model imposes significant restraints on government, especially on the police.

Second, advocates of the DP Model question the reliability of informal systems of criminal justice. Whereas the CC system pictures police officers as skilled investigators likely to ascertain the truth if obstacles are not placed in their way, the DP Model emphasizes the risks of human error and bias in informal investigative processes.[17] For the DP advocate, reliability is enhanced by a process involving early intervention of judges and lawyers — and, thus, of formality — in the justice system.

---

10. Roach, Note 3, *supra*, at 678.

11. Packer, Note 3, *supra*, at 159.

12. *Id.* at 160.

13. The "center of gravity [in the CC Model] ... lies in the early, administrative fact-finding stages." *Id.* at 162.

14. *Id.* at 160.

15. Alan M. Dershowitz, The Best Defense xxi (1982) (stating that two rules of "the justice game" are: (1) "[a]lmost all criminal defendants are in fact guilty"; and (2) "[a]ll defense lawyers, prosecutors and judges understand and believe" the first rule).

16. Packer, Note 3, *supra*, at 165.

17. *E.g.*, Saul M. Kassin, *On the Psychology of Confessions*, 60 Am. Psychologist 215 (2005) (summarizing recent research that demonstrates that police investigators not infrequently commit false-positive errors, therefore presuming innocent suspects guilty; and also showing that police officers in the interrogation room are not good at distinguishing between uncorroborated true and false confessions).

Third, while the CC Model is predicated on the assumed *factual* guilt of suspects, the DP system focuses on the doctrine of *legal* guilt. That is, a criminal suspect is not legally guilty of a crime unless and until the prosecutor proves the defendant's guilt beyond a reasonable doubt in the courtroom, through the adversarial process, on the basis of legally admissible evidence, or the defendant concedes it through a guilty plea in a carefully monitored formal courtroom process.[18] The legal presumption of innocence, like the CC Model's belief in the factual guilt of the suspect, represents a mood, a way of thinking about criminal cases: by thinking of suspects as innocent persons, DP Model advocates believe that we are more apt to appreciate the value of setting limits on governmental power ("How would I, an innocent person, want to be treated?"). Moreover, the presumption of innocence decreases the likelihood of conviction of innocent persons, although it increases the possibility that factually guilty persons will escape conviction.

Fourth, the models differ in their evaluation of the importance of redressing economic inequality in the criminal justice system. Adherents of the DP Model assert that "[t]here can be no equal justice where the kind of trial a man gets depends on the amount of money he has."[19] Therefore, to the extent possible, they seek to place indigent individuals in the same position as more wealthy suspects. In contrast, in the efficiency-driven CC system, an indigent is entitled to an adequate, but not necessarily equal, opportunity to demonstrate his factual innocence. Likewise, the DP model would devise rules to reduce the likelihood and effects of other forms of inequality, such as racial discrimination. This is not an express priority of the CC Model.

Finally, the judiciary has a more active role to play in the DP Model than in the CC system, which favors legislative supremacy. Judicial activism is appropriate in the DP Model because its advocates believe that the "central purpose of our written Constitution, and more specifically of its unique creation of a life-tenured federal judiciary, [is] to ensure that certain rights [i.e., those included in the Bill of Rights] are firmly secured *against* possible oppression by the Federal or State Governments."[20]

Thus, all else being equal, a system modeled on DP values will be less efficient, more inclined to favor an active judiciary *vis-à-vis* the legislature, more apt to protect individual liberties, more interested in bringing about equality in the justice system, less likely to convict innocent persons, and more likely to allow the guilty to go free, than one based on CC values.

---

18. Packer's factual/legal guilt distinction is too simplistic. Packer assumes that factual guilt is merely an empirical question: did the suspect (and not some unidentified person) commit the acts that constitute the offense, e.g., did the accused kill/rob/rape the victim? This is a matter that may, indeed, often be provable through informal investigatory processes. The trial process, then, appears accordingly to consist, simply, of rules for proving factual guilt to a high degree of certainty. But factual guilt is more than an empirical judgment: to be *guilty* of a *crime*—and not simply to have done a harmful act—a person must commit the *actus reus* of an offense with the statutorily requisite degree of moral culpability and accountability. In short, a *normative* judgment must often (some would say, always) be made before it may properly be said that a person is factually guilty of a crime. Quite simply, even factual guilt *cannot* be determined informally. *See* Arenella, Note 3, *supra*, at 214.

19. Griffin v. Illinois, 351 U.S. 12, 19 (1956) (plurality opinion).

20. Florida v. Meyers, 466 U.S. 380, 385 (1984) (Stevens, J., dissenting) (emphasis added).

§ 2.03 The Role of "Truth" in the Criminal Justice System[21]

Everyone agrees that truth—reliable trial outcomes, in which the guilty are convicted and the innocent are acquitted—is a critical goal of any legitimate criminal justice system. All else being equal, the criminal process should advance, rather than retard, the truth-seeking process.

Nonetheless, controversies abound in this field. First, there is disagreement regarding the best methods for enhancing reliability. For example, as noted in § 2.02, some people believe that the formalities of the adjudicatory process diminish reliability, whereas others believe that formality promotes truth-finding better than the more informal fact-finding processes of the police.

A second and vital question of policy—indeed, one implicating fundamental moral values—is whether erroneous convictions and erroneous acquittals are equally undesirable. That is, once we accept that no human system of fact-adjudication is error-free, one must determine whether a justice system should be indifferent to the direction of the error.

The civil law uses a "guilt-innocence neutral"[22] approach to error allocation. In contrast, the traditional view of American criminal justice, reflected by the constitutional presumption of innocence and by other doctrines such as the constitutional rule against double jeopardy (being tried twice for the same offense) and privilege against compulsory self-incrimination, is that an "innocence-weighted" approach is preferable: "it is far worse to convict an innocent man than to let a guilty man go free."[23] Blackstone went so far as to claim that "the law holds than it is better that ten guilty persons escape, than that one innocent suffer."[24] In short, there is particular evil in infliction of undeserved pain; and there may also be utilitarian reasons for the special protection of the innocent, in that "the moral force of the criminal law [is] diluted by a [legal process] that leaves people in doubt whether innocent men are being condemned."[25] According to this view, a process that devises an even playing field is, in fact, improperly balanced; rather, the law should place a heavy thumb "on the defendant's side of the scales of justice."[26]

---

21. *See generally* William T. Pizzi, Trials Without Truth (1999); Albert W. Alschuler, *The Search for Truth Continued, The Privilege Retained: A Response to Judge Frankel*, 54 U. Colo. L. Rev. 67 (1982); William J. Brennan, Jr., *The Criminal Prosecution: Sporting Event or Quest for Truth?*, 1963 Wash. U. L.Q. 279; Marvin E. Frankel, *The Search for Truth: An Umpireal View*, 123 U. Pa. L. Rev. 1031 (1975); Monroe H. Freedman, *Judge Frankel's Search for Truth*, 123 U. Pa. L. Rev. 1060 (1975); Henry J. Friendly, *Is Innocence Irrelevant? Collateral Attack on Criminal Judgments*, 38 U. Chi. L. Rev. 142 (1970); Gary Goodpaster, *On the Theory of American Adversary Criminal Trial*, 78 J. Crim. L. & Criminology 118 (1987); Klein, Note 4, *supra*; A. Kenneth Pye, *The Role of Counsel in the Suppression of Truth*, 1978 Duke L.J. 921; Tom Stacy, *The Search for the Truth in Constitutional Criminal Procedure*, 91 Colum. L. Rev. 1369 (1991); Thomas Weigend, *Criminal Procedure: Comparative Aspects* in 1 Encyclopedia of Crime and Justice 444 (Joshua Dressler, ed., 2d. ed. 2002).

22. Stacy, Note 21, *supra*, at 1407.

23. In re Winship, 397 U.S. 358, 372 (1970) (Harlan, J., concurring).

24. 4 William Blackstone, Commentaries on the Laws of England 358 (1765).

25. In re Winship, 397 U.S. at 364.

26. Barbara D. Underwood, *The Thumb on the Scales of Justice: Burdens of Persuasion in Criminal Cases*, 86 Yale L.J. 1299 (1977).

This position may be less in vogue today than in centuries past.[27] From a purely retributive perspective, it can be claimed that the two forms of error are equally wrong: it is wrong to punish an innocent person, but it is equally unjust for a guilty person to avoid paying his debt to society. From a utilitarian viewpoint, a system of rules that makes it easier for guilty people to go free may send a dangerous message to would-be offenders; and the wrongful release of particularly dangerous individuals may result in more societal pain than is imposed by the infliction of punishment on an equal number of innocent persons.[28]

Professor and Judge Richard Posner contends that "unless the resources devoted to determining guilt and innocence are increased, the only way to reduce the probability of convicting the innocent is to reduce the probability of convicting the guilty as well."[29] That is, with finite resources, every dollar spent to protect the innocent is money not spent to convict the guilty. If one starts from the assumption that most people charged with crime are factually guilty, the reasoning continues, concern for protecting innocence will result in a less reliable outcome than a process that is evenly balanced. Indeed, if one accepts Posner's view, a guilt-weighted system is preferable: the principle that we should give the fox — under this view, most persons suspected of crime — a chance of surviving the hunt "makes for good sports, but in a criminal investigation we should be seeking truth rather than entertainment."[30]

This debate brings us close to a third serious controversy: *Is* the truth of a defendant's guilt or innocence the only value that should be considered in the criminal justice system? Some commentators suggest as much: subordination of the truth to *any* other value is indefensible; when the truth is not discovered, or its implications ignored, the system necessarily fails in its mission. One scholar has argued that, properly interpreted, the constitutional provisions relating to criminal procedure exist only "to protect the innocent. The guilty, in general, receive . . . protection only as an incidental and unavoidable byproduct of protecting the innocent *because* of their innocence."[31] It follows from this view, for example, that a rule of law that requires the exclusion at trial of trustworthy evidence because it was illegally secured by the police is an unwise rule.

The contrary position is that the criminal justice system should not focus exclusively on the truth-finding process. As one English court put it, "[t]ruth, like all other good things, may be loved unwisely — may be pursued too keenly — may cost too much."[32] From this perspective, "truth must find its place in the context of a larger concern to do justice."[33] "Justice" in this context means more than, simply, a reliable result in a particular prosecution. Under this view, "the truth" is too expensive if it is obtained by governmental use of torture or violation of other important human rights. Thus, it is preferable to allow a potentially guilty party to go free — out of respect for the accused's human rights, concern about the moral integrity of the justice system, or as a means of deterring

---

27. *See especially* Stacy, Note 21, *supra* (contending that the Supreme Court's emerging view is that wrongful acquittals are as bad as wrongful convictions).

28. For debate on this subject, *see* Jeffrey Reiman & Ernest van den Haag, *On the Common Saying that it is Better that Ten Guilty Persons Escape than that One Innocent Suffer: Pro and Con*, 7 Soc. Phil. & Policy, Spring, 1990, at 226.

29. Richard A. Posner, The Problems of Jurisprudence 216 (1990).

30. Joseph D. Grano, *Selling the Idea to Tell the Truth: The Professional Interrogator and Modern Confessions Law*, 84 Mich. L. Rev. 662, 677 (1986).

31. Akhil Reed Amar, The Constitution and Criminal Procedure: First Principles 154 "1997).

32. Pearse v. Pearse, 63 Eng. Rep. 957, 970 (1846).

33. Law Reform Commission of Canada, Our Criminal Procedure (Report 32) 10 (1988).

future official abuses — than to use the tainted evidence to obtain a conviction.[34] In particular in regard to the constitutional law of criminal procedure, many would agree that "the pursuit of truth . . . is not the only, or even, perhaps, the most important, principle at work. . . ."[35]

§ 2.04 Accusatorial Versus Inquisitorial Systems of Justice[36]

Judges often state that "ours is an accusatorial and not an inquisitorial system"[37] of criminal justice. But, is it? And, more significantly for present purposes, *should* it be accusatorial?

In its pure form, an accusatorial system of criminal justice is one founded on the belief that "to respect the inviolability of the human personality, . . . the government seeking to punish an individual [must] produce the evidence against him by its own independent labors."[38] The government must "shoulder the entire load."[39] It may not convict a person by obtaining evidence of guilt involuntarily from the accused. As one scholar has explained, the defendant in the accusatorial system is treated "*as if* he is innocent and need lend no aid to those who would convict him."[40]

At trial, the accusatorial system is founded on the adversarial theory of trial practice. The adversarial system is "a regulated storytelling contest between champions of competing, interpretive stories."[41] That is, the parties in dispute, normally represented by attorneys, present their conflicting versions of the events to a passive and impartial decisionmaker.

---

34. *See* Sawyer v. Whitley, 505 U.S. 333, 356 (1992) (Blackmun, J., concurring in the judgment) (criticizing the Court's "single-minded focus" on truth-finding, and stating that "[t]he accusatorial system of justice adopted by the Founders affords a defendant certain process-based protections that do not have accuracy of truth-finding as their primary goal"); *see also* Rumsfeld v. Padilla, 542 U.S. 426, 465 (2004) (dissenting opinion) (whether information obtained through normal techniques "is more or less reliable than that acquired by more extreme forms of torture is of no consequence. For if this Nation is to remain true to the ideals symbolized by its flag, it must not wield the tools of tyrants even to resist an assault by the forces of tyranny").

35. Klein, Note 4, *supra*, at 534.

36. *See generally* Miriam Damaska, *Adversary System*, in 1 Encyclopedia of Crime and Justice (Joshua Dressler ed., 2d ed. 2002); Abraham S. Goldstein, *Reflections on Two Models: Inquisitorial Themes in American Criminal Procedure*, 26 Stan. L. Rev. 1009 (1974); Abraham S. Goldstein & Martin Marcus, *The Myth of Judicial Supervision in Three "Inquisitorial" Systems: France, Italy, and Germany*, 87 Yale L.J. 240 (1977); Goodpaster, Note 21, *supra*; John H. Langbein & Lloyd L. Weinreb, *Continental Criminal Procedure: "Myth" and Reality*, 87 Yale L.J. 1549 (1978); Myron Moskovitz, *The O.J. Inquisition: A United States Encounter With Continental Criminal Justice*, 28 Vand. J. Transnat'l L. 1121 (1995); Gregory W. O'Reilly, *England Limits the Right to Silence and Moves Towards an Inquisitorial System of Justice*, 85 J. Crim. L. & Criminology 402 (1994); Weigend, Note 21, *supra*.

37. Rogers v. Richmond, 365 U.S. 534, 541 (1961).

38. Miranda v. Arizona, 384 U.S. 436, 460 (1966).

39. *Id.* (quoting 8 Wigmore, Evidence 317 (McNaughton rev. 1961)).

40. Goldstein, Note 36, *supra*, at 1017.

41. Goodpaster, Note 21, *supra*, at 120.

In contrast, an inquisitorial system in its most extreme form permits the government to obtain evidence of a defendant's guilt through the "simple expedient of compelling it"[42] from the accused party, such as by coercive interrogation or, more reliably, by requiring a suspect to furnish his DNA, blood, or fingerprints. During the trial, the judge (as inquisitor), conducts the factual and legal investigation himself, rather than leaving the matter to attorneys to present the facts in a competing manner. The trial is an investigation rather than a competition, and the judge is the lead investigator rather than the referee. In this system, the judge may also compel the defendant to be a witness against himself.

Sloganeering aside, it is not true that the American system of criminal justice is purely accusatorial in character, just as few, if any, countries on the European continent today perfectly fit the inquisitorial mold. Indeed, the Supreme Court has stated that "[o]ur system of justice is, and has always been, an inquisitorial one at the investigatory stage . . ."[43] Although this is surely an overstatement as well, it is true that the government is *not* required to "shoulder the entire load" to convict a suspect. For example, a suspect may constitutionally be compelled to participate in a lineup, to be fingerprinted, and to have his blood extracted from his veins against his will,[44] all of which procedures may assist in his conviction and punishment. On the other hand, the Supreme Court has sometimes taken steps to "even the playing field" in the police station (in accordance with an adversarial model), such as by allowing defense lawyers to be present during post-indictment lineups, and to permit suspects to request the assistance of counsel during police interrogations.[45]

If the investigatory phase contains inquisitorial features, the adjudicatory phase of the criminal justice system—with the adversarial process fully in play, and the recognized Fifth Amendment right of a defendant not to be "compelled in any criminal case to be a witness against himself"—is mostly accusatorial in nature. But, even here, some non-accusatorial features may be found, such as the rule that the government may require a defendant to notify the prosecutor regarding his intended trial defenses,[46] a rule that makes it easier for the government to prepare and win its case.

The critical question is whether the justice system should be more (or less) accusatorial than it presently is. To the extent that truth-production is the goal of the criminal process, some have argued that the adversarial trial system is appropriate because "truth is best discovered by powerful statements on both sides of the question."[47] Only this way, it is asserted, will an arbiter avoid the tendency to judge a controversy too swiftly.

Other commentators claim that the adversarial process is not conducive to a reliable verdict.[48] They would agree with the view of one jurist who complained that the adversary process achieves truth "only as a convenience, a byproduct, or an accidental

---

42. Miranda v. Arizona, 384 U.S. at 460.

43. McNeil v. Wisconsin, 501 U.S. 171, 181 n.2 (1991).

44. *See* § 23.04[D][1], *infra.*

45. *See* §§ 24.04 (custodial interrogations) and 26.02 (post-indictment lineups), *infra.*

46. *See* 2 Joshua Dressler & Alan C. Michaels, Understanding Criminal Procedure § 7.08 (4th ed. 2006).

47. United States v. Cronic, 466 U.S. 648, 655 (1984) (quoting Lord Eldon in Kaufman, *Does the Judge Have a Right to Qualified Counsel?*, 61 A.B.A. J. 569, 569 (1975) (internal quotation marks omitted)).

48. *See* Goodpaster, Note 21, *supra*, at 121–22.

approximation."[49] If what we want is the truth, they assert, the judge should take a more active role at trial, and there should be no bar to the production of reliable evidence, including the defendant's own trial testimony, simply because it was obtained involuntarily from the accused.

An alternative defense of the adversary system, one that is particularly aimed at the pretrial investigatory phase, is that such a system places a needed protective barrier between the accused, a potentially innocent person, and the far more powerful government. In this context, an observation by the Supreme Court may be relevant:

> We have learned the lesson of history, ancient and modern, that a system of criminal law enforcement which comes to depend on the "confession" [and other evidence secured from the accused] will, in the long run, be less reliable and more subject to abuses than a system which depends on extrinsic evidence independently secured through skillful investigation.[50]

However, even if the accusatorial system can be justified on this ground, the question remains whether more truth-enhancing techniques can safely be permitted in the adversarial system.

§ 2.05 Race, Gender, and Economic Class in the Law[51]

Issues related to race, gender, and economic class (and, less often, sexual orientation[52]) are very often at the center of attention in criminal procedure. For example, a rich person can hire an attorney and, if convicted, pay to file an appeal. An indigent cannot afford a private attorney or to pay court filing costs. Therefore, courts and legislatures must determine *whether* (and, if so, *how*) to ensure that indigent defendants obtain access to the criminal process on the same basis as non-indigent persons, and obtain representation of similar quality and energy as that which can be secured by a wealthy individual.[53]

Gender issues also arise, such as whether legislatures should be allowed to permit women to seek release from jury duty on more lenient grounds than are available to

---

49. Frankel, Note 21, *supra*, at 1037.

50. Escobedo v. Illinois, 378 U.S. 478, 488–89 (1964) (footnotes omitted).

51. *See generally* David Cole, No Equal Justice (1999); Randall Kennedy, Race, Crime and the Law (1997); Feminist Legal Theory: Readings in Law & Gender (Katherine T. Bartlett & Rosanne Kennedy, eds. 1991); Richard Delgado & Jean Stefancic, *Critical Race Theory: An Annotated Bibliography*, 79 Va. L. Rev. 461 (1993); Symposium, *Racial Blindsight and Criminal Justice*, 5 Ohio St. J. Crim. L. 1–159 (2007).

52. E.g., David Alan Sklansky, *"One Train May Hide Another": Katz, Stonewall, and the Secret Subtext of Criminal Procedure*, 41 U.C. Davis L. Rev. 875 (2008) (arguing that a largely forgotten achievement of one of the most important Fourth Amendment cases, *Katz v. United States*, discussed fully in Chapter 6, *infra*, is that it helped restrict the common practice of governmental spying on men in toilet stalls to catch homosexuals).

53. *See generally* Chapter 28, *infra*, and 2 Dressler & Michaels, Note 46, *supra*, at chapter 9 (discussing the risk that innocent indigents, represented by harried lawyers, may be compelled to plead guilty).

males,[54] and whether lawyers should be permitted to exclude prospective jurors solely on the basis of a person's sex.[55]

Perhaps most tragically of all, racism has long permeated the criminal justice system on many levels. Studies have shown, for example, that minority youths are treated more harshly than non-minority youths in the juvenile justice system,[56] jurors are influenced by the race of defendants in criminal cases;[57] and there is conceded evidence of so-called "racial profiling," in which police officers stop, question, and often search African-Americans (and other minorities) and their automobiles based on racial stereotypes.[58] And, the complexity of the profiling issue has grown in light of the September 11 attacks on the United States: for example, was it inappropriate racial profiling or sensible law enforcement to single out Middle-Eastern-looking persons for special searches and questioning at airports and elsewhere in the days and months following the attacks?[59]

---

54. Taylor v. Louisiana, 419 U.S. 522 (1975) (holding that a statute permitting women, but not men, to file a written declaration of their desire not to be subject to jury service violated the Sixth Amendment right of a defendant to a jury pool that is a representative cross-section of the community).

55. J.E.B. v. Alabama ex rel. T.B. 511 U.S. 127 (1994) (holding that exercise of peremptory challenges based solely on gender violates the Equal Protection Clause of the Fourteenth Amendment; therefore, a party's efforts to remove male jurors in a child custody and paternity action cannot properly be based on the assumption that men (or women) will decide such cases solely on the basis of their sex); see 2 Dressler & Michaels, Note 46, supra, at chapter 10.

56. Fox Butterfield, *Racial Disparities Seen as Pervasive in Juvenile Justice*, New York Times, April 26, 2000, at A1 (reporting on findings compiled by the Department of Justice and six national foundations).

57. Samuel R. Sommers & Phoebe C. Ellsworth, *Race in the Courtroom: Perceptions of Guilt and Dispositional Attributions*, 26 Personality & Soc. Psych. Bulletin 1367 (2000) (among the findings is that in cases in which race was not a salient factor, white jurors rated African-American defendants more guilty, aggressive, and violent than they did white defendants).

58. *E.g.*, State v. Soto, 734 A.2d 350 (N.J. Super. 1996) (citing statistical evidence that New Jersey State Police engaged in racial discrimination in its enforcement of traffic laws); Iver Peterson, *Whitman Concedes Troopers Used Race in Stopping Drivers*, New York Times, April 21, 1999, at A1 (the Governor of New Jersey conceded that state troopers singled out African-American and Hispanic motorists on the highway for stops, and then searched their vehicles three times more often than in the case of white motorists); Albert J. Meehan & Michael C. Ponder, *Race and Place: The Ecology of Racial Profiling African American Motorists*, 19 Justice Q. 399 (2002) (finding that African-Americans are subject to disproportionate surveillance and detentions by police when driving through white areas, a finding not explained by any higher criminality rates among African-Americans); see also Bureau of Justice Statistics, *Special Report: Contacts between Police and the Public, 2005* (April 2007, NCJ 215243) (reporting that, in year 2005, "white, black, and Hispanic drivers were stopped by police at similar rates," but that "blacks and Hispanics were more likely than whites to be searched by police"; the report indicates that (the apparent disparities documented in this report . . . might be explained by countless other factors [than treating people "differently along demographic lines"]. *See generally* David A. Harris, Problems in Injustice: Why Racial Profiling Cannot Work (2002); David A. Harris, *"Driving While Black" and All Other Traffic Offenses: The Supreme Court and Pretextual Traffic Stops*, 87 J. Crim. L. & Criminology 544 (1997); Tracey Maclin, *Race and the Fourth Amendment*, 51 Vand. L. Rev. 333 (1998); David A. Sklansky, *Traffic Stops, Minority Motorists, and the Future of the Fourth Amendment*, 1997 Sup. Ct. Rev. 271. *See also* §§ 2.07[B], 8.02[F], and 17.03[B][5], *infra*.

59. *Compare* Sherry F. Colb, *Profiling With Apologies*, 1 Ohio St. J. Crim. L. 611 (2004) (defending some law enforcement profiling in the post-9/11 era) *with* Sharon L. Davies, *Profiling Terror*, 1 Ohio St. J. Crim. L. 45 (2003) (critiquing arguments offered by some scholars in favor of some forms of "ethnic profiling").

Ultimately, legislators, courts and federal and local law enforcement agencies have struggled to determine how to deal with these sensitive issues.

But even as courts, lawyers, and scholars seek to find ways to develop a more race- and gender-blind criminal justice system, other commentators believe that, in some regards, the law should take race and gender *more* into account. For example, in determining what conduct may be expected of a "reasonable person" in a confrontation with a police officer, Professor Tracey Maclin has argued that "the dynamics surrounding an encounter between a police officer and a black male are quite different from those that surround an encounter between an officer and the so-called average, reasonable person."[60] If this is correct, the issue arises whether the "reasonable person" standard should be race- and gender-specific, rather than race- and gender-neutral.[61]

Issues of race, gender, economic status call on society—and lawyers—to ask difficult and sensitive questions. Because these matters affect the contours of the law, and the way it is enforced, they should be kept in mind.

§ 2.06 Who Should Devise the Rules of Criminal Procedure?[62]

The United States Supreme Court unabashedly took the leading role in formulating rules of criminal justice during the 1950s, continuing through the early 1970s. In the last three decades, however, the Court has been far more reluctant to formulate new procedural rules, particularly for the police, thereby leaving many matters of criminal procedure to legislative bodies or, at least, to state courts for resolution.

Which approach is better? That is, should the judiciary, or should some other institution, formulate criminal procedural rules? As noted earlier,[63] advocates of the so-called Due Process Model of criminal justice generally favor an active judiciary in formulating criminal procedure law. Advocates of a strong judicial role consider it unrealistic to expect legislatures to develop rules limiting police and prosecutorial powers and, worse, they fear that any legislative solution would be shaped more by politics than thoughtful reform. When issues of individual rights are implicated, legislative dominance is apt to result in subordination of the rights of individuals accused of crime. Courts—especially life-tenured federal judges—are better equipped to dispassionately develop rules of criminal procedure.

In contrast, advocates of the Crime Control Model favor fewer rules and, where rules are required, believe they should be formulated by the police and local legislative

---

60. Tracey Maclin, *"Black and Blue Encounters" (Some Preliminary Thoughts About Fourth Amendment Seizures: Should Race Matter?*, 26 Val. U. L. Rev. 243, 250 (1991); *see also* Tracey Maclin, *Terry v. Ohio's Fourth Amendment Legacy: Black Men and Police Discretion*, 72 St. John's L. Rev. 1271 (1998).

61. *See* § 17.03[B][5], *infra.*

62. *See generally* Craig M. Bradley, The Failure of the Criminal Procedure Revolution 38–94 (1993); Anthony G. Amsterdam, *The Supreme Court and the Rights of Suspects in Criminal Cases*, 45 N.Y.U. L. Rev. 785 (1970); Dripps, Note 8, *supra*; Henry J. Friendly, *The Bill of Rights as a Code of Criminal Procedure*, 53 Cal. L. Rev. 929 (1965).

63. *See* § 2.02[C], *supra.*

bodies, which are better equipped to evaluate local needs. Moreover, some commentators prefer a legislative solution precisely because, unlike federal judges, legislators are elected by their constituents: police powers and limitations should be developed through the democratic process. Additionally, some courts and scholars advocate a limited federal judicial role because, in the words of Justice Louis Brandeis, "[i]t is one of the happy incidents of the federal system that a single courageous state may, if its citizens choose, serve as a laboratory"[64] that experiments on ways to improve the justice system. In contrast, a Supreme Court decision based on the Constitution necessarily announces a national rule of criminal procedure, which inevitably stifles local ingenuity.[65]

However one resolves the preceding debate, there is a pragmatic point that merits attention. Most conflicts between the police and private individuals never reach the courts, much less can be resolved by the Supreme Court. Thus, although Supreme Court pronouncements may be valuable because "they have vast mystical significance" and "state our aspirations,"[66] society cannot rely on the high court to regulate the activities of the police, prosecutors, and courts of the 50 states. As Professor Anthony Amsterdam ruefully observed four decades ago, as a practical matter, the hard work "must be done . . . by local legislators, executives, the police command structure and citizens in their communities. In light of past performance—or, rather, nonperformance—by all of these persons, this may seem a vain hope."[67]

§ 2.07 Formulating the Rules of Criminal Procedure: Some Overarching Controversies

[A] Bright-Line Rules versus Case-by-Case Adjudication[68]

An ongoing and critically important issue in criminal procedure is this: Should courts (and other lawmaking institutions) develop bright-line rules of criminal procedure, or should they formulate "blurry line" rules—general standards—the implementation of which requires case-by-case adjudication?

Both types of rules abound in the criminal law. For example, in police interrogation law, the Supreme Court has held that, pursuant to the Due Process Clause, a statement

---

64. New State Ice Co. v. Liebmann, 285 U.S. 262, 311 (1932) (dissenting opinion).

65. Friendly, Note 62, *supra*, at 954–55.

66. Amsterdam, Note 62, *supra*, at 793.

67. *Id.* at 810.

68. *See generally* Albert W. Alschuler, *Bright Line Fever and the Fourth Amendment*, 45 U. Pitt. L. Rev. 227 (1984); Craig M. Bradley, *Two Models of the Fourth Amendment*, 83 Mich. L. Rev. 1468 (1985); Edwin J. Butterfoss, *Bright Line Breaking Point: Embracing Justice Scalia's Call for the Supreme Court to Abandon an Unreasonable Approach to Fourth Amendment Search and Seizure Law*, 82 Tulane L. Rev. 77 (2007); Joseph D. Grano, *Miranda v. Arizona and the Legal Mind: Formalism's Triumph Over Substance and Reason*, 24 Am. Crim. L. Rev. 243 (1986); Wayne R. LaFave, *Being Frank About the Fourth: On Allen's "Process of 'Factualization' in the Search and Seizure Cases"*, 85 Mich. L. Rev. 427 (1986); Wayne R. LaFave, *The Fourth Amendment in an Imperfect World: On Drawing "Bright Lines" and "Good Faith"*, 43 U. Pitt. L. Rev. 307 (1982); Wayne R. LaFave, *"Case-by-Case Adjudication" Versus "Standardized Procedures": The Robinson Dilemma*, 1974 Sup. Ct. Rev. 127.

obtained from a suspect by means of police coercion, i.e., obtained involuntarily, is inadmissible at the suspect's criminal trial.[69] However, the voluntariness of a confession is assessed from the totality of the circumstances. There is "no talismanic definition of 'voluntariness'"[70]: the court looks at all of the circumstances surrounding the confession (e.g., the length of detention, the physical conditions in the interrogation room, the interrogation techniques used, the age and mental state of the suspect, etc.) in order to determine whether the statement was freely given. Under a totality-of-the-circumstances standard, "everything [is] relevant but nothing [is] determinative."[71] In short, there is no bright-line rule.

On the other hand, the Supreme Court has also announced bright-line interrogation rules. The so-called "*Miranda*[72] rule" is bright-line in nature, in that any statement obtained during custodial interrogation is inadmissible against the speaker during the government's case-in-chief, unless the police initially informed the suspect of certain specified constitutional rights. Subject to certain exceptions, this rule is absolute: in the absence of the warnings, *any and all* statements are inadmissible, *regardless* of whether the suspect was aware of his rights, and *regardless* of how the statement was secured.

Fourth Amendment jurisprudence, as well, contains both types of rules. For example, when the police arrest an occupant of a home, they may search the "area 'within [the arrestee's] immediate control'" — the so-called grabbing area — without a search warrant.[73] The quoted language states a blurry-line rule requiring case-by-case adjudication, because the size of the grabbing area depends on the particular circumstances of the case, including the nature and contents of the room in which the arrest occurs, and the dexterity of the arrestee.[74] In contrast, when a police officer makes a custodial arrest, he may *always* search the arrestee for weapons and evidence, even if the officer has no reason to believe he will find any.[75] This latter rule is bright-line.

Which approach to rule-making is preferable? Advocates of case-by-case adjudication argue that their approach is more apt to lead to the "correct" result, i.e., to the result that is most consistent with the underlying justification for the rule. They contend that bright-line rules can do no more than be right much of the time, whereas the goal of case-by-case adjudication is to be correct all of the time. For example, the Supreme Court has frequently expressed a preference for police officers to secure warrants before they conduct searches, in order to protect citizens' privacy concerns.[76] The justification for *warrantless* searches incident to arrests, notwithstanding this preference, is to protect an arresting officer's safety by letting him look for weapons that an arrestee might secure, and to prevent destruction of any criminal evidence in the arrestee's proximity. The grabbing-area rule, therefore, fits this justification by allowing the police to search the

---

69. *See generally* Chapter 22, *infra.*

70. Schneckloth v. Bustamonte, 412 U.S. 218, 224 (1973).

71. Grano, Note 68, *supra*, at 243.

72. Miranda v. Arizona, 384 U.S. 436 (1966). *See generally* Chapter 24, *infra.*

73. Chimel v. California, 395 U.S. 752 (1969). *See* § 12.03, *infra.*

74. *See also* Missouri v. McNeely, 133 S. Ct. 1552, 1559, 1559 n.3 (2013) (stating that "[t]o determine whether a law enforcement officer faced an emergency that justified acting without a warrant, this Court looks to the totality of circumstances"; and "the general exigency exception [to the warrant requirement], which asks whether an emergency existed that justified a warrantless search, naturally calls for case-specific inquiry").

75. *See* § 12.04, *infra.*

76. *See* § 10.01, *infra.*

area within the suspect's physical control, but to go no further. The rule, if you will, fits like a glove. However, if that principle is converted to a bright-line rule (for example, the right to search all of the premises where the arrest occurred), the police will be permitted to conduct warrantless searches when the need to act in the absence of a search warrant is often lacking.[77] The rule would now fit more like a hand-me-down.

Advocates of bright lines point to the fact that law enforcement officers must make split-second constitutional determinations. Therefore, they contend, "[a] single, familiar standard is essential to guide police officers, who have only limited time and expertise to reflect on and balance the social and individual interests involved in the specific circumstances they confront."[78] Put another way, those who enforce the law need clear guidance, rather than rules that are "qualified by all sorts of ifs, ands, and buts [that] requir[e] the drawing of subtle nuances and hairline distinctions."[79]

Professor Anthony Amsterdam has reasoned that although a blurry-line rule (case-by-case adjudication) may be "splendid in its flexibility," it is apt to be "awful in its unintelligibility, unadministrability, and . . . general ooziness."[80] Therefore, the argument proceeds, it is preferable to have a clear rule that can be obeyed nearly all of the time, even if it will lead to a correct result in, perhaps, only 90 percent of the cases, than it is to implement *unclear* rules that should lead to the correct result *all* of the time, but which well-intentioned officers are able to apply correctly in only 75 percent of the cases.[81]

It may not be the case, however, that police officers implement bright-line rules better than they do non-bright-line ones.[82] Moreover, even assuming their virtue, do bright-line rules remain bright? Justice William Rehnquist has observed that lawyers are "trained to attack 'bright lines' the way hounds attack foxes."[83] Lawyers want rules to be "responsive to every relevant shading of every relevant variation of every relevant complexity" that might arise in a criminal case.[84] The tendency of courts, forced to confront real-world gray issues with black-and-white rules, is to develop technical distinctions and exceptions that dim the virtues of the once-bright lines.[85]

---

77. Thornton v. United States, 541 U.S. 615, 628 (2004) (Scalia, J., dissenting) (stating that "[r]eported cases involving . . . a motorist handcuffed and secured in the backseat of a squad car"—and, thus, not realistically in position to grab a weapon or evidence inside the arrestee's vehicle—"when the search takes place[,] are legion.").

78. Dunaway v. New York, 442 U.S. 200, 213–14 (1979); *see also* Atwater v. Lago Vista, 532 U.S. 318, 347 (2001) ("Often enough, the Fourth Amendment has to be applied on the spur (and in the heat) of the moment, and the object in implementing its command of reasonableness is to draw standards sufficiently clear and simple to be applied with a fair prospect of surviving judicial second-guessing months and years after an arrest or search is made.").

79. LaFave, *"Case-by-Case Adjudication" . . .* , Note 68, *supra*, at 141.

80. Anthony G. Amsterdam, *Perspectives on the Fourth Amendment*, 58 Minn. L. Rev. 349, 415 (1974).

81. LaFave, *The Fourth Amendment in an Imperfect World . . .* , Note 68, *supra*, at 321.

82. William C. Heffernan & Richard W. Lovely, *Evaluating the Fourth Amendment Exclusionary Rule: The Problem of Police Compliance with the Law*, 24 U. Mich. J.L. Ref. 311, 356 (1991) (in a study of four mid-sized police departments, the authors found that officers were no more likely to understand bright-line search-and-seizure rules than non-bright-line rules).

83. Robbins v. California, 453 U.S. 420, 443 (1981).

84. Amsterdam, Note 79, *supra*, at 375; *see* Georgia v. Randolph, 547 U.S. 103, 125 (2006) ("[T]he Fourth Amendment does not insist upon bright-line rules. Rather, it recognizes that no single set of legal rules can capture the ever changing complexity of human life.") (Breyer, J., concurring).

85. *See* Bradley, Note 62, *supra*, at 77–81.

Some commentators take a middle position in the debate.[86] They favor bright lines, but only if certain conditions are met. First, a bright-line rule should be implemented only when there is evidence of a genuine need for it, i.e., when case-by-case adjudication provides inadequate guidance. Second, a bright-line rule should parallel the result that would be reached in a high percentage of cases if case-by-case adjudication were involved — in short, if there must be a bright line, make sure it is the *right* bright line. Third, the bright-line rule should not readily be susceptible to abuse by those enforcing it.

[B] Subjectivity versus Objectivity: Rule-Making to Avoid Pretextual Conduct[87]

Should the legitimacy of police conduct depend on the subjective state of mind of a law enforcement officer, i.e., his actual beliefs or reasons for acting? Or, should courts disregard an officer's hidden motivations, even if they are malicious, and measure police performance solely on objective grounds?

The Supreme Court has formulated both subjective and objective rules of criminal procedure. For example, in the interrogation field, the Court has held that a police officer violates the Sixth Amendment right to counsel if the officer "deliberately and designedly" — a subjective standard, because it seeks to determine the actual state of mind of the officer — sets out to elicit information in the absence of the accused's counsel.[88] On the other hand, the Court has crafted an objective standard to determine whether police conduct, short of actual questioning, constitutes the functional equivalent of "interrogation" for purposes of requiring *Miranda* warnings ("words or actions on the part of the police . . . that the police *should know* are *reasonably likely* to elicit an incriminating response from the suspect").[89]

Fourth Amendment jurisprudence, too, includes both subjective and objective standards, although the clear emphasis is on the latter. The Court has stated that "evenhanded law enforcement is best achieved by the application of objective standards of conduct, rather than standards that depend upon the subjective state of mind of the officer."[90] As a consequence, the justices have held that detention of a motorist, if probable cause exists to believe that the driver committed a traffic violation, does not violate the Fourth Amendment even if the officer may have been subjectively motivated to stop

---

86. *E.g.*, LaFave, *The Fourth Amendment in an Imperfect World . . .* , Note 68, *supra*, at 325–33.

87. *See generally* Symposium, *Programmatic Purpose, Subjective Intent, and Objective Intent: What is the Proper Role of "Purpose" Analysis to Measure the Reasonableness of a Search or Seizure?*, 76 Miss. L.J. 339–622 (2006); John M. Burkoff, *The Pretext Search Doctrine Returns After Never Leaving*, 66 U. Det. L. Rev. 363 (1989); Butterfoss, Note 68, *supra*; Edwin J. Butterfoss, *Solving the Pretext Puzzle: The Importance of Ulterior Motives and Fabrications in the Supreme Court's Fourth Amendment Pretext Doctrine*, 79 Ky. L.J. 1 (1990); Andrew D. Leipold, *Objective Tests and Subjective Bias: Some Problems of Discriminatory Intent in the Criminal Law*, 73 Chi-Kent L. Rev. 559 (1998); see also the citations in the second paragraph of Note 58, *supra*.

88. Brewer v. Williams, 430 U.S. 387, 389 (1977). *See* § 25.05, *infra*.

89. Rhode Island v. Innis, 446 U.S. 291, 301 (1980) (emphasis added) (footnotes omitted). *See* § 24.08, *infra*.

90. Horton v. California, 496 U.S. 128, 138 (1990); *see also* Ashcroft v. Al-Kidd, 563 U.S. 731, 739 (2011). ("Efficient and evenhanded application of the law demands that we look to whether the arrest is objectively justified, rather than to the motive of the arresting officer.").

the motorist for reasons other than a desire to enforce traffic laws.[91] On the other hand, sometimes an officer's state of mind will affect the legitimacy of the conduct. For example, although the police may inventory an automobile that they have impounded, as long as they apply standardized procedures, the police may *not* use such procedures as a ruse for investigating suspected criminal activity.[92]

Which approach — taking into consideration the subjective motivations of the official or disregarding them — is preferable? Most commonly, this question is characterized in the criminal investigatory field in terms of how to deal with "pretextual" police conduct, i.e., a situation in which "the officer does not have the state of mind which is hypothecated by the reasons which provide the legal justification for the officer's action."[93] Reconsider the example above: An officer issues a traffic ticket to a speeding motorist, not because he really thought that the traffic violation merited the officer's attention, but rather so that he has an opportunity to look inside the car on the hunch that the driver might be in possession of illegal narcotics (a hunch, perhaps, based on racial profiling). Similarly, an officer might delay a valid arrest until the suspect is at a friend's home. The delay might be motivated by the officer's desire to search the third person's residence, in the absence of probable cause, in the hope of linking the resident to the crime.

The most obvious way to deal with a claim of pretext is to consider each claim on a case-by-case basis, in order to determine whether the officer acted for proper or improper reasons. The primary difficulty with this approach is that "the catch is not worth the trouble of the hunt when courts set out to bag the secret motivations of policemen."[94] People rarely act of a single mind: conflicting motivations, some proper and others not, often inspire action. Even the most truthful officer may be unable to testify with certainty regarding his thought processes on an earlier occasion; and a dishonest officer has a strong incentive to perjure himself if his subjective beliefs will control the admissibility of the evidence. Realistically, a judge, forced to divine a police officer's motivations, is likely to give the officer the benefit of the doubt.

Alternatively, the Supreme Court might devise constitutional rules that, in general, limit police power in those circumstances in which the risk of pretext is especially high. Occasionally, the Court has taken this approach. For example, the Supreme Court has ruled that a police officer may not ordinarily enter a person's home to arrest a guest unless he is also armed with a warrant, supported by probable cause, to search the third person's premises.[95] The Court observed that if a search warrant were not required, an arrest warrant might "serve as the pretext for entering a home in which the police have a suspicion, but not probable cause to believe, that illegal activity is taking place."[96]

---

91. Whren v. United States, 517 U.S. 806 (1996). Commentators have criticized the Court's focus on the objective justification for police activity. *See, e.g.,* Gabriel J. Chin and Charles Vernon, *Reasonable but Unconstitutional: Racial Profiling and the Radical Objectivity of* Whren v, United States, 83 Geo. Wash. L. Rev. 882 (2015) (arguing that any search or arrest that is subjectively motivated by race is "unreasonable" under the Fourth Amendment).

92. *See* Colorado v. Bertine, 479 U.S. 367, 375–76 (1987); South Dakota v. Opperman, 428 U.S. 364, 376 (1976). *See* § 15.01[B], *infra.*

93. Scott v. United States, 436 U.S. 128, 138 (1978).

94. Amsterdam, Note 79, *supra,* at 436 (footnote omitted).

95. Steagald v. United States, 451 U.S. 204 (1981). *See* § 9.05[D], *infra.*

96. *Id.* at 215; *see also* Maine v. Moulton, 474 U.S. 159, 180 (1985) (the police inadvertently obtained incriminating statements from *M* about Crime X, in violation of *M*'s right to counsel, while they were *legitimately* asking *M* questions about Crime Y; held: the statements about Crime X were

Far more often, however, the Court has refused to draft rules to limit the risk of pretext. Put simply, the Court has said, "[s]ubjective intentions play no role in ordinary, probable-cause Fourth Amendment analysis."[97]

---

inadmissible, despite the officers' possible good faith; "[t]o allow the admission of evidence obtained from the accused in violation of his Sixth Amendment rights whenever the police assert an alternative, legitimate reason for their surveillance invites abuse . . . in the form of fabricated investigations . . .").

97. Whren v. United States, 517 U.S. 806, 813 (1996).

Chapter 3

Incorporation of the Bill of Rights

§ 3.01 Incorporation: Overview[1]

[A] Nature of the Issue

The first 10 amendments to the United States Constitution — the so-called Bill of Rights — were adopted contemporaneously with the ratification of the Constitution. These provisions were designed to limit the power of the federal government. They were not intended as restrictions on the actions of state government.[2] The vast majority of criminal prosecutions, however, originate in state courts as the result of criminal investigations conducted by state or local police officers. Consequently, the provisions of the Bill of Rights that pertain to criminal procedure — primarily, the Fourth, Fifth, Sixth, and Eighth Amendments — do not directly apply in the vast majority of criminal cases arising in this country.

The Fourteenth Amendment, adopted in 1868, imposes limits on *state* action. Section 1 of that amendment limits the states in three ways:

> No State shall [1] make or enforce any law which shall abridge the privileges or immunities of citizens of the United States; [2] nor shall any State deprive any person of life, liberty, or property, without due process of law; [3] nor deny to any person within its jurisdiction the equal protection of the laws.[3]

The relationship between the Fourteenth Amendment and the Bill of Rights has been vigorously disputed. The legal battle, commonly called the "incorporation debate,"

---

1. *See generally* Akhil Reed Amar, *The Bill of Rights and the Fourteenth Amendment*, 101 Yale L.J. 1193 (1992); William Winslow Crosskey, *Charles Fairman, "Legislative History," and the Constitutional Limitations on State Authority*, 22 U. Chi. L. Rev. 1 (1954); Charles Fairman, *Does the Fourteenth Amendment Incorporate the Bill of Rights? The Original Understanding*, 2 Stan. L. Rev. 5 (1949); Barry Latzer, *Toward the Decentralization of Criminal Procedure: State Constitutional Law and Selective Disincorporation*, 87 J. Crim. L. & Criminology 63 (1996); Gary L. McDowell & Judith A. Baer, *The Fourteenth Amendment: Should the Bill of Rights Apply to the States? The Disincorporation Debate*, 1987 Utah L. Rev. 951; George C. Thomas III, *When Constitutional Worlds Collide: Resurrecting the Framers' Bill of Rights and Criminal Procedure*, 100 Mich. L. Rev. 145 (2001); George C. Thomas III, *The Riddle of the Fourteenth Amendment: A Response to Professor Wildenthal*, 68 Ohio St. L.J. 1627 (2007); Bryan H. Wildenthal, *The Lost Compromise: Reassessing the Early Understanding in Court and Congress on Incorporation of the Bill of Rights in the Fourteenth Amendment*, 61 Ohio St. L.J. 1051 (2000); Bryan H. Wildenthal, *The Road to Twining: Reassessing the Disincorporation of the Bill of Rights*, 61 Ohio St. L.J. 1457 (2000); Bryan H. Wildenthal, *Nationalizing the Bill of Rights: Revisiting the Original Understanding of the Fourteenth Amendment in 1866–67*, 68 Ohio St. L.J. 1509 (2007); Symposium, *The Fourteenth Amendment and the Bill of Rights*, 18 J. Contemp. Legal Issues 1–533 (2009).

2. Barron v. Baltimore, 32 U.S. (7 Pet.) 243 (1833).

3. U.S. Const. amend. XIV, § 1 (numbers in brackets added).

centers on the second clause of section 1, namely, the Due Process Clause.[4] The essential question is this: To what extent does the Fourteenth Amendment Due Process Clause "incorporate" (or "absorb") the Bill of Rights and, as a consequence, impose upon the states the same restrictions the Bill of Rights imposes on the federal government? As discussed below, some courts and scholars believe that the Fourteenth Amendment was intended to incorporate all of the Bill of Rights, but others disagree. A related question is whether the Fourteenth Amendment guarantees any rights *not* enumerated in the Bill of Rights.

[B] Importance of the Debate

The incorporation debate is important for several reasons. First, the extent to which individuals are protected from overreaching by state agents depends in large measure on the extent to which the Fourteenth Amendment incorporates the Bill of Rights.[5] At one extreme, if none of the rights found in the Bill of Rights apply to the states, citizens may be subjected, for example, to warrantless invasions of the home by local police, coercive interrogation techniques, and felony trials without the assistance of counsel.[6] On the other hand, if the Due Process Clause incorporates the Bill of Rights in its entirety, the latter charter becomes a national code of criminal procedure—federal and state action would be identically restricted.

Second, as the latter observation suggests, values of federalism are at stake in the incorporation debate. The broader the interpretation of the scope of the Fourteenth Amendment Due Process Clause, the less free the states are to develop their own rules of criminal procedure, and to adapt them to an individual state's particular social and political conditions.

Third, the incorporation debate raises important questions regarding the proper role of the judiciary in the enforcement of constitutional rights. In particular, if the Due Process Clause of the Fourteenth Amendment incorporates some, but not all, of the Bill of Rights, then judges must use some standard to decide which doctrines apply against the

---

4. Early on, the Supreme Court rejected the plausible claim that the Fourteenth Amendment Privileges and Immunities Clause prohibits states from abridging the rights set out in the Bill of Rights. The Court ruled that this clause only bars states from abridging privileges and immunities *inherent in national citizenship*, which the Court determined did not include the provisions of the Bill of Rights. *See* Slaughter-House Cases, 83 U.S. (16 Wall.) 36 (1873). In *McDonald v. Chicago*, 130 S. Ct. 3020 (2010), the Supreme Court was asked to overrule its earlier decisions and hold that the Privileges and Immunities Clause incorporates the Bill of Rights. Both the four-justice plurality and three of the justices in dissent expressly declined the invitation, thereby reaffirming that questions of rights-protection "by the Fourteenth Amendment against state infringement . . . [are] analyzed under the Due Process Clause of that Amendment and not under the Privileges and Immunities Clause." *Id.* at 3030–31; *see also id.* at 3089 (Stevens, J., dissenting); *id.* at 3132 (Breyer, J., dissenting). Only Justice Thomas advocated using the Privileges and Immunities Clause for this purpose. *See id.* at 3059 (Thomas, J., concurring).

5. Usually unstated in the incorporation debate is the belief of many advocates of incorporation that states are "chronically . . . backward" in their protection of individual rights. Without incorporation, the argument goes, states would trample on citizens' rights. There is historical support for this view (particular in Southern states in regard to the rights of African-Americans). According to some modern commentators, however, "the state courts are no longer rights-antediluvians, and that therefore an entire set of assumptions underlying incorporation has eroded." Latzer, Note 1, *supra*, at 66.

6. A state constitution or statute, however, may prohibit such conduct.

states and which do not, thereby increasing the risk that judges will make these determinations based on personal policy predilections rather than on a legitimate and principled constitutional basis.

§ 3.02 Incorporation Theories

[A] Full Incorporation

According to Justice Hugo Black, the judicial architect and chief proponent of so-called "full" or "total" incorporation, "one of the chief objects that the provisions of the [Fourteenth] Amendment's first section, separately, and as a whole, were intended to accomplish was to make the Bill of Rights, applicable to the states."[7] In other words, the Fourteenth Amendment in general, and the Due Process Clause in particular, incorporates all of the rights included in the Bill of Rights, nothing more and nothing less.

[B] Fundamental Rights

"Fundamental rights" doctrine gained ascendency in the 1930s with the influential support of Justices Benjamin Cardozo[8] and Felix Frankfurter.[9] The essence of this doctrine is that the Fourteenth Amendment "neither comprehends the specific provisions by which the founders deemed it appropriate to restrict the federal government nor is it confined to them. The Due Process Clause . . . has an independent potency . . ."[10]

According to fundamental rights advocates, the Due Process Clause does not incorporate *any* of the provisions of the Bill of Rights. Instead, the Fourteenth Amendment Due Process Clause requires states to honor "'principle[s] of justice so rooted in the traditions and consciences of our people as to be ranked as fundamental'."[11] These fundamental rights "might indeed happen to overlap wholly or in part with some of the rules of the Bill of Rights, but [they] bear no logical relationship to those rules."[12]

Notice that this means that a right may be included in the Bill of Rights (and thus be protected against encroachment by the *federal* government) and yet *not* be deemed fundamental (and, therefore, *not* be protected against *state* overreaching). By the same token, a right may be fundamental, and yet not expressly protected by the Bill of Rights. Thus, the Fourteenth Amendment potentially provides both more and less than the Bill of Rights.

Over the years, the Supreme Court has articulated in a variety of ways the test by which the "fundamentalness" of a right is determined. These have included whether the right

---

7. Adamson v. California, 332 U.S. 46, 71–72 (1947) (Black, J., dissenting); see also Rochin v. California. 342 U.S. 165, 174–77 (1952) (Black, J., concurring).

8. *See* Palko v. Connecticut, 302 U.S. 319 (1937), *overruled* in Benton v. Maryland, 395 U.S. 784 (1969).

9. *E.g., Adamson*, 332 U.S. at 59–68 (concurring opinion); *Rochin*, 342 U.S. at 166–74 (majority opinion).

10. *Adamson*, 332 U.S. at 66 (Frankfurter, J., concurring).

11. *Palko*, 302 U.S. at 325 (*quoting* Snyder v. Massachusetts, 291 U.S. 97, 105 (1934)).

12. Amar, Note 1, *supra*, at 1196.

"is among those fundamental principles of liberty and justice which lie at the base of all our civil and political institutions; whether it is basic in our system of jurisprudence; . . . whether it is a fundamental right, essential to a fair trial . . . [, and whether it] is fundamental to the American scheme of justice."[13]

[C] Full-Incorporation-Plus

Justices Frank Murphy, Wiley Rutledge, and William Douglas posited the broadest interpretation of the Fourteenth Amendment. According to these justices, the Due Process Clause incorporates the Bill of Rights in its entirety (full incorporation), as well as any fundamental rights that fall outside the express language of the Constitution (a component of fundamental rights doctrine).[14]

[D] Selective Incorporation

Selective incorporation includes features of both fundamental rights theory and total incorporation, without following the logic of either doctrine. According to one judicial critic, it represents "an uneasy and illogical compromise"[15] between the two doctrines.

Selective incorporationists agree with fundamental rights theorists that not all rights included in the Bill of Rights are inevitably absorbed by the Fourteenth Amendment. On the other hand, contrary to fundamental rights theory, and more in keeping with full incorporation, selective incorporationists believe that once a right *is* deemed to be fundamental, it is "applicable to the States with all the subtleties and refinements born of history and embodied in case experience developed in the context of federal adjudication."[16]

The latter quotation is critical to understanding how selective incorporation differs from full incorporation and the fundamental rights theory. The point of "fundamental rights" is that a right is protected by the Due Process Clause because it is crucial to the maintenance of justice; its inclusion in the Bill of Rights is not a logical requisite. It follows, therefore, that the constitutional case law that has developed regarding the *federal* right is not determinative (under "fundamental rights" doctrine) of the scope of the *state* version of the analogous right emanating from the Fourteenth Amendment. For example, freedom from unreasonable searches and seizures is expressly guaranteed by the Fourth Amendment and considered a fundamental right under the Fourteenth Amendment.[17] To advocates of fundamental rights doctrine, however, it is logically possible that what constitutes an *unreasonable* search or seizure according to the Fourth Amendment might be *reasonable* under the Fourteenth Amendment, or vice-versa. In contrast,

---

13. Duncan v. Louisiana, 391 U.S. 145, 148–49 (1968) (citations and internal quotations omitted).

14. *See Adamson*, 332 U.S. at 123–25 (Murphy and Rutledge, JJ., dissenting); Poe v. Ullman 367 U.S. 497, 516 (1961) (Douglas, J., dissenting).

15. *Duncan*, 391 U.S. at 172 (Harlan, J., dissenting).

16. Williams v. Florida, 399 U.S. 78, 130–31 (1970) (Harlan, J., concurring) (explaining the theory).

17. Wolf v. Colorado, 338 U.S. 25 (1949), *overruled on other grounds* in Mapp v. Ohio, 367 U.S. 643 (1961).

selective incorporation absorbs "all of the bag and baggage"[18] of the Bill of Rights. Once a Bill of Rights provision is determined to be fundamental, *every* feature of the federal right applies to the states.

§ 3.03 The Incorporation Debate

[A] Overview of the Debate

The incorporation debate has focused on several issues. Some discourse turns on matters of textualism (i.e., which approach is more consistent with the language of the Fourteenth Amendment?) and/or originalism (i.e., which approach most closely approximates the intent of the framers of the provision?).

Two other important considerations arise in the incorporation debate: libertarianism (i.e., which due process approach is more protective of individual liberties?); and structuralism (i.e., which theory is more consistent with concepts of federalism and separation-of-powers?). A brief review of the debate follows.

[B] What Did the Framers Intend?

Justice Black and some scholars have accumulated evidence that purports to support their assertion that the framers of the Fourteenth Amendment intended to incorporate the entirety of the Bill of Rights.[19] Other scholars,[20] however, and Supreme Court justices have disputed this claim. Justice Frankfurter obliquely questioned the full incorporation position by observing that all but one ("an eccentric exception"[21]) of the Supreme Court justices who had previously considered the question had rejected full incorporation. Frankfurter doubted that state legislators, by ratifying the Fourteenth Amendment, believed that they were agreeing to dismantle their own systems of justice and replace them with the federal system.

Although most scholars today reject Justice Black's historical claims, one commentator concluded that the framers' intent is "to a considerable degree . . . shrouded in the mists of history. There is simply no clear answer [to the historical question]."[22] Indeed, it is entirely possible that among the legislators who voted to adopt and ratify the Fourteenth Amendment, some thought it applied the Bill of Rights to the states and others did not.[23]

---

18. Duncan v. Louisiana, 391 U.S. at 213 (Fortas, J., concurring).

19. Justice Black provided a 31-page appendix to his dissent in *Adamson, supra*, in support of his claim; *see also* Crosskey, Note 1, *supra*; Wildenthal, Note 1, *supra* (all cited articles).

20. *E.g.*, Fairman, Note 1, *supra*. While not accepting "Black's brand of mechanical incorporation," Professor Amar is critical of Professor Charles Fairman's "130 pages of Black-bashing." Amar observes that "Fairman spent so much energy attacking Justice Black that he failed to offer any sustained narrative in support of an alternative reading of the Fourteenth Amendment." Amar, Note 1, *supra*, at 1238.

21. *Adamson*, 332 U.S. at 62.

22. McDowell & Baer, Note 1, *supra*, at 956–57 (statement of McDowell in debate with Baer).

23. Timothy S. Bishop, *Comment, The Privileges or Immunities Clause of the Fourteenth Amendment: The Original Intent*, 79 Nw. U. L. Rev. 142, 145–84 (1984) (detailing the variety of viewpoints).

[C] Textual Claims: What Does "Due Process" Mean?

Opponents of full incorporation frequently point out that if the words "due process of law" are meant to incorporate the Bill of Rights, as Justice Black asserts, "it is a strange way of saying it."[24] If the framers sought full incorporation, why did they not say so directly? Why would they have used this oblique shorthand? Indeed, since the phrase "due process of law" also rests in the Fifth Amendment, why would the phrase mean one thing in the Fourteenth Amendment and another in the Fifth?[25]

Those who reject full incorporation are not out of the textual woods, either. "Due process of law" is also an odd way of saying, for example, "principle[s] of justice so rooted in the traditions and consciences of our people as to be ranked as fundamental." Moreover, the Due Process Clause has been interpreted to protect fundamental substantive rights not mentioned expressly in the Constitution, such as a right of privacy;[26] it is difficult to see how *substantive* rights can be textually defended with language that speaks merely of providing due *process.*[27]

[D] Which Doctrine Is More Libertarian?

On its face, full incorporation is more libertarian than selective incorporation or fundamental rights because, with one sweep of the wand, the entire Bill of Rights is nationalized. In contrast, the fundamental rights doctrine in theory is like an accordion: it can "periodically ... expand and contract ... to conform to the Court's conception of what at a particular time constitutes 'civilized decency' and 'fundamental liberty and justice.'"[28]

This perspective is somewhat misleading. Fundamental rights doctrine allows for the recognition of rights not specified in the Constitution. Indeed, Justice Black and other followers of full incorporationism have rejected any effort to "discover" rights not expressly found in the Constitution itself.

[E] Which Theory Is Structurally Preferable?

Full incorporation runs afoul of traditional views of federalism because it compels states to uproot their established methods for prosecuting crimes and fastens upon them the federal version of due process. Fundamental rights doctrine potentially permits states to run their criminal justice systems more freely because they need only recognize those rights essential to fundamental justice.

Fundamental rights doctrine, however, is subject to criticism on separation-of-powers grounds. Advocates of full incorporation argue that one need only look at the various

---

24. *Adamson*, 332 U.S. at 63 (Frankfurter, J., concurring).

25. In other words, under full incorporation, "due process of law" is a shorthand for freedom of speech, freedom of religion, the right to bear arms, and so on; yet, in the Fifth Amendment, the words "due process of law" could not logically have this meaning because these other rights are enumerated elsewhere in the Bill of Rights.

26. *See* Griswold v. Connecticut, 381 U.S. 479 (1965).

27. John Hart Ely, *Constitutional Interpretivism: Its Allure and Impossibility*, 53 Ind. L.J. 399, 419–20 (1978) ("[T]here is simply no blinking the fact that the word that follows 'due' is 'process.'").

28. *Adamson*, 332 U.S. at 69 (Black, J., dissenting).

tests of "fundamental rights" to conclude that this doctrine invites judges "to roam at large in the broad expanses of policy and morals and to trespass, all too freely, on the legislative domain of the States as well as the Federal Government."[29] It permits federal judges, unelected and serving life appointments, to behave like "dictators or philosopher kings,"[30] as they determine whether a "fair and enlightened system of justice" would be possible in the absence of a particular protection.

§ 3.04 Which Theory Has "Won" The Debate?

The full incorporation position has lost the rhetorical war in the Supreme Court. No majority opinion of the Court has ever accepted the principle, nor does it have support of even a single justice on the Court today.

The Court has instead considered specific provisions of the Bill of Rights on a right-by-right basis, determining whether a particular right is fundamental to an American system of justice. Once the Court has determined that a right *is* fundamental, it has nearly always concluded that the provision of the Bill of Rights should "be enforced against the States under the Fourteenth Amendment according to the same standards that protect those personal rights against federal encroachment."[31] That is, with the exception of the unanimity requirement of the right to a jury trial,[32] it appears that all of the incorporated rights relating to criminal procedure include all of the "baggage" from the federal system. Thus, in this regard, the Court seems to have followed the selective incorporation approach rather than fundamental-rights doctrine.[33]

But wait. As a practical matter, Justice Black's goal of incorporating the entirety of the Bill of Rights has nearly been realized. In the realm of criminal procedure, all but

---

29. *Id.* at 90 (Black, J., dissenting).

30. Ely, Note 27, *supra*, at 445.

31. Malloy v. Hogan, 378 U.S. 1, 10 (1964).

32. In *Apodaca v. Oregon*, 406 U.S. 404 (1972), the Court split 4–4 on whether the Sixth Amendment requires that jury verdicts be unanimous. Justice Powell, an opponent of "bag and baggage" incorporation, concluded that the Sixth Amendment requires unanimous verdicts, but that the Fourteenth Amendment does not impose this requirement on the states. This led to the anomalous result that, although eight of the justices would have applied the same constitutional rule regarding jury unanimity to the states and to the federal government, the unanimity requirement in fact applies to the latter but not to the former.

33. The Court recently had a return foray into the incorporation issue in *McDonald v. City of Chicago*, 130 S. Ct. 3020 (2010), in which the Court had to decide whether the individual right to bear arms for the purpose of self-defense, a right it had first recognized two years earlier, applied to the states. While the case did not produce a majority opinion regarding incorporation through the Due Process Clause, the conclusion that selective incorporation "won" the methodological debate was reaffirmed. The four-justice plurality concluded that the right was "fundamental to our scheme of ordered liberty" and applies to the states in the same manner it applies to the federal government. (A fifth justice, Justice Thomas, also found the Second Amendment fully incorporated, but under the Privileges and Immunities Clause, rather than the Due Process Clause). The three dissenting justices who addressed the incorporation question, while reaching a different conclusion on the ultimate question, also seemed to follow a selective incorporation analysis. While the Court was fractured on the proper methodology, as usual the right at issue was incorporated and incorporated "bag and baggage."

one provision of the Bill of Rights applies to the states.[1] Moreover, the Court has held that rights not mentioned in the Constitution, such as a right of privacy, are mandated by "due process." In the criminal procedure context, the Court has stated that, although the Due Process Clause has only "limited operation" "[b]eyond the specific guarantees enumerated in the Bill of Rights,"[2] that "limited operation" does encompass some important unenumerated protections, for example, the right of a criminal defendant to disclosure by the prosecution of evidence that is favorable to the defendant and material to guilt or punishment.[3]

Ironically, therefore, if practical "winners" are to be declared, they may be those few justices, all now deceased, who favored full-incorporation-plus.

---

1. The exception is the Fifth Amendment provision that no person shall be held to answer for a serious crime except by indictment or presentment of a grand jury, which does not apply to the states. Hurtado v. California, 110 U.S. 516 (1884). In addition, two Eighth Amendment provisions — the Excessive Fines Clause and the Excessive Bail Clause — have been the subject of dicta, rather than holdings. As to excessive fines, the Court has contradicted its own dicta. *Compare* Cooper Industries v. Leatherman Tool Group, 532 U.S. 424, 433–34 (2001) (citing a 1972 case involving the "cruel and unusual punishment" provision of the Eighth Amendment for the proposition that the "Due Process Clause . . . makes the Eighth Amendment's prohibition on excessive fines . . . applicable to the States"), and Browning-Ferris Industries of Vermont, Inc. v. Kelco Disposal, Inc., 492 U.S. 257, 276 n.22 (1989) (expressly leaving open the question whether the "Eighth Amendment's prohibition on excessive fines applies to the several States through the Fourteenth Amendment"). As to bail, the Court's repeated statement that "the Eighth Amendment's proscription of excessive bail has been assumed [by the Court] to have application to the States through the Fourteenth Amendment," *Baker v. McCollan*, 443 U.S. 137, 145 n.3 (1979) (citation and internal quotation omitted), has never been essential to a holding. *See also* Baze v. Rees, 553 U.S. 35, 47 (2008) (in which Chief Justice Roberts, joined by Justices Kennedy and Alito, stated in their plurality opinion that "[t]he Eighth Amendment . . . [is] applicable to the States through the Due Process Clause of the Fourteenth Amendment," citing *Robinson v. California*, 370 U.S. 660, 666 (1962) for this proposition).

2. Dowling v. United States, 493 U.S. 342, 352 (1990).

3. Brady v. Maryland, 373 U.S. 83 (1963).

Chapter 4

Fourth Amendment: Overview

§ 4.01 A Warning before Beginning the Fourth Amendment Journey[1]

According to one commentator, the Fourth Amendment contains "both the virtue of brevity and the vice of ambiguity."[2] Another scholar has stated that the amendment is "brief, vague, general, [and] unilluminating."[3] For almost a century the text remained "largely unexplored territory."[4] It did not take "full flower"[5] until 1961, when the Supreme Court extended the provision's judicially implied exclusionary rule to the states.[6]

Many years ago, Justice Felix Frankfurter observed that "[t]he course of true law pertaining to [the Fourth Amendment] . . . has not . . . run smooth."[7] Today, this is a gross understatement. "Almost no one has a kind word to say about fourth amendment

---

1. Citations to Fourth Amendment sources will be provided throughout the Text. By far the most cited Fourth Amendment source is Professor Wayne LaFave's six-volume lawyer's treatise, Search and Seizure (4th ed. 2004). For discussion of the Amendment's history and its modern significance, *see generally* Andrew E. Taslitz, Reconstructing the Fourth Amendment: A History of Search and Seizure, 1789–1868 (2006); Akhil Reed Amar, *Fourth Amendment First Principles*, 107 Harv. L. Rev. 757 (1994); Thomas Y. Davies, *Recovering the Original Fourth Amendment*, 98 Mich. L. Rev. 547 (1999); Carol S. Steiker, *Second Thoughts About First Principles*, 107 Harv. L. Rev. 820 (1994).

For general discussion of Fourth Amendment jurisprudence, *see generally* Anthony G. Amsterdam, *Perspectives On The Fourth Amendment*, 58 Minn. L. Rev. 349 (1974); Susan Bandes, *"We the People" and our Enduring Values*, 96 Mich. L. Rev. 1376 (1998); Gerard V. Bradley, *The Constitutional Theory of the Fourth Amendment*, 38 DePaul L. Rev. 817 (1989); Thomas K. Clancy, *The Framers' Intent: John Adams, His Era, and the Fourth Amendment*, 86 Indiana L.J. 979 (2011); Thomas K. Clancy, *What Does the Fourth Amendment Protect: Property, Privacy, or Security?*, 33 Wake Forest L. Rev. 307 (1998); Thomas K. Clancy, *The Purpose of the Fourth Amendment and Crafting Rules to Implement that Purpose*, 48 U. Rich. L. Rev. 479 (2014); Morgan Cloud, *Pragmatism, Positivism, and Principles in Fourth Amendment Theory*, 41 UCLA L. Rev. 199 (1993); Sherry F. Colb, *Innocence, Privacy, and Targeting in Fourth Amendment Jurisprudence*, 96 Colum. L. Rev. 1456 (1996); Tracey Maclin, *When the Cure for the Fourth Amendment Is Worse than the Disease*, 68 S. Cal. L. Rev. 1 (1994); David A. Sklansky, *The Fourth Amendment and Common Law*, 100 Colum. L. Rev. 1739 (2000); William J. Stuntz, *Privacy's Problem and the Law of Criminal Procedure*, 93 Mich. L. Rev. 1016 (1995); Scott E. Sundby, *"Everyman's" Fourth Amendment: Privacy or Mutual Trust Between Government and Citizen?*, 94 Colum. L. Rev. 1751 (1994); and Silas J. Wasserstrom & Louis Michael Seidman, *The Fourth Amendment as Constitutional Theory*, 77 Geo. L.J. 19 (1988).

2. Jacob W. Landynski, Search and Seizure and the Supreme Court: A Study in Constitutional Interpretation 42 (1966).

3. Amsterdam, Note 1, *supra*, at 353–54.

4. Landynski, Note 2, *supra*, at 49.

5. Wayne R. LaFave, *The Fourth Amendment Today: A Bicentennial Appraisal*, 32 Vill. L. Rev. 1061, 1064 (1987).

6. Mapp v. Ohio, 367 U.S. 643 (1961). For discussion of the exclusionary rule, *see* § 4.04[B] and Chapter 20, *infra*.

7. Chapman v. United States, 365 U.S. 610, 618 (1961) (concurring opinion).

jurisprudence."[8] According to one critic, "[t]he Fourth Amendment today is an embarrassment."[9] And, whether or not one agrees with the observation that "Fourth Amendment case law is a sinking ocean liner—rudderless and badly off course,"[10] it is true that criticism of Fourth Amendment law comes from widely divergent, and even opposite, political and philosophical poles.

Put simply, the single sentence that constitutes the Fourth Amendment has resulted in billions of words of interpretive text by the Supreme Court, state and lower federal courts, and commentators. The goal of anyone studying Fourth Amendment law, therefore, is to make as much sense of it as possible, as well as to consider ways to improve upon what has been constructed (or, to continue one metaphor, to save the ocean liner before it sinks).

§ 4.02 The Text and Some (Hopefully) Useful Initial Observations[11]

The Fourth Amendment to the United States Constitution is a mere 54 words long. It reads:

> The right of the people to be secure in their persons, houses, papers, and effects, against unreasonable searches and seizures, shall not be violated, and no Warrants shall issue, but upon probable cause, supported by Oath or affirmation, and particularly describing the place to be searched, and the persons or things to be seized.

In reading the text, one can divide the Fourth Amendment into two general parts. The first portion of the Fourth Amendment tells us what the amendment seek to prohibit (or, if you will, it states the constitutional right we hold against the government). In this portion, the text states *who* is covered ("the people"); *what* is covered ("persons, houses, papers, and effects"); and the nature of the protection ("to be secure . . . against unreasonable searches and seizures"). This portion of the Fourth Amendment, in particular the latter language, is sometimes described as the "Reasonableness Clause" (or "reasonableness requirement") of the Fourth Amendment.

Many sub-issues are raised by these initial words of the Fourth Amendment, about which all practicing lawyers must be sensitive: (1) Who are "the people" whose rights are covered by the Fourth Amendment?;[12] (2) Is there anything that is *not* a "person, house, paper, or effect," which (therefore) falls outside the scope of the Fourth

---

8. Wasserstrom & Seidman, Note 1, *supra*, at 19.

9. Amar, Note 1, *supra*, at 757.

10. *Id.* at 759.

11. For shorthand purposes, this Text speaks of the provisions of the Fourth Amendment as if they applied directly to the states, although it is the Fourteenth Amendment Due Process Clause that recognizes the fundamental right to be secure from unreasonable searches and seizures by state agents. Wolf v. Colorado, 338 U.S. 25 (1949), *overruled on other grounds*, Mapp v. Ohio, 367 U.S. 643 (1961).

12. There is relatively little law on this subject, but *see* § 4.04[E], *infra*.

Amendment?;[13] (3) What is a "search" and/or "seizure" in Fourth Amendment terms?;[14] and, of course, (4) What makes a search or seizure unconstitutionally "unreasonable"?[15]

The second portion of the Fourth Amendment expressly relates to warrants. It tells us what is required for a warrant to be issued ("probable cause [for the search or seizure], supported by oath or affirmation"), and tells us something about the form of the warrant itself ("particularly describing the place to be searched, and the persons or things to be seized"). This portion of the text is often described as the "Warrant Clause," with its "particularity requirement." Here, too, there are sub-issues, most especially: (1) What constitutes "probable cause"?;[16] and (2) How particular must the warrant state the "place to be searched" and "persons or things to be seized" to satisfy the particularity requirement?[17]

The preceding sub-issues relating to each portion of the Fourth Amendment, as important as they are, are dwarfed in importance by a greater debate: the connection, if any, between the Reasonableness Clause and the Warrant Clause, which clauses you will notice are separated by a comma, and not a semi-colon. If the framers had used a semi-colon, it would be easier to argue textually that the two clauses are independent of each other, but in light of the comma, one may sensibly ask whether the second clause informs the first? *That is, in view of the Warrant Clause, should we conclude that any search or seizure conducted without a valid warrant is unreasonable (or, at least, presumptively unreasonable) and, thus, impermissible, in view of the reasonableness requirement of the Fourth Amendment? Or, instead, is the Warrant Clause independent of the Reasonableness Clause?* That is, does the Warrant Clause tell us, simply, *how* warrants should be issued (with probable cause, etc.), but tell us nothing whatsoever about *whether* or *when* warrants must be issued?

The debate on this critical question is summarized elsewhere in this Text,[18] and is at the center of much of the controversy in Fourth Amendment case law.

§ 4.03 What Does the Fourth Amendment Seek to Protect?: An Overview

[A] The Supreme Court's View

The text of the Fourth Amendment tells us that our "persons, houses, papers and effects" should be free from "unreasonable searches and seizures." But *why* are we entitled to this protection? Is it, in a sense, a property right that the framers intended to enforce? Or is the Fourth Amendment intended to guarantee us some level of privacy from governmental intrusion? Or did the drafters of the Fourth Amendment have some other intention?

---

13. *See* Chapter 5, *infra*.

14. These terms have very specialized — and, at times, surprising — definitions. *See* Chapter 6 ("search") and 7 ("seizure"), *infra*.

15. This question — the ultimate issue in Fourth Amendment analysis — is covered, directly or indirectly, by Chapters 10–18, *infra*.

16. *See* Chapter 8, *infra*.

17. *See* § 10.03[C], *infra*.

18. *See* § 10.01, *infra*.

The Supreme Court has observed that "the Fourth Amendment's commands grew in large measure out of the colonists' experience with the writs of assistance and their memories of the general warrants formerly in use in England."[19] Specifically, writs of assistance authorized the use of "assistants"—local officials, such as the sheriff—to aid the Crown's agents to forcibly enter and search a colonist's home (or any other place), virtually at will, for smuggled goods. Similarly, general warrants were used in England to ferret out supposed seditious publications. Search warrants empowered agents of the Crown, on very little basis, to forcibly enter and search (indeed, ransack) homes for books and papers for use in seditious libel prosecutions.[20]

Although house searches under general warrants and writs of assistance constituted the immediate evils that the framers sought to prohibit (the "aboriginal subject of the fourth amendment"[21]), the Supreme Court has since asserted "that the evil the Amendment was designed to prevent was broader than the[se] abuse[s]."[22] What other evils may the framers have had in mind? According to one scholar, in a classic article on the Fourth Amendment, the amendment is properly viewed as "quintessentially a regulation of the police—that, in enforcing the fourth amendment, courts *must* police the police."[23]

In one historical survey of the subject, Professor Thomas Davies determined that, although the statements of the framers focused almost exclusively on their concerns about abusive warrants—thus, their attention was directed at the role judges, not the police, should play—this fact is misleading. He explains that the framers

> saw no need for a constitutional standard to regulate the warrantless officer because they did not perceive the warrantless officer as being capable of posing a significant threat to the security of person or house. This was so because the *ex officio* authority of the peace officer was still meager in 1789.[24]

Ultimately, therefore, Davies concludes that "any attempt to return to the literal original meaning—that is, to an understanding that the text only banned general warrants but did not address warrantless intrusions—would subvert the larger purpose for which the Framers adopted the text; namely to curb the exercise of discretionary authority by officers."[25]

The latter quotation raises another point. For some scholars and justices, the drafters' intent is the predominant, perhaps exclusive, basis for interpreting the Fourth Amendment: we should determine the framers' eighteenth century intent and enforce it. Other members of the Court and commentators, however, have expressed doubt that the framers' intent, whatever it is, can or should serve as the sole criterion for enforcing the Fourth Amendment in the twenty-first century.[26] For those who do not feel constrained by framers' intent, the goal is to determine how to ensure the viability of the Fourth Amendment in modern times while remaining reasonably faithful to constitutional text and history.

---

19. United States v. Chadwick, 433 U.S. 1, 7–8 (1977).

20. Osmond K. Fraenkel, *Concerning Searches and Seizures*, 34 Harv. L. Rev. 361, 362–63 (1920).

21. Amsterdam, Note 1, *supra*, at 363.

22. Payton v. New York, 445 U.S. 573, 585 (1980).

23. Amsterdam, Note 1, *supra*, at 371.

24. Davies, Note 1, *supra*, at 552.

25. *Id.* at 556.

26. *Id.; see also* Susan R. Klein, *Enduring Principles and Current Crises in Constitutional Criminal Procedure*, 24 Law & Social Inquiry 533, 542–43 (1999); *see also* George C. Thomas III, *Stumbling Towards History: The Framers' Search and Seizure World*, 43 Tex. Tech. L. Rev. 199 (2010).

One way to strive for both historical faithfulness and modern relevance is to ask and answer the following question: Beyond the specific *means* of intrusion historically barred by the Fourth Amendment (intrusion of homes, by means of general warrants or writs), what broad overriding *values* inspired the framers of the Fourth Amendment? Originally, the Supreme Court claimed that the Fourth Amendment was intended to prevent violations of the "sacred and incommunicable" right to private property, which was described as "[t]he great end for which men entered into society."[27] Thus, the amendment was seen as a means to prevent unfettered physical intrusions — trespasses — on private property in order to obtain information. More recently, the Supreme Court suggested that the framers also intended to "assur[e] preservation of that degree of privacy against government that existed when the Fourth Amendment was adopted."[28]

Under both the property- and privacy-oriented historical interpretations, the Court has suggested that "physical entry of the home [without a valid warrant] is the chief evil against which the . . . Fourth Amendment is directed."[29] The unwarranted "breach of the entrance to an individual's home"[30] is the clearest violation of Fourth Amendment values, whether those values are primarily property or privacy based. As will be seen, even as the Court's devotion to search warrants has ebbed and flowed, the justices have remained comparatively firm in their commitment to the protection of the home — even from some modern technological "invasions" that do not require physical intrusion[31] — and, to a somewhat lesser extent, other "privately owned building[s]."[32]

[B] The Reflections of Some Scholars

Some contemporary scholars believe that the Court's approach to the Fourth Amendment has been wrong-footed. For example, the late Professor William Stuntz has written that the modern law of criminal procedure has focused too much on informational privacy — on the right to keep information hidden from the government — rather than on human dignitary interests. According to Stuntz:

> [C]riminal procedure would be better off with less attention to privacy, at least as privacy is defined in the doctrine today. Were the law of criminal procedure to focus more on force and coercion [used by the government] and less on information gathering . . . , it would square better with other constitutional law and better protect the interests most people value most highly.[33]

---

27. Boyd v. United States, 116 U.S. 616, 627 (1886) (quoting Lord Camden).

28. Kyllo v. United States, 533 U.S. 27, 34 (2001). As is developed in Chapter 6, it appeared to most legal observers that the Supreme Court shifted in the 1960s from a property-rights to a privacy-oriented view of the Fourth Amendment. (However, even then, the Court warned that the Fourth Amendment "cannot be translated into a general constitutional 'right to privacy.'" Katz v. United States, 389 U.S. 347, 350 (1967).) However, in 2012, the Supreme Court stated that the privacy-oriented approach to the Fourth Amendment did not displace — it merely augmented — the previous property-oriented interpretation. United States v. Jones, 132 S. Ct. 945 (2012).

29. United States v. United States District Court, 407 U.S. 297, 313 (1972).

30. Payton v. New York, 445 U.S. 573, 589 (1980).

31. Kyllo v. United States, 533 U.S. 27 (2001) (holding that the Fourth Amendment protects persons from indiscriminate use of "thermal imaging devices," which can be used on public land to detect relative amounts of heat escaping private homes).

32. California v. Acevedo, 500 U.S. 565, 585 (1991) (Scalia, J., concurring).

33. Stuntz, Note 1, *supra*, at 1020.

Another approach to the Fourth Amendment has been suggested by Professor Scott Sundby. He would choose a new "constitutional metaphor" by which to think about the amendment: "Justice Brandeis's famous image of 'the right to be let alone,' no longer fully captures the values that are at stake. . . . [T]he animating principle . . . is the idea of reciprocal government-citizen trust."[34] According to Sundby, government action draws its legitimacy from the trust that the people place in their representatives by choosing them to govern. This mandate is not valid, however, unless there is voluntary consent of the governed, which only occurs if the government acts in a manner manifesting its trust in the people to exercise liberty responsibly. That trust, however, "is jeopardized when the government is allowed to intrude into the citizenry's lives without a finding that the citizenry has forfeited society's trust to exercise its freedoms responsibly."[35]

Sundby believes that the value of the metaphor of trust is not that it offers a simple rule for evaluating police conduct in specified circumstances, but rather that it directs attention beyond the privacy expectations of the individual, and beyond the short-term justifications for the government intrusion, to the broader normative question of what relationship should exist between citizens and their government in a democratic society. In essence, Professor Sundby would have us (and the courts) think more about "the long-term dangers attendant to not protecting the citizen's independence from the government."[36]

Or, consider the ideas of Professor Sherry Colb.[37] She argues that the Fourth Amendment right against unreasonable searches is intended to protect two distinct interests: a right of privacy, but also a right to be free from unreasonable governmental targeting. She argues that the former interest should be considered from the perspective of the person being searched and, therefore, should not protect one using his private space in order to conceal illegal activities. In contrast, the targeting interest should be evaluated from the government's perspective — even persons involved in criminal activities should be protected from being singled out ("targeted"), without proper justification, by the government. This latter interest may be of critical importance in considering the legitimacy of governmental targeting of racial, religious, or ethnic minorities.[38]

§ 4.04 Some Things to Know at the Outset

[A] Standing to Raise Fourth Amendment Claims

A defendant in a criminal prosecution may not raise a claim of a Fourth Amendment violation unless *he*, personally, is the purported victim of the unreasonable search or seizure. In other words, Fourth Amendment rights are personal; they may not be vicariously asserted. This is sometimes called the "standing" requirement, a subject discussed in detail in Chapter 19.

Conceptually, standing to raise a Fourth Amendment claim is a threshold issue. A defense lawyer who believes evidence seized by the police should be suppressed at trial

---

34. Sundby, Note 1, *supra*, at 1754.
35. *Id.* at 1777.
36. *Id.* at 1809.
37. Colb, Note 1, *supra*. *See also* Clancy, *Purpose of the Fourth Amendment*, Note 1, *supra*.
38. *See* §§ 2.05 and 2.07[B], *supra*; and 8.02[F] and 17.03[B][5], *infra*.

pursuant to the Fourth Amendment "exclusionary rule" (discussed immediately below) must initially demonstrate that his client—and not, instead, someone else—was the supposed victim of the unreasonable search or seizure.

The Supreme Court no longer treats the issue of standing separately from the substantive merits of the defendant's Fourth Amendment claim.[39] Nonetheless, it is usually preferable (and judges often continue) to treat "standing" as a distinct inquiry. This is because it is conceptually possible for a person to have authority to raise a claim ("standing") and yet ultimately lose on the Fourth Amendment merits, just as there are cases in which Fourth Amendment interests *have* been violated, but the particular person who brings the claim is not the proper one to do so.

[B] Exclusionary Rule

The *right* guaranteed by the Fourth Amendment—to be free from unreasonable searches and seizures—must be distinguished from the *remedy* for a Fourth Amendment violation. Since 1914 in federal criminal proceedings,[40] and since 1961 in state criminal trials,[41] the primary Fourth Amendment remedy has been the so-called "exclusionary rule." In very (stress, very) general terms, this rule provides that evidence seized by the police in violation of the Fourth Amendment may not be introduced by the government at the criminal trial of the victim of the unreasonable search or seizure.

The Fourth Amendment exclusionary rule is controversial because it often prevents the government from introducing at trial reliable evidence of a defendant's guilt. As a result, significant limits, and exceptions to it, have been placed on the scope of the rule. Indeed, Justice Scalia, writing for four other justices in 2006, hinted that the exclusionary rule, whatever its value "in different contexts and long ago," may no longer be needed.[42]

The significant limits on the exclusionary rule, and the arguments for and against it, are surveyed in Chapter 20.

[C] Pretrial Nature of Fourth Amendment Issues

In light of the exclusionary rule, the ultimate Fourth Amendment issue in criminal proceedings will almost always be whether evidentiary matters seized by the police relating to the crime charged—tangible items, as well as potentially incriminating statements—are admissible at the defendant's trial. The admissibility issue is typically raised by the defense prior to trial in the form of a motion to suppress the evidence on the ground that it was obtained as a result of an unreasonable search or seizure, which issue is resolved, also prior to trial, by a judge. Jurors are not involved in this determination.

There is some historical irony in this judicial procedure. As Professor Akhil Amar has noted, in the eyes of the framers of the Constitution, judges were "the heavies, not

---

39. Rakas v. Illinois, 439 U.S. 128 (1978).

40. Weeks v. United States, 232 U.S. 383 (1914).

41. Mapp v. Ohio, 367 U.S. 643 (1961).

42. Hudson v. Michigan, 547 U.S. 586, 597 (2006) ("That would be forcing the public today to pay for the sins and inadequacies of a legal regime that existed almost a half century ago.").

the heroes, of our [Fourth Amendment] story,"[43] because it was they who authorized the abusive general warrants and writs of assistance that the amendment sought to abolish.[44] Traditionally, as well, reasonableness is "a classic question of fact for the jury."[45] But would jurors be willing to rule that incriminating evidence—for example, large quantities of illegal drugs or weapons discovered in the defendant's possession—should be excluded from the defendant's trial, regardless of police misconduct? According to some scholars, the current approach of "having judges decide what police conduct violates the Fourth Amendment reflects a distrust of society's ability or willingness to apply the Fourth Amendment properly."[46]

Some scholars have argued for jury participation in the process.[47] Currently, however, trial judges make all findings of fact and rulings of law on Fourth Amendment matters. A judge decides whose version of the facts—the police version or the defendant's description of the events—should be believed and, based on the court's findings of fact, renders a legal ruling on the constitutional reasonableness of the police conduct. In any subsequent appeal of the trial judge's determination, an appellate court must accept the lower court's factual findings, absent an abuse of discretion.

[D] "Private" Searches and Seizures[48]

The Fourth Amendment limits *governmental* action.[49] It does not restrict the actions of private parties, i.e., persons who are not directly or indirectly acting for the government. Put starkly, the Fourth Amendment has nothing to say regarding private searches and seizures. Therefore, evidence secured by a private individual—no matter how unreasonable, or even illegal, the methods used to obtain it—is constitutionally admissible in a criminal proceeding against the victim of the improper conduct.[50] Thus, if a private security guard searches an office without cause, or if one neighbor breaks into the house of another, or a computer hacker stumbles on child pornography on another's computer hard drive,[51] these actions do not violate the Fourth Amendment even if they violate federal or state criminal laws.

The Fourth Amendment does apply, however, if a private person acts "as an instrument or agent of the Government."[52] For example, a Fourth Amendment violation may be found if, at the request of a law enforcement officer, a private individual conducts surveillance of a citizen or opens a package belonging to another. Whether a private person should be deemed an agent of the government for Fourth Amendment purposes depends

---

43. Akhil R. Amar, *The Bill of Rights as a Constitution*, 100 Yale L.J. 1131, 1179 (1991).

44. *See* § 4.03, *supra.*

45. Amar, Note 43, *supra*, at 1179.

46. George C. Thomas III & Barry S. Pollack, *Saving Rights from a Remedy: A Societal View of the Fourth Amendment*, 73 B.U. L. Rev. 147, 149 (1993).

47. *E.g., id.*; Amar, Note 1, *supra*, at 817–19.

48. *See generally* 1 LaFave, Note 1, *supra*, at § 1.8.

49. Although most Fourth Amendment litigation involves searches and seizures by police officers, the amendment applies to other public employees, such as firefighters, *e.g.*, Michigan v. Tyler, 436 U.S. 499 (1978), public school teachers, *e.g.*, New Jersey v. T. L. O., 469 U.S. 325 (1985), and housing inspectors, *e.g.*, Camara v. Municipal Court, 387 U.S. 523 (1967).

50. *See* Burdeau v. McDowell, 256 U.S. 465 (1921).

51. United States v. Jarrett, 338 F.3d 339 (4th Cir. 2003).

52. Skinner v. Railway Labor Executives' Ass'n, 489 U.S. 602, 614 (1989); *see* United States v. Jacobsen, 466 U.S. 109, 113–14 (1984).

on the degree of governmental involvement in the situation, and is determined by the totality of the circumstances.[53]

[E] The "Silver Platter" Doctrine

The United States has a federalist system of government, with each state (and the federal government) allowed to set its own rules to regulate police conduct. The United States Constitution applies to all state and federal proceedings, but beyond that minimum standard, states and the federal government are free to give the police more or less power in any given situation. For example, the federal rule for executing search warrants tends to be stricter than most state rules, while certain states interpret their own constitution as granting their citizens greater privacy rights than are created by the federal constitution.

This means that in order to take advantage of more lenient rules, occasionally law enforcement will have an incentive to argue that officers from a more forgiving jurisdiction carried out the investigation.[54] For example, if both state and federal agents are acting together to investigate a crime, they will structure the investigation so that the federal officers are the ones who conduct the search, because generally their actions will not be as constrained as the state officers. Once the federal officers obtain the evidence, they may be able to hand it over for use in a state prosecution, even though that same evidence would have been inadmissible if the state officers had conducted the search. Critics of this practice argue that the first set of law enforcement officers is offering up the evidence on a "silver platter." In theory, these hand-offs are illegal if the two agencies are coordinating their efforts, but in practice, courts occasionally still allow these silver platter hand-offs.[55]

[F] Who Are "the People" Protected by the Fourth Amendment?[56]

The Fourth Amendment guarantees "the people" the right to be free from unreasonable searches and seizures. But who are "the people"? Does the Fourth Amendment apply to *any* person, regardless of citizenship or location, if the search or seizure is conducted by United States law enforcement officers? For example, would an Afghan citizen whose home is searched by United States military or civilian officials have a cognizable Fourth Amendment claim if evidence so obtained was used against him in a criminal proceeding in this country? What about the search of an American in Afghanistan? What about a non-American visitor to California whose property is searched during a brief vacation

---

53. *Skinner*, 489 U.S. at 614.

54. *See* Wayne A. Logan, *Dirty Silver Platters: The Enduring Challenge of Intergovernmental Investigative Illegality*, 99 Iowa L. Rev. 293 (2013).

55. *Id.* at 307–16. Before the 1960s, the exclusionary rule did not apply to many of the states; thus, law enforcement officers often used the silver platter doctrine to allow state officers to conduct searches and then hand the evidence over to federal agents. Today, state rules are apt to be stricter than federal rules, and so the silver platter doctrine usually works in the opposite direction.

56. *See generally* 1 LaFave, Note 1, *supra*, at § 1.8(h).

in this country? How about an undocumented immigrant who has lived for years in the United States?

The United States Supreme Court has said relatively little about these Fourth Amendment issues, although recent events—the international scope of the so-called "war on drugs," American military interventions in foreign countries, and present-day immigration controversies in this country—could result in more litigation in the future.

Here is what is known. The Fourth Amendment does not restrict the conduct of *foreign* law enforcement officers acting *outside* the United States. Therefore, United States citizens (and, of course, others) cannot assert Fourth Amendment protection in such circumstances. Evidence independently secured by a foreign officer, therefore, if turned over to an American court, may be admitted against the victim of the search. On the other hand, if there is sufficient American involvement in an extraterritorial search of an *American* citizen, the Fourth Amendment applies.

A different question arises when U.S. law enforcement officers participate in an extraterritorial search of a *non*-U.S. citizen. In *United States v. Verdugo-Urquidez*,[57] the United States Drug Enforcement Agency (DEA), in conjunction with Mexican police, without a warrant, searched the Mexican property of *D*, a Mexican citizen and resident, who was temporarily in custody in an American correctional facility at the time of the extraterritorial search. The Supreme Court held, by a vote of 6–3, that the Fourth Amendment was not implicated in these circumstances.

Beyond this bare holding, it is difficult to determine the broader significance of *Verdugo-Urquidez*. Chief Justice Rehnquist, ostensibly writing for a five-justice majority, stated that the words "the people" in the Fourth Amendment text "refer[] to a class of persons who are part of a national community or who have otherwise developed sufficient connection with this country to be considered part of that community." Thus, nonresident aliens located outside the United States or its territories, as well as those temporarily and involuntarily in the country (such as *D* here, who was transported to the United States by Mexican police officers at U.S. request), seemingly are not protected by the Fourth Amendment against foreign searches, even if those searches are conducted by U.S. officers.

The preceding observation by the Court "majority" is undermined, however, because one of the five justices—Justice Kennedy—while joining the Court's opinion, wrote a concurrence that departed from the opinion he joined in one fundamental respect. According to Justice Kennedy,

> I cannot place any weight on the reference to "the people" in the Fourth Amendment as a source of restricting its protections. . . . I submit these words do not detract from its force or reach. Given the history of our Nation's concern over warrantless and unreasonable searches, explicit recognition of "the right of the people" to Fourth Amendment protection may be interpreted to underscore the importance of the right, rather than restrict the category of persons who may assert it.[58]

Instead, for Justice Kennedy, *D* could not object to the warrantless search because

> [t]he conditions and considerations of this case . . . make adherence to the Fourth Amendment's warrant requirement impracticable and anomalous. . . .

---

57. 494 U.S. 259 (1990).
58. *Id.* at 276.

The absence of local [Mexican] judges or magistrates available to issue warrants, the differing and perhaps unascertainable conceptions of reasonableness and privacy that prevail abroad, and the need to cooperate with foreign officials all indicate that the Fourth Amendment's warrant requirement should not apply in Mexico as it does in this country.[59]

A sixth justice (Justice Stevens) concurred in the judgment, but not in the Chief Justice's opinion. He and the three dissenters would have held that *D*, who did not enter the country unlawfully, was among "the people" protected by the Fourth Amendment. (Thus, apparently, five justices believed that *D* was among "the people" governed by the Fourth Amendment.) Stevens narrowly concluded that the Warrant Clause does not apply to extraterritorial searches.

Based on the split opinion, Professor Wayne LaFave has observed that "the *most* that can be definitely concluded [from the case] is that the Fourth Amendment's warrant clause is inapplicable to a search conducted under the circumstances present" in this case.[60] And, it should be noted, only two justices involved in the case (Scalia and Kennedy) are still sitting on the Court.

Various issues were expressly left open by the Court. First, does the Fourth Amendment apply (and, if so, how) to a non-citizen whose involuntary presence in the country is prolonged (such as a non-citizen serving a terms of years in a state or federal prison)? Does such a person, in the Chief Justice's language, have sufficient connection with the country to be entitled to raise Fourth Amendment claims? Second, and more significantly, the Court merely assumed, but did not decide, that undocumented immigrants living *voluntarily* in the United States, but who "presumably have accepted some societal obligations," possess Fourth Amendment rights.

§ 4.05 Fourth Amendment Checklist

In criminal prosecutions, Fourth Amendment issues arise in an evidentiary context. That is, the question that normally must be considered is this:

> *Should a particular tangible object or oral communication, secured by government agents, and which the prosecutor intends to introduce at trial against the defendant (D) in the government's case-in-chief, be excluded because it was obtained in violation of the Fourth Amendment?*

Answering this question is almost never simple. Nor is there any foolproof way to go about determining the answer. Nonetheless, the following checklist of questions may help clarify matters. It may be useful to return to it multiple times as you proceed through the Fourth Amendment thicket.

In answering the evidentiary question stated above, one should focus on the police activity that resulted in discovery of the particular item evidence at issue, and consider as many of the following questions as are relevant. If there are multiple items of evidence to consider, it is preferable to consider them in chronological order, i.e., in the order in which the evidence was secured by the police.

---

59. *Id.* at 278.
60. 1 LaFave, Note 1, *supra*, at 325–326.

1. *Does D have standing to raise a Fourth Amendment challenge to the specific item of evidence in question?* If the answer is "no," the evidence is admissible, insofar as the Fourth Amendment is concerned. If the answer is "yes," the analysis continues. In a multi-defendant criminal prosecution, *this question must be asked separately as to each defendant.* One person may have standing to raise the claim, while another does not.

2. *Is D among "the people" protected by the Fourth Amendment?* If the answer is "yes," proceed to the next question.

3. *Did the police activity in question implicate a "person, house, paper, or effect"?* If the answer to this question is "no," which is rare, the Fourth Amendment does not apply.

4. *Did the police activity constitute a "search" and/or "seizure"?* These words have specialized meanings in Fourth Amendment jurisprudence. If the police activity in question does not constitute either a search or seizure, the Fourth Amendment does not apply. If the activity constitutes either a search or seizure, the analysis continues.

5. *Was the search and/or seizure reasonable or unreasonable?* This is the ultimate substantive issue: it indicates whether the Fourth Amendment was violated. Nonetheless, one cannot answer this question without considering various sub-issues, including the following:

A. *Did the police have adequate grounds to conduct the search and/or seizure?* For searches and seizures, the police traditionally must have "probable cause," a constitutional term of art. Many searches and seizures, however, are permitted on a lesser ground, called "reasonable suspicion." And, the Supreme Court has approved suspicion-free searches and/or seizures in a few cases. In light of the different applicable standards, one must look at the particular search and/or seizure in question, and determine whether it is the type for which probable cause is required (many cases), whether it is the type for which reasonable suspicion is sufficient (many cases), or whether this is one of the few cases in which the police may act at random. Then, assuming some level of cause *is* required, a lawyer must determine whether the police possessed the requisite "probable cause" or "reasonable suspicion," as the case may be. If the police did not have sufficient grounds, the search or seizure was unreasonable, in violation of the Fourth Amendment.

B. *Even if the police acted on the basis of probable cause, did the police obtain a search warrant or arrest warrant, as the case may be?* If the answer to question is "yes," a number of sub-issues arise: (I) *Did the police obtain the warrant in a proper manner?*; (ii) *Was the party issuing the warrant a "neutral and detached magistrate"?*; (iii) *Was the warrant in proper form, e.g., does it satisfy the constitutional particularity requirement?*; and (iv) *Did the police execute the warrant properly?*

If the police did *not* secure a warrant, the sub-question is: *Did the police have a valid reason for not obtaining the warrant?* As will be explained in the Text, *arrest* warrants are constitutionally required only in very limited circumstances. *Search* warrants are required more often, but many "exceptions" to a so-called "search warrant requirement" exist. If no valid exception existed, however, a warrantless search or seizure would be considered unreasonable and, therefore, in violation of the Fourth Amendment.

6. Assuming that the preceding questions justify the conclusion that the police conducted an unreasonable search or seizure in violation of *D*'s rights, the Fourth Amendment exclusionary rule comes into potential play as to the particular item of evidence in question. However, there are still questions to be asked and answered:

A. *Does the exclusionary rule apply in the particular situation?* In light of relatively recent case law, the scope of the exclusionary rule has been limited. There are certain categories of unconstitutional searches or seizures to which the exclusionary does not apply; as well, the degree of culpability of the police officers who violated the Fourth Amendment must also be considered.

B. Assuming the exclusionary rule applies, then the evidence obtained in direct violation of the Fourth Amendment is inadmissible. Then ask: *Does the government seek to introduce any other evidence that is a fruit of the poisonous tree—that is, evidence causally linked to the initial illegality?* If the answer is "yes," these "fruits" are also inadmissible, subject to two limiting doctrines, explained elsewhere: (i) the inevitable-discovery doctrine; and (ii) the attenuated-connection doctrine.

As this checklist suggests, Fourth Amendment law is exceptionally complicated. This Text seeks to clarify the complicated law, step-by-step, in Chapters 5–20.

Chapter 5

Fourth Amendment: "Persons, Houses, Papers, and Effects"

§ 5.01 Significance of the Constitutional Phrase

The Fourth Amendment provides that the "right of the people to be secure in their *persons, houses, papers, and effects*, against unreasonable searches and seizures, shall not be violated . . ."[1]

There are two plausible ways to interpret the relationship between the italicized words and the prohibitory phrase, "unreasonable searches and seizures." First, the text can be interpreted to mean that governmental activity that does not impinge upon a "person, house, paper, or effect" is not a "search" or "seizure" within the meaning of the Fourth Amendment. Alternatively, and more plausibly as a textual matter, the language may inform us that the Fourth Amendment only prohibits "unreasonable searches and seizures" *of* "persons, houses, papers, and effects." In this second interpretation, the latter phrase tells us *what* is protected by the Fourth Amendment, while the former phrase describes the nature of the protection provided.

Either interpretation leads to the same conclusion: police activity that does *not* involve a person, house, paper, or effect is not barred by the Fourth Amendment — regardless of whether the police activity is reasonable or unreasonable, conducted with or without a warrant, and whether supported by probable cause, some lesser suspicion, or no credible evidence at all.

Very few cases have turned on the meaning of this constitutional phrase. Occasionally, however, the Supreme Court defines a component of the phrase narrowly and, thus, rules that the contested governmental action falls outside the scope of the Fourth Amendment.

§ 5.02 "Persons"

The word "person" in the Fourth Amendment phrase implicates searches and seizures that involve: (1) *D*'s body, as a whole, such as when she is arrested;[2] (2) the exterior of *D*'s body, including her clothing, such as when she is patted down for weapons or when the contents of her clothing are searched;[3] and (3) the interior of *D*'s body, such as when blood is extracted to test for alcohol content.[4]

---

1. Emphasis supplied.
2. *See, e.g.*, Chimel v. California, 395 U.S. 752 (1969).
3. *See, e.g.*, Terry v. Ohio, 392 U.S. 1 (1968).
4. *See, e.g.*, Schmerber v. California. 384 U.S. 757 (1966).

61

Early in the twentieth century, the Supreme Court held that the Fourth Amendment applied only to searches and seizures of material things.[5] Based on that interpretation, oral communication was not considered a "person, house, paper, or effect"; therefore, warrantless electronic surveillance of conversations did not violate the Fourth Amendment.[6] The Court subsequently reversed itself,[7] and has construed the amendment's protection of "persons" to encompass electronic eavesdropping of their conversations.[8]

§ 5.03 "Houses"

"House" is broadly construed. It includes virtually all structures that people commonly use as a residence, whether on a temporary basis, such as a hotel room,[9] or on a long-term basis, such as an apartment.[10] It also encompasses buildings attached to the residence, such as a garage.[11]

For constitutional purposes, the word "house" also includes the *curtilage* of the home, that is, "the area to which extends the intimate activity associated with the 'sanctity of a man's home and the privacies of life.' "[12] In contrast, so-called "open fields" — "any unoccupied or undeveloped area outside of the curtilage"[13] of a home — are excluded.[14]

Offices, stores, and other commercial buildings are included within the term "houses,"[15] a conclusion that the Supreme Court stated has "deep roots in the history of the Amendment."[16] However, this does not mean that the *scope* of Fourth Amendment coverage of such "houses" is the same: commercial structures are treated differently from residential property, primarily because one's expectations of privacy in the former are less than in homes.[17]

§ 5.04 "Papers and Effects"

The term "papers" encompasses personal items, such as letters and diaries, as well as impersonal business records.[18]

---

5. Olmstead v. United States, 277 U.S. 438 (1928).

6. *Id.*

7. Katz v. United States, 389 U.S. 347 (1967).

8. Oliver v. United States, 466 U.S. 170, 176 n.6 (interpreting *Katz*).

9. *See, e.g.*, Stoner v. California, 376 U.S. 483 (1964).

10. *See, e.g.*, Clinton v. Virginia, 377 U.S. 158 (1964) (per curiam).

11. *See, e.g.*, Taylor v. United States, 286 U.S. 1 (1932).

12. Oliver v. United States, 466 U.S. at 180 (quoting Boyd v. United States, 116 U.S. 616, 630 (1886)).

13. *Id.* at 180 n.11.

14. Hester v. United States, 265 U.S. 57 (1924); Oliver v. United States, 466 U.S. 170 (1984); see generally 1 Wayne R. LaFave, Search and Seizure § 2.4(a) (4th ed. 2004). The factors that distinguish a curtilage from an open field are considered at § 6.06[B], *infra*.

15. *See, e.g.*, See v. City of Seattle, 387 U.S. 541 (1967); see generally 1 LaFave, Note 14, *supra*, at § 2.4(b).

16. Oliver v. United States, 466 U.S. at 178 n.8.

17. Minnesota v. Carter, 525 U.S. 83, 90 (1998); New York v. Burger, 482 U.S. 691, 700 (1987).

18. *See, e.g.*, Andresen v. Maryland, 427 U.S. 463 (1976) (business records).

The word "effects" represents the residual component of the constitutional phrase. For example, "effects" include automobiles, luggage and other containers, clothing, weapons, and even the fruits of a crime.[19] The term is less inclusive, however, than the word "property." For example, the Supreme Court has determined that an "open field," which is not a "house," is also not an "effect."[20]

---

19. *See, e.g.,* United States v. Chadwick, 433 U.S. 1 (1977) (automobile); Bond v. United States, 529 U.S. 334 (2000) (luggage); United States v. Edwards, 415 U.S. 800 (1974) (clothing); Warden v. Hayden, 387 U.S. 294 (1967) (weapons, money from a robbery).

20. Oliver v. United States, 466 U.S. at 177.

Chapter 6

Fourth Amendment Terminology: "Search"

§ 6.01 Why "Search" Law Matters

[A] Constitutional Significance of the Term "Search"

The Fourth Amendment prohibits unreasonable searches and seizures. This chapter considers the meaning of the word "search" in the Fourth Amendment.[1]

As the preceding sentence suggests, "search" is a technical term of art in Fourth Amendment jurisprudence. The word is not employed in its ordinary and popular sense. Indeed, the difference between the lay and legal meaning of the word is so substantial that lawyers, including those sitting on the Supreme Court, sometimes describe particular police activity as a "search," even as it is judged to be a "non-search" in the Fourth Amendment context.[2] In order to avoid this confusion, our discussion will refer to any police investigative activity generally as "surveillance" and use the term "search" only if the surveillance is covered by the Fourth Amendment.

If the police surveillance at issue is not a "search" (or a "seizure," as that term is explained in the next chapter), *the Fourth Amendment simply does not apply.* Put more starkly, if a court determines that no search (and no seizure) has occurred, Fourth Amendment analysis immediately ceases. As one judge bluntly put it, "the law does not give a constitutional damn" about non-search and non-seizure police activity.[3]

Consequently, in considering the law discussed in this chapter, do not lose sight of the fact that the question, "Was the Fourth Amendment satisfied?" is preceded by the critical threshold question, "Does the Fourth Amendment even apply to the police conduct at issue?" If a court answers the threshold question negatively, any claim that the police acted without a warrant or without probable cause—or even if the police acted maliciously—may properly be answered with the remark, "So what?" Indeed, "[w]hen the fourth amendment is inapplicable [because no "search" or "seizure" has occurred], good and evil have no relevance."[4]

---

1. *See* John M. Burkoff, *When Is a Search Not a "Search?": Fourth Amendment Doublethink*, 15 U. Toledo L. Rev. 515 (1984).

2. *See, e.g.,* Oliver v. United States, 466 U.S. 170, 173 (1984) (in which the Court framed the issue to be whether the "open fields" doctrine "permits police officers to . . . search a field," although the Court went on to hold, in part, that inspection of an open field is not a Fourth Amendment "search").

3. Charles E. Moylan, *The Fourth Amendment Inapplicable vs. The Fourth Amendment Satisfied: The Neglected Threshold of "So What?"*, 2 So. Ill. U.L.J. 75, 76 (1977).

4. *Id.* at 75.

[B] An Important Question for Further Consideration

In light of the cynical observation at the end of subsection [A], it is submitted here that the Supreme Court might have done itself and the law a service if it had chosen to define the term "search" in a common-sense dictionary-meaning manner,[5] thus treating virtually every police investigative technique as a "search." If this were the case, courts could immediately turn to what is, after all, the ultimate Fourth Amendment issue: Is the contested law enforcement technique reasonable or unreasonable (and why)?[6]

This is not to suggest that there is a simple answer to the latter reasonableness question. A scholar once observed that "[l]egal description is blind without the guiding light of a theory of values,"[7] and "obtaining anything approaching consensus on a 'theory of values' in the United States . . . seems quite unlikely . . ."[8] But this might be a more intellectually honest way to confront most Fourth Amendment litigation.[9]

§ 6.02 "Search": Original "Trespass" Analysis

Fourth Amendment "search" analysis is divisible into three historical periods. During the early period, the Court held that government surveillance was a search under the Fourth Amendment if the government action trespassed on the defendant's property interests. This period ended in 1967 when the Supreme Court announced its landmark decision in *Katz v. United States*.[10] *Katz* rejected the property-based test and instead focused on whether or not the government action violated the defendant's "reasonable expectation of privacy." That period ended in 2012, when the Supreme Court decided *United States v. Jones*,[11] which revived the "trespass" test of the earlier period and

---

5. Justice Antonin Scalia recently pointed out that "[w]hen the Fourth Amendment was adopted, as now, to 'search' meant '[t]o look over or through for the purpose of finding something; to explore; to examine by inspection; as, to *search* the house for a book; to *search* the wood for a thief.' N. Webster, An American Dictionary of the English Language 66 (1828) (reprint 6th ed. 1989)." Kyllo v. United States, 533 U.S. 27, 32 n.1 (2001).

6. *See generally* Daniel J. Solove, *Fourth Amendment Pragmatism*, 51 B.C. L. Rev. 1511 (2010) (arguing for a pragmatic approach to the Fourth Amendment in which the "Coverage Question"— whether the Fourth Amendment is implicated—is broadly interpreted, so as to focus instead on the question of whether the Fourth Amendment bars the particular activity in question).

7. Felix S. Cohen, *Transcendental Nonsense and the Functional Approach*, 35 Colum. L. Rev. 809, 849 (1935).

8. George C. Thomas III, *Law's Social Consequences*, 51 Rutgers L. Rev. 845, 847 (1999).

9. A myriad of sub-issues arise in any "reasonableness" analysis, such as: (1) Should the reasonableness of particular police activity be resolved on a case-by-case basis, or should the Court try to provide generalizable answers?; (2) To what extent is the presence or absence of a search warrant relevant?; (3) To what extent should the reasonableness inquiry be governed by the framers' intent and seventeenth-century common law history?; and (4) To what extent is the appropriate inquiry what "citizens in a civilized society are entitled to expect [from] their government"? Jeffrey Rosen, *Here's Looking At You*, The New Republic, Oct. 16, 2000, at 24, 26. This latter issue, of course, is unabashedly normative in nature, which insures vigorous debate. But these questions and others are an inevitable feature of constitutional adjudication of a text that prohibits "*unreasonable* searches and seizures."

10. 389 U.S. 347 (1967).

11. 132 S. Ct. 945 (2012).

held that surveillance is a search if it violates a defendant's reasonable expectation of privacy *or* infringes on the defendant's property interests.

The first period began with *Boyd v. United States*,[12] which laid the seeds for a property-rights interpretation of the Fourth Amendment.[13] According to *Boyd*, the "odious" English practice of issuing general warrants[14] was "fresh in the memories" of the drafters of the Fourth Amendment. The Court quoted extensively from the "memorable discussion" and condemnation of general warrants set out in *Entick v. Carrington*,[15] in which Lord Camden stated that "every invasion of private property, be it ever so minute, is a trespass."

Under *Boyd*, the Fourth Amendment did not apply in the absence of a physical intrusion—a trespass—by government agents into a "constitutionally protected area,"[16] in order to "find something or to obtain information."[17]

Olmstead v. United States[18] provides the most famous example of the Court's pre-*Katz* property rights/trespass approach to the Fourth Amendment. In *Olmstead*, federal officers, without obtaining a search warrant, used wiretaps to intercept the conversations of *O* and others, conducted by telephone from their homes and offices. The Court ruled that this conduct fell outside the reach of the Fourth Amendment.

The explanatory portion of the opinion was brief and unrevealing. The reasoning, however, came down to this: because they are intangible, conversations are not "persons, house, papers, or effects," so they are unprotected;[19] the houses and offices from which the conversations arose *are* protected by the Fourth Amendment, but only from physical intrusions or trespasses; eyes and ears cannot "search" or "seize," since neither can trespass; and, the wiretaps used to listen to the conversations, which *can* trespass, did not do so here because they were installed on telephone lines *outside* *O*'s property.

In other pre-*Katz* decisions applying the trespass doctrine, the Supreme Court concluded that the use of a searchlight was not a "search," in essence because light cannot trespass.[20] It also held that no "search" occurs when an undercover agent consensually enters a criminal suspect's premises with a hidden transmitter[21] or tape recorder[22] on the agent's body, and there engages the suspect in incriminating conversations, since the invited agent is not a trespasser.

On the other hand, in *Silverman v. United States*,[23] a "search" occurred when a spike-microphone inserted into a party wall intruded minutely into the speakers' side of the wall. The justices observed, however, that the decision was not based on the fact that there

---

12. 116 U.S. 616 (1886).

13. Ironically, *Boyd* also provided support for the privacy-oriented view of the Fourth Amendment that ultimately developed. *See* Tom Bush, *A Privacy-Based Analysis for Warrantless Aerial Surveillance Cases*, 75 Cal. L. Rev. 1767, 1789–91 (1987).

14. *See* § 4.03, *supra*.

15. 19 Howell St. Tr. 1029, 1066 (1765) (Eng.).

16. Lanza v. New York, 370 U.S. 139, 142 (1962).

17. United States v. Jones, 132 S. Ct. 945, 951 n.5 (2012).

18. 277 U.S. 438 (1928), *overruled by* Katz v. United States, 389 U.S. 347 (1967).

19. *See especially* § 5.02, *supra*.

20. United States v. Lee, 274 U.S. 559 (1927).

21. On Lee v. United States, 343 U.S. 747 (1952).

22. Lopez v. United States, 373 U.S. 427 (1963).

23. 365 U.S. 505 (1961).

was a "technical trespass under . . . local property law." The Supreme Court was preparing to look beyond trespass analysis.

§ 6.03 "Search": *Katz v. United States* and the "Privacy" Analysis[24]

[A] An Overview

In *Katz v. United States*,[25] federal officers conducted warrantless surveillance of *K*'s conversations by attaching an electronic listening device to the outside of a telephone booth *K* used to conduct conversations. In light of the Court's original jurisprudence, the parties pressed their Fourth Amendment claims in terms of whether the telephone booth, like a house, was a "constitutionally protected area," and whether a physical intrusion of it was necessary to raise a Fourth Amendment "search" claim.

The Court rejected this line of analysis. With the advent of modern technology as it existed in the 1960s — and, thus, with the government's capacity electronically to intercept conversations without physical intrusion into any enclosure — the Court arrived at the view that the trespass doctrine constituted "bad physics as well as bad law."[26] Consequently, the Court announced "that the 'trespass' doctrine . . . can no longer be regarded as controlling." Instead, the Court created a new test: whether the government surveillance violated the defendant's "reasonable expectation of privacy."

[B] Majority Opinion: In Search of a New Test

Justice Potter Stewart wrote the Court's opinion in *Katz*. One scholar has described the Stewart opinion as an "efficient dismantler, but neglectful reconstructor."[27] That is, *Katz* seemingly buried the trespass doctrine, but the majority opinion offered no evident test in its place. Although *Katz* "bestowed a controlling role upon privacy,"[28] it rejected "privacy" as a new talisman. In fact, Stewart warned that "the Fourth Amendment cannot be translated into a general constitutional 'right to privacy.' That Amendment

---

24. *See generally* Symposium, *Katz v. U.S.: 40 Years Later*, 41 U.C. Davis L. Rev. 775-1325 (2008); Anthony G. Amsterdam, *Perspectives On The Fourth Amendment*, 58 Minn. L. Rev. 349 (1974); Burkoff, Note 1, *supra*; William C. Heffernan, *Fourth Amendment Privacy Interests*, 92 J. Crim. L. & Criminology 1 (2001); Lewis R. Katz, *In Search of a Fourth Amendment for the Twenty-First Century*, 65 Ind. L.J. 549 (1990); Harvey A. Schneider, *Katz v. United States: The Untold Story*, 40 McGeorge L. Rev. 13 (2009) (describing the author's involvement in legal representation of Katz before the Supreme Court); David Alan Sklansky, *"One Train May Hide Another": Katz, Stonewall, and the Secret Subtext of Criminal Procedure*, 41 U.C. Davis L. Rev. 875 (2008); Solove, Note 6, *supra*; James J. Tomkovicz, *Beyond Secrecy for Secrecy's Sake: Toward an Expanded Vision of the Fourth Amendment Privacy Province*, 36 Hastings L.J. 645 (1985); Peter Winn, *Katz and the Origins of the "Reasonable Expectation of Privacy" Test*, 40 McGeorge L. Rev. 1 (2009); Note, *A Reconsideration of the Katz Expectation of Privacy Test*, 76 Mich. L. Rev. 154 (1977).

25. 389 U.S. 347 (1967).

26. *Id.* at 362 (Harlan, J., concurring).

27. Tomkovicz, Note 24, *supra*, at 650–51.

28. *Id.* at 651.

protects individual privacy against certain kinds of governmental intrusion, but its protections go further, and often have nothing to do with privacy at all."

Justice Stewart stated that "the Fourth Amendment protects people, not places." Although this statement is surely true—the Amendment begins, after all, with the phrase "[t]he right of the people"—it is less helpful than it might seem because, as Justice Harlan wisely observed in his concurring opinion, the ultimate "question . . . is what protection [the Fourth Amendment] affords to those people. Generally, . . . the answer to that question requires reference to a 'place.'"

Although Justice Stewart offered no bright-line definition of a "search," he did state in language that has been cited frequently in post-*Katz* cases—if there is anything like a "test" in the majority opinion, it is this—that "[w]hat a person knowingly exposes to the public, even in his own home or office, is not a subject of Fourth Amendment protection," whereas "what he seeks to preserve as private, even in an area accessible to the public, may be constitutionally protected."

In this "knowing public exposure"/"seek to preserve as private" context, Stewart distinguished, in *K*'s situation in the telephone booth, between the uninvited ear (the electronic bug) and intruding eyes. Because the telephone booth was made of glass, *K*'s physical actions were knowingly exposed to the public, but what he sought to exclude when he entered the booth was the uninvited ear. Therefore, by shutting the door on the booth[29] and paying the toll, *K* was "surely entitled to assume that the words he utter[ed] . . . [would] not be broadcast to the world." As a result, "the Government's activities . . . violated the privacy upon which he justifiably relied . . ."

[C] Concurring Opinion: A New "Search" Test

If Justice Stewart's opinion lacked a definition of a Fourth Amendment "search," Justice John Harlan's concurring opinion filled the void. He interpreted the case "to hold only" that a telephone booth, like a home, and unlike an open field, is an area in which "a person has a constitutionally protected 'reasonable expectation of privacy' . . ." Although Justice Harlan asserted that this holding "emerged from prior decisions," it is this language that has survived as the operative definition under *Katz* of a Fourth Amendment "search."

As Justice Harlan explained, the "reasonable expectation of privacy" standard has a subjective and an objective component. First, the individual must have "exhibited an actual (subjective) expectation of privacy." Second, he must prove[30] that the expectation

---

29. It bears mention that nearly all telephone booths today—themselves a vanishing structure in the modern world of cell phones—are open. Few booths have doors that users can close to bar "the uninvited ear." This is just another reason why technology has quite arguably left *Katz* and its analysis outdated.

30. *Katz* did not consider the question of who has the burden of proof in search cases. However, in *Florida v. Riley*, 488 U.S. 445 (1989), four justices inferentially, *id.* at 451, and a fifth justice (Justice O'Connor) expressly, *id.* at 455, suggested that the defendant must provide facts that would support the claim that his expectation of privacy was reasonable. Four justices dissented on this issue. *Id.* at 465. In issues of standing, which the Court has equated to the "search" question, *see* § 19.04[A], *infra*, the Court has expressly held that the defendant "bears the burden of proving . . . that he had a legitimate expectation of privacy" in the area searched. Rawlings v. Kentucky, 448 U.S. 98, 104 (1980).

he exhibited is one that "society is prepared to recognize as 'reasonable'" or — to use the Court's variants — "legitimate"[31] or "justifiable."[32]

Police conduct does not constitute a "search" — and, thus, the Fourth Amendment is not triggered — if either prong of the test is lacking. For example, if *K* in *Katz* had spoken "in the open" (e.g., on a busy public sidewalk) where he could have been overheard, rather than in the closed telephone booth that shut out the uninvited ears of others,[33] *K*'s subjective expectation of privacy would have been unreasonable under the circumstances. Therefore, *K* could not have successfully claimed that he was the subject of a Fourth Amendment "search."

Similarly, *K* would not have had a valid "search" claim if he had realized that the telephone booth was bugged. Thus, although people *in general* may have a reasonable expectation of privacy in their telephone conversations conducted in private, an individual's *subjective* realization that his conversations were not private would eviscerate his Fourth Amendment claim.

[D] Analysis and Critique of the *Katz* Test

[1] Overview

Professor Anthony Amsterdam once observed that Justice Stewart's opinion "was written to resist captivation in any formula."[34] The Court seemingly abandoned the prior law because it had become too rigid: thoughtful analysis had given way to formulas and talismans, such as "trespass," which did not take into account technological advances. Therefore, according to Amsterdam, Harlan's "search" test violated the essence of *Katz* because it substituted one talisman for another.

Justice Harlan came to agree, at least in part, with this criticism. He later acknowledged that his expectations formula, although "an advance over the unsophisticated trespass analysis of the common law," also had its "limitations and can, ultimately, lead to the substitution of words for analysis."[35] Based on a survey of post-*Katz* Supreme Court decisions, especially the Court's treatment of the objective prong of his "search" standard, some critics of *Katz* would maintain that Harlan's warning about his own test has proved prescient. At a minimum, as another critic of *Katz* has observed, Harlan's

---

31. *E.g.*, Illinois v. Andreas, 463 U.S. 765, 771 (1983).

32. Smith v. Maryland, 442 U.S. 735, 740 (1979); *see also Katz*, 389 U.S. 347, 353 (1967) ("The Government's activities . . . violated the privacy upon which [*D*] justifiably relied . . .").

33. Suppose, in *Katz*, that *X*, a lip reader, had stood outside the booth and "listened" to *K*'s conversation? If *K* had observed *X* watching his lips, would he have had a reasonable expectation of privacy regarding *this* mode of interception of his conversation? Perhaps not, at least if *K* had understood that *X* was reading his lips. Under such circumstances, it may be said that *K* "knowingly exposed" (to use Justice Stewart's language) his words to *X*; his conversations were "in the open" (to use Justice Harlan's words) insofar as *X* was concerned. As well, Stewart explicitly distinguished between "intruding eyes" and "uninvited ears." One could reason, therefore, that *Katz* stands for the proposition that a person may have a reasonable expectation of privacy regarding one mode of intrusion, and yet have none if the same information is intercepted in a different manner. *See* § 6.04[B], *infra*.

34. Amsterdam, Note 24, *supra*, at 385.

35. United States v. White, 401 U.S. 745, 786 (1971) (dissenting opinion).

"reasonable expectation of privacy test has led to a contentious jurisprudence that is riddled with inconsistencies and incoherence."[36]

Potential problems with the "reasonable expectation of privacy" test are set out below.

[2] Should We Have the Subjective Prong?

Many commentators fault Justice Harlan for including a subjective prong in his expectations formula.[37] Their thesis is that if the subjective component is taken seriously, the government can eliminate privacy expectations—and, thus, render the Fourth Amendment inapplicable—by the simple act of announcing its intention to conduct Orwellian surveillance.[38] If citizens know that their government is reading their electronic mail,[39] listening to their conversations, and generally intruding on their privacy—as increasingly is possible[40]—many people will ultimately possess no subjective expectation of privacy.

Beyond this, *non*-governmental intrusions potentially undermine our right to be free of governmental intrusions. Modern technology makes it possible—even inexpensive[41]—for private individuals to observe their neighbors from long distances, even at night, or to track their movements electronically, as well as for corporations to discover previously private information about people who use the Internet. As a result, few of us believe that we possess as much privacy today as we did even a decade ago. In light of our lesser subjective expectations of privacy, under *Katz*, our Fourth Amendment protections from governmental overreaching recede further.[42]

---

36. Solove, Note 6, *supra*, at 1511.

37. *E.g.*, Amsterdam, Note 24, *supra*, at 384; Burkoff, Note 1, *supra*, at 537–39; Wayne R. LaFave, *The Fourth Amendment Today: A Bicentennial Appraisal*, 32 Vill. L. Rev. 1061, 1080–81 (1987); Note, Note 24, *supra*, at 157–58.

38. Raymond Shih Ray Ku, *The Founders' Privacy: The Fourth Amendment and the Power of Technological Surveillance*, 86 Minn. L. Rev. 1325, 1327 (2002) ("[T]he Supreme Court's current Fourth Amendment doctrine allows government to determine for itself the scope of its own powers."); in this regard *see* Joel Brinkley, *Israel in Uproar Over TV Report Confirming Existence of Secret Army Unit*, New York Times, June 24, 1991, at A3 (a military security film showing two Israeli soldiers disguised as Arabs catching a "Palestinian suspect" was shown on Israeli television; the stated purpose was "simply to scare the Arabs"; according to an Army spokesman, "Now they will be aware of the fact that nothing is secured.... [T]hat's exactly [the atmosphere] we are trying to create.").

39. Consider Rosen, Note 9, *supra*, at 26 ("[T]he FBI's unfortunately named Carnivore system . . . invisibly searches everyone's e-mail but alerts law enforcement only when it finds the particular messages it has been programmed to look for.").

40. Kyllo v. United States, 533 U.S. 27, 36 n. 3 (2001) ("The ability to 'see' through walls and other opaque barriers is a clear, and scientifically feasible, goal of law enforcement research and development.").

41. Christopher Slobogin, *Peeping Techno-Toms and the Fourth Amendment: Seeing Through Kyllo's Rules Governing Technological Surveillance*, 86 Minn. L. Rev. 1393, 1402–04 (2002) (applying what he calls the "Wal-Mart test," the author describes some of the devices readily accessible to large segments of the public for intruding on the privacy of others).

42. The same criticism applies to Justice Stewart's "*knowing* exposure to the public" test. In view of modern technology and other incursions into citizens' private lives, virtually everyone *knowingly* exposes intimate and private details of their lives to others. Had Stewart simply substituted the word "purposely" for "knowingly," his standard would have resulted in much broader constitutional protection: "Purposeful" exposure only occurs when it is the conscious objective of the individual to expose the information to others. Today we *knowingly* expose a great deal of private information that we do not *desire* to expose. *Contra*, Sherry F. Colb, *What Is a Search? Two Conceptual Flaws in Fourth Amendment Doctrine and Some Hints of a Remedy*, 55 Stan. L. Rev. 119,

Justice Harlan ultimately agreed with this criticism of his test. He concluded that the critical focus should be on *objective* expectations. Privacy analysis, he concluded, should "transcend the search for subjective expectations" because "[o]ur expectations . . . are in large part reflections of laws that translate into rules the customs and values of the past and present."[43] The task of the law, he noted, is "to form and project," and not simply to "mirror and reflect."

The Court has acknowledged the risk inhering in the subjective prong. It has stated that if the situation should ever occur that a person's subjective expectations were "conditioned by influences alien to well-recognized Fourth Amendment freedoms," the subjective element "obviously could play no meaningful role."[44] And in fact, an empirical study of more than 500 Fourth Amendment cases decided in 2012 determined that only 12 percent even applied the subjective prong of the test, and in no case did the subjective prong affect the outcome.[45] Thus, we may already be at the point at which the subjective prong plays "no meaningful role" in the Fourth Amendment analysis.

[3] The Objective Prong: What *Precisely* Is the Standard?[46]

Justice Harlan stated in *Katz* that, in order for the Fourth Amendment to apply, the expectation exhibited by an individual must be one that "society is prepared to recognize as 'reasonable.'" In the majority opinion, Justice Stewart stated that the electronic surveillance in that case violated the privacy upon which *K* "justifiably" relied in the telephone booth. In stating or applying the objective prong, some post-*Katz* cases have also used the word "justifiable," and still others have employed the word "legitimate." The Court treats these words interchangeably, and yet a distinction arguably could be drawn between, on the one hand, "reasonable" expectations and, on the other hand, "legitimate" or "justifiable" ones. The potential distinction merits notice.

---

124 (2002) (characterizing the "knowing exposure" concept as "basically sound," but arguing that the Supreme Court has given improper content to the concept).

43. United States v. White, 401 U.S. 745, 786 (1971) (dissenting opinion).

44. Smith v. Maryland, 442 U.S. 735, 740 n.5 (1979). Although the Court, in a majority opinion, has not elaborated on this remark, five justices recently have. In *United States v. Jones*, 132 S. Ct. 945 (2012), the Court considered the question of whether the attachment of a Global-Positioning-System (GPS) tracking device to a suspect's automobile, and subsequent monitoring of his movements for 28 days, constituted a Fourth Amendment search. Justice Alito, writing as well for Justices Ginsburg, Breyer, and Kagan, observed that "the *Katz* test rests on the assumption that [there is] a well-developed and stable set of privacy expectations. But technology can change those expectations. Dramatic technological change may . . . produce significant changes in popular attitudes." Thus, it would seem Alito is stating in part that the subjective expectations of members of the public are apt to be affected—reduced—as a result of technological "advances."Justice Sotomayor, as well, expressed her concern that "the same technological advances that have made possible nontrespassory surveillance techniques will also affect the *Katz* test by shaping the evolution of societal privacy expectations." She indicated that she is open to reconsidering some post-*Katz* case law because of her concern that modern surveillance techniques are tools "so amenable to misuse, especially in light of the Fourth Amendment's goal to curb arbitrary exercises of police power. . . ."

45. Orin Kerr, Katz *Has Only One Step: The Irrelevance of Subjective Expectations*, 82 U. Chi. L. Rev. 113 (2015).

46. *See generally* Christopher Slobogin & Joseph E. Schumacher, *Reasonable Expectations of Privacy and Autonomy in Fourth Amendment Cases: An Empirical Look at "Understandings Recognized and Permitted by Society"*, 42 Duke L.J. 727 (1993).

Typically, to say that a person's belief or expectation is "reasonable" means that his belief or expectation is one that an ordinary person might possess. In the privacy context, this would mean that an expectation of privacy is "reasonable" when a "reasonable person" would not expect his privacy is at serious risk. So understood, "reasonableness" contains a significant empirical component, a "matter[] of statistical probability"[47] that there will be a privacy incursion.

In contrast, to say that a person has a "legitimate" or "justifiable" expectation of privacy is to draw a normative conclusion—a value judgment—that the individual has a right to the privacy expectation.[48] As one court has put it, the privacy protected by the Fourth Amendment under this view "is not the privacy that one reasonably *expects* but the privacy to which one has a *right*."[49] Professor Amsterdam has asked the normative question this way:

> [W]hether, if the particular form of surveillance practiced by the police is permitted to go unregulated by constitutional restraints, the amount of privacy and freedom remaining to citizens would be diminished to a compass inconsistent with the aims of a free and open society.[50]

Based on this distinction, a privacy expectation could be empirically "reasonable" and yet normatively "illegitimate" or "unjustifiable"; on the other hand, an "unreasonable" expectation of privacy could be "justifiable" or "legitimate." For example, suppose that *D* commits a crime in a secluded spot in a park during the middle of the night after carefully ascertaining that the area is frequented at that hour only once every 672 days. Based on this information, *D* expects that his actions will not be observed. That expectation would seem to be "reasonable" in the sense that most persons would expect, as a matter of statistical probability, to be free from observation. Nonetheless, if a police officer happened by and observed the criminal conduct, commentators would likely agree with the conclusion that *D*'s subjective privacy expectation should not be protected. This is because *D*'s expectations, although perhaps "reasonable," were "unjustifiable" or "illegitimate." As a normative matter, people arguably should have no right to expect privacy if they conduct criminal activities in the open, even if it is very unlikely they will be discovered on any particular occasion.

On the other hand, suppose that *D* lives in a high-crime area in which police helicopters routinely hover at a very low altitude over the backyards of homes, scanning the area. On a particular occasion, suppose that a police helicopter hovers sufficiently low that the pilot observes a marijuana plant growing in *D*'s fenced-in and heavily-treed backyard, or he sees the homeowners having sexual intercourse next to their pool. As a matter of foreseeability, it is unreasonable for people in a heavily surveyed area to expect privacy in their backyard. As a value judgment, however, it is at least an open issue as to whether this type of governmental surveillance should be approved.[51]

Which form of analysis—empirical or normative—did Justice Harlan intend by his test? In *Katz*, he described the objective component in terms of an expectation "that

---

47. LaFave, Note 37, *supra*, at 1081.

48. Note, Note 24, *supra*, at 155–56.

49. State v. Campbell, 759 P.2d 1040, 1044 (Or. 1988).

50. Amsterdam, Note 23, *supra*, at 403; *see also* Rosen, Note 9, *supra*, at 26 ("The question is whether citizens in a civilized society are entitled to expect that their government isn't lurking in front of their homes and peering through their walls without proper cause.").

51. For the Court's judgment in this regard, *see* § 6.07, *infra*.

society is prepared to recognize as 'reasonable'." The italicized words may connote a normative inquiry. Harlan's view, however, became clearer after *Katz*. In a reflective post-*Katz* opinion, he placed himself definitively on the side of a normative interpretation of the objective prong. He stated that judges must determine "the desirability of saddling" people with particular risks to their privacy. He wrote that "[t]he critical question . . . is whether under our system of government, as reflected in the Constitution, we should impose on our citizens . . . [particular privacy] risks . . . without at least the protection of a warrant requirement."[52]

Justice Harlan's views notwithstanding, the Court's approach to the issue has been mixed. At least in some circumstances, it has stated that a normative inquiry is proper.[53] Usually, however, the Court has treated the empirical fact of privacy incursions — e.g., that people trespass,[54] conduct aerial surveillance of residential backyards,[55] or look through other people's trash[56] — as justification for concluding that subjective expectations of privacy were empirically unreasonable and, therefore, unprotected by the Fourth Amendment.[57]

It is submitted here that Justice Harlan was correct in treating the issue normatively.[58] If so, the critical question that remains is whether courts should attempt to determine *society's* normative judgments in regard to particular forms of surveillance, or whether it is the responsibility of the judges themselves (in the words of Justice Harlan) "to form and project" privacy expectations.[59] The benefit of researching public attitudes is that the normative judgment will not consist solely of the views of nine (or even five) justices on the United States Supreme Court.[60] The detriment in this approach is that the law may end up merely mirroring current attitudes, which have themselves been conditioned by prior incursions authorized by the courts, rather than projecting a twenty-first century view of the proper relationship between the government and citizenry.[61]

---

52. United States v. White, 401 U.S. 745, 786 (1971) (dissenting opinion).

53. Smith v. Maryland, 442 U.S. 735, 740 n.5 (1979).

54. *See* §6.06[A], *infra.*

55. *See* §6.07, *infra.*

56. *See* §6.08, *infra.*

57. *See also* United States v. Jones, 132 S. Ct. 945, 962 (2012) (Alito, J., concurring in judgment) (stating that societal expectations of privacy are not stable and that "popular expectations [of privacy] are in flux," thus implying that the reasonable-expectation-of-privacy test is determined empirically and not normatively).

58. *See, e.g.,* Orin Kerr, *Four Models of Fourth Amendment Protection,* 60 Stan. L. Rev. 503 (2007) (arguing that the term "reasonable" in the objective test is generally normative, though in some cases the normative test ends up being empirical in nature).

59. At least one scholar has suggested allowing *juries* to decide these questions, since they are better equipped than judges in determining what constitutes society's "reasonable expectation of privacy." *See* Meghan J. Ryan, *Juries and the Criminal Constitution,* 65 Ala. L. Rev. 849 (2014).

60. *See* Minnesota v. Carter, 525 U.S. 83, 97 (1998) (Scalia and Thomas, JJ, concurring) ("In my view, the only thing the past three decades have established about the *Katz* test . . . is that, unsurprisingly, those 'actual (subjective) expectation[s] of privacy' 'that society is prepared to recognize as "reasonable"' bear an uncanny resemblance to those expectations of privacy that this Court considers reasonable.").

61. The Supreme Court has never sought to use reliable social science literature to determine public expectations of privacy. One study in this regard suggests that "the Supreme Court's conclusions about the scope of the Fourth Amendment are often not in tune with commonly held attitudes about police investigative techniques." Slobogin & Schumacher, Note 46, *supra,* at 774.

[E] *Jones* and the Resurrection of the "Trespass" Test

Forty-five years after the *Katz* test apparently buried the "trespass" test once and for all, the Supreme Court resurrected the test. In *Jones v. United States*,[62] the Court reviewed the warrantless use of a Global Positioning System (GPS) tracking device in public areas, and a majority of the Court held that the government surveillance constituted a Fourth Amendment search because the government action infringed on the defendant's property rights.

In *Jones*, federal officers attached a GPS device to the undercarriage of a suspect's Jeep and then monitored his movements for 28 days without a valid search warrant.[63] The issue, as the Court put it, was "whether the attachment of a * * * [GPS] tracking device to an individual's vehicle, and subsequent use of that device to monitor the vehicle's movements on public streets, constitutes a search or seizure within the meaning of the Fourth Amendment."[64]

The government defended its actions on the ground that the agents had conducted no Fourth Amendment search (thus requiring no warrant). In support of its position, the government reasoned that Jones had no "reasonable expectation of privacy in the area of the Jeep accessed by government agents (its underbody) and in the locations of the Jeep on the public roads, which were visible to all."

Notwithstanding this argument, and case law arguably supporting the government's position,[65] the Court unanimously held that the installation and use of the GPS tracking device for 28 days constituted a Fourth Amendment "search." The justices divided sharply, however, in their reasoning. Justice Scalia, writing for the Chief Justice and Justices Kennedy, Thomas, and Sotomayor, stated that "we need not address the Government's contentions, because Jones's Fourth Amendment rights do not rise or fall with the *Katz* formulation."

How can this be? The answer, according to Scalia, is that "for most of our history the Fourth Amendment was understood to embody a particular concern for government trespass upon the areas ('persons, houses, papers, and effects') that it enumerates. *Katz did not repudiate that understanding.*"[66] According to the Court, "the *Katz* reasonable-expectation-of-privacy test has ... *added to*, not *substituted for*, the common-law trespassory test." The Court stated that "[w]hatever new methods of investigation may be devised, our task, *at a minimum*, is to decide whether the action in question would have constituted a 'search' within the original meaning of the Fourth Amendment. Where, as here, the Government obtains information by physically intruding on a constitutionally protected area, such a search has undoubtedly occurred."[67]

---

62. 132 S. Ct. 945; *see generally* Thomas K. Clancy, *United States v. Jones: Fourth Amendment Applicability in the 21st Century*, 10 Ohio St. J. Crim. L. 303 (2012); Orin S. Kerr, *The Mosaic Theory of the Fourth Amendment*, 111 Mich. L. Rev. 311 (2012); Erin Murphy, *United States v. Jones*, 10 Ohio St. J. Crim. L. 325 (2012).

63. The officers obtained a District of Columbia warrant authorizing them to attach the GPS within 10 days and to conduct surveillance. However, agents installed the device in Maryland (rendering the warrant invalid) and too late (on the eleventh day).

64. 132 S. Ct. at 948.

65. *See* Section 6.10[C] below.

66. *Id.* at 950 (emphasis added).

67. *Id.* at 951, n.3; *see also id.* at 955 (Sotomayor, J., concurring) ("[T]he trespassory test ... reflects an irreducible constitutional minimum: When the Government physically invades personal property to gather information, a search occurs.").

In understanding the *Jones* test, it is important to focus on two aspects of the preceding sentence. First, government action will only constitute a search under the *Jones* test if the purpose of the government action was to find something or obtain information.[68] If a police officer trespasses onto a suspect's home for a different purpose—perhaps to render emergency aid, or to sell tickets to a police charity event—the trespass will not constitute a search under *Jones*. Second, the *Jones* test is not triggered by *any* type of trespass; rather, it is triggered only if the government trespasses into a "constitutionally protected area"—that is, a "person, house, paper, or effect." Specifically, trespassing onto the defendant's land alone will not implicate the Fourth Amendment.[69]

Thus, *Jones* returned the law to the pre-*Katz* trespass doctrine *without rejecting the Katz test*. Either test can now be used to establish that the government surveillance constituted a Fourth Amendment search.

This was not the view of Justice Alito, who wrote a concurrence that included Justices Ginsburg, Breyer, and Kagan. The concurring justices rejected the majority opinion because "[i]t strains the language of the Fourth Amendment; it has little if any support in current Fourth Amendment case law; and it is highly artificial."[70] They would exclusively apply the *Katz* test. Instead, the concurrence adopted a new doctrine known as the "mosaic theory," in which it recognizes that large amounts of public information can potentially reveal private details about a person. We discuss the mosaic theory in more detail in Section 6.10[D] below.

So where do we stand now? The *Katz* "reasonable expectation of privacy" test is still alive and well, but the *Jones* "trespass" test is now also used by courts. The Supreme Court has applied the trespass test in two other cases since *Jones*, holding that the government conducted a Fourth Amendment search when it brought a drug-sniffing dog onto the defendant's porch,[71] and that it conducted a Fourth Amendment search when it attached a tracking device to the body of a sex offender.[72] Thus, government surveillance will constitute a search if it *either* violates the defendant's reasonable expectation of privacy *or* it trespasses on the defendant's property rights.

Having said that, the *Katz* test is still by far the most common test that courts will apply, for a number of reasons. First, the *Katz* test has been around for many decades, and so there are dozens of Supreme Court cases and thousands of lower-level appellate court cases that have applied the test in a variety of different contexts, so there is a rich history of jurisprudence for courts to turn to when determining whether a search occurred. Second, many of the more modern surveillance techniques involve using electronic surveillance methods (such as intercepting cell phone data or copying a computer's hard drive) that lend themselves quite naturally to a "reasonable expectation of privacy" analysis but are a poor fit with a "trespass" analysis. For these reasons, we will focus on the *Katz* test for most of this chapter. Keep in mind, however, that it is now one of two ways in which the defendant can establish that a "search" has taken place.

---

68. *Id.* at 951 n.5.
69. *See* Section 6.06.
70. *Id.* at 958.
71. Florida v. Jardines, 569 U.S. 1 (2013).
72. Grady v. North Carolina, 135 S. Ct. 1368 (2015).

§ 6.04 Post-*Katz* "Search" Jurisprudence: An Overview[73]

[A] What Has *Katz* Wrought?

Katz was decided during the peak of the Warren Court's so-called "criminal procedure revolution." By the time the Court began to interpret *Katz* with some regularity, however, Earl Warren and various others members of the *Katz* Court had retired and been replaced by more "crime control"-oriented justices. As a consequence, *Katz* has not had the impact on law enforcement that civil libertarians desired or police departments feared.

As will be seen in the remaining sections of this chapter, more often than not, the Supreme Court has ruled that controversial police investigative techniques—for example, use of undercover agents to acquire information, trespassing into open fields, aerial surveillance of the backyards of homes, use of dogs to sniff for contraband in public places, inspection of garbage, and use of some electronic tracking devices—fall outside the scope of the Fourth Amendment, i.e., no "search" has occurred. Indeed, many post-*Katz* rulings, although ostensibly based on reasonable-expectation-of-privacy grounds, have reached the same outcome one would expect from applying pre-*Katz* property-rights trespass analysis. And, at times, the Court has used language in its opinions reminiscent of the pre-*Katz* era.

That said, Fourth Amendment "search" law might be at an important crossroad. Justice Harlan observed in *Katz* that the trespass doctrine represented "bad physics as well as bad law." The remarkable technological developments of recent years make that observation far more relevant today. The Court, therefore, has sought, albeit cautiously, to place some constitutional limits on the use of modern and future sense-enhancing technology.[74] Ironically, it has done so most recently by returning to pre-*Katz* property-rights trespass doctrine.[75]

In terms of reasonable-expectation-of-privacy analysis, the following summary is possible.

[1] Subjective Prong

In Supreme Court Fourth Amendment "search" jurisprudence, the Court has more often than not found that the Fourth Amendment claimant possessed an expectation of

---

73. *See generally* Burkoff, Note 1, *supra*; Thomas K. Clancy, *What Is a "Search" Within the Meaning of the Fourth Amendment?*, 70 Albany L. Rev. 1 (2006); Colb, Note 47, *supra*; Melvin Gutterman, *A Formulation of the Value and Means Models of the Fourth Amendment in the Age of Technologically Enhanced Surveillance*, 39 Syracuse L. Rev. 647 (1988); Heffernan, Note 23, *supra*; Stephen E. Henderson, *Beyond the (Current) Fourth Amendment: Protecting Third-Party Information, Third Parties, and the Rest of Us Too*, 34 Pepperdine L. Rev. 975 (2007); Katz, Note 23, *supra*; Christopher Slobogin, *Technologically-Assisted Physical Surveillance: The American Bar Association's Tentative Draft Standards*, 10 Harv. J. L. & Techn. 383 (1997); Slobogin & Schumacher, Note 50, *supra*; Scott E. Sundby, *"Everyman"'s Fourth Amendment: Privacy or Mutual Trust Between Government and Citizen?*, 94 Colum. L. Rev. 1751 (1994); Tomkovicz, Note 24, *supra*.

74. *See* § 6.10, *infra*.

75. United States v. Jones, 132 S. Ct. 945 (2012). *See* § 6.03[A], *supra*, and § 6.10[E], *infra*.

privacy, was willing to assume that he did, or simply moved to the objective prong with-out significant discussion of the subjective factor.[76]

However, on occasion the Court has suggested that the claimant's subjective expec-tation was not, or might not have been, present. In one case,[77] the Court did not seek to determine the defendant's subjective expectations, but rather expressed doubt that people "in general" possess a subjective expectation of the sort claimed by the defendant. In another case,[78] the Court distinguished between a subjective "intent" or "hope" for pri-vacy (which the Court conceded the defendant "clearly" possessed) and a subjective "ex-pectation" (which the Court said was "not entirely clear" from the circumstances).

[2] Objective Prong

Most "search" litigation has focused on the objective component of Justice Harlan's *Katz* test. At least three interrelated factors have proved particularly important in "ob-jective prong" analysis. First, *the site or nature of the property inspected.* Although Justice Stewart observed in *Katz* that the Fourth Amendment "protects people, not places," in fact the extent to which a person has a reasonable expectation of privacy is significantly tied to the place where the police activity occurred or the citizen is located, and/or the nature of the property being inspected. For example, "open fields" fall outside the pro-tection of the Fourth Amendment, but the "curtilage" of a person's home is entitled to somewhat greater protection, and activities within the home are most strictly protect-ed.[79] At the same time, the Court is especially disinclined to state that an expectation of privacy in contraband—property that one has no lawful right to possess—can be legitimate.[80]

A second factor is *the extent to which a person has taken measures to keep information, his property, or an activity private.* In this context, two rules are frequently asserted by the Court: (1) drawn from Justice Stewart's opinion in *Katz*, it is said that a person cannot possess a reasonable expectation of privacy in that which he knowingly exposes to the public or is otherwise in open view; and (2) one who voluntarily conveys information or property to another person "assumes the risk" that the latter individual is a government agent or will transmit the information or property to the government. The effect of the latter doctrine is, as one critic has put it, that "the fourth amendment is eliminated from a great many aspects of modern life. The Court requires the individual who seeks full . . . protection to live an isolated life within his house with the shades drawn."[81]

---

76. *E.g.*, California v. Greenwood, 486 U.S. 35, 39 (1988) ("It may well be that respondents did not expect that the contents of their garbage bags would become known to the police or other members of the public."); Oliver v. United States, 466 U.S. 170, 177 (1984) (not discussing the sub-jective prong, and simply stating that "[t]he Amendment does not protect the merely subjective expectation of privacy. . . ."); United States v. White, 401 U.S. 745, 751 (1971) ("Very probably, indi-vidual defendants neither know nor suspect that their colleagues have gone or will go to the police or are carrying recorders or transmitters. Otherwise, conversation would cease. . . .").

77. Smith v. Maryland, 442 U.S. 735 (1979). *See* §6.10[B], *infra.*

78. California v. Ciraolo, 476 U.S. 207 (1986). *See* §6.07[B], *infra.*

79. *See* Payton v. New York, 445 U.S. 573, 590 (1980) (the Fourth Amendment draws "a firm line at the entrance to the house"); Kirk v. Louisiana, 536 U.S. 635 (2002) (per curiam) (reaffirming *Payton*'s "firm line"); Kyllo v. United States, 533 U.S. 27, 34 (2001) (noting that that the interior of a home "is a ready criterion, with roots deep in the common law, of the minimal expectation of pri-vacy that *exists* and that is acknowledged to be *reasonable*.").

80. *See* §6.09, *infra.*

81. *Katz*, Note 24, *supra*, at 568.

Third, *the degree of intrusion experienced* is relevant. For example, whether very low-altitude aerial surveillance of the backyard of a person's home by helicopter constitutes a "search" may depend on whether the helicopter causes noise and dust, thereby disrupting legitimate activities therein.[82] Similarly, police surveillance that provides only very limited information to the government—e.g., that a locked suitcase contains illegal drugs, but which provides no further information as to its contents—is more likely to be considered a "non-search" than surveillance techniques that provides intimate information about the individual.

[B] Lurking Issues

Assuming the Court does not redraft its definition of a Fourth Amendment "search," various questions relating to *Katz* are worthy of consideration in evaluating the Supreme Court's post-*Katz* jurisprudence. First, how should the Court resolve the issue raised earlier[83] regarding the difference between an empirically "reasonable" expectation of privacy and a normatively "legitimate" or "justifiable" one?

Second, to what extent should the *mode* of governmental intrusion matter to "search" analysis? Should the Court conclude that a citizen may have a reasonable expectation of privacy regarding one form of intrusion or mode of surveillance, even if he does not, or cannot, have such an expectation as to another? For example, suppose that two persons are performing a sexual act in an open stall in a public restroom. Should the law be that they have no reasonable expectation of privacy if an officer enters the bathroom and observes them, but that they maintain a legitimate expectation that the government will not observe them from a more clandestine vantage point, such as through a peephole in the back wall or by use of a hidden overhead camera?[84]

The Court's consideration of this issue has been inconsistent. For example, in one case,[85] the Supreme Court suggested, in part, that a person does not have an objectively reasonable expectation of privacy from visual observations made by officers trespassing into an open field because the same observations could have been made by lawful aerial surveillance. And yet the Court has expressly drawn a "search" distinction between "visual, as opposed to tactile, observation" of particular property,[86] and even more recently stated that "[t]he fact that equivalent information could sometimes be obtained by other means does *not* make lawful the use of means that violate the Fourth Amendment."[87]

---

82. *See* § 6.07[C], *infra.*

83. *See* § 6.03[D][3], *supra.*

84. *E.g.,* People v. Triggs, 506 P.2d 232 (Cal. 1973) (police observation from a hidden "plumbing access area" of activities in a doorless public toilet stall constitutes a "search"), *overruled on other grounds,* People v. Lilienthal, 587 P.2d 706 (Cal. 1978); *see* State v. Bonnell, 856 P.2d 1265 (Haw. 1993) (in which the court applying the state constitution, but defining "search" in *Katz*-ian terms, stated that the mode of governmental intrusion is a relevant factor in determining whether a person maintains a reasonable expectation of privacy; therefore, the police conducted a "search" when they secretly videotaped activities in a room used by public employees during their work breaks, although the room was not private and could be entered freely by anyone). *See generally* Sklansky, Note 24, *supra* (arguing that one of the great but ignored achievements of *Katz* is that it restricted the then-common practice of police spying on men in toilet stalls to catch homosexual conduct).

85. Oliver v. United States, 466 U.S. 170 (1984); *see* § 6.06, *infra.*

86. Bond v. United States, 529 U.S. at 337.

87. Kyllo v. United States, 533 U.S. at 35 n.2 (emphasis added); *see also* § 6.07[C], *infra* (potentially distinguishing between airplane and helicopter surveillance).

Indeed, in *Katz*, it will be remembered, Justice Stewart distinguished between the metaphorically uninvited ear in the telephone booth and intruding eyes.

Third, should it matter *who* intrudes on our privacy? Should we say that a person may have a legitimate expectation of privacy from governmental intrusion, even though he may not have a similar expectation of freedom from private invasions? For example, should we be permitted to assume that police agents will not inspect our garbage without a warrant, even if we know that homeless persons might sift through our trash?[88] Or, should a property owner who knows that his land is often the subject of unlawful trespass by private individuals be allowed to maintain a legitimate expectation of privacy from similar criminal trespasses by police officers?

§ 6.05 Surveillance of Conversations by "False Friends"[89]

[A] "False Friends" versus *Katz*

Katz v. United States[90] involved electronic monitoring by the government of private conversations to which neither of the speakers consented. That is, while K and X spoke on the telephone, unbeknownst to either, government agents listened to their conversations. *Katz* concluded that the speakers had a reasonable expectation of privacy in their conversations. Therefore, the government was required to conduct the surveillance—a Fourth Amendment "search"—in a constitutionally reasonable manner by obtaining a search warrant.

Katz must be distinguished from cases in which the police acquire a suspect's statements without electronically monitoring his conversations, or by monitoring them with the consent of a conversational participant. Two categories of cases of this sort are considered here. Both involve situations in which X, a police informant or covert ("undercover") police agent, insinuates himself into D's confidence in order to elicit incriminating information from D. In such circumstances, X might be termed a "false friend" of D, essentially a visible "bug" with an invisible purpose.

In the first category of false-friend cases—the pure version—D makes statements to X, or makes statements to another person in X's known presence. X gathers the information from D by listening, and then reports the statements to other law enforcement personnel. The second category might be termed the "wired false friend" cases, which differ from the first scenario in that the "friend," X, also has in his possession a hidden transmitter that permits the police simultaneously to monitor their conversations, or has a hidden tape recorder that registers D's words.

---

88. For the Court's answer to this question, *see* § 6.08, *infra*.

89. *See generally* Tracey Maclin, *Informants and the Fourth Amendment: A Reconsideration*, 74 Wash. U.L.Q. 573 (1996); Geoffrey R. Stone, *The Scope of the Fourth Amendment: Privacy and the Police Use of Spies, Secret Agents, and Informers*, 1976 Am. B. Found. Res. J. 1193; H. Richard Uviller, *Evidence from the Mind of the Criminal Suspect: A Reconsideration of the Current Rules of Access and Restraint*, 87 Colum. L. Rev. 1137 (1987).

90. 389 U.S. 347 (1967).

[B] False Friends

No "search" occurs if *X*, a police informant or undercover agent who is visibly present but is masquerading as *D*'s friend, business associate, or colleague in crime, listens to and reports to the government *D*'s statements to *X* or to another person in *X*'s presence. Prior to *Katz*, the Supreme Court invoked an "assumption of the risk" doctrine to reach this conclusion; after *Katz*, it reaffirmed this rule but framed its reasoning in expectation-of-privacy terms.

In the leading pre-*Katz* false-friend case, *Hoffa v. United States*,[91] *H* conversed with *X* in *H*'s hotel suite. *X* was an acquaintance of *H*, but at the time of their conversations the Supreme Court assumed that *X* was serving as a paid government informant. The government sought to introduce *D*'s statements to *X* at *H*'s later trial.

The Court rejected *H*'s claim that his statements were obtained in violation of the Fourth Amendment. The justices held that although the hotel room in which the conversations arose was a constitutionally protected area, "no interest legitimately protected by the Fourth Amendment [was] involved" because *H* "was not relying on the security of the hotel room; he was relying upon his misplaced confidence that [*X*] would not reveal his wrongdoing."

The lesson of *Hoffa* is that when a person voluntarily speaks to another, i.e., deliberately reveals his mental impressions to a second person, he assumes the risk that the listener is not whom he claims to be—a friend—or is a friend who will later betray the speaker. According to the Court, such a possibility is "inherent in the conditions of human society. It is the kind of risk we necessarily assume whenever we speak."

Hoffa was reaffirmed after *Katz* in *United States v. White*.[92] According to *White*, *Katz* left the holding and assumption-of-risk analysis of *Hoffa* "undisturbed," but the Court also restated *Hoffa* in "*Katz*-ian" terms, by stating that a person does not have "a justifiable and constitutionally protected expectation that a person with whom he is conversing will not then or later reveal the conversation to the police." (This result may also be explained by invoking Justice Stewart's language from *Katz*: There is no Fourth Amendment protection because, by speaking, a person knowingly exposes his thoughts to another and, therefore, to the public.)

Hoffa and *White* may be defended on this ground: Whereas a person can control the extent to which he gives up his privacy in his home by admitting one person but excluding all others, he cannot similarly ensure privacy regarding his thoughts once he discloses them to another. That is, *D* can admit *X* into his home, and yet remain fully protected from unreasonable entry by others. When *D* discloses his thoughts by talking to *X*, however, *D* cannot selectively surrender them. He "necessarily entrust[s] the recipient with complete control over their dissemination, relying wholly on [the] listener's discretion."[93] That the listener turns out to be a false friend is a risk that the speaker assumes by talking.

Despite this justification, *Hoffa* and *White* are controversial for various reasons. First, people doubtlessly must assume the risk that their friends will later betray them, as this possibility exists in all interpersonal relations. It does not necessarily follow, however,

---

91. 385 U.S. 293 (1967).
92. 401 U.S. 745 (1971).
93. Uviller, Note 80, *supra*, at 1198.

that people should be expected to assume the risk in a free society that their "friends" are government agents at the moment they speak.

Second, Professor Geoffrey Stone has warned that "[t]he ability of the individual to rely on the confidentiality of his private conversations is necessary for the maintenance of personal autonomy and the development of creative individuality."[94] Moreover, if one cannot trust in the security of one's private conversation—even worse, if one must worry that one's friend is really a government informant—"the development of intimate, personal and informal social relationships" are jeopardized. Arguably, therefore, government-initiated seizure of conversations should ordinarily be forbidden unless a search warrant is obtained.

Notwithstanding these policy concerns, and the fact that some police informants fabricate conversations,[95] the Supreme Court has consistently affirmed the use of undercover police agents to conduct conversational surveillance. The justices' tolerance of this investigative technique is likely founded on their pragmatic recognition of the fact that use of "false friends" is often essential to the detection of otherwise inaccessible information about crime.[96]

[C] "Wired" False Friends

Prior to *Katz*, the fact that a false friend was "wired" with a transmitter or tape recorder was irrelevant to "search" analysis. As long as the agent did not trespass, no search occurred.

Katz left this rule undisturbed. In *United States v. White*,[97] the Court held that there is no constitutional difference between the pure false-friend case, in which *X* converses

---

94. Stone, Note 89, *supra*, at 1233.

95. Fabrication occurs because, as one prosecutor observed about police informants, "[t]hey are scum, the underbelly of the system. Informants will not testify because they are nice guys. . . . [W]e are trading something for something." Robert Reinhold, *California Shaken Over an Informer*, New York Times, Feb. 17, 1989, at 1; *e.g., A Snitch's Story: In L.A., an Informer Blows the Whistle—On Himself*, Time Magazine, Dec. 12, 1988, at 32 (informant admitted to concocting false confessions in as many as 120 criminal cases resulting in convictions).

96. In a companion case to *Hoffa*, the Supreme Court ruled that the Fourth Amendment was not violated when *X*, a federal agent, misrepresented his identity and purpose and thereby obtained an invitation to *L*'s home, where an illegal narcotics sale occurred in *X*'s presence. Lewis v. United States, 385 U.S. 206 (1966). The Court held that *X*'s testimony regarding the sale was admissible because his activities inside *L*'s premises remained within the scope of *L*'s invitation. Chief Justice Warren observed that "[w]ere we to hold the deceptions of the agent in this case constitutionally prohibited, we would come near to a rule that the use of undercover agents in any manner is virtually unconstitutional *per se*." *Id.* at 210.

97. 401 U.S. 745 (1971) (plurality opinion); *contra under the state* constitution, State v. Goetz, 191 P.3d 489 (Mont. 2008) (warrantless electronic monitoring and recording of defendant's conversations with a police informant in the defendant's home or automobile is prohibited); State v. Allen, 241 P.3d 1045 (Mont. 2010) (warrantless recording of cell phone conversations is also unconstitutional even if one of the participants to the conversation consents); State v. Mullens, 650 S.E.2d 169 (W. Va. 2007) (the police may not surreptitiously use an electronic device to record conversations between the defendant and a police agent in the defendant's home without a warrant); State v. Blow, 602 A.2d 552 (Vt. 1991) (electronic participant-monitoring of conversations conducted in a person's home ordinarily requires a search warrant); State v. Geraw, 795 A.2d 1219 (Vt. 2002) (police must obtain a warrant before surreptitiously tape recording a face-to-face conversation in a suspect's home).

with *D* and then testifies at trial as to *X*'s recollection of the conversation, and the situation in which *X* uses the more reliable technique of recording the conversation, or where *X* carries a microphone that transmits the conversation to other agents who can then corroborate *X*'s testimony. To the *White* Court, the "wired" false-friend doctrine follows almost inevitably from the false-friend doctrine: "If the law gives no protection to the wrongdoer whose trusted accomplice is or becomes a police agent [as in *Hoffa*], neither should it protect him when the same agent has recorded or transmitted the conversations which are later offered in evidence to prove the State's case."

Justice Harlan dissented in *White*. He accepted the *Hoffa* false-friend doctrine, but he believed that the practice of participant-monitoring of conversations was a matter of greater concern: Such monitoring undermined "that confidence and sense of security with one another that is characteristic of individual relationships between citizens in a free society." Harlan worried that police use of electronic devices to monitor conversations "makes technologically feasible the Orwellian Big Brother."

Justice Harlan predicted that people, fearful that their conversations may be transmitted to third persons, will measure their words more carefully than they would in ordinary false-friend situations. The fear of bugging, he worried, will "smother that spontaneity—reflected in frivolous, impetuous, sacrilegious, and defiant discourse—that liberates daily life." Balancing the utility of the law enforcement practice against "its impact on the individual's sense of security . . . I am of the view that more than self-restraint by law enforcement officials is required." For Harlan, participant monitoring of conversations constituted a Fourth Amendment search for which "at the least warrants should be necessary."

§ 6.06 Open Fields[98]

[A] Rule and Rationale

Entry into and exploration of so-called "open fields"[99] does not amount to a search within the meaning of the Fourth Amendment. This "open-fields doctrine," first announced by the Supreme Court prior to *Katz*,[100] was reaffirmed after *Katz* in *Oliver v. United States.*[101]

Oliver involved two cases in which officers without search warrants entered private property, ignored "No Trespassing" signs, walked around either a locked gate or a stone wall, and there observed marijuana plants not visible from outside the property. The

---

98. 1 Wayne R. LaFave, Search and Seizure § 2.4(a) (4th ed. 2004).

99. *See* subsection [B] for clarification of what constitutes an "open field."

100. Hester v. United States, 265 U.S. 57 (1924).

101. 466 U.S. 170 (1984); *contra under the state constitution*, Barnard v. State, 124 So. 479 (Miss. 1929) (an open field is subject to state constitutional protection); People v. Scott, 593 N.E.2d 1328 (N.Y. 1992) (same); Welch v. State, 289 S.W. 510 (Tenn. 1926) (same); State v. Kirchoff, 587 A.2d 988 (Vt. 1991) (same); State v. Myrick, 688 P.2d 151 (Wash. 1984) (same); *see also* State v. Bullock, 901 P.2d 61 (Mont. 1995) (holding that a person may have an expectation of privacy in an open field, and that where that expectation is evidenced by fencing, a "no trespassing" sign, or by some other means that unmistakably indicates that entry is not permitted, entry by law enforcement requires consent or a warrant); State v. Dixson, 766 P.2d 1015 (Or. 1988) (same).

Supreme Court, by a 5–3 vote, stated that people do not have a legitimate expectation of privacy in activities occurring in open fields, even if the activity occurring there could not be observed from the ground except by trespassing in violation of civil or criminal law. In short, trespassing by law enforcement officers into open fields does not constitute a Fourth Amendment "search."[102]

Why is it not a "search"? According to *Oliver*, the Fourth Amendment reflects the constitutional framers' belief that certain "enclaves," such as a house, should be free from governmental interference. In contrast, "open fields do not provide the setting for those intimate activities that the Amendment is intended to shelter from government interference or surveillance." The Court stated that "[t]here is no societal interest in protecting the privacy of those activities, such as cultivation of crops, that occur in open fields."[103]

Furthermore, as a practical matter, open fields usually are accessible to the public and the police in ways that homes and offices are not. The Court observed that "No Trespassing" signs do not effectively bar intruders. Moreover, the same activities that police officers observe unlawfully by trespassing can be observed lawfully by air. Therefore, any expectation that a homeowner may have in his open fields is not one that society is prepared to recognize as reasonable.

[B] "Open Field" versus "Curtilage"

In Fourth Amendment analysis, lawyers must distinguish between: (1) a "house," which is provided full Fourth Amendment protection; (2) the "curtilage" to a house, which is said to be encompassed within the term "houses" in the Fourth Amendment text, but which receives somewhat less Fourth Amendment protection than the interior of the house itself; and (3) an "open field," entry into which falls outside the Fourth Amendment.

Oliver did not define the term "open fields," but it did state that it "may include any unoccupied or undeveloped area outside the curtilage." It also stated that it "need be neither 'open' nor a 'field' as those terms are used in common speech." The "curtilage" is "the land immediately surrounding and associated with the home." At common law it

---

102. This portion of *Oliver* may be considered dictum because the Court, 6–3, first disposed of the case on an alternative ground, albeit in just two paragraphs. (Justice White refused to concur in the "search" portion of the opinion because it was dictum.) It quoted Justice Holmes, in *Hester v. United States*, Note 100 *supra*, that "the special protection accorded by the Fourth Amendment to the people in their 'persons, houses, papers, and effects' is not extended to the open fields. The distinction between the latter and the house is as old as the common law." The Court also held that an open field is not an "effect" within the meaning of the Fourth Amendment, as the latter does not encompass real property. *See* §§ 5.03, 5.04, *supra*.

103. The dissenters strenuously disagreed. They suggested that "[m]any landowners like to take solitary walks on their property," and they speculated that landowners may use their open fields "to meet lovers, others to gather together with fellow worshippers, still others to engage in sustained creative endeavors." Perhaps most tellingly, the dissenters reminded the majority that the cultivation of crops, which the majority did not believe merits constitutional privacy protection, constitutes landowners' agricultural business. The Court accords constitutional protection to *urban* businesses by treating office buildings as "houses" within the meaning of the Fourth Amendment. *See* § 5.03, *supra*. The dissent questioned why an open field, a potential rural "office," is "less deserving of the benefits of the Fourth Amendment."

is the "area to which extends the intimate activity associated with the 'sanctity of a man's home and the privacies of life.' "[104]

As set out in *United States v. Dunn*,[105] four factors are relevant in determining whether land falls within or outside the curtilage: (1) the proximity of the land to the home; (2) whether the area is included within enclosures surrounding the house; (3) the nature of the use to which the area is put; and (4) the steps taken by the resident to protect the land in question from observation.

For example, in *Dunn*, *D* owned a ranch enclosed by a fence. Another fence surrounded *D*'s ranch house. Approximately 50 yards beyond the latter fence were two barns, each enclosed by its own fence. A federal officer, who had received information that *D* was producing illegal drugs on his property, climbed over *D*'s perimeter fence and an interior fence. The officer smelled an acidic odor commonly associated with drug production emanating from the barns. He climbed over the barn fences and, without entering the structures, peered in. He observed incriminating evidence in one barn.

The Court determined that the barns were not within the curtilage of the ranch house: they were 60 yards from the house and 50 yards outside the fence surrounding it; the officer had objective evidence that the barns were not being used for intimate, home-related, activities; and the Court did not believe that *D* took sufficient steps to prevent observation into the barn from the open-field vantage point.[106]

Note that the open fields cases were decided after 1967 but before 2012 — in other words, they were decided at a time when the Court was applying the *Katz* "reasonable expectation of privacy" test, but not the *Jones* "trespass" test. Given this fact, one might expect that the Court would reconsider the open fields doctrine once *Jones* revived the trespass test. But remember that the trespass test does not mean that *any* invasion of property rights constitutes a search; only an invasion of property rights with regard to the items listed in the Fourth Amendment ("persons, houses, papers, and effects"). The *Jones* case itself made this point clear:

> Quite simply, an open field, unlike the curtilage of a home, is not one of those protected areas enumerated in the Fourth Amendment. The government's physical intrusion on such an area — unlike its intrusion on the "effect" at issue here — is of no Fourth Amendment significance.[107]

So does this mean that police officers must have a warrant to enter the curtilage of someone's property without a warrant? Not exactly. A police officer can still walk up to a front door, knock, and ask questions of the resident of the house (this is commonly known in police parlance as the "knock and talk.") The resident of the house would expect members of the general population — including the police — to walk up and use the front door in order to talk to the resident. In other words, the resident does not have a reasonable expectation of privacy that nobody will come to the front door; nor does a

---

104. *Oliver*, 466 U.S. at 180 (quoting Boyd v. United States, 116 U.S. 616, 630 (1886)).

105. 480 U.S. 294 (1987).

106. An issue not decided by the Court in *Oliver* or since is whether a person may retain a reasonable expectation of privacy regarding the interior of a structure, such as the barn in *Dunn*, found in an open field. The Court in *Dunn* only assumed *arguendo* that a search would have occurred if the federal officer had entered the structure and there observed matters or activities not visible from the open field.

107. Jones v. United States, 132 S. Ct. 945, 953 (2012).

person who walks up to the front door to knock infringe on the resident's property interests.[108] However, if an officer lingers at the front door,[109] or approaches the front door with a purpose other than conversing with the resident—with a drug dog, for example, or other equipment that is designed to detect illegal activity—then the officer is conducting a search and a warrant is required.[110]

[C] Criticism of the Open-Fields Doctrine

Oliver is a controversial decision. Various criticisms of the opinion merit note because they raise broader questions about Fourth Amendment jurisprudence. First, notice that the Court resolved the issue by providing a bright-line rule—i.e., an expectation of privacy in an open field is *never* legitimate. It might have chosen to resolve the question on a case-by-case basis, by holding that a person may have a legitimate expectation of privacy in an open field in some cases, depending on such circumstances as the use to which the land is being put, and the methods taken to protect privacy.[111] The justices rejected this approach because they believed it would provide police insufficient guidance.

However, even if a bright-line rule is preferable to case-by-case adjudication, a matter of considerable importance and controversy,[112] the Court could have drawn an alternative bright line. The dissenters suggested that a better rule would have been: "Private land marked in a fashion sufficient to render entry thereon a criminal trespass under the law of the state in which the land lies is protected by the Fourth Amendment. . . ." It bears reminder that such a rule would not bar police entry onto open fields; it would simply render the Fourth Amendment applicable to the case. The police could still enter with a search warrant, good reason not to secure a warrant, or consent.

Second, the Court justified its conclusion that an expectation of privacy in an open field is unreasonable in part on the ground that people frequently trespass on open fields.[113] But, this raises an important question: Should the foreseeability or fact of criminal wrongdoing undercut the privacy rights of citizens? Are we to say that when our neighbors or others invade our privacy, we have a lesser (or, perhaps, no) expectation of privacy against the government? At a minimum, perhaps the appropriate question the Court ought to have asked is whether people have a right to expect that law enforcement officers, as distinguished from private persons, will obey criminal laws and respect property rights.

Third, *Oliver* is founded in part on the basis that, because the police can observe activities in an open field lawfully from the air,[114] the Fourth Amendment is not violated even if the observation occurred unlawfully on land. In short, the Court did not distinguish here between the *means* of governmental intrusion. Yet such a distinction might

---

108. *See* Florida v. Jardines, 133 S. Ct. 1409 (2013).
109. Once an officer leaves the front door after talking to the resident, he may not linger in the curtilage but must move back out into public spaces. *See, e.g.,* Commonwealth v. Dixon, 482 S.W.3d 386 (Ky. 2016).
110. *See* § 6.09[B] below.
111. After all, the arguments raised by the dissent, *see* Note 103, *supra*, might be true in some cases, but not all.
112. *See* § 2.07[A], *supra*.
113. This is not the only time the Court has used other people's intrusive conduct as a reason for limiting Fourth Amendment protections. *See* § 6.09, *infra*.
114. *See* 6.07, *infra*.

have been intended in *Katz* when Justice Stewart distinguished between "the intruding eye . . . [and] the uninvited ear." And, the Court has drawn this mode-of-intrusion distinction in other contexts.[115]

§ 6.07 Aerial Surveillance[116]

[A] Rule

As explained more fully below, non-sense-enhanced aerial surveillance by the government of activities occurring within the curtilage of a house does not constitute a Fourth Amendment search if the surveillance: (1) occurs from public navigable airspace; (2) is conducted in a physically nonintrusive manner; and (3) does not reveal intimate activities traditionally connected with the use of a home or curtilage.

[B] Surveillance by Airplanes

In *California v. Ciraolo*,[117] O, a police officer, received an anonymous tip that C was growing marijuana in his backyard. O attempted to observe C's yard from ground-level but was thwarted by a six-foot-high outer fence and a 10-foot-high inner fence. Therefore, O obtained a private plane to fly over the backyard at an altitude of approximately 1,000 feet, which was within public navigable airspace according to Federal Aviation Administration (FAA) regulations. From that vantage point, O observed marijuana plants in C's backyard.

The Supreme Court held that this aerial surveillance of C's backyard, an area that the Court agreed was within the curtilage of the house, did not constitute a search. Regarding the subjective prong of the *Katz* test, Chief Justice Warren Burger stated that "[c]learly . . . [C] has met the test of manifesting his own subjective intent and desire to maintain privacy as to his unlawful agriculture." Remarkably, however, this did not necessarily satisfy the subjective prong, for all that the 10-foot-high fence demonstrated to the Court is C's "intent and desire" to maintain privacy; it did not necessarily demonstrate his *expectation* of such privacy.

The Court pointed out that the fence "might not shield these plants from the eyes of a citizen or a policeman perched on the top of a truck or a 2-level bus."[118] Therefore, the Court stated that it was "not entirely clear" whether C maintained a "subjective expectation of privacy from *all* observations of his backyard," or only from ground-level observations. The implication from this comment may be that one cannot satisfy the first

---

115. *See* §6.04[B], *supra*, and §6.07[C] and 6.010[D], *infra*.

116. *See generally* 1 LaFave, Note 98, *supra*, at §2.3(g); Bush, Note 13, *supra*; Clifford S. Fishman, *Technologically Enhanced Visual Surveillance and the Fourth Amendment: Sophistication, Availability, and the Expectation of Privacy*, 26 Am. Crim. L. Rev. 315 (1988); David E. Steinberg, *Making Sense of Sense-Enhanced Searches*, 74 Minn. L. Rev. 563 (1990).

117. 476 U.S. 207 (1986).

118. There were no such buses in the community in which the surveillance occurred. Wayne R. LaFave, *The Forgotten Motto of Obsta Principiis in Fourth Amendment Jurisprudence*, 28 Ariz. L. Rev. 291, 298 (1986).

prong of *Katz* unless the person has an expectation of privacy regarding all modes of surveillance possible under the circumstances.

In any case, the Court held that the objective prong of the expectation-of-privacy standard was not satisfied here. The Chief Justice observed that police officers need not shield their eyes from information or activities knowingly exposed to them,[119] even in the curtilage of a house. And the fact that a person has taken measures to restrict some views of her activities within the curtilage does not preclude the police from observing them from a public vantage point where they have a right to be.

According to *Ciraolo*, a person is not entitled to assume that what is grown in the backyard will not be observed in a nonintrusive manner by passing aircraft in public airspace or, for that matter, "by a power company repair mechanic on a pole overlooking the yard." The Court stated that "[i]n an age where private and commercial flights in the public airways is routine," it was unreasonable for C to expect privacy from the air.

Ciraolo has been criticized on various grounds. First, this case points up the problem of determining privacy expectations in an empirical, rather than normative, manner.[120] The Court essentially holds that the Fourth Amendment does not protect citizens from aerial snooping in public airspace because airplane flights over private property are common. This fact of modern life, however, does not answer the independent question of whether a person should have a *right* to expect privacy in this regard from government surveillance.

Second, the Court equates the unfocused, momentary, and unintentional observations of a private party sitting in the window seat of a commercial airplane with the focused, purposeful, and less-brief observations—indeed, surveillance—by a trained police officer involved in a criminal investigation. There seems little doubt that the two cases are not similar to the average person; the degree of privacy intrusion is much greater in the latter case than in the former.

Third, the practical message of the case is that one who wishes to retain Fourth Amendment privacy rights in her backyard must cover or enclose it. Yet this destroys the value and purpose of the curtilage, which is to maintain the privacies of the home, but in an outside venue.

[C] Surveillance by Helicopters

In *Florida v. Riley*,[121] the Supreme Court applied the reasoning of *Ciraolo* to inspections by helicopter, which allow for much lower-altitude surveillance. In *Riley*, O, an officer in a police helicopter, observed marijuana plants growing in R's within-the-curtilage greenhouse, which was missing two roof panels. In order to observe the inside of the structure, O descended to an altitude of 400 feet, which would have been impermissible under FAA regulations if the flight had occurred in a fixed-wing aircraft, but which was lawful for helicopter flights.

---

119. Notice here the use of Justice Stewart's "knowing exposure to the public" standard from *Katz*.

120. *See* § 6.03[D][3], *supra*.

121. 488 U.S. 445 (1989); *contra under the state constitution*, State v. Bryant, 950 A.2d 467 (Vt. 2008) (stating in the context of a helicopter surveillance that the Vermont constitution provides broader protection than the Fourth Amendment).

The Supreme Court held, 5–4, that this surveillance was not a search. Justice White's four-justice plurality opinion stated that R knowingly exposed his greenhouse to the surveillance because "any member of the public could legally have been flying over [R's] property in a helicopter at the altitude of 400 feet and could have observed [his] greenhouse." He observed that private and commercial helicopter flights in public airways are routine, and R offered no evidence—the burden was on R to prove—"that such flights [were] unheard of" in the vicinity of his house.

The plurality opinion, however, contained limiting language. Justice White indicated that it "would have [been] a different case if flying at that altitude had been contrary to law or regulation." The implication of this remark is that the surveillance would have constituted a search if an airplane rather than a helicopter had surveyed R's greenhouse from precisely the same vantage point. In short, the mode of intrusion—the type of flying machine used—would have mattered in this case.

Justice White also warned that "an inspection of the curtilage of a house from an aircraft will [not] always pass muster under the Fourth Amendment simply because the place is within navigable airspace specified by law." He suggested that the result might have been different if there had been "any intimation that the helicopter interfered with [R's] normal use of the greenhouse or of other parts of the curtilage." The plurality considered it significant that the record did not reveal that "intimate details connected with the use of the home or curtilage were observed, and there was no undue noise, no wind, dust, or threat of injury."

This language is intriguing. Why should it matter whether the officer spots marijuana crops or, instead, observes "intimate" activities in the curtilage of the home?[122] Does the Court mean that if the same helicopter had observed the contents of the greenhouse as well as consensual but illegal sexual acts in the backyard, the surveillance would have been a "search" of one but not of the other activity? This seems strange because, as the Court frequently observes, the police need not shield their eyes to activities visible to them from vantage points where they have a right to be. Nor is it clear why helicopter-caused dust, as an example, triggers a privacy right that is not otherwise implicated. This harkens back, as the dissenters pointed out, to the pre-*Katz* "intrusion" and "trespass" concepts of the Fourth Amendment.

Justice O'Connor, who concurred in the judgment, along with the four dissenters in *Riley*, minimized the significance of the lawfulness of the helicopter flight. The issue to them was not whether the flight was lawful, or even whether *police* helicopter flights at 400 feet were common, but rather whether, as Justice O'Connor phrased the issue, "members of the public travel with sufficient regularity [at such low altitudes] that [R's] expectation of privacy from aerial observation" was unreasonable. In other words, five justices in *Riley* apparently believed that a person may have a reasonable expectation of privacy regarding *police* aerial surveillance, regardless of its frequency, if *non-police* helicopter flights (in general, as distinguished from flights over the specific individual's curtilage) are rare.

---

122. Kyllo v. United States, 533 U.S. 27 (2001), discussed at § 6.09[C], *infra*, teaches that *in the home* "all details are intimate details." In the curtilage, however, the Court apparently may draw such distinctions.

§ 6.08 Inspection of Garbage[123]

The Supreme Court held in *California v. Greenwood*[124] that a person has no reasonable expectation of privacy in garbage enclosed in a closed bag and left for collection outside the curtilage of the home. No search occurs, therefore, when an officer opens a trash bag left at the curb and sifts through its contents.

In *Greenwood*, the Court conceded that *G*, the homeowner whose garbage was inspected by the police, might have had a subjective expectation that the trash bag would not be opened by the police or the public. However, it concluded that *G*'s Fourth Amendment claim failed on objective grounds, because "it is common knowledge" that plastic garbage bags left on the curb for pickup "are readily accessible to animals, children, scavengers, snoops, and other members of the public."

In light of this common knowledge, the Court invoked two related "search" rules. First, applying *Katz* and the aerial surveillance decisions,[125] it stated that the Fourth Amendment does not protect information knowingly exposed to the public. Second, citing *Smith v. Maryland*,[126] a case in which the police learned what phone numbers a home-dweller had called by seeking the information from the telephone company, the Court noted that one cannot have a reasonable expectation of privacy in information voluntarily turned over to others.

However, *Greenwood* goes further than the cases the Court cited. In those cases, the individuals exposed *information* to others "by conducting activities in an area visible to aircraft, and by making telephone calls, the numbers of which were being recorded by the telephone company). In *Greenwood*, *G* only knowingly exposed the *container* that enclosed the information. As the dissent pointed out, *G* did not "flaunt[] his intimate activity" by exposing the contents of his trash.

Essentially, under *Greenwood*, *G*'s expectation of privacy is considered illegitimate because of, as the dissent put it, the "mere *possibility* that unwelcome meddlers [might] open and rummage through the containers." Because private persons *might* snoop, individuals have no constitutionally recognized reasonable expectation of privacy when and if the police—not private persons—*in fact* snoop. If that is enough to render the Fourth Amendment inapplicable, the dissenters asked rhetorically, would the Court suggest that "the possibility of a burglary negates an expectation of privacy in the home[?]"

---

123. *See generally* 1 LaFave, Note 98, *supra*, at § 2.6(c).

124. 486 U.S. 35 (1988); *contra under the state constitution*, State v. Tanaka, 701 P.2d 1274 (Haw. 1985) (a person maintains a reasonable expectation of privacy in opaque, closed trash bags left at curbside for garbage collection); State v. Goss, 834 A.2d 316 (N.H. 2003) (*id.*); State v. Hempele, 576 A.2d 793 (N.J. 1990) (police may *seize* a garbage bag left for collection without a warrant or probable cause, but a warrant is required to *search* its contents); State v. Granville, 142 P.3d 933 (N.M. App. 2006) (inspection of garbage bags placed in trash cans left outside for collection constitutes a "search" requiring a warrant); State v. Galloway, 109 P.3d 383 (Or. App. 2005) (a person maintains privacy and possessory interests in the contents of garbage cans left at curb for collection); State v. Boland, 800 P.2d 1112 (Wash. 1990) (a citizen's private affairs are unreasonably intruded upon by police officers who remove trash from a garbage can, at curbside, and transport it the police station for inspection, without a search warrant).

125. *See* § 6.07, *supra*.

126. 442 U.S. 735 (1979), discussed at § 6.10[B], *infra*.

§ 6.09 Use of Dogs and Other "Binary" Investigative Techniques to Discover Contraband[127]

[A] In General

Many Fourth Amendment cases involve police investigations to determine whether a person is in possession of contraband, most particularly illegal drugs. This section, however, deals exclusively with investigative techniques that can *only* identify the presence (or absence) of contraband and provide the police with no other information about the suspect. These searches are frequently known as "binary searches," because the result of the surveillance produces only one of two results: that contraband is present, or that contraband is not present.

The Supreme Court has held that binary searches do not implicate the Fourth Amendment, because individuals have no Fourth Amendment right to keep illegal activity secret. In other words, the *Katz* test only protects activity in which the suspect has a reasonable *and legitimate* expectation of privacy. The Court gave an example of unprotected illegitimate activity: suppose that a burglar were to break into a summer home to steal some items, and while he was inside, the police officers entered the home without a warrant and observed his activity.[128] This action would not violate the burglar's Fourh Amendment rights because he had no legitimate expectation of privacy while burgling someone else's home. Thus, a defendant cannot object to a search if the only information it uncovers is evidence of illegal activity.

The vast majority of surveillance techniques, of course, reveal (or have the potential to reveal) much more than just evidence of illegal activity; when the police search a home, or a purse, or a car, they may find contraband, but they will also almost certainly find items that are not illegal in which the suspect has a legitimate expectation of privacy. Thus, true binary searches—in which the *only* possible result is learning about the absence or presence of illegal activity—are rare. So far, there are only two contexts in which it has applied: dog sniff cases and field tests for drugs. However, police may soon be able to use technology to create newer forms of binary searches, especially in the context of digital surveillance.[129]

[B] Dog-Sniffs

In *United States v. Place*,[130] Drug Enforcement Administration (DEA) agents seized luggage belonging to *P*, a deplaning airline passenger whom they suspected of drug

---

127. *See generally* 1 LaFave, Note 98, *supra*, at § 2.2(g); Lewis R. Katz & Aaron P. Golembiewski, *Curbing the Dog: Extending the Protection of the Fourth Amendment to Police Drug Dogs*, 85 Neb. L. Rev. 735 (2007); Ric Simmons, *The Two Unanswered Questions of Illinois v. Caballes: How to Make the World Safe for Binary Searches*, 80 Tulane L. Rev. 411 (2005); Steinberg, Note 116, *supra*.

128. Rakas v. Illinois, 439 U.S. 128, 143 n.12 (1978).

129. *See, e.g.,* Lawrence Rosenthal. *Binary Searches and the Central Meaning of the Fourth Amendment*, 22 Wm. & Mary Bill Rts. J. 881, 882 (2014).

130. 462 U.S. 696 (1983); *contra under the state constitution*, Pooley v. State, 705 P.2d 1293 (Alaska Ct. App. 1985) (dog sniff of luggage constitutes a search, requiring reasonable suspicion);

possession, and subjected it to a "sniff test" by a dog trained to discover narcotics. The dog "reacted positively" to one piece of luggage.

The Supreme Court was anxious to resolve the validity of this type of investigatory procedure. Although resolution of the issue was unnecessary to the decision, and the matter had not been briefed or argued in the Court, the justices declared that the dog sniff in this case—critically limited to "exposure of [P's] luggage, which was located in a public place, to a trained canine"—did not constitute a search.

The Court focused on two facts. First, the information was obtained in a comparatively nonintrusive manner: the luggage, observed in a public area, was not opened and, thus, its contents were never exposed to the public eye. Second, the information revealed by the test was extremely limited, as "the sniff discloses only the presence or absence of narcotics, a contraband item."

This latter factor is of particular significance to the Court. In *Illinois v. Caballes*,[131] the Supreme Court again upheld as a "non-search" the use of a narcotics-trained dog— this time to walk around an automobile lawfully stopped on the highway for speeding— to sniff for drugs. Justice Stevens, for the Court, stated that "any interest in possessing contraband cannot be deemed 'legitimate,' and thus, governmental conduct that *only* reveals the possession of contraband 'compromises no legitimate privacy interest.'" As he further put it, a "dog sniff conducted during a concededly lawful traffic stop that reveals no information other than the location of a substance that no individual has any right to possess does not violate the Fourth Amendment."

Place and *Caballes* involved the use of a dog to smell for contraband in a container (luggage, or an automobile) lawfully encountered in a public area. These decisions left open the question of whether use of a dog to sniff the exterior of private enclaves, such as a home, for contraband also falls within the no-search principle. Various state courts, applying their own constitutions, have rejected *Place* in such circumstances.[132]

In the past, the Supreme Court has sent mixed signals on this question. In *Kyllo v. United States*,[133] the Court ruled that police use, outside a home, of sense-enhancing technology, to secure information regarding activities inside a home—information that could not otherwise be obtained without physical intrusion into the dwelling— constitutes a search (at least where the technology in question is not in general public

---

People v. Haley, 41 P.3d 666 (Colo. 2001) (dog sniff of the exterior of an automobile stopped on the highway is a search requiring reasonable suspicion); People v. Boylan, 854 P.2d 807 (Colo. 1993) (same; dog sniff of a private express courier package); People v. Cox, 782 N.E.2d 275 (Ill. 2002) (dog sniff of a vehicle is a search, requiring reasonable suspicion); State v. Davis, 732 N.W.2d 173 (Minn. 2007) (reasonable suspicion strikes the "appropriate balance" under state constitution for dog sniff of a common hallway outside defendant's apartment); State v. Tackitt, 67 P.3d 295 (Mont. 2003) (dog sniff of automobile is a search, requiring reasonable suspicion); State v. Pellicci, 580 A.2d 710 (N.H. 1990) (same); People v. Devone, 931 N.E.2d 70 (N.Y. 2010) (same); Commonwealth v. Martin, 626 A.2d 556 (Pa. 1993) (dog sniff of a person is a search, requiring probable cause).

131. 543 U.S. 405 (2005); *see generally* Simmons, Note 114, *supra*.

132. *See* McGahan v. State, 807 P.2d 506 (Alaska Ct. App. 1991) (dog sniff of the exterior of a commercial building is a search, requiring reasonable suspicion); State v. Rabb, 881 So.2d 587 (Fla. App. 2004) (dog sniff of odors coming from the closed door of a home is a search); State v. Ortiz, 600 N.W.2d 805 (Neb. 1999) (*id.*, dog sniff of an apartment residence from the hallway); People v. Dunn, 564 N.E.2d 1054 (N.Y. 1990) (*id.*); Commonwealth v. Johnston, 530 A.2d 74 (Pa. 1987) (*id.*, dog sniff of a storage place); State v. Dearman, 962 P.2d 850 (Wash. 1998) (use of a trained narcotics dog to detect marijuana growing in the defendant's garage constitutes a search).

133. 533 U.S. 27 (2001). *Kyllo* is discussed in detail in § 6.10[D], *infra*.

use). "Dog sniffing," of course, is not "technology," but it *is* sense-enhancing, in that specially trained dogs can smell contraband in circumstances in which humans cannot. The *Kyllo* Court's strong language about the sanctity of the home—most especially its assertion that, in the home, "*all* details are intimate details"—suggests that use of a dog outside a home, to sniff for contraband *inside* a residence, could constitute a Fourth Amendment search.

On the other hand, the reasoning of *Caballes*, which placed great emphasis on the nature of the information secured—the presence of contraband—could well suggest that the Court will not protect home-dwellers from dog sniffs outside their front doors. Indeed, in *Caballes*, the Court distinguished *Kyllo*, stating that "[c]ritical to that decision was the fact that the [technological] device [used] was capable of detecting lawful activity—in that case, intimate details in a home. . . . The legitimate expectation that information about perfectly lawful activity will remain private is categorically distinguishable from [a person's] hopes or expectations concerning the nondetection of contraband in the trunk of his car."

You will notice that the Court applied reasonable-expectation-of-privacy analysis in *Place* and *Caballes*. However, as noted in Section 6.03[E], the Supreme Court now applies both the *Katz* reasonable-expectation-of-privacy doctrine and the *Jones* trespass analysis in determining whether police activity constitutes a Fourth Amendment search. If the activity is a "search" under *either* approach, it triggers Fourth Amendment scrutiny. This dual approach is seen in the Supreme Court's recent treatment, in *Florida v. Jardines*,[134] of a "dog sniff" outside a person's home.

In *Jardines*, the police responded to an unverified tip that marijuana was being grown in J's home by approaching the front porch with a dog trained to detect the scent of marijuana, cocaine, heroin, and several other drugs. The dog's behavioral changes alerted his handler to the presence of illegal narcotics inside the home.

Did this use of the dog constitute a "search," although the use of trained dogs in *Place* and *Caballes* did not? Justice Scalia, writing for a five-justice majority, held that this police activity *did* constitute a search, but he reached this conclusion on "trespass" rather than expectation-of-privacy grounds. Applying pre-*Katz* language and reasoning, Justice Scalia held that the police conduct constituted a physical intrusion of a constitutionally protected area. The front porch was within the curtilage"[135] of the house. According to the Court, "when it comes to the Fourth Amendment, the home is first among equals. At the 'very core' stands 'the right of a man to retreat into his home and there be free from unreasonable governmental intrusion.'" And, the Court reasoned, that right "would be of little practical value if the State's agents could stand in a home's porch or side garden and trawl for evidence with impunity."

But how was this an "intrusion"? People—neighbors, mail carriers, Girl Scout cookie-sellers, trick-or-treaters, peddlers, and even police—come to the front doors of homes all the time.[136] Are *they* trespassing? Justice Scalia stated that such people ordinarily have an implicit license to come to the door, "knock promptly, wait briefly to be received, and then (absent invitation to linger longer) leave." Here, however, "introducing a trained police dog to explore the areas around the home in hopes of discovering incriminating evidence is something else. There is no customary invitation to do *that*."

---

134. 133 S. Ct. 1409 (2013).

135. See §6.06[B], *supra*, for the definition of "curtilage."

136. *See* §6.06()b) above.

Justice Kagan, joined by Justices Ginsburg and Sotomayor, while joining the Scalia opinion, wrote a concurring opinion. They stated that the same result would apply using reasonable-expectation-of-privacy analysis. Justice Kagan asked us to hypothesize a stranger coming to our front door carrying "super-high-powered binoculars," and not knocking, but instead using the binoculars to peer through the window "into your home's furthest corners. . . . In just a couple of minutes, his uncommon behavior allows him to learn details of your life you disclose to no one." To the concurring justices, this conduct is not only a trespass but an invasion of our reasonable expectations of privacy. For the concurring justices, therefore, *Place* and *Caballes* do not apply here because this was Jardines' home and not luggage in a public airport or a car on a public road.[137]

Justice Alito, writing for the Chief Justice, and Justices Kennedy and Breyer, dissented. He reasoned that dogs have been domesticated for "about 12,000 years," were "ubiquitous" in this country and Britain at the time of the adoption of the Fourth Amendment, and "their acute sense of smell has been used in law enforcement for centuries. Yet the Court has been unable to find a single case . . . that supports the rule on which its decision is based." Alito observed that the police activity took only "a minute or two" and occurred on the front porch, not in the backyard or in another presumably forbidden area. According to the dissenters, trespass analysis is not based on whether the person knocks at the door (mail carriers frequently don't) or whether the person on the front porch is, for example, a tolerable or intolerable peddler ("Girl Scouts selling cookies versus adults selling aluminum siding").

As for the concurring opinion's privacy analysis, Justice Alito stated: "I see no basis for concluding that the occupants of a dwelling have a reasonable expectation of privacy in odors that emanate from the dwelling and reach spots where members of the public may lawfully stand."

[C] Beyond Dogs

The Court in *Place* observed that "the canine sniff is *sui generis*. We are aware of no other investigative procedure that is so limited both in the manner in which the information is obtained and in the content of the information revealed by the procedure." Dog sniffs, however, soon proved *not* to be *sui generis*. In *United States v. Jacobsen*,[138] a DEA agent conducting a drug investigation came upon white powder in a plastic bag belonging to J. Because the agent suspected that it was cocaine, he conducted an on-the-scene test: he placed a small amount of the powder in three test tubes containing liquids; the liquids took on a certain sequence of colors, which confirmed that the powder was cocaine.

The Supreme Court, in a conclusion it stated was "dictated" by *Place*, ruled that any chemical test that "merely discloses whether or not a particular substance is cocaine does not compromise any legitimate interest in privacy," and is, therefore, not a search.

---

137. A few years after *Jardines* was decided, the Seventh Circuit adopted Justice Kagan's reasoning and held that using drug-sniffing dogs at the door of an apartment building is a "search" under *Jardines*. This was true even though under Seventh Circuit law the defendant had no reasonable expectation of privacy in the hallway of his apartment building (the circuits are split on how *Katz* applies to the common areas of an apartment building, but the Seventh Circuit's is the majority view). Nonetheless, the defendant had the right to preclude "persons in the hallway snooping into his apartment using sensitive devices not available to the general public." United States v. Whitaker, 820 F.3d 849 (7th Cir. 2016).

138. 466 U.S. 109 (1984).

As Congress has determined that private possession of certain items is illegitimate, "government conduct that can reveal whether a substance is [contraband], and no other arguably "private" fact, compromises no legitimate privacy interest." In contrast, if a substance is not tested to determine if it is contraband, but rather to find out whether it contains evidence of a person's prior *use* of contraband, the test *is* a search.[139]

As surveillance technology becomes more sophisticated, law enforcement officials may be able to devise newer types of binary searches. What about a computer program that monitors Internet traffic and alerts law enforcement only if it detects a known photo of child pornography that is being sent? Or perhaps an X-ray machine that can identify the exact shape of a handgun and only return a signal to its user if it detects the presence of a firearm?[140] Under the binary search doctrine, police officers could use these tools indiscriminately, without implicating the Fourth Amendment, because they reveal nothing about the individual who is being searched unless the individual is engaging in illegal activity.

§ 6.10 Technological Information Gathering[141]

[A] In General

The Supreme Court shifted away from the trespass doctrine in *Katz v. United States* in considerable part because, as Justice Harlan put it then, the trespass doctrine constituted "bad physics as well as bad law."[142] Technology had reached the point by 1967 that the trespass doctrine no longer seemed to serve as a meaningful limitation on governmental intrusion. By that time, it was possible, and even easy and relatively inexpensive, for the police to intercept conversations without ever trespassing on private property. The technology of 1967, however, pales in comparison to that which has developed in the past few decades, thus placing increasing pressure on *Katz*'s reasonable-expectation-of-privacy doctrine.[143] The Supreme Court has focused on two questions in determining whether a new type of surveillance technology constitutes a "Fourth Amendment search."

---

139. Skinner v. Railway Labor Executives' Ass'n, 489 U.S. 602 (1989) (tests of blood and urine for evidence of drug usage is a "search").

140. This "gun detector" would only count as a binary search if it is used in a jurisdiction or in a context where concealed carry of a firearm is illegal—otherwise it could inform the officer that the person is carrying a legal firearm, which would violate the person's legitimate and reasonable expectation of privacy.

141. *See generally* Fishman, Note 116, *supra*; Gutterman, Note 64, *supra*; Slobogin, Note 64, *supra*; Steinberg, Note 103, *supra*; Symposium, *The Effect of Technology on Fourth Amendment Analysis and Individual Rights*, 72 Miss. L. Rev. 1-564 (2002).

142. 389 U.S. 347, 362 (1967) (Harlan, J., concurring).

143. The speed at which technology is advancing has made the Court cautious in setting out new rules for evaluating new surveillance technology. The Court observed in *City of Ontario v. Quon*, 130 S. Ct. 2619 (2010), that it "must proceed with care when considering the whole concept of privacy expectations in communications. The judiciary risks error by elaborating too fully on the Fourth Amendment implications of emerging technology before its role in society has become clear." The Court contrasted the days of *Katz*, when justices could rely on their own knowledge and experience "to conclude that there is a reasonable expectation of privacy in a telephone booth," with the current "[r]apid changes in the dynamics of communication and information transmission" that cause difficulty in "predicting how . . . privacy expectations will be shaped . . . or the degree to which society will be prepared to recognize those expectations as reasonable."

First, is the device used in the surveillance a technology that is in "general public use"? If so, people's reasonable expectation of privacy will take into account the fact that many members of society use the technology, and therefore the police will have a lot more leeway in using the technology to conduct surveillance. For example, an individual in the early nineteenth century might have had a reasonable expectation of privacy in his activity in a public park in the middle of the night, because he could reasonably assume that nobody could see what he was doing. In modern times, however, the "surveillance technology" of flashlights is commonly used by the public, so a person cannot reasonably expect those actions will be private.

In contrast, a person in a public park *does* have a reasonable expectation of privacy in the contents of their pockets. If the police developed a new device that allowed them to see through clothing, using that device would be a Fourth Amendment search, because such a device is not in general public use. If in the future these devices became ubiquitous, and everyone commonly used them to look through people's clothing and see inside their pockets, then at that point people would no longer have a reasonable expectation of privacy in the inside of their pockets and the use of these devices by the police would no longer be a Fourth Amendment search.

The second question the Court looks to is the nature of the information that the police obtain when using the surveillance technology. If the device does nothing more than allow the police to gather otherwise public information more easily or efficiently (sometimes referred to as a "sense-enhancing device"), using the device will not usually constitute a Fourth Amendment search. (If the device is gathering massive amounts of public information, which can be processed to reveal private information, using the device could be considered a Fourth Amendment search under the mosaic theory, as described below in Section 6.10[D].) But if the device allows the police to access information that they otherwise could not obtain, then using the device will always constitute a search.

For example, assume the police set up two dozen surveillance cameras in a public park and assign an officer to monitor the video feed from all of the cameras. This surveillance tool will not constitute a search because the police officer is not observing anything that he could not ordinarily observe without the help of the technology — he is merely able to see it more efficiently than before. In contrast, when the police place a wiretap on a telephone, they are conducting a Fourth Amendment search because that surveillance technology reveals information that they could not otherwise have known.

The Supreme Court affirmed these principles in the foundational 2001 case *Kyllo v. United States*.[144] In *Kyllo*, a federal agent, suspicious that *K* was using high-intensity lamps in his home to grow marijuana, used a thermal imager to scan the triplex in which *K* lived. A thermal imager is a device that can "detect infrared radiation, which virtually all objects emit but which is not visible to the naked eye. The imager converts radiation into images based on relative warmth. . . . [I]n that respect, it operates somewhat like a video camera showing heat images." The agent in *Kyllo* conducted the imaging from his vehicle across the street from *K*'s residence. The scanning showed that the roof of the garage and a side wall of *K*'s home were substantially warmer than the rest of the building. Based on this information and other evidence, the agent obtained a warrant to search the residence. The issue in *Kyllo*, as Justice Scalia put it for the Court, was "whether the use of a thermal-imaging device aimed at a private home from a public street to detect

---

144. 533 U.S. 27 (2001). *See generally* Symposium, *Searching for the Meaning of Fourth Amendment Privacy After* Kyllo v. United States, 86 Minn. L. Rev. 1325–1438 (2002).

relative amounts of heat within the home constitutes a 'search' within the meaning of the Fourth Amendment."

By a vote of 5–4, the Court answered the question in the affirmative and, in the process, announced a new rule to deal with technological advances in existence or in development[145] that impinge on the privacy of home dwellers. The majority, quoting language from the pre-*Katz* era *Silverman*[146] case, stated that:

> [w]e think that obtaining by sense-enhancing technology any information regarding the interior of the home that could not otherwise have been obtained without physical "intrusion into a constitutionally protected area," . . . , constitutes a search—at least where (as here) the technology in question is not in general public use.

Later, the majority stated the holding of the case this way:

> Where, as here, the Government uses a device that is not in general public use, to explore details of the home that would previously have been unknowable without physical intrusion, the surveillance is a "search" and is presumptively unreasonable without a warrant.[147]

Although the *Kyllo* Court did not specifically define what it meant by "general public use," it did provide the following footnote:

> The dissent argues that we have injected potential uncertainty into the constitutional analysis by noting that whether or not the technology is in general public use may be a factor. That quarrel, however, is not with us but with this Court's precedent. . . . Given that we can quite confidently say that thermal imaging is not "routine," we decline in this case to reexamine that fact.

Justice Scalia used the *Kyllo* case again to criticize the *Katz* test[148] as "circular, and hence subjective and unpredictable," and—presaging his subsequent position in the *Jones* case—one that may answer the wrong question.[149] He stated that it is "difficult" to refine the *Katz* test in the context of telephone booths, curtilages of homes, and automobiles, but "in the case of the search of the interior of homes . . . there is a ready criterion, with roots deep in the common law." Again quoting pre-*Katz Silverman*, the majority stated that—"[a]t the very core" of the Fourth Amendment 'stands the right of a man

---

145. Justice Scalia conceded that the technology used in the present case was "relatively crude." But, citing a Department of Justice website, he noted that the "ability to 'see' through walls and other opaque barriers is a clear, and scientifically feasible, goal of law enforcement research and development."

146. Silverman v. United States, 365 U.S. 505 (1961).

147. Although the text of the Fourth Amendment seems to require that search warrants be granted only upon a finding by the issuing magistrate of probable cause (the text of the Fourth Amendment provides that ". . . no Warrants shall issue, but upon probable cause . . ."), there is a difference of opinion among federal courts as to whether the warrant required for a thermal scan may be based on a lesser standard than probable cause. *Compare* United States v. Huggins, 299 F.3d 1039 (9th Cir. 2002) (requiring ordinary probable cause) with United States v. Kattaria, 503 F.3d 703 (8th Cir. 2007) (requiring reasonable suspicion, a lesser standard than probable cause). The concepts of "probable cause" and "reasonable suspicion" are discussed in the text at §§ 8.02 (probable cause) and 17.03 (reasonable suspicion).

148. *See* Note 60, *supra*.

149. "One might think that . . . examining the portion of a house that is in plain public view, while it is a 'search' despite the absence of trespass, is not an 'unreasonable' one under the Fourth Amendment. . . . But in fact we have held that visual observation is no 'search' at all. . . ."

to retreat into his own home and there be free from unreasonable governmental intrusion.'"

But what about the fact that thermal imagers only detect relative heat emanations from the home and not intimate details about life inside the dwelling? The Court's answer was: "In the home . . . *all* details are intimate details, because the entire area is held safe from prying government eyes."[150] According to Scalia, "[t]he Fourth Amendment's protection of the home has never been tied to measurement of the quality or quantity of information." A "search" occurs if there is "any physical invasion of the structure of the home, 'by even a fraction of an inch',"[151] or if a police officer "barely cracks open the front door and sees nothing but the nonintimate rug on the vestibule floor."

The dissenters would have distinguished between "through-the-wall" surveillance— the type Justice Scalia fears in the future—and "off-the-wall" surveillance. Justice Stevens, author of the dissent, explained:

> [T]his case involves nothing more than off-the-wall surveillance . . . to gather information exposed to the general public from the outside of petitioner's home. All that the infrared camera did . . . was passively measure heat emitted from the exterior surfaces of [K's] home. . . . [N]o details regarding the interior of [K's] home were revealed. Unlike an x-ray scan, or other possible "through-the-wall" techniques, the detection of infrared radiation emanating from the home did not accomplish "an unauthorized physical penetration into the premises," nor did it "obtain information that it could not have obtained by observation from outside the curtilage of the house."

Justice Stevens explained that with "ordinary use of the senses" a neighbor could observe the heat emanating from the building, if (as here) it was vented; furthermore, "any member of the public might notice that one part of a house is warmer than another part . . . if, for example, rainwater evaporates or snow melts at different rates across its surfaces."[152] Thus, to the dissent, the imager provided information to the police that came "off the wall" and not through it; all the police did is use that information (and tips they had received elsewhere) to *infer* what was taking place inside.

The *Kyllo* dissent was correct in one sense: as long as a police officer is present in a lawful vantage point, anything he observes with his naked eye is not a Fourth

---

150. It is difficult to see how *Kyllo* and *Smith v. Maryland*, 442 U.S. 735 (1979), the pen register case discussed in subsection [B], can coexist. There, it will be remembered, the Court distinguished between the *contents* of private conversations—which *Katz* protects—and the supposedly more limited information (the phone numbers called from within a home) provided by a pen register. If the police may use a pen register, a device situated outside the house, to obtain phone numbers being called inside the house by a resident, it would seem that is permissible to use a thermal-imaging device to determine relative house heat emanations (which, it should be pointed out, are *outside* the home when the device records it). Or, put the opposite way, if the Court intends to stand by *Kyllo*, the Court might need to reconsider *Smith*.

151. The Court again cited *Silverman* for this proposition.

152. Justice Scalia responded in *Kyllo* that "[t]he fact that equivalent information could sometimes be obtained by other means does not make lawful the use of means that violate the Fourth Amendment. The police might, for example, learn how many people are in a particular house by setting up year-round surveillance; but that does not make breaking and entering to find out the same information lawful." Thus, Scalia is drawing a mode-of-intrusion distinction. *See* §6.04[B], *supra*. In contrast, the Supreme Court in *Oliver v. United States, see* §6.06, *supra*, justified trespassing in open fields, in part on the ground that the police could have obtained the same information lawfully by aerial surveillance.

Amendment search. Thus, a police officer on a public sidewalk who looks through a window into a private home and observes illegal activity has not violated the Fourth Amendment. This is even true if the police officer uses a device to magnify his observations, such as binoculars or a telescope.[153] As long as the device is merely "sense-enhancing," use of the device does not constitute a Fourth Amendment search.

A good example of this principle is the pre-*Kyllo* case *Dow Chemical Co. v. United States*.[154] In *Dow Chemical*, agents of the Environmental Protection Agency (EPA) sought evidence against Dow by photographing its 2,000-acre industrial complex from altitudes of 1,200 to 12,000 feet with the use of what the Court described as a "standard, floor-mounted, precision aerial mapping camera." The Court did not treat this surveillance as a search because "[h]ere, EPA was not employing some unique sensory device that, for example, could penetrate the walls of buildings and record conversations in Dow's plants, offices, or laboratories, but rather [was using] a conventional, albeit precise, commercial camera commonly used in mapmaking." The Court stated in dicta, however, that "surveillance of private property by using highly sophisticated surveillance equipment not generally available to the public . . . might be constitutionally proscribed absent a [search] warrant."

Where the majority and the dissent disagree in *Kyllo*, then, is in the nature of the information obtained by the thermal imager. The dissent argued that the thermal imager did nothing more than "enhance" the senses of the police—an ordinary police officer is able to detect heat, and the device did nothing more than enhance the ability of the officer to detect heat that was emanating into public space. The majority took a less formalistic view of the device and held that for all practical purposes the thermal imager gave the police information about the inside of the house that the police could not realistically have obtained in any other way (aside from, of course, actually entering the house, which would clearly be a Fourth Amendment search).

The subsections below consider the Court's treatment of various forms of modern technology, some used to provide information to the police about activities going on in private residences, and other times to survey less private areas.

The case law in this area is considered in chronological order.

[B] Pen Registers, Metadata, and the Third Party Doctrine[155]

A "pen register" is an old device that attached to a telephone line and detected the telephone number that was being dialed. Although pen registers are no longer in widespread use, the term is now commonly used for any investigative technique that reveals the "metadata" of an electronic communication—the telephone number being dialed on a phone call, or the address of an e-mail or text.

---

153. *See, e.g.,* On Lee v. United States, 343 U.S. 747, 754 (1952) ("[t]he use of bifocals, field glasses or the telescope to magnify the object of a witness' vision is not a forbidden search or seizure, even if they focus without his knowledge or consent upon what one supposes to be private indiscretions.") Although *On Lee* predated the *Katz* test, its principle is consistent with *Katz*.

154. 476 U.S. 227 (1986).

155. 1 LaFave, Note 98, *supra*, at § 2.7(b).

The Supreme Court considered the question of pen registers in the 1979 case of *Smith v. Maryland*.[156] The *Smith* Court held that installation and use of a pen register by the telephone company, at the behest of the government, to record the telephone numbers dialed from a private residence is not a "search" within the meaning of the Fourth Amendment. The Court rested its holding on two separate points, both of which are still good law, but both of which are being cast into doubt by subsequent case law and by changing technology. As noted below, *Smith*'s continued vitality is in some doubt as a result of subsequent case law.

First, the *Smith* Court distinguished pen registers from the electronic surveillance that occurred in *Katz* based on the type of information that the government obtained. In *Katz*, a telephone booth was bugged in order to permit the police to acquire the *contents* of private communications. Pen registers, however, have a more limited capacity, in that they only disclose metadata: the telephone numbers that were dialed and the length of the phone call. Metadata does not inform its user what was said, or even if a conversation occurred; nor are the identities of the persons called disclosed. Thus, the narrow issue, as the *Smith* Court framed it, was whether the defendant "had a 'legitimate expectation of privacy' regarding the numbers he dialed on his phone."

The Court expressed doubt "that people in general entertain any actual expectation of privacy in the numbers they dial." The Justices reasoned that telephone users know that they convey the numbers they are dialing to the telephone company, and they know that the phone company has the capacity to record this information, because customers see a list of toll calls on their monthly bills. Also, the Court observed, "[a]lthough most people may be oblivious to a pen register's esoteric functions, they presumably have some awareness" — from notices in phone books — "of one common use: to aid in the identification of persons making annoying or obscene calls." Therefore, the Court inferred that, "[a]lthough subjective expectations cannot be scientifically gauged, it is too much to believe" that telephone users harbor subjective privacy expectations regarding the numbers they call. Consequently, the Court concluded, "in all probability" the defendant entertained no actual expectation of privacy in the numbers he dialed.

Although the majority considered the information disclosed by pen registers relatively non-intrusive — merely phone numbers called, and not the conversations themselves — the dissenters found the "prospect of unregulated governmental monitoring ... disturbing even to those with nothing illicit to hide. Many individuals, including members of unpopular political organizations or journalists with confidential sources, may legitimately wish to avoid disclosure of their personal contacts."[157]

This part of *Smith*'s holding is known as the "address/content" distinction: the theory that individuals have no expectation of privacy in the *address* of their communications, only in the *content* of their communications. In this sense, a telephone call can

---

156. 442 U.S. 735 (1979); *contra under the state constitution*, People v. Sporleder, 666 P.2d 135 (Colo. 1983); State v. Rothman, 779 P.2d 1 (Haw. 1989); State v. Thompson, 760 P.2d 1162 (Idaho 1988); State v. Hunt, 450 A.2d 952 (N.J. 1982); Commonwealth v. Melilli, 555 A.2d 1254 (Pa. 1989); Richardson v. State, 865 S.W.2d 944 (Tex. Crim. App. 1993); State v. Gunwall, 720 P.2d 808 (Wash. 1986).

157. As noted above in the text, *Smith*'s continued vitality is in some doubt. Further evidence of this assertion is Justice Sotomayor's statement in a concurring opinion in *United States v. Jones*, 132 S. Ct. 945, 957 (2012), that "it may be necessary to reconsider the premise that an individual has no reasonable expectation of privacy in information voluntarily disclosed to third parties," citing *Smith* and *Miller*.

be analogized to a traditional letter. The outside of the envelope, which contains the address, is open for all to see, including law enforcement, and so individuals have no reasonable expectation of privacy in the name of the person with whom they are communicating. But the actual letter is sealed inside the envelope, and it would plainly be a search if the government ripped open the envelope to read the contents. As we will see in Section [E] below, this distinction becomes harder to make in the era of digital communications.

The second argument put forward by the *Smith* Court was the third party doctrine. Citing the false-friend conversational surveillance cases[158] and *United States v. Miller,*[159] it concluded that a person has no legitimate expectation of privacy in any information that the individual voluntarily turns over to third parties. By knowingly exposing information (the numbers dialed) to a third party (here, the telephone company), the telephone user assumes the risk that it will be transmitted to law enforcement agents.

The dissenters distinguished the false-friend cases from pen registers. They argued that a person can "exercise some discretion in deciding who should enjoy his confidential communications." In contrast, people have no choice in modern society but to use telephones. Moreover, the dissent reasoned that "[p]rivacy is not a discrete commodity, possessed absolutely or not at all." The rule should not be, the dissenters argued, that if one discloses information to a telephone company, that the individual assumes the risk that this information will be disclosed to the rest of the world for other purposes.

The third party doctrine is still good law today, but its continued validity is under attack, and it is almost uniformly condemned by legal scholars.[160] In 1971, when *Smith* was decided, it was relatively rare for individuals to entrust information to third parties. But even back then, as the dissenters pointed out, nobody is really "choosing" to share information with third parties—in order to participate in society, a person had to have a telephone and thereby "share" certain information with the phone company. Today, the application of the third party doctrine has far greater consequences. In the digital age, we share almost all of our personal information with third parties—our e-mails are stored on third-party servers; our data is stored in the cloud; search engines record the search terms we enter and the websites we visit. Furthermore, that data is all easily accessible by the government, who can obtain it merely by issuing a subpoena to the company that stores the information.

---

158. *See* § 6.05, *supra.*

159. 425 U.S. 435 (1976). In *Miller,* the Court held that a bank customer has no legitimate expectation of privacy in financial information that he "voluntarily conveys" to bank employees in the ordinary course of business. No search occurs, therefore, if the bank hands over the customer's financial records to the government. *Contra under the state constitution,* People v. Jackson, 452 N.E.2d 85 (Ill. 1983); State v. McAllister, 875 A.2d 866 (N.J. 2005); Commonwealth v. De John, 403 A.2d 1283 (Pa. 1979); State v. Thompson, 810 P.2d 415 (Utah 1991).

160. *See, e.g.,* 1 Wayne R. LaFave, Search and Seizure: A Treatise on the Fourth Amendment § 2.7(c) at 747 (4th ed. 2004) (describing the doctrine as "dead wrong;" Christopher Slobogin, Privacy at Risk: The New Government Surveillance and the Fourth Amendment 151–64 (2007). *But see* Orin Kerr, *The Case for the Third Party Doctrine,* 107 Mich. L. Rev. 561 (2007) (arguing in favor of the doctrine).

[C] Electronic Tracking Devices: The "Beeper Cases"[161]

In the past—especially before the advent of Global Positioning System (GPS) satellite devices—police officers used electronic devices ("beepers") to track the movements of suspects. A "beeper" is a small battery-operated device that can be installed in or on a suspect's vehicle, or in some object that the suspect will have in his possession, which emits periodic radio signals that can be picked up by officers in police cars, airplanes, or helicopters. *Installation* of such a device in or on the suspect's property potentially raises a "seizure" issue.[162] *Use* of the device to monitor the suspect's movements raises a "search" question.

In *United States v. Knotts*,[163] federal officers suspected *K* of manufacturing drugs. Without obtaining a warrant, they installed a beeper in a chemical drum that they asked a merchant to sell to *K*. With the assistance of the beeper, the officers followed *K*'s automobile as he drove from one state to another. At one point, due to *K*'s evasive maneuvers, the police lost visual surveillance of the vehicle. They also temporarily lost the signal from the beeper, but they later regained contact with it by helicopter. The signal indicated that the chemical drum was located outside a certain cabin. Based on this information, the police secured a warrant to search the cabin. *K* reasoned that the warrant was invalid because critical information used to obtain the warrant was secured unconstitutionally, i.e., as the result of electronic surveillance conducted without a warrant.

The Supreme Court held that use of the beeper did not constitute a search and, therefore, no warrant was required to monitor *K*'s movements. The Court focused on two interrelated factors. First, the beeper did not provide the police with any information that they could not have secured by visual surveillance from public places along the route. In essence, *K* knowingly exposed to others the information of his movements by driving on public roads. The fact that a beeper was used instead of visual surveillance did not alter the analysis. The mode of surveillance here was irrelevant. Second, the beeper had "limited use" in this case: It did not reveal information as to *K*'s movements within any private place, such as within the cabin.

The latter distinction proved dispositive in *United States v. Karo*.[164] In *Karo*, the beeper allowed the police to monitor the movement of a container of chemicals inside various homes as well as in public places. The information secured in this manner was used to obtain a warrant to search a house for drug-related evidence. The Court held that the Fourth Amendment protected against use of the beeper located inside the house. It observed that "[i]ndiscriminate monitoring of property that has been withdrawn from public view would present far too serious a threat to privacy interests in the home to escape entirely some sort of Fourth Amendment oversight."

Knotts and *Karo* suggest a few intriguing points about Fourth Amendment "search" analysis. First, the implication of *Knotts* is that as long as monitoring is limited to movements of persons in non-private areas, the government is free to conduct constant surveillance of citizens. The *Knotts* Court, aware of this troubling implication, observed that "if such dragnet-style . . . practices . . . should eventually occur, there will be time enough

---

161. 1 LaFave, Note 98, *supra*, at §2.7(e).
162. *See* §7.02[B], *infra*.
163. 460 U.S. 276 (1983); *contra under the state constitution*, State v. Campbell, 759 P.2d 1040 (Or. 1988).
164. 468 U.S. 705 (1984).

then to determine whether different"—stress, different—"constitutional principles may be applicable."

Second, the suggestion in *Knotts* that *K* did not have a legitimate expectation of privacy because the officers could have obtained the same information by visual surveillance, obscures the fact that "to learn what the beeper revealed . . . would have taken an army of bystanders in ready and willing communication with one other" along the route traveled.[165] The implication of *Knotts* is that as long as it is hypothetically conceivable (although, in some cases, nearly impossible practically) to obtain information in a non-technologically-enhanced manner from a lawful vantage point, it is irrelevant that, instead, the government uses an electronic tracking device to obtain the same information.

To many observers, *Knotts-Karo* suggested that the police could place GPS devices on automobiles and track suspects' movements as long as the information they obtained did not include surveillance of movements inside a home. As we see in the next section, that turns out not to be the case.

[D] Massive Data Collection and the Mosaic Theory

Under *Knotts* and *Karo*, the Court established that a person does not have any reasonable expectation of privacy in information that they knowingly expose to the public. This includes where they travel on public roads. Thus, when the Court considered the question of whether the police could use a GPS device to track a suspect's car while it traveled along public roads, a strict application of *Knotts* would mean that the surveillance did not implicate the Fourth Amendment.

As we saw in Section 6.05[E] above, the Supreme Court did not follow this course when it considered the use of GPS devices in *Jones v. United States*. Instead, a majority of the Court revived the old "trespass" test and held that the government conducted a search because it trespassed on the defendant's property when it attached a GPS device to the car. Four Justices rejected the trespass test and applied the *Katz* test—and those Justices also agreed that the use of the GPS was a Fourth Amendment search.

To reach this conclusion, Justice Alito and the three other Justices in the concurring opinion applied what is known as the "mosaic theory." Just as a mosaic is made up of individual meaningless points that resolve themselves into a meaningful picture when combined together, the mosaic theory holds that aggregating many public pieces of information could result in a "mosaic" that reveals private information. Thus, even if a person does not have a reasonable expectation of privacy in an individual piece of information (such as one trip along a public road), a person could have a reasonable expectation of privacy in all of his trips along public roads over an extended period. By aggregating all of these individual trips, the police are able to spot patterns and potentially deduce intimate information about the suspect that they would not be able to deduce after monitoring one trip.

Thus, according to Justice Alito's concurrence, "relatively short-term monitoring of a person's movements on public streets accords with expectations of privacy that our

---

165. LaFave, Note 37, *supra*, at 1082.

society has recognized as reasonable." However, "the use of longer term GPS monitoring in investigations of most offenses impinges on [reasonable] expectations of privacy."[166]

The mosaic theory is somewhat controversial. On the one hand, the *Jones* concurrence is correct in stating that modern technology has allowed the police to conduct surveillance of public places on a scale vastly different from what could have been envisioned when *Katz* and *Knotts* were decided. Thus, courts did not have to worry about regulating massive amounts of data collection, because "[t]raditional surveillance for any extended period of time was difficult and costly and therefore rarely undertaken. The surveillance at issue in this case—constant monitoring of the location of a vehicle for four weeks—would have required a large team of agents, multiple vehicles, and perhaps aerial assistance."[167] But that is no longer the case. GPS devices make continuous, long-term monitoring relatively inexpensive, and in the absence of legislative action, courts must decide whether to allow constant surveillance of this kind or subject it to the *Katz* test.

The problem is not limited to GPS tracking. Constant video surveillance of a person's property can also create privacy concerns that may lead to the application of the mosaic doctrine.[168] And the rise of "big data analytics"—the ability to gather and process mass quantities of data to learn new information—has altered the way law enforcement conducts investigations. The government can track our Internet search history, learn whom we are calling on our phones, and subpoena all of our credit card charges. Under the third party doctrine described in Section [B] above, we have no reasonable expectation of privacy in any of this information because we have voluntarily turned it over to third parties (search engine companies, telecommunication companies, credit card companies). The government can easily track years of our social networking communications because that is information we have knowingly exposed to the public.[169] If this type of surveillance is unregulated by the Fourth Amendment, law enforcement will be able to discover significant amounts of private information about us without implicating the Fourth Amendment. The mosaic theory is a mechanism by which courts can take a more holistic and less formalistic view of the government's actions and examine what the government is *really* learning about us when it collects and processes massive amounts of data.

On the other hand, the mosaic theory has attracted widespread criticism from courts and commentators.[170] Critics note that the theory is doctrinally suspect: it asserts that multiple numbers of "non-searches" can somehow be added together to become a search, which is akin to saying that multiplying zero by a large enough number results in a non-zero number. It is also problematic to implement: at what point do large amounts of

---

166. United States v. Jones, 132 S. Ct. 945, 964 (Alito, J., concurring). *See also* Commonwealth v. Rousseau, 465 Mass. 372, 990 N.E.2d 543 (Mass. 2013) (under the state constitution, even where the police have not trespassed on the defendant's property, holding that "a person may reasonably expect not to be subjected to extended GPS electronic surveillance by the government, targeted at his movements, without judicial oversight and a showing of probable cause").

167. Jones v. United States, (Alito, J., concurring).

168. *See* United States v. Vargas (No. No. CR-13-6025-EFS; W.D. Wash. Dec 15, 2014) (six weeks of continuous video surveillance of the defendant's front lawn from a camera on a nearby utility pole is a Fourth Amendment search); *Contra* United States v. Houston, 813 F.3d 282 (6th Cir. 2016).

169. *See* Monu Bedi, *Social Networks, Government Surveillance, and the Fourth Amendment Mosaic Theory*, 94 B. U. L. Rev. 1809 (2014).

170. *See, e.g.*, Orin Kerr, *The Mosaic Theory and the Fourth Amendment*, 111 Mich. L. Rev. 311 (2012).

public information suddenly become private? The *Jones* concurrence acknowledged this challenge but then dodged the question, stating that it "need not identify with precision the point at which the tracking of this vehicle became a search, for the line was surely crossed before the 4-week mark." It conceded that later cases will present more difficult questions.[171] Finally, widespread adoption of the mosaic theory will force courts to answer a number of novel questions:[172] Does the theory apply when law enforcement gathers the information, or only when it processes the information in certain ways that reveal private information? Do courts aggregate information that is obtained by different officers, or even different agencies? Should courts apply different standards for aggregated location information than they do for telephone metadata or social media posts? The mosaic theory has the potential to further complicate an already complex area of Fourth Amendment law.

[E] Computers and Electronic Transmissions

As more and more information is stored and transmitted digitally, law enforcement officers frequently conduct searches of computer hard drives or monitor Internet searches, e-mails, or other electronic communications. Courts often struggle to apply language that was written in the eighteenth century or case law that was decided in the 1960s to modern technology.

A preliminary point about digital surveillance: this area of surveillance law is highly regulated by statute. The Pen Register Act sets standards for law enforcement officials who seek any kind of "address" information, whether it is the numbers dialed from a telephone or the address line of an e-mail. This is a very low standard: the police need only demonstrate that the information that is likely to be obtained is "relevant to an ongoing investigation."[173] The Stored Communication Act covers any opened e-mails that are stored by Internet service providers, and generally requires law enforcement to show "specific and articulable facts showing that there are reasonable grounds to believe" that the information being sought is relevant to an ongoing investigation.[174] And the Electronic Communications Privacy Act regulates the interception of the content of electronic communications while in transit, requiring the government to show not just probable cause, but also that no other investigative procedures are feasible and that the surveillance will be conducted in a way that minimizes the interception of irrelevant information.[175]

These statutes all create higher standards than those imposed by the Fourth Amendment: as we saw in Section B above, the Fourth Amendment does not cover the address information regulated by the Pen Register statute, and the third party doctrine means

---

171. Lower courts have also struggled to define the scope of *Jones'* plurality decision in cases where the government engaged in long-term monitoring of public places. In one case, the government installed a camera on a public utility pole near the suspect's house and monitored the suspect's home continuously for 10 weeks; the Sixth Circuit held that this was a search. United States v. Houston, 813 F.3d 282 (2016). In a nearly identical case, however, a district court held that it was *not* a search when the government used a similar camera to monitor the suspect's front lawn for six weeks. United States v. Vargas, CR-13-6025-EFS (E.D. Wash. 2014).

172. Kerr, note 170, *supra*, at 334–336.

173. *See* 18 U.S.C. §§ 3122, 3123.

174. *See* 18 U.S.C. §§ 2702-2703. The Stored Communication Act also sets different standards for unopened e-mails and customer records.

175. *See* 18 U.S.C. § 2518.

that the Fourth Amendment does not protect e-mails that are stored on a third-party server. However, there are many other types of digital surveillance that are unregulated by statutes where the Fourth Amendment is still relevant, or where lower courts are aggressively pushing for a change in Fourth Amendment doctrine in response to new technology.

Courts treat searches of computers just like searches of any other "container." Thus, in the same way that it is a Fourth Amendment search to open up a briefcase or a file cabinet, it is also a search to look through the files on a computer or to copy the hard drive and examine it later.[176] A more complicated issue arises when police want to monitor a defendant's Internet searches. The Supreme Court has not yet ruled on this question, but lower courts have held that the IP addresses of the sites that an individual visits on the Internet are merely "address" information (akin to pen register information) and so are not subject to the Fourth Amendment.[177]

Some lower courts have even gone so far as to challenge the third party doctrine when it is applied to stored electronic communications. As noted above, there is some statutory protection for opened e-mails that are stored on a third-party server, but it is relatively weak protection — all that is required are specific and articulable facts showing that there are "reasonable grounds to believe" that the information being sought is relevant to an ongoing investigation. In *United States v. Warshak*,[178] the Sixth Circuit ruled that the Fourth Amendment applied to the defendant's opened e-mails even though they were stored on a third-party server. In this case the police suspected W of massive fraud in his running of a mail-order scheme. In order to prove this fraud, the police approached N Communications, W's Internet service provider, with an order to turn over all of W's e-mails that they had stored for W over a three-year period. N Communications complied with the order and ultimately gave the government more than 27,000 of W's e-mails. The government never obtained a warrant for these e-mails and W never received notice that his e-mails were being handed over to the government.

Under a strict application of the third party doctrine, the government had every right to obtain these e-mails from the third-party company, because W forfeited any reasonable expectation of privacy when he shared them with the third party. But the Sixth Circuit disagreed, saying that the content of e-mails contained too much private information to be obtained without a warrant: "By obtaining access to someone's e-mail, government agents gain the ability to peer deeply into his activities."[179] The lower courts are divided on this issue, however, with some circuits freely applying the third party doctrine to stored e-mails and other digital information.[180] Until the Supreme Court

---

176. *See* Wayne R. LaFave, Search and Seizure, § 2.6(f) (4th ed. 2004); State v. Rodgers, 240 Ariz. 245 (Ariz. 2016) (police officers conducted a Fourth Amendment search when they looked through defendant's cell phone even though he was not in possession of the phone and did not have it password protected.

177. *See* United States v. Forrester, 495 F.3d 1041 (2007).

178. 631 F.3d 266 (6th Cir. 2010).

179. This philosophy was echoed later by Justice Sotomayor of the Supreme Court in her concurrence in *United States v. Jones*, in which she stated that given the amount of information routinely given to third parties, courts should no longer "assume that all information voluntarily disclosed to some member of the public for a limited purpose is, for that reason alone, disentitled to Fourth Amendment protection." United State v. Jones, 132 S. Ct. 945, 957 (2012) (Sotomayor, J., concurring).

180. *See, e.g.*, Rehburg v. Paulk, 598 F.3d 1268 (11th Cir. 2010) (third party doctrine applies to e-mails because they are shared with the Internet service provider; United States v. Ciara, 833 F.3d

resolves this issue, the extent to which the third party doctrine applies to digital information that is routinely shared with third-party companies is still an open question.

[F] Cell Phone Information

A related question arises when the government tracks a suspect's location using the suspect's cell phone signal. One common method the government uses to locate an individual is to obtain "historical cell cite information" from the suspect's cell phone service provider. This is essentially a record of which cell towers were used by the suspect's telephone when the cell phone was in use. The government can use this information to triangulate the suspect's position at specific times in the past; for example, the location information could show that the suspect was near the scene of the crime at the time the crime occurred.[181]

Although the Supreme Court has not yet ruled on this issue, lower courts have so far held that individuals do not have a reasonable expectation of privacy in the location information that their cell phones send to their service providers.[182] Courts base this conclusion on three principles. First, the suspect is voluntarily sharing the location information with a third party—the cell phone service provider—and so under the third party doctrine of *Smith v. Maryland*,[183] the suspect has no reasonable privacy interest in the information. Second, the location information is not "content" information, which is given broad protection, but merely "address" information, which receives almost no protection. And finally, courts distinguish these cases from the GPS cases like *Jones* because the location information obtained by this method is much less precise—generally only telling the government the suspect's location within a mile-long area. Thus, the government is unlikely to learn the kind of intimate details about the suspect's life that concerned the *Jones* plurality.[184]

These decisions are not without controversy. The idea that the suspect is "voluntarily" sharing his location information with a third party seems to ignore the realities of the modern world, in which the vast majority of Americans use a cell phone. The courts' argument implies that if we "choose" to use a cell phone (essentially a modern-day necessity), then we are conceding that the government gets to track all of our movements throughout the day. And although current historical cell site information is imprecise, the government will soon be able to refine this technique to locate the cell phone user

---

803 (7th Cir. 2016) (third party doctrine applies to suspect's login history and the Internet protocol address he logs in from).

181. *See generally* Kyle Malone, *The Fourth Amendment and the Stored Communications Act: Why the Warrantless Gathering of Historical Cell Site Location Information Poses No Threat to Privacy,* 39 Pepp. L. Rev. 701 (2013).

182. *See, e.g.,* In re Application of U.S. for an Order Directing Provider of Elec. Commc'n Serv. to Disclose Records to Gov't, 620 F.3d 304, 313 (3d Cir. 2010); In re Application of the U.S. for Historical Cell Site Data, 724 F.3d 600, 612–13 (5th Cir. 2013); United States v. Davis, 785 F.3d 498, 511 (11th Cir. 2015) (en banc); United States v. Carpenter, 819 F.3d 380 (6th Cir. 2016); Taylor v. State, 2016 BL 127001, *4 (Nev. 2016).

183. *See* subsection [B], *supra* (explaining that a defendant does not have a reasonable expectation of privacy in the phone numbers that he dials, because he knows the telephone company keeps a record of those numbers).

184. This does not mean that this information is completely unprotected; under the Stored Communication Act, the government must show "specific and articulable facts" before obtaining information stored by third parties. *See* 18 U.S.C. § 2703(d).

with much greater precision. This could mean the government could track our location while we are inside our homes or other private property, which runs contrary to decisions such as *Kyllo v. United States*[185] and *United States v. Karo,*[186] which create a clear public place/private place distinction.

Notwithstanding these concerns, lower courts have nearly unanimously held that historical cell site information is not protected by the Fourth Amendment. However, other government uses of cell phone information may require a warrant. For example, sometimes the government is seeking "prospective" location information—essentially real-time information about a suspect's location. Or the government may ask the service provider to "ping" the suspect's cell phone, thus forcing the cell phone to reveal its location even if the suspect is not using it at the time. Some courts have held that these actions are "searches" that require a warrant.[187] And finally, the government can use a tool called an IMSI catcher or "Stingray" device that imitates a cell phone tower and can thus intercept all of the data sent by the suspect's phone (as well as all the other phones in the area). Stingrays can be used to obtain the identification information from a telephone, or even the content of the messages being sent. So far, courts have held that the government does not need a warrant if it uses a Stingray to obtain a cell phone's identification information, but the Department of Justice has instructed all of its agents to obtain a warrant before using these devices.

---

185. 533 U.S. 27. *See* subsection [D], *supra.*
186. 468 U.S. 705. *See* subsection [C], *supra.*
187. *See* In re Application for Historical Cell Cite Information, 509 F. Supp. 2d 64, 75 (D. MA. 2007); Tracey v. State, 152 So. 3d 504 (Fla. 2014). Other state courts have applied their own state constitutions to conclude that real-time tracking using cell phone information is a search. *See, e.g.,* State v. Earls, 70 A.3d 630 (N.J.2013). These cases raise similar, if not identical, issues as the GPS tracking cases discussed in § 6.10[E].

Chapter 7

Fourth Amendment Terminology: "Seizure"

§ 7.01 Constitutional Significance of the Term "Seizure"

This chapter defines the term "seizure." Unlike the word "search," which has a single constitutional definition, the word "seizure" requires multiple definitions, one relating to property, and a different definition for seizure of persons. As is the case with searches, the issue of whether police conduct constitutes a seizure is a matter of threshold significance: Unless the police action is a "seizure" (or a "search"), the various restrictions of the Fourth Amendment do not apply.

If police conduct *does* constitute a seizure, the remaining constitutional issue is whether the seizure was reasonable. With property, this means that the police must often have a search warrant, based on probable cause, or a justification for not securing the warrant.[1] In the case of seizure of persons, the police must have adequate cause to seize the individual. In the case of an arrest, the police must have probable cause to make the arrest;[2] and if the arrest occurs in the home, an arrest warrant is usually required.[3] With personal seizures less intrusive than arrests, a lesser standard—reasonable suspicion— is satisfactory;[4] and in relatively few circumstances, the police may briefly seize a person without any suspicion at all.[5]

§ 7.02 Seizure of Property

[A] General Rule

In contrast to a search, which affects a person's privacy interest, a seizure of property invades a person's possessory interest in that property.[6] Tangible[7] property is "seized" in

---

1. *See especially* Chapter 10, *infra*.
2. "Probable cause" is explained in Chapter 8, *infra*.
3. *See* § 9.05, *infra*.
4. *See* § 17.03, *infra*.
5. *See, e.g.,* 18.04[B][1], *infra*.
6. Texas v. Brown, 460 U.S. 730, 747 (1983) (Stevens J., concurring).
7. The Supreme Court originally ruled that the Fourth Amendment applied only to searches and seizures of material things, which excluded conversations, but the word "person" in the constitutional phrase "persons, houses, papers and effects" is now interpreted to encompass an

Fourth Amendment terms "when there is some meaningful interference with an individual's possessory interests in that property."[8]

A "seizure" occurs when a police officer exercises control over *D*'s property by destroying it,[9] or by removing it from *D*'s actual or constructive possession.[10] A house or office and its contents are "seized" when an officer secures the premises, i.e., prevents persons from entering or taking away or destroying personal property.[11] On the other hand, no "seizure" occurs when an officer merely picks up an object to look at it or moves it a small distance, because any interference with *D*'s possessory interest in such circumstances is not "meaningful."[12]

[B] Special Issue: Installation of Electronic Devices on or in Personal Property

The installation of an electronic device on or in personal property, in order to monitor a person's movements or to intercept conversations, can raise "seizure" issues.[13] At least in some contexts, installation of such a device is not a seizure. For example, in *United States v. Karo*,[14] federal agents learned that *K* intended to obtain ether from *M*, a merchant, for use in the production of illegal drugs. With *M*'s consent, the agents installed an electronic "beeper" inside an ether can that *M* agreed to transfer to *K*, so that the agents could monitor *K*'s movements as he transported the can in an automobile.

The Court held that placement of the device in the can was not a seizure, since the container at the moment of installation did not belong to *K*, and thus did not invade *his* possessory interests in it.[15] More controversially, the Court also held that no seizure occurred when the "beeper"-infested can was transferred to *K* by *M*. According to the Court, "[a]lthough the can may have contained an unknown and unwanted foreign object, it cannot be said that anyone's possessory interest was interfered with in a meaningful way."[16]

---

individual's conversations. *See* § 5.02, *supra*. Current law treats the act of monitoring a conversation as both a search and seizure of the words. *See* Berger v. New York, 388 U.S. 41 (1967).

8. United States v. Jacobsen, 466 U.S. 109, 113 (1984).

9. *Id.* at 124–25.

10. *E.g.*, United States v. Place, 462 U.S. 696 (1983) (detention of *P*'s luggage for 90 minutes in order to take it from La Guardia Airport to JFK Airport to permit a trained narcotics dog to smell it constitutes a seizure).

11. Illinois v. McArthur, 531 U.S. 326 (2001).

12. *See, e.g.*, Arizona v. Hicks, 480 U.S. 321 (1987) (officer slightly moved stereo equipment in order to read a serial number on the back: no "seizure" issue raised); New York v. Class, 475 U.S. 106 (1986) (officer slightly moved a piece of paper in *C*'s car to see underneath: no "seizure" issue raised); Texas v. Brown, 460 U.S. 730 (1983) (officer moved a balloon a few feet in order to better view its contents: no "seizure" issue raised).

13. The installation and, in particular, monitoring of a person's movements by means of an electronic device, can also raise major "search" issues. *See* § 6.10[C] and [E], *supra*.

14. 468 U.S. 705 (1984).

15. Of course, there was no meaningful interference with the *merchant's* possessory interest in the property, as he consented to the installation.

16. Justice Stevens, joined by Justices Brennan and Marshall, dissented from this conclusion. They contended that a possessory interest in property includes the right to exclude others from it, which was meaningfully interfered with the moment the can was transferred to *K* with the monitoring

A different result would seem to apply if the electronic device were installed *inside* a person's property in a manner that meaningfully interferes with her property. For example, if the police break open the lock of a car or suitcase, thereby damaging the property, in order to install a beeper, this should constitute a seizure of the property in question.

§ 7.03 Seizure of Persons[17]

[A] Overview

The arrest of a suspect uncontroversially constitutes a seizure of that person.[18] The Court has also held that circumstances short of an arrest may constitute a seizure, so the high court has had to provide a working definition of a "seizure" of a person.

Recently, the Court provided this summary of what constitutes a seizure of a person:

> A person is seized by the police ... when the officer, by means of physical force or show of authority, terminates or restrains his freedom of movement *through means intentionally applied.* Thus, an unintended person may be the object of the detention, so long as the detention is willful and not merely the consequence of an unknowing act. A police officer may make a seizure by a show of authority and without the use of physical force, but there is no seizure without actual submission. ...

intentional seizure

> When the actions of the police do not show an unambiguous intent to restrain or when an individual's submission to a show of governmental authority takes the form of passive acquiescence ... a seizure occurs if in view of all of the circumstances surrounding the incident, a reasonable person would have believed that he was not free to leave. ... [W]hen a person "has no desire to leave" for reasons unrelated to the police presence, the [test for a seizure is] whether "a reasonable person would feel free to decline the officers" requests or otherwise terminate the encounter."[19]

unintentional seizure

This summary, although reasonably concise, is not useful without elaboration, to which the Text now turns.

---

device secreted inside. As the dissent put it, "the character of the property is profoundly different when infected with an electronic bug than when it is entirely germ free."

17. *See generally* 4 Wayne R. LaFave, Search and Seizure § 9.4 (4th ed. 2004); Ronald J. Bacigal, *In Pursuit of the Elusive Fourth Amendment: The Police Chase Cases*, 58 Tenn. L. Rev. 73 (1990); Thomas K. Clancy, *The Future of Fourth Amendment Seizure Analysis after Hodari D. and Bostick*, 28 Am. Crim. L. Rev. 799 (1991); Wayne R. LaFave, *Pinguitudinous Police, Pachydermatous Prey: Whence Fourth Amendment "Seizures"?*, 1991 U. Ill. L. Rev. 729 (1991); Tracey Maclin, *"Black and Blue Encounters"—Some Preliminary Thoughts About Fourth Amendment Seizures: Should Race Matter?*, 26 Val. U. L. Rev. 243 (1991); Janice Nadler, *No Need to Shout: Bus Sweeps and the Psychology of Coercion*, 2002 Sup. Ct. Rev. 153.

18. *E.g.*, Henry v. United States, 361 U.S. 98 (1959).

19. Brendlin v. California, 551 U.S. 249, 254–255 (2007) (internal citations and ellipses omitted).

[B] The *Terry* Definition

The Supreme Court first defined "seizure" (of persons) in *Terry v. Ohio*:[20] "Obviously, not all personal intercourse between policemen and citizens involves "seizures" of persons. Only when the officer, by means of physical force or show of authority, has in some way restrained the liberty of a citizen may we conclude that a "seizure" has occurred."

The *Terry* rule has been slightly restated by later Court decisions this way: A person is seized when the officer by one of the means noted in *Terry*—use of physical force or show of authority—either terminates or restrains the individual's freedom of movement through means intentionally applied.[21] According to this definition, *D* is "seized" by an officer when, for example: she is physically restrained or ordered to stop so that she can be frisked or questioned on the street;[22] she is intentionally shot by the officer;[23] she is taken into custody and brought to a police station for questioning[24] or fingerprinting;[25] she is the driver or passenger in a car ordered to pull off the highway for questioning or to receive a traffic citation;[26] or she is intentionally forced to stop her car by means of a roadblock.[27] She is *not* seized, however, if she is a driver of a motorcycle whom a police officer accidentally strikes during a high-speed pursuit.[28]

[C] The *Mendenhall* "Reasonable Person" Test

[1] In General

Some police-citizen encounters are not as clear-cut as the examples set out in subsection [B], because the officer's intention to restrain a person's freedom of movement is externally ambiguous or the citizen's submission to authority occurs through passive acquiescence.

For example, in *United States v. Mendenhall*,[29] two male federal drug agents approached *M*, an African-American woman, in an airport concourse. They identified themselves as federal agents, and asked to see her identification and airline ticket, which she handed to them. Did this brief encounter constitute a seizure of *M*? If so, the agents needed to have reasonable cause for approaching her and requesting her identification and ticket; if it was *not* a seizure, they could approach her at will to make such a request.

Justice Stewart announced the judgment of the Court, and in a portion of the opinion in which only Justice Rehnquist joined, but which now commands the support of the full Court,[30] he added an objective component to the "seizure" definition: "We conclude that a person has been "seized" within the meaning of the Fourth Amendment

---

20. 392 U.S. 1 (1968).
21. Brendlin v. California, 551 U.S. at 254.
22. Terry v. Ohio, 392 U.S. 1 (1968).
23. Tennessee v. Garner, 471 U.S. 1 (1985).
24. Dunaway v. New York, 442 U.S. 200 (1979).
25. Hayes v. Florida, 470 U.S. 811 (1985).
26. United States v. Hensley, 469 U.S. 221 (1985) (driver); Brendlin v. California, 551 U.S. 249 (2007) (passenger).
27. Brower v. Inyo County, 489 U.S. 593 (1989).
28. County of Sacramento v. Lewis, 523 U.S. 833 (1998).
29. 446 U.S. 544 (1980).
30. The test was adopted as the majority rule in *I.N.S. v. Delgado*, 466 U.S. 210 (1984).

only if, in view of all of the circumstances surrounding the incident, a reasonable person would have believed that he was <u>not free to leave</u>."

The implication of the *Mendenhall* objective test is that, in determining whether a seizure has occurred, the subjective intention of a police officer to forcibly detain a suspect if she attempts to leave is irrelevant, except insofar as that intention is conveyed to the suspect and, thus, might affect the impressions of a reasonable person in the suspect's shoes. It follows, as well, that the subjective impressions of the person accosted is irrelevant, except to the extent that a reasonable person in that individual's situation would have the same concerns.

[2] Some Applications of the Test

[a] Seizure by Questioning?

The Court stated in *Terry v. Ohio* that "[o]bviously, not all personal intercourse between policemen and citizens involves "seizures" of persons." In the simplest case, if an officer asks a person on the street for the time of day, no reasonable person would believe that her freedom of movement is restricted because of the question. Under *Terry-Mendenhall*, no seizure has occurred.

However, even when a law enforcement agent questions an individual about suspected criminal activity, brief questioning in a public place *by itself* does not amount to a seizure.[31] The Court's reasoning is frankly pragmatic: "[C]haracterizing every street encounter between a citizen and the police as a "seizure," while not enhancing any interest secured by the Fourth Amendment, would impose wholly unrealistic restrictions upon a wide variety of legitimate law enforcement practices."[32]

The Supreme Court has determined that the police have considerable Fourth Amendment leeway in conducting criminal investigations: "Even when law enforcement officers have no basis for suspecting a particular individual, they may pose questions, ask for identification, and request consent to search luggage—provided they do not induce cooperation by coercive means."[33] In this context, consider the Court's treatment of the facts in *Mendenhall*. Justices Stewart and Rehnquist concluded that, based on the totality of circumstances in that case, no seizure occurred when the agents first accosted *M* and requested her identification and airline ticket. It was irrelevant that the officers might have physically restrained *M* or ordered her to remain in their custody had she refused to cooperate. In the view of these two justices—a view that seems unrealistic to many people and may best be explained on the pragmatic ground noted in the last paragraph— a reasonable person in *M*'s situation would have believed that she was free to leave.[34] Justice Stewart explained, "[t]he events took place in the public concourse. The agents wore no uniforms and displayed no weapons. They did not summon [*M*] to their

---

31. United States v. Drayton, 536 U.S. 194, 200 (2002) ("Law enforcement officers do not violate the Fourth Amendment's prohibition of unreasonable seizures merely by approaching individuals on the street or in other public places and putting questions to them if they are willing to listen.").

32. United States v. Mendenhall, 446 U.S. 544, 554 (1980).

33. *Drayton*, 536 U.S. at 201.

34. Three justices in *Mendenhall* did not determine whether she was seized, stating only that the question was "extremely close." The four dissenters pointed out that the "seizure" question had not been raised below; therefore they would have remanded to the district court for an evidentiary hearing on the question.

presence, but instead approached her. . . . They requested, but did not demand to see [her] identification and ticket. . . ."

What *would* have converted the encounter into a seizure? Justice Stewart stated:

> Examples of circumstances that might indicate a seizure, even where the person did not attempt to leave, would be the threatening presence of several officers, the display of a weapon by an officer, some physical touching of the person of the citizen, or the use of language or tone of voice indicating that compliance with the officer's request might be compelled.

The line between a finding of "no seizure" and "seizure," therefore, is exceedingly thin. Contrast *Mendenhall* to the facts in *Florida v. Royer*.[35] In *Royer*, two detectives accosted R, an embarking airline passenger, identified themselves, and asked to see his ticket and driver's license, which he provided them. When the officers spotted a discrepancy in the documents, they informed him that he was suspected of transporting narcotics. Without returning his ticket and license, they requested that he accompany them to a small airport office to be searched. R agreed.

As in *Mendenhall*, the Supreme Court held that the initial encounter — when the officers asked R for identification — was not a seizure, but the plurality opinion stated that R *was* seized when the agents asked him to accompany them to the room for a search. And yet, in *Mendenhall*, the Court held that a similar request by federal agents that M accompany them to a nearby airport office for a search was *not* a seizure. The *Royer* Court explained the difference and, in doing so, showed how careful one must be in studying the facts:

> The case before us differs in important respects [from *Mendenhall*]. Here [R]'s ticket and identification remained in the possession of the officers throughout the encounter; the officers also seized and had possession of his luggage. As a practical matter, [R] could not leave the airport without them. In *Mendenhall*, no luggage was involved, the ticket and identification were immediately returned, and the officers were careful to advise that the suspect could decline to be searched. Here, the officers had seized [R]'s luggage and made no effort to advise him that he need not consent to the search.[36]

[b] Factory Sweeps

The Supreme Court applied the *Terry-Mendenhall* rule strictly in *Immigration and Naturalization Service v. Delgado*.[37] *Delgado* involved a so-called "factory sweep," in which INS agents, without warning, enter a factory or other employment site where the agents believe they might find undocumented workers, and question them. In this case, the agents entered *en masse*. While several agents stood at the building exits, other agents dispersed throughout the factory to question workers. The agents were armed, displayed badges, and carried walkie-talkies. When they confronted an employee, they asked one to three questions relating to citizenship. During the sweep, which lasted between one and two hours, employees continued their work and were free to walk about the factory.

The Supreme Court, per Justice Rehnquist, held that such factory sweeps did not constitute seizure of all of the workers inside the factory. The Court reasoned that when

---

35. 460 U.S. 491 (1983).
36. *Id.* at 503 n.9.
37. 466 U.S. 210 (1984).

people are at work, "their freedom to move about has been meaningfully restricted, not by the actions of law enforcement officials, but by the workers' voluntary obligations to their employers." Second, the workers could move about the factory freely. Third, individual employees were subjected to "nothing more than a brief encounter."

This reasoning is questionable. First, although a worker's freedom of action *is* restricted by the employment relation, as the Court itself noted, this restriction is the result of the *voluntary* obligations of the employees. Ordinarily, if a worker wants to leave the job site during the day, she may do so; she might lose her job or, more likely, be docked some salary, but she *can* leave. During the factory sweep, however, armed agents blocked the way.

Second, in view of the near-military method of entrance, it is unrealistic to think that a factory worker, even a United States citizen or documented immigrant, would believe, as a reasonable person, that she could discontinue her contact with the INS agents. Yet, as manifested in *Mendenhall*, the Court assumes that a reasonable person has considerable fortitude, and that such a person not only could, but would, discontinue an encounter with government agents if that were her wish.

[c] Bus Sweeps

The Supreme Court has also demonstrated its unwillingness to seriously limit law enforcement agents conducting other types of "sweeps," most notably bus sweeps for narcotics. In *Florida v. Bostick*,[38] for example, two sheriff's deputies, one of whom was armed, boarded an interstate bus while it was temporarily stopped to pick up passengers, in order to intercept drug traffickers who might be aboard. Dressed in "raid" jackets bearing the department's insignia, the deputies approached *B*, who was sitting in the back of the bus, identified themselves as narcotics agents, and questioned him. The deputies requested and received permission to search *B*'s luggage. The search turned up illegal drugs.

The state supreme court ruled that a reasonable person in *B*'s position would not have felt free to leave the bus and, therefore, that *B* was "seized," and, consequently, that *B*'s subsequent consent to search his luggage was invalid.

The United States Supreme Court, per Justice Sandra O'Connor, reversed.[39] Justice O'Connor stated that "[o]ur cases make it clear that a seizure does not occur simply because a police officer approaches an individual and asks a few questions," and that there was "no doubt that if this same encounter had taken place before [*B*] boarded the bus or in the lobby of the terminal, it would not rise to the level of a seizure."

The fact that the encounter occurred on a cramped bus, about to depart, obviously reduced the passengers' impression that they could leave, but that did not change the result. Although Justice O'Connor conceded that "[w]here the encounter takes place is one factor, . . . it is not the only one." As with the workers in the *Delgado* factory-sweep case discussed in the last subsection, the bus passengers' freedom of movement "was restricted by a factor independent of police conduct"—their voluntary status as passengers. In such a case, the Court concluded, "the degree to which a reasonable person [in

---

38. 501 U.S. 429 (1991).

39. The Court did *not* determine whether *B* was seized. It remanded the case to the state court to evaluate the matter "under the correct legal standard." Nonetheless, the Court's reasoning left no doubt as to its view that, on the facts developed, *B* was not seized. On remand, the state supreme court affirmed the finding of the trial court that no seizure occurred. Bostick v. State, 593 So. 2d 494 (Fla. 1992).

B's position] would feel that he or she could leave is not an accurate measure of the coercive effect of the encounter." The proper test in such circumstances is whether "a reasonable person would feel free to decline the officers' requests or otherwise terminate the encounter."[40] Absent coercion in that process, no seizure occurs. In the latter regard, the Court identified two facts "particularly worth noting": although an officer who confronted B was armed, he did not remove his weapon from his pouch; and the officers advised B that he could refuse consent to the search.

The Court seemingly extended *Bostick* in *United States v. Drayton*,[41] a second bus-sweep case. In *Drayton*, one police officer knelt on the driver's seat facing the rear of the bus while a second stood at the back of the bus facing forward. A third officer walked forward from the back of the bus, stopping next to or just behind each passenger to whom he spoke. Although the officers here, unlike in *Bostick*, did *not* tell the passengers that they had the right not to cooperate, the Court concluded that "[t]he officers gave the passengers no reason to believe that they were required to answer the officers' questions": The interrogating officer "did not brandish a weapon or make any intimidating movements. He left the aisle free so [passengers] could exit. He spoke to passengers one by one and in a polite, quiet voice." In short, nothing was done by the officers that "would suggest to a reasonable person that he or she was barred from leaving the bus or otherwise terminating the encounter."

Drayton arguably goes beyond *Bostick* because the Court found no seizure even though the officers failed to inform passengers of their right to refuse consent to a search. In contrast, the *Bostick* Court considered it "particularly worth noting" that the officers advised passengers of their rights. Interestingly as well, the *Drayton* Court stated that the fact that the agents were *not* in uniform nor visibly armed—circumstances one might have thought the Court would have emphasized in support of its "no seizure" conclusion here—"should have little weight in the analysis." According to Justice O'Connor, "[o]fficers are often required to wear uniforms and in many circumstances this is cause for assurance, not discomfort." As for the fact that the officers were visibly armed in *Bostick*, but not here, this did not carry much weight either, because "most law enforcement officers are armed . . . [and this] is well known to the public. The presence of a holstered firearm thus is unlikely to contribute to the coerciveness of the encounter absent active brandishing of the weapon." It seems, therefore, that the fact that an officer is uniformed (or not) and/or visibly armed (or not) carries little weight in the "seizure" analysis in the bus-sweep context (as long as no weapon is brandished).

[3] An Issue of Importance: The Nature of the "Reasonable Person"[42]

The *Mendenhall* portion of the "seizure" test is evaluated on the basis of the perceptions of a "reasonable person," so it is critical to determine the nature of this fictional character. The Supreme Court has made clear that the "reasonable person" standard

---

40. The Court subsequently applied this "terminate the encounter" test outside the bus sweep context, indicating that it is the preferred standard "when a person has no desire to leave for reasons unrelated to the police presence." Brendlin v. California, 551 U.S. 249, 255 (2007) (using this test to conclude that an automobile passenger is seized when the police stop the car in which the passenger is riding) (citations and internal quotation marks omitted).

41. 536 U.S. 194 (2002).

42. *See generally* Susan F. Mandiberg, *Reasonable Officers vs. Reasonable Lay Persons in the Supreme Court's Miranda and Fourth Amendment Cases*, 14 Lewis & Clark L. Rev. 1481 (2010).

"presupposes an innocent person."[43] Thus, in determining whether a person accosted by the police is seized, a court will evaluate the situation on the assumption that the individual has nothing illegal to hide, rather than to ask whether a reasonable law violator would believe that she is free to terminate the encounter.

Beyond this, to what extent does—or *should*—the "reasonable person" possess the subjective characteristics of the individual accosted by the police? For example, was it relevant in *Mendenhall* that *M* was a woman and that the agents were male? Should the test be whether a reasonable *woman* accosted by two *male* federal agents would feel free to leave? Is it relevant that *M* was 22 years old rather than 50 years old or, on the other hand, a teenager?

The Supreme Court has only occasionally confronted this issue in the Fourth Amendment context. In *Mendenhall*, however, Justices Stewart and Rehnquist stated that "these factors"—her age and gender, and the agents' gender—"were not irrelevant" in determining whether a reasonable person, in view of all of the circumstances surrounding the incident, would have believed that she was not free to leave.[44]

A touchier issue, but one of even greater practical significance, is whether the racial characteristics of the parties should be considered in determining how a reasonable person would behave. In *Mendenhall*, the federal agents were white and *M* was African-American. Professor Tracey Maclin has argued that "the dynamics surrounding an encounter between a police officer and a black male are quite different from those that surround an encounter between an officer and the so-called average, reasonable person."[45]

Maclin contends that the ordinary encounter between a black male suspect and the police, even when the suspect is middle-class or professional, involves a degree of coercion ordinarily absent in other encounters. Therefore, he reasons, courts should "abandon a naive theory of the Fourth Amendment, and consider the real world that exists on the street,"[46] including the fact that racial minorities, especially black males, are not treated the same as white people in day-to-day encounters with the police.

Empirically, it would seem difficult to deny the accuracy of Maclin's observations. Many African-Americans, especially black males, have been the victims of racial profiling by police officers.[47] And, at least some justices on the United States Supreme Court have observed that in the minority community, even an innocent person may often "believe[] that contact with the police can itself be dangerous."[48] Therefore, the ordinary African-American is likely to treat encounters with the police with more-than-ordinary trepidation; compared to non-minority persons, she is more likely to believe that her

---

43. Florida v. Bostick, 501 U.S. 429, 438 (1991).

44. Professor Susan F. Mandiberg argues that the "reasonableness" standard as applied by the courts assumes that the suspect belongs to a community "whose experiences with government officials leads to the conclusion that it is safe to assert one's rights." In fact, Mandiberg argues, suspects will call upon their own experiences or those of their own community, thus perhaps leading them to act "unreasonably" when they interact with police. Susan F. Mandiberg, *Reasonable Officers vs. Reasonable Lay Persons in the Supreme Court's* Miranda *and Fourth Amendment Cases*, 14 Lewis & Clark L. Rev. 1481, 1502 (2010).

45. Maclin, Note 17, *supra*, at 250.

46. *Id.* at 279.

47. *See* §2.05, *supra*, and §§8.02[F] and 17.03[B][5], *infra*.

48. Illinois v. Wardlow, 528 U.S. 119, 132 (2000) (Stevens J., with whom Souter, Ginsburg, and Breyer, JJ, joined, dissenting).

freedom of movement is significantly curtailed.[49] Again, the two-justice *Mendenhall* opinion indicated that the racial characteristics of the parties in the case "were not irrelevant" to the "seizure" issue, although it concluded that the racial aspects of the case at bar were not determinative, and the Court has never found them determinative in the decades since.

[D] Embellishment on the *Terry-Mendenhall Test*: The Submission-to-Authority Problem

There is a bit more to the *Terry-Mendenhall* test than was explained in subsections [B] and [C]. An embellishment on the *Terry-Mendenhall* test most often arises when a police officer pursues a fleeing suspect. The question in such cases is this: When, if at all, does pursuit of a suspect constitute a seizure of the person? For example, suppose that *O*, a police officer, observes *D* standing on the sidewalk. *D* notices *O*'s attention and flees. If *O* pursues *D* by car or on foot, is *D* "seized" the moment the pursuit begins, or only if and when she is captured, i.e., when the pursuit is over? Or, might a "seizure" occur at some intermediate stage on a case-by-case basis?

This issue is significant. If the pursuit itself is *not* a seizure, then the police may chase anyone, even if they have no basis for believing that the individual is involved in wrongdoing, without violating the Fourth Amendment. Furthermore, if the pursued not-yet-seized party discards an object during such a chase, the police may retrieve the object without the latter police action constituting a fruit of an unlawful seizure.

Hodari D

The Supreme Court provided a resolution of the pursuit-seizure issue in *California v. Hodari D.*[50] In doing so, it explained (or, some would say, changed) the *Terry-Mendenhall* standard. Speaking for the majority in *Hodari D*, Justice Scalia stated that the latter definition "says that a person has been seized 'only if,' not that he has been seized 'whenever'" a reasonable person would have believed that she was not free to leave. That is, the *Terry-Mendenhall* test "states a *necessary*, but not a *sufficient*, condition for seizure—or, more precisely, for seizure effected through a 'show of authority.'"

To explain: The *Terry* definition of "seizure" set out at the start of subsection [B] notes two ways in which a police officer can seize a person: by use of physical force or by show of authority. In light of *Hodari D.*, lawyers must now distinguish between these two methods of seizure. Specifically, in show-of-authority circumstances, a seizure is not proven simply by showing that a reasonable person in the suspect's situation would have believed

---

49. This is not to under-emphasize the fact that social science literature demonstrates that most people, even members of the majority race, feel strong pressures to comply with the requests of authority figures. Nadler, Note 17, *supra*, at 155, 165–97.

50. 499 U.S. 621 (1991); *contra, interpreting state constitutional law,* Hall v. State, 145 P.3d 605 (Alaska App. 2006) (defining "seizure" exclusively by means of the *Mendenhall* test); State v. Oquendo, 613 A.2d 1300 (Conn. 1992) (same); Jones v. State, 745 A.2d 856 (Del. 1999) (same); State v. Quino, 840 P.2d 358 (Haw. 1992) (same); Commonwealth v. Stoute, 665 N.E.2d 93 (Mass. 1996) (same); In re Welfare of E.D.J., 502 N.W.2d 779 (Minn. 1993) (same); State v. Clayton, 45 P.3d 30 (Mont. 2002) (same); State v. Beauchesne, 868 A.2d 972 (N.H. 2005) (same); State v. Tucker, 642 A.2d 401 (N.J. 1994) (same); State v. Garcia, 217 P.3d 1032 (N.M. 2009); People v. Madera, 596 N.Y.S.2d 766 (App. Div. 1993), *aff'd*, 624 N.E.2d 675 (N.Y. 1993) (same); State v. Puffenbarger, 998 P.2d 788 (Or. App. 2000) (same); Commonwealth v. Matos, 672 A.2d 769 (Pa. 1996) (same); State v. Randolph, 74 S.W.3d 330 (Tenn. 2002) (same); and Commonwealth v. Young, 957 P.2d 681 (Wash. 1998) (same).

that she was not free to end the encounter. More must be shown to constitute a seizure. Speaking for the Court, Justice Scalia explained:

> The word "seizure" readily bears the meaning of a laying on of hands or application of physical force to restrain movement, even when it is ultimately unsuccessful. ("She seized the purse-snatcher, but he broke out of her grasp.") It does not remotely apply, however, to the prospect of a policeman yelling "Stop, in the name of the law!" at a fleeing felon that continues to flee. That is no seizure.... [A seizure] requires *either* physical force ... *or*, where that is absent, *submission* to the assertion of authority.

For example, if O, a police officer, chases D, a suspect, and grabs her, a seizure occurs at that instant, even if D pulls away from O's grasp and flees. However, if O does not touch D, but instead orders her to stop, or if O fires a warning shot in the air, D is not seized (although a reasonable person in D's situation would very likely believe that she is not free to end the encounter as she wishes) unless and until D *actually* submits to O's authority.

Justices Stevens and Marshall dissented in *Hodari D.* They attacked the ruling as "profoundly unwise." The dissenters' worry relates to the potentially "significant time interval between the initiation of the officer's show of [authority] and the complete submission by the citizen." Applying the majority's approach, the police may now lawfully chase a person—even if the pursuit includes a command to "freeze," the use of police car sirens, or other coercive actions—without reasonable suspicion of wrongdoing (indeed, on *no* basis at all, or on a malicious basis) in the hope that during the pursuit the citizen's response, e.g., a furtive motion, will give the police a legitimate basis to seize the individual. Indeed, the flight itself may often provide the requisite justification for seizing the fleeing party.[51] Yet, anomalously, if an officer barely touches the suspect in an effort to detain her, and she immediately escapes, such "laying on of hands" is a seizure, and the subsequent furtive behavior by the citizen cannot justify the prior seizure.[52]

Hodari D. does not indicate when the requisite "submission to authority" occurs. Has a fleeing suspect, for example, submitted to authority (and, thus, been seized) as soon as she stops running, or only when she indicates by words or action (e.g., raising her hands above her head) that she has submitted? Or, when does the driver of a car, ordered to pull over on the highway, submit to authority? Is it as soon as the driver sees the officer's red lights flashing in the rear view mirror, slows down, and begins to change lanes to pull over, or only when the vehicle comes to a complete stop?[53] The bright-line rule of *Hodari D.*, therefore, will require further judicial clarification.

---

51. This is because flight from the police in many circumstances may itself create "reasonable suspicion," the requisite basis for justifying a subsequent brief seizure. *See* § 17.03[B][4], *infra*.

52. Only somewhat tongue-in-cheek, Professor Wayne LaFave has suggested that the message of *Hodari D.* to police departments is that when they chase a person on a wild and unsupported hunch, a "fat cop" is preferable to one who is "slim, trim, and of athletic build," because the latter officer is too likely to catch up to the suspect and grab him "by the scruff of the neck *before* the [contraband is] ditched." LaFave, *Pinguitudinous Police* ..., Note 17, *supra*, at 730, 731.

53. *Brendlin v. California*, 551 U.S. 249 (2007), provides dictum on the subject. In *Brendlin*, the police ordered a vehicle, in which a passenger was riding, to pull over. The Court held that the passenger, and not just the driver, was seized; however, the precise moment at which the seizure occurred was not an issue in the case. Nonetheless, in describing the holding, the opinion stated that "[the passenger] was seized from the moment ... [the] car came to a halt on the side of the road." *Id.* at 263.

Chapter 8

Fourth Amendment: "Probable Cause"

§ 8.01 The Constitutional Role of "Probable Cause"[1]

One clause of the Fourth Amendment prohibits "unreasonable searches and seizures." Another clause provides that "no Warrants shall issue, but upon probable cause." The interrelationship of these two clauses is a matter of considerable dispute,[2] but what is not in dispute is that "probable cause" is a critical feature of Fourth Amendment jurisprudence. One scholar has observed that "the concept of probable cause lies at the heart" of the Amendment.[3] As the Supreme Court has suggested, the "rule of probable cause is a practical, nontechnical conception affording the best compromise that has been found" for balancing competing needs: "safeguard[ing] citizens from rash and unreasonable interferences with privacy and from unfounded charges of crime" while, at the same time, "giv[ing] fair leeway for enforcing the law in the community's protection."[4]

The importance of "probable cause" in Fourth Amendment jurisprudence is evident from three general constitutional principles. First, the text of the Fourth Amendment itself provides that arrest and search warrants may *only* be issued if supported by probable cause. Second, *all* arrests (even those that do *not* require a warrant) require probable cause. That is, an arrest — which is one form of "seizure" of a person — on less than probable cause is *always* constitutionally *unreasonable*.[5] Third, in computer terms we might say that "probable cause" is the default position for searches and seizures of property: with rare exceptions, searches and seizures are reasonable if they are conducted *with* probable cause;[6] although subject to more exceptions, many searches and seizures conducted *without* probable cause are constitutionally *unreasonable*.

---

1. *See generally* Akhil Reed Amar, *Fourth Amendment First Principles*, 107 Harv. L. Rev. 757, 782–85 (1994); Fabio Arcila, Jr., *In the Trenches: Searches and the Misunderstood Common-Law History of Suspicion and Probable Cause*, 10 U. Pa. J. Constit. L. 1 (2007); Tracey Maclin, *When the Cure for the Fourth Amendment Is Worse Than the Disease*, 68 S. Cal. L. Rev. 1, 25–32 (1994).

2. *See* §§ 4.02–.03, *supra*, and § 10.01, *infra*.

3. Albert W. Alschuler, *Bright Line Fever and the Fourth Amendment*, 45 U. Pitt. L. Rev. 227, 243 (1984). Not everyone agrees with this appraisal. Professor Akhil Amar, see Note 1, *supra*, at 785, points out that the "probable cause" standard is found only in the Warrant Clause of the Fourth Amendment; therefore, he argues, "probable cause" is central only to cases in which the police apply for a warrant. As for warrant*less* searches and seizures, Amar reasons from the text and history of the Fourth Amendment that police conduct need only be "reasonable," a much more flexible standard than "probable cause." For a vigorous response to Professor Amar's views, *see* Maclin, Note 1, *supra*.

4. Brinegar v. United States, 338 U.S. 160, 176 (1949).

5. *See* Henry v. United States, 361 U.S. 98, 100–101 (1959).

6. Whren v. United States, 517 U.S. 806, 817 (1996). On rare occasions a finding of probable cause seemingly is insufficient to render a search or seizure reasonable. This is the case when the

121

§ 8.02 Probable Cause: General Principles[7]

[A] "Probable Cause": Definition

"Probable cause" is traditionally to defined to exist when the facts and circumstances within an officer's personal knowledge, and of which he has reasonably trustworthy information, are sufficient in themselves to warrant a person of reasonable caution in the belief that: (1) in the case of an arrest, an offense has been committed and the person to be arrested committed it; or (2) in the case of a search, a specifically described item subject to seizure will be found in the place to be searched.[8]

A shorthand way to make the same point is this: A law enforcement officer, as a reasonable person, must have a "good reason" — enough reliable information — to reasonably believe that (in the case of arrest) the person to be arrested committed a crime or (in the case of a search) that the search will uncover evidence relating to a crime.[9]

[B] "Probable Cause": Objective versus Subjective

"Probable cause" is an objective concept. An officer's subjective belief, no matter how sincere, that he has good cause to arrest a person or to conduct a search does not by itself constitute probable cause.[10] It also follows that an officer's *lack* of belief that he has probable cause does not foreclose a finding to the contrary.[11] And, especially controversially, if there is objective probable cause, the officer's subjective motivations for making the arrest or search — even if they are pretextual or malicious — are irrelevant to the "probable cause" finding.[12]

On the other hand, in determining what a so-called "person of reasonable caution" would believe, a court will take into account the expertise of the officer whose actions are under scrutiny. For example, an officer's specialized knowledge of the appearance or odor of a narcotic is relevant in determining whether an officer has probable cause to make an arrest or drug search.[13] Likewise, an officer's personal experience assigned to patrol a particular area of town, or his many years of detective work, may render his

---

Fourth Amendment activity is "conducted in an extraordinary manner, unusually harmful to an individual's privacy or even physical interests — such as, for example, seizure by means of deadly force, unannounced entry into a home, entry into a home without a warrant, or physical penetration of the body." *Id.* at 818 (internal citations omitted). One scholar has also proposed that probable cause should not be sufficient to justify an arrest, and that a court should ensure that an arrest is both supported by probable and general reasonableness. One measure of the reasonableness of the arrest would be the cost to the dignity of the arrestee. *See* Josh Bowers, *Probable Cause, Constitutional Reasonableness, and the Unrecognized Point of a "Pointless Indignity,"* 88 Stan. L. Rev. 987 (2014).

7. *See generally* 2 Wayne R. LaFave, Search and Seizure § 3.2 (4th ed. 2004); Akhil Reed Amar, *Terry and Fourth Amendment First Principles*, 72 St. John's L. Rev. 1097 (1998); Craig S. Lerner, *The Reasonableness of Probable Cause*, 81 Tex. L. Rev. 951 (2003); Ronald M. Gould & Simon Stern, *Catastrophic Threats and the Fourth Amendment*, 77 S. Cal. L. Rev. 777 (2004).

8. Brinegar v. United States, 338 U.S. 160, 175–76 (1949).

9. Gould & Stern, Note 7, *supra*, at 786.

10. Beck v. Ohio, 379 U.S. 89, 97 (1964).

11. Florida v. Royer, 460 U.S. 491, 507 (1983).

12. Wren v. United States, 517 U.S. 806 (1996). *See* subsection [F], *infra*.

13. *E.g.*, Johnson v. United States, 333 U.S. 10 (1948).

belief that crime is afoot reasonable,[14] even though a reasonable layperson would not have good reason to draw the same conclusion.

[C] "Probable Cause": Arrests versus Searches

The methodology for making a probable cause determination is the same for arrests as it is for searches. However, the result need not be the same in a particular case: that is, an officer might have probable cause to arrest a person but not to conduct a search, or vice-versa. For example, O might have probable cause to believe that he will find contraband in D's automobile, and yet lack probable cause to arrest D, because he may lack sufficient evidence that D is aware of the contraband, a required element of the offense. Conversely, O might have probable cause to arrest D for manufacturing drugs, but if D's arrest occurs at X's house, about which O has no evidence of drug activity, O might lack probable cause to search X's residence for drugs.

Furthermore, evidence that would justify a search is apt to become "stale" sooner than information that is used to justify an arrest. For example, information obtained on January 1 that a small quantity of drugs will be found in D's bedroom might be insufficient to warrant a search on February 1, because the drugs might have been moved or consumed by then. In contrast, if an officer has probable cause to arrest D for possession of drugs on January 1, the arrest will be valid a month later—the "probable cause" is still fresh—unless intervening information casts doubt on the trustworthiness of the earlier information. For example, "probable cause" might no longer exist if the officer subsequently learned that the informant who implicated D had a motive to lie.

Staleness

[D] "Probable Cause": With or Without Warrants

A central feature of traditional Fourth Amendment jurisprudence is that the constitutionally preferable arbiter of probable cause is a "neutral and detached magistrate," rather than a police officer "engaged in the often competitive enterprise of ferreting out crime."[15]

Even when the police are justified in acting without prior judicial authorization—that is, without a warrant—probable cause usually is required. If an officer acts without a warrant, a court subsequently called on to determine whether the officer's actions were reasonable must determine whether the officer had probable cause at the time of the Fourth Amendment activity (i.e., whether a magistrate *would* have issued a warrant if one had been sought).

In view of "the Fourth Amendment's strong preferences for searches conducted pursuant to a warrant,"[16] the Supreme Court has indicated that "the resolution of doubtful or marginal cases [of probable cause] . . . should be largely determined by the preference to be accorded to warrants."[17] That is, in close probable-cause cases, a search conducted *with* a warrant should be upheld where a warrantless search might be rejected for want of probable cause.

---

14. *E.g.*, Terry v. Ohio, 392 U.S. 1 (1968).
15. Johnson v. United States, 333 U.S. at 13–14. *See generally* §§ 10.01 and 10.03, *infra*.
16. Illinois v. Gates, 462 U.S. 213, 236 (1983).
17. United States v. Ventresca, 380 U.S. 102, 109 (1965).

[E] "Probable Cause": Search for and Seize What?

Originally, a search was unjustifiable unless there was probable cause to believe that it would result in the seizure of one of three categories of evidence: (1) a "fruit" of a crime (e.g., money obtained in a robbery); (2) an instrumentality of a crime (e.g., the gun used to commit a robbery, or the car used in the get-away); or (3) contraband (e.g., illegal narcotics). So-called "mere evidence," that is, items that have only evidentiary value in the apprehension or conviction of a person for an offense, could not be seized.[18]

The so-called "mere evidence rule" was founded on property-based concepts consistent with the original understanding of the Fourth Amendment. The justification for the rule was that the government could search for and seize property only if it asserted an interest in the property superior to that of the person from whom it would be seized. Such a superior right was said to exist in relation to fruits, instrumentalities, and contraband, but not as to "mere evidence."

The superior-interest theory was largely a fiction, but it was based on the following assumptions. In the case of fruits, the government, representing the true owner, had a greater interest in the stolen items than did the alleged criminal. Regarding contraband, the government had a superior property right because a private person has no right whatsoever to possess such property. In the case of a criminal instrumentality, the property was considered forfeited to the government because of its use in criminal activities (and to prevent its use in later crimes). Regarding "mere evidence" of crime, however, no justification existed for subordinating the individual's property rights to the government.

The Supreme Court abolished the mere-evidence rule in *Warden v. Hayden*.[19] Police officers may now seize not only fruits, instrumentalities, and contraband, but also "mere evidence," i.e., an article for which there is a nexus between it and criminal activity. According to *Hayden*, this nexus exists if there is probable cause "to believe that the evidence sought will aid in a particular apprehension or conviction."[20]

The *Hayden* Court abolished the mere evidence rule because it believed that the doctrine was indefensible in light of modern Fourth Amendment privacy principles. It concluded that a search for evidence disturbs privacy no more than one directed at fruits, instrumentalities, or contraband because, in all of these cases, a magistrate can intervene, "and the requirements of probable cause and specificity [in the warrant] can be preserved intact."

The Court also concluded that nothing in the nature of property seized as "mere evidence" is more private than other types of property. Indeed, the same item that constitutes evidence in one case might be a fruit or instrumentality in another. For example, a diary seized in one case because it includes evidence that ties the defendant to the crime might be a fruit of a theft in another case.

In general, the reasoning of *Hayden* is unexceptionable. Nonetheless, abolition of the mere evidence rule was not without significant privacy repercussions. First, persons who possess the fruits of a crime, criminal instrumentalities, or contraband are often guilty of wrongdoing. Innocent persons, however, may unwittingly come into possession of

---

18. *See* Gouled v. United States, 255 U.S. 298 (1921).

19. 387 U.S. 294 (1967).

20. Some jurisdictions also provide for warrants to be issued to search for and seize any "person . . . who is unlawfully restrained." *E.g.*, Fed. R. Crim. P. 41(c)(4). This provision is justified on the ground that the person seized, e.g., a kidnap victim, is evidence of a crime.

evidence that relates to a criminal investigation or, in the modern world of computer records, have their information intermingled with evidence of someone else's crime. As a practical matter, therefore, *Hayden* enlarged the class of persons who may be subjected to searches.[21]

Second, although *Hayden* involved seizure of clothing as evidence of a crime, the implication of the case is that private papers, including highly personal diaries and letters, are no longer immune from search and seizure as "mere evidence." Yet, as the Supreme Court has acknowledged, "there are grave dangers inherent in executing a warrant authorizing a search and seizure of a person's papers that are not necessarily present in executing a warrant to search for physical objects whose relevance is more easily ascertainable."[22] One "grave danger" is that in searching for evidentiary papers, the police must often examine innocent-but-private documents in order to find the incriminating material.

Despite the special privacy concerns relating to searches of papers, the Supreme Court has approved the seizure of business records as long as the police seek to minimize unnecessary intrusions on privacy.[23] There is no reason to believe greater protections are constitutionally required for personal papers.[24]

[F] Special Issue: "Probable Cause" and Pretextual Police Conduct[25]

In *Whren v. United States*,[26] one of the Supreme Court's most controversial and perhaps far-reaching Fourth Amendment decisions, Justice Antonin Scalia stated for

---

21. *E.g.*, Zurcher v. Stanford Daily, 436 U.S. 547 (1978) (police obtained a warrant to search the files of a student newspaper for photographs revealing the identity of persons who attacked police officers during a demonstration).

22. Andresen v. Maryland, 427 U.S. 463, 482 n.11 (1976).

23. *Id.*

24. Arguably, a heightened level of probable cause for searches and seizures of personal papers *should* be demanded. The concept of a sliding scale of probable cause is considered at § 8.07[C], *infra*.

25. *See generally* David A. Harris, Problems in Injustice: Why Racial Profiling Cannot Work (2002); Kami Chavis Simmons, *Beginning to End Racial Profiling: Definitive Solutions to an Elusive Problem*, 18 Wash. & Lee J. Civil Rts. and Soc. Just. 25 (2011); Sherry F. Colb, *Profiling with Apologies*, 1 Ohio St. J. Crim. L. 611 (2004); Sharon L. Davies, *Profiling Terror*, 1 Ohio St. J. Crim. L. 45 (2003); Samuel R. Gross & Debra Livingston, *Racial Profiling Under Attack*, 102 Colum. L. Rev. 1413 (2002); David A. Harris, *"Driving While Black" and All Other Traffic Offenses: The Supreme Court and Pretextual Traffic Stops*, 87 J. Crim. L. & Criminology 544 (1997); Andrew D. Leipold, *Objective Tests and Subjective Bias: Some Problems of Discriminatory Intent in the Criminal Law*, 73 Chi.-Kent. L. Rev. 559 (1998); Tracey Maclin, *Race and the Fourth Amendment*, 51 Vand. L. Rev. 333 (1998); David A. Sklansky, *Traffic Stops, Minority Motorists, and the Future of the Fourth Amendment*, 1997 Sup. Ct. Rev. 271; William Stuntz, *Local Policing After the Terror*, 111 Yale L.J. 2137 (2002); Anthony C. Thompson, *Stopping the Usual Suspects: Race and the Fourth Amendment*, 74 N.Y.U. L. Rev. 956 (1999); Daniel B. Yeager, *The Stubbornness of Pretexts*, 40 San Diego L. Rev. 611 (2003). *See also* §§ 2.05, 2.07[B], *supra* and § 17.03[B][5], *infra*, for further consideration of racial profiling, an important sub-issue of the pretext controversy.

26. 517 U.S. 806 (1996); *contra, under state constitution*, State v. Sullivan, 74 S.W.3d 215 (Ark. 2002) (an arrest that would not have been made but for the officer's wish to investigate a different offense is unreasonable); State v. Ladson, 979 P.2d 833 (Wash. 1999) (pretextual traffic stops are made without "authority of law" and, therefore, prohibited).

a unanimous Court that "[s]ubjective intentions play no role in ordinary, probable-cause Fourth Amendment analysis."[27] That is, generally speaking, if probable cause objectively exists to make an arrest or conduct a search, the Court will look no further:[28] It is of no Fourth Amendment consequence that the officer may subjectively have had an ulterior motive—even, for example, a racially or religiously biased reason—for his actions.[29]

Notice the implications of *Whren*, particularly in the context of searches and arrests conducted on the highway. In the words of one of the briefs to the *Whren* Court, "the use of automobiles is so heavily and minutely regulated that total compliance with traffic and safety rules is nearly impossible." Thus, virtually every person who drives a car sooner or later (often sooner!) violates one or more traffic laws. If an officer has the inclination to do so, therefore, he can observe almost anyone long enough to develop probable cause to issue a traffic citation. Thus, an officer who has a hunch, unsupported by probable cause, that the driver may be involved in some form of criminal activity (for example, drug possession) can use the traffic violation for which he has probable cause—for example, driving 58 miles per hour in a 55 zone[30]—as a pretext to stop the car and conduct an investigation based on his hunch. This does not run afoul of the Fourth Amendment, as interpreted by *Whren*.[31] Likewise, an officer may make a full custodial arrest for a minor traffic offense based on probable cause,[32] even if the arrest is a mere pretext to conduct a search of the arrestee incident to the arrest, for evidence unrelated to the arrest.

Whren is founded on the current Court's dislike for Fourth Amendment rules that are based on subjective considerations.[33] Can a court ever determine with any reasonable level of confidence the hidden motivations of a police officer? Can we trust police officers to tell the truth about their motivations in court? For that matter, it may be naive to think that any person acts from a single motive: A police officer may stop a speeding driver in part for pretextual reasons, but also because he truly considers it appropriate

---

27. *Whren*, 517 U.S. at 813.

28. *See* Virginia v. Moore, 553 U.S. 164, 171 (2008) ("[W]hen an officer has probable cause to believe a person committed even a minor crime in his presence, the balancing of private and public interests is not in doubt. The arrest is constitutionally reasonable.").

29. If he can prove intentional discrimination, a victim of racial bias may assert a claim on the basis of the Fourteenth Amendment Equal Protection Clause, but the Fourth Amendment is not violated thereby.

30. United States v. Roberson, 6 F.3d 1088 (5th Cir. 1993).

31. The *Whren* Court conceded that it has occasionally suggested that an officer's pretextual motivations *may* be relevant in Fourth Amendment analysis, for example, in inventory search cases. *See* §15.01[B][1], *infra*. But *Whren* said, "only an undiscerning reader would regard these cases as endorsing the principle that ulterior motives can invalidate police conduct that is justifiable on the basis of probable cause to believe that a violation of law has occurred. . . . [W]e were addressing [in those other cases] the validity of a search conducted in the *absence* of probable cause." *See also* City of Indianapolis v. Edmond, 531 U.S. 32 (2000) (in which the Court treated as relevant the motivation behind a drug interdiction checkpoint program in determining the constitutionality of suspicionless vehicle stops; the Court distinguished *Whren* on the ground that *Whren* "expressly distinguished cases where we had addressed the validity of searches conducted in the absence of probable cause").

32. The Fourth Amendment does not prohibit a state from authorizing the police to take a person into custody for minor offenses, even for violation of a highway safety rule. Atwater v. Lago Vista, 532 U.S. 318 (2001). States differ over whether to provide their police with this authority. *See* §9.03, *infra*.

33. *See* §2.06[B], *supra*, for general discussion of whether subjective or objective rules of criminal procedure are preferable.

to issue the ticket. All of that said, those who would like courts to consider the subjective motivations of the police point out that courts and juries are required to determine the *mens rea* of criminal defendants, so why not here?[34]

§ 8.03 Determining "Probable Cause": Overview

[A] Types of Information: In General

When a police officer wishes to conduct a search or seizure that must be supported by probable cause, the preferred constitutional approach is for the officer to seek a warrant from a "neutral and detached" magistrate.[35] Thus, initially, if the preferred approach is taken, it is the magistrate who determines if there is the requisite probable cause to issue the warrant.[36]

When a magistrate is required to make a "probable cause" determination, he must ask two questions: (1) Is the information being offered sufficiently trustworthy to be considered? and (2) If it is, is the quantum of evidence sufficient to constitute probable cause? The first question is the subject of this section and Sections 8.04 and 8.05. The second question in considered in Section 8.07.

In general, a police officer may furnish a magistrate with two types of information when he applies for a warrant: (1) "direct information," i.e., information the officer secured by personal observation; and (2) "hearsay information," i.e., information he received from another person who is not present for questioning by the magistrate. Because the officer provides his information under oath by affidavit, he is commonly described in probable cause nomenclature as the "affiant," whereas one whose hearsay information is tendered in the affidavit is the "informant."

A magistrate may consider hearsay for purposes of determining probable cause, as long as the information is reasonably trustworthy.[37] Moreover, the informant's identity need not be disclosed to the magistrate unless the court doubts the affiant's credibility regarding the hearsay.[38] For example, disclosure may be compelled if the magistrate has reason to believe that the affiant lied regarding the informant's existence or misstated the nature of the information received.

[B] "Bald and Unilluminating" Assertions

A "bald and unilluminating assertion of suspicion" is entitled to no weight in the probable cause determination.[39] For example, a magistrate should not consider an

---

34. It should be noted that the defendants in *Whren* were only asking for a special probable cause rule in the context of enforcement of traffic regulations, where the risk of pretextual conduct is especially high.

35. *See* § 10.03[A], *infra*.

36. If the officer acts without a warrant, the defendant may later seek a magistrate's *post hoc* determination that the police lacked probable cause at the time of the search.

37. Brinegar v. United States, 338 U.S. 160, 173–74 (1949).

38. *See* McCray v. Illinois, 386 U.S. 300 (1967).

39. Spinelli v. United States, 393 U.S. 410, 414 (1969); Nathanson v. United States, 290 U.S. 41, 47 (1933); *see* Illinois v. Gates, 462 U.S. 213, 239 (1983).

officer-affiant's assertion that he "has cause to suspect and does believe" that seizable articles will be found in a particular place, unless the officer provides the reasons for his belief.[40] In view of the fact that a neutral and detached magistrate, rather than the police officer, is the preferred arbiter of probable cause, this rule makes sense. If a magistrate were to consider wholly conclusory statements made in an affidavit, he "would be serving simply as the rubber stamp of the source's conclusion."[41]

[C] Direct Information

Unless a magistrate has reason to believe that the affiant has committed perjury or recklessly misstated the truth,[42] the court may consider all direct information (as distinguished from "bald and unilluminating" assertions) provided by the affiant. The affiant's information is considered reasonably trustworthy because the oath he takes affirms his honesty,[43] and the fact that the information was personally observed by him attests to the firsthand basis of his knowledge.[44]

Of course, the fact that the magistrate may consider direct information provided by the affiant does not mean that there is probable cause to issue a warrant based on it. The magistrate must still determine whether the information, alone or in conjunction with any trustworthy hearsay information provided,[45] satisfies the probable cause standard, i.e., that the *quantum* of evidence is sufficient.

[D] Hearsay ("Informant") Information

An informant's assertions raise special concerns. First, by definition, such assertions are hearsay. Therefore, even if the affiant has presented the hearsay accurately, the magistrate cannot personally question the out-of-court informant and, through such questioning, make credibility determinations. Credibility determinations are especially useful

---

40. *Nathanson*, 290 U.S. 41 (1933).

41. Charles E. Moylan, Jr., *Illinois v. Gates: What It Did and What It Did Not Do*, 20 Crim. L. Bull. 93, 101 (1984).

42. In such circumstances, see § 10.03[B], *infra*.

43. However, Ninth Circuit federal judge Alex Kozinski has been quoted as saying that: "[i]t is an open secret long shared by prosecutors, defense lawyers and judges that perjury is widespread among law enforcement officers." Stuart Taylor, Jr., *For the Record*, Am. Law., Oct. 1995, at 72. This problem prevails throughout the criminal justice process, and not simply at probable-cause hearings. Generally speaking, however, despite the "open secret," judges apparently often accept police testimony they suspect is perjurious. The reasons for this vary, including the wish to help law enforcement officers convict persons whom the judge believes is guilty. Other reasons include a desire not to be portrayed in the media as "soft on crime," thus jeopardizing re-election. Andrew J. McClurg, *Good Cop, Bad Cop: Using Cognitive Dissonance Theory to Reduce Police Lying*, 32 U.C. Davis L. Rev. 389, 405 (1999). For general discussion of the problem of policy perjury (or what has come to be called "testilying"), as well as consideration of the ethical issues relating to police deceit, *see generally* Gabriel J. Chin & Scott C. Wells, *The "Blue Wall of Silence" as Evidence of Bias and Motive to Lie: A New Approach to Police Perjury*, 59 U. Pitt. L. Rev. 233 (1998); McClurg, *supra*; Robert P. Mosteller, *Moderating Investigative Lies by Disclosure and Documentation*, 76 Or. L. Rev. 833 (1997); Margaret L. Paris, *Lying to Ourselves*, 76 Or. L. Rev. 817 (1997); Christopher Slobogin, *Testilying: Police Perjury and What to Do About It*, 67 U. Colo. L. Rev. 1037 (1996).

44. *Spinelli*, 393 U.S. at 423 (White, J., concurring).

45. If the direct evidence alone constitutes probable cause, hearsay information is "redundant and can simply be factored out." Moylan, Note 41, *supra*, at 101.

here because—and this is a related, second point—probable-cause hearsay often comes from untrustworthy sources. As one commentator has observed, the ordinary police informant is not a former Boy Scout and present-day prince of the church.[46] Typically, an informant is a person involved in criminal activities, perhaps as a small-time drug pusher, or a low- or medium-level member of a criminal terrorist organization, or a middle- or even high-level member of an organized crime syndicate. Frequently, as well, the tipster provides the information in consideration of some benefit offered by the police or the prosecutor (e.g., money or immunity from criminal prosecution), which calls into question his motives.

Not only are some informants untrustworthy by nature, but the source of *their* information varies. In some cases, the informant's knowledge of the facts he relates to the officer arises from firsthand participation in, or observations of, the criminal activities reported, while in other cases the informant may be relating no more than a vague rumor heard on the streets.

The most difficult question that must be answered in probable cause determinations, then, is this: Under what circumstances is information obtained from an informant sufficiently trustworthy to justify its consideration by the magistrate? The Supreme Court has wrestled mightily with this question. At one time it applied the so-called "*Aguilar*" (or "*Aguilar-Spinelli*") two-pronged test. In 1983, it abandoned this test for the *Gates* "totality-of-the-circumstances test." However, the full import of the prevailing *Gates* test cannot be fully appreciated without an understanding of the *Aguilar* test. The old and new tests are discussed in the two sections that follow.

§ 8.04 The *Aguilar* Two-Pronged Test[47]

[A] In General

The original two-pronged test for determining the trustworthiness of hearsay information from an informant was stated in *Aguilar v. Texas*,[48] a case in which the validity of a warrant to search for drugs was at issue:

> Although an affidavit may be based on hearsay information and need not reflect the direct personal observations of the affiant, . . . the magistrate must be informed of some of the underlying circumstances from which the informant concluded that the narcotics were where he claimed they were, and some of the underlying circumstances from which the officer concluded that the informant . . . was "credible" or his information "reliable."

---

46. Charles E. Moylan, Jr., *Hearsay and Probable Cause: An Aguilar and Spinelli Primer*, 25 Mercer L. Rev. 741, 758 (1974). Stephen Trott, a former prosecutor, now federal judge, has warned that informants' "willingness to do anything [to help themselves] includes not only truthfully spilling the beans on friends and relatives, but also lying, committing perjury, manufacturing evidence, soliciting others to corroborate their lies with more lies, and double-crossing anyone with whom they come into contact, including . . . the prosecutor." Mark Curriden, *Secret Threat to Justice*, National Law Journal, Feb. 20, 1995, at 1A.

47. *See generally* Moylan, Note 46, *supra*.

48. 378 U.S. 108 (1964).

This statement, more fully explained in *Spinelli v. United States*,[49] suggested two inquiries regarding hearsay evidence: (1) "How did the informant get the information?"; and (2) "Why should I [the magistrate] believe this person?" These two questions represented the two prongs of *Aguilar:* (1) the *basis-of-knowledge* prong; and (2) the *veracity* prong, of which there were two alternative spurs, the "credibility-of-the-informant spur" and the "reliability-of-the-information spur."[50]

Under *Aguilar*, if both prongs of the test were satisfied, the informant's assertions were sufficiently trustworthy to be considered by the magistrate in his probable cause determination. If either of the prongs was not satisfied, however, the hearsay evidence standing alone was insufficiently trustworthy to be considered. Its trustworthiness, however, could be resuscitated by at least partial corroboration of the informant's tip, as discussed in subsection [D].

[B] Basis-of-Knowledge Prong

[1] In General

The point of the basis-of-knowledge prong—"How did the informant get the information?"—is that the tipster might be passing along information based on personal knowledge, which is good, but it is also possible that he is reporting nothing more reliable than "an offhand remark heard at a neighborhood bar."[51]

This prong is satisfied by a showing that the informant obtained his information first-hand, for example by observing reported events, overhearing criminal planning activities, or even participating in the reported criminal activities. For example, the basis of knowledge is surely proved if *I*, the informant, tells *O*, the officer-affiant, that "*D* is using her house to sell drugs. *I know this because I bought drugs from her at her house yesterday.*" The italicized words demonstrate *I*'s first-hand knowledge.[52]

On the other hand, suppose that *I* tells *O*, "A friend of mine told me that *D* is selling drugs at her home." Here, *I* has his own informant. In that case, under *Aguilar*, the two-pronged test must be applied one step further down the hearsay chain, and the magistrate must ascertain how *I*'s informant got *his or her* information, and how reliable *that* informant is.

[2] "Self-Verifying Detail"

If an informant does not indicate how he obtained his information, and the officer fails to question him regarding this omission, the officer might be unable to satisfy the magistrate's need for sufficient underlying information to ascertain the basis of the informant's knowledge. For example, if *I* tells *O* only that "*D* is using her house to sell drugs," neither *O* nor the magistrate can ascertain the basis of *I*'s knowledge. Without clarification, the basis-of-knowledge prong is not met.

---

49. 393 U.S. 410 (1969).
50. Moylan, Note 46, *supra*, at 755.
51. *Spinelli*, 393 U.S. at 417.
52. Of course, the informant could be lying, but this goes to the veracity prong.

In some circumstances, however, the Court has allowed indirect proof of this prong, on the basis of so-called "self-verifying detail."[53] In this regard, the Court stated that the facts in *Draper v. United States*,[54] a pre-*Aguilar* case, "provide a suitable benchmark."[55] In *Draper, I*, without stating how he obtained his information, told the police that *D* had gone to Chicago on a specified date by train, that he would return by train with three ounces of heroin on one of two particular dates, that he would be wearing specifically described clothing, that he would carry a tan zipper bag, and that he walked "habitually fast." The police later corroborated some of this information before they conducted a search of *D*.

Although the *Draper* Court focused on the police corroboration of *I*'s information (a matter considered in subsection [D] below), the *Spinelli* Court provided an alternative approach to the case: Although *I* had not disclosed the basis of his information, "the tip [itself] describe[d] the accused's criminal activity in sufficient detail that the magistrate may know that he is relying on something more substantial than a casual rumor . . . or an accusation based merely on an individual's general reputation." From this premise, the Court concluded that it was reasonable to infer that *I*'s information was obtained firsthand.

Justice Byron White, concurring in *Spinelli*, did not rule out the possibility that there might be "limited special circumstances in which an 'honest' informant's report, if sufficiently detailed, will in effect verify itself," but he went on to observe that "if it may be so easily inferred from the affidavit that the informant has himself observed the facts . . . no possible harm could come from requiring a statement to that effect, thereby removing the difficult and recurring questions which arise in such situations." In short, an officer who receives detailed information from an informant ought to ask the informant how he obtained the reported information, and then disclose the informant's answer to the magistrate in the affidavit.

Justice White's suggestion seems justified. In *Draper*, even if *I* was not a liar (a veracity issue), the richness of detail demonstrates at most that *someone* had firsthand knowledge of *D*'s plans, but the detail suggests no reason to assume that the person with firsthand knowledge was *I*. *I* might just have been passing along the detailed information of *X*, a third person, whose own veracity would then be at issue. In such a circumstance, a magistrate's assumption, on an ambiguous record, that *I* was reporting his own firsthand information inappropriately short-circuits all inquiry about *X*—a problem, as Justice White pointed out, that could easily be cured by the officer asking his informant a simple question ("How did you learn this?").

[C] Veracity Prong

Even if an informant states that his information was obtained firsthand, he may be lying or his information-gathering skills might be poor. For these reasons, evidence was required under *Aguilar* to demonstrate either that *I* is a credible person (the credibility

---

53. Moylan, Note 46, *supra*, at 749.
54. 358 U.S. 307 (1959).
55. *Spinelli*, 393 U.S. at 416.

spur of the veracity prong) or, if that cannot be shown, that his information in the present case is nonetheless reliable (the reliability spur).[56]

The Supreme Court has provided relatively little guidance regarding how an affiant should demonstrate an informant's veracity. Lower federal and state courts have exercised primary responsibility to fashion an answer. *Aguilar* itself states only that reliability *cannot* be proved on the ground of a mere assertion by the affiant that the informant is reliable.

Typically, an affiant proves the informant's veracity by providing the magistrate with the informant's "track record" or "batting average." For example, an assertion that the informant's prior tips have led to arrests culminating in convictions is an especially suitable way to prove *I*'s credibility.[57] Of course, if the affiant informs the magistrate regarding the tipster's successes, he should also report any failures. That is the only way to measure the informant's batting average.

The veracity prong may also be satisfied through the reliability-of-the-information spur. This approach is apt to be necessary in circumstances in which the informant has a questionable (or no) track record. This spur typically involves circumstances that suggest that it is unlikely the informant was lying when making the particular statement, regardless of his veracity in general. For example, in *United States v. Harris*,[58] the police affiant declared that the informant "has personal knowledge of and has purchased illicit whiskey from within the residence described, for a period of more than 2 years, and most recently within the past 2 weeks." Chief Justice Burger observed from this declaration against the informant's penal interest that (a prudent and disinterested observer' would "credit these statements. People do not lightly admit a crime and place critical evidence in the hands of the police. . . ."[59]

[D] Corroboration

A tipster's information that would not otherwise satisfy the two-pronged *Aguilar* test may be considered by a magistrate if the police verify aspects of the informant's facts, as long as it can "fairly be said that the [corroborated] tip . . . is as trustworthy as a tip which would pass *Aguilar*'s tests without independent corroboration."[60]

Draper v. United States[61] again provides a benchmark. In that case, after *I* provided detailed information regarding *D*'s activities, the police corroborated some of *I*'s assertions, including *D*'s presence at the train station on one of the dates predicted, his clothing, and his fast gait. Verification was "the present-tense equivalent of a good past track record."[62]

---

56. Courts do not carefully attend to the veracity prong if the informant was the victim of the offense or an ordinary citizen who personally witnessed the crime. Although such persons are "informants" (they are sometimes called "citizen-informers" in an effort to distinguish them from the unsavory characters who ordinarily provide tips), courts typically assume their reliability absent special circumstances. *See generally* 2 LaFave, Note 7, *supra*, at § 3.4.

57. *See* McCray v. Illinois, 386 U.S. 300 (1967).

58. 403 U.S. 573 (1971).

59. But is an incriminating statement of this sort realistically a declaration against penal interest in light of the fact police officers often reward informants by not prosecuting them for their admitted offenses?

60. *Spinelli*, 393 U.S. 410, 415 (1969).

61. 358 U.S. 307 (1959). *See* the text following Note 55, *supra*.

62. Moylan, Note 41, *supra*, at 101.

In contrast, in *Spinelli* the police "corroborated" an informant's claim that *D* was a gambler using a particular residence for bookmaking by learning independently that the residence had two telephone numbers. Corroboration of this "one small detail" was deemed insufficient.

§ 8.05 The *Gates* "Totality of the Circumstances" Test[63]

The *Aguilar* two-pronged standard, explained above, has been replaced by the totality-of-circumstances test discussed below.

[A] The Test Explained

In *Illinois v. Gates*,[64] Bloomingdale, Illinois, police officers received an anonymous letter that accused a married couple of selling drugs at a specified address. The letter described in detail the couple's alleged *modus operandi*, including the fact that they usually bought drugs in Florida and brought them to Illinois by car. The letter also stated that on a specified date the wife would drive to Florida, drop off the car and fly home, and the husband would fly down a few days later and drive back alone with a large quantity of drugs in the trunk.

The police and federal agents verified facts alleged in the letter, including the Florida trip. The letter was wrong, however, in predicting that the wife would fly home immediately after dropping off the car; instead, she remained and accompanied her husband on the trip north. As they began driving north "on an interstate frequently used by travelers to the Chicago area," the police sought and secured a warrant to search the suspects' automobile and home.

All of the justices in *Gates* were in agreement that the anonymous tip, standing alone, did not satisfy the two-pronged *Aguilar v. Texas*[65] standard,[66] although it is arguable that the police department's partial corroboration of the tip was sufficient to permit a finding of probable cause under *Aguilar*.[67] Nonetheless, the Court, per Justice Rehnquist, abandoned *Aguilar* and what it described as "the elaborate set of legal rules" that

---

63. *See generally* Joseph D. Grano, *Probable Cause and Common Sense: A Reply to the Critics of Illinois v. Gates*, 17 U. Mich. J.L. Ref. 465 (1984); Roger S. Hanson, *The Aftermath of Illinois v. Gates and United States v. Leon: A Comprehensive Evaluation of Their Impact Upon the Litigation of Search Warrant Validity*, 15 West. St. U.L. Rev. 393 (1988); Yale Kamisar, *Gates, "Probable Cause," "Good Faith," and Beyond*, 69 Iowa L. Rev. 551 (1984); Moylan, Note 41, *supra*.

64. 462 U.S. 213 (1983); *but see, continuing to apply the Aguilar test under the state constitution*: State v. Jones, 706 P.2d 317 (Alaska 1985); Commonwealth v. Upton, 476 N.E.2d 548 (Mass. 1985); State v. Cordova, 784 P.2d 30 (N.M. 1989); People v. Griminger, 524 N.E.2d 409 (N.Y. 1988); and State v. Jackson, 688 P.2d 136 (Wash. 1984).

65. 378 U.S. 108 (1964); *see* § 9.04, *supra*.

66. The letter writer was unknown to the police, so there was no way to judge his or her veracity. The Court also stated that "we are inclined to agree" that the letter gave "absolutely no indication of the basis for the writer's predictions regarding the criminal activities."

67. This was the position taken by Justice White, who concurred in the judgment. He would not have overruled the *Aguilar-Spinelli* standard.

developed from it. In its place, the Court substituted "the totality-of-the-circumstances analysis that traditionally has informed probable cause determinations." On the basis of that standard, the *Gates* Court held that the warrant was supported by probable cause.[68]

According to *Gates*, a magistrate must conduct a "balanced assessment of the relative weights of all the various indicia of reliability (and unreliability) attending an informant's tip." The factors enunciated in *Aguilar*—basis-of-knowledge and veracity—remain "highly relevant" in determining the value of an informant's tip. However, the prongs are no longer treated as separate, independent requirements. Now, the strength of one prong or some other indicia of reliability may compensate for weakness in the other prong.

The Court justified abandonment of *Aguilar* on the ground that "probable cause" is a "fluid," nontechnical, commonsense conception, based on "the factual and practical considerations of everyday life on which reasonable and prudent men, not legal technicians, act." According to *Gates*, "probable cause" is not "reduc[ible] to a neat set of legal rules" supposedly developed under *Aguilar*.[69]

Justice Rehnquist also defended the change on the ground that the earlier test's alleged rigidity seriously impeded effective law enforcement. The Court further contended that this inflexibility tempted officers to avoid the warrant process entirely, thereby reducing the desired influence of magistrates in the search-and-seizure process.

[B] Criticism of *Gates*

Gates has been criticized by many,[70] but not all,[71] commentators and rejected by a few state courts.[72] Critics especially question the essence of the opinion, which is that the two-pronged *Aguilar* "test relied too much on logic and not enough on experience to decide what the reasonably cautious police officer would and should do under the

---

68. Justices Stevens, Brennan, and Marshall dissented in two separate opinions, but they were in agreement that, at the time the police sought the warrant, probable cause was lacking (even applying the new, totality-of-the-circumstances test) for a search of the house. Justice Stevens was troubled by the informant's incorrect prediction that the wife would fly home immediately after dropping the car off in Florida, which she did not do. According to Stevens, this discrepancy was "significant." First, the informant's description of events always placed one person at the Gates home at all times, the inference from this being that "the Gates did not want to leave their home unguarded because something valuable [illegal drugs] were hidden within." Second, "the discrepancy made the Gates' conduct seem substantially less unusual than the informant had predicted it would be." Finally, "the fact that the anonymous letter contained a material mistake undermined the reasonableness of relying on it as a basis for making a forcible entry into a private home." Justice Stevens also pointed out that, prior to seeking the warrant, the police did not confirm that the Gateses were returning home after a suspiciously short stay in Florida. The highway on which they were spotted, he noted, was one commonly used by travelers to Disney World, Sea World, the circus, Cocoa Beach, Cape Canaveral, and other tourist spots.

69. *See also* Florida v. Harris, 133 S. Ct. 1050, 1055–1056 (2013) ("We have rejected rigid rules, bright-line tests, and mechanistic inquiries in favor of a more flexible, all-things-considered approach.").

70. *E.g.*, Wayne R. LaFave, *The Fourth Amendment Today: A Bicentennial Appraisal*, 32 Vill. L. Rev. 1061, 1065–70 (1987); Kamisar, Note 63, *supra*.

71. *E.g.*, Grano, Note 63, *supra*.

72. *See* Note 64 *supra*.

circumstances."[73] They believe that *Aguilar* worked well, and they deny that logic is a bad source for a rule.

More specifically, some critics disagree with *Gates* that the strength of one prong can logically compensate for the weakness of the other. Let's consider this objection. First, Justice Rehnquist asserts in *Gates* that if an informant, is "known for the unusual reliability of his predictions . . . his failure, in a particular case, to thoroughly set forth the basis of his knowledge surely should not serve as an absolute bar to a finding of probable cause based on his tip." Great strength in the veracity prong, in other words, may make up for lack of evidence regarding the informant's basis of knowledge.

To critics of *Gates*, this conclusion is not self-evident. Suppose that *A*, a person of great trustworthiness—for example, a nun or rabbi—claims that *D* is a murderer. As a matter of logic, critics maintain, there is no more reason to believe *A*'s claim than that of an unproven stranger, unless and until we know how *A* came to her conclusion. If she obtained incriminating information about *D* from an unreliable source, e.g., from a pathological liar, then the assertion of *D*'s guilt is no more trustworthy than the liar whose claims were filtered through the nun or rabbi.

Moreover, as Justice White argued in his concurring opinion in *Gates*, if Justice Rehnquist is correct in the view that the veracity of an informant may compensate for the lack of information regarding the tipster's basis of knowledge, then it follows that a conclusory assertion by an honest and experienced police officer should also be acceptable. Yet, the Supreme Court has repeatedly held that the wholly unsupported ("bald and unilluminating") assertions of an officer do not satisfy the probable cause requirement.[74]

Defenders of *Gates* respond with some force that if an informant has provided, for example, 10 reliable reports in the past, but in the present case does not indicate how he obtained his information, "it may be reasonable to infer that [he] . . . does not report information unless it has been reliably obtained."[75] Likewise, our common experiences tell us that we *are* apt to believe the nun or rabbi, even without knowing how she obtained her information, because we trust her *not* to accept and repeat the claims of unreliable persons.

Perhaps, then, the defenders of *Gates* are correct in this regard, but in light of the constitutional interests at stake, it seems preferable for courts to require magistrates to question affiants carefully to determine the sources of their information and, likewise, for police officers to question *their* informants, so that magistrates are not tempted to infer a reliable basis of knowledge that might not exist.

Whether one agrees with Justice Rehnquist or his critics on this matter, the *Gates* majority is probably wrong in its other assertion, namely, that strength in the basis-of-knowledge prong can make up for weakness in the informant's veracity. On this matter, Justice Rehnquist states: "[E]ven if we entertain some doubt as to an informant's motives, his explicit and detailed description of alleged wrongdoing, along with a statement that the event was observed first-hand, entitles his tip to greater weight than might otherwise be the case."

---

73. Grano, Note 63, *supra*, at 469.

74. *See* § 8.03[B], *supra*.

75. Grano, Note 63, *supra*, at 513.

Even taking into consideration the soft language used—"entitles the tip to *greater* weight than *might* otherwise be the case"—Justice Rehnquist provides no support whatsoever for a notion that Professor Wayne LaFave has rightly described as "bizarre."[76] In computer lingo, the answer to Justice Rehnquist is "garbage in, garbage out." That is, a liar can just as easily provide specific non-existent "details"—including a false claim that he obtained his information firsthand—as he can give a more general statement. Indeed, it is probably reasonable to assume that a liar, to appear more credible, will be as specific as his creativity allows. It is submitted here that an informant's claims should not be considered by a magistrate unless the veracity prong is independently satisfied.

§ 8.06 Probable Cause in "Administrative Searches": The Reasonableness Standard and the *Camara* Principle[77]

The Fourth Amendment was once considered a "monolith."[78] It was assumed, for example, that all searches required probable cause, and that "probable cause" had the same meaning in every context.

Such a monolith no longer exists, if it ever did. Not all searches require probable cause.[79] And, it is fair to say that, today, "probable cause" is a "somewhat variable concept."[80] This variability is considered further in § 8.07, but an important starting point for understanding the issue is *Camara v. Municipal Court*.[81]

In *Camara*, housing inspectors wanted to conduct a routine annual administrative inspection of *C*'s apartment in order to ascertain whether the municipal housing code was being honored. The inspectors lacked suspicion of any criminal law or administrative code violation on *C*'s premises. Application of traditional "probable cause" standards, therefore, would have prevented their entry onto *C*'s premises without his consent, which he refused to grant. The Supreme Court's response to this situation was to retain the Fourth Amendment warrant requirement in this case,[82] but to recognize a different kind of "probable cause" for issuance of a search warrant in what has come to be known as an "administrative search" case.

The Court, per Justice White, started out by stating that "probable cause is the standard by which a particular decision to search is tested against the constitutional mandate of reasonableness." In turn, "there can be no ready test for determining reasonableness

---

76. 2 LaFave, Note 7, *supra*, at 109.

77. *See generally* Ronald J. Bacigal, *The Fourth Amendment in Flux: The Rise and Fall of Probable Cause*, 1979 U. Ill. L.F. 763; Wayne R. LaFave, *Administrative Searches and the Fourth Amendment: The Camara and See Cases*, 1967 Sup. Ct. Rev. 1; Scott E. Sundby, *A Return to Fourth Amendment Basics: Undoing the Mischief of Camara and Terry*, 72 Minn. L. Rev. 383 (1988).

78. Anthony G. Amsterdam, *Perspectives On the Fourth Amendment*, 58 Minn. L. Rev. 349, 388 (1974).

79. *See especially* Chapters 17–18, *infra*.

80. LaFave, Note 70, *supra*, at 1070.

81. 387 U.S. 523 (1967).

82. Warrants are not required for all administrative searches. *See* § 18.02, *infra*.

other than by balancing the need to search against the invasion which the search entails." In other words, "probable cause" is variable, in the sense that what constitutes a reasonable search or seizure, based on probable cause, requires a balancing of the competing public and individual interests.

The Court proceeded to balance the competing interests. On the side of permitting housing-code inspections was the public's long acceptance of such programs, and the Court's realization that their effectiveness would be seriously threatened if inspectors could not readily enter premises in order to check for violations not visible from public vantage points. Weighed against this was "a relatively limited invasion of the urban citizen's privacy," because such inspections "are neither personal in nature nor aimed at the discovery of evidence of crime."

Based on this balancing approach, the Court developed a special "probable cause" standard to apply in such administrative-search circumstances: Probable cause exists to issue a warrant to inspect premises for administrative code violations as long as there are "reasonable legislative or administrative standards for conducting an area inspection [that] are satisfied with respect to a particular dwelling." That is, unlike traditional "probable cause," which requires *individualized* suspicion that *criminal* evidence will be found in the area to be searched, administrative "probable cause" may be founded on the basis of more generalized factors, such as the passage of time since the last inspection, the nature of the building in question, and the condition of the entire area to be searched; and there is no requirement of suspicion of criminal wrongdoing as distinguished from the possibility of finding administrative code violations based on the factors just noted.

Camara's modified version of "probable cause" is critical in the distinct but important area of administrative law. *Camara's* significance in Fourth Amendment jurisprudence, however, is also great. As discussed elsewhere,[83] the balancing approach first applied in *Camara* is now at the core of Fourth Amendment analysis in criminal (non-administrative) investigations, even outside the realm of "probable cause." More to the immediate point, *Camara* brings into the open the plausible argument that what constitutes "probable cause," even in the traditional criminal law context, should be variable, based on the societal interest at stake, on the one hand, and the potential intrusion on the security or privacy of the individual, on the other hand. This possibility is considered in subsection [C] of the next chapter section.

§ 8.07 How Probable Is "Probable Cause"?[84]

[A] Governing Law

Suppose that *O*, a police officer, observes *A* and *B* standing over *V*'s body. Assume further that *O* has reason to believe, nearing 100% certainty, that *A* or *B*, but not both,

---

83. *See* Chapters 17–18, *infra*.

84. *See generally* Alschuler, Note 3, *supra*, at 243–56; Amar, Note 1, *supra*, at 782–85; Ronald J. Bacigal, *Making the Right Gamble: The Odds on Probable Cause*, 74 Miss. L.J. 279 (2004); Grano, Note 63, *supra*; Maclin, Note 1, *supra*, at 25–32; Christopher Slobogin, *The World Without a Fourth Amendment*, 39 UCLA L. Rev. 1, 38–78 (1991).

murdered *V.* The odds, however, are equal as to which one is guilty. Or, suppose that, after a car accident, *O* determines that both occupants of the car were intoxicated, but each accuses the other of being the driver.[85] May *O* constitutionally arrest *both* suspects in these cases, knowing that one is innocent?[86] Is the answer different if three, rather than two, suspects are at the scene, and only one is guilty? Or, what if *O* is virtually certain that a murder suspect is hiding in one of two (or three) houses. May the police simultaneously search both (or all three) houses to find the suspect? The essential question raised by these scenarios is this: How certain must the "person of reasonable caution" be before arresting a suspect or conducting a search and seizure, or before a magistrate authorizes such activity?

The Supreme Court has never quantified "probable cause." To the contrary, it has described probable cause as a "fluid concept,"[87] "incapable of precise definition or quantification into percentages because it deals with probabilities and depends on the totality of the circumstances."[88] Instead, the Court uses phrases such as "fair probability," "substantial basis," and "reasonable grounds" to articulate the quantum of evidence necessary to prove "probable cause."

While the Court eschews a precise quantification of the concept, this much is known: Less evidence is required to justify an arrest or search based on probable cause than to convict a person at trial, but more is required than "bare" or "mere" or even "reasonable suspicion."[89] More specifically, the "probable cause" standard "does *not* demand any showing that such a belief be correct or more likely true than false."[90] In other words, whatever else it may mean, "probable cause" involves less than a "50%+" likelihood of accuracy.

Consequently, in the hypotheticals described above, *O* has probable cause to arrest (or search) two suspects, even if *O* knows that one of the suspects is innocent;[91] or, it would seem counter-intuitively, *O* could flip a coin and arrest (or search) one of two suspects even based on the knowledge that there is a 50 percent chance that he picked the wrong person. On the other hand, Supreme Court dictum, albeit in a very old case, implies that the arrest of three persons, only one of whom could be guilty, is unconstitutional for want of probable cause.[92]

---

85. People v. Sutherland, 683 P.2d 1192 (Colo. 1984).

86. The assumption here is that the two suspects are not acting jointly. If *O* has reason to believe that *A* and *B* are acting jointly, the problem raised in the text disappears. *See also* Note 92, *infra.*

87. Illinois v. Gates, 462 U.S. 213 (1983).

88. Maryland v. Pringle, 540 U.S. 366, 371 (2003).

89. Brinegar v. United States, 338 U.S. 160, 175 (1949) ("bare suspicion"); Mallory v. United States 354 U.S. 449, 454 (1957) ("mere suspicion"). "Reasonable suspicion" is a term of art that justifies less-than-ordinarily-intrusive searches and seizures. *See* Chapter 17, *infra.*

90. Texas v. Brown, 460 U.S. 730, 742 (1983).

91. *See, e.g.,* State v. Horton, 625 N.W.2d 362, 365–66 (Iowa 2001).

92. Mallory v. United States, 354 U.S. at 456 (condemning "arrests at large," in which one of three suspects was arrested in order to interrogate him). Do not confuse the issue raised in the text—in which the police have reason to believe that one, *but only one,* of two (or more) suspects is guilty (or subject to search)—with the case in which the police have reason to believe that both or all the suspects are guilty of the offense. For example, in *Maryland v. Pringle,* 540 U.S. 366 (2003), *O* lawfully discovered cocaine and cash in a vehicle containing three occupants. *O* questioned the three men about ownership of the contraband, and he warned them that he would arrest all three if they did not provide ownership information. When the men offered no assistance, *O* arrested all

[B] Reflections on the Issue

Precedent and dictum aside, is the Court justified in permitting arrests and searches on less than a preponderance of the evidence? One plausible answer is, "It depends." That is, "probable cause" might be determined on a sliding scale, in which the degree of suspicion required would depend on a balancing of the individual and societal interests implicated in the particular case. This possibility is discussed in subsection [C]. However, even if the degree of "probable cause" were to vary depending on the circumstances, one question would persist: How probable *should* "probable cause" be in the ordinary, run-of-the-mill, arrest or search case, before one looks at the exceptional cases that justify a heightened or reduced level of probability?

In an ideal world, problems such as those hypothesized in subsection [A] would not occur. For example, O might be able to avoid the dilemma of arresting A and B by briefly detaining both suspects at the scene rather than arresting them, and questioning them long enough to determine which person is (even slightly) more likely guilty. But, even if he did so, A and B might refuse to answer O's questions, or their answers might not assist in focusing suspicion on one of them, in which case O would be back where we started.

The question that ultimately must be answered is this: In what type of society do we wish to live? Do we think it is better that both persons, one of whom is nearly certainly guilty of an offense, remain free while the police seek more evidence, than that O arrest them both, knowing that one of them is innocent, and seek post-arrest evidence that incriminates one and/or exculpates the other?

The conclusion that O may arrest A *and* B for a crime that O knows only one committed is troubling, but arguably is correct. To permit O to arrest both suspects provides society needed leeway without "leav[ing] law-abiding citizens at the mercy of the officers' whim or caprice."[93] After all, it may be said that "the function of arrest [is not] merely to produce persons in court for purposes of the prosecution. . . . [T]here is also an investigative function" — time to determine which suspect is guilty — "which is served by the making of arrests."[94]

An officer who acts on a 50% likelihood that the person arrested is guilty has arguably conducted a reasonable seizure of the person, at least if the alternative is to arrest neither suspect and, thus, knowingly allow a criminal to be free. As the Court has observed in a different context, "what is generally demanded of the many factual determinations that must regularly be made by agents of the government . . . is not that they always be correct, but that they always be reasonable."[95]

---

three car occupants. The Court held that the arrest of P, one of the occupants, was founded on probable cause, but its basis was stated, at 373, as follows:

> Here we think it was reasonable for the officer to infer a common enterprise among the three men. The quantity of drugs and cash in the car indicated the likelihood of drug dealing, an enterprise to which a dealer would be unlikely to admit an innocent person with the potential to furnish evidence against him.

Thus, "a reasonable officer could conclude that there was probable cause to believe [P] committed the crime of possession of cocaine, either solely or jointly." *Id.*, at 372.

93. Brinegar v. United States, 338 U.S. 160, 176 (1949).
94. State v. Horton, 625 N.W.2d 362, 366 (Iowa 2001).
95. Illinois v. Rodriguez, 497 U.S. 177, 185 (1990).

Even if an arrest or search based on a 50% chance of accuracy satisfies us, this only shifts the debate to the more difficult question: How much lower likelihood of accuracy are we prepared to accept? At what point does the interest in protecting the community from crime give way to the Fourth Amendment interest in safeguarding citizens from rash and unreasonable interferences with their personal security or privacy?

One scholar, Joe Grano, has gone so far as to contend that an officer who suspects 10 persons of a crime, but who has no way of distinguishing among them, should be permitted in some circumstances to arrest all 10, and then seek evidence later to clear the nine innocent parties.[96] According to him, focusing on the 10% accuracy figure "distorts our perspective." We should instead concentrate on the fact that the police have successfully narrowed their investigation "from the universe of all possible suspects, which may include much of the population, to 10 individuals."

But, what about those nine innocent persons? Why are they not justified in demanding that the police narrow their investigation further before they are arrested (or, for example, before their houses are searched)? According to Professor Grano, the answer is that we should construct a model of criminal justice premised on the view that individuals cannot act "oblivious to the community's needs." According to this model, even in a society "traditionally and properly dedicated to individual rights," the community may legitimately demand that the nine innocent individuals sacrifice "some liberty or privacy in order to unmask the offender."

This view of the proper balance between the individual and society is one that some people would reject on the ground that it unduly minimizes the interests of the nine innocent persons arrested. An arrest — even one that lasts just a few days or weeks before release of the apparently innocent parties — entails more than trivial liberty and privacy loss. An arrest results in loss of liberty, stigmatization, personal humiliation (such as when the arrestee is compelled to undergo a strip search prior to incarceration), any physical or mental trauma that occurs in the jail system (hardly a rarity), as well as collateral harm, such as legal fees, possible loss of employment, and a permanent arrest record. And, all of this is multiplied times nine innocent persons.

The demand that police meet relatively high standards of probable cause may result in them catching fewer criminals or, more likely, having to work harder before making arrests and conducting searches. But, this may be "the price the framers anticipated and were willing to pay to ensure the sanctity of the person, the home, and property against unrestrained governmental power."[97]

None of this discussion ultimately tells us where the probable cause line ideally should be drawn once we agree (or accept, as we must, the precedent) that the doctrine falls below the civil preponderance-of-evidence standard, and that "probable cause" is a fluid concept. If it *is* fluid, however, why not say so expressly and develop a sliding-scale version of probable cause. That idea is considered next.

---

96. Grano, Note 63, *supra*, at 496–97. Apparently, Professor Grano would allow the police to hold the suspects until their first appearance before a magistrate, which usually occurs within a day or two of arrest, *see* § 1.03[C][3], *supra*, or until a preliminary hearing is conducted, usually within two weeks after the first appearance, *see* § 1.03[C][4], *supra*, at which point the prosecutor would be required to meet a somewhat higher standard of proof.

97. Potter Stewart, *The Road to Mapp v. Ohio and Beyond: The Origins, Development and Future of the Exclusionary Rule in Search-and-Seizure Cases*, 83 Colum. L. Rev. 1365, 1393 (1983).

[C] "Probable Cause" as a Sliding Scale?[98]

[1] *Is* There a Sliding Scale?

Camara v. Municipal Court[99] demonstrated that there are different *kinds* of "probable cause": one that applies to criminal investigations and another that is used in administrative search cases. But, are there also different *degrees* of "probable cause"? Is there, in other words, a sliding scale of "probable cause"? After all, if it's proper to weigh society's interest in an administrative-search case against an individual's interest to be free from intrusion, why shouldn't this balancing process apply across the board?

The Supreme Court has never stated that there is a sliding-scale concept of probable cause, but it *has* developed an alternative sliding-scale approach to searches and seizures: It has said that some searches and seizures may be conducted on a lesser level of suspicion than probable cause. In the watershed case of *Terry v. Ohio*,[100] the Supreme Court held that searches and seizures that are less-than-ordinarily intrusive may be conducted on the basis of a lesser quantum of evidence than "probable cause." That lesser amount is termed "reasonable suspicion." Furthermore, in a few circumstances, where the intrusion on privacy is especially slight, and society's interest in conducting the search or seizure is unusually great, government officers may act without *any* individualized suspicion.[101]

Does the sliding-scale slide in the other direction? Do *more*-than-ordinarily intrusive searches and seizures require a quantum of evidence greater than probable cause? Logic would suggest that they should; and the Supreme Court has on occasion recognized that a greater-than-ordinary justification may be required in some especially intrusive situations. For example, in *Schmerber v. California*,[102] a physician, at the direction of a police officer, extracted blood from a suspect to test for alcohol content. This bodily intrusion "implicated . . . [the] most personal and deep-rooted expectations of privacy,"[103] and the Court held that this form of search required "a clear indication" that the desired evidence would be found. The precise meaning of the phrase "clear indication" is in some doubt; however, in *Winston v. Lee*,[104] a case in which the government sought authority to conduct invasive surgery on an individual in order to extract evidence of a crime (a bullet), the Court held that "more substantial [than ordinary] justification"—indeed, a "compelling need"—was required to "intrude upon an area in which our society recognizes a significantly heightened privacy interest."[105]

[handwritten margin note: More intrusive searches require more than po]

---

98. *See generally* Amar, Note 7, *supra*; Ronald M. Gould & Simon Stern, *Catastrophic Threats and the Fourth Amendment*, 77 So. Cal. L. Rev. 777 (2004); Christopher Slobogin, *Let's Not Bury Terry: A Call for Rejuvenation of the Proportionality Principle*, 72 St. John's L. Rev. 1053 (1998); Scott E. Sundby, *An Ode to Probable Cause: A Brief Response to Professors Amar and Slobogin*, 72 St. John's L. Rev. 1133 (1998).

99. 387 U.S. 523 (1967). See § 8.06, *supra*.

100. 392 U.S. 1 (1968). *See generally* Chapter 17, *infra*.

101. *E.g.*, Mich. Dept. of State Police v. Sitz, 496 U.S. 444 (1990) (permitting brief random seizures of drivers at sobriety checkpoints).

102. 384 U.S. 757 (1966).

103. Winston v. Lee, 470 U.S. 753, 760 (1985).

104. *Id.*

105. On the other hand, in *Zurcher v. Stanford Daily*, 436 U.S. 547 (1978), the Court justified the search of a newspaper office for photographic evidence of a crime on the basis of ordinary probable cause, although a heightened cause requirement might have been justified on either of two grounds: that the police searched the premises of individuals not personally suspected of crime; or that the

[2] *Should* There Be a Sliding Scale?

The summary of the law in subsection [1] demonstrates that, although the Supreme Court has not explicitly implemented an overall sliding-scale of "probable cause," it *has* developed a downward-directed sliding-scale of "reasonable" searches and seizures, i.e., those that require probable cause, and those that require less than probable cause ("reasonable suspicion" or no individualized suspicion); and, on rare occasions, it has required something more than ordinary probable cause to conduct highly intrusive bodily searches.

It may be too late to change direction now, but perhaps the Supreme Court should expressly recognize a sliding-scale of "probable cause," and reject other doctrines not textually included in the Fourth Amendment, such as "reasonable suspicion." Justice Robert Jackson once advocated what essentially was a sliding-scale version of probable cause.[106] He conceded that he would "strive hard" to justify a roadblock around a neighborhood in which all outgoing automobiles were searched if its purpose was to prevent a kidnapper from leaving with his victim, but that he would not justify the same conduct, based on the same information, in order "to salvage a few bottles of bourbon and catch a bootlegger."

Or, consider this all-too-modern hypothetical: The government has reliable evidence that a weapon of mass destruction small enough to fit in a suitcase has been smuggled into New York City, and is secreted in a one-square-mile area that includes 1,000 homes.[107] Although the odds of discovering the weapon in any particular residence is just one-tenth of one percent, should we conclude that the government has sufficient cause to conduct highly intrusive searches of as many as 1,000 homes?[108] Whatever our answer, it seems hard to resist the argument that the government should be given more leeway in *this* case than if the police want to search 1,000 — or even 10 — houses in order to find a small quantity of drugs.

Professor Akhil Amar contends that the Supreme Court went wrong when it decided that the concept of "probable cause" was at the heart of the Fourth Amendment. He reasons that the probable cause requirement is found only in the Warrant Clause of the amendment. In *that* context — when the police seek to obtain a warrant — he would require "a standard akin to more than fifty percent." However, with *warrantless* searches and seizures — which are *not* textually linked to the probable cause requirement — all that should be required (in his view) is that the search or seizure be "reasonable," a concept that "obviously . . . require[s] different levels of cause in different contexts, and not always a high probability of success." Alternatively, one might say that *all* searches, even those conducted *without* a warrant, require "probable cause," but that this doctrine is, indeed, *highly* variable, and should permit searches and seizures based on different degrees of likelihood of success, as long as there is a reasonable, albeit small, likelihood of success.

---

police conduct threatened First Amendment values. *See also* New York v. P.J. Video, Inc., 475 U.S. 868 (1986) (providing that a warrant application authorizing the seizure of materials presumptively protected by the First Amendment is evaluated by traditional standards of "probable cause").

106. Brinegar v. United States, 338 U.S. 160, 182–83 (1949) (Jackson, J., dissenting).

107. Gould & Stern, Note 98, *supra*, at 779.

108. Notice that the searches here will be exceptionally intrusive: not only is a person's "castle" — the home — invaded, but the police will have to conduct extensive searches inside the residence, because the weapon may be hidden in a small container.

Critics of this approach argue that once a sliding-scale approach is recognized, the Fourth Amendment becomes "one immense Rorschach blot."[109] One potential effect of the sliding scale is a "graduated fourth amendment . . . splendid in its flexibility, [but] awful in its unintelligibility, unadministrability, unenforceability and general ooziness."[110] Given its "ooziness," a second effect of a sliding scale is that it is likely to "produce more slide than scale," because "courts are seldom going to say that what [the police] did was unreasonable."[111]

---

109. Amsterdam, Note 78, *supra*, at 393.
110. *Id.* at 415.
111. *Id.* at 394. *See generally* § 2.07[A], *supra*.

Chapter 9

Arrests

§ 9.01 "Arrest": Overview[1]

[A] Definition

The term "arrest" is often used in court opinions and statutes, but is rarely defined. Indeed, the word "arrest" is sometimes modified by adjectives such as "formal,"[2] "custodial,"[3] and "traditional,"[4] from which one may infer that some arrests are "informal," "noncustodial," and "nontraditional."

Operationally (and in the traditional sense of the term), a person is "arrested" when she is taken into custody by lawful authority, for the purpose of holding her in order to answer for a criminal charge. Nonetheless, a few states by statute or judicial opinion characterize the temporary detention of a person for the purpose of issuing a summons or to write a traffic citation as an arrest, albeit a non-custodial one.[5] This use of the term is uncommon. Unless otherwise specified in this Text, the term "arrest" is used in the operational taken-into-custody sense of the term.

[B] "Arrest" versus "Seizure"

An arrest, which must always be founded on probable cause,[6] constitutes a "seizure" of the person, as that term is used in Fourth Amendment jurisprudence.[7] However, although all arrests are Fourth Amendment seizures, not all seizures constitute arrests. Use of the word "arrest" ordinarily implies that the individual's freedom of movement has been curtailed for an indefinite period—at least long enough so that she can be taken to police headquarters for formal booking—whereas a person can be detained against her will for a brief time—and, thus, be seized—without being "arrested" as explained here.

---

1. *See generally* David A. Moran, *Traffic Stops, Littering Tickets, and Police Warnings: The Case for a Fourth Amendment Non-Custodial Arrest Doctrine*, 37 Am. Crim. L. Rev. 1143 (2000).

2. *E.g.,* Berkemer v. McCarty, 468 U.S. 420, 425 (1984).

3. *E.g.,* United States v. Robinson, 414 U.S. 218, 235 (1973).

4. *E.g.,* Dunaway v. New York, 442 U.S. 200, 212 (1979).

5. *E.g.,* People v. Bland, 884 P.2d 312, 315–16 (Colo. 1994); Thomas v. State, 614 So. 2d 468, 470–71 (Fla. 1993).

6. *See* Dunaway v. New York, 442 U.S. 200 (1979); Henry v. United States, 361 U.S. 98 (1959).

7. *See* § 7.03, *supra*.

§ 9.02 Arrests: Common Law and Statutory Arrest Rules

At common law, a police officer could not arrest a person for an offense unless the officer had reasonable grounds to believe that a crime had been committed and that the person to be arrested committed it.[8] The common law term "reasonable grounds" is equivalent to the constitutional term "probable cause."[9]

Today, most statutes[10] provide that the police may make a felony arrest without a warrant. However, a warrant is required for a misdemeanor arrest unless the offense occurs in the officer's presence.[11] As discussed below,[12] however, warrantless arrests in some circumstances are unconstitutional, notwithstanding common law and statutory precedent.

§ 9.03 Custodial Arrests for Minor Offenses[13]

As noted above, an arrest traditionally involves taking an individual into custody, rather than merely issuing a citation at the scene and requiring that person to appear in court on the charge at a later date. Citations are usually implemented when dealing with very minor criminal offenses and so-called "civil" offenses (e.g., ordinary motor vehicle code provisions), which typically involve a monetary fine but no term of imprisonment. But does it violate the Fourth Amendment for a state or local community to authorize police officers to take a person into custody (and not simply issue a citation), based on probable cause to believe that the individual has violated a minor, fine-only offense?

In *Atwater v. Lago Vista*,[14] the Supreme Court held, 5–4, that the Fourth Amendment does *not* forbid the police from making custodial arrests, rather than issuing citations, if they have probable cause to believe that the person has committed an offense, even an exceedingly minor one—in this case, a seat belt violation punishable by a small fine.

---

8. *See generally* Joshua Dressler, Understanding Criminal Law § 21.02[A][1] (6th ed. 2012).

9. Draper v. United States, 358 U.S. 307, 310 n.3 (1959).

10. *See, e.g.,* Cal. Penal Code § 836 (2012).

11. For the common law meaning of the phrase "in the presence," *see* 3 Wayne R. LaFave, Search and Seizure § 5.1(c) (4th ed. 2004).

12. *See generally* § 9.05, *infra.*

13. *See generally* Thomas Y. Davies, *The Fictional Character of Law-and-Order Originalism: A Case Study of the Distortions and Evasions of Framing-Era Arrest Doctrine in Atwater v. Lago Vista,* 37 Wake Forest L. Rev. 239 (2002); *see also* Richard S. Frase, *What Were They Thinking? Fourth Amendment Unreasonableness in Atwater v. City of Lago Vista,* 71 Fordham L. Rev. 329 (2002); Arnold H. Loewy, *Cops, Cars, and Citizens: Fixing the Broken Balance,* 76 St. John's L. Rev. 535, 559–563 (2002).

14. 532 U.S. 318 (2001); *contra under state constitution,* State v. Bauer, 36 P.3d 892 (Mont. 2001) (in the absence of special circumstances, custodial arrest for a nonjailable offense violates the state constitution); State v. Brown, 792 N.E.2d 175 (Ohio 2003) (a custodial arrest for a minor misdemeanor offense violates the state constitution).

Atwater involved a remarkable set of facts, some of which are not found in Justice David Souter's majority opinion, but instead are gleaned from Justice Sandra Day O'Connor's dissent and from the Circuit Court opinions below.[15] Gail Atwater was driving her pickup truck in Lago Vista, Texas, with her three-year-old son and five-year-old daughter, looking for a toy attached to her pickup that had fallen off while she was driving her children home from soccer practice. She permitted her children to unbuckle their seat belts while they looked, and she herself did not have her seat belt on, in violation of a motor vehicle ordinance.

Lago Vista officer Bart Turek, who had previously stopped Atwater because he had believed (incorrectly) that Atwater's son had not been seat-belted, again stopped Atwater, yelled at her, frightened her young children, and told her she was under arrest and would be taken into custody (although he had discretion to issue a traffic citation and let her go). He refused Atwater's request that she be permitted to leave her children with a neighbor before being taken to jail.[16] Turek then handcuffed Atwater, placed her in his police vehicle, and drove her to the police station (ironically, without securing her seat belt), where she was required to remove her shoes, eyeglasses, and jewelry, and empty her pockets. She was photographed and placed in a jail cell for approximately an hour, after which she was taken before a magistrate and released on bond. (Atwater later paid a $50 fine for the seat-belt violations.)

Why did Officer Turek's conduct not constitute an unreasonable seizure of Gail Atwater? The answer to this question must start with Justice Souter's remarkable concession:

> If we were to derive a rule exclusively to address the uncontested facts of this case, Atwater might well prevail. She was a known and established resident of Lago Vista with no place to hide and no incentive to flee, and common sense says she would almost certainly have buckled up as a condition of driving off with a citation. In her case, the physical incidents of arrest were merely gratuitous humiliations imposed by a police officer who was (at best) exercising extremely poor judgment. Atwater's claim to live free of pointless indignity and confinement clearly outweighs anything the City can raise against it specific to her case.

Essentially, Atwater *was* the victim of an unreasonable seizure. But the Supreme Court observed that "we have traditionally recognized that a responsible Fourth Amendment balance is not well served by standards requiring sensitive case-by-case determinations of government need, lest every discretionary judgment in the field be converted into an occasion for constitutional review." In short, the Court preferred a bright-line rule — applicable to *all* custodial arrests for minor offenses — over case-by-case adjudication based on general standards.[17] As one scholar put it succinctly, "the arrest of Ms. Atwater, though considered individually unreasonable, was held to be constitutionally reasonable."[18]

---

15. *See especially* Atwater v. City of Lago Vista, 195 F.3d 242 (5th Cir. 1999) (Garza, J., dissenting; and Wiener, J., dissenting).

16. Luckily for Atwater's children, a friend learned of the situation, arrived, and took custody of them before Atwater was taken to the police station.

17. *See generally* § 2.07[A], *supra*.

18. Loewy, Note 13, *supra*, at 560.

The majority based its Fourth Amendment holding in great part on its historical survey of pre-Constitutional English common law, statutes enacted by the Parliament before the founding of the United States, and its examination of American history during the constitutional framing era. The Court concluded from this survey that, although history is not unequivocal, the Fourth Amendment did not bar custodial arrests for minor "fine-only" offenses.

The Court also concluded that it was impractical to devise a constitutional line between jailable offenses (for which custodial arrests are reasonable) and "fine-only" offenses (for which custody is not reasonable), because "we cannot expect every police officer to know the details of frequently complex penalty schemes," and because "penalties for ostensibly identical conduct can vary on account of facts difficult 'if not impossible' to know at the scene of an arrest." Justice Souter worried:

> Often enough, the Fourth Amendment has to be applied on the spur (and in the heat) of the moment, and the object in implementing its command of reasonableness is to draw standards sufficiently clear and simple to be applied with a fair prospect of surviving judicial second-guessing months and years after an arrest or search is made. Courts attempting to strike a reasonable Fourth Amendment balance thus credit the Government's side with an essential interest in readily administrable rules.

Atwater is significant when considering some general Fourth Amendment issues. First, a majority of the justices are now increasingly inclined to resolve Fourth Amendment issues on historical grounds (or, at least, *their* reading of history), rather than on the basis of modern policy considerations. Second, *Atwater* represents one of many examples of the Court's current inclination to devise bright-line rules rather than develop general standards requiring case-by-case adjudication.

The specific holding in *Atwater* also has important policy implications once one considers other Fourth Amendment rules that invite the enhanced possibility of governmental abuse.[19] The Court has held[20] that the police may constitutionally make probable-cause-based traffic (and other) arrests, even if the reason for doing so is pretextual, e.g., so that they can harass the individual (as perhaps was the case in *Atwater*) or gain an opportunity to look inside a vehicle. Once a person, like Atwater, is subjected to custodial arrest, the arresting officer has lawful authority, *not available if she only issues a citation*, to search the arrestee without probable cause.[21] As well, the police may have authority to search the trunk of the vehicle later as part of a routine car inventory at the police station.[22] Since nearly all persons who drive a vehicle are, at one time or another, liable to violate a traffic or motor vehicle ordinance, *Atwater* opens the door, if lawmakers choose to give their police the authority to take traffic violators into custody, to widespread warrantless, suspicionless searches of persons and, sometimes, their vehicles.[23]

---

19. For more details, *see* Frase, Note 13, *supra*.

20. Whren v. United States, 517 U.S. 806 (1996); *see* § 8.02[F], *supra*.

21. United States v. Robinson, 414 U.S. 218 (1973); *see* § 12.04, *infra*.

22. *See* § 15.01, *infra*.

23. As an antidote to what many consider to be police overreach in cases like *Atwater*, one scholar has proposed that probable cause be considered a necessary but not sufficient ground for an arrest. Under this proposal, a court would have to find that there was probable cause and then also determine that the arrest was reasonable (that is, that an objectively reasonable police officer "in

§ 9.04 Grounds for Arrest: "Stop and Identify" Statutes

Nineteen states in 2004 had so-called "stop-and identify" statutes. In general, these statutes make it an offense for a person to refuse to provide her name—and, in some statutes, a driver's license or other form of identification—to a police officer upon request. In *Brown v. Texas*,[24] two police officers stopped a man, B, on the street even though they lacked any objective grounds to believe that he was engaged in criminal conduct. They demanded that he identify himself. When he refused, they arrested B pursuant to a Texas statute that obligates a person to give his name and address to a police officer "who has lawfully stopped him and requested the information." The Court unanimously overturned B's conviction because the officers lacked valid Fourth Amendment grounds to seize him in order to request identification. In short, B had not been *lawfully* stopped as a constitutional matter, so the provisions of the stop-and-identify statute could not constitutionally be applied.

But what if they had *lawfully* stopped B, and *then* arrested him for failing to identify himself? That is essentially the issue in *Hiibel v. Sixth Judicial Dist. Court*,[25] in which an officer lawfully stopped H, based on reasonable suspicion (but less than probable cause to believe) that H had been involved in an earlier assault of a woman. The officer asked H to identify himself, and when H repeatedly failed to do so, arrested H for obstructing the officer in the discharge of his lawful duties, under the authority of a Nevada statute that requires a person lawfully stopped to disclose her name to an officer upon request.

The Court held that the Nevada statute did not violate the Fourth Amendment.[26] It stated that dicta in prior opinions, which suggested that a person who is questioned is "not obliged to answer . . . and refusal to answer furnishes no basis for an arrest,"[27] were not controlling. The Court explained that, "the Fourth Amendment does not impose obligations on the citizen but instead provides rights against the government. As a result, the Fourth Amendment itself cannot require a suspect to answer questions. . . . Here, the source of the legal obligation [to identify oneself] arises from Nevada state law, not the Fourth Amendment."

According to *Hiibel*, although "an officer may not arrest a suspect for failure to identify himself if the request for identification is not reasonably related to the circumstances justifying the stop," in this case that standard was satisfied. *H* was lawfully stopped in an assault investigation; requiring him to provide his name (it should be noted that the holding here is limited to statutes that only require a person to disclose one's name) did not "alter the nature of the stop itself: it [did] not change its duration." The request for

---

the same circumstances would have made the arrest for the reason given." See Josh Bowers, *Probable Cause, Constitutional Reasonableness, and the Unrecognized Point of a "Pointless Indignity,"* 88 Stan. L. Rev. 987, 1018–19 (2014).

24. 443 U.S. 47 (1979).

25. 542 U.S. 177 (2004).

26. The Court also held that the statute did not violate the Fifth Amendment bar on compelled self-incrimination. *See* §23.04[D][2], *infra*.

27. Terry v. Ohio, 392 U.S. 1, 34 (1968) (White, J., concurring); *see also* Berkemer v. McCarty, 468 U.S. 420, 439 (1984) (in which the Court, explaining *Terry*, observed that a person detained "is not obliged to respond" to questions).

identification was "reasonably related in scope to the circumstances which justified" the original detention.

More legislatures may be inclined to enact stop-and-identify laws in light of *Hiibel.* The limitation set out in the case (that the request for identification be reasonably related to the circumstances justifying the stop) is a trivial one, as a request for identification is reasonable in almost any lawful criminal investigation.

§ 9.05 Arrest Warrants: Constitutional Law

[A] Overview

[1] General Rules

All custodial arrests must be founded on probable cause. An arrest not founded on probable cause constitutes an unreasonable seizure of the person, in violation of the Fourth Amendment.

The law regarding arrest *warrants* is less categorical. As a *constitutional* matter, a police officer: (1) may arrest a person in a public place without a warrant, even if it is practicable to secure a warrant; but (2) may *not* arrest a person in her home without an arrest warrant, absent exigent circumstances or valid consent; and (3) absent exigent circumstances or valid consent, may not arrest a person in another person's home without a search, and perhaps an arrest, warrant. These rules are discussed in detail below.

Rules for Arrests

[2] How Arrest Warrant Issues Arise

An arrest that is invalid because it was executed without a required warrant does not render unlawful the continued custody of the suspect and, therefore, does not by itself void a conviction.[28] Instead, the constitutionality of a warrantless arrest arises as an issue in a criminal prosecution in an evidentiary context, that is, *when the arrest results in the seizure of evidence that the government wishes to use against the arrestee at her criminal trial.*

For example, if the police seek to justify a warrantless *search* of *D*'s home for evidence on the basis that it was an incident to *D*'s *lawful* arrest in the residence, or if the police claim that the evidence was in *lawful* "plain view" at the time of *D*'s arrest, then the lawfulness of *D*'s arrest that gave rise to the search and/or seizure is brought into question. In such circumstances, the absence of an arrest warrant, if one is constitutionally required, serves as the basis for potentially excluding the seized evidence.

---

28. *See* United States v. Crews, 445 U.S. 463 (1980); Gerstein v. Pugh, 420 U.S. 103 (1975); Frisbie v. Collins, 342 U.S. 519 (1952).

[B] Arrest in a Public Place: The No-Warrant Rule[29]

In *United States v. Watson*,[30] federal postal inspectors arrested *W* in a restaurant for possession of stolen credit cards. The agents possessed probable cause for the arrest, but they acted without an arrest warrant, under authority of a federal statute, similar to those in nearly all states, that permits warrantless arrests on the basis of probable cause that the suspect "has committed or is committing a felony."

The Supreme Court upheld the constitutionality of the statute in the context of felony arrests in public places. The Court largely grounded its ruling on its reading of history. The majority observed that warrantless felony arrests were permitted at common law, and that this rule "survived substantially intact" thereafter in nearly every state, as well as in the federal system. The Court particularly noted the 1792 passage by Congress of a statute providing federal marshals with, in the words of the original statute, "the same powers in executing the laws of the United States, as sheriffs and their deputies in the several states have by law." Since sheriffs at that time had authority to arrest felons *without* a warrant, this legislation demonstrated that contemporaries of the drafters of the Constitution saw no inconsistency between the Fourth Amendment and legislation authorizing warrantless felony arrests.

Justice Powell concurred in the opinion, but with reservations. He conceded that the Court's holding "create[d] a certain anomaly." The anomaly is that seizures of persons in public places are subject to less judicial scrutiny than searches and seizures of property, which generally require a warrant. As he observed:

> There is no more basic constitutional rule in the Fourth Amendment area than that which makes a warrantless search unreasonable except in a few "jealously and carefully drawn" exceptional circumstances.... [¶] Since the Fourth Amendment speaks equally to both searches and seizures, and since an arrest, the taking hold of one's person, is quintessentially a seizure, it would seem that the constitutional provision should impose the same limitations upon arrests that it does upon searches. Indeed, as an abstract matter an argument can be made that the restrictions upon arrest perhaps should be greater. A search may cause only annoyance and temporary inconvenience to the law-abiding citizen.... An arrest, however, is a serious personal intrusion regardless of whether the person seized is guilty or innocent.... [¶] But logic sometimes must defer to history and experience.

The dissenters questioned the Court's reliance on common law authority. They noted that only the most serious crimes were identified as felonies at common law. In contrast, many modern-day felonies were common law misdemeanors and, therefore, required an arrest warrant. The holding in *Watson*, therefore, "result[ed] in contravention of the common law."

---

29. *See generally* 3 LaFave, Note 11, *supra*, at § 5.1(b); Thomas Y. Davies, *Correcting Search-and-Seizure History: Now-Forgotten Common-Law Warrantless Arrest Standards and the Original Understanding of "Due Process of Law,"* 77 Miss. L.J. 1 (2007).

30. 423 U.S. 411 (1976); *contra, under the state constitution,* Campos v. State, 870 P.2d 117 (N.M. 1994) (the validity of a warrantless arrest in a public place depends on exigent circumstances).

[C] Arrest in the Arrestee's Home: The Warrant-Requirement Rule[31]

[1] In General

The Supreme Court ruled in *Payton v. New York*[32] that the Fourth Amendment prohibits warrantless, nonconsensual entry into a suspect's home in order to make a "routine" (non-exigent) felony[33] arrest.[34]

In *Payton*, police officers had probable cause to arrest *D1* for a felony. They came to *D1*'s home to arrest him without a warrant. They heard music playing inside the home, and knocked, but received no reply. After a brief wait, they broke in with the assistance of a crowbar. Nobody was inside, but they seized evidence in plain view. In a companion case, again with probable cause but without a warrant, the police knocked at *D2*'s door, his three-year-old son opened it, and the officers, observing *D2* inside, entered and arrested him without a warrant.

The Supreme Court, per Justice Stevens, held that the Fourth Amendment prohibited the warrantless entries in these two cases. The Court stated that, absent exigent circumstances, which it did not define, *nonconsensual* entry into a suspect's home in order to make an arrest requires an arrest warrant and "reason to believe the suspect is within."[35] If the officer is armed with a warrant, however, she has implicit authority to search anywhere in the home that the person named in the warrant might be found, until she is taken into custody.[36]

The *Payton* Court justified the warrant requirement primarily on the ground that "physical entry of a home is the chief evil against which the wording of the Fourth Amendment is directed." The purpose of the arrest warrant, in other words, is not to protect the suspect from unreasonable seizure, but rather is to safeguard the integrity of the home from entry, and the occupants' privacy therein, in the absence of a prior determination of probable cause by a magistrate.[37]

Justice Stevens pointed out that general warrants and writs of assistance were the immediate evils that motivated the adoption of the Fourth Amendment.[38] However, he said, "[i]t is ... perfectly clear that the evil the Amendment was designed to prevent was broader than the abuse of a general warrant." A broader purpose of the Amendment is to protect against governmental intrusion into "the sanctity of a man's home and the

---

31. *See generally* 3 LaFave, Note 11, *supra*, at § 6.1.

32. 445 U.S. 573 (1980).

33. Although *Payton* concerned felony arrests and, consequently, the rule was stated in those terms, the doctrine applies to misdemeanor arrests in the home as well. *See* Welsh v. Wisconsin, 466 U.S. 740 (1984).

34. *See also* Kirk v. Louisiana, 536 U.S. 635 (2002) (per curiam) (stating that "police officers need either a warrant or probable cause plus exigent circumstances in order to make a lawful entry into a home").

35. Lower courts are split on whether this quoted language means that the police must have probable cause to believe that a suspect is inside the residence, or whether a lesser standard will do. *See* State v. Smith, 90 P.3d 221 (Ariz. App. 2004) (and collecting cases).

36. Maryland v. Buie, 494 U.S. 325, 330 (1990). Under limited circumstances, arresting officers may also conduct a "protective sweep" of the home for *other* persons who might pose a danger to the officers or others. See § 17.08, *infra*.

37. Minnesota v. Olson, 495 U.S. 91, 95 (1990) (explaining *Payton*).

38. See § 4.03, *supra*.

privacies of life." According to the Court, absent an emergency or consent, the Fourth Amendment bars (in crucial language) the warrantless "breach of the entrance to an individual's home." Although the Amendment protects privacy in various settings, "[i]n none is the zone of privacy more clearly defined than when bounded by the unambiguous physical dimensions of an individual's home."

The dissenters found the majority's historical argument faulty. They argued that at the time of the adoption of the Fourth Amendment, law enforcement officers had broad inherent power to arrest without a warrant. The evil of general warrants and writs of assistance was that they gave *magistrates* power to expand upon this inherent authority, and it was *this* judicial expansion that the Fourth Amendment sought to prohibit. As one scholar has put it, in the framers' minds, "judges and warrants are the heavies, not the heroes, of our story."[39] On this view, the framers would have considered it perverse to require a judicial warrant to make *any* kind of arrest.

[2] Scope of the Rule

[a] "Home" versus "Public Place"

An arrest warrant is required (absent consent) for a routine arrest of the defendant in her home (*Payton*), including her temporary residence (e.g. a motel room). However, warrantless arrests in public places are constitutional (*Watson*). It is critical, therefore, to distinguish between a "home" and a "public place" for Fourth Amendment purposes.

Clearly, an arrest on the street, in a public park, or in any other public site, falls within the *Watson* no-warrant-requirement rule. It is also clear that "public place" includes the inside of a privately owned commercial building open to the public, since the arrest in *Watson* occurred in a restaurant during working hours. There is a split of lower court authority, however, on whether *Watson* or *Payton* applies to the entry of a commercial facility not open to the general public.[40]

The *Watson-Payton* distinction is sometimes difficult to draw, even when an arrest occurs in the context of an arrestee's home. For example, in *United States v. Santana*,[41] the arresting officer testified that he found S standing directly in the open doorway of her house when he arrived without a warrant to arrest her. The Court stated that "one step forward would have put her outside [the house], one step backward would have put her in the vestibule of her residence." The *Santana* Court stated that although the threshold of her dwelling is "private" in the same way that her yard is, for purposes of the arrest-warrant rule S was standing in a "public place." According to the Court, she was standing in open view; as such, she was as "exposed to public view, speech, hearing, and touch as if she had been standing completely outside her house."

In *Santana*, S retreated into her home after she spotted the officers, who followed her inside. The Court justified the police entry on the independent ground of hot pursuit, an exception to *Payton* discussed below. However, if D had stood motionless in the

---

39. Akhil Reed Amar, *The Bill of Rights as a Constitution*, 100 Yale L.J. 1131, 1179 (1991). *See generally* § 10.01, *infra*.

40. *Compare* United States v. Ponce, 488 F. Supp. 226 (S.D.N.Y. 1980) (permitting entry of a warehouse through an ajar door) *with* United States v. Driver, 776 F.2d 807 (9th Cir. 1985) (requiring a warrant to enter a closed office inside a warehouse).

41. 427 U.S. 38 (1976).

doorway, her warrantless arrest would have been constitutional, as much so as if she had been standing on a public street.

A more difficult and controversial question relates to the following common scenario: In a non-emergency situation, *O*, a police officer, comes to *D*'s home without an arrest warrant; *O* knocks at the door; *D* opens the door; *O* arrests *D*. Here, unlike *Santana*, the arrestee is in her home, with the door shut, when the officer arrives. Under these circumstances, is a warrantless arrest valid? Does it matter whether part of *D*'s body— perhaps her toes—are minutely outside the home when she opens the door? Or, what if it is *O*'s toes that are, ever-so-slightly, *inside* the doorway of *D*'s premises? Or, suppose that *O* asks *D* to come outside, *D* obeys, at which moment the arrest occurs?

Lower courts are divided on how to deal with these and related scenarios.[42] Some courts take the view that if the arrestee is fully within the house, a warrantless arrest is invalid, even if the officer accomplishes the arrest without entering the home, on the ground that the critical issue is "not the location of the arresting officer," but rather is "the location of the arrestee."[43] But it should be remembered that *Payton* made much of the fact that there should not be a "breach of the entrance to an individual's home." As a consequence, some courts allow warrantless home arrests if the arrest can be effectuated without such a breach.[44] The latter approach allows police officers to avoid the strictures of *Payton* by careful planning,[45] but can also result in Fourth Amendment violations of a very technical nature.[46]

[b] Exigencies Justifying Warrantless Entry[47]

[i] Hot Pursuit

Warrantless entry of a home is permitted in hot pursuit of a fleeing felon. As the Court explained in *United States v. Santana*,[48] "hot pursuit" involves "some sort of chase [of the suspect], but it need not be an extended hue and cry 'in and about [the] public streets.'"

In *Santana*, police officers had probable cause, but no warrant, to arrest *S* for a felony. They arrived at *S*'s house, where they observed her standing in the doorway. Constitutionally speaking, this placed her in a "public place." When she observed the officers,

---

42. *See* 3 LaFave, Note 11, *supra*, at 301–309 (and cases cited therein).

43. State v. Holeman, 693 P.2d 89, 91 (Wash. 1985).

44. *E.g.*, State v. Santiago, 619 A.2d 1132 (Conn. 1993); *see* United States v. Berkowitz, 927 F.2d 1376, 1386 (7th Cir. 1991) ("*Payton* prohibits only a warrantless *entry* into the home, not a policeman's use of his voice to convey a message of arrest from outside the home.").

45. *E.g.*, People v. Gillam, 734 N.W.2d 585 (Mich. 2007) (the police, lacking an arrest warrant, did not "constructively enter" a home in violation of *Payton* by positioning themselves outside *G*'s apartment and repeatedly asking, but not coercing, him to step outside, at which point they arrested him; held: the arrest was constitutional); *but see* United States v. Reeves, 524 F.3d 1161 (10th Cir. 2008) (at 3:00 a.m., four officers, without an arrest warrant, went to a motel room where *R* was living; they knocked loudly on the door and windows for 20 minutes until *R* opened the door and stepped outside, at which time he was formally arrested; held: opening the door to one's home when ordered to do so constitutes a seizure of the homeowner inside the home and, therefore a de facto warrantless arrest in violation of *Payton*).

46. *E.g.*, State v. Johnson, 501 N.W.2d 876 (Wis. Ct. App. 1993) (the Fourth Amendment is violated if an officer, without a warrant, positions herself in the suspect's doorway, with her "toenails" to the "balls of [the] feet" inside the home).

47. *See also* § 11.04, *infra*.

48. 427 U.S. 38 (1976).

she retreated into her home, although she left the door open. The officers entered to arrest her.

The police entry of the home took the case outside of the *Watson* "public place" rule. Nonetheless, the Court justified the entry and warrantless arrest according to the hot pursuit doctrine: that is, the pursuit to arrest began in a public place and ended, albeit quickly, in the home.[49]

[ii] Other Exigencies

The Supreme Court has rarely indicated what exigencies, beyond hot pursuit, justify a warrantless entry of a home to make an arrest. However, in *Minnesota v. Olson*,[50] the Court said that the Minnesota Supreme Court "applied essentially the correct standard" for determining what circumstances justify a warrantless entry of a home to make an arrest.

Based on *Olson*, apparently the police may nonconsensually enter a home without a warrant not only in hot pursuit of a felon, but also if they have reasonable cause to believe that if they do not enter immediately: (1) evidence will be destroyed; (2) the suspect will escape; or (3) harm will result to the police or others either inside or outside the dwelling. In assessing the exigency, the gravity of the crime and the likelihood that the suspect is armed must be considered.

The gravity of the crime is sometimes a critical factor. *Olson* involved a felony arrest. The Supreme Court indicated in *Welsh v. Wisconsin*,[51] however, that "application of the exigent-circumstances exception in the context of a home entry should rarely be sanctioned when there is probable cause to believe that only a minor offense . . . has been committed." In *Welsh*, the Court declared unconstitutional the warrantless entry of *W*'s home in order to arrest *W* for driving his car under the influence of alcohol, an offense which constituted a noncriminal violation for which *W* only could have been fined $200. The Court rejected the government claim that the entry was necessary because evidence of the crime—the alcohol in *W*'s bloodstream—would have been imminently "destroyed" by bodily processes if the police could not enter quickly in order to test *W*'s blood-alcohol content. The Court stopped short of deciding whether the Constitution "impose[s] an absolute ban on warrantless home arrests for certain minor offenses." However, it observed that "it is difficult to conceive of a warrantless home arrest that would not be unreasonable . . . when the underlying offense is extremely minor."[52]

---

49. Sometimes the hot pursuit doctrine is invoked in questionable circumstances. For example, in *Warden v. Hayden*, 387 U.S. 294 (1967), the police had probable cause to believe that *H* had committed an armed robbery moments earlier and had entered a particular house. The Court upheld the officers' warrantless entry of the house to search for and arrest *H* on the basis of the "exigencies of the situation." Because the officers did not chase *H* from the scene of the crime to the house, *Hayden* did not "involve a "hot pursuit" in the sense that that term would normally be understood." *Santana*, 427 U.S. at 43 n.3. Nonetheless, the Court often treats *Hayden* as if it were a "hot pursuit" case. *E.g.*, Welsh v. Wisconsin, 466 U.S. 740, 750 (1984) (citing *Hayden* as a hot pursuit case). It would seem, therefore, that "hot pursuit," as a justification for entering a home, has come to mean either that the police started the pursuit or attempted the arrest while the person was in a public place or, in some circumstances, where the crime was committed moments earlier in a public place.

50. 495 U.S. 91 (1990).

51. 466 U.S. 740 (1984).

52. In *Welsh*, although the police claimed exigent circumstances, the police did not enter the home after "hot pursuit" (i.e., immediate or continuous pursuit from the scene of the crime) of

[D] Arrest in a Third Person's Home

Payton teaches that when the police seek to enter a person's own home in order to arrest her, they must (absent consent or an emergency) have an *arrest* warrant. A search warrant is not required. Therefore, if the police search *D*'s home looking for *D*, for whom they have an arrest warrant, any evidence they find in plain view[53] may be seized and used against *D*, although they lack a search warrant.

Suppose, however, that the police have reason to believe that the person whom they wish to arrest is not at home, but is a guest in another person's residence. Does the *arrest* warrant provide the police with the limited authority to enter the third party's residence and search for the arrestee, or do they now need a *search* warrant? *Payton* left this question unanswered. *Steagald v. United States*[54] answered it.

In *Steagald*, the police had information that *L*, for whom they had an arrest warrant, could be "reached during the next 24 hours" at *S*'s home. The officers did not go to *S*'s premises for a few days. When they did, they entered without consent, did not find *L*, but observed illegal drugs that resulted in *S*'s arrest. The Supreme Court held that the arrest warrant for *L* was an inadequate safeguard of *S*'s independent Fourth Amendment right to privacy in his own home. The *arrest* warrant served to prevent *L*'s arrest on less than probable cause; it did not protect *S*'s right to reasonable security in his home.

The Court ruled that a person whose home is searched for the presence of a guest is entitled, absent an emergency or consent, to a prior judicial determination of probable cause to search the premises for the person to be arrested. Without this protection, the Court observed, there would be a "significant potential for abuse," in that the police, armed only with an arrest warrant, "could search all the homes of that individual's friends and acquaintances" in the speculative hope of finding evidence against the latter parties.[55]

Steagald creates line-drawing problems. When the residence that is entered is, as *Payton* put it, the "dwelling in which the suspect lives," an arrest warrant is required, but a search warrant need not be obtained. When a person is a "guest" in another person's home, a search warrant is required. The line between a householder (*Payton*) and a guest (*Steagald*) can be thin.

Some cases are easy to decide. After all, in *Payton* itself, other people—*D2*'s three-year-old son, for example—lived with *D2*. The son's (and other family members") privacy rights were threatened by the police entry, but an arrest warrant would have been sufficient. It follows, therefore, that where *D* and *X* are co-residents of a home, *Payton*

Welsh. That fact may be significant. Recently, in a case involving hot pursuit of a misdemeanant to his home, the Supreme Court observed that *Welsh* "did not lay down a categorical rule for all cases involving minor offenses, saying only that a warrant is 'usually' required [in such cases]." Stanton v. Sims, 134 S. Ct. 1, 6 (2013) (*per curiam*). *Stanton* further observed (without announcing any new rule) that "despite our emphasis in *Welsh* on the fact that the crime at issue [in that case] was minor . . . nothing in the opinion establishes that the seriousness of the crime is equally important *in cases of hot pursuit*."

53. *See* Chapter 14, *infra*, regarding the plain view doctrine.

54. 451 U.S. 204 (1981).

55. As noted in the text, in *Steagald*, the intended arrestee, *L*, was not present. Had he been present and arrested pursuant to the valid arrest warrant, however, *L* would *not* have been able to have any evidence seized at *S*'s home suppressed in *L*'s prosecution, because *L*'s Fourth Amendment rights (as opposed to those of the homeowner) were not infringed. *See generally* Chapter 19, *infra*, regarding the "standing" doctrine.

applies. At the other extreme, where a person is a short-term daytime guest of another, *Steagald* applies.

What about an overnight guest? In *Steagald*, *L* was expected to be at *S*'s house "during the next 24 hours," which would suggest he was staying overnight. Furthermore, the police did not enter for a few more days, which suggests that they may have assumed that he was still living there. Yet, on these facts, the majority required a search warrant. Thus, a brief stay, even if this includes sleeping on the premises, apparently does not convert a guest into a householder for *Payton-Steagald* purposes.

§ 9.06 Beyond Warrants: Executing an Arrest[56]

[A] Arrests in the Home: When and How Entry of the Residence Is Permitted

The Fourth Amendment "require[s] that police actions in execution of a warrant be related to the objectives of the authorized intrusion."[57] This means that a valid arrest warrant "carries with it the limited authority to enter a dwelling in which the suspect lives *when there is reason to believe the suspect is within*."[58] In the absence of such a reasonable basis, the police may not justify entry of a home on the basis of an arrest warrant.

Even if an officer has reason to know the suspect is inside a residence, the pre-constitutional common law provided that an officer was not generally permitted to enter a home by force to execute a warrant, unless he knocked, announced his purpose for entering, requested admittance, and was not granted entry. As discussed more fully elsewhere,[59] the Supreme Court ruled in *Wilson v. Arkansas*[60] that this common law "principle forms a part of the reasonableness inquiry under the Fourth Amendment." Specifically, a police officer—even one armed with a warrant—may not ordinarily enter a residence without satisfying this so-called "knock-and-announce" requirement. Although *Wilson* involved entry to conduct a search, this rule presumably applies to arrests, as well.

[B] Force in Making an Arrest

The Fourth Amendment prohibits unreasonable seizures of persons (and property). As a consequence, police officers must not only possess probable cause to make an arrest, but they must not use excessive—i.e., unreasonable—force in seizing a person, whether to arrest or temporarily detain her. This statement of generality, however, obscures considerable detail and evolution in the Supreme Court's approach to the issue.

The Court's first significant Fourth Amendment decision in the "excessive force" field concerned deadly force. Until the fourteenth century, agents of the Crown were permitted to use deadly force to kill fleeing felons, regardless of the felony, and

---

56. *See also* § 10.04, *infra*.
57. Wilson v. Layne, 526 U.S. 603, 611 (1999).
58. Payton v. New York, 445 U.S. 573, 603 (1980) (emphasis added).
59. See § 10.04[C], *infra*.
60. 514 U.S. 927 (1995).

regardless of whether such force was necessary in order to prevent the escape. Eventually a necessity component was added to the rule, but it remained the case that deadly force was permissible to prevent any felon, even a non-violent one, from avoiding arrest.[61]

In *Tennessee v. Garner*,[62] the Supreme Court held that this common law rule, codified in many states, is unconstitutionally broad.[63] In *Garner*, O, an officer, was dispatched to a home on a "prowler inside call." He observed G fleeing in the direction of a six-foot-high chain-link fence. By use of his flashlight, O could tell that G was young, 5′5″ to 5′7″ tall, and apparently unarmed. He ordered G to halt; when the youth began to scale the fence, O shot him in the back of the head, killing him.

The Supreme Court, per Justice Byron White, held that O's use of deadly force (typically defined as force intended or likely to cause death or grievous bodily harm) to prevent the escape of G, an apparently unarmed felon, violated the Fourth Amendment. It stated that "[t]he use of deadly force to prevent the escape of all felony suspects, whatever the circumstances, is constitutionally unreasonable. It is not better that all felony suspects die than that they escape."

Garner seemingly announced a rule applicable to all cases of deadly force used to prevent a suspect from escaping arrest: Deadly force is unreasonable, even if there is probable cause for the arrest, unless two conditions are met: (1) the officer must have "probable cause to believe that the suspect poses a significant threat of death or serious physical injury to the officer or others"; and (2) the officer must reasonably believe that deadly force is necessary to make the arrest or prevent escape.

The Court would later announce that *Garner*'s reasoning is not confined to deadly-force cases. In *Graham v. Connor*,[64] the Court, stating that it was making "explicit what was implicit in *Garner*'s analysis," held "that *all* claims that law enforcement officers have used excessive force—deadly or not—in the course of an arrest, investigatory stop, or other 'seizure' of a free citizen should be analyzed under the Fourth Amendment . . . 'reasonableness' standard." Among the relevant factors to be considered, the Court stated, are the seriousness of the crime, the extent to which the suspect poses an immediate threat to the safety of others, and the extent to which the suspect is resisting arrest or attempting to escape.

In 2007, in *Scott v. Harris*,[65] the justices returned to the issue of police use of deadly force. In doing so, however, it effectively reconstructed the lesson of *Garner*. In *Harris*, police officers rammed a fleeing motorist's car from behind during a high-speed chase that began when they sought to ticket the motorist for speeding. The motorist survived the incident and brought suit against the police under *Garner*, asserting that the officers failed to meet the two preconditions to use of deadly force set out in that case.

---

61. See Dressler, Note 8, *supra*, at §21.03[B].

62. 471 U.S. 1 (1985); *see generally* Abraham N. Tennenbaum, *The Influence of the Garner Decision on Police Use of Deadly Force*, 85 J. Crim. L. & Criminology 241 (1994); H. Richard Uviller, *Seizure by Gunshot: The Riddle of the Fleeing Felon*, 14 N.Y.U. Rev. L. & Soc. Change, 705 (1986).

63. In most cases, as in *Garner*, the issue of alleged use of unnecessary force arises in the context of a civil suit against the officer for the wrongful death of the suspect or violation of the citizen's constitutional rights under 42 U.S.C. §1983. The rule announced in *Garner* only raises potential Fourth Amendment exclusionary rule issues if the suspect survives the excessive force, and the prosecutor seeks to introduce evidence obtained from the arrestee as the result of the purportedly unreasonable police conduct.

64. 490 U.S. 386 (1989).

65. 550 U.S. 372 (2007).

The *Scott* Court agreed that the police action here "posed a high likelihood of serious injury or death" to the motorist and, thus, constituted deadly force. They further acknowledged that the police could have avoided the risk of killing the motorist by terminating pursuit of him. Nonetheless, in an opinion authored by Justice Scalia, the Court held that the officers' action did not violate the Fourth Amendment, and further stated:

> *Garner* does not establish a magical on/off switch that triggers rigid preconditions whenever an officer's actions constitute "deadly force." *Garner* was simply an application of the Fourth Amendment's "reasonableness" test . . . to the use of a particular type of force in a particular situation. . . . Whatever *Garner* said about the factors that *might have* justified shooting the suspect in that case, such "preconditions" have scant applicability to this case, which has vastly different facts.[66]

Although the Court did not back off from its specific holding in *Garner*, it warned that "in the end we must still slosh through the fact-bound morass of 'reasonableness.'" And, in that sloshing process, the Court added an additional factor to those set out in *Graham*, to be weighed in the "reasonableness" analysis: the "relative culpability" of the persons who lives are put at risk. That is, in evaluating the reasonableness of the police action here, Justice Scalia stated that it was appropriate to treat the life of the motorist, whose choice to flee put himself and innocent persons at physical risk, as a less weighty interest than that of an innocent person.

The Court reinforced this principle in *Plumhoff v. Rickard*, in which the suspect led police on a high-speed chase that at some points exceeded 100 miles per hour.[67] At one point the police appeared to have the car cornered, but the driver continued to use the accelerator, even as his car was flush against a police car. At that point the officers fired three shots into his car, and then as the car began to speed away, the officers fired 12 more shots at the car, causing it to crash, killing the driver and a passenger. The Court held that the use of force was reasonable, and quoted *Scott*: "A police officer's attempt to terminate a dangerous high-speed car chase that threatens the lives of innocent bystanders does not violate the Fourth Amendment, even when it places the fleeing motorist at risk of serious injury or death."[68] Although the driver in *Plumhoff* appeared to be trapped at one point, the police reasonably concluded that the chase was not over and that the driver still posed a serious threat to bystanders.

§ 9.07 Beyond Warrants: Use of Force after Arrest

After a suspect is arrested, he is often held in custody before trial. During that period, police officers may need to use force (or believe they need to use force) to ensure

---

66. *Id.* at 382. *But see* Karen M. Blum, *Scott v. Harris: Death Knell for Deadly Force Policies and Garner Jury Instructions*, 58 Syracuse L. Rev. 45, 59 (2007) (describing this statement of the Court's as "simply wrong, or, at best misguided, and reflects an exercise in reconstruction of a case that has clearly stood for more than its particular facts for over twenty years").

67. 134 S. Ct. 2012 (2014).

68. *Scott,* 550 U.S. at 385.

that he complies with their commands. What are the limits of this use of force? In *Kingsley v. Hendrickson*,[69] the Supreme Court held that a pretrial detainee can prove that the use of force against him was excessive if he can show that the force "purposely or knowingly used against him was objectively unreasonable" under the circumstances. K was in jail awaiting trial on a drug charge, and he refused to leave his cell when police officers ordered him to do so. The officers forcibly handcuffed him, removed him from the cell, and then placed him face down on a bunk. The officers alleged that when they tried to remove the handcuffs he continued to be uncooperative, so they placed a knee on his back and then stunned him with a Taser gun for five seconds. K ultimately sued the officers for excessive use of force, arguing that their actions violated the Due Process Clause of the Fourteenth Amendment.

The Court held that there were two steps in evaluating a claim for excessive force in the pretrial detention context. First, the detainee must prove that the officers "purposely or knowingly" used force against him — in other words, "if an officer's Taser goes off by accident or if an officer unintentionally trips and falls on a detainee," there is no way to prove an excessive force claim.[70] Second, the detainee must prove that the use of force was unreasonable under the circumstances. There is no need to prove that the officer using the force believed it to be unreasonable or was even aware of a risk that it was unreasonable.

---

69. 135 S. Ct. 2466 (2015).
70. *Id.* at 2472.

Chapter 10

Search Warrants: In General

§ 10.01 The Constitutional Role of Search Warrants: The Debate[1]

[A] Nature and Significance of the Debate

The first clause of the Fourth Amendment (the Reasonableness Clause) provides that "the right of the people to be secure . . . against unreasonable searches and seizures shall not be violated." The Amendment's second clause (the Warrant Clause) states that "no Warrants shall issue, but upon probable cause, supported by Oath or affirmation, and particularly describing the place to be searched, and the persons or things to be seized." The relationship, if any, of these two clauses is a "syntactical mystery,"[2] and is a matter of considerable controversy.

There are two schools of thought regarding the relationship of the two clauses. One view is that they are vitally linked; specifically, "the Warrant Clause defines and interprets the Reasonableness Clause."[3] According to this view, "[t]he command of the Fourth Amendment to the American police officer and the American prosecutor is simple: 'You always have to get a warrant—UNLESS YOU CAN'T.'"[4] Or, as one scholar put it, "a warrant is *always* required for *every* search and seizure when it is practicable to obtain one."[5]

---

1. *See generally* Akhil Reed Amar, *Fourth Amendment First Principles*, 107 Harv. L. Rev. 757 (1994); Craig M. Bradley, *Two Models of the Fourth Amendment*, 83 Mich. L. Rev. 1468 (1985); Sherry F. Colb, *The Qualitative Dimension of Fourth Amendment "Reasonableness*," 98 Colum. L. Rev. 1642 (1998); Thomas Y. Davies, *Recovering the Original Fourth Amendment*, 98 Mich. L. Rev. 547 (1999); Thomas Y. Davies, *Correcting Search-and-Seizure History: Now-Forgotten Common-Law Warrantless Arrest Standards and the Original Understanding of "Due Process of Law*," 77 Miss. L.J. 1 (2007); Joseph D. Grano, *Rethinking the Fourth Amendment Warrant Requirement*, 19 Am. Crim. L. Rev. 603 (1982); William W. Greenhalgh & Mark J. Yost, *In Defense of the "Per Se" Rule: Justice Stewart's Struggle to Preserve the Fourth Amendment's Warrant Clause*, 31 Am. Crim. L. Rev. 1013 (1994); Tracey Maclin, *When the Cure For the Fourth Amendment Is Worse Than the Disease*, 68 S. Cal. L. Rev. 1 (1994); Carol S. Steiker, *Second Thoughts About First Principles*, 107 Harv. L. Rev. 820 (1994); James J. Tomkovicz, *California v. Acevedo: The Walls Close In on the Warrant Requirement*, 29 Am. Crim. L. Rev. 1103 (1992); H. Richard Uviller, *Reasonability and the Fourth Amendment: A (Belated) Farewell to Justice Potter Stewart*, 25 Crim. L. Bull. 29 (1989); Oren Bar-Gill & Barry Friedman, *Taking Warrants Seriously*, 106 Nw. U. L. Rev. 1609 (2012).

2. Uviller, Note 1, *supra*, at 33.

3. Maclin, Note 1, *supra*, at 20.

4. Dyson v. State, 712 A.2d 573, 577 (Md. App. 1997), *rev'd*, Maryland v. Dyson, 527 U.S. 465 (1999).

5. Bradley, Note 1, *supra*, at 1471. *See also* Bar-Gill & Friedman, Note 1, *supra*, at 1614 (contending that search warrants "should be required any time obtaining a warrant is feasible or, in other words, any time exigent circumstances are not present;" applying social science literature to defend the proposition that such a bright-light rule would have positive results in deterring constitutional violations).

The Supreme Court expressed this "warrant requirement" (or, perhaps more accurately, "warrant preference") rule in *Katz v. United States*,[6] when it provided that "searches conducted outside the judicial process, without prior approval by judge or magistrate, are *per se* unreasonable under the Fourth Amendment — subject only to a few specifically established and well-delineated exceptions." Advocates of this rule believe that exceptions to the warrant requirement should be "jealously and carefully drawn,"[7] and permitted only on "a showing . . . that the exigencies of the situation [make] that course imperative."[8]

The competing position is that the preference for search warrants was "judicially created"[9] and is not constitutionally required. According to this view, the Warrant Clause does not inform the Reasonableness Clause; the clauses — although it should be noted that they are separated by a comma, and not a semi-colon — are independent of each other. Advocates of this model believe that the first clause of the Fourth Amendment "speaks globally to all searches and seizures,"[10] and provides simply that they must be reasonable, taking into consideration all relevant factors.[11] As the Supreme Court put it in *United States v. Rabinowitz*,[12] the appropriate test of police conduct "is not whether it is reasonable to procure a search warrant, but whether the search is reasonable." According to this view, the purpose of the Warrant Clause is to tell us "when warrants may *not* issue, not when they may, or must."[13] It informs us that "any warrant that *does* issue is per se unreasonable if not supported by probable cause, particular description, and the rest."[14]

The practical significance of the debate is enormous. Strict enforcement of a warrant requirement would compel police officers to apply for warrants in the vast majority of cases. In such a system, judges, rather than the police, would make nearly all probable-cause determinations. On the other hand, warrants would be a comparative rarity under the alternative model. The police would determine whether to impose on a citizen's privacy, and the judiciary would have the more limited role of determining, after the incursion, whether the police conduct was reasonable.

[B] The Substance of the Debate

[1] Historical Debate

Years ago, Professor Telford Taylor claimed that those "who have viewed the fourth amendment primarily as a requirement that searches be covered by warrants, have stood the amendment on its head."[15] Opponents of a warrant requirement reason that

---

6. 389 U.S. 347 (1967).
7. Jones v. United States, 357 U.S. 493, 499 (1958).
8. McDonald v. United States, 335 U.S. 451, 456 (1948).
9. Robbins v. California, 453 U.S. 420, 438 (1981) (Rehnquist, J., dissenting).
10. Amar, Note 1, *supra*, at 762.
11. *See* Terry v. Ohio, 392 U.S. 1, 21 (1968) (quoting Camara v. Municipal Court, 387 U.S. 523, 536–37 (1967)) ("there is 'no ready test for determining reasonableness other than by balancing the need to search [or seize] against the invasion which the search [or seizure] entails'"); Bradley, Note 1, *supra*, at 1471 ("[a] search or seizure must be reasonable, considering all relevant factors on a case-by-case basis").
12. 339 U.S. 56 (1950), *overruled on other grounds*, Chimel v. California, 395 U.S. 752 (1969).
13. Amar, Note 1, *supra*, at 774 (emphasis added).
14. *Id.* at 762 (emphasis added).
15. Telford Taylor, Two Studies in Constitutional Interpretation 46–47 (1969).

the framers of the Fourth Amendment were not concerned that the executive branch of government, including the police, would usurp its authority; instead, they feared the judiciary, which in the colonial era authorized abusive general warrants and writs of assistance.[16] In short, in the framers' eyes, judges were "the heavies, not the heroes, of our story."[17] It makes no sense, therefore, to think that the Fourth Amendment is intended to compel the police to seek judicial approval before they conduct searches.

In further support of this reading of history, opponents of a warrant requirement point out that, at common law, warrantless arrests were permissible in many circumstances, and warrantless searches incident to arrests were also allowed. Moreover, the First Congress, which proposed the Fourth Amendment, passed legislation authorizing federal naval inspectors to enter and conduct warrantless searches of ships.[18] According to Professor Akhil Amar, "[i]f any members of the early Congresses objected to or even questioned these warrantless searches and seizures on Fourth Amendment grounds, supporters of the so-called warrant requirement have yet to identify them."[19]

In response, proponents of the warrant-requirement rule contend that the preceding arguments are wrong or go too far. They agree that the drafters of the Fourth Amendment intended for the Warrant Clause to prevent abusive warrants, but they do not believe that this was the sole purpose of the clause. They make a textual claim: "On any fair reading, this language appears to assume that searches and seizures will be conducted, at least sometimes, pursuant to warrants."[20] Were it otherwise, a legislature could evade the probable cause and particularity requirements of the Warrant Clause by the simple expedient of abolishing all warrants. Thus, unless there is at least *some* warrant requirement, a legislature could render the constitutional text useless.

Moreover, the history of the Fourth Amendment is not as clear as opponents of the warrant requirement suggest. According to Professor Joseph Grano, "[w]hile the colonists did not object to warrantless searches, the reason for the absence of such objection was that such searches, except perhaps in the context of lawful arrests, simply did not exist."[21] Indeed, Telford Taylor concluded from his historical survey that the correct principle of law in colonial time was that "searches incident to arrests [were] permissible, and in exceptional cases, *if authorized by warrant*, searches independent of arrest [could] be carried out."[22]

According to some advocates of a warrant requirement, the "history of the Fourth Amendment is about controlling executive power."[23] Professor Anthony Amsterdam has suggested that "the fourth amendment is quintessentially a regulation of the police — that, in enforcing the fourth amendment, courts *must* police the police."[24]

---

16. *See* § 4.03, *supra.*

17. Akhil Reed Amar, *The Bill of Rights as a Constitution*, 100 Yale L.J. 1131, 1179 (1991).

18. Professor Thomas Davies contends that ship search legislation does *not* reveal the framers' view of the Fourth Amendment, because ships were not viewed as "effects" that enjoyed common law security in 1789. Thomas Y. Davies, *The Fictional Character of Law-and-Order Originalism: A Case Study of the Distortions and Evasions of Framing-Era Arrest Doctrine in Atwater v. Lago Vista*, 37 Wake Forest L. Rev. 237, 262, 265 (2002).

19. Amar, Note 1, *supra*, at 766–67.

20. Grano, Note 1, *supra*, at 617.

21. *Id.*

22. Taylor, Note 15, *supra*, at 49.

23. Maclin, Note 1, *supra*, at 5 (emphasis added).

24. Anthony G. Amsterdam, *Perspectives on the Fourth Amendment*, 58 Minn. L. Rev. 349, 371 (1974).

So, who is right? Professor Thomas Davies's recent research suggests that the "Framers' complaints were not about warrantless intrusions but were almost exclusively about . . . searches of houses under general warrants."[25] Nonetheless, Davies contends that the "warrant-preference construction [of the Fourth Amendment] is more faithful to the Framers' concerns than the generalized-reasonableness construction. *In fact, the latter is nearly the antithesis of the Framers' understanding.*"[26] Davies believes that the framers' lack of attention to warrantless police action was a function of historical factors irrelevant in modern times:

> [I]t made sense for the Framers to focus only on clarifying warrant standards because the *ex officio* authority of the framing-era officer was still rather meager. For example, the framing-era constable's arrest authority was much narrower than is generally supposed, and nowhere near that of a modern police officer. Likewise, the justifications available for a warrantless entry of a house were especially limited. At common law, controlling the warrant *did* control the officer for all practical purposes.[27]

As Davies reads the historical evidence, the immediate purpose of the Fourth Amendment was to prohibit general warrants and their like, but "the larger purpose for which the Framers adopted the text . . . [was] to curb the exercise of discretionary authority by officers."[28]

[2] Policy Debate

Proponents of a warrant-requirement rule also argue that even if history conclusively supported the claims of opponents, this would not resolve the debate. Many of them favor "constitutional dynamism—the principle that interpretations of the Constitution will and should change over time to accommodate the needs of different historical ages."[29] Current needs, warrant advocates contend, provide compelling reasons for demanding that a police officer ordinarily obtain a warrant before conducting a search.

In *Johnson v. United States*,[30] the Supreme Court explained the policy in favor of warrants this way:

> The point of the Fourth Amendment, which often is not grasped by zealous officers, is not that it denies law enforcement the support of the usual inferences which reasonable men draw from evidence. Its protection consists in requiring that those inferences be drawn by a neutral and detached magistrate instead of being judged by the officer engaged in the often competitive enterprise of ferreting out crime. Any assumption that evidence sufficient to support a magistrate's disinterested determination to issue a search warrant will justify the

---

25. Davies, *Recovering*, Note 1, *supra*, at 553.

26. *Id.* at 556 (emphasis added).

27. *Id.* at 554.

28. *Id.* at 556.

29. Steiker, Note 1, *supra*, at 825–26; *see* Maclin, Note 1, *supra*, at 11 (the Fourth Amendment "states an ideal; it is not a constitutional wrench that 'locks-in' search and seizure practices of a vanished era"); *see also* Davies, *Recovering*, Note 1, *supra*, at 556 ("I . . . doubt[] that the original meaning [of the Amendment] can be directly applied to address modern issues. . . . [I]t would be inappropriate to employ framing-era doctrines selectively to answer specific modern issues because historic doctrines often do not accomplish the same ends in the modern context as they did during the framing era.").

30. 333 U.S. 10 (1948).

officers in making a search without a warrant would reduce the Amendment to a nullity and leave the people's homes secure only in the discretion of police officers.

Essentially, the argument is this: The Fourth Amendment "is designed to prevent, not simply to redress, unlawful police action."[31] Therefore, if people are going to be secure in their persons, houses, papers, and effects from unreasonable searches and seizures, as the Fourth Amendment guarantees, a neutral party—the judge, and not the police officer (nor, for that matter, the person whose privacy or security is at risk)—should make the initial determination whether there is sufficient basis to intrude on an individual's security. Warrant advocates also suggest that a magistrate's intervention between the police and a citizen is more important today than in the eighteenth century, in light of the enhanced authority claimed by government over the lives of individuals, the more intrusive crime prevention tools available to law enforcement, and racial divisions.[32]

In response, opponents of the warrant requirement contend that "if taken seriously, a warrant requirement makes no sense."[33] Professor Akhil Amar defends this position by noting that nobody believes that warrants are *always* required. For example, there must be an exception for exigent circumstances. It also makes no sense to him that the police should be barred from conducting a warrantless search if they receive consent to do so. Moreover, nobody would seriously claim that a warrant is required before an officer seizes an object in plain view, or before guards x-ray luggage at an airport. He contends that, in view of the "vast number of real-life, unintrusive, non-discriminatory searches and seizures to which modern day Americans are routinely subjected,"[34] the warrant requirement, as an absolute, cannot withstand scrutiny.

Advocates of a warrant requirement concede that there are exceptions.[35] In essence, the argument is that there is not a constitutional warrant *requirement*, but rather a constitutional *preference* for, or *presumption* of, warrants. Professor Amar contends, however, that since there are no exceptions to the supposed warrant requirement in the text of the Fourth Amendment—the courts just make them up as they go along—this "modification seems to concede that the ultimate touchstone of the Amendment is not warrants, but reasonableness."[36] Our common sense tells us, he suggests, that "reasonableness" is the proper rule: if the Supreme Court accepted this proposition, it and lower courts would not have to play "word games" to avoid the Warrant Clause, such as by suggesting that some searches are not really searches at all,[37] and that "probable cause" does not really mean "probable."[38]

But, if reasonableness *is* the touchstone, what then? Amar concedes that, if "reasonableness" is going to be evaluated on a case-by-case basis,[39] this standard involves a

---

31. Chimel v. California, 395 U.S. 752, 766 n.12 (1969).

32. *See* Steiker, Note 1, *supra*, at 830–44.

33. Amar, Note 1, *supra*, at 767–68.

34. *Id.* at 769.

35. However, some advocates argue that these exceptions should be shrinking in number, since new technology has increased the speed and convenience of warrant applications. For example, Professors Oren Bar-Gill and Barry Friedman propose that warrants should be required any time exigent circumstances are not present: "[f]easibility and exigency are both functions of technology, which operates in today's world to favor warrants." Bar-Gill & Friedman, Note 1, *supra*.

36. *Id.* at 771.

37. *See* § 6.01[A], *supra*.

38. *See* § 8.07[A], *supra*.

39. But perhaps it should not be. See Note 51, *infra*.

"complex equation" that demands of police officers and the courts that they balance a myriad of factors, including the probability of finding the evidence in question, "the intrusiveness of the search, the identity of the search target, the availability of other means of achieving the purpose of the search, and so on."[40] Just as noted in the context of "probable cause,"[41] "reasonableness" converts the Fourth Amendment into "one immense Rorschach blot,"[42] which would be "splendid in its flexibility, [but] awful in its unintelligibility, unadministrability, unenforceability and general ooziness."[43] In view of the vagueness — ooziness — of the standard, proponents of the warrant requirement fear that "courts are seldom going to say that what [the police] did was unreasonable."[44]

[C] Who Has "Won" the Debate?

The Supreme Court's Fourth Amendment "jurisprudence [has] lurched back and forth between imposing a categorical warrant requirement and looking to reasonableness alone."[45] In the early years of Fourth Amendment law, a long line of cases suggested that searches had to be conducted "pursuant to a warrant or . . . fall within one of the exceptions to the warrant requirement."[46] The Court's position became muddy in the late 1940s and 1950s, however, and remained so until the Supreme Court's *Katz*[47] decision in 1967.

The warrant-requirement rule re-emerged forcefully with *Katz*. During the next 15 years or so, the Court fairly consistently reaffirmed the supremacy of the Warrant Clause. Yet, even as it did so, it approved new and broader exceptions to the "warrant requirement." As a consequence, "the Supreme Court . . . created a jurisprudential mare's nest,"[48] in which the exceptions to the "requirement" seemingly gobbled up the rule. A leading judicial advocate of the warrant requirement during this era was Justice Potter Stewart, who retired in 1981. Justice Byron White was a leading advocate of the competing "reasonableness" interpretation of the Fourth Amendment.

With Justice Stewart's departure, the Supreme Court increasingly moved away from the principle of a warrant requirement. "Warrant requirement" language is now typically found in dissenting opinions.[49] Majority opinions now state that "[t]he touchstone

---

40. Amar, Note 1, *supra*, at 801.

41. *See* § 8.07[C][2], *supra*.

42. Amsterdam, Note 24, *supra*, at 393.

43. *Id.* at 415.

44. *Id.* at 394.

45. California v. Acevedo, 500 U.S. 565, 582 (1991) (Scalia, J., concurring in the judgment).

46. Greenhalgh & Yost, Note 1, *supra*, at 1041.

47. Katz v. United States, 389 U.S. 347 (1967).

48. Hulit v. State, 982 S.W.2d 431, 436 (Tex. Crim. App. 1998).

49. Sometimes, however, a majority opinion — perhaps when the author wants to muster additional votes — will express a softened version of the "warrant requirement." For example, in *Kentucky v. King*, 563 U.S. 452, 459 (2011), Justice Alito, writing for all of the Court except Justice Ginsburg (who is herself a "warrant requirement" advocate), stated that "[a]lthough the text of the Fourth Amendment does not specify when a search warrant must be obtained, this Court has inferred that a warrant must generally be secured." Later, Justice Alito stated that "the warrant requirement is subject to certain reasonable exceptions." *E.g.*, Fernandez v. California, 134 S. Ct. 1126, 1139 (2014) (Ginsburg, J., dissenting) (stating that the "Court has . . . declared warrantless searches, in the main, '*per se* unreasonable'"; and stating that "[i]f this main rule is to remain hardy, . . . exceptions to the warrant requirement must be 'few in number and carefully delineated'").

of the Fourth Amendment is reasonableness."[50] Indeed, it now appears that a majority of the justices sitting on the Supreme Court believe not only that the reasonableness rule should predominate, but that courts should look initially to pre-constitutional common law for an understanding of what constitutes a reasonable search or seizure. In *Wyoming v Houghton*,[51] the Court stated:

> In determining whether a particular governmental action violates [the Fourth Amendment], we inquire first whether the action was regarded as an unlawful search or seizure under the common law when the Amendment was framed. Where that inquiry yields no answer, we must evaluate the search or seizure under traditional standards of reasonableness by assessing, on the one hand, the degree to which it intrudes upon an individual's privacy and, on the other hand, the degree to which it is needed for the promotion of legitimate governmental interests.[52]

This sea-change in the Court's attitude may also be seen in the following justification for dispensing with a warrant requirement for the search of containers found in automobiles:

> To the extent that the [warrant-requirement] rule protects privacy, its protection is minimal. Law enforcement officers may seize a container and hold it until they obtain a search warrant. . . . "Since the police, by hypothesis, have probable cause to seize the property, we can assume that a warrant will be routinely forthcoming in the overwhelming majority of cases."[53]

The Court's conclusion that warrants would be "routinely forthcoming" when the police seize a container they wish to search demonstrates that the Court no longer believes that there is a pressing need to impose a neutral arbiter between the police and the citizenry before searches are conducted. In light of this reasoning, one scholar has predicted that "the Court is 'substantively,' if not 'formally,' headed toward" the conclusion that "the warrant rule is unsound or [at least] that it has no application outside the home."[54]

The latter proposition—that the Court might retain a warrant requirement, albeit subject to various exceptions, in the limited context of the home[55]—seems more likely than that the Court will abandon warrants entirely. Indeed, Justice Scalia, an advocate

---

50. *E.g.*, Florida v. Jimeno, 500 U.S. 248, 250 (1991). *See also* Riley v. California, 134 S. Ct. 2473, 2482 (2014); Fernandez v. California, 134 S. Ct. 1126, 1132 (opinion by Justice Alito). Indeed, in *Fernandez*, the facts that the police very likely had probable cause to conduct the search and a warrant was readily available, were deemed "beside the point."

51. 526 U.S. 295, 299–300 (1999); *see generally* David A. Sklansky, *The Fourth Amendment and Common Law*, 100 Colum. L. Rev. 1739 (2000).

52. In *Houghton, supra*, as well as in various other Fourth Amendment cases (e.g., Atwater v. Lago Vista, 532 U.S. 318 (2001), discussed in § 9.03, *supra*), the Supreme Count has eschewed fact-intensive case-by-case "reasonableness" analysis in favor of a "reasonableness" rule that applies to an entire category of cases.

53. California v. Acevedo, 500 U.S. at 575 (quoting the dissenting opinion in Arkansas v. Sanders, 442 U.S. 753, 770 (1979)).

54. Tomkovicz, Note 1, *supra*, at 1176–77.

55. Where would such a rule leave the homeless? Indeed, do the homeless have a reasonable expectation of privacy in their belongings, or are they shut out of Fourth Amendment protection entirely? This issue has rarely been considered by the courts. *But see* State v. Mooney, 588 A.2d 145 (Conn. 1991) (involving a search of a homeless person's belongings left unattended under a bridge); *see generally, e.g.*, Mark A. Godsey, *Privacy and the Growing Plight of the Homeless: Reconsidering the Values Underlying the Fourth Amendment*, 53 Ohio St. L.J. 869 (1992); Peter Mancini, *Mooney and Privacy: Some Tough Questions*, 72 B.U. L. Rev. 425 (1992); Kevin Royer, *The Mooney Blues:*

of the "reasonableness" rule, has indicated that he believes that warrants *are* required in limited circumstances—"where the common law required a warrant [presumably, in searches of homes]; and . . . [if] changes in the surrounding legal rules . . . make a warrant indispensable to reasonableness where it once was not."[56]

In any event, for the time being, lawyers and courts must frequently talk about a "warrant requirement" or, more accurately, about "exceptions" to the "warrant requirement." This is because the Supreme Court has not cleared the deck of many of its rulings from the earlier era. Thus, there are many explicit "exceptions" to the "warrant requirement" that were formulated in the middle of the twentieth century that remain good law today, even if the underlying reasoning may increasingly seem dated.

§ 10.02 The Warrant Application Process[57]

An investigating officer who seeks a warrant prepares an application for a search (or arrest) warrant; an affidavit sworn under oath or by affirmation setting out the facts supporting the warrant; and the warrant itself.[58] Often, the officer then seeks approval of the documents from a police supervisor or, in some jurisdictions, an assistant prosecutor.

Once approval is obtained, the officer goes to the courthouse or, if necessary, to the home of a judge.[59] When choices are available, such as in large urban areas, judge-shopping is common: the officer seeks a judge known to issue warrants liberally.[60] During the daytime, the officer ordinarily presents the application to the judge while he is on the bench or in chambers, during a court recess.

Ideally, the judge carefully reads the officer's documents and questions him regarding any ambiguities in the materials. When the application includes hearsay information, which is common, the judge should be expected to question the officer, if needed, to determine whether the informant's basis of knowledge was good and his veracity high.

Homelessness and Constitutional Security from Unreasonable Searches, 72 B.U. L. Rev. 443 (1992). As for people who live in their vehicle, *see* § 13.04, *infra*.

56. California v. Acevedo, 500 U.S. at 583 (concurring in the judgment).

57. *See generally* Laurence A. Benner & Charles T. Samarkos, *Searching for Narcotics in San Diego: Preliminary Findings from the San Diego Search Warrant Project*, 36 Cal. West. L. Rev. 222 (2000); Richard Van Duizend et al., The Search Warrant Process: Preconceptions, Perceptions, and Practices (National Center for State Courts ed. 1984); Abraham S. Goldstein, *The Search Warrant, the Magistrate, and Judicial Review*, 62 N.Y.U. L. Rev. 1173 (1987).

58. Increasingly, police departments use a computer program to construct search warrants and supporting affidavits. *E.g.*, Benner & Samarkos, Note 57, *supra*, at 242.

59. In many jurisdictions, a warrant may now be issued on sworn oral testimony via telephone or by electronic means. *E.g.*, Fed. R. Crim. P. 41(d)(3). Indeed, "[w]ell over a majority of States allow police officers or prosecutors to apply for search warrants remotely through various means, including telephonic or radio communication, electronic communication such as e-mail, and video conferencing." Missouri v. McNeely, 133 S. Ct. 1552, 1562 (2013). Thus, as the Court recently stated, "technological advances . . . have . . . made the process of obtaining a warrant . . . more efficient." Riley v. California, 134 S. Ct. 2473, 2493 (2014). Courts have so far rejected challenges that claim that an electronic warrant application lacks the formality and solemnity required by the Fourth Amendment. *See, e.g.*, State v. Gutierrez-Perez, 323 P.3d 1017 (Utah 2014).

60. Benner & Samarkos, Note 57, *supra*, at 227–28.

Although it is exceedingly rare, the judge may require the informant to be identified or produced, if necessary to the probable cause determination.[61]

In practice, warrant proceedings are brief. According to one study, the average time taken by a reviewing magistrate to consider an application was two minutes, 48 seconds; the median time was two minutes, 12 seconds. Ten percent of all applications were reviewed in less than one minute. Fewer than 10 percent of all applications were rejected.[62]

After a warrant is approved and signed by the judge, he gives the original warrant and a copy to the officer, and retains a copy and the supporting documentation. Frequently, a clerk will establish a file for the case. After execution of the warrant, the officer files a "return" with the court, indicating when the search occurred and what, if anything, was seized.

§ 10.03 Search Warrant Requirements

No warrant is valid unless it is supported by probable cause, a requirement considered in detail in Chapter 8. What follows are other warrant requirements.

[A] "Neutral and Detached Magistrate"

Although the Fourth Amendment does not expressly so require, a warrant must be issued by a "neutral and detached magistrate."[63] This requirement is not satisfied if the person issuing the warrant is a member of the executive branch, such as the state attorney general, rather than a member of the judiciary.[64]

Even if a warrant is issued by a member of the judiciary, the magistrate must be neutral and detached, rather than a "rubber stamp for the police."[65] Thus, an unsalaried magistrate who receives a fee for each warrant issued, but no compensation for applications denied, lacks the requisite institutional detachment.[66] A warrant is also invalid if the issuing magistrate, by behavior in a particular case, manifests a lack of neutrality. For example, a judge who accompanies officers to a bookstore suspected of selling obscene material, and who there inspects the materials to determine which ones are obscene, is "not acting as a judicial officer but as an adjunct law enforcement officer."[67]

On the other hand, the magistrate or judge issuing a warrant need not be a lawyer. In *Shadwick v. City of Tampa*,[68] the Supreme Court approved the issuance of misdemeanor arrest warrants by non-lawyer court clerks. Although *Shadwick* dealt only with misdemeanor arrests, the Court cited felony search warrant cases in support of its holding.

---

61. McCray v. Illinois, 386 U.S. 300 (1967).
62. Van Duizend et al., Note 57, *supra*, at 25–32. The cited study, although dated, remains the most thorough study of its kind.
63. Johnson v. United States, 333 U.S. 10, 14 (1948).
64. Coolidge v. New Hampshire, 403 U.S. 443, 453 (1971).
65. United States v. Leon, 468 U.S. 897, 914 (1984).
66. Connally v. Georgia, 429 U.S. 245 (1977).
67. Lo-Ji Sales, Inc. v. New York, 442 U.S. 319, 327 (1979).
68. 407 U.S. 345 (1972).

Indeed, the Supreme Court in *Illinois v. Gates*[69] observed without criticism that "search and arrest warrants long have been issued by persons who are neither lawyers nor judges, and who certainly do not remain abreast of each judicial refinement of the nature of 'probable cause.'"

[B] "Oath or Affirmation"

The Fourth Amendment provides that warrants must be "supported by Oath or affirmation." Therefore, a warrant defective for want of probable cause cannot be saved by post-warrant proof that the police had additional information that they failed to disclose to the judge.[70]

A more complex situation arises when an officer provides false information, under oath, to the magistrate.[71] Under limited circumstances outlined in *Franks v. Delaware*,[72] a defendant may mount a post-search attack on a facially valid warrant on the ground that, but for the falsity in the affidavit, a warrant would not have been issued.

According to *Franks*, an affidavit supporting a search warrant is presumed valid. A defendant is not entitled to a hearing to attack the affidavit (and, thus, the warrant) unless he makes a "substantial preliminary showing"[73] that: (1) a false statement was included in the affidavit (e.g., the affiant did not observe the events that he swore to have seen, did not have the conversations he claimed to have had, or fabricated the existence of a confidential informant);[74] (2) the affiant made the false statement "knowingly and intentionally" or with reckless disregard for the truth;[75] and (3) the false statement was necessary to the magistrate's finding of probable cause.

If these allegations are proved by a preponderance of the evidence, the warrant is void, and the fruits of the search would be excluded from evidence at the criminal trial. As

---

69. 462 U.S. 213, 235 (1983).

70. Whiteley v. Warden, 401 U.S. 560 (1971).

71. For general discussion of the problem of policy perjury (or what has come to be called "testilying"), *see* Gabriel J. Chin & Scott C. Wells, *The "Blue Wall of Silence" as Evidence of Bias and Motive to Lie: A New Approach to Police Perjury*, 59 U. Pitt. L. Rev. 233 (1998); Andrew J. McClurg, *Good Cop, Bad Cop: Using Cognitive Dissonance Theory to Reduce Police Lying*, 32 U.C. Davis L. Rev. 389 (1999); Christopher Slobogin, *Testilying: Police Perjury and What to Do About It*, 67 U. Colo. L. Rev. 1037 (1996).

72. 438 U.S. 154 (1978).

73. Such a showing is made in the form of specific allegations and an offer of proof, including the use of affidavits or other reliable statements of witnesses.

74. *E.g.*, Allan R. Gold, *Dead Officer, Dropped Charges: A Scandal in Boston*, N.Y. Times, March 20, 1989, at A12 (charges were dropped in a homicide case due to "egregious misconduct" by the prosecutor and the police, including the fact that a police officer applied for several warrants based on hearsay information from "John," who did not exist). Professor Donald Dripps has suggested that when the outcome of a suppression hearing depends on the credibility of witnesses, "the court should inquire whether either party is willing to supplement the record with a polygraph examination of the party's witness or witnesses." Although the trial court would not be bound by the results of the polygraph examinations, it could consider them along with the other evidence, and the results would become part of the record to be considered, as appropriate, by an appellate court. Donald A. Dripps, *Police, Plus Perjury, Equals Polygraphy*, 86 J. Crim. L. & Criminology 693, 694 (1996).

75. In other contexts the Court has defined "reckless disregard for the truth" to mean that the person "in fact entertained serious doubts as to the truth" of the statement made. St. Amant v. Thompson, 390 U.S. 727, 731 (1968).

stated in *Franks*, "it would be an unthinkable imposition upon [the magistrate's] authority if a warrant affidavit, revealed after the fact to contain a deliberately or recklessly false statement, were to stand beyond impeachment."

Franks does not authorize similar impeachment of a "nongovernmental informant." Therefore, a warrant is not voidable if an informant lies to the affiant, who then innocently or negligently passes this false information along to the magistrate. The rationale for drawing this distinction is that the credibility of the *informant* must be shown in the probable-cause determination process,[76] whereas the veracity of the *affiant* ordinarily is assumed because he takes an oath of truthfulness.

[C] "Particularity"

[1] In General

The Fourth Amendment provides that warrants must "particularly describ[e] the place to be searched, and the persons or things to be seized." Particularity is required in order to avoid the abuses exemplified by the general warrants and writs of assistance used in the English and colonial common law.[77] A warrant that lacks particularity permits police officers too much discretion in its execution and, thereby, also undercuts the probable cause requirement.

[2] "Place to be Searched"

The place to be searched must be described in the warrant with sufficient clarity that the officer executing the warrant can identify it with reasonable effort.[78] For example, it is sufficient if the search warrant provides the street address of a single-unit house to be searched. If the structure is a multiple-unit building, additional information, such as an apartment number, is required.

If the officer who applies for a warrant has reason to believe that the building to be searched is a single-unit structure, so that a street address is sufficient, but the officer *executing* the warrant discovers that the structure contains multiple units, the warrant itself is *not* invalid for want of particularity, because its validity "must be assessed on the basis of the information that the officers disclosed, or had a duty to discover and to disclose, to the issuing Magistrate."[79] The more difficult problem in such a case relates to the *execution* of the facially valid warrant. If the warrant directs the police to search "the home belonging to *D*, who lives at 123 Main Street," and upon arriving there the officers learn (or should have learned) that the building at that address is a duplex, the officers are obligated to limit their search to *D*'s unit, which they may ascertain by reasonable effort, such as by checking names on the mailbox or by asking neighbors.[80]

---

76. *See* § 8.04, *supra*.

77. *See* § 4.03, *supra*.

78. Steele v. United States, 267 U.S. 498, 503 (1925).

79. Maryland v. Garrison, 480 U.S. 79, 85 (1987).

80. However, a search of the wrong premises may still be reasonable. In *Garrison, id.*, the officers executed a warrant on a "third floor apartment" at a particular address. The officers did not learn (and had no reason to know) until after they had entered the "third floor apartment" and seized evidence that the "third floor apartment," in fact, was a two-apartment unit and that they were in the wrong apartment. The Court admitted the evidence seized, however, observing that it must "allow some latitude for honest mistakes that are made by officers in the dangerous and

A warrant to search an automobile is sufficient if it describes the vehicle in a manner that reasonably assists the officer in determining what car may be searched. For example, the license or vehicle identification number of the vehicle is adequate. So, too, it could be sufficient simply to identify it by its location, if the location is a one-car personal garage, but not if it is a two-car garage or public parking lot.

[3] "Persons or Things to be Seized"

The phrase "persons . . . to be seized" primarily relates to arrest warrants, because an arrest is a seizure of a person.[81] Obviously, an arrest warrant must identify the person to be arrested.

The "things to be seized" should be described in search warrants with sufficient particularity that "seizure of one thing under a warrant describing another [cannot occur]. As to what is to be taken, nothing is left to the discretion of the officer executing the warrant."[82] This requirement of particularity, which mandates identification of the "things" in the warrant, assures that the magistrate approves the scope of the search and that the person whose property is being searched can also ascertain that scope.[83]

In practice, neither the Supreme Court nor lower courts have applied the preceding test strictly. In his treatise, Wayne LaFave has helpfully summarized the general principles that he has distilled from the numerous cases in the field.[84] Among the principles he identified are: (1) vagueness in the warrant description is tolerated to a greater degree when the police have described the item with as much particularity as can reasonably be expected;[85] and (2) less specificity is required regarding contraband[86] than is required regarding stolen goods[87] or items, such as books and papers, which retain special First Amendment protection.[88]

---

difficult process of making arrests and executing search warrants." Once they became aware of their error, however, the officers were required to desist from further searching the wrong apartment.

81. Some jurisdictions permit the seizure of a person "who is unlawfully restrained," such as a kidnap victim, as "evidence" of the crime. *E.g.*, Fed. R. Crim. P. 41(c)(4).

82. Marron v. United States, 275 U.S. 192, 196 (1927).

83. *E.g.*, Groh v. Ramirez, 540 U.S. 551 (2004) (a federal agent prepared an application for a warrant to search *R*'s ranch for specified weapons, explosives, and records; the agent also prepared a detailed affidavit setting forth the agent's belief that the specified items were on the ranch; the agent prepared a warrant to be signed by the judge, but in the portion calling for a description of the "person or property" to be seized, he failed entirely to list the items to be seized; the magistrate signed the warrant without correcting it; held: the warrant was "plainly invalid" in that it "failed altogether" to comply with the particularity requirement of the Fourth Amendment; the Court left for another day the question of whether the particularity requirement is satisfied if the warrant incorporates by reference another document that particularizes the items to be seized).

84. 2 Wayne R. LaFave, Search and Seizure §4.6 (4th ed. 2004).

85. *E.g.*, Andresen v. Maryland, 427 U.S. 463, 479 (1976) (a warrant authorizing the seizure of items pertaining to a real estate fraud, but which included a residual clause authorizing the seizure of "fruits, instrumentalities, and evidence of crime at this [time] unknown," was upheld by the Court, in part because of the complexity of the real estate scheme, and the inability of the police to be more specific).

86. *E.g.*, it is satisfactory for the warrant to direct the officers to seize "gambling paraphernalia," "controlled substances," or "drugs unlawfully possessed."

87. *E.g.*, it is insufficient to describe the item to be seized as "the stolen automobile" or "the jewelry," if a more specific description is possible.

88. Stanford v. Texas, 379 U.S. 476, 485 (1965) ("[T]he constitutional requirement [of particularity] . . . is to be accorded the most scrupulous exactitude when the 'things' are books, and the basis for their seizure is the ideas which they contain.").

§ 10.04 Execution of Search Warrants[89]

[A] In Anticipation of Execution

In the ordinary course of events, the police will obtain a search warrant and then proceed to the site of the search and execute it according to the principles laid out in this chapter section. On occasion, however, the police may find themselves in a situation in which an exigency justifying an immediate warrantless search does not yet exist,[90] but in which they have reason to fear that such an exigency will develop while they apply for the warrant. In such circumstances, the police may wish to cordon off the area in anticipation of securing the warrant. Such an action, however, may itself constitute a warrantless seizure of the property in question.

For example, in *Illinois v. McArthur*,[91] police officers had probable cause to believe that *M* had hidden illegal drugs in his trailer home. They went to *M*'s home and asked for permission to search it, but *M* refused. One officer immediately sent a second officer to apply for a search warrant. In the meantime, *M* had left his trailer and was standing on the porch. The officer informed him that, until a warrant was obtained, *M* could not reenter his trailer unaccompanied by an officer. During the wait for the warrant, *M* reentered his home to get cigarettes and make telephone calls, but each time the officer stood guard just inside the door. Two hours later, warrant in hand, the police searched the trailer and discovered the contraband.

The Court upheld the police action here. Although the Court said that in "the ordinary case" a warrantless *seizure* of personal property, just like a warrantless *search*, is unreasonable, the Court believed that the warrantless temporary seizure of the premises here was reasonable.[92] The Court pointed to the following cumulative circumstances: (1) the police had probable cause to conduct the search for contraband; (2) the police "had good reason to fear that, unless restrained, [*M*] would destroy the drugs"; (3) "the police made reasonable efforts to reconcile their law enforcement needs with the demands of personal privacy" (e.g., they avoided significant intrusions into the house until the warrant was obtained); and (4) the length of time of the restraint was limited.

McArthur is a narrow opinion and does not justify all anticipatory warrantless seizures of personal premises. But a temporary seizure, supported by probable cause, "designed to prevent the loss of evidence while the police diligently obtain[] a warrant in a reasonable period of time" is permissible.

[B] Time of Execution

Some jurisdictions, by statute or rule of procedure, require that search warrants be executed within a specified period of time, often within 10 days or two weeks,[93] from the date that the warrant was signed by the magistrate. This rule reduces the risk that

---

89. *See generally* 2 LaFave, Note 84, *supra*, at §§ 4.7–4.12.

90. *See generally* § 11.04, *infra* (when a warrantless entry of a home is justified on exigent grounds).

91. 531 U.S. 326 (2001).

92. The police action constituted a seizure of the house because it resulted in a meaningful interference with *M*'s possessory interest in his trailer. *See* § 7.02[A], *supra*.

93. *E.g.*, Fed. R. Crim. P. 41(e)(2)(A)(i).

the justification for the search—the basis for the finding of probable cause—will become stale.

Some jurisdictions bar nighttime execution of warrants, "unless the judge, for good cause, expressly authorizes" the nighttime execution.[94] The Supreme Court has approved non-exigent nighttime warrant executions,[95] but only as a matter of statutory interpretation, without expressly addressing whether such an approach is constitutionally reasonable.

[C] Means of Entry

[1] Knock-and-Announce Rule

At common law, absent special circumstances, an officer was not permitted to enter a home forcibly to execute a warrant, unless he knocked at the door (or otherwise indicated his presence), identified himself as an officer, stated his purpose for entering, requested admittance, and was refused admission.

In *Wilson v. Arkansas*,[96] the Supreme Court, per Justice Clarence Thomas, unanimously held that the common law knock-and-announce "principle forms a part of the reasonableness inquiry under the Fourth Amendment." Justice Thomas stated that this common law rule "was woven quickly into the fabric of early American law," because most states that ratified the Fourth Amendment also enacted statutes or constitutional provisions incorporating English common law. History, therefore, "leaves no doubt that the reasonableness of a search of a dwelling may depend in part on whether law enforcement officers announced their presence and authority prior to entering."

In *Hudson v. Michigan*,[97] the Court identified three interests protected by the knock-and-announce rule. First, the rule protects "human life and limb, because an unannounced entry may provoke violence in supposed self-defense by the surprised resident." Second, the rule protects property by giving someone whose home will be searched the opportunity to open the door and thereby avoid damage to the home that could result from a forcible entry. Third, the rule "protects those elements of privacy and dignity that can be destroyed by a sudden entrance," for example by giving a person the opportunity to put on some clothes or to get out of bed.

Justice Breyer, dissenting for four members of the *Hudson* Court, objected that this list did not "fully describe the constitutional values, purposes and objectives underlying the knock-and-announce requirement."[98] The knock-and-announce rule, no less than the warrant requirement, Justice Breyer argued, offers "special protection for the privacy of the home" by assuring "that government agents will not enter . . . without complying with [rules] that diminish the offensive nature of any such intrusion."

As explained elsewhere in the Text,[99] the Supreme Court ruled in *Hudson* that the Fourth Amendment exclusionary rule does not apply to evidence discovered as the result of a search conducted in violation of the knock-and-announce rule if the search was

---

94. *E.g.*, Fed. R. Crim. P. 41(e)(2)(A)(ii).
95. Gooding v. United States, 416 U.S. 430 (1974).
96. 514 U.S. 927 (1995).
97. 547 U.S. 586 (2006).
98. *Id.* at 620.
99. *See especially* § 20.05[B][2][c], *infra*.

otherwise authorized by a valid warrant. According to the *Hudson* dissent, this ruling, "by destroy[ing] the strongest legal incentive to comply with the Constitution's knock-and-announce requirement[,] . . . weakens, perhaps destroys, much of the practical value of the Constitution's knock-and-announce protection."

[2] Exceptions to Rule

The knock-and-announce rule is qualified; there are exceptions to the requirement. Justice Thomas, in *Wilson v. Arkansas*,[100] did not provide a comprehensive list of circumstances in which no-knock entries are permitted, choosing instead to leave the matter initially to lower courts for determination. Nonetheless, he cited cases that have acknowledged the authority of the police to enter without notice: (1) "under circumstances presenting a threat of physical violence"; (2) in hot-pursuit cases ("in cases where a prisoner escapes . . . and retreats to his dwelling"): (3) and, of most frequent relevance, "where police officers have reason to believe that evidence would likely be destroyed if advance notice were given."

Although the Supreme Court has avoided case-by-case adjudication in various other Fourth Amendment realms, the Court has determined that, in applying the exceptions to the knock-and-announce rule, case-by-case analysis is required. That is, the police are not permitted to justify their failure to satisfy the knock-and-announce requirements by simply categorizing a case as, for example, a drug investigation.[101] As the Court explained in *Richards v. Wisconsin*,[102] "[i]f a *per se* exception were allowed for each category of criminal investigation that included a considerable—albeit hypothetical—risk of danger to officers or destruction of evidence, the knock-and-announce element of the Fourth Amendment's reasonableness requirement would be meaningless."

Nonetheless, *Richards* did create a substantial loophole in the knock-and-announce rule. In order to satisfy one of the exceptions to the requirement set out above, the police need only possess reasonable suspicion, rather than probable cause, "that knocking and announcing their presence, under the particular circumstances, would be dangerous or futile, or that it would inhibit the effective investigation of the crime by, for example, allowing the destruction of evidence."[103]

The Court stated that the reasonable suspicion standard "strikes the appropriate balance between the legitimate law enforcement concerns . . . and the individual privacy interests." Because "reasonable suspicion" requires only a little more than a hunch,[104] the likely effect of *Richards* is that the exceptions will gobble up the knock-and-announce requirement.

[3] After the Knock: What Then?

How long must the police wait before they enter premises after they knock and announce their presence and purpose, and does it matter what method they use to enter

---

100. 514 U.S. 927 (1995).

101. *See* United States v. Banks, 540 U.S. 31, 36 (2003).

102. 520 U.S. 385, 394 (1997).

103. *Contra under the state constitution*, Commonwealth v. Macias, 711 N.E.2d 130 (Mass. 1999) (unannounced entry into a residence, founded on police officers' belief that evidence will be destroyed if they comply with the knock-and-announce rule, is not justified unless the belief satisfies the probable cause standard).

104. *See* § 17.03, *infra*.

forcibly? The Court provided some answers to these questions in *United States v. Banks*.[105] In *Banks*, law enforcement officers, armed with a warrant to search B's two-bedroom apartment for cocaine, knocked loudly and called out "police search warrant." They waited about 15 to 20 seconds. Hearing nothing (as it turned out, B was in the shower and testified that he did not hear the knocking), the officers broke open the door with a battering ram, entered, and executed the warrant.

The Court unanimously held that although the "call is a close one, . . . we think that after 15 or 20 seconds without a response, police could fairly suspect that cocaine would be gone if they were reticent any longer," thus justifying the forcible entry. The fact that B was in the shower was irrelevant: "it is enough to say that the facts known to the police are what count in judging reasonable waiting time." Essentially, as the Court saw it, if B had *not* been in the shower, this length of time would have been sufficient to cause a reasonable officer to suspect that B, aware of the officers' purpose for entry, would begin flushing the cocaine down a toilet or otherwise disposing of the contraband. As the Court put it, such a length of time "does not seem an unrealistic guess about the time someone would need to get in a position to rid his quarters of cocaine." Thus, although no bright-line exists, the knock-and-announce rule does not bar very rapid forcible entry after the warning is given, if the police reasonably suspect—apparently, have a "realistic guess"—that exigent circumstances require entry, which they usually will in drug-search cases.

The Court made another important point in *Banks*. Assuming (as here) the existence of an exigency justifying immediate entry, the police "may damage premises so far as necessary for a no-knock entrance without demonstrating the suspected risk in any more detail than the law demands for an unannounced intrusion simply by lifting the latch." Put differently, if the police are at the point at which immediate *forcible* entry is constitutionally reasonable, the police do *not* need a heightened justification to enter, nor must they wait longer, merely because they will have to damage the premises in order to enter. However, the Court stated that if an exigency does *not* yet exist, "the reasonable wait time [before entering] may well be longer when police [must] make a forced entry" and thereby damage property, than if the door to the house is open. As Justice Souter for the unanimous Court put it,

> [s]uffice it to say that the need to damage property in the course of getting in is a good reason to require more patience than it would be reasonable to expect if the door were open. Police seeking a stolen piano may be able to spend more time to make sure they really need the battering ram.

[D] Search of Persons While Executing a Warrant

[1] In Premises Open to the Public

A search warrant may properly authorize the search of a named individual who is expected to be found on the premises to be searched, as long as probable cause exists to search that person at the time the warrant is issued. On the other hand, a warrant authorizing the search of "all persons found on the premises," without identifying the individuals, is unconstitutionally broad except in the unlikely event that there is probable cause to believe that anyone and everyone who might be present at the time of the search will be in possession of seizable criminal evidence.

---

105. 540 U.S. 31 (2003).

There is a related question. Under what circumstances, if any, may an officer executing a valid search warrant of premises open to the public search persons found at the scene who are *not* named in the warrant? *Ybarra v. Illinois*[106] provides insights into this question. In *Ybarra*, officers possessed a warrant to search a tavern, and a specifically named bartender, for heroin. Eight officers executing the warrant entered the bar while it was open to the public and frisked each of the customers for weapons. While frisking *Y*, who was not acting suspiciously, an officer felt something in *Y*'s pocket, which seemed to be "a cigarette pack with objects in it." Later, the officer pulled out the object, which was a cigarette pack as predicted, and opened it to find tin foil packets of heroin.

The Supreme Court concluded in *Ybarra* that "a person's mere propinquity to others independently suspected of criminal activity does not, without more, give rise to probable cause to search that person." That is, every customer on the premises in *Ybarra* had individualized Fourth Amendment protection. A warrantless search of a person on the premises, therefore, requires independent probable cause and a justification for dispensing with the warrant requirement (e.g., consent or exigent circumstances).

This does not mean that officers executing a warrant on public premises must necessarily bypass people present at the scene. Based on the principles of *Terry v. Ohio*,[107] an officer executing a warrant may pat down (frisk) an occupant for weapons if the officer has reasonable suspicion, based on specific articulable facts, that the person to be frisked is armed and dangerous. If the officer conducting the pat-down feels what appears to be a weapon, he may then conduct a full search in order to seize the object. In *Ybarra*, however, the officer lacked reasonable suspicion to believe that *Y* was armed and dangerous; therefore, even the initial pat-down was unconstitutional.

[2] In Private Homes

Ybarra involved the execution of a search warrant on premises open to the general public, in a circumstance in which there was no evidence that any customer was linked to the criminal activities that brought the officers to the tavern. What should the rule be, however, when the police execute a valid warrant to search a private residence? May they search anyone found on the premises?

The Supreme Court has not answered this question directly. A few lower courts permit the police, while executing a search warrant of a home for narcotics, automatically to frisk all occupants for weapons. Other courts require particularized suspicion that the person frisked is armed and dangerous.[108]

Even if reasonable suspicion is required, it should usually be much easier to justify a limited pat-down search in a residence than in a building open to the public. As the Supreme Court has observed in the context of arrests, "an in-home arrest puts the officer at the disadvantage of being on his adversary's "turf."[109] Moreover, a private home,

---

106. 444 U.S. 85 (1979).

107. 392 U.S. 1 (1968). *See* § 17.02, *infra*.

108. 2 LaFave, Note 84, *supra*, at 715–717.

109. Maryland v. Buie, 494 U.S. 325, 333 (1990). In *Buie*, the Court ruled that the police may conduct a protective visual sweep of a home while they are completing an in-home arrest, but only if they possess reasonable suspicion that the area to be swept harbors a dangerous person. *See* § 17.08, *infra*. The Court did not indicate in *Buie* what the police may do if they find a person during such a sweep.

unlike the *Ybarra* bar, "does not attract casual visitors off the street."[110] Therefore, officers in a residence will frequently have good reason to fear that the occupants are connected to the suspected criminal activity or, at least, have an incentive to protect the criminal interests of the residents by using force against the police.

[E] Detention of Persons During Searches

In *Michigan v. Summers*,[111] police officers encountered *S* as he descended the front steps of a house the officers had a warrant to search for narcotics. They requested and obtained *S*'s assistance in entering the premises, after which they forcibly detained (seized) him while they searched the house.

The search proved fruitful. After the officers learned that *S* was the owner of the house, they arrested and searched him incident to the arrest. More drugs were found on his person, and it was *this* evidence that *S* sought to exclude at his trial on the ground that it was a fruit of his unlawful detention in his home.

The Court held that *S*'s temporary seizure was reasonable. It noted three justifications for the detention of persons during the execution of a search warrant: (1) to avoid flight of an occupant with the evidence sought; (2) to reduce the risk of bodily harm to the officers or others; and (3) to facilitate the search by inducing the detained occupants to open locked containers or doors.

Although the police did not prove that any of the above-stated reasons applied in *Summers*, the Court chose to provide a bright-line rule, rather than invite case-by-case adjudication: A warrant to search for contraband includes the limited authority to detain all occupants of the premises to be searched while the warrant is executed. This right of detention "does not require law enforcement to have particular suspicion that an individual [seized under the rule] is involved in criminal activity or poses a specific danger to the officers."[112] The right is automatic. On the other hand, because the right of detention is automatic and can result in a relatively lengthy detention while a search is conducted, the *Summers* rule is limited to the detention of occupants of the residence and ones discovered "immediately outside a residence at the moment the police officers executed the search warrant. . . . Once an individual has left the immediate vicinity of the premises to be searched, detentions must be justified by some other rationale" than the *Summers* rule.[113]

The potential limits of *Summers* should be noted. First, the Court did not determine whether the rule also applies to *warrantless* residential searches. The Court stated in a footnote, however, that its holding does not "preclude the possibility that comparable police conduct may be justified by exigent circumstances in the absence of a warrant."

Second, the *Summers* rule, as stated, was limited to searches for contraband. In a footnote, the Court left open the issue of whether the police may detain persons during

---

110. People v. Thurman, 257 Cal. Rptr. 517, 520 (Cal. App. 1989).

111. 452 U.S. 692 (1981).

112. Bailey v. United States, 133 S. Ct. 1031, 1037–1038 (2013).

113. *Id.* at 1042, 1043. In *Bailey*, *B* left the residence that the police had a warrant to search, but he was not detained until he was about a mile away from the residence. Because this detention was beyond "any reasonable understanding" of the term "immediate vicinity" of the premises, his seizure fell outside the scope of *Summers*.

searches for evidence of a crime. Subsequent cases, however, demonstrate that there is no "contraband" limitation to the *Summers* rule.[114]

Third, the Court used the word "occupants" in the holding and elsewhere in the opinion. But the Court also used the word "residents," and further observed in that context that "we may safely assume that most citizens ... would elect to remain in order to observe the search of their possessions." So, did the Court mean to limit the scope of its holding to persons who have a possessory connection to the premises searched, or may the police detain anyone coincidentally present when the warrant is executed? The Court has not expressly answered this question, although one expert, perhaps overly optimistically, suggests that "it would seem that the word 'occupants' is not to be loosely construed as covering anyone present . . ."[115]

It should also be noted that the right of the police under *Michigan v. Summers* to detain an occupant during a warranted search of a residence includes the right to use reasonable means to secure the detention, including handcuffing of the detainee. For example, in *Muehler v. Mena*,[116] officers, armed with a warrant to search a house for deadly weapons and evidence of gang membership, handcuffed a female occupant whom they discovered in bed when they entered the premises. The detention, with handcuffs, lasted two to three hours while the warrant was executed.

The Court, per Chief Justice Rehnquist, held that "[i]nherent in *Summers*' authorization to detain an occupant of the place to be searched is the authority to use reasonable force to effectuate the detention." Although the handcuffing "undoubtedly" constituted a "separate intrusion in addition to detention"—which, therefore, required its own justification—the majority held that "[t]he governmental interests in not only detaining, but using handcuffs, are at their maximum when, as here, a warrant authorizes a search for weapons and a wanted gang member [not the person handcuffed] resides on the premises. In such inherently dangerous situations, the use of handcuffs minimizes the risk of harm to both officers and occupants."

Seemingly, all nine justices agree that handcuffing can be reasonable in some residential searches. Only five of the justices, however, were prepared to hold that the duration of its use here was reasonable. And Justice Kennedy, while joining the majority opinion, wrote separately to warn that it is "a matter of first concern that excessive force is not used on persons detained, especially when those persons, though lawfully detained under *Michigan v. Summers*, are not themselves suspected of any involvement in criminal activity." Furthermore, Kennedy warned that "[i]f the search extends to the point when the handcuffs can cause real pain or serious discomfort, provision must be made to alter the conditions of detention at least long enough to attend to the needs of the detainee."

Justice Stevens, writing for Justices Souter, Ginsburg, and Breyer, believed that it was "clear that the jury could properly have found [as it did] that this 5-foot-2-inch young lady [who was handcuffed] posed no threat to the officers at the scene, and that [the officers] used excessive force in keeping her in handcuffs for up to three hours."

---

114. Muehler v. Mena, 544 U.S. 93 (2005) (*Summers* applied to a warranted search of a residence for weapons and evidence of gang membership); Los Angeles County, California v. Rettele, 550 U.S. 609 (2007) (*Summers* applies to a warranted search of a residence for computer files and other documents in a fraud and identity-theft crime-ring investigation).

115. 2 LaFave, Note 84, *supra*, at 726–727.

116. 544 U.S. 93 (2005).

[F] Scope of the Search

A search warrant must satisfy the particularity requirement of the Fourth Amendment. However, assuming that a warrant describes the place to be searched with adequate precision, the authority to search that place includes the entire area in question, including containers found within it, as long as the containers are large enough to contain the object of the search.[117] For example, in a search of a bedroom for stolen jewelry, the police may open dresser drawers and jewelry boxes that could hold the fruits of the crime. If they were searching for a stolen large-screen television set, however, they would not be justified in opening those containers for such a large object.

Police may constitutionally *seize* any item (even if it is not described in the warrant) if: (1) they observe the item while searching a place which they have authority to search; (2) the item is located in such an area; and (3) police have probable cause to believe the item is subject to seizure.[118]

Once the articles particularly described in a warrant are discovered and seized, the search must cease.[119]

---

117. United States v. Ross, 456 U.S. 798, 820–21 (1982).
118. *See generally* Chapter 14, *infra* (explaining the "plain-view doctrine").
119. Horton v. California, 496 U.S. 128, 141 (1990).

Chapter 11

Warrantless Searches: Exigent Circumstances

§ 11.01 Exigency Exception: Explained

Many exceptions to the "warrant requirement" of the Fourth Amendment are based on exigent circumstances, that is, on the ground that time constraints make it impracticable for the officer to seek a warrant. Because an exigency is a situation that requires immediate action, it is reasonable for an officer in emergent circumstances to search without a warrant.

Some exigent circumstances commonly recur. For example, an arrest triggers a threat to the police officer that the arrestee might use a concealed weapon or destroy evidence hidden on her person or in the area of her control before the officer can obtain a search warrant. Thus, there is a "search incident to lawful arrest" exception to the warrant requirement. Similarly, the mobility of an automobile makes it difficult to secure a warrant to search a car discovered on the highway. Therefore, there is an "automobile" warrant exception. These and other specific exceptions to the "warrant requirement" are considered in coming chapters of this Text.

Other exigencies occur less frequently, however, or arise in such disparate factual circumstances that courts have not generally classified them under a specific warrant exception. Therefore, these cases tend to be grouped together under the general umbrella of an "exigency" exception to the search warrant requirement, the subject of this chapter.

Certain generalizations regarding the "exigency" warrant exception are possible. First, cases that fall within this exception typically involve situations in which the police act without a warrant because they reasonably believe that criminal evidence will be destroyed or a suspect will avoid capture if they take the time to seek a warrant.

Second, the exigency that justifies the warrantless action should restrict the scope of the resulting search. For example, if the exigency is that a large box containing criminal evidence in a particular house may imminently be destroyed, the right to search for the box should extend only to those places in the residence that could reasonably conceal the box.

Third, the "exigent circumstances" exception lasts no longer than the exigency. That is, once the exigency ends, the police may no longer search without a warrant or they must justify their continued warrantless conduct on the basis of a different exception to the warrant requirement.

Fourth, although an exigency justifies the absence of a search warrant, it does not dispense with any underlying requirement of probable cause that may exist. In short— and this is a point worth keeping in mind when considering *all* warrant exceptions—the issue of whether a warrant is required is independent of the question of whether suffi-cient cause exists for the warrantless search or seizure.

Fifth, the exigency exception to the warrant requirement does *not* apply if the police "create the exigency by engaging or threatening to engage in conduct that violates the Fourth Amendment."[1] Thus, if a police officer comes to a home in *non-exigent* circum-stances and demands, in violation of the Fourth Amendment, that the occupants allow her to enter without a warrant, she cannot then claim that an exigency (for example, that after her unlawful demand for admittance, she heard an occupant inside apparently destroying criminal evidence) justifies a warrantless entry. On the other hand, if the officer — with probable cause to search, but without a warrant — arrives at the scene, knocks, announces her identity to the occupants, and requests that the door be opened, all of which is in conformity with the Fourth Amendment,[2] the police may enter without a warrant if the knock-and-announce triggers the threat of imminent destruction of evidence. This is so, even if the police could have sought a warrant before arriving at the scene.[3]

Finally, it is important to keep in mind that the search warrant exception now under discussion relates to criminal investigations. In contrast, the Court has indicated that law enforcement officers may enter a home (and, it follows, less private confines) without a warrant "to render emergency assistance to an injured occupant or to protect an oc-cupant from imminent injury."[4] The Court has sometimes described such activities as "community caretaking functions, totally divorced from the detection, investigation or acquisition of evidence relating to the violation of a criminal statute."[5] In such circum-stances, different principles apply: not only are search warrants — intended for crimi-nal investigations — inapplicable, but "probable cause," which is a criminal investigatory concept, is not required; instead, there need only be reasonable grounds to believe emer-gency assistance is needed. And, any criminal evidence discovered in plain view during the non-criminal community caretaking activity may lawfully be seized and used in a subsequent criminal investigation.[6] Unfortunately, the line between a criminal investi-gation and the community caretaking function can be difficult to discern.[7] Remember also that the subjective intent of the police officers is irrelevant in this context, so even

---

1. Kentucky v. King, 563 U.S. 452, 462 (2011); *see also id.* at 1858 n.4 ("There is a strong argu-ment to be made that, at least in most circumstances, the exigent circumstances rule should not apply where the police, without a warrant or any legally sound basis for a warrantless entry, threaten that they will enter without permission unless admitted.").

2. See § 10.04[C], *supra.*

3. *King*, 563 U.S. at 466 (2011). *King* is considered in greater detail in § 11.04, *infra.*

4. Brigham City, Utah v. Stuart, 547 U.S. 398, 403 (2006).

5. Cady v. Dombrowski, 413 U.S. 433, 441 (1973). Examples of such "caretaking functions" in-clude: restraining an occupant of a house who is observed hurting another individual, Brigham City, Utah v. Stuart, 547 U.S. 398 (2006); opening the door of an automobile, parked on the side of the highway with the lights off but motor running at 3:00 a.m., after the apparently asleep driver did not respond to a knock on the window, State v. Lovegren, 51 P.3d 471 (Mont. 2002); detaining a person near an apartment complex because he was swaying and walking unsteadily, which sug-gested he might need medical care, Commonwealth v. Waters, 456 S.E.2d 527 (Va. Ct. App. 1995); and entering a private residence when a trail of blood led to the door of the residence and there was blood on the outside of the door, State v. Matalonis, 875 N.W.2d 567 (Wis. 2016). In regard to non-criminal investigations generally, *see* Chapters 15 (inventory searches) and 18 (various "special needs" circumstances), *infra.*

6. *See generally* Chapter 14, *infra.*

7. In this regard, *see generally* John F. Decker, *Emergency Circumstances, Police Responses, and Fourth Amendment Restrictions*, 89 J. Crim. L. & Criminology 433 (1999).

if the police may have a subjective intent to find evidence of criminal activity, they are permitted to conduct the warrantless search as long as it is justified under the community caretaking function.

§ 11.02 Intrusions Inside the Human Body[8]

The Supreme Court has wrestled with the question of whether, and under what circumstances, the government may compel a search that involves intrusion inside the body of a suspect. In some cases, police methods to obtain evidence in this manner may "offend 'a sense of justice,' "[9] and consequently violate the Due Process Clause. However, in the Fourth Amendment context: (1) the fact that a search will involve intrusion inside a person's body does not in itself bar the government, in appropriate circumstances, from proceeding without a warrant; but (2) *with or without a warrant*, a search inside the body is not reasonable unless special criteria are met.

Schmerber v. California[10] demonstrates both of these points. *S* was arrested at a hospital for driving under the influence of alcohol. On the order of the arresting officer, a physician took a blood sample from *S* to test for alcohol content. Although the Court stated that there was "plainly probable cause" for the arrest, the search and seizure of blood were without a warrant. The Court held that the warrantless taking of the blood sample was justifiable on the ground that the evidence—the alcohol in the bloodstream—would have been lost if the police had been required to obtain a warrant: The evidence was in the process of being "destroyed" as *S*'s body eliminated it from its system. In short, an exigency justified dispensing with the warrant requirement.[11]

---

8. *See generally* Michael G. Rogers, Note, *Bodily Intrusion in Search of Evidence: A Study in Fourth Amendment Decisionmaking*, 62 Ind. L.J. 1181 (1987).

9. Rochin v. California, 342 U.S. 165, 173 (1952), discussed at § 20.01[C][2], *infra*.

10. 384 U.S. 757 (1966).

11. The Supreme Court recently made clear that the right of the police to conduct a warrantless blood test in a drunk-driving investigation is not automatic. That is, the fact that there is a natural dissipation of alcohol in the bloodstream — and, thus, that there is an inevitable gradual destruction of evidence in the bloodstream—does not justify a categorical right of the police to dispense with the warrant requirement. Missouri v. McNeeley, 133 S. Ct. 1552 (2013). In *McNeeley*, the trial court ruled that, based on the facts of that case, "there were no circumstances suggesting the officer faced an emergency in which he could not practicably obtain a warrant." The Court, per Justice Sotomayor, concluded that because a blood test involves "a compelled physical intrusion beneath [a person's] skin and into his veins," courts should conduct a "finely tuned approach" to the warrant issue by looking to the totality of the circumstances. The Court agreed that a "significant delay in testing will negatively affect the probative value of . . . [blood test] results" and, therefore, there are circumstances when securing a warrant will be impractical, but it determined that each case should be decided on its own facts.

Similarly, a state cannot pass a law that makes it a crime for a suspected drunk driver to refuse a blood test. Birchfield v. North Dakota, 136 S. Ct. 1241 (2016). Because breath tests are far less intrusive and provide police with essentially the same information as a blood test, police cannot conduct a blood test on a suspected drunk driver unless they obtain a warrant or prove that securing a warrant would be impractical in the specific case at hand.

Of course, police can still turn to the exigent circumstances exception if they have sufficient facts specific to the case that indicates that the evidence will likely disappear in the time that it takes to obtain a warrant. *See, e.g.*, State .v Parisi, 875 N.W.2d 619 (Wis. 2016) (holding that exigent circumstances existed given the rapid rate of dissipation of heroin in the bloodstream, combined

Although the warrantless search here was permissible, the Court warned that any intrusive bodily search would violate the Fourth Amendment unless: (1) the police are justified in requiring the individual to submit to the test; and (2) the means and procedures employed to conduct the test are reasonable. The first requirement was met here: the officer had, in *Schmerber*'s words, "plainly probable cause" to arrest *S* for driving under the influence of alcohol; the blood test, therefore, was not conducted "on the mere chance" that alcohol would be found in the bloodstream, but rather on the basis of a "clear indication" that such evidence would be discovered.

The second requirement was also met here. The procedure involved—extraction of blood—is highly effective, commonplace, and rarely painful or traumatic. Also, the test was performed in a reasonable manner: by a physician, in a hospital environment, under accepted medical practices. Therefore, the warrantless search was reasonable.

The Court has since considered this second (reasonableness) requirement more fully and demonstrated that searches that extend under the skin, even with probable cause for the procedure, should only be authorized with caution. In *Winston v. Lee*,[12] the police sought a court order directing *L*, who had been arrested for attempted robbery, to undergo surgery to remove a bullet lodged under his left collarbone (the robbery victim had returned fire at the suspect).

The Court concluded that the "reasonableness of surgical intrusions beneath the skin depends on a case-by-case approach, in which the individual's interests in privacy and security are weighed against society's interests in conducting the procedure." In *Winston*, notwithstanding probable cause for the search, the Supreme Court affirmed a federal court injunction prohibiting the surgery without *L*'s consent. The Court noted a number of factors that distinguished *Winston* from *Schmerber*: here general anesthesia was required; the procedure would be an "extensive" intrusion on *L*'s bodily integrity; the medical risks of the operation, "although apparently not extremely severe, [were] a subject of considerable dispute"; and the government failed to prove that it had a "compelling" need for the bullet to prove its case.

On the other hand, when the intrusion is nonsurgical, it may more easily be found to be reasonable. In *Maryland v. King*,[13] the Court approved a process of taking a "buccal swab," which "involves wiping a small piece of filer paper or a cotton swab similar to a Q-tip against the inside cheek of an individual's mouth to collect some skin cells," from *all* arrestees booked on "serious offenses" in order to obtain a DNA identification.

§ 11.03 External Searches of the Body

External searches of the body are sometimes permitted without a warrant due to exigent circumstances. The facts in *Cupp v. Murphy*,[14] if not the express reasoning of the Court, provide a good example. In *Cupp*, the police had probable cause to arrest *M* for the strangulation murder of his wife. *M* voluntarily appeared at the police station for

---

with the unstable health condition of the defendant and the "multiple unknown facts" regarding how much heroin the defendant had consumed and when he had consumed it).

12. 470 U.S. 753 (1985).

13. 133 S. Ct. 1958 (2013) (discussed more fully § 12.02, *infra*).

14. 412 U.S. 291 (1973).

questioning, after which he was released. During the questioning, the officers observed a dark spot on *M*'s finger, which they suspected was dried blood from the murder. When they asked for permission to take a small scraping for testing, *M* refused and rubbed his fingers together, and then put his hands in his pocket. The police heard a "metallic sound, such as keys or change rattling," which further suggested that *M* was destroying the evidence that connected him to the crime. Therefore, an officer forcibly took scrapings from underneath *M*'s fingernails.

The Supreme Court approved the warrantless police action. Justice Potter Stewart's opinion for the Court concluded that in view of "the existence of probable cause, the very limited intrusion undertaken . . . , and the ready destructibility of the evidence," the search was reasonable. Although the Court did not use the language of "exigency," it certainly could have done so. The police concededly had probable cause to arrest *M*. That probable cause, coupled with *M*'s actions in their presence, almost certainly gave them probable cause to believe that *M* was destroying criminal evidence. That exigency would justify the warrantless limited search they conducted.

§ 11.04 Entry and Search of a Home

The Supreme Court has stated in ringing terms that "physical entry of the home is the chief evil against which the wording of the Fourth Amendment is directed."[15] Indeed, in no other circumstance is the requirement of a search warrant as jealously guarded. Nonetheless, exigent circumstances can justify a warrantless entry of a dwelling to make a felony arrest or to conduct a search related to a serious offense.

In *Minnesota v. Olson*,[16] the Supreme Court concluded that a state court "applied essentially the correct standard" when it identified the following exigencies as circumstances justifying warrantless entry of a home: (1) hot pursuit of a fleeing felon; (2) imminent destruction of evidence; (3) the need to prevent a suspect's escape; or (4) risk of harm to the police or others, inside or outside the dwelling.

Warden v. Hayden[17] provides a good example of how entry into a home and a full-scale search of the premises may be justified on exigency grounds. In *Hayden*, police officers had probable cause to believe that *H*, a man involved in an armed robbery, had moments earlier entered a particular house. An unspecified number of officers hurried to the address, knocked at the door, and were allowed to enter "without objection" by a woman living in the house. The officers spread out on both floors of the house and the basement looking for the suspect, in order to arrest him. *H* was discovered feigning sleep in a bedroom, where he was arrested. At the same time, other officers came upon and seized items related to the crime in other parts of the house.

The officers' warrantless conduct was justified by the Supreme Court because "the exigencies of the situation made the course imperative." The officers were in hot pursuit

---

15. United States v. United States District Court, 407 U.S. 297, 313 (1972); *see also* Brigham City v. Stuart, 547 U.S. 398, 403 (2006) ("It is a 'basic principle of Fourth Amendment law' that searches and seizures inside a home without a warrant are presumptively unreasonable.") (quoting Groh v. Ramirez, 540 U.S. 551, 559 (2004)). In turn, this language was quoted in Kentucky v. King, 563 U.S. 452, 459 (2011).

16. 495 U.S. 91 (1990).

17. 387 U.S. 294 (1967).

of an armed robber and speed was essential. This justified their warrantless entry of the house in order to make an arrest. Once they entered and began their search for the suspect, "only a thorough search of the house for persons and weapons could have insured that [*H*] was the only man present and that the police had control of all weapons which could be used against them or to effect escape."

In short, the exigency justified the warrantless entry, and the nature of the exigency defined the legitimate scope of the warrantless search after the entry. In this case, at a minimum, the police had the right to search any place in the home where the armed robber, anyone else who might interfere with the arrest, and/or weapons, might be found.[18] But the right to conduct the exigency search ended as soon as the robber was discovered and the threat to the officers' safety ended.[19]

A recent case, *Kentucky v. King*,[20] may make it easier for the police to justify warrantless home entries on exigency grounds. In *King*, the police smelled recently burnt marijuana emanating from an apartment door. Seemingly, this gave the police probable cause to search the premises for drugs. Rather than seek a warrant, however, the officers knocked loudly on the door and announced their presence ("This is the police" or "Police, police, police"), at which point they "could hear people inside moving" and "[i]t sounded as [though] things were being moved inside the apartment," all of which "led the officers to believe that drug-related evidence was about to be destroyed." Based on the sounds, the police entered without a warrant. The Court, 8–1, held that the entry was constitutional.

It should be noted that the Supreme Court of Kentucky assumed *arguendo*, as did the United States Supreme Court, that exigent circumstances existed on these facts. One could certainly question that assumption. Does hearing people inside moving, and sounds that *might* be "things being moved inside the apartment" provide ample grounds to believe that destruction of drug-related evidence was imminent? If so, the exigency doctrine may turn out to be a paper-thin exception. But, beyond that, here the basis for the warrantless entry—an exigency—did not exist until the police chose to knock loudly on the door and announce their presence rather than first seek a warrant. To the *King* Court, however, as long as the exigency is not the result of the police "engaging or threatening to engage in conduct that violates the Fourth Amendment," the police may enter without a warrant.

---

18. The Court did not decide in *Hayden* whether the police would have been justified in searching for evidence of the crime, other than weapons, that might be destroyed before they discovered *H*. Although *Olson*, *supra*, concerns the exigencies that justify a warrantless *entry* of a home, the reasoning of that case would justify the search and seizure of criminal evidence, while the police are in hot pursuit of a felon.

19. *See also* Mincey v. Arizona, 437 U.S. 385 (1978) (officers, inside a home when a homicide occurred, secured the premises and searched for other victims; 10 minutes later, homicide investigators arrived and searched the entire premises without a warrant; held: the initial warrantless search for possible victims by the police was justifiable; the subsequent warrantless search by the homicide investigators—now that the emergency was over—was unconstitutional). It should be kept in mind that, just as an exception to the warrant requirement no longer applies once the circumstances justifying the warrant exception no longer exist, the new circumstances may trigger a different warrant exception. For example, in *Warden v. Hayden*, once *H* was arrested, a different warrant exception (search incident to a lawful arrest, *see* Chapter 12, *infra*) came into play.

20. 563 U.S. 452 (2011).

To Justice Ginsburg, the sole dissenter, this ruling "arms the police with a way routinely to dishonor the Fourth Amendment warrant requirement in drug cases." She objected that, under *King*, "police officers may now knock, listen, then break the door down, nevermind that they had ample time to obtain a warrant." Ginsburg would only permit use of the exigency warrant exception if the exigency exists "when the police come on the scene, not subsequent to their arrival, prompted by their own conduct."[21]

---

21. *Id.* at 474.

Chapter 12

Searches Incident to Lawful Arrests

§ 12.01 Warrant Exception: In General[1]

[A] Rule

A police officer who makes a lawful *full custodial arrest*[2] may conduct a contemporaneous[3] warrantless search of: (1) the arrestee's person; and (2) the area within the arrestee's immediate control (sometimes called the "grabbing" or "lunging" area).[4] There are two additional aspects to the rule, which depend on the site of the arrest: (3) if the arrest occurs in a home, the police may also conduct a warrantless search of "closets and other spaces immediately adjoining the place of arrest from which an attack could be immediately launched";[5] and (4) if the police arrest a recent occupant of a vehicle, they may search the passenger compartment of the vehicle, even if the arrestee does not have immediate access to it, if the officers have reason to believe that evidence relevant to the crime of arrest might be discovered there.[6]

This rule, *subject to substantial clarification in § 12.02*, constitutes the "search incident to lawful arrest" (or, for short, "SILA") exception to the search warrant requirement.

[B] Rationale of the Warrant Exception

The leading SILA cases were handed down during a period in which the Supreme Court typically declared that there was a "warrant requirement," i.e., that warrantless searches are unreasonable in the absence of a compelling justification for permitting the police to act without prior judicial authorization.[7] In the SILA cases, the Court's "compelling justification" for dispensing with the warrant requirement was explained in *Chimel v. California*[8] as follows: A custodial arrest provides the suspect with the incentive to use any available weapon to resist the officer or to flee, and to destroy or conceal evidence of the

---

1. *See generally* 3 Wayne R. LaFave, Search and Seizure §§ 5.2, 6.3, 6.4, 7.1 (4th ed. 2004); Myron Moskowitz, *A Rule in Search of a Reason: An Empirical Reexamination of Chimel and Belton*, 2002 Wisc. L. Rev. 657.
2. Regarding the meaning and significance of the italicized words, *see* § 12.02[A][1], *infra*.
3. The arrest must *precede* the search. Sibron v. New York, 392 U.S. 40, 63 (1968) ("It is axiomatic that an incident search may not precede an arrest and serve as part of its justification.").
4. Chimel v. California, 395 U.S. 752 (1969).
5. Maryland v. Buie, 494 U.S. 325 (1990).
6. Arizona v. Gant, 556 U.S. 332 (2009).
7. For a review of the Court's treatment of the Warrant Clause of the Fourth Amendment, *see* § 10.01, *supra*.
8. 395 U.S. 752 (1969).

crime.[9] Further, an in-home arrest "puts the officer at the disadvantage of being on his adversary's 'turf,'"[10] because the arrest creates the risk that an accomplice, relative, or friend of the arrestee might attack the officer. In view of these risks, it is reasonable for arresting officers immediately—without a warrant—to search a suspect and his "grabbing area" (the areas to which he could lunge) for weapons or destructible evidence, and (if in a house) to search the immediately adjoining spaces for dangerous persons.

Searches outside these areas cannot be justified on these grounds. Therefore, as to searches outside these areas, the ordinary rule—that searches should be conducted *with* warrants—comes back into play (unless another warrant exception applies). In modern terms, we may say that the requirement of a warrant is the constitutional "default position": It applies until a compelling justification for acting without a warrant is present, and it applies again once that justification is absent.

[C] Probable Cause

[1] For the Search

The recognition of an exception to a search warrant requirement normally does not in itself dispose of the ordinary rule that a full search may not be conducted in the absence of probable cause. However, in the SILA context, the right of an officer to search the person of the arrestee and the area within his immediate control for weapons and evidence, and the right to search closets and other spaces adjoining the place of arrest for persons who might launch an attack, flows automatically from the arrest itself.[11] That is, the police may conduct such a warrantless search *even if there is no reason to believe that weapons, evidence, or dangerous persons will be discovered.*

There is one critical clarification to the preceding statement, in the special context of the arrest of a recent occupant of a car. Even if the arrestee is no longer able to get inside his vehicle to destroy evidence or seize a weapon—and, thus, an automatic search is *not* permissible—a search of at least the passenger compartment of the vehicle is still permitted if it is "reasonable to believe" evidence relating to the crime of arrest might be found there.[12] Whether this standard is the same as "probable cause" or something less is uncertain. If one reconsiders the definition of "probable cause,"[13] a case can be made for

---

9. *See* Moskowitz, Note 1, *supra*, at 697:

> An arrest is often a traumatic event for a suspect. One moment he is free, and the next moment he is in the custody of the police. And he might realize that this custody can turn into a lengthy prison term if the police obtain more evidence to convict or add further charges. In this emotional state, the arrestee might seek to harm the arresting officers in order to escape, and he might try to dispose of any evidence that might enhance this likelihood of conviction or lead to further charges.

10. Maryland v. Buie, 494 U.S. at 333.

11. United States v. Robinson, 414 U.S. 218 (1973) (search of the arrestee); Arizona v. Gant, 556 U.S. 332 (2009) (search of the passenger compartment of a vehicle); Maryland v. Buie, 494 U.S. 325 (1990) (search of the adjoining area of a home for dangerous persons). Police authority to conduct a SILA does *not*, however, extend to searches of data on cell phones discovered as part of a search. Riley v. California, 134 S. Ct. 2473 (2014) (discussed more fully in 12.06, *infra*). Instead, "officers must generally secure a warrant before conducting such a search." *Id.* at 2485.

12. Arizona v. Gant, 556 U.S. 332, 346, 351 (2009).

13. *See* § 8.02[A], *supra*.

the view that "reason to believe" or "reasonable belief," on the one hand, and "probable cause," on the other hand, are synonyms. However, the Court did not use the term "probable cause," and talks only of a "reasonable belief" that evidence "might" be in the vehicle, which suggests that it will permit the search on a lesser standard, possibly on the basis of "reasonable suspicion," a concept considered in Section 17.03 of this Text.

[2] For the Seizure of Evidence

A separate issue relates to the *seizure* question. As to this, the rule is that an officer, without a warrant, may *seize* any article discovered during a lawful SILA search, even if it relates to a crime unrelated to the arrest,[14] but only if the officer has probable cause to believe the object constitutes constitutionally seizable evidence,[15] i.e., that it is contraband, or is an instrumentality, fruit, or evidence of a crime.[16] In short, the officer need not have probable cause to conduct the ordinary SILA *search*, but must have probable cause to *seize* the evidence found in the search.

§ 12.02 Warrant Exception: In Greater Detail

[A] The Arrest

[1] "Full Custodial"

The SILA rules apply to arrests in which the officer takes the suspect into "full custody," i.e., transports the arrestee to the police station for booking.[17]

Do the SILA rules discussed in this chapter also apply when an officer temporarily detains a suspect in order to issue a traffic citation or other summons? The Supreme Court has answered this question. In *Knowles v. Iowa*,[18] *O*, an Iowa police officer, stopped *K* for speeding. *O* had statutory authority to take *K* into custody for the minor offense and immediately transport him to a magistrate. Instead, however, *O* issued *K* a traffic citation. Then, pursuant to statute, *O* conducted a full search of the car, during which he discovered marijuana under the driver's seat.

The Court unanimously held that this warrantless search could not be justified on SILA grounds. The Court stated that neither of the reasons for permitting warrantless searches at the time of an arrest—to disarm a suspect or to discover and preserve evidence—justifies a search of a car when an officer merely issues a speeding ticket. The Court stated that although officer safety is a "legitimate and weighty" interest, the physical threat to an officer when issuing a citation "is a good deal less" than when he takes

---

14. *E.g.,* United States v. Robinson, 414 U.S. 218 (1973) (holding that the arresting officer properly seized heroin discovered during the search of a traffic violator).

15. *See* § 8.02[E], *supra.*

16. *See* Warden v. Hayden, 387 U.S. 294, 307 (1967) (stating that there must be "a nexus . . . between the item to be seized and criminal behavior"); Arizona v. Hicks, 480 U.S. 321, 326 (1987) (the police must have probable cause to seize items found in plain view).

17. *E.g.,* United States v. Robinson, 414 U.S. 218 (1973) (dealing expressly with a "full custody arrest").

18. 525 U.S. 113 (1998).

the individual into custody.[19] In the latter circumstance, he will be in close proximity to the arrestee for an extended period.

As for discovering evidence, the *Knowles* Court stated that "[a]s for the destruction of evidence relating to [the driver's] identity, if a police officer is not satisfied with the identification furnished by the driver, this may be a basis for arresting him rather than merely issuing a citation." And regarding the possibility that the driver might destroy evidence of an *unrelated* offense, the Court said that such possibility "seems remote."

On its face, *Knowles* is a victory for advocates of limitations on police authority when dealing with citizens in "minor offense" contexts. But it must be kept in mind that the Iowa statute in question gave the police authority to issue a traffic citation to a speeder, as occurred in *Knowles, or* to take the driver into custody and then conduct a warrantless search incident to the lawful custodial arrest. What if *O*, in *Knowles*, had chosen the option of taking *K* into custody?

That is precisely what happened in *Atwater v. Lago Vista*.[20] In *Atwater, O* stopped *A* in her pickup truck because she and her two young children did not have their seatbelts on, a misdemeanor punishable by a small fine. *O* could have issued a traffic citation, but instead he took *A* into custody, which was also authorized by statute. The Court ruled, 5–4, that the Fourth Amendment does not prohibit the custodial arrest of a person for a minor, "fine-only" offense.[21] And once such a custodial arrest is made, the arresting officer is authorized to search the driver and the area within the driver's immediate control. Thus, when officers have the option of taking minor offenders into custody, the conjunction of *Knowles* and *Atwater* creates an incentive for an officer, if he has a hunch that a traffic violator has criminal evidence in his possession or in the passenger compartment of the car, to make a full custodial arrest in order to obtain constitutional authority to search incident to the custodial arrest.[22]

[2] Lawfulness of the Arrest

The SILA doctrine applies to a search conducted after a constitutionally *lawful* arrest. Therefore, if an arrest is constitutionally unlawful, the warrantless search cannot be justified on the basis of this warrant exception. To be constitutionally lawful the police must have probable cause and, in limited circumstances, an arrest warrant.

Notice that the text immediately above speaks of a *constitutionally* lawful arrest. That distinction is important in light of *Virginia v. Moore*.[23] According to *Moore*, an arrest based on probable cause, although in violation of state law, is "lawful" for purposes of the Fourth Amendment, i.e., it is a constitutionally lawful arrest. A search conducted as

---

19. The Court noted that an officer may be justified in non-custodial circumstances to take *some* precautions against the potential use of a weapon by a traffic violator, but a full car search is not required. As to those other precautions, see §§ 17.04[C][2], and 17.07, *infra.*

20. 532 U.S. 318 (2001).

21. See § 9.03, *supra*, for further details on *Atwater.*

22. In the case of a warrantless search of the driver himself, the incentive of a police officer to make a full custodial arrest is substantial, because the right to search the person is automatic in full-custody SILA circumstances. In the case of a search of the vehicle, however, an officer will have less ability to manipulate the situation: If he handcuffs the traffic violator and moves him away from the car, the officer will lose the right to search the interior of the car on SILA grounds except in the very unlikely event that there is reason to believe evidence of the traffic violation can be discovered in the car. See § 12.01[C][1], *supra.*

23. 553 U.S. 164 (2008).

an incident of *that* arrest, therefore, satisfies the Fourth Amendment rules discussed in this chapter.

Thus, in *Moore*, an officer arrested *M* for a minor driving offense and took him into custody. The arrest was supported by probable cause, but under state law the officer should have issued a summons rather than take *M* into custody, so the arrest was "unlawful" according to state law. The Court unanimously held that the arrest was constitutionally lawful because it was supported by probable cause. The search incident to this "lawful" arrest, therefore, was also valid.

Notice that *Moore* may create an incentive for a bad-faith officer, who has probable cause to issue a citation, to instead take that person into custody — even if doing so is in violation of state law — if the officer has a hunch that the search of the person incident to the *constitutionally* lawful arrest might turn up criminal evidence, as occurred here (the search yielded crack cocaine).

[B] Contemporaneousness of the Search

[1] Area within Arrestee's Immediate Control

An officer's right to conduct a search of the area within the immediate control of an arrestee is limited to searches conducted contemporaneously with the arrest. For example, if an officer does not search the car of an arrestee until it is towed to the police garage, this search cannot be justified on SILA grounds.[24] Quite simply, the search is no longer an "incident" of the arrest. This rule is reasonable in light of the SILA doctrine's stated purpose: Once the arrestee is taken into custody and separated from his car at the police station, there is no risk that he can grab any weapons or destroy any evidence that previously were in the lunging area.

[2] Closets and Other Spaces Adjoining the Place of Arrest

Once a person arrested in his home is removed from it, the justification vanishes for a search of closets and other spaces immediately adjoining the place of arrest. Therefore, although the Supreme Court has not yet dealt with a non-immediate search of such areas incident to an arrest, the contemporaneousness limitation should apply.

[3] Of the Person

The contemporaneousness limitation might *not* apply to searches of the person or, perhaps more to the point, the SILA exception merges nearly seamlessly into another warrant exception in most non-contemporaneous searches of custodial arrestees.

Consider *United States v. Edwards*:[25] *E* was arrested at night and jailed for an attempted burglary. Soon after the arrest the police learned that the burglar had attempted to enter the building by prying open a window. Therefore, the police suspected that paint chips might be found on *E*'s clothing. The next morning, about 10 hours after the arrest, the

---

24. Preston v. United States, 376 U.S. 364 (1964). But such a search could, under proper circumstances, be justified under the "inventory search" warrant exception. *See* Chapter 15, *infra*.

25. 415 U.S. 800 (1974).

police purchased new clothing for *E* and seized what he was wearing, which they inspected and held as evidence of the crime.

The Supreme Court upheld the warrantless search. Although the holding appears to be based on various warrant-exception rules,[26] the Court apparently had the SILA rule in mind when it stated that a search of a person "that could be made on the spot at the time of arrest may legally be conducted later when the accused arrives at the place of detention."

Edwards is controversial. In support of the holding is the fact that, as the Court said, *E* "was no more imposed upon than he could have been at the time and place of arrest or immediately upon arrival at the place of detention." If the police could have inspected his clothing, even vacuumed it, at the time of the arrest, *E*'s privacy was not more seriously invaded when the search occurred 10 hours later. Furthermore, any paint chips that were on *E*'s clothing remained in his grabbing area in the jail cell, and the incentive to conceal or destroy the evidence existed throughout the night. Finally, the delay in the search was reasonable, as the police needed time to obtain replacement clothing. On the other hand, the police had 10 hours to secure a warrant, which distinguishes *Edwards* from the ordinary SILA case. Moreover, to the extent that *E* had the inclination to destroy evidence on his clothing, he already had ample time to do so.

Cases like *Edwards* are rare. As a practical matter, when an arrestee is incarcerated the right to search his person incident to the arrest is followed quickly by the right of the police or jail authorities to conduct an arrest inventory,[27] which is likely to be *at least* as thorough as the search incident to the arrest.

[C] Scope of the Search

[1] Search of the Person

The right to search a person incident to a lawful arrest includes the right to search the pockets of the arrestee's clothing, and to open containers found therein,[28] as well as to search containers "immediately associated"[29] with the person, such as a purse or shoulder bag, as long as the containers are large enough to conceal a weapon or evidence of crime.

The right to search the arrestee is not unlimited in scope. For example, because a warrantless search involving penetration of the bodily surface, such as testing a person's blood for evidence of alcohol, implicates the "most personal and deep-rooted expectations of privacy,"[30] it may not be justified under ordinary SILA doctrine, although it may

---

26. Some language in *Edwards* supports the proposition that the search could be justified on principles analogous to the "arrest inventory" exception to the warrant requirement. *See* § 15.02, *infra*. The Court also said that another "closely related consideration" that justified the examination of the clothing was the "plain view" principle, *see* Chapter 14, *infra*, that "the police . . . are normally permitted to seize evidence of crime when it is lawfully encountered."

27. *See* § 15.02, *infra*.

28. *E.g.*, United States v. Robinson, 414 U.S. 218 (1973) (cigarette package in pocket of arrestee). The right to open containers does not, however, include the right to review data on cell phones. *See* Riley v. California, 134 S. Ct. 2473 (2014) (discussed more fully in § 12.06, *infra*).

29. United States v. Chadwick, 433 U.S. 1, 15 (1977).

30. Winston v. Lee, 470 U.S. 753, 760 (1985).

be justifiable on other grounds.[31] However, police may conduct a warrantless breath test for alcohol under the search incident to arrest doctrine, since the level of intrusion for a Breathalyzer test is slight, and the need for an effective and immediate test for blood-alcohol level is significant. In fact, states may pass laws that impose criminal penalties on a motorist who is suspected of drunk driving and refuses to take a Breathalyzer test.[32]

The Supreme Court has not determined under what Fourth Amendment circumstances, if any, a strip search or body-cavity search can be conducted as an incident to an arrest (as distinguished from a search before an arrestee is confined to a jail). At a minimum, however, searches incident to arrest, or even incarceration, must not "violate the dictates of reason . . . because of . . . their manner of perpetration."[33]

[2] Area within the Arrestee's Immediate Control

[a] In General

The area within the "immediate control" of an arrestee is the area into which the person might lunge for a weapon or for evidence to destroy. Accordingly, the arrest of a person in his three-bedroom home does not justify a search of the entire premises,[34] but it might justify the search of much or all of the room in which the arrest occurs, including containers found in the room that could hold a weapon or evidence.

In principle, the scope of the grabbing area depends on the circumstances of the individual case. There is no bright-line rule. Among the factors that may properly affect the scope of the arrestee's grabbing area are: whether he is handcuffed (and, if so, whether he is cuffed in front or behind his back); the size and dexterity of the arrestee; the size of the area to be searched; whether containers in the area are open or shut, and if shut, whether they are locked or unlocked; and the number of police officers relative to suspects.

Notwithstanding the Supreme Court's rejection of a bright-line rule in this context, as a practical matter, some lower courts apply a bright-line "one-room rule" to a search incident to a lawful arrest in a home, i.e., they permit a search of the entire room in which the arrest occurred, regardless of the room size or other circumstances.[35] Improperly, but commonly, as well, some courts treat the arrestee as "a combination acrobat and Houdini who might well free himself from his restraints and suddenly gain access to some distant place."[36]

---

31. In Schmerber v. California, 384 U.S. 757 (1966), the Supreme Court upheld a blood test of a person arrested for driving under the influence of alcohol, but it required that there be a "clear indication" that the test would discover alcohol, and the Court required that the search be performed in a reasonable manner. Although this warrantless search occurred shortly after arrest, *Schmerber* is more obviously justified as an "exigency exception" case. *See generally* § 11.02, *supra*. Given the high level of intrusion involved in a blood test, states are prohibited from passing laws that criminalize a suspect's refusal to take a blood test. Birchfield v. North Dakota, 136 S. Ct. 1241 (2016).

32. Birchfield v. North Dakota, 136 S. Ct. 1241 (2016).

33. United States v. Edwards, 415 U.S. 800, 808 n.9 (1974) (quoting Charles v. United States, 278 F.2d 386, 389 (9th Cir. 1960)).

34. Chimel v. California 395 U.S. 752 (1969).

35. 3 LaFave, Note 1, *supra*, at 352.

36. *Id.* at 304; *see also* Thornton United States, 541 U.S. 615, 626 (Scalia & Ginsburg, JJ., concurring in judgment) (quoting United States v. Frick, 490 F.2d 666, 673 (5th Cir. 1973), which describes a hypothetical arrestee as "possessed of the skill of Houdini and the strength of Hercules").

It should be kept in mind that the grabbing area of a suspect changes if the arrestee moves. The Supreme Court has held that it is not unreasonable for an officer, "as a matter of routine, to monitor the movements of an arrested person, as his judgment dictates, following the arrest."[37] For example, if *D* is arrested in his bathrobe in his living room, it is not unreasonable for the officer to allow *D* to enter the bedroom to get dressed before being taken to the police station. In such circumstances, the officer has "a right to remain literally at [*D*'s] elbow,"[38] and to search the new grabbing area, which includes the clothes *D* intends to wear.

[b] Automobiles

SILA law, specifically relating to automobiles, has taken a particularly complicated, controversial, and meandering path. It is described in detail in Section 12.05.

[3] Protective Searches for Dangerous Persons

The traditional purpose of a search incident to a lawful arrest is to look for weapons or evidence that the arrestee might grab. However, in *Maryland v. Buie*,[39] the Supreme Court stated that as an incident to an arrest in a home, police officers may "as a precautionary matter and without probable cause or reasonable suspicion, look in closets and other spaces immediately adjoining the place of arrest from which an attack could be immediately launched" before the police have time to depart.[40]

Buie provides no clues as to the meaning of the phrase "immediately adjoining the place of arrest." Presumably, this language authorizes the police to look in places outside the arrestee's immediate grabbing area. After all, the purpose of this search is not to prevent the person in custody from grabbing a weapon or evidence, but rather is to look for people who might threaten the officers' safety. On the other hand, because a *Buie* search is for persons, and not for weapons or evidence, the spaces in which the police may look must be large enough to contain a human being.

Buie does not state what an officer may do if he finds a person during such a search. However, especially if the arrest is for a crime of violence, it must certainly be the case that the police, at a minimum, may conduct a limited pat-down for weapons of any person discovered in a closet or other space adjoining the place of the arrest.[41]

[4] DNA Swabs: *Maryland v. King*[42]

In *Maryland v. King*, the Court held that the police may take and analyze a DNA sample from an arrestee as part of a standard booking procedure, provided the arrest was for a "serious offense" supported by probable cause. In *King*, *K* was arrested and charged with first-degree assault for menacing a group of people with a shotgun. On the day of his arrest, as part of processing *K* for detention, the police used a "cheek swab" to take a

---

37. Washington v. Chrisman, 455 U.S. 1, 7 (1982).

38. *Id.* at 6.

39. 494 U.S. 325, 334 (1990).

40. Under more limited circumstances, they may also conduct a protective sweep of other parts of the home, but this action is not based on the SILA exception to the warrant requirement. *See* § 17.08, *infra*.

41. *See* Terry v. Ohio, 392 U.S. 1 (1968).

42. 133 S. Ct. 1958 (2013).

DNA sample from *K*, pursuant to the state's DNA collection statute, which authorized collection of DNA samples from anyone charged with a crime of violence. After *K*'s arraignment, his DNA was uploaded to a database, and it was discovered that his DNA tied him to an unsolved rape case from six years earlier. *K* was subsequently convicted for that rape and sentenced to life in prison without the possibility of parole.

In considering the constitutionality of taking and using *K*'s DNA, every member of the Court agreed that the cheek swab procedure constituted a "search" for the purposes of the Fourth Amendment, but the agreement ended there.

Justice Kennedy, writing for a 5–4 majority, placed the scrutiny of the search's constitutionality "within the category of cases this Court has analyzed by reference to the proposition that the 'touchstone of the Fourth Amendment is reasonableness, not individualized suspicion.'"[43] Accordingly, the majority weighed the "legitimate government interest" served by taking a DNA sample from arrestees charged with serious crimes against the resulting intrusion on privacy. The Court highlighted identification, broadly understood, as a "critical" government interest. The Court cited a number of values of DNA identification: unambiguous knowledge of who the arrestee is, knowledge of the arrestee's criminal history (to assess his dangerousness and likelihood of flight), and, "in the interests of justice," determination of whether the arrestee is "the perpetrator of some [other] heinous crime." For these purposes, the Court described DNA identification as a contemporary analogue of fingerprinting. Balanced against this "substantial interest," the Court found the intrusion of the swabbing procedure "minimal," particularly given the diminished expectation of privacy of an individual "arrested on probable cause for a dangerous offense," and the statutory limitation of the use of the DNA sample to identification purposes. So, the majority held, the Fourth Amendment permits the procedure.

Justice Scalia, writing for the four dissenters, described an ironclad rule: "[t]he Fourth Amendment forbids searching a person for evidence of a crime" without individualized suspicion. When the Court has allowed searches without suspicion, the dissent noted, it has always required a motive at least formally separate from investigation of a crime. Because the dissenters found it "obvious that no such non-investigative motive" was present—because the whole point of the DNA swab was to investigate whether *K* had committed some other crime for which he was not yet under suspicion—the dissenters would rule the "search" of *K* for DNA a violation of the Fourth Amendment.

King's impact beyond the immediate context of DNA testing of arrestees is uncertain. As the dissent points out, the purpose of such programs is quite plainly to determine whether arrestees committed other crimes. The Court had previously held that, under the "special needs" doctrine, only searches ostensibly conducted for non-law enforcement purposes could take place without individualized suspicion.[44] If suspicionless searches for the purpose of criminal investigation are now authorized whenever "reasonable," the expansion of state power would be substantial. On the other hand, and perhaps for this reason, the majority insisted on the "identification" rationale for the search in *King*—perhaps as distinct from criminal investigation—and placed great weight on those searched being arrestees, who are already subject to searches

---

43. *Id.* at 1970 (quoting *Samson v. California*, 547 U.S. 843 (2006)).
44. These searches and their constitutional history are discussed in Chapter 18, *infra*.

with only paper-thin non-criminal justifications, such as searches "incident to arrest," discussed in this Chapter, and "inventory searches."[45] So perhaps the power to take DNA samples will be limited to this specific context.

Even if so, that context itself is substantial: according to the Court, 28 states and the federal government already have statutes similarly authorizing DNA searches of arrestees in certain circumstances, and, as the dissent points out, there is little in the opinion to suggest that the law could not be expanded to cover most arrestees. In 2011, there were more than half a million arrests for violent crimes in the United States, and a total of more than 12 million arrests for non-traffic offenses.[46] Apart from this broad scope, a troubling aspect of gathering evidence from arrestees without suspicion is the very strong evidence that, at least in some contexts, African-Americans are arrested disproportionately to their rate of offending relative to whites. The impact of such discrimination would be multiplied by the enhanced investigation of arrestees.[47]

§ 12.03 *Chimel v. California*: Setting the Rule's Contours[48]

Chimel v. California[49] is the benchmark search-incident-to-lawful-arrest case. In *Chimel*, the police, armed with an arrest warrant but without a search warrant, arrested C in his three-bedroom home for burglary. After the arrest, the officers searched the entire premises, including the attic, garage, and a small workshop, for evidence connected to the crime. Various items were seized. The police contended that the warrantless search should be permitted on the ground that it was incident to the lawful arrest.

Justice Potter Stewart delivered the opinion of the Court. He conceded that the prior law bearing on the issue was "far from consistent." Stewart detailed the Court's four decades of twists and turns in SILA, including twists—*Harris v. United States* and *United States v. Rabinowitz*[50]—in which the Court authorized searches as broad in scope as that which occurred in *Chimel*. In *Chimel*, the Court took another turn. It ruled, 7–2, that, as incident to an arrest, the police may conduct a warrantless search of the arrestee and the area in his immediate control, but that they may *not* search the entire house without a warrant.

The majority's treatment of the issue is illustrative of the Supreme Court's approach to search warrant cases generally in the 1960s and early 1970s.[51] The analysis centered on the Fourth Amendment Warrant Clause and the majority's belief that, in general,

---

45. *See* § 15.02, *infra*.
46. *Crime in the United States, 2011* 1 (U.S. Dep't of Justice 2012), available at http://www.fbi.gov/about-us/cjis/ucr/crime-in-the.u.s/2011/crime-in-the.u.s.-2011/persons-arrested.
47. It is worth noting that some state courts have struck down similar DNA collection schemes by relying on their state constitutions. *See, e.g.,* State v. Medina, 102 A.3d 661 (Vt. 2014); People v. Buza, 231 Cal. App.4th 1446 (Cal. 2014).
48. Moskowitz, Note 1, *supra*.
49. 395 U.S. 752 (1969).
50. *Harris*, 331 U.S. 145 (1947); *Rabinowitz*, 339 U.S. 56 (1950). Both cases were overruled by *Chimel*.
51. *See* § 10.01[B]–[C], *supra*.

warrantless searches are per se unreasonable ("the Constitution requires a magistrate to pass on the desires of the police before they violate the privacy of the home"[52]). Accordingly, a warrantless search is prohibited unless the government demonstrates that an exigency made the warrantless conduct imperative. As the Court stated, "the burden is on those seeking [an] exemption [from the requirement] to show the need for it. . . ." Justice Stewart also stated that when a warrant exception *is* recognized, it "must be "strictly tied to and justified by" the circumstances which rendered its initiation permissible."[53] Put somewhat differently, an exception to the warrant requirement should be defined as narrowly as possible, and the exception should not apply to situations in which the justification for the exception is absent.

In the case of a search incident to an arrest, the Court concluded that a warrantless search of an arrestee is justified in order to remove any weapons that he might seek to use in order to resist arrest or to effect an escape, as well as to seize any evidence that might be destroyed or concealed. For the same reasons, the scope of the search must include the "area within the immediate control" of the arrestee, which the Court defined as "the area into which an arrestee might reach in order to grab a weapon or evidentiary items."

On the other hand, the Court concluded that it is unreasonable to expand the scope of the search to the remainder of the premises on which a suspect is arrested. Such a rule would expand the exception beyond its stated justification of protecting the arresting officer from harm and of preventing the destruction of evidence by the person arrested. Justice Stewart also expressed concern that if a full search of the premises of an arrestee were allowed, the police could pretextually avoid the warrant requirement "by the simple expedient of arranging to arrest suspects at home rather than elsewhere."[54]

Justice Byron White, with whom Justice Hugo Black joined, dissented. The dissent started from a different Fourth Amendment jurisprudential perspective. According to Justice White, there is no Fourth Amendment "warrant requirement"; instead, the Reasonableness Clause of the Fourth Amendment governs search-and-seizure law. In his view, the issue in *Chimel* was not whether an exigency made it impracticable to secure a warrant, but rather was whether a search beyond the area of the arrestee's immediate control, if founded on probable cause, is reasonable.

The dissent reasoned that a search of an arrestee's home incident to an arrest, *if supported by probable cause*, is reasonable. An arrest in a home, he argued, often creates exigent circumstances, including the risk that a family member (for example, *C*'s wife, who was present at the time of his arrest) or an accomplice will seek to destroy evidence after the police depart. "This must so often be the case," Justice White concluded, that it is "unreasonable to require a warrant for the search of the premises" of a person taken into custody in the home. That is, because many or most in-home arrests create an exigency, a bright-line rule should be announced permitting a search of the *entire* premises in *every* case (even one not involving an exigency), as long as the police have probable cause for the warrantless search beyond the grabbing area.

---

52. Chimel v. California, 395 U.S. at 761 (quoting McDonald v. United States, 335 U.S. 451, 455–56 (1948)).

53. *Id.* (quoting Terry v. Ohio, 392 U.S. 1, 19 (1968)).

54. Regarding the general issue of pretextual police conduct, *see* § 2.07[B], *supra*.

§ 12.04 *United States v. Robinson*:
The Traffic Arrest Case[55]

[A] The Holding

Only four years after the high court handed down its opinion in *Chimel v. California*,[56] but also after four changes in personnel on the Supreme Court, the justices decided *United States v. Robinson*.[57] *Robinson* focused on the issue of whether the police, as an incident to a lawful custodial arrest for a routine traffic violation, may search an arrestee although they have no reason to believe that weapons or criminal evidence will be found on him.

In *Robinson*, *O*, a District of Columbia police officer, observed *R* driving his automobile on a public road. Based on prior information, *O* had probable cause to believe that *R* was driving with a revoked operator's permit. *O* ordered *R* to pull over, after which he informed *R* that he was under arrest for "operating after revocation," an offense that required *R*'s custodial arrest, pursuant to police department regulations.

Because District police procedures required him to do so, *O* searched *R*. First, *O* patted down the outside of *R*'s clothing. *O* felt an object in *R*'s breast pocket that he could not identify, but which he pulled out. It was a crumpled up cigarette package inside of which were objects that did not feel like cigarettes. *O* opened the package and found 14 gelatin capsules that contained heroin, which *O* seized, and which served as the basis for *R*'s prosecution on drug possession charges.

The Court of Appeals ruled that the officer acted unconstitutionally by conducting the full search. It focused on the fact that the arrest was for a minor traffic offense, rather than for a serious crime. The court reasoned that *O* had no basis for believing that *R* was in possession of destructible evidence relating to the offense of driving with a revoked license. As for a concern for weapons, the Court of Appeals concluded that with a traffic offense a limited pat-down frisk was sufficient. As the frisk here did not disclose any object that felt like a weapon, the subsequent full searches (pulling out the cigarette package, and then opening it) were impermissible.

The Supreme Court, per Justice Rehnquist, rejected this analysis. It discounted as speculative the assumption that people who violate traffic laws are less likely to possess dangerous weapons than those arrested for more serious crimes. However, its "more fundamental disagreement" with the lower court was with the latter's view that, as the Supreme Court put it, "there must be litigated in each case the issue of whether or not there was present one of the reasons supporting the authority for a search of the person incident to a lawful arrest."

According to *Robinson*, the authority to search a person incident to a lawful custodial arrest does not depend on "what a court may later determine was the probability in

---

55. *See generally* Albert W. Alschuler, *Bright Line Fever and the Fourth Amendment*, 45 U. Pitt. L. Rev. 227, 256–60 (1984); Craig M. Bradley, *The Court's "Two Model" Approach to the Fourth Amendment: Carpe Diem!*, 84 J. Crim. L. & Criminology 429 (1993); Wayne R. LaFave, *"Case-by-Case Adjudication" Versus "Standardized Procedures": The Robinson Dilemma*, 1974 Sup. Ct. Rev. 127; Moskowitz, Note 1, *supra*; James B. White, *The Fourth Amendment as a Way of Talking About People: A Study of Robinson and Matlock*, 1974 Sup. Ct. Rev. 165.

56. 395 U.S. 752 (1969).

57. 414 U.S. 218 (1973).

a particular arrest situation that weapons or evidence would in fact be found upon the person of the suspect." That is, "[a] custodial arrest of a suspect based on probable cause is a reasonable intrusion under the Fourth Amendment; *that intrusion being lawful, a search incident to the arrest requires no additional justification.*"[58] According to *Robinson*, "in the case of a lawful custodial arrest, a full search of the person is not only an exception to the warrant requirement . . . , but is also a 'reasonable' search under [the Fourth] Amendment."

[B] *Robinson* versus *Chimel*

Robinson's holding is not inconsistent with that of *Chimel*. *Chimel* was concerned with the scope of the SILA exception; the Court was not called upon in that case to determine whether probable cause (or any other level of suspicion) was required for searches that occurred within the scope of the exception. Nonetheless, the *Robinson* Court's Fourth Amendment analysis differs from the *Chimel* Court's reasoning and, therefore, is worthy of attention.

In *Chimel*, the Court majority focused on the Warrant Clause of the Fourth Amendment, placed the burden of proof on the government to justify *any* exception to the warrant requirement and, in light of the presumption against warrantless searches, refused to announce an exception broader than was absolutely necessary to meet the circumstances of the situation. In contrast, the *Robinson* Court did not require the government to show that a full warrantless search in the present case (as distinguished from a more limited pat-down) was needed; it did not demand (as *Chimel* did) proof of facts, *particular to the case*, that justified dispensing with the warrant requirement. While noting the existence of a warrant requirement of the Fourth Amendment, the *Robinson* Court primarily focused on its view that a full search of a person custodially arrested for an offense—any offense—is a reasonable search.

In this vein, notice how the *Robinson* Court gave short shrift to the search of *R*'s cigarette package after it was removed from his pocket. That is, even granting the right of officers to search all arrestees for possible weapons and evidence, a remaining question is whether police officers should have the automatic right to open containers found on the person of the arrestee. If warrant exceptions are tied to the exigencies that justify them (as *Chimel* said), an officer should *seize* such a container without a warrant, place it in a safe place outside the arrestee's grabbing area, and thereby avoid the additional privacy intrusion of a warrantless *search* of the container. Justice Rehnquist's analysis of this issue in *Robinson* consisted simply of the statement that "the Fourth Amendment does not require [the officer's judgment] to be broken down in each instance into an analysis of each step in the search." Yet *Chimel*'s reasoning would suggest just such a step-by-step process.

Finally, notice the Court's treatment of the problem of pretextual conduct. In *Chimel*, the Court worried that a rule allowing a full search of the premises of an arrestee would invite police officers pretextually to make arrests in private residences.[59] But, in a case such as *Robinson* there is a significant risk that a police officer will use a minor violation of a vehicle ordinance—an ordinance that requires the officer to take the driver into

---

58. 414 U.S. at 235 (emphasis added).
59. *See* the text immediately preceding Note 54, *supra*.

custody—as a pretext to conduct a full search of someone whom the officer suspects, but has less than probable cause to believe, is in possession of criminal evidence.

Indeed, in *Gustafson v. Florida*,[60] a companion case of *Robinson*, the Supreme Court upheld a search factually similar to that in *Robinson*, except that in *Gustafson* there was no police departmental policy requiring that traffic violators be taken into custody or that full-body searches be conducted. In other words, the officer in *Gustafson* had the opportunity to choose whether to issue a traffic ticket and permit the driver to leave unsearched or, instead, to take the violator into custody and conduct a search incident to the custodial arrest. The Supreme Court in *Gustafson* was not troubled by the possibility that an officer, exercising discretion, might choose to take the driver into custody simply so that he could conduct a search that would not otherwise be constitutionally permitted. In essence, the Court did not consider the problem of pretextual conduct sufficiently serious to justify developing a rule that limited potential police overreaching.[61]

Whichever approach to the Fourth Amendment—that of *Chimel* or *Robinson*—is better, there is considerable basis for asserting that the two opinions do not fit comfortably with each other in terms of general Fourth Amendment jurisprudence.

§ 12.05 Searches of Automobiles Incident to Arrest[62]

[A] *New York v. Belton*

The Supreme Court's approach to searches of automobiles incident to arrest has resulted in controversy and, as a result, change in constitutional interpretation in recent years. The starting point to understanding this aspect of SILA law is *New York v. Belton*.[63] In this case, *O*, a police officer, arrested four occupants of an automobile that he had

---

60. 414 U.S. 260 (1973).

61. *See also* Whren v. United States, 517 U.S. 806, 812 (1996) (observing that the Court's cases, including *Robinson* and *Gustafson*, foreclose the argument "that an officer's [improper] motive invalidates objectively justifiable behavior under the Fourth Amendment").

62. *See generally* Alschuler, Note 55, *supra*; Bradley, Note 55, *supra*; Moskowitz, Note 1, *supra*; David M. Silk, *When Bright Lines Break Down: Limiting New York v. Belton*, 136 U. Pa. L. Rev. 281 (1987).

63. 453 U.S. 454 (1981); *contra, under the state constitution*, State v. Hernandez, 410 So. 2d 1381 (La. 1982) (in dictum, rejecting the bright-line *Belton* rule and requiring case-by-case adjudication of the proper scope of a car SILA); State v. Pierce, 642 A.2d 947 (N.J. 1994) (*Belton* rule does not apply to a warrantless custodial arrest for a motor vehicle offense); Camacho v. State, 75 P.3d 370 (Nev. 2003) (probable cause and exigent circumstances are required to conduct a warrantless SILA); State v. Pittman, 127 P.3d 1116 (N.M. App. 2005) (warrantless SILA of an automobile must be justified by likelihood of physical harm or loss of evidence, and finding neither justification present when defendant was handcuffed and secured in patrol car); People v. Belton, 432 N.E.2d 745 (N.Y. 1982) (warrantless car SILA only allowed when the police have reason to believe that the car contains a weapon or evidence of a crime); State v. Kirsch, 686 P.2d 446 (Or. Ct. App. 1984) (requiring case-by-case adjudication of the grabbing area); Commonwealth v. White, 669 A.2d 896 (Pa. 1995) (absent exigent circumstances, the police may not conduct a warrantless car SILA once occupants are arrested, removed from the car, and in police custody); State v. Bauder, 924 A.2d 38 (Vt. 2007) (*Belton* rule does not apply when car occupant has been arrested, handcuffed, and placed in a police cruiser, eliminating concerns regarding officer safety and protecting evidence); State v.

stopped for speeding, after he smelled burnt marijuana in the vehicle and observed an envelope on the floor of the car marked "Supergold," a term that he associated with marijuana. O removed the occupants from the car and separated them from each other "so they would not be in physical touching area of each other." He returned to the vehicle, opened the envelope, and discovered marijuana. He then searched the remainder of the passenger compartment. In the backseat he found a jacket. He unzipped a pocket of it, in which he found cocaine.

In an opinion written by Justice Stewart, the author of *Chimel*, the Supreme Court approved the warrantless search, including that of the jacket, as an incident to the lawful arrest of the occupants. In doing so, the Court lamented the lack of a "straightforward rule" respecting the question of what constitutes the grabbing area of persons arrested in automobiles. And yet, the Court reported, "[o]ur reading of the cases suggests the generalization that articles inside the relatively narrow compass of the passenger compartment of an automobile are in fact generally, if not inevitably," within the arrestee's grabbing area. Therefore, the Court generated a supposed[64] bright-line rule for automobiles: In all cases, an officer may conduct a contemporaneous warrantless search of the passenger compartment of a vehicle, including all containers therein, incident to a lawful custodial arrest of the occupants. For purposes of this rule, a "container" is defined as "any object capable of holding another object." Under *Belton*, the glove compartment, consoles "or other receptacles," as well as luggage, clothing, boxes, "and the like" found in the passenger compartment are subject to warrantless search. The trunk and engine compartment fall outside the scope of the bright-line *Belton* rule.[65]

It is almost impossible to rationalize *Belton* in light of *Chimel*, and particularly perplexing is the fact that Justice Stewart wrote both opinions. As discussed earlier, *Chimel* was based on the principle that, in view of the constitutional importance of warrants, the scope of a search should be "strictly tied" to the circumstances that render the warrantless action permissible. In *Belton*, however, the bright-line rule seemingly permits the police to dispense with the warrant requirement in many cases in which no genuine exigency exists. For example, if the doors of the passenger compartment of a car are closed and the arrestee is handcuffed, or if he is a considerable distance from the vehicle, or if the arrestee is in custody in the police car, it is hard to imagine that the interior of the vehicle is within the "immediate control" of the arrestee. Yet, the *Belton* bright-line rule seemingly covers such fact patterns. As dissenting Justice Brennan put it, "[i]n its attempt to formulate a single familiar standard . . . to guide police officers . . . the Court disregard[ed] [earlier Fourth Amendment principles], and instead adopt[ed] a fiction— that the interior of a car is *always* within the immediate control of an arrestee who has recently been in the car."[66]

Stroud, 720 P.2d 436 (Wash. 1986) (a warrant is needed to search a locked glove compartment or locked container of car incident to lawful arrest); Vasquez v. State, 990 P.2d 476 (Wyo. 1999) (accepting the scope of a *Belton* search, but only if it is reasonable under the circumstances of the individual case).

64. Arnold H. Loewy, *Cops, Cars, and Citizens*, 76 St. John's L. Rev. 535, 550 (2002) (*Belton* "failed on its own terms to create a true bright line decision"). Some of the interpretive problems are noted in the next footnote.

65. The rule is not as bright-line as it may first appear. Does the rule, which permits the police to open *closed* containers, apply as well to *locked* containers? If the police may search the passenger compartment of a car incident to an arrest, what is the rule if the "car" is a motor home? Also unsettled is the law relating to the "trunk" in a hatchback vehicle.

66. *Belton*, 453 U.S. at 466 (omitting internal quotation marks).

If *Belton*'s approach had been followed in *Chimel*, the search condemned in *that* case—a search of the entire house, while the arrestee and his wife were on the premises—might have been upheld. At the very least, a bright-line "one room" or "one floor" rule (such as lower courts have implicitly adopted[67]), rather than the vague "area of immediate control" rule, would likely have been formulated in the home-arrest context. Put simply, if *Belton* is right in devising a bright-line rule to assist the police and courts in car cases, the case-by-case adjudication called for by *Chimel* in home arrests is hard to justify. If *Chimel* is right, however, *Belton* is hard to fathom.

Even if bright-line rules *are* desirable, a matter of considerable dispute,[68] a strong case can be made that *Belton* is not the proper bright-line rule. Such rules ought to produce results fairly similar to those that would occur by case-by-case adjudication.[69] It is implausible to believe now—and should have been implausible even when *Belton* was decided—that in the majority of cases in which a car occupant is arrested, the entire passenger compartment of the vehicle is in the arrestee's grabbing area *after he is removed from the vehicle, when the search occurs.*[70] Most police training manuals instruct that when a car occupant is arrested, he should be removed from the vehicle, handcuffed, and placed in the police car before any car search occurs. Therefore, if a bright-line rule is desired, it would be closer to reality to declare that the interior of a vehicle is *never* in the arrestee's immediate control once he is removed from it or, at least, once he is placed in the police car.

As will be seen, these weaknesses in *Belton*, expressed by scholars, the many state courts that refused to follow *Belton*,[71] and of course the dissenters in *Belton* itself, would cause the Supreme Court to reconsider and narrow *Belton*.

[B] The Change Comes: *Arizona v. Gant*

In 2009, as a result of *Arizona v. Gant*,[72] the *Belton* "bright-line" rule became less bright, narrower, and arguably more consistent with the Fourth Amendment principles underlying *Chimel v. California*.[73] As Justice Stevens, writing for the five-justice majority, candidly put it, "[t]he chorus that has called for us to revisit *Belton* includes courts, scholars, and Members of this Court who have questioned that decision's clarity and its fidelity to Fourth Amendment principles. We therefore granted the State's petition for certiorari."

In *Gant*, G parked his car in a driveway and exited his vehicle. He then was lawfully arrested (based on prior information) for driving on a suspended license. The officers handcuffed G and locked him in a patrol car, after which they searched his car and discovered cocaine in the pocket of a jacket in the backseat. Thus, the scope of the search was uncontroversial—the drugs were found in a container in the passenger compartment of the car. And G was a "recent occupant" of the vehicle. G argued, however, that

---

67. *See* the text accompanying Note 35, *supra*.

68. *See* § 2.07[A], *supra*.

69. Wayne R. LaFave, *The Fourth Amendment in an Imperfect World: On Drawing "Bright Lines" and "Good Faith,"* 43 U. Pitt. L. Rev. 307, 325–26 (1982).

70. *See* Moskowitz, Note 1, *supra*, at 692 (stating that cases of arrestees gaining access to their car at the time of the search are "very unusual" in practice).

71. See Note 63, *supra*.

72. 556 U.S. 332 (2009).

73. 395 U.S. 752 (1969).

the *Belton* rule did not apply because "he posed no threat to the officers after he was handcuffed in the patrol car and because he was arrested for a traffic offense for which no evidence could be found in the vehicle."

The trial judge denied the motion to suppress, understandably interpreting *Belton* as authority to conduct the warrantless search. The Arizona Supreme Court, however, reversed. According to it, *Belton* announced a bright-line rule as to the *scope* of a car search incident to arrest, but it did not answer the "threshold question whether the police may conduct a search incident to arrest at all once the scene is secure."

The Supreme Court conceded that the predominant approach of lower courts had been to interpret *Belton* as the Brennan dissent in that case had put it — on the "fiction . . . that the interior of a car is *always* within the immediate control of an arrestee who has recently been in the car."[74] As the Court now observed (much as *Belton*'s critics had already pointed out), "[u]nder this broad reading of *Belton*, a vehicle search would be authorized incident to every arrest of a recent occupant notwithstanding that in most cases the . . . passenger compartment will not be within the arrestee's reach at the time of the search." In turn, this would "untether the rule from the justifications underlying the *Chimel* exception."

The Court rejected this reading of *Belton*, although it was clearly the most reasonable one, and announced instead that "we . . . hold that the *Chimel* rationale authorizes police to search a vehicle incident to a recent occupant's arrest only when the arrestee is unsecured and within reaching distance of the passenger compartment at the time of the search." However, after announcing this considerably narrower reading of *Belton*, the Court added a new feature of SILA law, drawn explicitly from Justice Scalia's concurrence in a previous case, *Thornton v. United States*[75]: "Although it does not follow from *Chimel*, we also conclude that circumstances unique to the vehicle context justify a search incident to a lawful arrest when it is 'reasonable to believe evidence relevant to the crime of arrest might be found in the vehicle.'"[76]

The Court not surprisingly held that the warrantless search of *G*'s vehicle was unconstitutional under this revised reading of *Belton*: While sitting handcuffed in a locked police car, he was not within the grabbing area of the passenger compartment of his vehicle; and there was no reason to believe evidence relating to the crime for which he was arrested (driving on a suspended license) might be found inside.

Justice Scalia concurred in the opinion. He would have preferred to:

> simply abandon the *Belton-Thornton* charade of officer safety and overrule those cases. I would hold that a vehicle search incident to arrest is *ipso facto* reasonable only when the object of the search is evidence of the crime for which the arrest was made, or of another crime that the officer has probable cause to believe occurred.

However, as he conceded, no one else on the Court "shares my view that application of *Chimel* in this context should be entirely abandoned." Therefore, Justice Scalia said, "[i]t seems to me unacceptable for the Court to come forth with a 4-to-1-to-4 opinion that

---

74. See the text to Note 66, *supra*.
75. 541 U.S. 615 (2004).
76. *Gant*, 556 U.S. at 343. Does this mean that the police need probable cause for such a search? See the text to Notes 12–13, *supra*.

leaves the governing rule uncertain." He preferred the "artificial narrowing of those cases" to the dissent's alternative, which would retain the law in its broad form and thereby justify "the greater evil" of "plainly unconstitutional searches."

Justice Alito dissented, joined by Chief Justice Roberts, Justice Kennedy, and, in most parts, Justice Breyer. Justice Alito stated that the Court's new approach will "confuse law enforcement officers and judges for some time to come," and will "cause the suppression of evidence gathered in many searches carried out in good-faith reliance on well-settled case law." Indeed, the essence of the dissent was that, "[a]lthough the Court refuses to acknowledge that it is overruling *Belton* . . . there can be no doubt that it does so."[77] And, in the dissent's view, departure from the usual rule of *stare decisis* was unjustified. It reached this conclusion based on five factors: (1) police reliance on the *Belton* rule; (2) the absence of changed circumstances justifying the change; (3) the workability of the original rule; (4) the consistency of later cases with *Belton*; and (5) the dissent's view that *Belton* was "only a modest—and quite defensible—extension of *Chimel*."[78]

The dissent pointed to certain anomalies or uncertainties in the new law. Of particular note is the Court's new rule that, even if the arrestee does not have access to the interior of the car, the police may nonetheless search the passenger compartment if they have reason to believe that it might contain evidence of the offense of arrest. Justice Alito asked: "[W]hy is this type of search restricted to evidence of the offense of arrest? . . . Nor is it easy to see why an evidence-gathering search incident to arrest should be restricted to the passenger compartment."

§ 12.06 *Riley v. California*: The Cell Phone Case

Times change, and the questions and controversy concerning the scope of police authority under the SILA exception change with them. In *Riley v. California*,[79] the Court faced the following question: May the police, under the SILA exception, conduct a warrantless search of digital information on a cell phone seized from an individual who has been arrested? The Court's unanimous answer was no.

Riley covered two different cases. In the first case, R was stopped for driving with expired registration tags and then arrested for firearm possession on the basis of guns the police found in the car R was driving. R was searched incident to his arrest, and the police removed his "smart phone" from his pants pocket. The police later discovered photos on R's phone showing R in front of a car the police suspected had been involved in a recent shooting. R was subsequently charged, convicted and sentenced to 15 years to life in prison in connection with those shootings, in part on the basis of the evidence from his cell phone.

In the second case, the police observed W making a drug sale from a car. W was arrested and, at the police station, the police took two cell phones from W's person. They

---

77. *Id.* at 356.
78. *Id.* at 361. Justice Breyer did not join the dissent as to this fifth point. In a separate dissent, he expressed his agreement with the majority that the *Belton* rule "can produce results divorced from its underlying Fourth Amendment rationale." *Id.* at 354.
79. 134 S. Ct. 2473 (2014).

used photo and contact information on the phone (a particular number was labeled "my house") to locate *W's* residence. On the basis of this information, the police obtained a search warrant for the residence. As a result of the subsequent search of the apartment, *W* was charged and convicted on three possession counts related to drugs and firearms and was sentenced to more than 20 years in prison.

Chief Justice Roberts, writing for eight members of the Court, began by reviewing the "search incident to arrest trilogy" of *Chimel*,[80] *Robinson*,[81] and *Gant*,[82] and noted that "a mechanical application of *Robinson* might well support the warrantless searches here." That "mechanical" reasoning would be: (i) the cell phones were properly taken from the arrestee's person under the SILA exception; (ii) police inspection of the contents of the cell phones was permissible because the SILA exception allows searching the inside of objects seized incident to arrest (such as the cigarette package in *Robinson*); and (iii) under *Robinson*, there is no case-by-case consideration of whether the underlying justifications for the SILA exception apply. Yet the Court rejected this path. Chief Justice Roberts wrote that while the "categorical rule strikes the appropriate balance in the context of physical objects, neither of its rationales have much force with respect to digital content on cell phones." Relying on *Gant* (which similarly departed from *Robinson's* automatic rule, although over Chief Justice Roberts' dissent), the *Riley* Court described the issue before it as whether applying the SILA "doctrine to this particular category of effects would 'untether the rule from the justifications underlying the *Chimel* exception.' "[83] Conducting that analysis, the Chief Justice dryly noted that once "an officer has secured a phone . . . data on the phone can endanger no one," and he was similarly dismissive of claims that searching a cell phone might be necessary to prevent the destruction of evidence.

In addition to finding the government interests described in *Chimel* inapplicable in the cell phone context, the Court importantly—probably crucially—also described a difference in the arrestee's privacy interest. The Court noted that it may make sense to conclude, in the context of "physical items," "that inspecting the contents of an arrestee's pockets" does not intrude much on privacy "beyond the arrest itself." But not so with cell phones. The government's assertion that searching the contents of a cell phone is indistinguishable from a search of physical items, "is like saying a ride on horseback is materially indistinguishable from a flight to the moon." The scope and volume of personal information stored on cell phones, the Court explained, "would typically expose to the government far *more* than the most exhaustive search of a house."[84]

The Court's decision in *Riley* provides a very clear rule, while simultaneously opening new questions. The clear rule: the police may not justify a search of the contents of a cell phone under the SILA exception; to view such data either a warrant must be obtained or a different warrant exception must apply. An immediate and perhaps continuing question will be the scope of police authority to search other technological devices under the SILA doctrine—tablets, e-readers, activity trackers, digital recorders, and more, including all the new devices to come. More broadly, will the Court's unanimous willingness to eschew "mechanical application" of existing Fourth Amendment tests in the face of new

---

80. Discussed in § 12.03, *supra*.
81. Discussed in § 12.04, *supra*.
82. Discussed in § 12.05[C], *supra*.
83. 134 S. Ct. at 2485 (quoting *Gant*, 556 U.S. 332, 343 (2009).
84. *Id*. at 2490 (emphasis in original).

technologies expand beyond the SILA exception? For example, will *Riley*'s "technology-is-different" approach apply in determining what constitutes a search (where the Court is already struggling)?[85] Will it matter to the application of the "plain view" exception[86] in the context of massive data aggregations? The Court will have ample opportunity to consider *Riley*'s implications in these and other contexts.

---

85. *See* § 6.10, *supra*.
86. *See* Chapter 14, *infra*.

Chapter 13

Searches of Cars and Containers Therein

§ 13.01 Automobile Search Warrant Exception: General Rules[1]

[A] Important Overview

A warrantless nonconsensual search of an automobile can be justified in various circumstances: as incident to a lawful arrest; in the police department's community caretaking function of inventorying a vehicle after it has been lawfully seized and towed from a public road; at international borders; and, in limited situations, when a driver is stopped on the highway for violating a traffic offense.[2] But there is also a specific "automobile[3] exception" to the Fourth Amendment search warrant "requirement," which is the subject of this chapter.

The automobile exception has broadened dramatically over time. The Supreme Court once stated that "[t]he word 'automobile' is not a talisman in whose presence the Fourth Amendment fades away and disappears."[4] Today, however, in nearly all circumstances, a citizen who enters an automobile surrenders the right to have the initial probable cause determination of a car search[5] made by a magistrate. Indeed, in many circumstances, the police may search or seize an *unoccupied* automobile without a warrant, as long as it is later determined that they possessed probable cause for the conduct.

The general rules are set out in the subsections that follow. But the rules that have developed are controversial. Therefore, to appreciate the controversies — and to fully understand the road that the Supreme Court has taken to its current destination — some of the most critical automobile cases are discussed in Section 13.02 through 13.04.

---

1. *See generally* 3 Wayne R. LaFave, Search and Seizure § 7.2(a)-(b) (4th ed. 2004); Lewis R. Katz, *The Automobile Exception Transformed: The Rise of a Public Place Exemption to the Warrant Requirement*, 36 Case W. Res. L. Rev. 375 (1986); Note, *Warrantless Searches and Seizures of Automobiles*, 87 Harv. L. Rev. 835 (1974).

2. *See* § 12.05, *supra* (search incident to a lawful arrest); § 15.01, *infra* (inventory search); § 17.07, *infra* (during traffic stop); and § 18.03 (border search).

3. As used in this chapter, the word "automobile" applies to all motorized vehicles, including trucks, airplanes, motor homes, and motor boats. *See* California v. Carney, 471 U.S. 386, 393 n.2 (1985).

4. Coolidge v. New Hampshire, 403 U.S. 443, 461–62 (1971) (plurality opinion).

5. The warrantless search of an occupant of a vehicle, as distinguished from the automobile itself, does not fall within the scope of the automobile search warrant exception. The justification for *that* search must be found elsewhere, e.g., as incident to an arrest.

A separate issue must also be considered in relation to automobiles. Often, a search of an automobile includes a search of a container, e.g., an occupant's purse or jacket, a paper bag, or a briefcase, found within the vehicle. This so-called container-in-car issue is considered in Section 13.05.

[B] Searches "At the Scene"

A police officer may conduct an immediate ("at the scene") warrantless search of an automobile that she has probable cause to believe contains contraband, or fruits, instrumentalities, or evidence of a crime, if: (1) she stops the car on the highway;[6] or (2) the vehicle is readily capable of use on the highway, is found "in a setting that objectively indicates that [the vehicle] is being used for transportation," and is discovered "stationary in a place not regularly used for residential purposes."[7]

Although early automobile cases were based on a requirement of exigency—that the vehicle could immediately be moved and, therefore, lost to the police—the current law provides that "the "automobile exception" has no separate exigency requirement."[8] It is now enough that "[i]f a car is readily mobile and probable cause exists to believe it contains contraband [or other seizable evidence], the Fourth Amendment . . . permits police to search the vehicle without more."[9]

It follows from this that, assuming probable cause to search, the police may conduct an immediate search of those portions of the vehicle for which the police have probable cause to search, when they stop the car on a public road,[10] or which they discover off the highway, at a gas station,[11] or parked in a public place, such as in a parking lot.[12] In contrast, there is possible support for the proposition that a warrantless search of an unoccupied car parked in the user's driveway or garage is not permitted if the police have time to secure a warrant prior to the search.[13]

---

6. Carroll v. United States, 267 U.S. 132, 153–54 (1925); *contra under the state constitution*, State v. Tibbles, 236 P.3d 885 (Wash. 2010) (the fact that a car is stopped on the highway and is inherently mobile, does not, by itself, justify a warrantless car search, even if there is probable cause for the search).

7. California v. Carney, 471 U.S. at 392, 394.

8. Maryland v. Dyson, 527 U.S. 465, 467 (1999); *contra under the state constitution*, State v. Miller, 630 A.2d 1315 (Conn. 1993); State v. Elison, 14 P.3d 456 (Mont. 2000); State v. Sterndale, 656 A.2d 409 (N.H. 1995); State v. Cooke, 751 A.2d 92 (N.J. 2000); State v. Kock, 725 P.2d 1285 (Or. 1986); State v. Larocco, 794 P.2d 460 (Utah 1990) (plurality opinion); State v. Patterson, 774 P.2d 10 (Wash. 1989) (all holding that, absent an exigency beyond the inherent mobility of a car or some other independent warrant exception, a warrant supported by probable cause is required to conduct a search of an *unoccupied* vehicle).

9. Pennsylvania v. Labron, 518 U.S. 938, 940 (1996).

10. *E.g.*, Carroll v. United States, 267 U.S. 132 (1925).

11. *See* Colorado v. Bannister, 449 U.S. 1 (1980) (per curiam) (the police observed the car on the road, but did not reach it until it had left the highway and entered a service station).

12. *E.g.*, California v. Carney, 471 U.S. 386 (1985) (vehicle was occupied). Many courts have justified warrantless searches of *unoccupied* cars parked on the street, often on the ground that the suspect linked to the car is at large, that accomplices might arrive and drive away the car, or even that a stranger might tamper with it. 3 LaFave, Note 1, *supra*, at 545–46, 559–60 (and cases cited therein).

13. *E.g.*, Coolidge v. New Hampshire, 403 U.S. 443 (1971) (plurality opinion). *Coolidge* is considered in Section 13.02[C], *infra*. Its questionable current vitality is considered in Section 13.04, *infra*.

As a corollary of the preceding rules, the Fourth Amendment does not require the police to secure a warrant to *seize* an automobile parked in a public place—even if they have time to obtain a warrant—when they have probable cause to believe that the vehicle itself constitutes forfeitable contraband under state law (e.g., there is probable cause to believe that the car was used on some prior occasion in the commission of a criminal offense).[14] The police may seize the vehicle on these grounds, although they have no reason to believe that it contains objects subject to seizure.[15]

[C] Searches "Away from the Scene"

A warrantless search of an automobile that would be valid if it were conducted at the scene, i.e., at the place where it was stopped or discovered, is also permitted if it takes place shortly thereafter away from the scene.[16] That is, if the police wish to do so—regardless of the reason for their decision[17]—they may seize a car without searching it, move it to another site (such as a police impoundment lot), and (presupposing probable cause) search it there without a warrant, on the day of the seizure,[18] or even a day[19] or a few days[20] later. On the other hand, a delay of a year to search an impounded vehicle without a warrant is unreasonable.[21]

[D] Probable Cause Requirement

As the preceding comments suggest, the police may conduct a search of an automobile without a warrant in most circumstances. But, the "automobile exception" to the Fourth Amendment is an exception only to the requirement of a search warrant; the probable cause requirement remains firm. The Supreme Court has explained that "[t]he scope of a warrantless search of an automobile . . . is defined by the object of the search and places in which there is probable cause to believe that it may be found."[22] Thus, it does *not* follow that "probable cause to search" *always* applies to an *entire* automobile. In most circumstances, the police will receive reliable information that criminal evidence is somewhere in (or, perhaps, throughout) the vehicle, in which case the right to search

---

14. Florida v. White, 526 U.S. 559 (1999).

15. After the seizure, the police may also be authorized to conduct a warrantless inventory *search* of the automobile. If so, evidence found during such a lawful inventory would be admissible at the car owner's trial. *See* § 15.01, *infra*.

16. Chambers v. Maroney, 399 U.S. 42 (1970).

17. Texas v. White, 423 U.S. 67 (1975) (per curiam).

18. *E.g.*, Chambers v. Maroney, 399 U.S. 42 (1970).

19. Cardwell v. Lewis, 417 U.S. 583 (1974) (plurality opinion).

20. *E.g.*, United States v. Johns, 469 U.S. 478, 487 (1985) (three-day delay was reasonable; however, the Court did not "foreclose the possibility" that a delay of that length could be deemed unreasonable if the owner proved that the delay "adversely affected [her] privacy or possessory interest" in the car or its contents).

21. *E.g.*, Coolidge v. New Hampshire, 403 U.S. 443 (1971) (the car was unconstitutionally searched without a warrant three times, two of which occurred more than a year after the car was seized); United States v. Johns, 469 U.S. at 487 (citing *Coolidge*, the Court observed that "police officers may [not] indefinitely retain possession of a vehicle and its contents before they complete a vehicle search").

22. United States v. Ross, 456 U.S. 798, 824 (1982).

will extend to the entire car. On the other hand, the police may possess more limited probable cause.

For example, in *California v. Acevedo*,[23] the police observed *A* place a small paper bag in the trunk of a vehicle and drive away. The officers had probable cause to believe that the bag contained drugs; they had no reason to believe that the car (beyond the bag) contained contraband. On these facts, the police had probable cause to search only the trunk to look for the paper bag.

A second point to understand is that once the police discover the criminal evidence for which they are searching, the search must cease, absent new information that would justify a new search. Thus, in *Acevedo*, once the paper bag was found in the trunk, the police could not lawfully continue to search the car (as distinguished from the paper bag), because there was no longer probable cause to search further.

Third, as with searches executed by warrant,[24] the police may not search any portion of a vehicle that could not contain the object of the search. For example, if the police have probable cause to search a car for a stolen large-screen television set, the police may not open the glove compartment. However, if they are looking for stolen jewelry, the glove compartment may be searched.

§ 13.02 Automobile Search Warrant Exception: The "Mobility" Rationale

[A] *Carroll v. United States*: True Mobility

In *Carroll v. United States*,[25] a Prohibition-era case, the Supreme Court first enunciated an automobile exception to the Fourth Amendment warrant requirement. In *Carroll*, federal officers stopped *C* and *X* in *C*'s automobile on the highway and searched it without a warrant for "bootleg" liquor. At the time *C*'s car was stopped, the officers had probable cause to search it for the contraband, but they lacked authority to arrest the occupants of the car unless and until they found the goods.[26]

The Court upheld the warrantless search for contraband.[27] In an opinion written by Chief Justice Taft, the Court stated that "[i]n cases where the securing of a warrant is reasonably practicable, it must be used." However, it also observed that "a necessary difference [exists] between a search of a . . . dwelling house or other structure in respect of which a proper official warrant readily may be obtained" and an automobile, because a

---

23. 500 U.S. 565 (1991).

24. *See* § 10.04[F], *supra*.

25. 267 U.S. 132 (1925).

26. Possession of the liquor was a misdemeanor, and the police could only arrest for a misdemeanor if the offense was committed in their presence, which required that they observe the liquor in the car.

27. *Carroll* only authorized a warrantless search of the automobile for contraband and property "subject to seizure and destruction." However, as Professor LaFave has observed, "the specific reference to contraband appears to be no more than recognition of the then extant 'mere evidence' rule, ultimately abolished. . . ." 3 LaFave, Note 1, *supra*, at 539. For discussion of the "mere evidence" rule, *see* § 8.02[E], *supra*.

"vehicle can be quickly moved out of the locality or jurisdiction in which the warrant must be sought."

The result in *Carroll* is unsurprising. Apparently, the police did not have probable cause to search the vehicle before they spotted it on the highway. Moreover, the police "were not looking for defendants at the particular time when they appeared." Therefore, the police could not be faulted for not possessing a warrant when they sighted the car. At that point, the car was clearly mobile; it was in transit on the highway. And, significantly, the occupants could not be arrested prior to the search, so the police could not prevent the suspects from driving out of the jurisdiction. Therefore, a genuine exigency existed. The only practical solution was to conduct a warrantless search.

[B] *Chambers v. Maroney*: A Controversial View of "Mobility"

In *Chambers v. Maroney*,[28] police officers had probable cause to stop *C*'s car because it fit the description of one involved in a robbery in the vicinity. When the officers approached the car and saw that the occupants fit the robbers' descriptions, the police lawfully arrested them. The police did not search the car at that time. Instead, they drove it and the suspects to the police station. Shortly thereafter, while the arrestees were in jail, the police searched the car without a warrant and found weapons and evidence of the crime concealed under the dashboard.

The Court, per Justice Byron White, upheld the warrantless search, ostensibly on the basis of the principles enunciated in *Carroll v. United States*. Essentially, *Chambers* stands for the proposition that, as the Court later explained, "police officers with probable cause to search an automobile at the scene where it was stopped [may] constitutionally do so later at the station house without first obtaining a warrant."[29]

Justice White stated that "[n]either *Carroll*, . . . nor other cases in this Court require or suggest that in every conceivable circumstance the search of an auto even with probable cause may be made without the extra protection for privacy that a warrant affords." Nonetheless, as in *Carroll* and the present case, "the circumstances that furnish probable cause to search . . . are most often unforeseeable; moreover, the opportunity to search is fleeting since a car is readily movable."

The Court reasoned that when an automobile is stopped on the highway, an effective search is possible only if the police search the car at the scene, or seize it without a warrant and hold it until one is obtained. Justice White conceded that "arguably," in view of the preference for a magistrate's determination of probable cause, the latter option should have been followed here, on the ground that "the 'lesser' intrusion [of the seizure] is permissible until the magistrate authorizes the 'greater' [intrusion of the search]." The Court rejected this "arguable" claim. It stated that the question of which is the greater intrusion "is itself a debatable question . . . the answer [to which] may depend on a variety of circumstances." Consequently, the Court concluded, there is no constitutional difference between the options: "Given probable cause to search, either course is reasonable under the Fourth Amendment."

---

28. 399 U.S. 42 (1970).
29. Texas v. White, 423 U.S. 67, 68 (1975).

But, the police in *Chambers* followed neither of these paths: they did *not* search the car at the scene without a warrant; and they did *not* seize it without a warrant and then submit the issue of probable cause to a neutral and detached magistrate. Instead, they seized the car without a warrant and searched it — again without a warrant — at the station. The Court justified the latter action on the ground that, "unless the Fourth Amendment permits a warrantless seizure of the car and the denial of its use to anyone until a warrant is secured," a car retains its mobility at the police station. Therefore, the officers' practical options at the stationhouse were the same as they were on the highway: search it immediately; or deny its use to others until a warrant could be obtained. Again, the Court ruled that there was no constitutional difference between these choices.

Two critical observations of *Chambers* are in order. First, "mobility," at least as it existed in *Carroll*, plainly was absent in *Chambers*. In *Carroll*, the police were unable to arrest the occupants, and thus the occupants might have driven the vehicle away before the police searched the vehicle. In *Chambers*, the occupants were in custody prior to the search, and the search occurred at the police station; therefore, there was no risk that the car would be quickly moved out of the jurisdiction or hidden. Nor did the government present any evidence that anyone who had a right to the car sought to take it while it was at the station. As one scholar has observed, the *Chambers* Court's rationale for the warrantless search, as one based on mobility, was "so transparently flimsy, that it is hard to take seriously."[30]

Second, the Court was almost certainly wrong when it concluded that there was no constitutional difference between the warrantless search of *C*'s car in *Chambers*, on the one hand, and its warrantless seizure until a magistrate could make the probable cause determination, on the other hand. The latter option surely constituted a lesser intrusion, as Justice Harlan argued in his dissent.

Why is this? When a car is stopped by police on the highway, various constitutionally recognized interests of its occupants are at stake.[31] First, the occupants have an interest in being permitted to continue their travel unimpeded. Second, the car owner has a possessory interest in her vehicle. Third, the occupants have a privacy interest in the contents of the car. In *Chambers*, however, neither *C* nor the others were in position to assert either of the first two interests. The occupants were in custody, so their right of uninterrupted travel had lapsed. Nor could they realistically expect the police to leave the car on the highway; the officers' caretaking function required them to move it to a safer site, so *C*'s interest in control over his car could not be enforced. Thus, *C*'s only substantial Fourth Amendment concern was his privacy interest in the contents of the car, which would be better protected by the requirement that the police apply for a search warrant.

Can *Chambers* be justified? The only way it can make sense on the basis of the mobility rationale is to define "mobility" differently than in *Carroll*. In the latter case, the car was considered "mobile" because it was occupied and in transit. Presumably, as well, a car is mobile if it is occupied and imminently will be on the road. In contrast, in *Chambers*, Justice White attached a much broader meaning to the concept of mobility: When he stated that an impounded automobile at a police station is "readily movable," he seemed to be focusing on the *inherent* nature of a motor vehicle. It follows from this that, after *Chambers*, the "exigency" that justifies a warrantless car search does not terminate

---

30. Arnold H. Loewy, *Cops, Cars, and Citizens: Fixing the Broken Balance*, 76 St. John's L. Rev. 535, 539 (2002).

31. Note, Note 1, *supra*, at 840–45.

simply because the car is unoccupied and the people to whom it belongs are in custody or otherwise unable to take the car.

This meaning of "mobility" applies nearly always to any motorized vehicle. The logic of this approach is that there is no real exigency requirement at all, separate from the fact that a car is a car (at least as long as it is in functioning condition). Cars, so understood, virtually fall outside the Fourth Amendment's warrant protection.

[C] *Coolidge v. New Hampshire*: Departing from *Chambers*

In *Coolidge v. New Hampshire*,[32] the police investigated *C*'s possible involvement in a recent murder. *C* and his wife fully cooperated with the police in the investigation. After three weeks, the authorities concluded that they had probable cause to arrest *C*, as well as probable cause to search his car for evidence related to the crime. The police arrested *C* at his home. His car was parked in the driveway. The police towed it to the police station, and thereafter searched it three times without a valid warrant, two days after it was seized, nearly a year later, and a third time 14 months after the original search.

Justice Potter Stewart delivered the opinion of the Court, but the portion of the opinion relating to the automobile exception to the warrant requirement mustered only four votes. The plurality held that the warrantless search of *C*'s car was unconstitutional. In an effort to distinguish the facts from *Carroll v. United States* and *Chambers v. Maroney*, where warrants were not required, Justice Stewart noted that, in the present case, "the police had known for some time of the probable role of the . . . car in the crime." Moreover, *C* "already had ample opportunity to destroy any evidence he thought incriminating." The Court also set out other facts it considered important, including that the vehicle was not stopped on the highway, as in the prior cases, but rather was "an unoccupied vehicle parked on the owner's private property."

These facts distinguish *Coolidge* from *Carroll*. The car in the earlier case, but not here, was in transit, and the police had to act quickly. But can this case truly be distinguished from *Chambers*? Although the car in that case started on the highway, and this one did not, in both cases the searches occurred after the vehicle was impounded, and after the suspect was in custody.

The difference between the cases really comes down to how the Court chooses to define the term "mobility." Justice White, the author of *Chambers*, stated in *Coolidge* that "the difference between a moving and movable vehicle is tenuous at best. It is a metaphysical distinction without roots in the commonsense standard of reasonableness governing search and seizure cases." In short, to Justice White and the *Chambers* majority, all functioning automobiles are "mobile," even as they sit unoccupied in a police impoundment lot. In contrast, consider Justice Stewart's remarks in *Coolidge*:

> It is frequently said that occupied automobiles stopped on the open highway may be searched without a warrant because they are "mobile," or "movable." . . . In this case, it is, of course, true that even though [*C*] was in jail, his wife was miles away in the company of two plainclothesmen, and the Coolidge property was under the guard of two other officers, the automobile was in a literal sense

---

32. 403 U.S. 443 (1971).

"mobile." . . . We attach no constitutional significance to this sort of mobility. . . . [A] good number of the containers that the police might discover on a person's property and want to search are equally movable, *e.g.*, trunks, suitcases, boxes, briefcases, and bags. How are such objects to be distinguished from an unoccupied automobile . . . sitting on the owner's property?

Whereas Justice White's view of mobility would leave automobiles nearly unprotected from warrantless searches,[33] Justice Stewart's approach seems intended to retain the logic of the mobility exception by placing limits on the concept. To him, "[t]he word 'automobile' is not a talisman in whose presence the Fourth Amendment fades away and disappears." And, as the quotation above suggests, Justice Stewart feared that the reasoning of *Chambers* could unwisely be expanded to justify warrantless searches of other containers.

Coolidge, it should be remembered, was only a plurality opinion. As seen below, Justice Stewart's conception of mobility has not gained majority approval, and its continued vitality even as a plurality holding is in question in light of subsequent case law, considered in the next two chapter sections.

§ 13.03 Automobile Search Warrant Exception: Lesser Privacy, a New Rationale

Coolidge v. New Hampshire[34] arguably made good sense from a mobility perspective, but it did not muster a majority vote. As to unoccupied vehicles no longer on the road at the time of the search, it was difficult for the Court after *Chambers v. Maroney*[35] to justify the automobile exception exclusively on the mobility principle. In 1982, the justices acknowledged in *Michigan v. Thomas*[36] that the right to search a car without a warrant does not "depend upon a reviewing court's assessment of the likelihood in each particular case that the car would have been driven away, or that its contents would have been tampered with, during the period required for the police to obtain a warrant."

In view of this acknowledgement, the Court needed a new theory to explain its willingness to permit warrantless car searches. The seeds of the new theory were sown in *Cady v. Dombrowski*.[37] In *Cady*, a car driven by *D*, an off-duty police officer, was involved in a traffic accident. *D* was arrested for drunk driving, and the car was towed to a private garage. Shortly thereafter, an officer investigating the accident learned that *D*'s service revolver was probably still in the car. Because the gun was vulnerable to theft in the parking lot, the officer searched the car for the weapon. Inadvertently, he discovered evidence that tied *D* to a homicide.

In a 5–4 opinion, the Court held that the warrantless search—"standard police procedure" in the department under such community caretaking circumstances—was

---

33. However, Justice White did not approve the second and third searches of the Coolidge car. He believed that *Chambers* only justified a relatively short detention of a vehicle in order to conduct a warrantless search.

34. 403 U.S. 443 (1971). *See* § 13.02[C], *supra*.

35. 399 U.S. 42 (1970). *See* § 13.02[B], *supra*.

36. 458 U.S. 259 (1982) (per curiam).

37. 413 U.S. 433 (1973).

reasonable. However, *Cady*'s long-term significance is found in the Court's discussion of the automobile exception to the warrant requirement. It conceded that although the original justification for the exception "was the [car's] vagrant and mobile nature," subsequent warrantless searches were upheld in cases in which mobility was "remote, if not non-existent." *Cady* provided an explanation of why, mobility aside, automobiles are different from houses:

> Because of the extensive regulation of motor vehicles and traffic, and also because of the frequency with which a vehicle can become disabled or involved in an accident on public highways, the extent of police-citizen contact involving automobiles will be substantially greater than police-citizen contact in a home or office.

A year later, in *Cardwell v. Lewis*,[38] a four-justice plurality developed this argument further. After noting the mobility of cars, the Court stated that "there is still another distinguishing factor," which is that:

> [o]ne has a lesser expectation of privacy in a motor vehicle because its function is transportation and it seldom serves as one's residence or as the repository of personal effects. A car has little capacity for escaping public scrutiny. It travels public thoroughfares where its occupants and its contents are in plain view.

A majority of justices later accepted the lesser-expectation-of-privacy rationale in *South Dakota v. Opperman*,[39] a car inventory case.[40] The rationale was adopted as part of the automobile exception to the warrant requirement in *California v. Carney*,[41] a case involving the search of a motor home. *Carney* is considered in Section 13.04.

Is the lesser-expectation-of-privacy rationale persuasive? First, the fact that a car is visible to the public on the road does not distinguish it from any object that a person might carry in open view, for example, a suitcase or valise. Additionally, although a car on the road is visible, its *contents* often are not, as they may be placed under the seat, in the glove compartment, or in the trunk.

Nor was the *Cardwell* Court accurate in stating that an automobile "seldom serves as one's residence or the repository of personal effects." People commonly use their cars, especially the trunk and glove compartment, to transport articles of considerable importance and of a personal nature. Although the car serves in such cases only as a temporary repository of these items, a car is as important a source of privacy as a hotel room, which receives full Fourth Amendment protection. Indeed, the Court appears to have accepted this point in some cases. It has conceded that "[c]ertainly the privacy interests in a car's trunk or glove compartment may be no less than those in a movable container."[42] Also, for homeless persons lucky enough to still have an automobile, and for people who live and travel in luxurious motor homes, the automobile may be their *only* repository for their treasured belongings.

Third, although cars are indeed the object of extensive governmental regulation, that fact does not wholly distinguish them from "fully" protected houses and offices, which are the subject of building, safety, and health code regulations and nonconsensual

---

38. 417 U.S. 583 (1974).
39. 428 U.S. 364 (1976).
40. *See* § 15.01, *infra.*
41. 471 U.S. 386 (1985).
42. United States v. Ross, 456 U.S. 798, 823 (1982).

inspections.[43] Perhaps in view of the fact that the government regulates so many aspects of our lives—and, therefore, reduces our "reasonable expectations"—the issue regarding cars ought to be whether we have a *right* to an undiluted expectation of privacy in our cars, regardless of the heavily regulated nature of automobile usage.

§ 13.04 *California v. Carney*: The Mobility and Lesser-Expectation-of-Privacy Rationales at Work

California v. Carney[44] involved a warrantless search of a "fully mobile 'motor home' located in a public place." The police received uncorroborated information that *C* was using his motor home as a site for exchanging drugs for sex. At the time, *C* was parked in a city lot, near a courthouse where a warrant could have been secured. The police put the motor home under surveillance for one and one-quarter hours, during which time they saw a youth enter the vehicle, and later leave with marijuana. The youth confirmed that he received the drugs in exchange for sexual contacts by *C*. Although there was no indication that the vehicle was about to depart, or even that *C* knew that he was under surveillance, the police entered the motor home without a warrant or consent, and seized drugs inside.

The Supreme Court, per Chief Justice Warren Burger, discussed both rationales for the automobile exception. Regarding mobility, it stated that the motor home was "obviously readily mobile by the turn of a switch key." This statement is true, of course, in the sense that the motor home had the capacity for movement; however, if that capacity had been utilized while an officer was seeking a warrant, the vehicle would doubtlessly have been immediately stopped. The Chief Justice's sense of "mobility" approximated Justice White's understanding of the term in *Chambers v. Maroney*,[45] and was contrary to the plurality analysis in *Coolidge v. New Hampshire*.[46] Except, perhaps, for a motor vehicle without wheels or a battery—which is not really a motorized vehicle—nearly any car is "mobile" in the sense explained here.

As for the lesser-expectation-of-privacy rationale, the Court stated that even when an automobile is not "immediately mobile, the lesser expectation of privacy resulting from its use . . . justifie[s] application of the vehicular exception." Chief Justice Burger conceded that *C*'s vehicle "possessed some, if not many of the attributes of a home." Nonetheless, "it is equally clear that the vehicle falls within the scope of the exception laid down [in the automobile] cases." And, critically perhaps, "the vehicle was so situated that an objective observer would conclude that it was being used not as a residence, but as a vehicle."

Of course, *C* might have been using his vehicle as *both* a residence and a mode of transportation. Even if this were the case, the automobile exception applies. The Court did not decide whether the exception applies, however, "to a motor home that is situated in

---

43. *See* § 18.02, *infra*.
44. 471 U.S. 386 (1985).
45. 399 U.S. 42 (1970). *See* § 13.02[B], *supra*.
46. 403 U.S. 443 (1971). *See* § 13.02[C], *supra*.

a way or place that objectively indicates that it is being used as a residence." According to Chief Justice Burger:

> Among the factors that might be relevant in determining whether a warrant would be required in such a circumstance is its location, whether the vehicle is readily mobile or instead, for instance, elevated on blocks, whether the vehicle is licensed, whether it is connected to utilities, and whether it has convenient access to a public road.

Ultimately and critically, the Court described the automobile exception this way: "When a vehicle is being used on the highways, or if it is readily capable of such use and is found stationary in a place *not regularly used for residential purposes* . . . the two justifications for the vehicle exception come into play" (emphasis added). The italicized language could allow the Court to reaffirm the plurality holding in *Coolidge* if it chooses to do so. Lower case law is divided on the vitality of *Coolidge* after *Carney*.[47] Except in this possible and limited situation, however, any vehicle "readily capable" of use for transportation purposes, which is not objectively being used solely as a residence, may be searched without a warrant (assuming probable cause for the search). And it is difficult to believe that *Coolidge* will remain good law: A car is no less mobile, as that concept is now used, just because it is situated in a private driveway; nor are most of the reasons for treating cars as less private any less applicable when the car is parked in the open in a driveway.

§ 13.05 Special Problem: Search of Containers Found in Cars[48]

[A] Clarification of the Issue

[1] In General

The "car cases" generally involve the issue of whether the police may search an automobile without a warrant, assuming they have probable cause for the inspection. But suppose that the officers come upon a container, e.g., a suitcase, briefcase, or paper bag, during the car search. May they open *it* without a warrant? Or, suppose that the police are validly searching the car (without a warrant) looking for a particular container that they have reason to believe contains contraband. If they find it, may they open that container without a warrant? These questions are considered here.

[2] What is a "Container"?

For current purposes, a "container" is "any object capable of holding another object."[49]

---

47. 3 LaFave, Note 1, *supra*, at 553 n.64.

48. *See generally* 3 LaFave, Note 1, *supra*, at § 7.2(d); Craig M. Bradley, *The Court's "Two Model" Approach to the Fourth Amendment: Carpe Diem!*, 84 J. Crim. L. & Criminology 429 (1993); Katz, Note 1, *supra*; James J. Tomkovicz, *California v. Acevedo: The Walls Close in on the Warrant Requirement*, 29 Am. Crim. L. Rev. 1103 (1992).

49. New York v. Belton, 453 U.S. 454, 460 n.4 (1981).

Containers are not all alike. Some containers are inexpensive, such as a simple paper bag, whereas others are expensive, such as an executive's attaché case. Furthermore, people protect the contents of containers in different ways. One person with a paper bag might fold it closed, and still another might staple it shut; luggage might be unlocked, locked, or even double-locked.

Given these distinctions, the Supreme Court could have developed myriad Fourth Amendment "container" rules. Instead, it has chosen the opposite approach: Observing that "[w]hat one person may put into a suitcase, another may put into a paper bag,"[50] the Supreme Court has ruled that, with one significant exception, all containers will be treated alike for Fourth Amendment purposes. That is, whatever rules regarding warrants apply—they are discussed below—the Court will not treat some containers as more deserving of protection than others.

The exception to this statement is that the Fourth Amendment does not provide full protection for containers which "by their very nature cannot support any reasonable expectation of privacy because their contents can be inferred from their outward appearance."[51] The Court's examples of such containers are a kit of burglar's tools and a gun case. In essence, if the contents of a container are in literal plain view because the container is open or transparent, a person cannot possess a reasonable expectation of privacy as to the observation of its contents. Likewise, contents are in figurative plain view if the container's "distinctive configuration . . . proclaims its contents."[52] Perhaps, as well—the Court has left the issue open[53]—one may not possess a reasonable expectation of privacy in a container the contents of which can be determined by its distinctive odor.

[B] General Rule

The rule, which did not come easily to the Court, is that containers—even ones belonging to a passenger of an automobile who is not suspected of criminal activity[54]—may be searched without a warrant during an otherwise lawful "automobile exception" search.[55] And, if the container may be searched at the scene, it may also be seized and searched without a warrant shortly thereafter, at the police station.[56]

This rule applies in either of two general circumstances. First, as part of a valid warrantless car search, the police may unforeseeably come across a container. If so, they may open it without a warrant, assuming (as always[57]) that the container is large enough to hold the criminal evidence for which the police are searching. In these circumstances, the existence of probable cause to search the car serves to justify the warrantless container search, even though the officer conducting the search lacks information regarding that particular container.

---

50. Robbins v. California, 453 U.S. 420, 426 (1981), *overruled on other grounds*, United States v. Ross, 456 U.S. 798 (1982).

51. Arkansas v. Sanders, 442 U.S. 753, 764–65 n.13 (1979), *overruled on other grounds*, California v. Acevedo, 500 U.S. 565 (1991).

52. Robbins v. California, 453 U.S. at 427.

53. United States v. Johns, 469 U.S. 478 (1985).

54. Wyoming v. Houghton, 526 U.S. 295 (1999). *See* Note 66, *infra*.

55. California v. Acevedo, 500 U.S. 565 (1991).

56. United States v. Johns, 469 U.S. 478 (1985).

57. *See* § 13.01[D], *supra*.

Second, the police may have probable cause to believe that a particular container holding criminal evidence will be found in a car. In such circumstances, the police may conduct a warrantless search of the car for the container (per the automobile exception), and then open the container, also without a warrant.

On the other hand, absent exigent circumstances, consent, or as part of a search incident to arrest, the police may not open a container found *outside* a motor vehicle without obtaining a search warrant.

[C] How the Container Rules Developed

[1] *United States v. Chadwick*

In *United States v. Chadwick*,[58] Amtrak officials observed two persons load an unusually heavy footlocker onto a train. One of the suspects fit a profile used to spot drug traffickers, and the footlocker was leaking talcum powder, a substance often used to mask the odor of illegal narcotics. The railroad employees transmitted this information to federal narcotics agents.

The agents put the suspects under surveillance when they got off the train two days later. Although the agents did not have a warrant, they came with a dog trained to detect marijuana. While the footlocker was sitting on the floor in the train station, the dog signaled the presence of an illegal narcotic inside. The agents then watched as C and two other persons lifted the double-locked footlocker into the trunk of a car. While the trunk was still open, and before the engine was started, the officers arrested the three persons, seized the footlocker, transported it to their headquarters, and there searched it 90 minutes later, still without a warrant.

At the trial court level, the government sought to justify the warrantless conduct on various grounds, including the automobile exception.[59] The trial court rejected this claim, because it "saw the relationship between the footlocker and [C's] automobile as merely coincidental." Presumably, the court meant by this that the police had probable cause to search the container before it was placed in the vehicle; moreover, the footlocker was seized only seconds after its placement in the car, before the engine was started. On appeal to the Supreme Court, the government abandoned this argument.

In the Supreme Court, the government offered two justifications for the warrantless search. First, in an argument that the dissent characterized as "extreme," the government asserted that the Fourth Amendment Warrant Clause "protects only interests traditionally identified with the home." Drawing on the history of the Fourth Amendment,

---

58. 433 U.S. 1 (1977).

59. The government also argued at the trial court level that the search was an incident to the lawful arrest. However, the Supreme Court stated that once police reduce "property not immediately associated with the person of the arrestee to their exclusive control" — as here, by taking the container to headquarters — and, therefore, there is no danger of the arrestee grabbing it, "a search of that property is no longer an incident of that arrest." A more difficult question is whether the search would have been justified under the search-incident-to-lawful-arrest warrant exception if the officers had opened the double-locked footlocker at the scene. Justices Blackmun and Rehnquist, who dissented in *Chadwick*, believed that the police could have lawfully opened the footlocker at the scene because it was in the grabbing area of the arrestees. Justice Brennan, who wrote a concurrence, believed it was "not at all obvious" that this was so, because he doubted that the *contents* of the "securely locked" container were in the grabbing area.

and the framers' concern about writs of assistance and general warrants,[60] the government argued that "only homes, offices, and private communications implicate interests which lie at the core of the Fourth Amendment." Therefore, since the footlocker was seized outside a home or office, it could be opened without a warrant, if the search was supported by probable cause.

The Court, per Chief Justice Burger, rejected this argument. Although general warrants and writs of assistance "deeply concerned the colonists" and were "foremost in the minds of the Framers, . . . it would be a mistake to conclude . . . that the Warrant Clause was therefore intended to guard only against intrusions into the home." The Chief Justice observed that the Warrant Clause does not distinguish between searches in private homes and elsewhere, and that the initial clause of the Fourth Amendment draws no distinctions among "persons, houses, papers, and effects" in barring unreasonable search and seizures. In essence, the container and its contents are "effects"; they are textually entitled to as much Fourth Amendment protection as persons, houses, and papers.

Beyond the textual and historical arguments, the Court noted that "we do not write from a clean slate." Quoting *Katz v. United States,*[61] it stated that the Fourth Amendment "protects people, not places." Therefore, it is wrong to assume that people are protected only in their homes. "Accordingly," the Chief Justice stated, "we have held warrantless searches unreasonable, and therefore unconstitutional, in a variety of settings." He also reasserted the traditional policy argument for warrants, stating that it is "far more likely that [a search] will not exceed proper bounds when it is done pursuant to a judicial authorization."

The government had a second, less broad, explanation for the warrantless search of the footlocker. Although it did not reassert the automobile exception, it used the "car search" cases to argue that "luggage is . . . analogous to motor vehicles for Fourth Amendment purposes." The apparent reasoning is that a footlocker or other container is as mobile as an automobile. Therefore, as with a motor vehicle, assuming probable cause for the search, a container should be subject to a warrantless search at the scene or, as in *Chambers v. Maroney,*[62] at police headquarters shortly thereafter.

The Supreme Court rejected this argument as well. It held that the warrantless *seizure* of C's footlocker was permissible, but that the warrantless *search* of it 90 minutes later was unconstitutional, as no exigency existed at the time of the search. According to the Chief Justice:

> Once the federal agents had seized [the container] at the railroad station and had safely transferred it to the Boston Federal Building under their exclusive control, there was not the slightest danger that the footlocker or its contents could have been removed before a valid search warrant could be obtained. . . . With the footlocker safely immobilized, it was unreasonable to undertake the additional and greater intrusion of a search without a warrant.

Of course, in terms of mobility, the same might have been said about the automobile in *Chambers.* If the car in that case remained "mobile" at the police station, why is a footlocker any different? The Court distinguished the cases on the ground that the seizure of a car does not necessarily guarantee that the vehicle will not be wrongfully moved,

---

60. *See* § 4.03, *supra.*
61. 389 U.S. 347 (1967).
62. Chambers v. Maroney, 399 U.S. 42 (1970). *See* § 13.02[B], *supra.*

since "[a]bsolutely secure storage facilities may not be available, . . . and the size and inherent mobility of a vehicle make it susceptible to theft or intrusion by vandals."

The Court drew another distinction between cars and containers: "The answer lies in the diminished expectation of privacy which surrounds the automobile. . . ." According to *Chadwick*:

> The factors which diminish the privacy aspects of an automobile do not apply to [*C's*] footlocker. Luggage[63] contents are not [ordinarily] open to public view . . . ; nor is luggage subject to regular inspections and official scrutiny on a continuing basis. Unlike an automobile, whose primary function is transportation, luggage is intended as a repository of personal effects. In sum, a person's expectations of privacy in personal luggage are substantially greater than in an automobile.

According to the Court, the privacy distinction also explains the difference between the *Chambers* car and the *Chadwick* footlocker: "It was the greatly reduced expectation of privacy in the automobile, coupled with the transportation function of the vehicle, which made the Court in *Chambers* unwilling to decide whether an immediate search of an automobile, or its seizure and indefinite immobilization, constituted a greater interference with the rights of the owner." In fact, however, *Chambers* never made this point: The lesser-expectation-of-privacy rationale of the "car search" cases had not yet developed. So, if the "privacy expectation" principle *did* motivate the *Chambers* Court, it was only at a subconscious level.

The lesson of *Chadwick* is this: People have a greater expectation of privacy in containers than in their cars. Therefore, when the police unexpectedly encounter a container that they believe holds criminal evidence, and assuming that no other warrant exception applies, the police may *seize* the container without a warrant. However, they may not open it until they convince a magistrate that they have probable cause to search it.

The extent to which this lesson of *Chadwick* remains good law is considered below.

[2] *Arkansas v. Sanders*

In significant respects, the facts in *Arkansas v. Sanders*[64] were similar to those in *Chadwick*. As in *Chadwick*, the police possessed probable cause to search a particular container (here, a green suitcase). As in *Chadwick*, the police did not seize the container until it was placed in a vehicle, in this case a taxicab at an airport. However, unlike the facts in *Chadwick*, the police here allowed the taxi to drive away, whereupon the officers gave pursuit, stopped the cab a few blocks away, seized the suitcase, and opened it immediately.

Because the search involved a container found in a car stopped on the public road, the government defended the warrantless police activity on the ground that it was permissible under the automobile exception. Thus, the issue was whether the principles of *Chadwick* or the car cases controlled.

Justice Lewis Powell delivered the opinion of the Court. He reasserted the primacy of the warrant requirement. He observed that "[t]he mere reasonableness of a search,

---

63. Despite the Court's use of the term "luggage," the principles enunciated in *Chadwick* apply to other types of containers. *See* § 13.05[A][2], *supra*.

64. 442 U.S. 753 (1979), *overruled by* California v. Acevedo, 500 U.S. 565 (1991).

assessed in the light of the surrounding circumstances, is not a substitute for the judicial warrant required under the Fourth Amendment." Although there are "some exceptions" to the warrant requirement, including one for automobiles, the Court concluded that the reasons justifying warrantless car searches—lesser expectation of privacy and mobility—do not apply to containers found in automobiles.

As to privacy, Justice Powell reasoned that "[o]ne is not less inclined to place private, personal possessions in a suitcase merely because the suitcase is to be carried in an automobile rather than transported by other means. . . ." Second, although the Court agreed that a suitcase in the trunk of an automobile is as mobile as the vehicle itself, "the exigency of mobility must be assessed at the point immediately before the search—after the police have seized the object to be searched and have it securely within their control." As the suitcase was in the officers' control when it was searched, it was not mobile. Therefore, Justice Powell stated, "as a general rule there is no greater need for warrantless searches of luggage taken from automobiles than of luggage taken from other places."

Notice the immediately preceding language, which was broader than was required to decide the case. *Sanders*, like *Chadwick*, involved a search of a container that the police had probable cause to seize and search *before* it was placed in a vehicle. In that sense, the container in *Sanders* was only (to use the trial court's language in *Chadwick*) "coincidentally" in a vehicle. Nonetheless, the general rule announced here seemed to be that containers found in cars *never* fall within the scope of the automobile exception. This expansive reading of the Warrant Clause of the Fourth Amendment, however, was short-lived.

[3] *United States v. Ross*

In *United States v. Ross*,[65] the police had probable cause to search an entire car for contraband. During the search, they discovered a closed paper bag in the trunk, which they opened without a warrant. Thus, *Ross* differed from *Chadwick* and *Sanders* in the following way: In *Ross* the probable cause focused on an automobile, in which a container coincidentally was discovered; in *Chadwick* and *Sanders*, the probable cause was directed at a container, later coincidentally placed in a car.

As it turned out, this distinction mattered. Justice John Stevens, speaking for the Court, held that the warrantless search here—including opening the paper bag—was constitutional. According to *Ross*, the permissible scope of a warrantless search "is defined by the object of the search and the places in which there is probable cause to believe that it may be found." In short, in *this* situation, the automobile exception took precedence: "If probable cause justifies the search of a lawfully stopped vehicle [under the "automobile exception"], it justifies the search of every part of the vehicle and its contents that may conceal the object of the search." And, the Court has since clarified, the *Ross* rule applies to *all* containers found in a car, even if the container belongs to a person not linked to the vehicle, such as a passenger of the suspect-driver or a person not in the vehicle at all.[66]

---

65. 456 U.S. 798 (1982).
66. Wyoming v. Houghton, 526 U.S. 295 (1999). In *Houghton*, the police had probable cause to search the car for drugs based on their contact with the driver after they lawfully stopped the vehicle for traffic violations. In the car search, the police found and opened a purse belonging to a female passenger, in which drug paraphernalia was found, resulting in her arrest. Justice Scalia, for

The Court compared the scope of a search of an automobile to that of a home. In the latter case, a warrant, supported by probable cause and that meets the particularity requirements of the Fourth Amendment, ordinarily is required. However, once the warrant is authorized, the police may search "the entire area in which the object of the search may be found and is not limited by the possibility that separate acts of entry or opening may be required to complete the search."

The same reasoning applies to a car search, according to *Ross*. Although a warrant is not required for the search of a car because of its mobility, the scope of the search should include all areas in the car that a magistrate, if it had been practicable to request a warrant, could have authorized.

Therefore, immediately after *Ross*, there were two lines of container cases. If the police had probable cause to search a container, which was then placed in an automobile, *Chadwick-Sanders* applied, and the police needed a warrant to search the container. (We might call this a "container-in-a-coincidental-car case.") In contrast, if the police had probable cause to search a car, and a container happened to be found during the lawful search, the automobile exception applied, and the container could be opened as part of the car search (assuming its size allowed for concealment of the criminal evidence). (We might call this a "car-with-a-coincidental-container case.") Then, along came *Acevedo*.

[4] *California v. Acevedo*

In *California v. Acevedo*,[67] the Supreme Court erased what it described as the "curious line between the search of an automobile that coincidentally turns up a container [*Ross*] and the search of a container that coincidentally turns up in an automobile [*Chadwick-Sanders*]."

Justice Blackmun, who dissented in both *Chadwick* and *Sanders*, delivered the Court's opinion. Stating that "[t]he protections of the Fourth Amendment must not turn on such coincidences," the Court expressly overruled *Sanders*. It announced the following rule: (The interpretation of the *Carroll* doctrine set forth in *Ross* now applies to all searches of containers found in an automobile. In other words, the police may search without a warrant if their search is supported by probable cause."

In *Acevedo*, as police looked on, *A* left a residence holding a closed paper bag that the officers had probable cause to believe contained illegal narcotics. *A* placed the bag in the trunk of a car, and drove away. The police stopped the car on the road, opened the trunk, and inspected the contents of the bag, which contained marijuana.

Thus, the case was factually similar to *Chadwick* and *Sanders* in a key respect: The police had probable cause to search a specific container before it was placed in the car. Moreover, as in *Sanders*, the container was not searched until the car was on the highway.

---

the Court, stated that "[p]assengers, no less than drivers, possess a reduced expectation of privacy with regard to the property that they transport in cars . . ." Moreover, a different rule would impair effective law enforcement as it might prevent the police from finding criminal evidence. Justice Scalia pointed out that a car passenger "will often be engaged in a common enterprise with the driver" and, therefore, will have the same interest in concealing contraband and other criminal evidence.

67. 500 U.S. 565 (1991); *contra under the state constitution*, State v. Savva, 616 A.2d 774 (Vt. 1991).

The present case was unlike *Ross* in one important respect: In *Ross*, the police had probable cause to search a car trunk for contraband, during which search they unexpectedly discovered a closed paper bag; in *Acevedo*, probable cause to search did not extend beyond the closed paper bag, i.e., the police had probable cause to search the trunk, *but only so that they could find the paper bag.*[68]

Why did the Court overrule *Sanders*? Justice Blackmun stated that "[t]he discrepancy between the two rules has led to confusion for law enforcement officers," thus failing to provide "clear and unequivocal" guidelines. But, Fourth Amendment jurisprudence rarely provides clear and unequivocal rules. Nor is it evident that the law in this area was especially difficult: the officers in *Chadwick* and *Sanders* knew full well that they wanted to search a container and not the car itself; and the rule announced there sent a fairly clear message—if the police believe there is criminal evidence in a particular container, they should seize it, but seek a warrant.

Second, the Court said that the separate rules "may enable the police to broaden their power to make warrantless searches and disserve privacy interests." Justice Blackmun worried that "[i]f the police know that they may open a bag only if they are actually searching the entire car, they may search more extensively than they otherwise would in order to establish the general probable cause required by *Ross.*" The apparent point of this statement is that, in the pre-*Acevedo* world in which the police only had probable cause to search a particular container (and, therefore, needed a warrant to open it), Blackmun feared that the police might search the rest of the vehicle in the hope of discovering contraband, so as to convert the situation into a *Ross*-like car search justifying a warrantless search of the container. Yet, as Professor LaFave has observed, this argument is "unmitigated poppycock," because "if any point is solidly grounded in Fourth Amendment jurisprudence, it is that the police cannot 'bootstrap' themselves into probable cause; a search may not be justified by what turns up in that search."[69]

Third, the majority maintained that, "[t]o the extent that the *Chadwick-Sanders* rule protects privacy, its protection is minimal." Why is this? Justice Blackmun observed:

> [Under *Chadwick-Sanders*] [l]aw enforcement officers may seize a container and hold it until they obtain a search warrant. *"Since the police, by hypothesis, have probable cause to seize the property, we can assume that a warrant will be routinely forthcoming in the overwhelming majority of cases"* (emphasis added).

The italicized language, which originated in Blackmun's own *dissent* in *Sanders*, is interesting, and disturbing to advocates of the warrant requirement. In essence, Justice

---

68. The italicized language is important. The police in *Acevedo* had the right to open *A*'s car trunk to search for the paper bag, but not to conduct a search of the trunk for contraband beyond that. Notice the significance of this distinction. *Scenario 1.* The police in *Acevedo* open the trunk and immediately spot the paper bag. According to this case, they may seize and search it without a warrant. The right to further search the trunk ceases. *Scenario 2.* The same as 1, except that when they open the trunk they see other criminal evidence in open view. They may seize *this* evidence under the plain view doctrine, see § 14.02, *infra*, as well as seize and search the paper bag, as before. Moreover, the newly found criminal evidence in the trunk *might* give the police independent probable cause to conduct a greater search of the trunk or, perhaps, the rest of the car. *Scenario 3.* The police in *Acevedo* open the trunk, and do not see the paper bag. They may now search the trunk until they find it. To do this, they may open *other* containers large enough to hold the paper bag. The police may seize any criminal evidence they find in plain view during the process.

69. 3 LaFave, Note 1, *supra*, at 582–83.

Blackmun is rejecting the statement in *Sanders*, which expresses the essence of the warrant requirement, that "[t]he mere reasonableness of a search . . . is not a substitute for the judicial warrant. . . ." The warrant requirement is based on the premise that, in the words of Justice Stevens's dissent in *Acevedo*, "the decision to invade the privacy of an individual's personal effects should be made by a neutral magistrate rather than an agent of the Executive."

Fourth, Justice Blackmun believed that the prior container rules resulted in an anomaly: The more likely the police are to discover drugs in a container, the less authority they have to search it. That is, under *Ross*, if the police are conducting a warrantless car search, and they stumble upon a container, they may open it, although they have no particularized reason to believe they will find evidence inside; yet, if they have solid probable cause to search a particular container, but no basis for searching the rest of the car, *Chadwick-Sanders* required a warrant to open the container. But, this "anomaly" mixes the issues of probable cause and the requirement of a warrant. As the dissenters observed, "even proof beyond a reasonable doubt will not justify a warrantless search that is not supported by one of the exceptions to the warrant requirement." In short, so long as a Fourth Amendment warrant requirement remains, those exceptions will always create "anomalies" of the kind to which Justice Blackmun pointed.

[5] What Is Left of *Chadwick*?

Acevedo overruled *Sanders*, but it did not expressly overrule *Chadwick*. What remains, then, of *Chadwick*? The majority opinion in *Acevedo* does not openly question *Chadwick*'s basic premise that a person possesses a legitimate expectation of privacy in closed containers outside the context of a vehicle.

However, what if (exactly as in *Chadwick*) the police conduct a warrantless search of a container the moment it is placed in a car, but before the vehicle is taken onto the highway? The reasoning of *Acevedo* strongly suggests that such a search now falls within the automobile exception to the warrant requirement. Language in *Acevedo* supports this conclusion: According to Justice Blackmun, "*Ross* now applies to all searches of containers found in an automobile." *Chadwick*, it will be remembered, was not argued to the Supreme Court in terms of the automobile exception. Therefore, if a case factually on all fours with *Chadwick* arises, and if the government invokes the automobile exception, the Court seems poised to overrule the holding of *Chadwick*.[70]

Assuming *Chadwick* remains good law as to containers found and searched *outside* an automobile, *Acevedo* creates its own anomaly. If a person walks along a street holding a briefcase that the police have probable cause to believe contains evidence of a crime, the police may seize, but not search, it without a warrant. However, once the person puts the briefcase, previously in open view, in an automobile, for example, in a locked car trunk, the police may search the trunk for the briefcase, and open it without a warrant. There is little to commend this distinction in terms of reasonable privacy expectations or mobility concerns.

It should be noted, however, that much of the reasoning of *Acevedo* undermines the "warrant requirement" of the Fourth Amendment. If it is true that warrants provide only minimal privacy protection, as the Court stated there, there is little reason to require a

---

70. Tomkovicz, Note 48, *supra*, at 1115.

warrant in the case of a container search outside an automobile. Therefore, the Court might be prepared to rethink the "extreme" government argument made and rejected in *Chadwick*, namely, that warrants are only needed to conduct searches inside a home or office. Perhaps outside a private building, the Court will declare that searches need only satisfy the reasonableness requirement of the Fourth Amendment.[71]

---

71. *See* Florida v. White, 526 U.S. 559, 565 (1999) (in part justifying the warrantless seizure of a car, parked in a public place, although its owner was already in custody, on the ground that "our Fourth Amendment jurisprudence has consistently accorded law enforcement officials greater latitude in exercising their duties in public places").

Chapter 14

"Plain View" and Related Doctrines

§ 14.01 Plain View: General Principles[1]

[A] Elements of the Doctrine

An object of an incriminating nature may be seized without a warrant if it is in "plain view" of a police officer lawfully present at the scene.

"Plain view" is a constitutional term of art. As explained more fully in Section 14.02, an article is in "plain view," and subject to warrantless seizure by a police officer, if: (1) he observes it from a lawful vantage point; (2) he has a right of physical access to it; and (3) it is immediately apparent to him that it is contraband or a fruit, instrumentality, or evidence of a crime.[2]

For example, suppose that O, a police officer, has a valid warrant to search D's garage for drug paraphernalia and illegal narcotics. As O is searching the garage pursuant to the warrant, he notices, to his surprise, that the automobile fits the description of one recently used in an unrelated murder. O seizes the car as evidence of the murder, although the warrant does not authorize him to do so.

Under the plain view doctrine, the warrantless seizure of the car would be permissible because: (1) O's entry into the garage (and, therefore, sighting of the car) was proper, as it was authorized by the warrant; (2) O's physical access to the car was lawful, as it was situated in the area O had a right to search pursuant to the warrant; and (3) when O observed the car it was immediately apparent to him that it was evidence of a crime.

[B] Rationale of the Doctrine

The plain view doctrine, as set out above, does *not* serve as an exception to the supposed rule that a warrant ordinarily is required to conduct a *search* of a person, house, paper, or effect. Instead, it functions as a justification for the police conducting a warrantless *seizure* of the evidence in plain view.[3]

A warrantless seizure of an object in plain view is not inconsistent with the purposes of the Fourth Amendment Warrant Clause. According to Justice Potter Stewart in *Coolidge v. New Hampshire*,[4] the Warrant Clause ensures that police officers, whenever practicable, seek a prior judicial determination of probable cause in order "to eliminate altogether searches not based on probable cause," as well as to prevent exploratory or

---

1. *See generally* 1 Wayne R. LaFave, Search and Seizure § 2.2(a) (4th ed. 2004).
2. Horton v. California, 496 U.S. 128 (1990); *see* Coolidge v. New Hampshire, 403 U.S. 443 (1971); Arizona v. Hicks, 480 U.S. 321 (1987); Texas v. Brown, 460 U.S. 730 (1983).
3. Horton v. California, 496 U.S. at 133–34.
4. 403 U.S. 443 (1971).

general searches. Thus, in the example in subsection [A], *O* obtained a prior judicial determination of probable cause to search the garage. Furthermore, the search did not become exploratory in nature by seizing the car: *O*'s presence in the garage was authorized by the warrant; and the seizure did not expand the lawful scope of the search.

Under such circumstances, a warrantless seizure of an object discovered in plain view is (in the words of *Coolidge*) only a "minor peril to Fourth Amendment protections, [but] . . . a major gain in effective law enforcement." To require an officer to obtain a warrant to seize what he discovers in plain view would be a "needless inconvenience, and sometimes [might be] dangerous—to the evidence or to the police themselves."

§ 14.02 "Plain View": Examining the Elements in Detail

[A] Element 1: Lawful Vantage Point

The first requirement of the plain view doctrine is that the officer must observe the object from a lawful vantage point. The Supreme Court has observed that "it is important to keep in mind that, in the vast majority of cases, *any* evidence seized by the police will be in plain view, at least at the moment of seizure."[5] Therefore, "an essential predicate to any valid warrantless seizure of incriminating evidence [is] that the officer did not violate the Fourth Amendment in arriving at the place from which the evidence could be plainly viewed."[6]

Generally speaking, there are four ways in which an officer might observe evidence from a lawful vantage point. First, he may discover the article during the execution of a valid search warrant. Second, the object may come into view during an in-home arrest pursuant to an arrest warrant. For example, an officer who enters *D*'s house armed with an arrest warrant might observe an incriminating object while looking for *D* inside the residence.

Third, criminal evidence might be discovered by an officer during a search justified under an exception to the warrant requirement. For example, an officer may come across an article of evidence while he is in a house in hot pursuit of a felon,[7] or while he is conducting a warrantless consent search. In such circumstances, the *search* that turned up the evidence is justified by an independent warrant exception; the plain view doctrine justifies the warrantless *seizure* of the evidence found.

Fourth, an officer's view of an object could arise from an activity that does not constitute a search and, therefore, falls outside the scope of the Fourth Amendment. For example, *O*, a police officer, walking down a public sidewalk might glance toward a residence and, from that vantage point, observe marijuana plants sitting in open view on a table near the window in *D*'s living room. In this example, as no "search" has occurred—*D* could hardly have a reasonable expectation of privacy in regard to the

---

5. *Id.* at 465.
6. Horton v. California, 496 U.S. at 136.
7. *E.g.*, Warden v. Hayden, 387 U.S. 294 (1967).

sighting—the first element of plain view is satisfied, but the second element presents a difficulty, as discussed below.

[B] Element 2: Right of Access to the Object

A police officer may observe an incriminating article from a lawful vantage point, but "she must also have a lawful right of access to the object itself."[8] Thus, in the example immediately above, the plain view doctrine does not allow O to enter D's home without a warrant to seize the marijuana visible from the street. Access to the living room requires a warrant or some search warrant exception.[9]

If an officer has a Fourth Amendment justification—not simply the fact that the article is visible to him—to enter a house, he may do so. For example, in *Washington v. Chrisman*,[10] O arrested C, a college student, in a public place for underage possession of alcohol. C claimed that he was over the minimum age for possession of the liquor. He sought permission to retrieve his identification from his dormitory room. O agreed and followed him to the room. While C was inside, O remained just outside the door, but from that spot he observed marijuana and drug paraphernalia inside the room. He entered and seized the items.

Because an arresting officer has the right to remain at an arrestee's elbow,[11] O had authority from the outset to follow C into the dormitory room. Consequently, the Court held that the warrantless entry after the objects came into his view was permissible. If the result were otherwise, the "perverse effect" would be to "penaliz[e] the officer for exercising more restraint than was required under the circumstances."

[C] Element 3: Right to Seize is "Immediately Apparent"

A police officer may not seize an article without a search warrant merely because he has a right of access to it from a proper vantage point. For example, the fact that O is lawfully in D's living room in order to make an arrest does not justify the seizure of every article that O observes in the room, regardless of its character. The Supreme Court stated in *Coolidge v. New Hampshire*[12] that seizure of an article in plain view is "legitimate only where it is immediately apparent to the police that they have evidence before them." As explained in *Arizona v. Hicks*,[13] "immediately apparent" means that the officer must have probable cause to seize the article in plain view.

The "immediately apparent"—or probable cause—requirement is consistent with the rationale of the doctrine of plain view. As explained in Section 14.01, the doctrine is

---

8. Horton v. California, 496 U.S. at 137.

9. Coolidge v. New Hampshire, 403 U.S. at 468 ("even where the object [in plain view] is contraband, this Court has repeatedly stated and enforced the basic rule that the police may not enter [private premises] and make a warrantless seizure").

10. 455 U.S. 1 (1982).

11. *See* § 12.02[C][2][a], *supra*.

12. 403 U.S. 443 (1971).

13. 480 U.S. 321 (1987).

meant only to free the police from the inconvenience of securing a warrant to seize that which is found in plain view during an otherwise lawful search or non-search activity. It does not purport to dispense with the probable cause requirement for the seizure. Justice Antonin Scalia reminds us, "[d]ispensing with the need for a warrant [in plain view circumstances] is worlds apart from permitting a lesser standard of *cause* for the seizure than a warrant would require, i.e., the standard of probable cause."[14]

§ 14.03 The Plain View Doctrine at Work: *Arizona v. Hicks*[15]

Arizona v. Hicks[16] provides an instructional, albeit controversial,[17] example of the interrelationship of the elements of the plain view doctrine. In *Hicks*, the police entered *H*'s apartment without a search warrant because a bullet had been fired through *H*'s floor into the apartment below it, wounding a man. The officers entered "to search for the shooter, for other victims, and for weapons."

While inside, *O*, one of the officers, observed two sets of expensive stereo components that seemed out of place in *H*'s "squalid" apartment. *O* reasonably suspected, but lacked probable cause to believe, that the components were stolen. Therefore, *O* either turned around or turned upside down a turntable in order to read and record its serial number. *O* reported the number to police headquarters, which confirmed that it had been taken in a robbery. *O* seized the turntable. Later, *O* secured a warrant to seize the remaining components.

The government sought to justify the warrantless seizure of the turntable on the basis of the plain view doctrine. Uncontroversially, the officers' warrantless entry into *H*'s apartment was proper due to the exigencies of the situation. Therefore, *O* had a right to be in a position in which the stereo components were visible and accessible to him as he looked for persons and weapons. Nonetheless, the Supreme Court, per Justice Scalia, held that the warrantless seizure of the turntable was unconstitutional.

The route that the Court took in reaching its conclusion merits careful attention. The difficulty in this case in the application of the plain view doctrine was with the third element of the rule, namely, the requirement that the incriminating nature of the article be immediately apparent to the police. To properly analyze this issue, and to see how this element relates to the other components of the plain view doctrine, it is useful to consider not only what occurred in *H*'s house but also what could have happened.

For example, if it had been immediately apparent to *O* as he looked at (without touching) the stereo components that they were stolen, it would have been proper for him to seize them under the plain view doctrine. But, as the situation actually materialized, *O* did not have probable cause to believe that the equipment was stolen when he first

---

14. Arizona v. Hicks, 480 U.S. 321, 327 (1987).
15. *See generally* 2 LaFave, Note 1, *supra*, at § 4.11(d); Denise Marie Cloutier, *Arizona v. Hicks: The Failure to Recognize Limited Inspections as Reasonable in Fourth Amendment Jurisprudence*, 24 Colum. J.L. & Soc. Probs. 351 (1991).
16. 480 U.S. 321 (1987).
17. *E.g.*, Cloutier, Note 15, *supra* (contending that *Hicks* should be overruled).

spotted the turntable. More was needed to bring his suspicion to the level of probable cause—he needed the serial number.

If *O* could have read the serial number without moving the equipment, there would have been no constitutional problem. His action—merely observing that which was in view from a place where he had a right to be—would not have constituted a search or seizure. Therefore, if this non-Fourth Amendment activity—the non-search and non-seizure inspection of the serial number—had provided *O* with probable cause to believe that the turntable was the fruit of a crime, *O* would have been acting lawfully if he had seized it without a warrant.

But in *Hicks* the facts were not as hypothesized. The turntable had to be moved to observe its serial number. Therefore, the question that the Court had to answer was whether *this* action—physically trivial as it was—constituted a new "search" or "seizure" that required an additional justification.

The slight movement of the turntable did not constitute a "seizure," as this action did not constitute a meaningful interference with *H*'s possessory interest in it.[18] But, the act of moving it was another "search" because it exposed to *O* matters not previously visible to him; on these facts, *H* had a reasonable expectation of privacy in the bottom of the turntable. As Justice Scalia explained, "a search is a search, even if it happens to disclose nothing but the bottom of a turntable."

The issue, therefore, was whether this new (warrantless) search was justified. To resolve this question the Court needed to reconsider the first element of the plain view doctrine. That is, in light of the original justification for the intrusion into the room—to look for the shooter, additional victims, and the weapon—was this additional search justified? If the answer had been yes—e.g., if a weapon could realistically have been underneath the turntable—the new search would have been permissible and, as it incidentally resulted in the information that gave *O* probable cause to believe that the turntable was stolen, he could lawfully have seized it. However, as Justice Scalia explained, the search was conducted for reasons "unrelated to the objectives of the authorized intrusion." Therefore, *O* was unable to justify his actions on the basis of plain view.

Justice Scalia's analysis is controversial. The dissent argued that the act of moving the turntable was a "cursory inspection" rather than a "full-blown search." As such, the dissent claimed, *O* should have been allowed to inspect it on the basis of "reasonable suspicion" (which *O* possessed) rather than "probable cause." Scalia rejected this argument, however, because he was "unwilling to send police and judges into a new thicket of Fourth Amendment law, to seek a creature of uncertain description."

However, the "cursory inspection" concept would not have sent the police and courts into a new Fourth Amendment "thicket." Long before this case, the Court recognized the general principle that searches that are less-than-ordinarily intrusive may be conducted on less than probable cause.[19] Nor is a "cursory inspection" inevitably a "creature of uncertain description": It might be defined, as Professor LaFave has suggested,[20] as the "picking up of an article to ascertain a serial number or other identifying characteristic on its exterior."

---

18. *See* § 7.02[A], *supra*.
19. *See* Chapter 17, *infra*.
20. 2 LaFave, Note 1, *supra*, at 795.

Justice Scalia defended his position by focusing on the importance of probable cause in Fourth Amendment jurisprudence. As he put it:

> [T]here is nothing new in the realization that the Constitution sometimes insulates the criminality of a few in order to protect the privacy of us all. Our disagreement with the dissenters pertains to where the proper balance should be struck; we choose to adhere to the textual and traditional standard of probable cause.

In recent years, this attitude regarding the importance of probable cause has frequently been ignored by the Supreme Court. In *Hicks*, it was not.

§ 14.04 "Inadvertent Discovery": The Plain View Debate[21]

In the typical "plain view" case, *O*, an officer, conducting a valid search, will discover incriminating evidence in open view that he did not anticipate finding. In such circumstances, *O* may seize this inadvertently discovered evidence. However, suppose that *O anticipated* finding the evidence in plain view. For example, suppose that *O* has probable cause to search *D*'s premises for articles A and B. *O* obtains a warrant to seize article A, but he does not request authorization to seize article B, although he expects that he will find it during the search, and he intends to seize it if he discovers it. If *O*, indeed, discovers article B during the execution of the warrant, may he seize it under the plain view doctrine?

In *Coolidge v. New Hampshire*,[22] Justice Stewart, author of the Court's four-justice plurality opinion, answered the question in the negative. He stated that if an officer anticipates discovery of a particular object, but fails to request a warrant to seize it, or if the officer fails to mention it in the application for a warrant to search for other articles, the subsequent search is analogous to an exploratory search, and the seizure of the anticipated articles "fl[ies] in the face of the basic rule that no amount of probable cause can justify a warrantless seizure." Thus, as the concept of plain view was explained in *Coolidge*, there was an inadvertency element—a fourth element—to the doctrine.

The inadvertency element was never accepted by a majority of the members of the Supreme Court. Nonetheless, after *Coolidge* was decided, virtually all of the states and lower federal courts endorsed the inadvertency rule.[23]

In *Horton v. California*,[24] the Supreme Court "revisited" the issue. In *Horton*, *O*, a police officer, obtained a warrant to search *H*'s home for the proceeds (jewelry) of a robbery. *O* anticipated finding the weapons used in the crime (including a machine gun and stun gun) during the search, and he intended to seize them, which he did, when they

---

21. *See generally* 3 LaFave, Note 1, *supra*, at § 6.7(c).

22. 403 U.S. 443 (1971).

23. Forty-six states, the District of Columbia, and 12 United States Courts of Appeals subscribed to the requirement. Horton v. California, 496 U.S. 128, 149–53 (1990) (appendices A and B to the dissenting opinion of Brennan, J.).

24. 496 U.S. 128 (1990); *contra under the state constitution*, State v. Meyer, 893 P.2d 159 (Haw. 1995) (inadvertency is a requirement of the plain view doctrine); Commonwealth v. Balicki, 762 N.E.2d 290 (Mass. 2002) (same).

were discovered in plain view in the home. *H* argued that the latter seizure was impermissible: The warrant did not provide for the seizure of the weapons and, because their discovery was not inadvertent, their seizure could not be justified under the plain view doctrine as set out in *Coolidge.*

The Supreme Court ruled, 7–2, per Justice John Stevens, that inadvertency, although "a characteristic of most legitimate 'plain view' seizures, . . . is not a necessary condition" of the doctrine. It concluded that "the absence of inadvertence was not essential to the Court's rejection of the State's 'plain view' argument in *Coolidge.*"

As *Horton* pointed out, the inadvertency requirement is not necessary "to prevent the police from conducting general searches, or from converting specific warrants into general warrants." These Fourth Amendment evils are prevented by scrupulous adherence to the Fourth Amendment requirement that no warrant be issued unless it particularly describes "the place to be searched and the persons or things to be seized," and by the judicial rule that warrantless searches must "be circumscribed by the exigencies which justify its initiation." In other words, the area and duration of a search is limited by the latter requirements; the inadvertency element adds no additional privacy protection.

For example, in *Horton,* the inadvertency element would not have offered *H* any privacy protection that was not already guaranteed: The warrant entitled the officer to be in *H*'s home in order to search for the fruits of a robbery; and the weapons were found in those areas of the home to which the officer had a constitutional right of access under the warrant. Furthermore, if the proceeds of the crime had been found before the weapons had been discovered, the search would have had to terminate at that time, so the omission of the weapons from the warrant did not lengthen the time the officers could legitimately stay on the premises.

The *Horton* Court additionally expressed its disinclination to apply a doctrine that requires courts to divine an officer's subjective state of mind, i.e., to determine whether the officer expected to find the evidence in question. According to Justice Stevens, "even-handed law enforcement is best achieved by the application of objective standards of conduct." He pointed out that if an officer has knowledge approaching certainty that certain evidence will be found during a search, there is no reason to believe that he "would deliberately omit a particular description of the item to be seized from the application for a search warrant."

On the other hand, if the officer has a warrant to search for one article, and merely suspects that he will find another item, whether or not the suspicion amounts to probable cause, the *Horton* Court did not believe that such a "suspicion should immunize the second item from seizure if it is found during a lawful search for the first." Borrowing from Justice White's dissent in *Coolidge,* the Court reasoned that there is no reason to draw a distinction between an article discovered inadvertently and one that is anticipated; the interference with the individual's possessory interest is the same in both cases, as is the inconvenience and danger of requiring the officer to depart and secure a warrant.

Justice Brennan, with whom Justice Marshall joined, dissented in *Horton.* The dissenters agreed with the majority that the inadvertency requirement furthers no privacy interests. But, they argued, this requirement *does* protect possessory interests: the message sent by the inadvertency requirement is that "we will not excuse officers from the general requirement of a warrant to seize if the officers know the location of the evidence, have probable cause to seize it, intend to seize it, and yet do not bother to obtain a warrant particularly describing that evidence." Exclusion of "evidence so seized will encourage officers to be more precise and complete in future warrant applications."

§ 14.05 Expanding on Plain View: Use of Other Senses[25]

[A] "Plain Hearing" and "Plain Smell" Doctrines

Courts have expanded on the "plain view" doctrine to recognize "plain hearing" and "plain smell" principles. These expansions make sense. What an officer observes from a lawful vantage point is not a search, because a person cannot maintain a reasonable expectation of privacy regarding anything visible to the naked eye from that position. For the same reason, a person cannot have a reasonable expectation of privacy regarding his oral communications, if they can he heard by someone, lawfully positioned, within ear shot ("plain hearing"); nor can he legitimately expect that an officer will not use his sense of smell to detect incriminating evidence from a lawful position.

[B] "Plain Touch" (or "Plain Feel") Doctrine[26]

In *Minnesota v. Dickerson*,[27] a unanimous Supreme Court recognized a "plain touch" or "plain feel" corollary to the plain view doctrine. Under this doctrine, the police may seize contraband detected solely through an officer's sense of touch if, analogously to plain view, the officer had a right to touch the object in question and, upon tactile observation, its identity as contraband was immediately apparent.

In *Dickerson*, O, a police officer, observed D acting suspiciously near a notorious "crack house." O frisked D for weapons as part of a *"Terry* stop,"[28] which permits an officer investigating possible criminal activity to pat down a suspect if, *but only if*, he is justified in believing that the person may be armed and presently dangerous. The *Dickerson* Court stated that if it had been immediately apparent to O during the lawful frisk that the object he was touching was contraband, O could properly have reached into the pocket and seized it without a warrant pursuant to the plain *touch* doctrine.

In this case, however, when O frisked D, he felt a "small lump," which he realized was not a weapon, but which he could not otherwise immediately identify. Under *Terry*, the weapons pat-down search of this part of D's clothing should have ended at that instant. Instead, O continued to examine the object with his fingers and determined that it was probably crack cocaine. O then reached into D's pocket and retrieved a small plastic bag containing cocaine.

The Court held that the warrantless seizure of the cocaine was unlawful. It reasoned that the second search—the act of examining the lump after the weapons search was completed—fell outside the scope of the original lawful intrusion. Therefore, O acted improperly under the plain touch doctrine when he seized the object. In essence, once O decided that D was unarmed, O's right to physical access to D ended; the second search should not have occurred.

---

25. *See generally* 1 LaFave, Note 1, *supra*, at 452–60.

26. *See generally* David L. Haselkorn, *The Case Against a Plain Feel Exception to the Warrant Requirement*, 54 U. Chi. L. Rev. 683 (1987); Anne Bowen Poulin, *The Plain Feel Doctrine and the Evolution of the Fourth Amendment*, 42 Vill. L. Rev. 741 (1997).

27. 508 U.S. 366 (1993).

28. Terry v. Ohio, 392 U.S. 1 (1968). *See* Chapter 17, *infra*.

Although the officer's conduct in *Dickerson* violated the Fourth Amendment, the line between a lawful and an unlawful search in such circumstances is extremely thin, even nearly nonexistent. Even putting aside the possibility of police perjury,[29] an officer may be unable to reconstruct the fast-moving events days or weeks later, when called upon to testify. Had O testified in *Dickerson*, for example, that he determined *simultaneously* that the object was not a weapon but that it was crack cocaine, the evidence would have been admissible under the plain touch doctrine.

---

29. Unfortunately, some magistrates "knowingly accept police perjury as truthful." Myron W. Orfield, Jr., *Deterrence, Perjury, and the Heater Factor: An Exclusionary Rule in the Chicago Criminal Courts*, 63 U. Colo. L. Rev. 75, 83 (1992) (study of Cook County criminal justice system).

Chapter 15

Inventory Searches

§ 15.01 Automobile Inventories[1]

[A] General Principles

Generally speaking, and subject to more detailed explanation in subsection [B], a routine inventory search ("inventory," for short) of a lawfully impounded automobile is reasonable under the Fourth Amendment even if it is conducted without a warrant and in the absence of probable cause to believe—indeed, in the absence of *any* basis for believing—that criminal evidence will be discovered. Consequently, if police discover criminal evidence during a valid inventory, they may seize it pursuant to the plain view doctrine, and introduce it in a criminal prosecution.

The Supreme Court first recognized this "automobile inventory" search warrant (and probable cause) exception[2] to the Fourth Amendment in *South Dakota v. Opperman.*[3] In *Opperman*, the police towed *O*'s unoccupied car to an impoundment lot after it had been ticketed twice on the same morning for being illegally parked in a tow-away zone. At the lot, a police officer observed a watch on the dashboard and other valuables sitting on the back seat and back floorboard. Pursuant to standard procedures in the jurisdiction, the police unlocked the car door, inventoried the contents of the passenger compartment, and removed them for safekeeping. During the inventory, the police discovered marijuana in the unlocked glove compartment. *O* was prosecuted for possession of this contraband.

The *Opperman* Court, 5–4, upheld the inventory search, notwithstanding the absence of probable cause or a warrant.[4] The Court drew on the fact that an inventory is not part of a criminal investigation, but rather is an administrative act, i.e., a feature of a police department's community caretaking function. According to *Opperman*, the "probable cause" concept of the Fourth Amendment is a standard for use in criminal investigations and, therefore, is "unhelpful when analysis centers upon the

---

1. *See generally* 3 Wayne R. LaFave, Search and Seizure §§ 7.4(a), 7.5(e) (4th ed. 2004).

2. Automobile inventories could reasonably fit under either the "administrative search" or "special needs" exceptions to the warrant and probable cause requirements of the Fourth Amendment. These exceptions are discussed in Chapter 18. Largely for historical reasons—the early "administrative search" cases focused on activities of *non*-police officials, and the "special needs" exception had not yet been devised—an independent "inventory exception" developed.

3. 428 U.S. 364 (1976); *contra under the state constitution*, State v. Sawyer, 571 P.2d 1131 (Mont. 1977), *overruled in part on other grounds by* State v. Long, 700 P.2d 153 (Mont. 1985) (only permitting warrantless inventories to secure objects in plain view from outside the vehicle); State v. Opperman, 247 N.W.2d 673 (S.D. 1976) (same).

4. *Opperman* dealt primarily with the "search" aspect of the inventory. The Court perfunctorily approved of the impoundment—seizure—of *O*'s car. It described as "beyond challenge" the right "of police to seize and remove vehicles impeding traffic or threatening public safety and convenience."

reasonableness of routine administrative caretaking functions, particularly when no claim is made that the protective procedures are a subterfuge for criminal investigations."[5]

With the probable cause component of the Fourth Amendment deemed irrelevant, the *Opperman* Court disposed of the need for search warrants in inventory cases by noting that the warrant requirement is "linked . . . textually . . . to the probable-cause concept." That is, because the Warrant Clause provides that "no Warrants shall issue, but upon probable cause," there is no need for a warrant if there is no reason for determining probable cause.

With the Warrant Clause out of the way, the Court looked exclusively at the Fourth Amendment reasonableness requirement. The Court stated that automobile inventories are a reasonable "response to three distinct needs": (1) to protect the police and the public from dangerous instrumentalities that might be hidden in the car; (2) to protect the police against claims of lost or stolen property; and (3) to protect the owner's property while it is in police custody. The Court concluded that these interests outweigh an owner's expectation of privacy in her automobile, which it described as "significantly less than that relating to one's home or office."[6]

Critics questioned the *Opperman* Court's analysis. First, before the terrorist attacks on the United States, critics contended that the assertion that inventories are needed in order to protect the safety of the police and the public from dangerous instrumentalities "border[ed] on the ridiculous."[7] Even today, cars rarely contain dangerous instrumentalities; and, in any case, there is little reason to believe that an unsearched car sitting in an impoundment lot constitutes a greater danger to the community than a nonimpounded car—which may not ordinarily be searched without probable cause or consent—that is parked on the street or in a public parking lot.

Second, protection of the police against claims of theft arguably does not justify warrantless inventories. Police departments, as involuntary bailees, usually have only limited liability for losses in such circumstances; and as concurring Justice Powell conceded in *Opperman*, inventories might not discourage false claims, because a car owner could fraudulently assert that an object was stolen prior to the inventory, or was purposely or negligently left off the inventory list.

Third, automobile inventories supposedly protect the owner's property from theft. In fact, of course, it is the act of securing the belongings, not the inventory itself, that reduces the risk of loss. It is unclear that the inventory process provides greater protection than the simpler and less intrusive procedure of rolling up the windows of an impounded car, locking its doors, and placing it in a secure place. Moreover, if the police are going to invade a car owner's privacy in order to protect her property, critics maintain that it is not unreasonable to suggest, as the dissenters did in *Opperman*, that an inventory should only be conducted after "the exhaustion and failure of reasonable efforts . . . to identify and reach the owner of the property in order to facilitate alternative means of security or to obtain [her] consent to the search." Since *Opperman* was decided, however, the Court has expressly discounted the relevance of alternative means of

---

5. The Court's conclusion was not inevitable. It might have formulated a different type of "probable cause" standard, relevant to administrative inventory searches. The Court has done this with other administrative inspections. *See* § 8.06, *supra*.

6. The lesser-expectation-of-privacy principle regarding cars is discussed at § 13.03, *supra*.

7. 3 LaFave, Note 1, *supra*, at 639.

protecting a car owner's property from theft. It has stated that "[t]he reasonableness of any particular governmental activity does not necessarily or invariably turn on the existence of alternative 'less intrusive' means.... [The Court is] hardly in a position to second-guess police departments as to what practical administrative method will best deter theft...."[8]

[B] The Inventory Exception: In Detail

[1] Administrative Non-Pretextual Nature of the Search

In upholding automobile inventories, the Supreme Court has noted at least twice that the inventories in question were true administrative searches, and not subterfuges for criminal investigations. A plausible implication from this is that evidence found during an inventory is inadmissible in a criminal trial if the administrative search is a pretext for a criminal investigation. This conclusion could have followed, as well, from the Court's reasoning in *Opperman* that the Warrant Clause is "unhelpful" in analyzing the reasonableness of "routine, administrative caretaking" activities by the police, "particularly when no claim is made that the protective procedures are a subterfuge for criminal investigations." Also, in *Colorado v. Bertine*, the Court noted that "there was no showing that the police ... acted in bad faith or for the sole purpose of investigation."[9] By definition, pretextual inventory searches are *not* routine administrative police activities; they *are* bad-faith subterfuges for criminal investigations.

On the other hand, this arguable "no pretext" limitation on inventories conflicts with the frequently expressed view of the Court in other contexts,[10] most notably in *Whren v. United States*,[11] that the validity of an officer's actions should be judged by objective criteria, without regard to her motivations. Moreover, in *Arkansas v. Sullivan*,[12] the Supreme Court ruled that the Fourth Amendment is *not* violated when a police officer lawfully, i.e., with objective probable cause, arrests an individual for traffic violations in order to have the opportunity to conduct an automobile inventory search for drugs.

Technically, *Sullivan* leaves open the "no pretext-based inventory" possibility, because the Court, which acted without full briefing or oral argument, only ruled that the *seizure*—the pretextual arrest—passed constitutional muster, without expressly addressing the constitutionality of the subsequent inventory *search*.[13] Indeed, the Court majority made no mention of the inventory cases in its decision. Nonetheless, the Court's eagerness to approve an arrest that, although supported by probable cause, was made for the purpose of capitalizing on the inventory search exception suggests that an argument

---

8. Illinois v. Lafayette, 462 U.S. 640, 647–48 (1983) (arrest inventory); *see also* Colorado v. Bertine, 479 U.S. 367, 374 (1987) ("[R]easonable police regulations ... administered in good faith satisfy the Fourth Amendment, even though courts might as a matter of hindsight be able to devise equally reasonable rules requiring a different procedure.").

9. 479 U.S. at 372.

10. *See, e.g.*, §§ 2.07[B], 8.02[B], 8.02[F], and 14.04, *supra*.

11. 517 U.S. 806 (1996).

12. 532 U.S. 769 (2001) (per curiam).

13. In further support of the view that the pretext limitation remains viable after *Sullivan* is that the Court in *Whren* acknowledged but distinguished the pretext language in the inventory cases by observing that the latter cases involved searches in the absence of probable cause; the pretext-is-irrelevant doctrine of *Whren* involved "police conduct that is justifiable on the basis of probable cause to believe that a violation of law has occurred." *Whren*, 517 U.S. at 811.

against pretext-based inventories may face an uphill battle with the currently constituted Supreme Court.

The no-pretextual-criminal-investigation limitation (assuming there is one) apparently applies only if the officer's "sole purpose"[14] in conducting the inventory is to investigate crime. An officer who hopes or even suspects that she will find criminal evidence during an inventory may nonetheless conduct one if she acts, at least in part, for legitimate administrative reasons.[15] Because humans rarely act from a single motive, this makes the pretext limitation of limited practical significance: assuming that an inventory is required by departmental regulations, a defendant will be hard put to argue convincingly that the officer's sole purpose was to investigate a crime.

[2] "Routine" Nature of the Inventory

[a] In General

A warrantless, suspicionless search of a car lawfully in police custody is not justifiable merely because it was conducted for administrative purposes. The inventory must be a "routine" or "standard" procedure of the department conducting it.[16] The purpose of this requirement is to reduce the risk that inventories will be conducted arbitrarily, discriminatorily, or (as noted above) as "a ruse for a general rummaging in order to discover incriminating evidence."[17]

Although there is language in *Opperman* that might suggest that a warrantless inventory is unreasonable unless it is triggered by police observation of valuables in plain view in the impounded car,[18] subsequent cases do not support such a limitation. If a departmental regulation authorizes that all impounded cars be inventoried, whether or not valuables are in plain view, the inventory may proceed.

[b] Nondiscretionary Inventories

Ideally, the regulations authorizing an inventory should be similar to those involved in *Opperman*, that is, they should provide no significant discretion to the individual officer. The procedures should require officers to "act more or less mechanically, according to a set routine."[19]

Nondiscretionary inventories are desirable because they "promote[] a certain equality of treatment.... [T]he minister's picnic basket and grandma's knitting bag [found in an automobile] are opened and inventoried right along with the biker's tool box and

---

14. Colorado v. Bertine, 479 U.S. 367, 372 (1987).

15. United States v. Frank, 864 F.2d 992, 1001 (3d Cir. 1988).

16. Colorado v. Bertine, 479 U.S. at 374 n.6 ("Our decisions have always adhered to the *requirement* that inventories be conducted according to standardized criteria.") (emphasis added). Of course, the fact that an inventory *is* conducted pursuant to standard departmental regulations is not by itself sufficient basis for upholding the police action. As one court has observed, "[u]nconstitutional searches cannot be constitutionalized by standardizing them as a part of normal police practice." State v. Jewell, 338 So. 2d 633, 640 (La. 1976).

17. Florida v. Wells, 495 U.S. 1, 4 (1990).

18. *Opperman*, 428 U.S. at 375, 376 & n.10 (in which the Court noted that the "inventory itself was prompted by the presence in plain view of a number of valuables inside the car," and that "once the policeman was lawfully inside the car to secure the personal property in plain view, it was not unreasonable to open the unlocked glove compartment . . .").

19. Commonwealth v. Sullo, 532 N.E.2d 1219, 1222 (Mass. App. Ct. 1989).

the gypsy's satchel."[20] Also, nondiscretionary inventories are less likely to function as a ruse for a criminal investigation, and further reduce the risk of arbitrary or discriminatory treatment.

[c] Discretionary Inventories

Although inventories conducted pursuant to regulations that allow individual officers considerable discretion in determining whether and how to conduct the search are problematic, the Supreme Court has upheld inventories that permit some police discretion. In *Colorado v. Bertine*,[21] the Court approved an inventory in which the regulations allowed officers in certain circumstances to choose whether to impound the car and conduct an inventory of it, on the one hand, or simply to park it in a public parking lot and lock it, on the other hand. Discretion regarding whether to conduct an inventory is allowed "as long as [it] ... is exercised according to standard criteria and on the basis of something other than suspicion of evidence of criminal activity." The standardized criteria in *Bertine* included provisions that prohibited the police from parking vehicles in lots vulnerable to theft or vandalism.

[3] Automobile Owner's Wishes

The right of the police to inventory an automobile does not depend on a finding that the car owner is unavailable to consent to the search, to take her belongings out of the car, or to waive any rights that she might have against the police for the theft of her property.

Originally, it was not implausible to interpret *Opperman* narrowly to permit warrantless inventories only when it was unreasonable for the police to contact the car owner. The majority in *Opperman* observed that the car owner in that case "was not present to make other arrangements for the safekeeping of his belongings."

Notwithstanding this language, the Supreme Court in *Bertine* upheld an inventory although the vehicle owner was in police custody and, therefore, could have been given the opportunity to make other arrangements to protect his property. Quoting from *Illinois v. Lafayette*,[22] an *arrest* inventory case, the *Bertine* Court stated that although such an alternative was possible, "the real question is not what 'could have been achieved,' but whether the Fourth Amendment *requires* such steps." The Court stated that the Fourth Amendment does not require the police to act in the least intrusive fashion possible.

[4] Scope of an Inventory

[a] Containers

The Supreme Court ruled in *Bertine* that as part of a valid automobile inventory, the police may open containers found in the car, without a warrant or probable cause. However, five justices in *Bertine* appeared to accept the rule that the police may open and search containers without a warrant only "if they are following standard police procedures that *mandate* the opening of such containers in *every* impounded vehicle."[23]

---

20. State v. Shamblin, 763 P.2d 425, 428 (Utah Ct. App. 1988).
21. 479 U.S. 367 (1987).
22. 462 U.S. 640 (1983). *See* § 15.03, *infra*.
23. Colorado v. Bertine, 479 U.S. at 377 (Blackmun, Powell, and O'Connor JJ., concurring) (emphasis added). Dissenting Justices Marshall and Brennan would have limited inventories of

Florida v. Wells[24] has clouded the picture. Chief Justice Rehnquist stated in dictum for five justices, over the strenuous objection of four dissenters, that "in forbidding un-canalized discretion to police officers conducting inventory searches, there is no reason to insist that they be conducted in a mechanical 'all-or-nothing' fashion." According to the Chief Justice, a "police officer may be allowed sufficient latitude to determine whether a particular container should or should not be opened in light of the nature of the search and characteristics of the container itself." This view contradicts the principle expressed in dictum in *Bertine*. As the quoted language from *Wells* is also dictum, and members of both the majority and dissent in *Wells* have left the Court, it is uncertain whether this language will become law.

[b] Locked Portions of the Automobile

Opperman approved an inventory search of an unlocked glove compartment because it was a customary place for persons to store valuables. The Court did not consider, nor has it since considered, the justifiability of an inventory of a *locked* glove compartment or of an automobile trunk. However, many courts have authorized such searches when they are a required part of a routine inventory.[25]

The lower court trend is likely to receive the Court's approval when and if it considers the issue. The *Opperman* car door was locked (although the glove compartment was not), yet the inventory was permitted; it is reasonable, therefore, to conclude that the fact that a glove compartment or the trunk is locked is not constitutionally significant, as long as the standard procedure in the jurisdiction requires (or, perhaps, authorizes under defined circumstances) the officer to open the locked portions of the car where valuables may reasonably be stored.

[c] Inspection of Papers

The Supreme Court has not determined whether or to what extent the police may read papers and documents found during an otherwise valid inventory. However, five justices in *Opperman* suggested that reading papers that touch upon intimate areas of a person's private life should not be routinely allowed.

Concurring Justice Powell observed in *Opperman* that "[u]pholding [inventory] searches . . . provides no general license for the police to examine all the contents of such automobiles." In particular, he noted that there was no evidence in the case that the police, who found "miscellaneous papers," a checkbook, and a social security card, read these personal papers. The four dissenters, as well, stated that the police "would not be justified in sifting through papers secured under the procedures employed here." This conclusion seems correct, as none of the Court's proffered justifications for an inventory justifies reading personal papers.

Lower courts have frequently barred the introduction of evidence secured as the result of inspection of private papers found during an inventory.[26] Line-drawing, however, is necessary. The police inevitably must handle papers found during an inventory, and they will often need to peruse them in order to identify them on an inventory sheet.

---

containers even further, so they would have accepted the limiting language in the concurring opinion.

24. 495 U.S. 1 (1990).

25. 3 LaFave, Note 1, *supra*, at 650.

26. *E.g.*, Commonwealth v. Sullo, 532 N.E.2d 1219 (Mass. App. Ct. 1989).

Therefore, although the police should not read the documents beyond what is absolutely necessary to complete the inventory, they cannot be expected to blind themselves to what they see in plain view in the process.

§ 15.02 Arrest Inventories[27]

In *Illinois v. Lafayette*,[28] the Supreme Court held that the police may search an arrested person, as well as her personal effects, including containers, as part of a routine[29] inventory at a police station, incident to her booking and jailing. Neither a search warrant nor probable cause is required for an arrest inventory.[30]

The Court's reasoning in *Lafayette* in support of arrest inventories parallels that pertaining to automobile inventories. The Court stated that an inventory is reasonable to prevent theft of the arrestee's property by inmates and jail employees, to protect the police from theft claims, and to prevent the arrestee from carrying dangerous instrumentalities or contraband into the jail.

In practice, the scope of an arrest inventory is broader than a search incident to an arrest. A search that would be impractical or embarrassing at the scene of the arrest can be conducted at the stationhouse. For example, as part of an arrest inventory, authorities are entitled not only to search the arrestee's clothing, but also to take the clothing and keep it in official custody.[31] The Court in *Lafayette* also left open the question of "the circumstances in which a strip search may or may not be appropriate" as part of the inventory process.

---

27. *See generally* 3 LaFave, Note 1, *supra*, at § 5.3(a).

28. 462 U.S. 640 (1983); *contra under the state constitution*, Reeves v. State, 599 P.2d 727 (Alaska 1979) (a warrantless arrest inventory may not be more intrusive than is absolutely necessary to prevent entry of weapons, drugs, or contraband inside the jail; therefore, any object taken from the arrestee's possession may not be further searched or opened, except pursuant to a warrant or valid warrant exception); State v. Perham, 814 P.2d 914 (Haw. 1991) (the police may not search the contents of an arrestee's wallet as part of an arrest inventory, in the absence of evidence that such an exploratory search was the least intrusive means of accomplishing the purposes of safeguarding the property and of protecting the police against fraudulent claims).

29. Regarding the requirement that inventories be routine, *see* § 15.01[B][2], *supra*.

30. Relying on a different justification from the inventory decisions, the Court has also approved obtaining a DNA sample by swabbing the inside of an arrestee's cheek as part of the routine booking procedure for those charged with "serious offenses." *See* Maryland v. King, 133 S. Ct. 1958 (2013) (discussed more fully at § 12.02, *supra*).

31. United States v. Edwards, 415 U.S. 800 (1974).

Chapter 16

Consent Searches

§ 16.01 Preliminary Observations: Pragmatism, the Police, and the Supreme Court[1]

If warrantless searches are *per se* unreasonable, as the Supreme Court has often maintained (although far less often recently), the most significant "exception" to the warrant "requirement" is probably the "consent search" exception. As one police officer explained:

> [T]here are a lot of warrants that are not sought because of the hassle. You just figure it's not worth the hassle. . . . I don't think you can forego a case because of the hassle of a search warrant, but you can . . . work some other method. If I can get consent, I'm gonna do it.[2]

Another police officer, frustrated at delays in getting a warrant, expressed the situation this way: "You say to yourself, 'My God, you know, if I'm putting you [the magistrate] out, you know, I'll run back to the house and *try bargaining for consent, you know, 'cause I can get that done.'"[3] Indeed, although there are no reliable figures on the number of warrantless searches justified on consent grounds, "consent" almost certainly represents the dominant category of lawful warrantless searches.[4] Put simply, there are few areas of Fourth Amendment jurisprudence of greater practical significance than consent searches.

One of the more interesting and, for some, potentially troubling, aspects of consent law, is how far the Supreme Court has bent to permit this form of warrantless activity. Justice Potter Stewart candidly explained the Court's attitude regarding consent searches in *Schneckloth v. Bustamonte:*[5]

> In situations where the police have some evidence of illicit activity, but lack probable cause to arrest or search, a search authorized by a valid consent may be the only means of obtaining important and reliable evidence. . . . And in those cases where there is probable cause to arrest or search, but where the police lack a

---

1. Tracey Maclin, *The Good and Bad News About Consent Searches in the Supreme Court*, 39 McGeorge L. Rev. 27 (2008); Janice Nadler, *No Need to Shout: Bus Sweeps and the Psychology of Coercion*, 2002 Sup. Ct. Rev. 153; Marcy Strauss, *Reconstructing Consent*, 92 J. Crim. L. & Criminology 211 (2002).

2. Richard Van Duizend et al., The Search Warrant Process: Preconceptions, Perceptions, and Practices 21 (National Center for State Courts 1984).

3. *Id.* at 95 (emphasis added).

4. One police detective has estimated that 98% of warrantless searches are "consensual." *Id.* at 21.

5. 412 U.S. 218, 227–28 (1973).

warrant, a consent search may still be valuable. If the search is conducted and proves fruitless, that in itself may convince the police that an arrest with its possible stigma and embarrassment is unnecessary, or that a far more extensive search pursuant to a warrant is not justified. In short, a search pursuant to consent . . . is a constitutionally permissible and wholly legitimate aspect of effective police activity.

Do these arguments hold up? In a situation in which the police believe they have probable cause to conduct a search, the primary justification for allowing them to act without a warrant — and, thus, to act without the supposedly preferred input of a neutral and detached magistrate — may be no more weighty than a claim of police efficiency or, less substantial still, police convenience. Why is that enough to justify a warrantless search? The answer may be, as the Supreme Court recently put it, that "[i]n a society based on law, the concept of agreement and consent should be given a weight and dignity of its own."[6] Put differently, a government agent should not have to go to the trouble of requesting a warrant when the person whose rights the Constitution is seeking to protect consents to the police action.

If this *is* the underlying justification, one would assume that courts would be very careful to assure themselves that the citizen's consent was properly — at a minimum, voluntarily — granted. And yet, in case after case, courts, including the Supreme Court, have characterized consent searches as "voluntary," notwithstanding the fact that common sense[7] often suggests what "empirical studies over the last several decades on the social psychology of compliance . . . have [shown]: the extent to which people feel free to refuse to comply is extremely limited under situationally induced pressures."[8]

An even greater challenge in justifying warrantless consent searches occurs when the police know or suspect that they do *not* have probable cause — when they could *not* obtain a warrant even if they sought one — and so they "bargain" for consent. Justice Stewart's concern is that, in such circumstances, "a search authorized by a valid consent may be the only means of obtaining important and reliable evidence." But, surely this pragmatic explanation, although candid, is conceptually weak *if* there *really* is a constitutional warrant requirement. As Justice Antonin Scalia has observed, "there is nothing new in the realization that the Constitution sometimes insulates the criminality of a few in order to protect the privacy of us all."[9]

As will be seen, consent law is more comfortably (although not necessarily satisfactorily) explained in the current constitutional era in which the Supreme Court speaks about the reasonableness of searches, rather than about warrant "requirements" and "exceptions" thereto.

---

6. United States v. Drayton, 536 U.S. 194, 207 (2002).

7. *See* Strauss, Note 1, *supra*, at 211 ("Every year, I witness the same mass incredulity. Why, 100 criminal procedure students jointly wonder, would someone 'voluntarily' consent to allow a police officer to search the trunk of his car, knowing that massive amounts of cocaine are easily visible there?").

8. Nadler, Note 1, *supra*, at 155.

9. Arizona v. Hicks, 480 U.S. 321, 329 (1987).

§ 16.02 Consent Searches: General Principles[10]

[A] General Rule

As explained in the remainder of this chapter, validly obtained consent justifies an officer in conducting a warrantless search, with or without probable cause. To be valid, consent must be: (1) granted voluntarily;[11] and (2) obtained from someone with real[12] or apparent[13] authority to give consent. Also, to be valid, (3) the scope of the search conducted must not exceed the consent granted.[14] Finally, even if these conditions are satisfied, permission to conduct a search of a residence does *not* give the police authority to do so if another person, with common authority over the property, is physically present and expressly refuses consent.[15]

If the officer discovers evidence during a valid consent search, he may seize it without a warrant, pursuant to the plain view doctrine.

[B] Rationale for the Rule

The Supreme Court has struggled to explain the "consent search" warrant exception.

[1] Waiver?

In comparatively early opinions, the Court justified consent searches on waiver principles, that is, on the ground that, by consenting, a person waives his right to be free from unreasonable searches and seizures.[16]

The Supreme Court no longer justifies consent searches on waiver principles. Indeed, if waiver were the basis for consent searches, a number of important rulings of the Court would need to be reconsidered. First, the Supreme Court has frequently stated that a waiver of a constitutional right is "an intentional relinquishment or abandonment of a *known* right or privilege."[17] The Supreme Court has held, however, that a warrantless search may be upheld even if the consenting party does not know that he may refuse.[18]

---

10. *See generally* 4 Wayne R. LaFave, Search and Seizure § 8.1(a)-(b) (4th ed. 2004); Maclin, Note 1, *supra*; Ric Simmons, *Not "Voluntary" but Still Reasonable: A New Paradigm for Understanding the Consent Search Doctrine*, 80 Ind. L.J. 773 (2005); Daniel R. Williams, *Misplaced Angst: Another Look at Consent-Search Jurisprudence*, 82 Ind. L.J. 69 (2007).

11. Schneckloth v. Bustamonte, 412 U.S. 218 (1973). *See* § 16.03, *infra*.

12. United States v. Matlock, 415 U.S. 164 (1974). *See* § 16.05, *infra*.

13. Illinois v. Rodriguez, 497 U.S. 177 (1990). *See* § 16.06, *infra*.

14. *See* Florida v. Jimeno, 500 U.S. 248 (1991). *See* § 16.04, *infra*.

15. Georgia v. Randolph, 547 U.S. 103 (2006). *See* § 16.05, *infra*.

16. *E.g.*, Amos v. United States, 255 U.S. 313, 317 (1921); Johnson v. United States, 333 U.S. 10, 13 (1948); Stoner v. California, 376 U.S. 483, 489 (1964).

17. Johnson v. Zerbst, 304 U.S. 458, 464 (1938) (emphasis added).

18. Schneckloth v. Bustamonte, 412 U.S. 218 (1973). Not all states agree with this rule, at least not in every circumstance. For example, the Washington Supreme Court held that when police arrive at a suspect's home and ask for entry to the house to search, they must inform the suspect of his right to deny the request or limit the scope of the search. The Court held that it is "inherently coercive" when police appear on a person's doorstep to talk about a criminal case. State v. Ferrier, 960 P.2d 927 (Wash. 1998).

Second, waiver principles conflict with the Court's so-called "third party" consent jurisprudence. For example, suppose that *A* and *B* jointly own and use certain premises, and *A* consents to a police search while *B* is absent. The Court has ruled that such consent is valid against "third party" *B*.[19] Yet, absent some agency relationship, *A* cannot waive *B*'s Fourth Amendment rights. For the same reason, waiver principles fail to explain the "apparent authority" doctrine, which provides that the police may conduct a search on the basis of consent granted by *X*, a stranger to the property, if the police reasonably believe that *X* has authority to give consent.[20] Quite obviously, *Stranger X* cannot waive the constitutional rights of a true owner, so the waiver principle also fails to explain this aspect of current consent law.

[2] Consent = No Search?

A second potential rationale of warrantless consent searches is that one who voluntarily consents to a search no longer has a reasonable expectation of privacy in the property in question. Under this view, a consent search is not really a "search" at all.

There is some support for this thesis in third-party consent cases. The Supreme Court has stated — in reasoning reminiscent of the "false friend" surveillance-of-conversation cases[21] — that one who shares authority over property with others "assume[s] the risk that one of their number might permit the common area to be searched."[22] As three members of the Court in *Illinois v. Rodriguez*[23] explained, "a person may voluntarily limit his expectation of privacy by allowing others to exercise authority over his possessions." However, this reading of consent law was rejected by the majority in *Rodriguez*. According to Justice Scalia, "[t]o describe a consented search as a non-invasion of privacy and thus a non-search is strange in the extreme."

[3] Reasonableness?

The Court's current explanation is that a consent search is a reasonable search. That is, "consent" is not really an exception to a warrant requirement. Instead, "[t]here are various elements . . . that can make a search . . . 'reasonable' — one of which is the consent of the person" whose premises or effects will be searched.[24]

But what makes a consent search reasonable? Perhaps the answer is that no cognizable harm of a privacy or dignitary nature occurs from a search that a person freely authorizes the government to conduct; if so, it is not unreasonable to search in such circumstances.[25] Or, perhaps the explanation lies in Justice Stewart's pragmatic observations in

---

19. United States v. Matlock, 415 U.S. 164 (1974).

20. Illinois v. Rodriguez, 497 U.S. 177 (1990).

21. *See* § 6.05, *supra*.

22. *Matlock*, 415 U.S. at 171 n.7.

23. 497 U.S. at 190 (Marshall, J., with whom Brennan and Stevens, JJ., joined, dissenting).

24. *Rodriguez*, 497 U.S. at 183–84. *See also* Fernandez v. California, 134 S. Ct. 1126 (2014) (in which the Court states that the "ultimate touchstone of the Fourth Amendment is 'reasonableness,'" and consent searches "occupy one of [the] categories" of permissible warrantless searches; "[i]t would be unreasonable — indeed, absurd — to require police officers to obtain a warrant when the sole owner or occupant of a house or apartment voluntarily consents to a search"; and, even if the police could obtain a warrant, this would be a "needless inconvenience [to] everyone involved").

25. Indeed, if one accepts the reasoning of the court in *United States v. Drayton*, 536 U.S. 194, 207 (2002), the agreement of a citizen to consent to a search by government agents "should be given

Schneckloth v. Bustamonte,[26] considered in Section 16.01, including his admission that, in some circumstances, "a search authorized by a valid consent may be the only means of obtaining important and reliable evidence." This argument is apt to be unpersuasive to those who favor a warrant requirement, but it can be justified as part of a reasonableness inquiry if one agrees that the consent was voluntarily granted.

There is another, newly expressed, explanation for justifying consent searches that might be placed under the "reasonableness" umbrella. According to the Supreme Court in *Georgia v. Randolph,*[27] "[t]he constant element in assessing Fourth Amendment reasonableness in the consent cases ... is the great significance given to widely shared social expectations, which are naturally ... influenced by the law of property, but not controlled by its rules." Thus, it may be reasoned, when consent is validly secured, the ensuing search by the government is consistent with "widely shared social expectations" in that situation and, therefore, reasonable.

Randolph is only a 5–4 opinion and, despite the majority's assertion that it was applying an approach (determining "widely shared social expectations") that has been a "constant element" in consent-to-search case law, in fact it is a new way to explain consent cases. It remains to be seen whether this explanation will retain vitality in coming years.

§ 16.03 Voluntary Consent[28]

[A] Voluntariness: In General

Consent is legally ineffective unless the person granting consent does so voluntarily, rather than as "the result of duress or coercion, express or implied."[29] The burden of proof is on the prosecutor to demonstrate by a preponderance of the evidence that consent was freely given.[30]

The Supreme Court has stated that there is "no talismanic definition of 'voluntariness.'"[31] "Voluntariness" is determined from the totality of circumstances of the individual case.[32] As with other applications of the totality-of-the-circumstances

---

a weight and dignity of its own."

26. 412 U.S. 218 (1973).

27. 547 U.S. 103, 111 (2006).

28. 4 LaFave, Note 10, *supra,* at § 8.2; Simmons, Note 10, *supra*; see also the sources in Note 1.

29. Schneckloth v. Bustamonte, 412 U.S. 218, 248 (1973).

30. Bumper v. North Carolina, 391 U.S. 543, 548–49 (1968).

31. Schneckloth v. Bustamonte, 412 U.S. at 224.

32. There is some intriguing language in *United States v. Drayton,* 546 U.S. 194, 207 (2002) that arguably conflicts with the statement in the text:

> In a society based on law, the concept of agreement and consent should be given a weight and dignity of its own. Police officers act in full accord with the law when they ask citizens for consent. It reinforces the rule of law for the citizen to advise the police of his or her wishes, and for the police to act in reliance on that understanding. When this exchange takes place, it dispels inference of coercion.

Taken literally, this statement—in particular, the last sentence—could suggest that *Drayton* stands for the proposition that "as a matter of law, ... when a police officer asks a citizen for consent to search, and the citizen responds positively, such consent is voluntary." Nadler, *supra* note 1, at 179. This would conflict with the totality-of-circumstances standard that the Court has regularly applied in consent cases.

test,[33] there is no limit to the factors that may be considered. Among the factors that arguably could demonstrate coerced consent are: (1) a show of force by the police, such as a display of guns, that would suggest to the person that he is not free to refuse consent; (2) the presence of a large number of officers, which may suggest to the person "that the police are contemplating an undertaking which does not depend upon the cooperation of the individual";[34] (3) repetitive requests for consent after an initial refusal; and (4) evidence relating to the consenting person's age, race,[35] sex, level of education, emotional state, or mental condition, that suggests that his will was overborne by the officers' conduct.

Despite the plethora of potentially relevant factors, courts rarely find consent involuntary. The probable reason for this is that courts do not view the voluntariness issue as an empirical one. That is, the *real* issue is *not* whether the particular defendant's will to refuse consent was overborne, even though many of the factors noted above would suggest that this *is* the issue. Nor is the test whether an average person in the defendant's shoes would have felt compelled.[36]

In reality, the concept of "voluntariness" is a normative one. The real issue is whether the police methods of obtaining consent are morally acceptable in light of law enforcement goals. This explains why the Court has observed that "voluntariness" is an "amphibian"[37] notion, "reflect[ing] an accommodation of the complex of values implicated"[38] in the police-citizen encounter. The perceived need for consent searches as a means of obtaining "important and reliable evidence"[39] of guilt colors the analysis: courts are prone to find that consent was voluntarily granted in the absence of police conduct that shocks judicial sensibilities.

[B] Claim of Authority by the Police

The Supreme Court held in *Bumper v. North Carolina*[40] that a state may not meet its burden of proof that consent was voluntarily granted "by showing no more than acquiescence to a claim of lawful authority." Specifically, *Bumper* states, consent is invalid when it "has been given only after the official conducting the search has asserted that he possesses a warrant." Such a situation "is instinct with coercion — albeit colorably lawful coercion."

On its face, *Bumper* provides a bright-line rule: If an officer asserts authority to conduct a search on the basis of a warrant, whether that warrant is valid, invalid, or nonexistent, consent granted as a result of that assertion is invalid. Such a per se rule, however, conflicts with the totality-of-circumstances doctrine ordinarily applied in consent cases.

---

33. *See* §§ 22.02[B][3] and 23.05[A][2], *infra*.

34. 4 LaFave, Note 10, *supra*, at 62.

35. On the matter of race, and the claim that a racial minority will feel more pressure to consent than a non-minority person, *see* § 7.03[C][3], *supra*. For the view that almost all people, regardless of race, treat "requests" for consent as commands, see the next Note.

36. If this *were* the standard, almost no consent would be voluntary. *See* H. Richard Uviller, Tempered Zeal 81 (1988) ("However gently phrased, [the police request for consent] is likely to be taken by even the toughest citizen as a command.").

37. Culombe v. Connecticut, 367 U.S. 568, 605 (1961).

38. Schneckloth v. Bustamonte, 412 U.S. 218, 224 (1973).

39. *Id*. at 227.

40. 391 U.S. 543 (1968).

And, indeed, lower courts have not usually treated the acquiescence-to-authority doctrine as if it were categorical.[41] For example, if *D* indicates to the officer asserting authority, "You needn't have brought a search warrant. You are welcome to search,"[42] the consent may be legally effective, on the ground that *D*'s statement indicates that his consent was not linked to the officer's claim of authority.

The ruling in *Bumper* has not been discredited, but it is worth observing that it was decided in 1968, during the peak of the Warren Court era, and the facts of the case—including the Supreme Court's description of the citizen as a "66-year-old Negro widow" confronted by four North Carolina (presumably white) law enforcement officials—suggests that this case may have been as much about civil rights as it was about Fourth Amendment consent law in the minds of the justices.

[C] Police Deception

Police officers sometimes use deception to obtain consent to search. Often the deception relates to the identity of the person seeking consent. That is, an undercover officer will actively misrepresent or fail to disclose his true identity in order to gain admission onto premises where he can observe activities or conduct a search. As discussed elsewhere,[43] the Supreme Court in a long line of cases, beginning in the pre-*Katz*[44] "trespass" era and continuing into modern times, has held that when *A* talks to *B* or invites him into an otherwise constitutionally protected area, *A* assumes the risk that *B* is not whom he purports to be. Put differently, consent is not vitiated by the fact that, but for the misrepresentation or nondisclosure of a police officer's identity, the person would not have granted consent to the undercover officer to enter the individual's premises.

A different form of deception occurs when an officer deceives an individual regarding the purpose of a requested police search. Sometimes, a court will invalidate consent given in such deceptive circumstances, but the deception itself may not actually explain the outcome. For example, in *United States v. Dichiarinte*,[45] the police obtained consent to search *D*'s premises by explaining that they wanted to search for narcotics; in fact, they intended to open and examine certain documents, which they did. The court invalidated the consent on the ground that police "may not obtain consent to search on the representation that they intend to look only for certain specified items and subsequently use the consent as a license to conduct a general exploratory search." However, as Professor LaFave has pointed out,[46] the search would have been invalid in any case—even if the police had been looking for narcotics as they claimed—on the ground that they exceeded the scope of the search to which consent had been granted (i.e., the citizen did not consent to the opening and examination of documents, because no drugs could be discovered this way).[47]

What if the police use deception, but do not exceed the legitimate scope of the search? For example, *O*, a police officer, might request consent to search *D*'s bedroom for

---

41. 4 LaFave, Note 10, *supra*, at 57–58.
42. *E.g.,* Earls v. State, 496 S.W.2d 464 (Tenn. 1973) (upholding the consent as voluntary).
43. *See* §§ 6.02 and 6.05[B], and most particularly Note 96 therein, *supra*.
44. Katz v. United States, 389 U.S. 347 (1967).
45. 445 F.2d 126 (7th Cir. 1971).
46. 4 LaFave, Note 10, *supra*, at 134.
47. Regarding scope-of-consent issues, *see* § 16.04, *infra*.

evidence relating to a jewelry theft, when in fact *O* is looking for a bloody shirt that is evidence of a recent murder. *D* might consent, knowing that he has no stolen jewelry, and assuming that *O* will not understand the significance of the bloody shirt if it is discovered. Does *O*'s deception vitiate *D*'s consent, although the search does not exceed the scope of consent (i.e., search of the bedroom)?

The Supreme Court has said little on the matter, and state and lower federal courts have reached mixed results in such cases. The law is sufficiently muddled that Professor LaFave has stated that "as unsettling as it may be to say," the test appears to be, simply, whether the police "deception [was] 'fair.'"[48] Even if "fair deception" is not an oxymoron, the concept is obviously value-laden—again, "voluntariness" is a value-laden, non-empirical concept[49]—and, therefore, requires courts to determine whether, and to what extent, agents of the government should "play fair" in trying to investigate the activities of persons whom they suspect of not "playing fair."

[D] Awareness of Fourth Amendment Rights[50]

In *Schneckloth v. Bustamonte*,[51] at 2:40 a.m., the police stopped a car containing multiple passengers because a headlight and license plate light were burned out. After the driver failed to produce his driver's license and only one passenger could provide identification, an officer asked for permission to search the car, which was granted. During the search, the police discovered evidence that connected one of the occupants to a crime. In the ensuing prosecution, the defendant asserted that the consent granted was invalid because the government did not prove that the consenting party knew that he had the right to refuse consent to the search.

The Supreme Court, per Justice Potter Stewart, framed the issue as follows: "[W]hat must the state prove to demonstrate that a consent was 'voluntarily' given[?]" To answer this question, Stewart sought guidance from the cases in which the Court had determined the voluntariness of a suspect's confession under the Fourteenth Amendment Due Process Clause.[52] As Stewart explained, "[t]hose cases yield no talismanic definition of 'voluntariness'"; to the question of "whether a defendant's will was overborne in a particular case, the Court has assessed the totality of all the surrounding circumstances." Therefore, in the Fourth Amendment context as well, the Court rejected the principle that "'voluntariness' requires proof of knowledge of a right to refuse as the *sine qua non* of an effective consent to search." Instead, a person's awareness (or lack thereof) of his right to refuse consent is merely one factor, among all of the surrounding circumstances, to be taken into account in determining the voluntariness of the consent granted.[53]

---

48. 4 LaFave, Note 10, *supra*, at 138.

49. *See* § 16.03[A], *supra*.

50. *See generally* Gerard E. Lynch, *Why Not a Miranda for Searches?*, 5 Ohio St. J. Crim. L. 233 (2007); Alan C. Michaels, *Rights Knowledge: Values and Tradeoffs*, 39 Texas Tech L. Rev. 1355 (2007).

51. 412 U.S. 218 (1973); *contra under the state constitution*, State v. Brown, 156 S.W.2d 722 (Ark. 2004) (an officer seeking consent to search a suspect's home without a warrant must warn the resident of the right to refuse consent); State v. Ferrier, 960 P.2d 927 (Wash. 1998) (same).

52. *See generally* Chapter 22, *infra*.

53. *See also* Ohio v. Robinette, 519 U.S. 33 (1996) (the Fourth Amendment does not require that a lawfully seized person, now free to go, be advised that he is free to leave before his consent to a car search will be recognized as voluntary; eschewing this bright-line rule, the Court followed the *Schneckloth* approach of treating voluntariness as a matter to be determined from all of the circumstances). *Contra under the state constitution*, State v. Pals, 805 N.W. 2d 767 (Iowa 2011) (adopting

Schneckloth has been criticized. Early critics maintained (as Justice Thurgood Marshall argued in dissent in the case) that the majority misstated the issue in the case. To them, the issue was not whether *A*'s consent was *voluntary*, but rather whether *A waived* his constitutional right to be free from unreasonable searches and seizures. This distinction is significant because the traditional waiver principle, enunciated in *Johnson v. Zerbst*,[54] is that the state must prove "an intentional relinquishment... of a known right or privilege." In *Schneckloth*, such knowledge was not proved; therefore, there seemingly was no valid waiver of the citizen's Fourth Amendment rights under this test. As Justice Stewart accurately pointed out, however, existing consent law is not based on waiver principles.[55]

Other critics maintain that, notwithstanding the fact that the government has the technical burden of proof in consent cases, *Schneckloth* demonstrates that "[t]he current law of consent searches [purposely] skews the balance against the citizen..."[56] They find it difficult to believe that any person in the shoes of the occupants of the *Schneckloth* car would have believed they could say no.[57] Therefore, if the Court had truly wanted to protect citizens in such circumstances, why would it not have created "*Schneckloth* warnings," much as the justices have devised *Miranda* warnings in the confession field?

This argument proceeds: *Miranda* warnings reduced the temptation of police officers to abuse their power in the interrogation room without significantly affecting the number of confessions secured. Likewise, a simple warning to a citizen that "You have a right to refuse..." could have a similar beneficial effect in the Fourth Amendment context without significantly reducing the number of consent searches granted.

The Supreme Court's refusal to take this route is probably a function of two factors.[58] First, *Miranda* warnings were part of the Supreme Court's efforts to deal with known abuses, including physical harm, that occurred in interrogation rooms in the first half of the twentieth century. In the Fourth Amendment context, as Justice Stewart wrote in *Schneckloth*, "there is no evidence of any inherently coercive tactics.... Indeed,... consent searches will normally occur on a person's own familiar territory," rather than in a police station.

Second, coerced confessions are inherently unreliable. In contrast, according to the *Schneckloth* Court, consent searches are not only a "wholly legitimate aspect of effective police activity," but they are sometimes "the only means of obtaining important"—*and, here may be the key*—"reliable evidence." That is, unlike constitutional rights that increase the reliability of the trial process (such as the bar on the admission of coerced confessions), the privacy protections of the Fourth Amendment have nothing to do with promoting an accurate determination of innocence or guilt at trial. The Court was unwilling in *Schneckloth*, therefore, to place obstacles in the way of police efforts to secure reliable evidence of guilt, even if this means that the police will not inform citizens of their constitutional right to refuse consent.

---

a seemingly stronger standard than *Robinette*, stating that the failure of police to inform a driver that he is free to leave "is, at a minimum, a strong factor cutting against the voluntariness of the [consent to] search" of the car).

54. 304 U.S. 458 (1938).

55. *See* § 16.02[B][1], *supra*.

56. Arnold H. Loewy, *Cops, Cars, and Citizens: Fixing the Broken Balance*, 76 St. John's L. Rev. 535, 553 (2002).

57. "Can anyone not thoroughly steeped in legal fiction really believe that they thought 'no' was one of their options?" *Id.* at 554.

58. Lynch, Note 50, *supra*, at 240–245.

§ 16.04 Scope of Search[59]

A warrantless consent search is invalid if an officer exceeds the scope of the consent granted. For example, if A consents to a search of his bedroom, the police may not search other parts of the house on the basis of the consent.[60] If A consents to a 10-minute search, the police may not invoke consent to justify the search after the consent expires.[61] Consent searches, however, are virtually never negotiated with the precision of a contract, so it is often unclear how extensively the police may search based on the permission granted.

In *Florida v. Jimeno*,[62] the Supreme Court provided guidance on the "scope of consent" issue. In *Jimeno*, O stopped J's car on the highway in order to issue a traffic citation. Because O had reason to suspect that J was carrying narcotics in the car, O requested permission to search the car for narcotics. J consented. During the search, O opened a folded paper bag, in which he discovered a kilogram of cocaine. The trial court suppressed the evidence on the ground that J had not expressly consented to a search of the container, only of "the car."

The Supreme Court reversed. Chief Justice Rehnquist declared that "[t]he standard for measuring the scope of a suspect's consent . . . is that of 'objective' reasonableness—what would the typical reasonable person have understood by the exchange between the officer and the suspect?" On the facts here, the Court maintained that "it was objectively reasonable for the police to conclude that the general consent to search [J's] car included consent to search containers within that car which might bear drugs." In other words, whether or not J *subjectively* thought about the container when he consented to the search, O acted *objectively* reasonably in interpreting J's consent to include the right to open the folded paper bag.

Jimeno does *not* stand for the proposition that the police may, in the absence of an express limitation, open *every* container discovered during *any* consent search of a residence or automobile. According to the Court, "[t]he scope of a search is generally defined by its expressed object." Therefore, it would be improper for the police to open a container too small to hide the object of the search. Potentially more significantly, the Court in dictum distinguished the case before it from one in which the police, pursuant to consent to search a car trunk, break open a locked suitcase found in the car trunk. In the latter situation, the Court opined, "[i]t is very likely unreasonable to think that a suspect, by consenting to the search of his trunk, has agreed to the breaking open of [the suitcase] . . ." Interestingly, the distinction drawn by this dictum—between a locked suitcase and a folded paper bag—is contrary to the Supreme Court's approach in other container cases, which treats all closed containers alike for Fourth Amendment purposes.[63]

---

59. *See generally* 4 LaFave, Note 10, *supra*, at § 8.1(c).

60. However, if the officer observes criminal evidence in view on the way to the bedroom, he may seize it pursuant to the plain view doctrine.

61. However, if criminal evidence is found during the 10 minutes, the police may be justified in arresting A, and conducting a separate search as incident to the arrest.

62. 500 U.S. 248 (1991).

63. *See* § 13.05[A][2], *supra*.

§ 16.05 Third-Party Consent[64]

More than one person may have an interest in real or personal property that the police want to search. A search of a residence, for example, typically intrudes on the privacy of several persons who inhabit it; a search of a container intrudes on the privacy interests of anyone who uses it as a depository of private effects.

In a criminal proceeding, no significant consent issue arises if X voluntarily consents to a search of premises or personal effects that also belong to D, as long as the evidence found during the search is introduced at trial only against X, the consenting party. The issue of "third-party consent" arises, however, when the person against whom the evidence is introduced (D) is not the one who granted consent (X).

Two factual scenarios must be distinguished in this area: (1) the case in which D is absent when X grants consent; and (2) the situation in which D and X are both present, X consents to the search, but D refuses consent.

The first scenario is seen in *United States v. Matlock*.[65] In the case, M was arrested in the front yard of a home in which he shared a room with X. The officers received consent from X to search the room. M's consent was not requested, although he was nearby in police custody. The Court declared the law to be "clear" that consent to a search "of one who possesses common authority over premises or effects is valid as against the absent nonconsenting person with whom the authority is shared."[66] According to *Matlock*, "it is reasonable to recognize that any of the co-inhabitants has the right to permit the inspection in his own right and that the others have assumed the risk that one of their number might permit the common area to be searched."

Although the holding of *Matlock* expressly was limited to cases in which the nonconsenting party was not physically present when consent was granted (although, it will be noted again, M could easily have been asked, as he was nearby in police custody), the underlying reasoning of the case did not seem so limited. After all, just as one who speaks to another assumes the risk that the other person will disclose the speaker's words to another person, *Matlock* seemingly suggests that, by living together or sharing property with another, one must accept the possibility that the other person will consent to give up their shared privacy to another person, including a police officer, even if the first person is present to object.

Nonetheless, when the Supreme Court confronted this second scenario, it took a different approach. The Supreme Court held, 5–3,[67] in *Georgia v. Randolph*,[68] that "a warrantless search of a shared dwelling for evidence over the express refusal of consent by

---

64. *See generally* 4 LaFave, Note 10, *supra*, at §§ 8.3–8.4; Mary I. Coombs, *Shared Privacy and the Fourth Amendment, or the Rights of Relationships*, 75 Cal. L. Rev. 1593 (1987); Maclin, Note 1, *supra*.

65. 415 U.S. 164 (1974).

66. The Court explained that "common authority" rests on "mutual use of the property by persons generally having joint access or control for most purposes." One who shares premises with another person may, however, retain exclusive control over a portion of the premises or over particular effects within them. For example, a particular room in an apartment shared by college roommates might be used exclusively by one person. In such circumstances, consent is ineffective unless it is granted by the person with exclusive control.

67. Justice Alito did not participate in the opinion.

68. 547 U.S. 103 (2006).

a physically present resident cannot be justified as reasonable as to him on the basis of consent given to the police by another resident."

In *Randolph*, police officers came to the home of Janet and Scott Randolph in response to a "domestic dispute" telephone call by Janet complaining that Scott had taken their child away. Shortly after police arrived, Scott returned. He explained that he had removed their son to a neighbor's house out of concern that Janet might take their son to Canada, where her parents lived, as she had done before. In the encounter, Janet told the officers that Scott was a cocaine user, which claim Scott denied. The officers asked Scott for permission to search the house. He refused, so one officer turned to Janet for consent, which she "readily" gave. A subsequent search turned up a straw with a powdery residue that the officers suspected was cocaine. Justice Souter, writing for the majority, stated:

> The constant element in assessing Fourth Amendment reasonableness in the consent cases . . . is the great significance given to widely shared social expectations, which are naturally enough influenced by the law of property, but not controlled by its rules. *Matlock* accordingly not only holds that a solitary co-inhabitant may sometimes consent to a search of shared premises, but stands for the proposition that the reasonableness of such a search is in significant part a function of commonly held understanding about the authority that co-inhabitants may exercise in ways that affect each other's interests.

As the preceding excerpt suggests, the Court shifted its analysis from the assumption-of-risk doctrine set out in *Matlock* to a widely shared social-expectation standard.[69] In this regard, Souter wrote:

> To begin with, it is fair to say that a caller standing at the door of shared premises would have no confidence that one occupant's invitation was a sufficiently good reason to enter when a fellow tenant stood there saying, "stay out." Without some very good reason, no sensible person would go inside under those conditions. Fear for the safety of the occupant issuing the invitation, or of someone else inside, would be thought to justify entry, but the justification then would be the personal risk, the threats to life or limb, not the disputed invitation.

> The visitor's reticence without some such good reason would show not timidity but a realization that when people living together disagree over the use of their common quarters, a resolution must come through voluntary accommodation, not by appeals to authority. Unless the people living together fall within some recognized hierarchy, like a household of parent and child or barracks housing military personnel of different grades, there is no societal understanding of superior and inferior, a fact reflected in a standard formulation of domestic property law. . . . In sum, there is no common understanding that one co-tenant generally has a right or authority to prevail over the express wishes of another, whether the issue is the color of the curtains or invitations to outsiders.[70]

---

69. Is there a *third* way to analyze these cases? In light of the Supreme Court's recent resuscitation of the pre-*Katz* trespass doctrine (*see* § 6.03[E]), Justice Scalia recently observed in dictum that the argument "that the search of [a person's] shared apartment violated the Fourth Amendment because he had a right under property law to exclude the police," is an argument that cannot "be . . . easily dismissed." Fernandez v. California, 134 S. Ct. 1126, 1137 (2014) (concurring opinion).

70. *In accord*, Lloyd L. Weinreb, *Generalities of the Fourth Amendment*, 42 U. Chi. L. Rev. 47, 63 (1974) ("[O]rdinarily, persons with equal 'rights' in a place would accommodate each other by not admitting persons over another's objection while he was present.").

The line drawn in this case, as Justice Souter conceded, is both thin and formalistic.[71] It does not apply if the co-occupant is not on the premises although perhaps nearby (as in *Matlock*), nor does the rule announced here apply if the co-occupant who would object fails to come to the door because, for example, he is napping on the couch, is in the shower, or is watching television.

Chief Justice Roberts wrote the primary dissent. He disagreed with the Court's new widely shared-social-expectation standard:

> The Court creates constitutional law by surmising what is typical when a social guest encounters an entirely atypical situation. The rule the majority fashions does not implement the high office of the Fourth Amendment to protect privacy, but instead provides protection on a random and happenstance basis. . . . And the cost of affording such random protection is great, as demonstrated by the recurring cases in which abused spouses seek to authorize police entry into a home they share with a nonconsenting abuser.

Chief Justice Roberts criticized the majority's "confident" assumptions ("confident enough to incorporate into the Constitution") about societal expectations:

> The fact is that a wide variety of differing social situations can readily be imagined, giving rise to quite different social expectations. A relative or good friend of one of two feuding roommates might well enter the apartment over the objection of the other roommate. The reason the invitee appeared at the door also affects expectations: A guest who came to celebrate an occupant's birthday, or one who has traveled some distance for a particular reason, might not readily turn away simply because of a roommate's objection. . . .
>
> The possible scenarios are limitless, and slight variations in the fact pattern yield vastly different expectations about whether the invitee might be expected to enter or go away. Such shifting expectations are not a promising foundation on which to ground a constitutional rule.

The Chief Justice, therefore, returned to the assumption-of-risk doctrine of *Matlock*:

---

71. Indeed, in *Fernandez v. California*, 134 S. Ct. 1126 (2014), the Supreme Court, 6–3, repeatedly described *Randolph* as a "narrow exception" to "our cases [that] firmly establish that police officers may search jointly occupied premises if one of the occupants consents." In *Fernandez*, F was arrested in an apartment he shared with R. At that time, he stated that "[y]ou don't have any right to come in here. I know my rights." After removing F and taking him to the police station for booking, an officer returned to the premises and requested and received consent from R to search the premises. The Court described this as a "very different situation," and noted that Justice Souter's opinion "went to great lengths to make clear that its holding was limited to situations in which the objecting occupant is present. Again and again, the opinion of the [*Randolph*] Court stressed this controlling factor."

Justice Alito, speaking for the Court, stated that R's prior objection "cannot be squared with the 'widely shared social expectations' or 'customary social usage' [approach] upon which the *Randolph* holding was based." He considered it "obvious that the calculus . . . would likely be quite different if the objecting tenant was not standing at the door . . . (and especially when it is known that the objector will not return during course of the visit)." This was a proposition that Justice Ginsburg, joined by Justices Kagan and Sotomayor, questioned. Quoting a Seventh Circuit dissent, she stated: " 'Only in a Hobbesian world,' . . . 'would one person's social obligations to another be limited to what the other[, because of his presence,] is . . . able to enforce.' " Moreover, she observed, even if sharing premises "entail[s] the prospect of visits by unwanted social callers while the objecting resident [is] gone, that unwelcome visitor's license would hardly include free rein to rummage through the dwelling in search of evidence and contraband."

The correct approach to the question presented is clearly mapped out in our precedents: The Fourth Amendment protects privacy. If an individual shares information, papers, *or places* with another, he assumes the risk that the other person will in turn share access to that information or those papers *or places* with the government. And just as an individual who has shared illegal plans or incriminating documents with another cannot interpose an objection when that other person turns the information over to the government, just because the individual happens to be present at the time, so too someone who shares a place with another cannot interpose an objection when that person decides to grant access to the police, simply because the objecting individual happens to be present.

Turning to policy, does the holding in *Randolph* threaten the safety of domestic abuse victims and other persons living where criminal activity is occurring? The Chief Justice said it does:

What does the majority imagine will happen, in a case in which the consenting co-occupant is concerned about the other's criminal activity, once the door clicks shut? The objecting co-occupant may pause briefly to decide whether to destroy any evidence of wrongdoing or to inflict retribution on the consenting co-occupant first, but there can be little doubt that he will attend to both in short order.

Justice Souter responded to this concern:

[T]his case has no bearing on the capacity of the police to protect domestic victims. . . . No question has been raised, or reasonably could be, about the authority of the police to enter a dwelling to protect a resident from domestic violence; so long as they have good reason to believe such a threat exists. . . . (And since the police would then be lawfully in the premises, there is no question that they could seize any evidence in plain view or take further action supported by any consequent probable cause.) Thus, the question whether the police might lawfully enter over objection in order to provide any protection that might be reasonable is easily answered yes.

In other words, although the police may not assert the "consent" exception to the warrant rule when a co-occupant objects to the officer's entry, the police may enter on the basis of a different warrant exception — here, the exigency exception.

Justice Breyer, who concurred in the majority opinion and represented the critical fifth vote, expressed his narrow reading of the situation. He stated that "the Fourth Amendment does not insist upon bright-line rules. Rather it recognizes that no single set of legal rules can capture the ever changing complexity of human life." He observed that "the 'totality of the circumstances' present here [did] not suffice to justify abandoning the Fourth Amendment's traditional hostility to police entry into a home without a warrant. I stress the totality of the circumstances, however, because, were the circumstances to change significantly, so should the result."[72]

---

72. It is noteworthy that two members of *Randolph* five-person majority, Justices Souter and Stevens, have since retired from the Court.

§ 16.06 "Apparent Authority"[73]

Suppose that *X*, a guest at *D*'s house, answers the door when the police arrive. The officers, believing that *X* lives at the residence, seek and receive consent from *X* to search the premises. Is such consent—consent based on apparent, not real, authority—effective? The issue cuts to the core of the rationale of consent searches.

In *Stoner v. California*,[74] the Supreme Court stated that "the rights protected by the Fourth Amendment are not to be eroded . . . by unrealistic doctrines of 'apparent authority.'" Ten years later, however, in *United States v. Matlock*,[75] the Court expressly left open the issue of whether "apparent authority" constitutes effective consent.

In *Illinois v. Rodriguez*,[76] the Court resolved the issue. It held, 6–3, that a warrantless entry of a residence is valid when it is based on the consent of a person whom the police, at the time of entry, reasonably (but incorrectly) believe has common authority over the premises.

In *Rodriguez*, *X* reported to the police that she had been severely beaten that day by *R* in a specified apartment. *X* stated that *R* was now asleep on the premises, and she offered to let the police in with her key so that they could arrest him. During her conversation with the police, *X* referred to *R*'s apartment as "our" apartment, and she stated that she had clothing and furniture there. In fact, however, although she had once shared the apartment with *R*, she had vacated it weeks earlier and had taken the key without *R*'s knowledge. With *X*'s consent, the police entered *R*'s apartment. Inside, they observed drug paraphernalia and cocaine in plain view. *R* was arrested and charged with possession of illegal drugs. The trial court granted *R*'s motion to exclude the evidence found in the apartment because *X* lacked common authority over the premises.

The Supreme Court, per Justice Scalia, reversed. According to *Rodriguez*, "what is at issue when a claim of apparent consent is raised is not whether the right to be free of searches has been *waived*, but whether the right to be free of *unreasonable* searches has been *violated*." Addressing the reasonableness issue, Justice Scalia wrote:

> It is apparent that in order to satisfy the "reasonableness" requirement of the Fourth Amendment, what is generally demanded of the many factual determinations that must regularly be made by agents of the government—whether the magistrate issuing a warrant, the police officer executing a warrant, or the police officer conducting a search or seizure under one of the exceptions to the

---

73. *See generally* 4 LaFave, Note 10, *supra*, at § 8.3(g).

74. 376 U.S. 483 (1964).

75. 415 U.S. 164 (1974).

76. 497 U.S. 177 (1990); *contra, under state constitution*, State v. Lopez, 896 P.2d 889 (Haw. 1995) (consent may not be based on apparent authority); State v. McLees, 994 P.2d 683 (Mont. 2000) (same); State v. Wright, 893 P.2d 455 (N.M. Ct. App. 1995) (same); *see also* Commonwealth v. Porter P., 923 N.E.2d 36 (Mass. 2010) (holding that, although Massachusetts recognizes an "apparent authority" doctrine, it applies it more narrowly than the federal constitutional doctrine; specifically, at least when the police seek to rely on consent of a landlord or other non-resident third party to search a home, they must see a written document purporting to give the consenting party authority to permit the search; in the absence of such a document, a claim of apparent authority in such circumstances fails as a matter of law).

warrant requirement—is not that they always be correct, but that they always be reasonable.[77]

In effect, therefore, a search based on a reasonable mistake of fact regarding the authority of the third person to give consent is a "reasonable" search within the meaning of the Fourth Amendment.[78]

The consent determination, as with other factual matters that arise under the Fourth Amendment, must be judged against an objective standard. The Court warned that an invitation by a person to conduct a search, even if accompanied by an explicit claim of authority to grant consent (e.g., "I live here"), is insufficient to justify a consent search if "the surrounding circumstances [are] . . . such that a reasonable person would doubt its truth."

Specifically, the objective test announced in *Rodriguez* is: "[W]ould the facts available to the officer at the moment . . . 'warrant a man of reasonable caution in the belief' that the consenting party had authority over the premises?" If the answer is "no," then "warrantless entry without further inquiry is unlawful unless actual authority exists." If the answer is "yes," the warrantless search is valid.

---

77. Notice the Court's inclusion of "exceptions to the warrant requirement" within the general rubric that the police need not be correct in their actions, only that they be reasonable. This language may have future impact on "warrant exception" case law. For example, suppose that a police officer conducts a search, ostensibly incident to a lawful arrest, but seizes evidence that a court later determines was slightly outside the arrestee's grabbing area. Under current law, that renders the warrantless search impermissible. In light of *Rodriguez*, however, the government would argue, perhaps successfully, that the officer's factual mistake was a reasonable one, thereby rendering the search reasonable.

78. What if a police officer acts on the basis of a reasonable mistake of *law*? According to the Supreme Court, this also satisfies the Fourth Amendment—though it is very rare for a police officer's mistake of law to be deemed reasonable. See § 17.03 *infra*.

Chapter 17

Terry v. Ohio: The "Reasonableness" Balancing Standard in Criminal Investigations

§ 17.01 *Terry v. Ohio*: An Overview to a Landmark Case[1]

The Fourth Amendment was once considered a monolith.[2] "Probable cause" had a single meaning, and "searches" and "seizures" were all-or-nothing concepts. The monolith was cracked by the Supreme Court in *Camara v. Municipal Court*.[3] In *Camara*, the justices recognized a different form of "probable cause,"[4] applicable in so-called administrative-search cases,[5] that does not require individualized suspicion of criminal wrongdoing and that is based on the general Fourth Amendment standard of "reasonableness." To determine "reasonableness," the *Camara* Court invoked a balancing test, in which the individual's and society's interests in the given type of administrative search were weighed against each other.

If *Camara* cracked the Fourth Amendment monolith, *Terry v. Ohio*[6] broke it entirely. Although the issue in *Terry* was described by the Court as "quite narrow" — "whether it is always unreasonable for a policeman to seize a person and subject him to a limited search for weapons unless there is probable cause to arrest" — the significance of the case to Fourth Amendment jurisprudence is, quite simply, monumental. In terms of the daily activities of the police, as well as the experiences of persons "on the street," there is probably no Supreme Court Fourth Amendment case of greater practical impact.

The significance of *Terry* will be seen in this chapter, but a brief overview is appropriate. First, *Terry* transported *Camara*'s "reasonableness" balancing test from the realm of administrative searches to traditional criminal investigations, and used it to determine

---

1. *See generally* 4 Wayne R. LaFave, Search and Seizure § 9.1 (4th ed. 2004); David A. Harris, *Frisking Every Suspect: The Withering of Terry*, 28 U.C. Davis L. Rev. 1 (1994); Wayne R. LaFave, *"Street Encounters" and the Constitution: Terry, Sibron, Peters, and Beyond*, 67 Mich. L. Rev. 39 (1968); Tracey Maclin, *The Decline of the Right of Locomotion: The Fourth Amendment on the Streets*, 75 Cornell L. Rev. 1258 (1990); Scott E. Sundby, *A Return to Fourth Amendment Basics: Undoing the Mischief of Camara and Terry*, 72 Minn. L. Rev. 383 (1988). *See also* the citations found in Note 15, *infra*.

2. Anthony G. Amsterdam, *Perspectives on the Fourth Amendment*, 58 Minn. L. Rev. 349, 388 (1974).

3. 387 U.S. 523 (1967).

4. *See* § 8.06, *supra*.

5. *See generally* § 18.02, *infra*.

6. 392 U.S. 1 (1968).

the reasonableness of certain warrantless searches and seizures, rather than merely to define "probable cause." The result has been a significant diminution in the role of the Warrant Clause in Fourth Amendment jurisprudence. That is, *Terry* provided the impetus, as well as the framework, for a move by the Supreme Court away from the proposition that "warrantless searches are *per se* unreasonable," to the competing view that the appropriate test of police conduct "is not whether it is reasonable to procure a search warrant, but whether the search was reasonable."[7] Warrantless police conduct became much easier to justify after *Terry*.

Second, *Terry* recognized that searches and seizures can vary in their intrusiveness. The Court no longer treats all searches and all seizures alike. As a result of this case, many police-citizen on-the-street encounters that do not involve arrests or full-blown searches come within the scope of the Fourth Amendment, but are considered lawful notwithstanding the absence of a warrant or probable cause.

Third, as a corollary of the last point, because of *Terry* the police may now conduct a wide array of searches and seizures that are considered less-than-ordinarily intrusive, on the basis of a lesser standard of cause than "probable cause," so-called "reasonable suspicion."[8]

Finally, although *Terry* does not require such a holding, the Supreme Court has applied the "reasonableness" balancing test that stems from it to hold that a limited number of seizures and searches of persons or property may be conducted without individualized suspicion of any kind.[9]

At least one other aspect of *Terry* deserves note here. Professor Akhil Amar suggests that this case may provide "one of the most open Fourth Amendment discussions of race to date."[10] Whether or not this assertion is accurate,[11] there is no gainsaying that when the police forcibly stop persons on the street to question them or to conduct full or cursory searches, highly sensitive issues of racial profiling (and issues of ethnicity, class, and gender) come to the fore.[12]

---

7. United States v. Rabinowitz, 339 U.S. 56, 66 (1950). *Terry* "established such a spongy test, one that allowed the police so much room to maneuver and furnished the courts so little bases for meaningful review, that the opinion must have been the cause for celebration in a goodly number of police stations." Yale Kamisar, *The Warren Court and Criminal Justice: A Quarter-Century Retrospective*, 31 Tulsa L.J. 1, 5 (1995).

8. *See, e.g.*, §§ 17.07 (weapons searches of automobiles), 17.08 (protective sweeps of residences), 18.05[B][1] (searches of public school students), and 18.05[B][2] (searches of public employees), *infra*.

9. *See* § 15.01, *supra* (car inventories), and §§ 18.03 (border searches), 18.04[B][1] (sobriety checkpoints), and 18.05[C] (drug and alcohol testing of public employees and public school children), *infra*.

10. Akhil Reed Amar, *Fourth Amendment First Principles*, 107 Harv. L. Rev. 757, 808 (1994).

11. His is not a universally held view. *E.g.*, Anthony C. Thompson, *Stopping the Usual Suspects: Race and the Fourth Amendment*, 74 N.Y.U. L. Rev. 956 (1999) (contending that the Supreme Court intentionally disguised the race-based aspects of the facts in *Terry*).

12. According to a New York County District Attorney *amicus* brief filed in the *Terry* case, 1,600 police reports of stop-and-frisks by the New York City Police Department "showed [a] disproportionate racial impact of those actions." Michael R. Juviler, *A Prosecutor's Perspective*, 72 St. John's L. Rev. 741, 743 (1998). This disparity apparently remains. Al Baker, *New York Minorities More Likely to be Frisked*, N.Y. Times, May 12, 2010 (reporting that New York City African-Americans and Latinos were nine times more likely than whites to be forcibly stopped by the police in 2009 and frisked, although they were *not* more likely to be arrested).

Some scholars believe that the *Terry* opinion (or, at least, the *Terry* doctrine as it has come to be interpreted over the years), and its move away from the warrant requirement, has done much to exacerbate racial tensions between the police and members of minority communities.[13] Others believe that the Court's movement in this case to a reasonableness standard is good, in part because it will force courts to confront issues, such as race and class, "honestly and openly."[14] Whoever is right in this regard, Chief Justice Earl Warren was surely correct when he observed in *Terry* that "[w]e would be less than candid if we did not acknowledge that this [case] thrusts to the fore, difficult and troublesome issues regarding a sensitive area of police activity."

§ 17.02 *Terry v. Ohio*: The Opinion[15]

[A] Majority Opinion

O,[16] a 39-year police veteran, became "thoroughly suspicious" when he observed two men walking back and forth repeatedly in front of a store, peering in. *O* testified that he suspected that the men were "casing a job," i.e., planning to commit an armed robbery. *O* also observed the two men talk to a third individual.[17]

---

13. Regarding the racial issues raised by *Terry*, *see generally* David A. Harris, *Factors for Reasonable Suspicion: When Black and Poor Means Stopped and Frisked*, 69 Ind. L.J. 659 (1994); Sheri Lynn Johnson, *Race and the Decision to Detain a Suspect*, 93 Yale L.J. 214 (1983); Tracey Maclin, *"Black and Blue Encounters"—Some Preliminary Thoughts About Fourth Amendment Seizures: Should Race Matter?*, 26 Val. U. L. Rev. 243 (1991); Adina Schwartz, *"Just Take Away Their Guns": The Hidden Racism of Terry v. Ohio*, 23 Fordham Urb. L.J. 317 (1996); *Developments in the Law, Race and Criminal Process: III. Racial Discrimination on the Beat: Extending the Racial Critique to Police Conduct*, 101 Harv. L. Rev. 1472, 1494 (1988); Randall S. Susskind, Note, *Race, Reasonable Articulable Suspicion, and Seizure*, 31 Am. Crim. L. Rev. 327 (1994).

14. Amar, Note 10, *supra*, at 808.

15. *See generally Terry v. Ohio 30 Years Later: A Symposium on the Fourth Amendment, Law Enforcement and Police-Citizen Encounters*, 72 St. John's L. Rev. 721–1524 (1998); Lewis R. Katz, *Terry v. Ohio at Thirty-Five: A Revisionist View*, 74 Miss. L.J. 423 (2004). For a fascinating study of how the Court reached its outcome in *Terry*, see especially John Q. Barrett, *Deciding the Stop and Frisk Cases: A Look Inside the Supreme Court's Conference*, 72 St. John's L. Rev. 749 (1998).

16. *O* was Cleveland Police Detective Martin McFadden. Attorney Louis Stokes (later an Ohio Congressman), who represented Terry (*T*), has described McFadden as follows:

> He was a real character—a tall, stately guy, and basically a good policeman. "Mac," as we called him, was really a guy that we really liked. He was straight. One thing about him— as a police officer, he came straight down the line. You did not have to worry about him misrepresenting what the facts were.

Louis Stokes, *Representing John W. Terry*, 72 St. John's L. Rev. 727, 729 (1998).

17. Although the *Terry* opinion is silent on the matter, *T* and the second suspect were African-American; the third individual was white. *T*'s defense counsel questioned *O* about his suspicions. According to the counsel's recollections three decades later:

> [Officer McFadden] said to us that he had seen these two fellows standing across the street from him, and he described them as being two Negroes, and then he talked of the white fellow who came up to them and talked with them. Then he [the third man] went on down the street. Mac then admitted to us they weren't doing anything, except one of the black fellows would leave the other one, walk down the street a little bit, turn around, peer into the window . . . , then walk back up to where the other fellow was. Then the other fellow would take a walk in a similar manner.

O approached the three suspects, identified himself as a police officer, asked for their names, and when he received only a mumbled reply from one, he grabbed *T*, spun him around, and patted down ("frisked") the outside of his clothing. *O* felt a pistol in the breast pocket of *T*'s overcoat, pulled it out, and arrested him for carrying a concealed weapon. At a hearing to determine the admissibility of the weapon, *O* testified that he frisked the suspects only to see whether they were armed, and that he put his hands in *T*'s clothing only after he felt the weapon. At the time of the pat-downs, *O* lacked probable cause to arrest the suspects or to search them.[18]

The Supreme Court, per Chief Justice Earl Warren, upheld *O*'s action. In doing so, however, it rejected the government's claim that the "stop-and-frisk" procedure fell outside the purview of the Fourth Amendment. This argument, the Court stated, "seeks to isolate from constitutional scrutiny the initial stages of the contact between the policeman and the citizen." The Chief Justice rejected this "rigid all-or-nothing" analysis. In considerable part, perhaps, the Court sought to bring the stop-and-frisk process within the scope of the Fourth Amendment because of "[t]he wholesale harassment by certain elements of the police community, of which minority groups, particularly Negroes, frequently complain."

For the first time, the Court stated that a person can be "seized"—and, thus, the Fourth Amendment is implicated—short of being arrested. The Chief Justice stated that a "seizure" occurs "whenever a police officer accosts an individual and restrains his freedom to walk away." In slightly different language, *Terry* also states that "[o]nly when the officer, by means of physical force or show of authority, has in some way restrained the liberty of a citizen may we conclude that a 'seizure' has occurred."[19] The Court stated that *T* was seized, although less intrusively than if he had been arrested, at least as soon as *O* initiated physical contact with *T* in order to search him.

Likewise, the Supreme Court held that the pat-down that *O* conducted was a "serious intrusion" on *T*'s privacy and, therefore, a "search," albeit "something less than a 'full'" one. Chief Justice Warren stated that "it is nothing less than sheer torture of the English language to suggest that a careful exploration of the outer surfaces of a person's clothing all over his or her body in an attempt to find weapons is not a 'search.'"[20]

[O] was asked specifically what attracted him to them. On one occasion he said, (Well, to tell the truth, I just didn't like "em." He was asked how long he'd been a police officer. "39 years." How long had he been a detective? "35 years." What did he think they were doing? "Well," he said, "I suspected that they were casing a joint for the purpose of robbing it." "Well," he was asked, "have you ever in your 39 years as a police officer, 35 as a detective, had the opportunity to observe anybody casing a place for a stickup?" He said, "No, I haven't." . . . "Then what attracted you to them?" He indicated he just didn't like them.

Id. at 729–30.

18. Subsequently, Terry was confined to an asylum for the criminally insane. By the time the case reached the high court, the second African-American suspect, who was also arrested, was killed in a robbery in Columbus, Ohio. Reuben M. Payne, *The Prosecutor's Perspective on Terry: Detective McFadden Had a Right to Protect Himself*, 72 St. John's L. Rev. 733, 733 (1998). The third suspect, although taken into custody, was not ultimately charged with any offense.

19. Since *Terry*, the Court has refined this definition of "seizure." *See generally* § 7.03, *supra*.

20. As the Court observed, a pat-down requires the officer to do a "thorough search" of the suspect's body, including "the groin and area about the testicles, and entire surface of the legs down to the feet." Indeed, although the Court did not say so, a pat-down could be considered *more* intrusive than, for example, a "full" search of the pocket of a person's shirt.

Although the stop-and-frisk conducted by *O* involved Fourth Amendment activity, the Court concluded that the Warrant Clause does not apply to this type of police practice. The Chief Justice stated that the Court would "not retreat" from the ordinary rule that the police must, whenever practicable, secure a search warrant, but, he said, "we deal here with an entire rubric of police conduct—necessarily swift action predicated upon the on-the-spot observations of a police officer on the beat—which historically has not been, and as a practical matter could not be, subjected to the warrant procedure."

Because the Warrant Clause was deemed inapplicable to this "entire rubric of police conduct," the Court held that the "probable cause" standard, which is textually tied to the warrant requirement in the Fourth Amendment, also does not apply.[21] Instead, the Court stated, the "central inquiry" is "the reasonableness in all the circumstances of the particular governmental invasion of a citizen's personal security." And, in determining whether the police activity was reasonable, the Court stated in critical and oft-quoted language that "our inquiry is a dual one—whether the officer's action was justified as its inception, and whether it was reasonably related in scope to the circumstances which justified the interference in the first place."[22]

---

21. This conclusion need not follow. When an exigency justifies an exception to the warrant requirement, the Court may retain the probable cause standard, as it has done, for example, in the case of searches of cars stopped on the highway. *See generally* Chapter 13, *supra*.

22. The implication of this language is that a search or seizure, although justified at its inception, becomes constitutionally unreasonable if subsequent police action is not reasonably related to the original justification for the interference or is excessive in its implementation. Recently, the Supreme Court diverged from the *Terry* requirement that the police action be reasonably related to the original reason for the seizure. In *Illinois v. Caballes*, 543 U.S. 405 (2005), the police conducted a lawful traffic stop to issue a warning citation, but took advantage of the time required to issue the citation to permit a dog to sniff the vehicle for possible drugs. Justice Stevens, for the Court, upheld the dog sniff, although the police had no reason to suspect the driver of drug possession. The six-justice majority defended the police action because the dog-sniff involved a relatively non-intrusive procedure (*see* § 6.09, *supra*) and, more significantly, because the procedure "reveal[ed] no information other than the location of a substance that no individual has the right to possess."

Justice Ginsburg and Souter dissented. They contended that "[e]ven if the drug sniff is not characterized as a Fourth Amendment "search," the sniff surely broadened the scope of the traffic-violation-related seizure." That is, as the dissent saw it, the original stop was justified at its inception, but the police action became constitutionally unreasonable once the officers converted the routine traffic stop into a drug investigation. *Contra, under the state constitution*, State v. Estabillio, 218 P.3d 749 (Haw. 2009) (state constitution forbids police from questioning motorists about offenses unrelated to the traffic violation, in the absence of reasonable suspicion, even if the questioning does not prolong the detention).

Although *Caballes* holds that the police may conduct investigations that go beyond the initial purpose of a seizure, the Court in that case *did* warn that a traffic stop may become unlawful if it is prolonged beyond the time reasonably required to complete the [traffic stop] mission. In *Caballes*, the dog sniff did not extend the length of the traffic stop, but in *Rodriguez v. United States*, 135 S. Ct. 1609 (2015), the facts were different. A routine traffic stop of a car containing two persons lasted 22 or 23 minutes, which was the time required for the officer to question the driver about the reason he had veered onto the highway shoulder, to gather the driver's license, registration, and proof of insurance and conduct a records check, and to receive the passenger's license for a similar records check. Only after the officer returned the documents and issued a warning ticket to the driver—and thus the purpose for the stop was completed—did he call for an officer to come with a trained dog to sniff the vehicle for drugs. (The officer lacked reasonable suspicion that the car contained narcotics.) This extended the time of the seizure by about eight minutes.

The Court, 6–3 per Justice Ginsburg, held that the dog sniff violated the Fourth Amendment because, per *Caballes*, it prolonged the stop beyond the time reasonably required to complete the traffic stop's initial mission. Justice Ginsburg explained that "[t]he critical question . . . is not

In terms of this dual inquiry, how does the Court go about determining whether a particular search or seizure is "reasonable"? Quoting *Camara v. Municipal Court*,[23] the Chief Justice observed that "there is 'no ready test for determining reasonableness other than by balancing the need to search [or seize] against the invasion which the search [or seizure] entails.'" The Court also warned in now oft-quoted language that "in justifying the particular intrusion, the police officer must be able to point to specific and articulable facts which, taken together with rational inferences from those facts, reasonably warrant the intrusion."

The Court proceeded to balance the competing interests. It focused first on the "nature and extent of the governmental interests involved." The Court pointed to the general interest of "effective crime prevention and detection" that would be impaired if the police could not confront suspects for investigative purposes on less than probable cause. It was this interest, the Chief Justice stated, that *O* was discharging when he decided to approach *T* and the other suspects to inquire about their activities.

The second governmental interest—what the Court deemed to be "[t]he crux of the case"—involved *O*'s frisk of *T* for weapons (the search). The Court stated that *O* had a legitimate immediate interest in assuring himself that the suspect was "not armed with a weapon that could unexpectedly and fatally be used against him." As the Chief Justice put it, "[c]ertainly it would be unreasonable to require that police officers take unnecessary risks in the performance of their duties. American criminals have a long tradition of armed violence. . . ."

Weighed against these interests, of course, were *T*'s interests in free locomotion on the street and freedom from police intrusion. The initial detention/seizure, however, was not as severe an intrusion as an arrest; and the pat-down "constitutes a brief, though far from inconsiderable, intrusion upon the sanctity of the person."

Based on this balancing approach, the Court announced certain principles. The Chief Justice concluded that when an officer has what has come to be known in later cases as "reasonable suspicion" that "the individual whose suspicious behavior he is investigating at close range is armed and presently dangerous to the officer or others," an officer has the constitutional authority to ascertain whether the person in fact is armed and, if necessary, disarm the suspect. The Court warned that, in determining whether an officer acted reasonably, "due weight must be given, not to his inchoate and unparticularized suspicion or 'hunch,' but to the specific reasonable inferences which he is entitled to draw from the facts in light of his experience."

---

whether the dog sniff occurs before or after the officer issues a ticket, . . . but whether conducting the sniff 'prolongs'—i.e., adds time to—'the stop.'"

If the police need to extend the stop beyond the time necessary to conduct a routine traffic stop, they must demonstrate reasonable suspicion that criminal activity is afoot. One state supreme court has ruled, for example, that claiming a package at the post office that smells of dryer sheets (a common masking agent for drugs) and using a false name when claiming the package did not give rise to reasonable suspicion to justify an additional 34-minute wait for a drug dog. MacKintrush v. State, 479 S.W.3d 14 (Ark. 2016).

Not all state constitutions agree with the *Rodriguez* decision. *See, e.g.,* State v. Alvarez, 138 Haw. 173 (2016) (even if bringing in a drug dog does not result in increased detention for the suspect, the drug dog represents an "escalation of the investigation" that requires "strong independent evidence of criminal activity,").

23. 387 U.S. 523 (1967).

Moreover, the self-protective procedure must be "strictly circumscribed [in manner] by the exigencies which justify its initiation." Specifically, the purpose of the *Terry* search is limited: to determine whether the suspect is armed, *and no more.* Unlike a search incident to an arrest, a *Terry*-type search "is not justified by any need to prevent the disappearance or destruction of evidence of crime."

The appropriate manner of the protective search depends on the facts of the case, but the Court approved the technique used here: a pat-down of the outside of the suspect's clothing that is reasonably designed to discover "guns, knives, clubs, or other hidden instruments for the assault of the police officer"; and, when a hard object that feels like a weapon is discovered during the pat-down, a full search under the clothing to remove it.

The majority opinion concluded with a carefully worded and narrow holding:

> We merely hold today that where a police officer observes unusual conduct which leads him reasonably to conclude in light of his experience that criminal activity may be afoot and that the persons with whom he is dealing may be armed and presently dangerous, where in the course of investigating this behavior he identifies himself as a policeman and makes reasonable inquiries, and where nothing in the initial stages of the encounter serves to dispel his reasonable fear for his own or others' safety, he is entitled for the protection of himself and others in the area to conduct a carefully limited search of the outer clothing of such persons in an attempt to discover weapons which might be used to assault him. Such a search is a reasonable search under the Fourth Amendment, and any weapons seized may properly be introduced in evidence against the person from whom they were taken.[24]

[B] Justice Harlan's Concurring Opinion

Justice Harlan, while "unreservedly agree[ing]" with the Court's holding, sought "to fill in a few gaps" in the majority opinion. In doing so, he provided two important insights into the stop-and-frisk process.

First, the majority opinion focused on the protective search — the pat-down — of T. But, as Justice Harlan rightly observed, the right to frisk ought to depend on whether an officer has authority in the first place to insist on the encounter that places her safety in jeopardy. In short, before the search, there is likely to be a seizure of the person, which logically must be justified first. This is because, just as an officer may ask a citizen a question, the "person addressed [absent reasonable suspicion] has an equal right to ignore his interrogator and walk away."[25] In this case, Justice Harlan believed that O had a right to seize T because he "observed circumstances that would reasonably lead an experienced, prudent policeman to suspect that [T] was about to engage in burglary or robbery."

---

24. *Terry*, 392 U.S. at 30–31.

25. Regarding the citizen's right to "ignore his interrogator," *see* § 9.04, *supra* (discussing Hiibel v. Sixth Jud. Dist. Ct., 542 U.S.177 (2004), which holds that state law may properly require a person subject to a lawful detention to provide her name to the police upon request, as long as the request is reasonably related to the purpose of the detention).

Second, Justice Harlan concluded that when a forcible stop is justified, "the right to frisk must be immediate and automatic if the reason for the stop is, as here, an articulable suspicion of a crime of violence." This comment is significant because the majority holding quoted above suggests that an officer, after seizing a suspect, needs to investigate further before conducting a pat-down. As discussed in § 17.06[A], however, the Supreme Court has implicitly acknowledged that Justice Harlan had the better side of this controversy.

§ 17.03 "Reasonable Suspicion"[26]

[A] In General

As discussed elsewhere,[27] the Supreme Court has never quantified the concept of "probable cause." The Court in *Illinois v. Gates*[28] described it as a "fluid concept" that is "not readily, or even usefully, reduced" to a mathematical formula. Basically, "probable cause" involves a "substantial basis" for concluding—a "fair probability" but less than a preponderance of the evidence—that a search will turn up criminal evidence or that the person seized is guilty of an offense.

In similar fashion, the Supreme Court in *Terry v. Ohio* did not indicate what quantum of evidence is required to justify a less-than-ordinarily-intrusive seizure of a person or to conduct a less-than-full search (pat-down) of a suspect, although Chief Justice Warren did make the rather obvious point in the context of a pat-down that the officer need not be "absolutely certain" that the suspect is armed. The Court has since stated that the "reasonable suspicion" standard applied in *Terry*[29] is "obviously less demanding than that for probable cause."[30] It requires "considerably less"[31] proof of wrongdoing than proof by a preponderance of the evidence. As the Court has recently put it, "*Terry* accepts the risk that officers may stop [and/or frisk] innocent people."[32] All that is required to justify a *Terry*-level search or seizure is "some minimal level of objective justification."[33]

---

26. *See generally* 4 LaFave, Note 1, *supra*, at § 9.5; David A. Harris, *Particularized Suspicion, Categorical Judgments: Supreme Court Rhetoric versus Lower Court Reality Under Terry v. Ohio*, 72 St. John's L. Rev. 975 (1998); Margaret Raymond, *Down on the Corner, Out in the Street: Considering the Character of the Neighborhood in Evaluating Reasonable Suspicion*, 60 Ohio St. L.J. 99 (1999).

27. *See* § 8.07[A], *supra*.

28. 462 U.S. 213 (1983).

29. A piece of trivia: The Court did not use the term "reasonable suspicion" in *Terry*, although it was used by a lower court, as quoted by the Supreme Court, in *Sibron v. New York*, 392 U.S. 40 (1968), a companion case to *Terry*. The Supreme Court apparently used the term itself, although in quotation marks, for the first time in a *Terry* context in *Almeida-Sanchez v. United States*, 413 U.S. 266, 268 (1973). The quotation marks were dropped in *Gustafson v. Florida*, 414 U.S. 260, 265 n.4 (1973), a non-*Terry* case, and later in *United States v. Brignoni-Ponce*, 422 U.S. 873, 882 (1975), a case involving a *Terry*-level seizure.

30. United States v. Sokolow, 490 U.S. 1, 7 (1989).

31. *Id.*

32. Illinois v. Wardlow, 528 U.S. 119, 126 (2000).

33. INS v. Delgado, 466 U.S. 210, 217 (1984).

Indeed, "reasonable suspicion," like "probable cause," can be based on an officer's reasonable mistake of fact[34] or law.[35]

Essentially, the police may not act on the basis of an "inchoate and unparticularized suspicion or hunch," which was expressly condemned in *Terry*; suspicion is "reasonable," however, if the officer can point to some (perhaps just a few) specific and articulable facts that, along with reasonable inferences from those facts, justify the intrusion.[36] And, in making the determination, police officers are entitled to draw on "their own experience and specialized training to make inferences from and deductions about the cumulative information available to them that 'might well elude an untrained person.'"[37]

As with probable cause, the Supreme Court has declared that the "reasonable suspicion" standard cannot be "readily, or even usefully, reduced to a neat set of legal rules."[38] Instead, the justifiability of a *Terry*-type seizure or search, like a seizure or search based on probable cause, is supposed to be evaluated on "the totality of the circumstances— the whole picture."[39]

[B] Types of Information

[1] Overview

As noted immediately above, the justifiability of a *Terry*-type seizure or search, like a seizure or search based on probable cause, is supposed to be evaluated on the totality of

---

34. Illinois v. Rodriguez, 497 U.S. 177 (1990) ("It is apparent that in order to satisfy the reasonableness requirement of the Fourth Amendment, what is generally demanded of the many factual determinations that must regularly be made by [the police] . . . is not that they always be correct, but that they always be reasonable." See also § 16.06, *supra*. More recently, the Court has noted that "[t]o be reasonable is not to be perfect, and so the Fourth Amendment allows for some mistakes on the part of government officials . . . . We have recognized that searches and seizures based on mistakes of fact can be reasonable." Heien v. North Carolina, 135 S. Ct. 530, 536 (2014).

35. Heien v. North Carolina, 135 S. Ct. 530 (2014). In *Heien*, a police officer observed that only one of a vehicle's brake lights was working, so he pulled the driver over. While issuing a warning ticket, he became suspicious of the conduct of the driver and passenger and their answer to questions. Therefore, the officer sought and obtained consent to search the vehicle, where cocaine was discovered. Heien sought to suppress evidence of the cocaine on the ground that his seizure—the stop of the vehicle—was unconstitutional. As it turned out, the applicable state code provision only required drivers to be equipped with one brake light. Thus, the officer did not have legal grounds to pull the vehicle over. Nonetheless, the Supreme Court, 8–1, held that, just as a search or seizure by a police officer can be reasonable based on an erroneous, but reasonable, mistake of fact, "reasonable men make mistakes of law, too, and such mistakes are no less compatible with the concept of reasonable suspicion [or probable cause]."

36. Critics of post-*Terry* case law have assumed that lower courts now routinely uphold police stop-and-frisks. However, according to one concededly incomplete (and now somewhat dated) sampling of federal district court and state appellate court opinions, defendants won suppression motions in 26% to 28% of the *Terry* cases. George C. Thomas III, *Terry v. Ohio in the Trenches: A Glimpse at How Courts Apply "Reasonable Suspicion,"* 72 St. John's L. Rev. 1025, 1029–1034 (1998).

37. United States v. Arvizu, 534 U.S. 266, 273 (2002) (quoting United States v. Cortez, 449 U.S. 411 (1981)).

38. United States v. Sokolow, 490 U.S. 1, 7 (1989) (quoting Illinois v. Gates, 462 U.S. 213, 232 (1983)).

39. United States v. Cortez, 449 U.S. 411, 417 (1981); *see also* United States v. Arvizu, 534 U.S. 266, 273 (2002); *contra under the state constitution*, Commonwealth v. Lyons, 564 N.E.2d 390 (Mass. 1990) (rejecting the totality-of-the-circumstances test in the context of probable cause/ reasonable suspicion in favor of the pre-*Gates* two-pronged approach).

the circumstances. However, according to some scholars, "lower courts have slowly and steadily created whole categories of cases which allow police to [stop and] frisk . . . , whatever the specific facts [of the individual case] are."[40] That is, certain observations (e.g., furtive behavior or flight by a suspect) or surrounding circumstances (e.g., the suspect is in a "high-crime area") can result in a virtual bright-line rule at the lower-court level that "reasonable suspicion" exists.[41]

Typically, as in *Terry*, a seizure of a person (and pat-down) will be based in whole or in considerable part on an officer's personal observations of the suspect and the surrounding circumstances. A police officer is entitled to make "common-sense conclusions about human behavior,"[42] and may draw upon her personal law enforcement expertise. More complex problems arise, however, when an officer claims that she acted on the basis of suspicions grounded at least in part on the observations or experiences of others.

The era of "Big Data," which refers to the collection and processing of vast amounts of information in order to predict outcomes, may signal new opportunities and challenges for police and courts as they try to determine reasonable suspicion. Many police officers routinely use big data analytics to determine where to focus their resources or which suspects may be dangerous; it is likely that police (and perhaps courts) will also use these tools to inform their decisions about whether reasonable suspicion exists.[43]

[2] Hearsay: When It Is and Is Not Sufficient

In *Terry*, the detaining officer acted on the basis of his own personal observations of the suspects. Three cases — *Adams v. Williams*,[44] *Alabama v. White*,[45] and *Florida v. J.L.*[46] — teach, however, that "reasonable suspicion," like "probable cause," may be based on hearsay. Furthermore, because "reasonable suspicion" is a less demanding standard than "probable cause," it may be satisfied not only on the basis of a lesser quantum of evidence, but also on the basis of "information that is less reliable than that required to show probable cause."[47] The same factors that apply to information supplied by an informant in the probable cause context — the informant's basis of knowledge and her veracity — apply in the *Terry* context, "although allowance must be made in applying them for the lesser showing required to meet that standard."[48] *Adams*, *White*, and *J.L.*, usefully suggest rough guidelines regarding how informants may (and may not) properly be used in the *Terry* context, and how courts should oversee the process.

In *Adams v. Williams*, the Supreme Court sustained a *Terry* stop-and-frisk based in part on an informant's tip that would not have justified an arrest or search based on

---

40. Harris, Note 26, *supra*, at 976.

41. *See also* Raymond, Note 26, *supra* (arguing that, in particular, the characterization of a neighborhood as crime- or drug-prone tends to dominate judicial analysis and push aside particularized facts that might result in a contrary outcome).

42. United States v. Cortez, 449 U.S. at 418.

43. *See* Andrew Guthrie Ferguson, *Big Data and Predictive Reasonable Suspicion*, 163 U. Penn. L. Rev. 327 (2015); Ric Simmons, *Quantifying Criminal Procedure: How to Unlock the Potential of Big Data in Our Criminal Justice System*, 2016 Mich. St. L. Rev. 947 (2016).

44. 407 U.S. 143 (1972).

45. 496 U.S. 325 (1990); *see generally* David S. Rudstein, *White on White: Anonymous Tips, Reasonable Suspicion, and the Constitution*, 79 Ky. L.J. 661 (1990–91).

46. 529 U.S. 266 (2000).

47. Alabama v. White, 496 U.S. at 330.

48. *Id.* at 328–29.

probable cause. In this case, a known informant told *O* that *W* was seated in a nearby car with narcotics in his possession and a gun concealed at his waist. The informant did not indicate the basis of his knowledge. *O* approached *W* and, on the basis of the tip, conducted a *Terry* procedure, which resulted in the seizure of a gun from *W*'s waist.

The Supreme Court, per Justice Rehnquist, conceded that the unverified tip might have been insufficient to justify any action that required probable cause. Nonetheless, the Court held that the tip "carried enough indicia of reliability" to justify a *Terry*-level seizure. The Court considered the tipster's information sufficiently reliable because he had provided the police with information on a prior occasion, and because he personally came to *O* with the present information, rather than making an anonymous report. As a result, the informant subjected himself to the (theoretical) risk of arrest for making a false complaint if the information he provided proved to be false. The Court was not dissuaded by the fact, pointed out by the dissenters, that the informant's prior track record consisted of a single tip, pertaining to a different type of conduct (alleged homosexual behavior in a railroad station), which did not result in an arrest. For purposes of reasonable suspicion, there were sufficient indicia of the informant's reliability.

The Court in *Adams* warned that "[s]ome tips, completely lacking in indicia of reliability, would either warrant no police response or require further investigation before a forcible stop of a suspect would be authorized." *Alabama v. White*[49] provides a good example of such an unsatisfactory tip, but one that was saved — although barely so — by independent police investigation. In *White*, the police received a telephone call from an anonymous informant who stated that *W* (a woman he named) would be leaving a specified apartment at a specified time, that she would get in a "brown Plymouth station wagon with the right taillight broken," and that she would drive to a specified motel, in possession of an ounce of cocaine in a brown attaché case.

The officers proceeded to the apartment building, where they observed an automobile fitting the informant's description, parked in front of the building. They spotted a woman, empty-handed, enter the car and drive in the direction of the motel. Before the car reached its destination, however, the officers stopped the vehicle and ordered the driver, *W*, out of the car. A search based on consent resulted in seizure of marijuana, found in an attaché case in the car.

The *White* Court held, 6–3, that the anonymous tip in this case, by itself, was insufficient to justify *W*'s forcible stop. Drawing language directly from *Illinois v. Gates*, the Court pointed out that the caller provided "absolutely no indication of the basis for the . . . predictions regarding [*W*'s] criminal activities"; furthermore, the call "provide[d] virtually nothing from which one might conclude that [the informant] . . . [was] either honest or his information reliable." Nonetheless, in what the Supreme Court crucially observed was "a close case," the majority concluded that "under the totality of the circumstances the anonymous tip, as corroborated, exhibited sufficient indicia of reliability to justify the investigatory stop of [*W*'s] car."

Notice here that the corroboration was incomplete and imperfect. First, it was not clear prior to the stop that the woman the police were following was the person named by the informant. Second, the police did not corroborate that the suspect left the apartment specified by the informant. Third, the police did not wait to see if *W* would drive her car to the motel, as predicted. Moreover, one fact not only was not corroborated but was false:

---

49. 496 U.S. 325 (1990).

W did not have the attaché case in her possession when she entered her car, as had been predicted.

Rather than dwell on these shortcomings, however, the Supreme Court focused on the fact that the informant predicted future conduct — that a particular person would come out of the apartment building and drive a particular automobile to a particular location — some of which was corroborated. According to Rehnquist, "[w]hen significant aspects of the caller's predictions were verified, there was reason to believe not only that the caller was honest but also that he was well informed, at least well enough to justify the stop." Of course, as the dissent noted, every fact the police corroborated in *White* involved innocent conduct that could fit the description of countless people each day. The majority was not dissuaded by the fact that, as Justice Stevens warned in his dissent, "[a]nybody with enough knowledge about a given person to make her the target of a prank, or to harbor a grudge against her, will certainly be able to formulate a tip about her like the one predicting" *W*'s actions. Again, to meet the lower standard of "reasonable suspicion" — to conduct a brief detention or frisk — the information, as corroborated, was adequate.

But, there is a point past which the Supreme Court will not go in justifying a *Terry* stop or frisk based on hearsay information. It must be kept in mind that the Court described *White* as a "close case" and relied heavily on the fact that the informant there accurately predicted some future behavior. Contrast this with *Florida v. J.L.*,[50] in which an anonymous telephone caller reported to police, simply, that a young black male wearing a plaid shirt and standing at a particular bus stop was carrying a gun. Two officers proceeded to the site where they observed three young black males "hanging out" at the bus stop. The officers saw no firearms, nor did J.L., dressed in a plaid shirt as stated, make any threatening or unusual movements. As the Court stated, "[a]part from the tip, the officers had no reason to suspect any of the three of illegal conduct." Nonetheless, the officers frisked J.L. (and the other two males) and seized a gun they discovered in J.L.'s pocket.

The Court unanimously held that the officers lacked reasonable suspicion that J.L. was armed. It observed that "[i]f [*Alabama v.*] *White* was a close case on the reliability of anonymous tips, this one surely falls on the other side of the line." Writing for the Court, Justice Ruth Bader Ginsburg rejected the government's claim that the police could act on the basis of the informant's tip because it provided an accurate description of a particular person at a particular location. Ginsburg declared that "[a]n accurate description of a subject's readily observable location and appearance is of course reliable in this limited sense: It will help the police correctly identify the person whom the tipster means to accuse." What the tip lacked — and what Ginsburg said was "essential" to the Court's holding in *White* — was predictive information that the police could corroborate.[51]

The government advanced a second argument in *J.L.*, namely, "that the standard *Terry* analysis should be modified to license a "firearm exception." Under such an exception, a tip alleging an illegal gun would justify a stop and frisk even if the accusation would fail standard pre-search reliability testing." The Court, again unanimously, declined to recognize such an exception, stating that it "would rove too far," by permitting an individual

---

50. 529 U.S. 266 (2000).

51. *J.L.* is also distinguishable from *Adams v. Williams*. Although the informant there, as here, only described a particular person at a particular location — he did not predict future conduct — the informant's reliability in *Adams* was stronger: he came to the police non-anonymously and had come to them before; therefore, his reputation could be better assessed and he could theoretically be held criminally responsible if his allegations proved to be fabricated. *See J. L.*, 529 U.S. at 270.

to harass another and to cause an intrusive search simply "by placing an anonymous call falsely reporting the target's unlawful carriage of a gun."[52]

[3] Drug-Courier Profiles[53]

The Supreme Court has stated that an officer's observations may properly be supplemented by "consideration of the modes or patterns of operation of certain kinds of lawbreakers."[54] In the drug-trafficking field, an officer's suspicions are sometimes based in part on her awareness that the suspect's conduct or appearance conforms to a so-called "drug-courier profile," which is a set of characteristics purportedly often associated with

---

52. The Court recently decided another case involving hearsay. In *Navarette v. California*, 134 S. Ct. 1683 (2014), the police stopped a vehicle exclusively on the basis of an anonymous 911 call from a driver who claimed that she had been driven off the road by a truck minutes earlier. She described the vehicle and provided a license plate number. Police officers spotted the vehicle approximately 15 minutes later. They followed the vehicle for about five minutes, but observed nothing unusual. Nonetheless, they stopped the vehicle. When they did they smelled marijuana. A subsequent search revealed 30 pounds of marijuana.

The Court, 5–4, upheld the stop, although it stated that, as with *White*, it was a "close case." Justice Thomas, writing for the majority, held that although an anonymous tip alone rarely justifies a stop, "under appropriate circumstances, an anonymous tip can demonstrate 'sufficient indicia of reliability to provide reasonable suspicion to make an investigatory stop.'" Here, Justice Thomas pointed out that the caller obviously had firsthand knowledge and, despite her anonymity, the Court found indicia of reliability: the "sort of contemporaneous report [as occurred here] has long been treated as especially reliable," because it tends to negate the likelihood of conscious misrepresentation; a "'statement relating to a startling event'—such as getting run off the road"—is treated as reliable; and furthermore, use of the 911 system enhances the caller's reliability because there are features today that "allow for identifying and tracing callers, and thus provide some safeguards against making false reports with immunity." Therefore, based on the 911 call, the Court concluded that the police had reasonable suspicion that the driver was driving while intoxicated.

Justice Scalia wrote a stinging dissent, criticizing virtually every aspect of the majority analysis. Among his arguments: "the peculiar fact that the accusation was anonymous" ("When does a victim complain to the police about an arguably criminal act . . . without giving his identity, so that he can accuse and testify when the culprit is caught?"); the fact that the report was not so immediate as to justify the majority's assumption of reliability; and, according to amicus briefs, it is often not possible to identify an anonymous 911 caller and, even if it were true, "it proves absolutely nothing unless the anonymous caller was *aware* of that fact." Beyond this, Justice Scalia stated that the claim that she was driven off the road hardly provides reasonable suspicion that a driver was intoxicated—there are too many other possible explanations—especially since the police observed the driver for five minutes and observed no signs of intoxication. According to the dissent,

> [t]he Court's opinion serves up a freedom-destroying cocktail consisting of two parts patent falsity: (1) that anonymous 911 reports of traffic violations are reliable so long as they correctly identify a car and its location, and (2) that s single instance of careless or reckless driving necessarily supports a reasonable suspicion of drunkenness. All the malevolent 911 caller need do is assert a traffic violation, and the targeted car will be stopped, forcibly if necessary, by the police.

> Drunken driving is a serious matter, but so is the loss of our freedom to come and go as we please without police interference . . . After today's opinion all of us on the road . . . are at risk of having our freedom of movement curtailed on suspicion of drunkenness, based upon a phone tip, true or false, of a single instance of careless driving.

53. Although this subsection deals with "profiling" of drug couriers—this is because profiling case law has centered on drug investigations, especially during the so-called "war on drugs" in the 1980s—the legal analysis discussed here would apply to any government effort to justify *Terry*-level, "reasonable suspicion" seizures of persons based on profiling, such as in terrorism investigations.

54. United States v. Cortez, 449 U.S. 411, 418 (1981).

drug traffickers, compiled by law enforcement agencies, such as the Drug Enforcement Administration.

Many litigated cases involving drug-courier profiles occur in the following context: law enforcement agents observe a person about to embark on, or disembarking from, an airplane, train, or bus; the individual's conduct is lawful in all respects, but it and the suspect's appearance fit a drug-courier profile; therefore, the officers stop the suspect in order to question her. If the investigation constitutes a *Terry*-level seizure, the police must possess reasonable suspicion for the forced encounter.[55]

The mere fact that a suspect's behavior and/or appearance conforms to a drug-courier profile does not, without more, constitute reasonable suspicion.[56] As one court has explained, "[m]ere mechanical matching of characteristics thought to be common to all drug couriers can never meet the rigorous requirements of the fourth amendment. To be reasonable, an officer's suspicion must be specific and, to some extent, individualized to the particular characteristics exhibited by a particular person."[57] On the other hand, the fact that the suspect's conduct conforms to a reliable drug-courier profile "does not . . . detract from [the] evidentiary significance [of the factors] as seen by a trained agent."[58]

Therefore, each drug-courier profile case must be decided on its own merits, and it is difficult to draw broad principles from the cases the Supreme Court has decided.[59] The Court took a comparatively strict view of the subject in an early pre-"war on drugs" case, *Reid v. Georgia*.[60] In *Reid*, the Court held that an officer lacked reasonable suspicion to justify detaining a suspect in an airport who fit a drug-courier profile in that he: (1) arrived from a "drug source" city; (2) arrived early in the morning, a time when law enforcement activity is reduced; (3) apparently tried to conceal the fact that he was traveling with another person; and (4) had no luggage except for shoulder bags. Notwithstanding the profile, the Court believed that, except for the third factor, the facts "describe[d] a very large category of presumably innocent travelers, who would be subject to virtually random seizures were the Court to conclude that as little foundation as there was in this case could justify a seizure." The Court disposed of the furtive conduct on the ground that the officer's suspicion that the suspect was concealing something was no more than an inchoate and unparticularized hunch. The Court did warn, however, that "there could . . . be circumstances in which wholly lawful conduct might justify the suspicion that criminal activity was afoot."

Three years later, the Court was presented with a case of lawful, but reasonably suspicious, conduct in *Florida v. Royer*.[61] In *Royer*, R, about to embark on an airplane, fit a drug-courier profile in that he: (1) was traveling from a major drug source city; (2) paid for his ticket in cash with a large number of small bills; (3) traveled under an assumed name; and (4) appeared to be nervous. For a four-justice plurality, Justice Byron White stated that when the police learned that R was traveling under an assumed name, "this fact, and the facts already known to the officers" justified a temporary detention.

---

55. Initial contact between an officer and a suspect will often fall short of a seizure of the person and, therefore, may lawfully take place in the absence of reasonable suspicion. *See* § 7.03, *supra*.

56. *See* Reid v. Georgia, 448 U.S. 438 (1980) (per curiam).

57. United States v. Hanson, 801 F.2d 757, 762 (5th Cir. 1986).

58. United States v. Sokolow, 490 U.S. 1, 10 (1989).

59. "[I]t cannot be said with assurance what combination of factors from the 'drug courier profile' will suffice to justify a *Terry* stop of a particular traveler." § 4 LaFave, Note 1, *supra*, at 506.

60. 448 U.S. 438 (1980) (per curiam).

61. 460 U.S. 491 (1983).

In *United States v. Sokolow*,[62] the conduct of S, a passenger disembarking from an airplane, fit a drug-courier profile in that: (1) he paid for airplane tickets totaling $2,100 with a roll of $20 bills; (2) he traveled under a name different from that listed for his telephone number; (3) his original destination was Miami, a major drug source city; (4) he stayed in the city, in July, for only two days, although his round-trip flight from Hawaii lasted 20 hours; (5) he appeared nervous; and (6) he did not check any of his luggage. The Court conceded that each of these factors was "quite consistent with innocent travel." On the other hand, it found factors (1) and (4) "out of the ordinary"; and it thought that the existence of factor (2) gave the police reasonable grounds for believing that S was traveling under an alias. Taken together, these three factors amounted to reasonable suspicion of drug trafficking.

Most drug-courier profile cases at the lower court level tend to be evaluated "in a common-sense fashion," based on the particular factors present in the case, "without accepting the profile itself as establishing that certain combinations of factors are inevitably sufficient to support a *Terry* stop."[63] Indeed, in the absence of statistical evidence presented to the trial court demonstrating the existence of a reasonable correlation between a profile and drug activity, courts have no logical basis for considering the drug-courier profile, as such.[64] As always, each case should be decided on its own merits.

One additional and serious concern with drug-courier (or, today, terrorism) profiles, if accepted uncritically, is that they can serve as a subterfuge for racial profiling, particularly if the profile includes a racial or ethnic factor, and the other factors are largely correlated with, rather than independent of, the racial or ethnic factor.[65] Racial profiling in the *Terry* context is considered in subsection [5], below.

[4] Flight in "High-Crime Areas"[66]

The existence of drug-courier profiles raises a related issue: Are there certain neighborhoods that are sufficiently riddled with crime that there is a statistically significant possibility (say, five percent chance) that *anyone* found in the area is involved in criminal activity—perhaps drug or weapons possession—at any given time? Even if the chances of criminal activity are not high enough to justify a search or arrest based on probable cause, what about a *Terry* stop of *anyone* found in such an area? The Supreme Court has ruled out such a conclusion, stating that "[t]he fact that [a person] was in a neighborhood frequented by drug users, standing alone, is not a basis for concluding that [he] himself was engaged in criminal conduct."[67] So, what more is needed?

In this regard, consider one possible common-sense inference about human behavior: A person who abruptly turns in the opposite direction and flees when she sees a police officer may have something unlawful to hide. Does such flight, standing alone,

---

62. 490 U.S. 1 (1989).

63. 4 LaFave, Note 1, *supra*, at 513.

64. Derricott v. State, 611 A.2d 592 (Md. 1992).

65. *E.g.*, United States v. Ornelas-Ledesma, 16 F.3d 714 (7th Cir. 1994) (the suspect was Hispanic, came from the "source" state of California, drove a two-door vehicle [which is supposedly preferred by drug traffickers], checked into a motel without a reservation at 4:00 a.m., and was accompanied by another man; the court was critical of the fact that these factors were correlated with the lower-income status of many innocent Hispanics on long-distance trips).

66. *See* Lenese C. Herbert, *Can't You See What I'm Saying? Making Expressive Conduct a Crime in High-Crime Areas*, 9 Geo. J. In Poverty L. & Pol'y 135 (2000); Raymond, Note 26, *supra*.

67. Brown v. Texas, 443 U.S. 47, 52 (1979).

constitute reasonable suspicion, regardless of the character of the neighborhood? In *California v. Hodari D.*,[68] Justice Scalia, writing for seven justices, hinted in dictum that unprovoked flight constitutes reasonable suspicion to stop a fleeing party by quoting the Bible, "The wicked flee when no man pursueth, *Proverbs* 28:1."

The Supreme Court directly confronted the unprovoked flight issue—and the relationship of flight to the character of a neighborhood—in *Illinois v. Wardlow*.[69] In *Wardlow*, officers in a police caravan converging on a Chicago area known for heavy drug trafficking observed *W* standing next to a building, in possession of an opaque bag. As the caravan arrived in his vicinity, *W* fled. Two officers in the last caravan vehicle pursued and ultimately seized *W*. At the suppression hearing, one of the pursuing officers testified that he was in uniform on that day, but he was not asked whether the other officers were in uniform, nor was he asked whether the caravan vehicles were marked.

The Supreme Court unanimously agreed in *Wardlow* that unprovoked headlong flight, *when coupled with other factors*, can constitute *Terry*-level suspicion justifying a seizure, but they split 5–4 on whether the facts here were sufficient. Although *Wardlow* provides no express *per se* rule regarding flight, the practical lesson of the case appears to be that the coupling of the two circumstances—unprovoked flight motivated by the presence of police, and a high-crime area—is sufficiently suspicious to justify the seizure of a fleeing individual, at least in the absence of special circumstances that render such flight innocent in appearance.

Chief Justice Rehnquist, writing for the majority, agreed that "there are innocent reasons for flight from police and that, therefore, flight is not necessarily indicative of ongoing criminal activity." But, under *Terry*, "the determination of reasonable suspicion must be based on commonsense judgments and inferences about human behavior." And, the majority said, "[h]eadlong flight—wherever it occurs—is the consummate act of evasion: it is not necessarily indicative of wrongdoing, but it is certainly suggestive of such." According to the Chief Justice, *Terry* demonstrates that ambiguous conduct, although susceptible of an innocent explanation, can justify a seizure to investigate the ambiguities: "*Terry* accepts the risk that officers may stop innocent people." Although an individual's presence in a high-crime area, standing alone, is insufficient to support *Terry*-level suspicion of criminal activity, the location of the events is a relevant factor; coupled with *W*'s unprovoked flight from the police, the majority held that the police acted lawfully here.

Justice Stevens, writing for four justices in a partial dissent, agreed that unprovoked flight is a relevant factor in determining reasonable suspicion, but warned that it "describes a category of activity too broad and varied to permit a *per se* reasonable inference regarding the motivation for the activity." Stevens pointed to many innocent motivations for rapid movement: "to catch up with a friend a block or two away, to seek shelter from an impending storm, to arrive at a bus stop before the bus leaves, . . . any of which might coincide with the arrival of an officer in the vicinity." He also suggested reasons why a person might innocently flee the police: to avoid being called as a witness to a crime; concern that the officers' presence indicates dangerous criminal activity nearby, which the citizen sensibly wishes to escape; and, perhaps most significantly, in the case of "minorities and those residing in high crime areas, there is . . . the possibility

---

68. 499 U.S. 621 (1991).
69. 528 U.S. 119 (2000).

that the fleeing person is entirely innocent, but, with or without justification, believes that contact with the police can itself be dangerous."[70]

According to the dissenters, unprovoked flight is not so rare as to be "aberrant" or "abnormal." Just as "innocent explanations surely do not establish that the Fourth Amendment is always violated whenever someone is stopped solely on the basis of an unprovoked flight, neither do the suspicious motivations establish that the Fourth Amendment is never violated when a *Terry* stop is predicated on that fact alone."

The dissenters were not impressed with the government's case here: the events occurred in the daytime; it was not even clear from evidence presented at the hearing that the address where *W* was spotted "was the intended [drug-infested] destination of the caravan" or was simply a building along the way; and it was uncertain whether *W* recognized the occupants of the vehicles as police officers. The testifying officer only stated, "[h]e looked in our direction and began fleeing." The dissenters believed that the prosecution failed to satisfy its burden of proof to justify the seizure.

Wardlow leaves various issues undecided. The Court spoke about "unprovoked flight," but what does this mean? Is flight "unprovoked" if, for example, a citizen runs away when she spots a police car with its lights on and sirens blaring? Just as critically, what are the parameters of the term "flight"? *Wardlow* supposedly involved "headlong flight," but what if an individual simply turns and walks quickly—or even slowly—in the opposite direction the moment she observes an officer? The Court also has thus far provided little insight into the meaning of "high-crime area." What features of a neighborhood are sufficiently suspicious that, coupled with flight or other suspicious conduct, they justify a forcible stop?

[5] Reflections on the Role of Race and Other Suspect Classifications in Determining "Reasonable Suspicion"[71]

A controversy receiving national attention at the turn of the twenty-first century was—and is—so-called racial profiling. As a result of the September 11, 2001 attacks on the United States, the profiling issue has received even greater public and scholarly attention, and is sometimes now characterized as "racial or ethnic profiling." Recent events arguably involve what might also constitute religious profiling, in which persons of the Islamic faith have become the focus of law enforcement attention.

The term "racial profiling" is defined in various ways, but one definition is "a decision to interdict or detain an individual [thus, triggering the Fourth Amendment] based solely on racial . . . assumptions about the individual's propensity toward criminality."[72] Perhaps the best known example of racial profiling is when a police officer stops an automobile driver solely on the basis of race, a procedure sufficiently common that it has come to be termed "driving while black" (DWB). As one court has observed,

---

70. *See* Herbert, Note 66, *supra*, at 143–44 ("[R]esidents or visitors of high-crime areas consistently characterize their interactions with police as overwhelmingly adversarial. . . . [Moreover,] [p]olice admit that their interactions with those encountered in such locations are much more aggressive, purportedly because aggression is required to establish police control and to squelch the higher levels of criminal activity.").

71. This subject is also considered at §§ 2.05, 2.07[B], and 8.02[F], *supra*. For excellent scholarly sources on the subject of racial "and ethnic" profiling, see the biographical citations at the beginning of § 8.02[F].

72. Sharon L. Davies, *Profiling Terror*, 1 Ohio St. J. Crim. L. 45, 53 (2003).

> [W]e cannot help but be aware that the burden of aggressive and intrusive po-
> lice action falls disproportionately on African-American, and sometimes Latino,
> males. . . . [A]s a practical matter neither society nor our enforcement of the
> laws is yet color-blind. Cases, newspaper reports, books, and scholarly writings
> all make clear that the experience of being stopped by the police is a much more
> common one for black men than it is for white men.[73]

The problem extends to African-Americans of all economic classes, including lawyers,
physicians, businesspeople, and academics.[74]

Some racial profiling cases arise in the probable cause context: An officer grows suspicious of an automobile driver on racial or ethnic grounds, waits until she has probable
cause to issue a traffic citation—which, given the plethora of driving regulations is only
a matter of time—and then uses that opportunity as a pretext to forcibly stop the car,
question the driver, observe the contents of the vehicle in plain view, and seek consent
to conduct a car search in the hope of finding illegal drugs or other criminal evidence.
According to *Whren v. United States*,[75] the pretextual nature of such stops is acceptable
under the Fourth Amendment.

But racial profiling issues also arise in the context of *Terry* stops on the street, as well
as in airports, and train and bus stations. Consider this hypothetical: Suppose federal
officers had ordered every person appearing to be of Middle Eastern descent (or, say, who
possessed a passport from Saudi Arabia) off airplanes in New York City flying to Saudi
Arabia, for brief questioning on September 15, 2001, the first day air flights resumed after
the terrorist attacks. Is this any different from DWB car stops? Would it—*should* it—
violate the Fourth Amendment to conduct such mass seizures? If "reasonable suspicion"
is required for such seizures, was this standard met on September 15, 2001? The issue
might more generally be framed this way: To what extent may a person's race, ethnicity,
or religious affiliation—so-called "suspect classifications" in the equal protection constitutional law context—serve as the "reasonable suspicion" basis for a *Terry* seizure of
a person?

A person's race (or any other fact) may legitimately be considered by the police in making "reasonable suspicion" determinations in some Fourth Amendment circumstances,
most obviously when the victim of, or witness to, a crime provides a description of the
alleged offender in terms of race, etc. If a witness identifies a bank robber as being a "black
male," these factors—race and gender—are relevant in narrowing the "circle of
suspicion."[76] It is reasonable for the officers to focus their attention on persons who appear to fit this description, assuming they trust the witness's identification.

Even here, however, there are limits. Consider *Brown v. City of Oneonta*,[77] in which a
77-year-old woman reported that a young black male, with a small wound on his hand,
had entered her home and attacked her. When a canine unit tracked the attacker to a
nearby university but was of no further help, the police obtained a list of all black male
students at the university and then sought to question and examine the hands of each of
them. When that effort failed to result in an arrest, the dragnet was extended to the entire Oneonta black community, with officers stopping, questioning, and inspecting the

---

73. Washington v. Lambert, 98 F.3d 1181, 1187 (9th Cir. 1996).
74. *Id.* at 1188.
75. 517 U.S. 806 (1996); *see* § 8.02[F], *supra*.
76. Davies, Note 72, *supra*, at 52.
77. 221 F.3d 329 (2d Cir. 2000).

hands of every young African-American male they observed. In a civil rights action brought against the police by African-Americans living in the community, the federal court not surprisingly observed that the government "would have difficulty demonstrating reasonable suspicion in this case, and indeed, they do not attempt to do so."[78] Even if what occurred in *Oneonta* is not "racial profiling" as defined above, race and gender alone—even race, gender, and general age (young)—can hardly constitute reasonable suspicion, because these facts do not significantly reduce the "circle of suspicion" in a diverse society such as ours (and Oneonta).

But, what if the victim in *Oneonta* had described her attacker as "a young black male with red hair, with a blond streak on the top of his head." Would the police be justified in seizing any person in Oneonta who fit *that* description? The circle of suspicion here is much smaller. Indeed, it is noteworthy, perhaps, that these characteristics narrow the circle so much that the police can be said to be looking for a particular described individual, not an individual number of persons belonging to a particular described group, as occurred in *Oneonta*.[79] In this context, the "a young black male with red hair, with a blond streak on the top of his head" description seems similar to the case of a witness to a bank robbery who says that the robber drove away in a "2004 blue Toyota Solara with a 'Vote for Jones for President' bumper sticker attached to the left back bumper, and with a small dent in the driver's door." It is submitted here that the police would be justified in stopping any person driving a car meeting that description in the general vicinity of the crime shortly after the robbery. If so, then it would seem that the same answer applies in the revised *Oneonta* hypothetical, although the description includes race, ethnicity, and/or other potentially suspect classifications.

That brings us back to the September 15, 2001 hypothetical. One might want more facts regarding why the Saudis were seized. Potential Scenario 1: The federal agents simply assume that any person of Arabic background is a potential future terrorist, so they decide it is worth investigating. This scenario may fairly be characterized as "flying while Arab," an obvious form of profiling.

Potential Scenario 2: The agents were trying to prevent a hijacking of the particular plane in question. Quite arguably, a Scenario 2 seizure should be impermissible if law enforcement agencies have no facts—just a hunch, or fear—that another hijacking might occur on that day on that plane. This is still ethnic profiling, because only Middle Eastern-looking persons are being singled out for seizure. (Did federal agents seize all white American males after the Oklahoma City bombing, after they learned that white males committed that offense?)

Potential Scenario 3: The agents were looking for possible conspirators in the 9/11 attacks who might be trying to escape the country at their first opportunity. Here we are dealing with a real crime, and the real possibility that other persons beyond those killed on 9/11 were involved in the attacks. And, it is not unreasonable to think that co-conspirators, if any, would try to leave the country. Moreover, unlike the case of DWB seizures, it is plausible to believe that most or all of any potential co-conspirators were of Middle Eastern descent and nationality.[80] Thus, the hypothetical action here does not seem as irrational with regard to group targeting as the seizure of African-Americans

---

78. The police argued instead that the contacts were consensual and, therefore, not Fourth Amendment seizures.

79. I thank Sharon Davies for drawing this distinction.

80. Sherry F. Colb, *Profiling With Apologies*, 1 Ohio St. J. Crim. L. 611, 616 (2004).

on the highway on the stereotypical belief that they are more likely than white persons to be in possession of drugs or other criminal evidence. But imagine the hypothetical seizures in this scenario: One might expect that nearly all of the passengers on the New York to Saudi Arabia flight would be of Arab background. Virtually everyone on the plane would thus be seized. Just a few non-Arabs would go through unmolested. Is this appreciably different from the facts in *Oneonta*? In both scenarios a group of people are selected for seizure based solely on their race, ethnicity, or appearance. If the police action in *Oneonta* violated the Fourth Amendment, must we also find a Fourth Amendment violation in Scenario 3?

These are important and difficult questions, made more urgent by the events of our time, which raise difficult questions about individual rights and societal protection.

§ 17.04 Distinguishing a "*Terry* Stop" from an Arrest[81]

[A] Overview to the Issue

An encounter between a police officer and a private citizen can be so non-intrusive that it does not constitute a "seizure" and, therefore, does not trigger Fourth Amendment scrutiny, a matter discussed earlier in this Text.[82] On the other hand, a detention can be so intrusive that it constitutes a de facto arrest and, therefore, requires probable cause, and not mere reasonable suspicion. The line between a *Terry*-level seizure and a de facto arrest, therefore, is a critical one. Unfortunately, the line is not bright. As with other *Terry* issues, courts consider the totality of circumstances surrounding the encounter. Various factors, however, deserve special note and are considered immediately below.

[B] Length of the Detention

Terry involved a very brief detention of persons suspected of criminal activity. The Court has more than once stated that the justifiability of a seizure on less than probable cause is predicated in part on the brevity of the detention.[83]

Nonetheless, there is no bright-line time limitation to a *Terry*-type seizure. A seizure based on reasonable suspicion may be permitted although it lasts longer than the seizures that occurred in *Terry*. For example, in *United States v. Sharpe*[84] the Court upheld a twenty-minute detention of suspects, stopped in their vehicles on a public highway, in order to investigate criminal activity. Although the Court upheld the seizures, their legitimacy was based on the presence of three critical temporal factors: (1) the officer

---

81. *See generally* 4 LaFave, Note 1, *supra*, at §9.8.

82. *See* §7.03, *supra*.

83. *See, e.g.*, Dunaway v. New York, 442 U.S. 200, 209 (1979) (*Terry* "involved a brief, on-the-spot stop on the street . . . , a situation that did not fit comfortably within the traditional concept of an 'arrest'"); United States v. Place, 462 U.S. 696, 706 (1983) ("the principles of *Terry* and its progeny would permit the officer to detain . . . briefly to investigate the circumstances that aroused his suspicion").

84. 470 U.S. 675 (1985).

"pursued his investigation in a diligent and reasonable manner"; (2) the method of investigation "was likely to confirm or dispel [the officers'] suspicions quickly"; and (3) the detention lasted no longer than was necessary to effectuate the purpose of the stop. A significant fact in *Sharpe* was that the length of detention was aggravated by evasive actions taken by the suspects in what otherwise would have been a briefer detention.

Sharpe should not be interpreted to mean that a seizure of *any* length may be justified on the basis of reasonable suspicion as long as the police pursue their investigation diligently. Indeed, *Sharpe* warned that even if the three conditions stated above are met, a detention that "continues indefinitely at some point . . . can no longer be justified" as a *Terry* stop.

Despite this warning, the Supreme Court in *United States v. Montoya de Hernandez*[85] upheld a seizure, based on reasonable suspicion, that lasted more than 16 hours. In the case, *M*, a woman whom customs agents reasonably suspected of concealing narcotics-filled balloons in her alimentary canal in order to smuggle them into the country, refused to undergo an x-ray. Therefore, the agents detained her in a small room, and told her that "if she went to the toilet she would have to use a wastebasket in the women's restroom," so that her stool could be inspected for balloons. The Court held that the seizure here "was not unreasonably long," in view of the fact the method of suspected smuggling did not allow for speedy determination, *M* refused the only alternative method of investigation (an x-ray), *M* made "heroic" efforts to avoid having the bowel movement, and (perhaps most importantly) it occurred at the international border.

[C] Forcible Movement of the Suspect

[1] In General

In *Terry,* the suspects were seized and searched where they were found, on the street. However, if the police move a suspect to another site for further investigation, a court may treat the seizure as tantamount to an arrest, requiring probable cause. This is especially likely to occur if the criminal investigation could have occurred where the detention arose.

For example, in *Dunaway v. New York,*[86] the police took *D* into custody at his neighbor's home, and transported him to a police station for questioning. Although *D* was told he was not under arrest, the Supreme Court treated the seizure as a de facto arrest, requiring probable cause. Likewise, in *Florida v. Royer,*[87] the police moved *R*, originally encountered in an airport concourse, to a small room forty feet away, where the investigation continued. Among the reasons given by the Court for treating this act as tantamount to an arrest was that there was no finding of a legitimate law enforcement purpose for moving the suspect.[88]

---

85. 473 U.S. 531 (1985).
86. 442 U.S. 200 (1979).
87. 460 U.S. 491 (1983).
88. *See also* Kaupp v. Texas, 538 U.S. 626 (2003) (per curiam) (on less than probable cause, three uniformed and two plainclothes officers came to the home of the 17-year-old suspect at 3:00 a.m., awakened him in his bedroom, and said, "we need to go and talk"; *K* was taken to the police station, handcuffed; held: the preceding events constituted an illegal seizure of the adolescent suspect, for want of probable cause).

[2] Special Problem: Removal from an Automobile After a Lawful Stop

The Supreme Court has held that whenever a police officer lawfully stops a vehicle on the road, even for a minor traffic violation, it is reasonable for the officer to order the driver out of the car, even if she does this as a matter of routine for purposes of safety. According to *Pennsylvania v. Mimms*,[89] once a driver is pulled over in her car, the incremental intrusion resulting from the order that she alight from the vehicle is *de minimis*. Therefore, the right to order the driver out of the car—again, assuming the initial seizure was lawful—is automatic, i.e., it requires no additional justification.[90]

Furthermore, the Supreme Court held, 7–2, in *Maryland v. Wilson* that an officer, making a valid traffic stop, may "as a matter of course" order *passengers*, and not simply the driver, out of the car pending completion of the detention.[91] The Court conceded that a passenger's interest in liberty is "in one sense stronger than that for the driver," because the police have grounds to stop the driver for a vehicular offense, whereas there is ordinarily no such basis for stopping or detaining passengers. Nonetheless, "as a practical matter, the passengers are already stopped by virtue of the stop of the vehicle." Therefore, the additional intrusion of being ordered out of the car is, again, *de minimis*, and is outweighed by an officer's interest in protecting herself from possible violence by passengers. In dissent, Justices Stevens and Kennedy stated that:

> the number of stops in which an officer is actually at risk is dwarfed by the far greater number of routine stops. . . . [¶] In contrast, the potential daily burden on thousands of innocent citizens is obvious. . . . [C]ountless citizens who cherish individual liberty and are offended, embarrassed, and sometimes provoked by arbitrary official commands may well consider the burden [of being ordered out of the car] to be significant.

In the dissenters' view, "wholly innocent passengers . . . have a constitutionally protected right to decide whether to remain comfortably seated within the vehicle rather than exposing themselves to the elements and the observation of curious bystanders."

The *Wilson* Court left open the issue of whether an officer may detain a passenger for the duration of the stop. More recently, the Supreme Court stated in *Arizona v. Johnson* that the "temporary seizure of driver and passengers ordinarily continues, *and remains reasonable*, for the duration of the stop."[92] This is true, *Johnson* stated, even if the officer uses the traffic stop to inquire "into matters unrelated to the justification for the traffic stop . . . so long as those inquiries do not measurably extend the duration of the stop." It should be noted, however, that the officer in *Johnson* had reason to question the car

---

89. 434 U.S. 106 (1977).

90. *Contra under the state constitution*, State v. Kim, 711 P.2d 1291 (Haw. 1985) (a police officer must have a reasonable basis to believe that a crime has been committed, to order a driver out of a car after a traffic stop); Commonwealth v. Gonsalves, 711 N.E.2d 108 (Mass. 1999) (a police officer must have a reasonable belief that her or another's safety is in danger before ordering a driver or other occupant out of a motor vehicle following a lawful stop of the vehicle); State v. Sprague, 824 A.2d 539 (Vt. 2003) (an officer must have "a reasonable basis to believe that the officer's safety, or the safety of others, is at risk or that a crime has been committed before ordering a driver out of a stopped vehicle").

91. 519 U.S. 408 (1997); *contra under the state constitution*, Commonwealth v. Gonsalves, 711 N.E.2d 108 (Mass. 1999) (requiring reasonable suspicion to order a passenger out of a vehicle); State v. Mendez, 970 P.2d 722 (Wash. 1999) (same).

92. 555 U.S. 323, 333 (2009) (emphasis added).

occupants about possible gang activity. The Fourth Amendment analysis might be different if, for example, the police stop a taxi driver for speeding and the passenger—about whom there is no suspicion of criminal activity or other legitimate reason to detain her—wishes to jump into a new cab in order to reach her destination. In such circumstances, it is *possible* that continued detention of the passenger would be considered unreasonable in light of the individual's interest in reaching her destination.

[D] Existence of "Less Intrusive Means"

In *Florida v. Royer*,[93] Justice White, author of the four-justice plurality opinion, but with the apparent support of Justice Brennan,[94] asserted that when a suspect is seized according to *Terry*, "the investigative methods employed should be the least intrusive means reasonably available to verify or dispel the officer's suspicions in a short period of time." In subsequent cases, however, the Court limited this principle to the length of a seizure, and has refused to apply it to the question of whether the seizure itself was necessary.

In *Royer*, the least-intrusive-means principle was violated when the police moved R, an embarking airplane passenger suspected of drug smuggling, from the public concourse to a small room nearby so that the police could retrieve his luggage and search it, a process that took 15 minutes. According to Justice White, the government did not "touch[] on the question whether it would have been feasible to investigate the contents of [R's] bag in a more expeditious way." In particular, he noted that "[t]he courts are not strangers to the use of trained dogs to detect the presence of controlled substances in luggage." Because there was no indication in this case that the latter investigatory technique "was not feasible and available," the officers' conduct was considered more intrusive than necessary.

Similarly, in *United States v. Place*,[95] another airport concourse case, the Court ruled that a ninety-minute detention of P's luggage, and implicitly of P, in order to get a dog to sniff the luggage, was unreasonable because the government agents had prior warning of P's intended arrival in New York and, therefore, "could have minimized the intrusion on [P's] Fourth Amendment interests," by having the dog available when he arrived.

In contrast to these length-of-detention cases, consider *United States v. Sokolow*,[96] in which S claimed that the police were constitutionally required, if they could do so, to verify their suspicions that he was smuggling narcotics *before* they seized him. The Court quickly disposed of this argument by stating that Justice White's "statement" in *Royer* "was directed at the length of the investigative stop, not at whether the police had a less intrusive means to verify their suspicions before stopping [the suspect]." According to *Sokolow*, "[t]he reasonableness of the officer's decision to stop a suspect does not turn on the availability of less intrusive investigatory techniques."[97]

---

93. 460 U.S. 491 (1983).

94. Justice Brennan concurred in the judgment. He stated that a *Terry* seizure must be so short in duration that it would be "difficult to conceive of a less intrusive means that would be effective to accomplish the purpose of the stop."

95. 462 U.S. 696 (1983).

96. 490 U.S. 1 (1989).

97. *See also* Michigan v. Long, 463 U.S. 1032, 1052 (1983) (a *Terry*-type search of a car for weapons is valid even if the police could have "adopt[ed] alternative means to ensure their safety in

Even in length-of-detention cases, the Court has tempered the force of the least-intrusive-means doctrine. In *United States v. Sharpe*,[98] S was detained for twenty minutes while the police sought to determine whether he was involved in transporting drugs in his pickup truck. The Court stated that in assessing whether this detention was too long to constitute a *Terry* stop, "[t]he question is not simply whether some other alternative was available, but whether the police acted unreasonably in failing to recognize or to pursue it." And, in answering the latter question, the Court warned reviewing courts "not [to] indulge in unrealistic second-guessing."

§ 17.05 Grounds for "*Terry* Stops"[99]

[A] Crime Prevention versus Crime Detection

Terry involved the brief seizure and limited search of a person suspected of imminent criminal activity. The brief seizure was reasonable in view of the government's interest in crime *prevention*. The Supreme Court unanimously held in *United State v. Hensley*,[100] however, that a *Terry*-level seizure may also be reasonable in order to investigate a crime that has already occurred. However, a seizure that is reasonable in the crime-prevention context will not necessarily be permissible in the crime-investigation setting.[101]

As the Court explained in *Hensley*, the factors that go into the *Terry* "reasonableness" balancing inquiry are not identical in the two contexts. The exigent circumstances that justify a brief detention when an officer reasonably suspects that serious crime is afoot may be missing in the crime-detection framework. Furthermore, in crime-detection cases, officers often can choose a time and place for the stop that is more convenient to the suspect than is possible when crime is afoot.

[B] Nature of the Offense

Most *Terry*-type seizures involve detention of persons suspected of involvement in violent crimes. The principles of *Terry* extend, however, beyond that narrow focus. For example, the police may seize a person for investigation of drug trafficking "or of any other serious crime."[102] And, the Supreme Court unanimously ruled that

---

order to avoid the intrusion involved in a *Terry* encounter."). *Long* is discussed in greater detail in § 17.07, *infra*.

    98. 470 U.S. 675 (1985).

    99. *See generally* 3 LaFave, Note 1, *supra*, at § 9.5.

    100. 469 U.S. 221 (1985).

    101. The Supreme Court has not been called upon to determine precisely when a seizure to investigate a completed offense is justified. Justice Thomas, writing for the Court, was recently able to avoid reaching that issue in *Navarette v. Calfornia*, 134 S. Ct. 1683 (2014), stating only that "we need not address under what circumstances a stop is justified by the need to investigate completed criminal activity." The four dissenters, per Justice Scalia, observed that "[t]he circumstances that may justify a stop under *Terry v. Ohio*, to investigate past criminal activity are far from clear (citing *Hensley*)."

    102. Florida v. Royer, 460 U.S. 491, 499 (1983).

in a traffic-stop setting, the first *Terry* condition—a lawful investigatory stop—is met whenever it is lawful for police to detain an automobile and its occupants pending inquiry into a vehicular violation. The police need not have, in addition, cause to believe any occupant of the vehicle is involved in criminal activity.[103]

[C] Fingerprinting

The Supreme Court considers fingerprinting a less serious intrusion on a person's security than most other police practices. First, fingerprinting (unlike interrogations and some searches) does not probe a person's private life and thoughts. Second, the process is more reliable than lineups and confessions, and "is not subject to such abuses as the improper [suggestive] line-up and the 'third degree' [interrogation]."[104] Third, fingerprinting can often be conducted at a time convenient to the suspect and need not be repeated.

In light of these differences, the transportation of a suspect to the police station for fingerprinting, if she is detained there only briefly, is permissible on the basis of probable cause or, the Court has hinted in dictum, "on less than probable cause" if it is "under judicial supervision."[105] The implication is that legislatures or courts could develop procedures for special "fingerprint search warrants," grounded on reasonable suspicion.

Also, the Court has indicated that there is support in its prior cases for the view that a brief detention of a suspect "in the field" for fingerprinting at the scene is permissible if: (1) the belief that the suspect has committed a crime meets the reasonable suspicion standard; (2) there is a reasonable basis for believing that fingerprinting will establish or negate the suspect's connection with that crime; and (3) the fingerprinting is conducted "with dispatch."[106]

§ 17.06 Weapons Searches: Of Persons[107]

[A] Permissibility

Terry v. Ohio authorizes, on the basis of reasonable suspicion, two categories of police actions: a brief seizure of a person for investigatory purposes *and*, after a lawful seizure, a "pat down" or frisk of the individual for weapons if certain conditions are met. As for the conditions, first, the officer must reasonably suspect that the person is "armed and

---

103. Arizona v. Johnson, 555 U.S. 323, 327 (2009). As the language quoted in the text indicates, the Court here was announcing a rule in "a traffic-stop setting." However, what if a *pedestrian* is detained to investigate a *completed* misdemeanor? Lower courts, at least prior to *Johnson*, have split on the answer. *E.g.*, Gaddis v. Redford Township, 364 F.3d 763 (6th Cir. 2004) (adopting bright-line rule barring *Terry*-level seizures to investigate completed misdemeanors); United States v. Hughes, 517 F.3d 1013 (8th Cir. 2008) (applying a case-by-case approach balancing personal security against governmental interests; here, the *Terry* seizure was unconstitutional in the investigation of a completed misdemeanor trespass).

104. Davis v. Mississippi, 394 U.S. 721, 727 (1969).

105. Hayes v. Florida, 470 U.S. 811, 816–17 (1985).

106. *Id.* at 817.

107. *See generally* 4 LaFave, Note 1, *supra*, at § 9.6.

presently dangerous."[108] Second, the *Terry* Court seemed to suggest that an officer must use the least intrusive means to protect himself: The officer must investigate first, and only frisk the suspect if "nothing in the initial stages of the encounter serves to dispel his reasonable fear for his own or others' safety."[109]

In contrast, Justice Harlan argued in his concurrence in *Terry* that the right to conduct a weapons search of a detained suspect is immediate and automatic if the basis for the seizure is that the officer believes that violent crime is afoot. In other words, assuming that an officer was justified in *seizing* the suspect for investigation of a *violent* crime, the officer should not be required to jeopardize her safety by questioning the suspect before she conducts a weapons search.

The Supreme Court's treatment of the facts in *Adams v. Williams*[110] suggests that Justice Harlan's view has been accepted. In *Williams*, an officer received information that *W* was sitting in a parked car, carrying narcotics, with a handgun concealed at his waist. The officer confronted *W*, after which he seized the gun without asking *W* any questions that might have dispelled his concern. The Court upheld the conviction, without commenting on the language in the *Terry* majority.

[B] Method

[1] Pat-Down (Frisk)

Terry did not mandate a particular weapons-search procedure, although it approved the one conducted in that case. In *Terry*, *O* patted down the exterior of *T*'s clothing. Upon feeling a weapon, *O* searched *T*'s pocket and pulled out the weapon. In contrast, in *Sibron v. New York*,[111] a companion case to *Terry*, the Court disapproved a search in which the officer thrust his hand into the suspect's pocket without first frisking him.

Notwithstanding *Sibron*, a pat-down is not always a prerequisite to a valid weapons search. Rather obviously, if a suspect whom the officer has reason to believe is armed and dangerous suddenly moves her hand into a pocket or under a piece of clothing that might contain a weapon, the officer need not jeopardize herself by conducting a pat-down.[112]

The facts in *Adams v. Williams*[113] provide another example of a valid weapons search that was not preceded by a pat-down. In *Williams*, the officer who had been informed that *W* was in his parked car with a weapon concealed at his waist, asked *W* to open his car door; when *W* opened his window instead, the officer reached into the car and, without frisking *W*, seized the gun from the suspect's waistband. The Court, without discussion of the procedure, approved the officer's actions. The officer's no-frisk approach can be justified on the ground that a pat-down in these circumstances—reaching into the car through the window—would have been difficult, even dangerous.

---

108. The Supreme Court now frequently drops the word "presently" from the description of the *Terry* frisk rule. *E.g.*, Knowles v. Iowa, 525 U.S. 113, 117 (1998); Arizona v. Johnson, 555 U.S. 323, 327 (2009).

109. *See* the text to Note 24, *supra*.

110. 407 U.S. 143 (1972).

111. 392 U.S. 40 (1968).

112. 4 LaFave, Note 1, *supra*, at 657.

113. 407 U.S. 143 (1972).

Because the officer reached only to the spot where he had been told the gun was concealed, his actions were reasonable.

[2] After the Pat-Down

If an officer feels no object during a pat-down, or she feels an object that does not appear to be a weapon, no further search is justifiable under *Terry*, which is based exclusively on the concern for the officer's safety. If the initial pat-down, with no further touching, provides the officer with probable cause for believing that an object felt in the clothing is contraband or other criminal evidence subject to seizure, she may pull out the object without a warrant, pursuant to the plain-touch doctrine.[114]

If the officer feels a hard object that she reasonably believes is a weapon, the officer may reach for the object. If the object she pulls out is a container, she may feel the container to see if it might contain a weapon inside. If her fears regarding the container are not reasonably dispelled by its size, weight, and feel, the officer may, at a minimum, retain possession of the container so as to separate the suspect from any weapon that might be inside. Although the Supreme Court has not definitively said so, probably the officer may even open the container and look inside, on the ground "that this is simply a continuation, in a sense, of the frisk of the person and thus may be carried out on the same terms."[115]

If the container pulled out by the officer could not reasonably contain a weapon (and assuming there is no independent probable cause to believe it contains contraband or other criminal evidence), the present rule is that it may not be kept or searched under *Terry*. Of course, if something else in the encounter gives rise to probable cause to arrest, the suspect may be searched incident to the arrest.

§ 17.07 Extending *Terry*:
Weapons Searches of Automobiles

A person may lawfully be frisked under certain circumstances, but what about cars? The Supreme Court ruled in *Michigan v. Long*[116] that, in some circumstances, the police may conduct a weapons search—a "frisk"[117]—of the passenger compartment of a lawfully stopped automobile.

In *Long*, police officers in a rural region of Michigan, at night, observed *L* drive his car erratically, at an excessive rate of speed, and swerve into a ditch. The officers stopped to investigate. As they did, *L* got out of his car and, leaving the door open, met the police at the rear of the automobile. *L* appeared to be intoxicated.

The officers requested *L*'s vehicle registration. After repeated requests, and no response, *L* began to walk toward the open door of the car. The officers followed him, and observed

---

114. Minnesota v. Dickerson, 508 U.S. 366 (1993). *See* § 14.05[B], *supra*.

115. 4 LaFave, Note 1, *supra*, at 672.

116. 463 U.S. 1032 (1983); *contra under the state constitution*, People v. Torres, 543 N.E.2d 61 (N.Y. 1989).

117. *See* Maryland v. Buie, 494 U.S. 325, 332 (1990) ("In a sense, *Long* authorized a 'frisk' of an automobile for weapons.").

a hunting knife on the floor of the driver's side of the car. At that point, the officers frisked *L*, but they felt no weapon. The officers then shone a light inside the car to look for other weapons. They noticed something, although they could not identify it, protruding from under the armrest on the front seat. One officer entered the car, lifted the armrest, and found an open pouch containing marijuana. *L* was arrested for possession of the contraband.

The Court upheld the car search for weapons. It observed that investigative detentions of persons in cars "are especially fraught with danger to police officers," and that the passenger compartment of a car is within the immediate control of a suspect. Therefore, it reasoned, if a weapon is inside a car, it represents a risk to the police. Although this reasoning might suggest that the police may conduct a weapons search of the passenger compartment of any automobile they lawfully stop, *Long*'s holding is narrower than this. The Court stated that "the search of the passenger compartment of an automobile, limited to those areas in which a weapon may be placed or hidden, is permissible if the police officer possesses a reasonable belief . . . that the suspect is dangerous and the suspect may gain immediate control of weapons."

In *Long*, the Court noted specific, articulable facts that, in its view, justified the officers in entering the car to search for weapons. These facts included: (1) it was late at night; (2) the area was rural; (3) *L* appeared to be intoxicated; (4) the officers had already observed a hunting knife in the vehicle; and (5) *L* intended to re-enter the vehicle.

Should these factors add up to reasonable suspicion that the suspect is dangerous? The Court did not explain the relevance of the hour of the night or the rural nature of the area, and neither seems to heighten the driver's dangerousness. Thus, the answer probably comes down to whether a drunk person with a hunting knife in his car presents a sufficient danger either during or in the immediate aftermath of the encounter to justify searching the entire passenger compartment of the car as opposed to, for example, just keeping the driver out of the car during the encounter. The Court's conclusion that the car "frisk" (more accurately, a full weapons search of the passenger compartment) was justified, while perhaps a stretch,[118] was not inconsistent with the thrust of its earlier *Terry* holdings.

§ 17.08 Extending *Terry*: Protective Sweeps of Residences[119]

As defined in *Maryland v. Buie*,[120] a "protective sweep" of a residence "is a quick and limited search of a premises, incident to an arrest and conducted to protect the safety of police officers or others. It is narrowly confined to a cursory visual inspection of those places in which a person might be hiding."

---

118. The Court pointed out that if *L* had not been arrested, he would have returned to the car to leave the scene, and thus could have reached the knife and any other weapon in the car. However, if he were not under arrest and no longer in temporary custody, *L* would have little incentive to use the knife against the officers.

119. *See generally* 3 LaFave, Note 1, *supra*, at § 6.4(c).

120. 494 U.S. 325 (1990).

As discussed elsewhere,[121] the Supreme Court ruled in *Buie* that, as an incident to an arrest of an individual, the police may automatically—i.e., without probable cause or reasonable suspicion—conduct a protective sweep of "spaces immediately adjoining the place of arrest" where people may be hiding. Moreover, *Buie* teaches that, beyond this limited area, the arresting officers may also conduct a warrantless protective sweep of other parts of the residence if there exists reasonable suspicion "that the area [to be] swept harbor[s] an individual posing a danger to the officer or others."

In *Buie*, six or seven officers entered *B*'s house with a warrant to arrest him for a crime allegedly committed by *B* and *X*. When they entered, they observed a basement; standing on the first floor, an officer ordered anyone in the basement to come out. Eventually, *B* emerged and was arrested and handcuffed on the main floor. Thereafter, an officer entered the basement to see if anyone else was present. Although he found no one, he discovered evidence in plain view related to the crime, which he seized. The Court stated that the officer acted properly in entering the basement if there were facts that warranted him in suspecting that a person posing a danger to him or others was downstairs.[122]

In announcing the new rule, the Supreme Court focused on the lessons to be learned from *Terry* and *Michigan v. Long*.[123] It applied the reasonableness balancing test set out in *Terry*. In regard to the governmental interest in permitting the warrantless search, the Court observed that both *Terry* and *Long* justified weapons searches out of concern for the safety of police officers. Here, too, there was a concern for police safety, perhaps even graver than that which confronted the officers in *Terry* and *Long*: "[U]nlike an encounter on the street or along a highway, an in-home arrest puts the officer at the disadvantage of being on his adversary's 'turf.' An ambush in a confined setting of unknown configuration is more to be feared than it is in open, more familiar surroundings."

In regard to the individual's privacy interests, the Court analogized protective sweeps to the limited intrusions allowed in *Terry* and *Long*. Although the Court conceded that a sweep of a home is not a *de minimis* intrusion, it is nonetheless a limited one, in that the sweep "may extend only to a cursory inspection of those spaces where a person may be found,"[124] and may "last[] no longer than is necessary to dispel the reasonable suspicion of danger and in any event no longer than it takes to complete the arrest and depart the premises." According to the Court, the interest in the arresting officers' safety outweighs the intrusion that protective sweeps may entail.

---

121. See § 12.02[C][3], *supra*.

122. The case was remanded to the state court to determine whether the requisite reasonable suspicion existed. In his concurrence, Justice Stevens expressed doubt that the police could justify this protective sweep. He reasoned that the police may only conduct a sweep if it will *reduce* the risk of harm to themselves or others: "in short, the search must be protective." He described the officer's decision to enter the basement after *B*'s arrest as "a surprising choice for an officer, worried about safety." On remand, however, the court found that the officers were justified in conducting the sweep. Buie v. State, 580 A.2d 167 (Md. 1990).

123. 463 U.S. 1032 (1983). See § 17.07, *supra*.

124. Notwithstanding the Court's observation, a protective search is far more extensive than the one approved in *Terry* in that every room and hallway closet in the residence may be entered. In that sense, the Court has approved a virtual *full* search of a residence based on reasonable suspicion, rather than probable cause.

§ 17.09 Extending *Terry*: Temporary Seizures of Property

In *United States v. Place*,[125] federal officers had advance information that *P* would disembark from an airplane with luggage containing narcotics. When *P* arrived, the officers seized his luggage and, ninety minutes later, subjected it to a "non-search"[126] sniff by a trained narcotics detection dog. The dog's response confirmed the officers' suspicions, after which they applied for and received a warrant to search the suitcase.

The Supreme Court, per Justice Sandra O'Connor, ruled that police officers may, without a warrant or probable cause, temporarily detain (seize) luggage on the basis of reasonable suspicion that it contains narcotics, in order to investigate the circumstances that aroused their suspicion. In short, *Terry* principles apply to seizures of property, and not simply to seizures of persons. However, the Court concluded that the 90-minute detention here was excessive, and therefore disapproved this seizure.

In reaching its conclusion, the Court applied the *Terry* reasonableness balancing test. It determined that the government's interest in seizing *P*'s personal property—detecting drug trafficking—was substantial. On the countervailing side, Justice O'Connor observed that "intrusion on possessory interests . . . can vary both in its nature and extent." She distinguished between a seizure of property "after the owner has relinquished control of the property to a third party or, as here, from the immediate custody and control of the owner." In the latter situation, the seizure not only intrudes upon a person's possessory interest in his property, but also on his "liberty interest in proceeding with his itinerary," because a person will ordinarily not feel free to leave an airport without his personal belongings. Consequently, the Court treated the seizure of the property in *Place* as if it included a seizure of *P* himself.

Under these circumstances, the Court concluded that the ninety-minute detention was excessive. Justice O'Connor noted the importance of brevity in *Terry* cases, and the fact that the police did not diligently pursue their investigation. With their prior knowledge that *P* would be arriving with suspicious luggage, the Court believed that the officers should have brought the trained dog to the scene in advance of *P*'s arrival.

---

125. 462 U.S. 696 (1983).
126. *See* § 6.09, *supra*.

Chapter 18

More "Reasonableness" Balancing: Searches and Seizures Primarily Conducted for Non-Criminal Law Purposes

§ 18.01 Overview[1]

With one exception,[2] previous chapters of this text have focused on searches and seizures conducted by police officers in criminal investigations (i.e., in pursuit of criminal evidence; of a person suspected of a crime already committed; or as part of a police effort to investigate crime that may be afoot). In contrast, this chapter centers on searches and seizures, sometimes performed by police officers but often conducted by other public officers, that are ostensibly conducted (at least, primarily) for non-penal, purposes—even if these "non-penal" searches or seizures might later result in criminal prosecutions.

As may be evident from the last sentence, and seen more clearly in later sections of this chapter, the line between a traditional criminal investigation, on the one hand, and a search or seizure designed primarily to serve *non*-criminal law enforcement goals, on the other hand, is thin and, quite arguably, arbitrary. Yet, it is also a line of considerable constitutional significance.

On the "criminal investigatory" side of the line, the Supreme Court once declared that search warrants, supported by probable cause, were presumptively required. Although warrants today are the exception rather than the rule, they are still required in various situations (e.g., the home), and probable cause remains the touchstone in criminal investigations. Moreover, when probable cause is not required, it remains the case that "[a] search or seizure is ordinarily unreasonable in the absence of *individualized* [reasonable] suspicion of wrongdoing."[3]

---

1. *See generally* Edwin J. Butterfoss, *A Suspicionless Search and Seizure Quagmire: The Supreme Court Revises the Pretext Doctrine and Creates Another Fine Fourth Amendment Mess*, 40 Creighton L. Rev. 419 (2007); Ronald M. Gould & Simon Stern, *Catastrophic Threats and the Fourth Amendment*, 77 So. Calif. L. Rev. 777 (2004); Stephen J. Schulhofer, *On the Fourth Amendment Rights of the Law-Abiding Public*, 1989 Sup. Ct. Rev. 87; William J. Stuntz, *Implicit Bargains, Government Power, and the Fourth Amendment*, 44 Stan. L. Rev. 553 (1992); Scott E. Sundby, *"Everyman's" Fourth Amendment: Privacy or Mutual Trust Between Government and Citizen?*, 94 Colum. L. Rev. 1751 (1994).

2. *See* Chapter 15, *supra* (inventory searches).

3. City of Indianapolis v. Edmond, 531 U.S. 32, 37 (2000). Notice the *Edmond* Court's use of the word "ordinarily." Even in the criminal investigation context, individualized suspicion is not *always* required. *See* Samson v. California, 547 U.S. 843 (2006) (upholding suspicionless searches of parolees by law. *See also* Maryland v. King, 133 S. Ct. 1958 (2013), discussed more fully in § 12.02,

In contrast, once one moves to the *non*-criminal investigatory side of the line, the analysis is quite different. Warrants, which are intended for criminal investigations, and "probable cause," which is textually linked to the warrant "requirement," are typically treated as irrelevant. And, the requirement of individualized suspicion of wrongdoing is "not an 'irreducible' component of reasonableness."[4] Suspicionless, warrantless searches and seizures are frequently permitted in the "non-criminal" realm.

An irony becomes evident once one compares the law on the two sides of the criminal-investigatory line. On the non-criminal law enforcement side of the line, the Supreme Court has often had the opportunity "to hear face-to-face, as Fourth Amendment claimants, those law-abiding citizens for whose ultimate benefit the constitutional restraints on public power were primarily intended."[5] And yet here the Court on occasion has required such law-abiding persons to open up their homes, businesses, papers, effects, and even bodies to *greater* scrutiny than occurs with criminal suspects.[6] This distinction seemingly ignores Justice Louis Brandeis's warning that "[e]xperience should teach us to be most on guard to protect liberty when the Government's purposes are beneficent."[7]

§ 18.02 Administrative Searches[8]

Modern "administrative search" law began in 1967 with companion cases *Camara v. Municipal Court*[9] and *See v. City of Seattle*.[10] *Camara* involved the attempt of an employee of the San Francisco Department of Public Health to enter *C*'s apartment without a warrant or consent in order to conduct a routine inspection of the residence for possible violations of the City's housing code. *See* involved a fire department employee's warrantless entry of a warehouse pursuant to a city ordinance that authorized entry into non-dwellings in order to inspect for fire code violations. In neither *Camara* nor *See* did the public employee who entered the building without a warrant possess probable cause to believe that evidence of a crime—or even of a code violation—would be found in the inspected area.

Camara and *See* are important cases for two reasons. First, as discussed elsewhere,[11] the Court in *Camara* developed an "administrative search" version of "probable cause" that does not require individualized suspicion of wrongdoing, and which requires only that administrative searches be "reasonable." To determine "reasonableness," *Camara*

---

supra (approving "searching" for a DNA sample by swabbing the inside of an arrestee's cheek as part of the routine booking procedure for those charged with "serious offenses").

4. *Edmond*, 531 U.S. at 37.

5. Schulhofer, Note 1, *supra*, at 88.

6. *Id.* at 89. Early on, the Court observed that "[i]t is surely anomalous to say that the individual and his private property are fully protected by the Fourth Amendment only when the individual is suspected of criminal behavior." Camara v. Municipal Court, 387 U.S. 523, 530 (1967).

7. Olmstead v. United States, 277 U.S. 438, 479 (1928) (dissenting opinion).

8. *See generally* 5 Wayne R. LaFave, Search and Seizure § 10.1-.02 (4th ed. 2004); Wayne R. LaFave, *Administrative Searches and the Fourth Amendment: The Camara and See Cases*, 1967 Sup. Ct. Rev. 1; Scott E. Sundby, *A Return to Fourth Amendment Basics: Undoing the Mischief of Camara and Terry*, 72 Minn. L. Rev. 383 (1988).

9. 387 U.S. 523 (1967).

10. 387 U.S. 541 (1967).

11. See § 8.06, *supra*.

implemented a balancing test, later used in criminal investigations,[12] in which "the need to search [is weighed] against the invasion which the search entails."

Second, *Camara* and *See* considered the question of whether the Fourth Amendment warrant requirement applies to health and safety code inspections of homes and commercial buildings. The Court held in both cases that, except in the case of an emergency or consent, the right of entry to conduct an administrative inspection requires a warrant, albeit one based on administrative, not ordinary, probable cause. The Court stated that "[i]t has nowhere been urged that fire, health, and housing code inspection programs could not achieve their goals within the confines of a reasonable search warrant requirement." This means that the legislature cannot pass a statute that requires businesses to submit to searches without allowing the business an opportunity for "individualized pre-clearance review" by a court.[13]

Post-*See* cases demonstrate, however, that under *many* circumstances, warrantless, non-exigent, nonconsensual administrative inspections of commercial premises *are* constitutional. As explained by the Court in *New York v. Burger*,[14] a "closely regulated" business[15] may be inspected without a warrant if three conditions are met. First, the administrative regulatory scheme must advance a "substantial interest," such as to protect the health and safety of workers.[16]

Second, warrantless inspections must be necessary to further the regulatory scheme. This element is met if there is a serious possibility that a routine warrant requirement would allow those regulated to conceal their violations of the rules, and thereby frustrate the administrative system.

Third, the ordinance or statute that permits warrantless inspections must, by its terms, provide an adequate substitute for the warrant, such as rules that limit the discretion of the inspectors, regarding the time, place, and scope of the search.

The line between administrative inspections and traditional criminal searches can be thin, as demonstrated by the facts and the Court's treatment of them, in *Burger*. In that case, police officers—not employees of an administrative agency—entered *B*'s automobile junkyard, a closely regulated business, without a warrant or probable cause of penal wrongdoing. Pursuant to a statute that authorized them to do so, they asked to inspect *B*'s business license and "police book," i.e., a record of automobiles and parts on the premises. *B* conceded that he had neither document, whereupon the officers searched the junkyard, found evidence of stolen vehicle parts, and arrested him for possession of stolen property.

---

12. Terry v. Ohio, 392 U.S. 1 (1968). *See* Chapter 17, *supra*.

13. *See* City of Los Angeles v. Patel, 135 S. Ct. 2443 (2015).

14. 482 U.S. 691 (1987).

15. A business is "closely regulated" if there is "a long tradition of close government supervision" of the business, Marshall v. Barlow's, Inc., 436 U.S. 307 (1978) or, in the case of new and emerging industries, if there is a "pervasiveness and regularity" of regulation. Donovan v. Dewey, 452 U.S. 594 (1981). Examples of "closely regulated businesses" are: liquor dealers, Colonnade Catering Corp. v. United States, 397 U.S. 72 (1970); gun dealers, United States v. Biswell, 406 U.S. 311 (1972); mining companies, Donovan v. Dewey, *supra*; and automobile junkyards, New York v. Burger, 482 U.S. 691 (1987). Hotels are not considered "closely regulated" businesses. City of Los Angeles v. Patel, 135 S. Ct. 2443 (2015).

16. Donovan v. Dewey, 452 U.S. 594 (1981) (mine workers).

The Court upheld the search.[17] It did not consider it fatal to the scheme that police officers, rather than administrative inspectors, conducted the search. The justices observed that many communities lack the resources to hire inspectors to enforce non-penal regulations.

More significantly, the Court considered it irrelevant to the Fourth Amendment aspects of the case that the regulations had the same ultimate purpose as criminal larceny laws, namely, to deter car thefts. The saving feature of the regulations was that they had "different subsidiary purposes and prescribe[d] different methods of addressing the problem." In this case, the Court concluded, the regulations established the conditions under which vehicle-dismantling businesses could be operated, including the institution of a requirement that the businesses be licensed and maintain certain records.

In regard to the line-drawing problem, *Burger* is troubling because *B* admitted to the police officers when they arrived that he was in violation of the regulations. Therefore, as soon as he made that admission, the ensuing search took on the obvious cast of a police effort to uncover evidence of criminal activity. But the Court did not focus on the motives of the specific officers in this case, but rather on the fact that the administrative regulations themselves were not "designed to gather evidence to enable convictions under the penal laws." As the Court has more recently explained *Burger*, the discovery of evidence of criminal wrongdoing there was "merely incidental to the purposes of the administrative search."[18]

§ 18.03 International Border Searches and Seizures[19]

[A] At the Border

The Supreme Court ruled in *United States v. Ramsey*[20] that people may be stopped (seized) at the international border or its "functional equivalent" (e.g., at an airport where an international flight arrives), and they and their belongings may be searched, without a warrant and in the absence of individualized suspicion of wrongdoing, "pursuant to the longstanding right of the sovereign to protect itself" from the entry of persons or objects dangerous to the nation. In short, relatively brief, warrantless, suspicionless searches and seizures are "reasonable simply by virtue of the fact that they occur at the border."

In the post-September 11 world, the Supreme Court is evidently prepared to authorize fairly substantial warrantless, suspicionless searches and seizures of property entering the country. For example, in *United States v. Flores-Montano*,[21] customs officials, without reasonable suspicion, seized *F*'s car at the international border, removed the gas tank, disassembled it, and thereafter seized 37 kilograms of marijuana they discovered inside

---

17. *Contra*, People v. Scott, 593 N.E.2d 1328 (N.Y. 1992) (holding that the regulatory scheme involved in *Burger* violated the state constitution).

18. Ferguson v. City of Charleston, 532 U.S. 67, 83 n. 21 (2001).

19. *See generally* 5 LaFave, Note 8, *supra*, at § 10.05.

20. 431 U.S. 606 (1977).

21. 541 U.S. 149 (2004).

the tank. The seizure and subsequent search took a little less than an hour. The Court unanimously approved the warrantless, suspicionless search and seizure. It remarked that "[t]he Government's interest in preventing the entry of unwanted persons and effects is at its zenith at the international border." It observed that "[i]t is difficult to imagine how the search of a gas tank, which should be solely a repository for fuel, could be more of an invasion of privacy than the search of the automobile's passenger compartment."[22]

The Court seemingly is somewhat more protective of the interests of persons, as distinguished from their property, at international borders (at least this was the case prior to 9/11). Thus, a person lawfully stopped at the border for routine inspection may be detained further *if the agents have reasonable suspicion of criminal activity*. But, perhaps again because it is an international border situation — the societal interests are so considerable — the Court has been willing to justify extended seizures in this context. For example, in *United States v. Montoya de Hernandez*,[23] the Court approved a 16-hour detention of *M*, a woman whom officers reasonably suspected of having swallowed balloons containing heroin in order to avoid detection. After *M* refused to undergo an x-ray (she falsely claimed she was pregnant), she was compelled to remain incommunicado in a small room furnished only with hard chairs and a table, while the authorities waited for her to defecate. The Court concluded that her seizure and extended detention was reasonable, although it conceded that *M* underwent a "long, uncomfortable, indeed, humiliating" detention. *M*'s interest in personal freedom was outweighed by the substantial national interest in preventing the importation of illegal drugs.

[B] Near the Border

[1] In General

Border officers frequently stop cars near, but not at, the Canadian and Mexican borders, in order to question occupants regarding their citizenship, and/or to search the vehicles for contraband or aliens being smuggled into the country. In such circumstances, the border agents may not know whether the car occupants came across the border. The reasonableness of these seizures and searches depends in part on whether they take place at a fixed checkpoint or as the result of a so-called "roving" border patrol.

[2] Roving Border Patrols

Roving border patrols present significant Fourth Amendment concerns. First, the patrols occur without notice, often at night on seldom-traveled roads, and their approach is apt to alarm motorists. Therefore, the subjective intrusion, measured by the surprise and alarm of lawful travelers, is significant. Second, roving border patrol agents have considerable discretion regarding whom to stop. Such unbridled discretion can result in discriminatory enforcement.

---

22. The Court left open the question of "whether, and under what circumstances, a border search might be deemed 'unreasonable' because of the particularly offensive manner it is carried out" (quoting dictum from *Ramsey, supra*). The Chief Justice observed that "[w]hile it may be true that some searches of property are so destructive as to require a different result, this was not one of them."

23. 473 U.S. 531 (1985).

As a consequence of these concerns, the Supreme Court has applied fairly traditional Fourth Amendment standards to searches and seizures conducted by roving border patrol agents. In *Almeida-Sanchez v. United States*,[24] A's car was stopped and searched approximately 25 air miles from the Mexican border. Marijuana was found inside the car. The patrol officers had no warrant and, concededly, no probable cause to conduct the search. The Supreme Court held, 5–4, that the search violated the Fourth Amendment according to ordinary car search principles.[25] The majority rejected the argument that the search was reasonable as a routine administrative search,[26] because the search here occurred solely at the "discretion of the official in the field," and not as the result of specified regulations.

The Court also applied traditional Fourth Amendment principles in *United States v. Brignoni-Ponce*,[27] a case in which roving border patrol agents briefly stopped a vehicle to question the occupants solely because they appeared to be of Mexican ancestry. The Court held that roving agents may not detain a person in a vehicle, even briefly for questioning, in the absence of reasonable suspicion of illegal presence in the country. The Court noted factors that may justify a brief seizure: information about recent illegal border crossings in the area; furtive behavior by the occupants of the vehicle; and evidence that the car has an "extraordinary number" of passengers. Reasonable suspicion may not be based, however, *exclusively* on the fact that occupants of the vehicle appear to be of foreign ancestry.

[3] Fixed Interior Checkpoints

Fixed interior checkpoints do not present the same Fourth Amendment concerns set out above. In this realm, therefore, the Supreme Court determined in *United States v. Martinez-Fuerte*[28] that vehicle occupants may be stopped at fixed checkpoints, and briefly detained for questioning, *without* individualized suspicion of wrongdoing.

The Court distinguished fixed checkpoints from roving patrols on two grounds. First, the subjective intrusion on the security of lawful travelers "is appreciably less in the case of a [fixed] checkpoint stop." In the latter circumstance, "the motorist can see that other vehicles are being stopped, he can see visible signs of the officers' authority, and he is much less likely to be frightened or annoyed by the intrusion." Second, fixed checkpoints involve less discretionary enforcement activity than roving patrols. The location of the fixed checkpoint is not determined by the officers, and they may only stop cars that pass through it.

In these circumstances, the Court balanced the government's interest in stopping cars near the border against the car occupants' interests in privacy and free locomotion. It determined that the objective intrusion was minimal as travelers were stopped only momentarily, and the subjective intrusion was less than with roving border patrols. Balanced against these minimal intrusions was the "substantiality of the public interest" in preventing the entry of illegal aliens. Furthermore, evidence was presented that a requirement that detentions be based on reasonable suspicion was impractical, and would "eliminate any deterrent to the conduct of well-disguised smuggling operations."

---

24. 413 U.S. 266 (1973).
25. *See* Chapter 13, *supra*.
26. *See* § 18.02, *supra*.
27. 422 U.S. 873 (1975).
28. 428 U.S. 543 (1976).

The holding in *Martinez-Fuerte* is expressly limited "to the type of stops described in [the] opinion." That is, any further detention beyond that which is necessary to conduct brief questioning regarding citizenship must be based on consent or probable cause.[29]

§ 18.04 Automobile Inspections and Checkpoints[30]

[A] Automobile License and Vehicle Registration Inspections

Automobiles have long been treated differently—and, from a Fourth Amendment perspective, less protectively—than homes and many other forms of personal property. The Supreme Court has stated that motorists have a lesser expectation of privacy in their automobiles, in part because motor vehicles are the subject of extensive regulation.[31] Every state, of course, requires vehicles to be registered and their operators to be licensed. Moreover, each state and most local communities have regulations regarding the use and maintenance of automobiles.

Police officers frequently stop motorists on the road to issue traffic citations, presumably based on probable cause. But, particularly in the second half of the twentieth century, police officers began to stop motorists without probable cause *or even reasonable suspicion* of wrongdoing, in order to conduct random driver's license and vehicle registration inspections.

The Supreme Court considered such vehicle-use inspections for the first time in *Delaware v. Prouse*.[32] In *Prouse*, an officer conducting a random driver's license and registration check, stopped *P*'s vehicle. After the stop, the officer observed marijuana in plain view inside the vehicle. The Supreme Court held that the search violated the Fourth Amendment because the officer did not have a right to order the driver to pull over to conduct the license/registration inspection. It reached this conclusion by balancing the intrusion on the driver's interests "against [the] promotion of legitimate governmental interests."

In the latter regard, the Court agreed "that the States have a vital interest in ensuring that only those qualified to do so are permitted to operate motor vehicles, that these vehicles are fit for safe operation, and hence that licensing, registration, and vehicle inspection requirements are being observed."[33] On the other side of the scale, the Court was

---

29. *See* United States v. Ortiz, 422 U.S. 891 (1975).

30. *See generally* 5 LaFave, Note 8, *supra*, at § 10.8; Wayne R. LaFave, *Controlling Discretion by Administrative Regulations: The Use, Misuse, and Nonuse of Police Rules and Policies in Fourth Amendment Adjudication*, 89 Mich. L. Rev. 442 (1990); Nadine Strossen, *Michigan Department of State Police v. Sitz: A Roadblock to Meaningful Judicial Enforcement of Constitutional Rights*, 42 Hastings L.J. 285 (1991); Scott E. Sundby, *Protecting the Citizen "Whilst He Is Quiet": Suspicionless Searches, "Special Needs" and General Warrants*, 74 Miss. L.J. 501 (2004).

31. *See* § 13.03, *supra*.

32. 440 U.S. 648 (1979).

33. The State suggested two other interests in such stops: apprehension of stolen cars; and identification of drivers under the influence of alcohol or narcotics. The Court responded in footnote: "The latter interest is subsumed by the interest in roadway safety, as may be the former interest to

troubled, first, by the fact that the officer "was not acting pursuant to any standards, guidelines, or procedures pertaining to document spot checks, promulgated by either his department or [the state]." Therefore, the risk of arbitrary and discriminatory enforcement was considerable.

Second, the Court questioned the wisdom of random stops. "Absent some empirical data to the contrary," the Court stated, "it must be assumed that finding an unlicensed driver among those who commit traffic violations [for which there is, therefore, probable cause to make the stop] is a much more likely event than finding an unlicensed driver by choosing randomly from the entire universe of drivers." The Court assumed in the absence of such data that the "contribution to highway safety made by discretionary stops selected from among drivers generally will . . . be marginal at best." In disapproving of the procedure in this case, the Court announced that:

> except in those situations in which there is at least articulable and reasonable suspicion that a motorist is unlicensed or that an automobile is not registered, or that either the vehicle or an occupant is otherwise subject to seizure for violation of law, stopping an automobile and detaining the driver in order to check his driver's license and the registration of the automobile are unreasonable under the Fourth Amendment.

The Court did not rule out the possibility that suspicionless license/registration inspections would be upheld under different circumstances. In important dictum, it stated that "[t]his holding does not preclude [a state] . . . from developing methods for spot checks that involve less intrusion or that do not involve the unconstrained exercise of discretion." The implication of this is that routine, warrantless, suspicionless checks *are* permissible if safeguards are devised to assure that "persons in automobiles on public roadways [do] not for that reason alone have their travel and privacy interfered with at the unbridled discretion of police officers." Specifically, according to *Prouse*, "[q]uestioning of all oncoming traffic at roadblock-type stops is one possible alternative."

[B] Automobile Checkpoints

[1] Sobriety Checkpoints

Are sobriety checkpoints—at which the police randomly, without individualized suspicion, stop motorists to check drivers for evidence of intoxication—constitutional? Law enforcement officials were once concerned that the Supreme Court might bar such suspicionless checkpoints. This concern seemed plausible in light of the Court's holdings in *Delaware v. Prouse*,[34] in which it invalidated a suspicionless driver's license and registration check, and *United States v. Brignoni-Ponce*,[35] in which the Court disapproved of suspicionless, roving border patrol stops of cars near the Mexican border.

Nonetheless, the Supreme Court upheld a suspicionless highway sobriety checkpoint in *Michigan Department of State Police v. Sitz*.[36] In *Sitz*, Michigan state police devised

---

some extent. The remaining governmental interest in controlling automobile thefts is not distinguishable from the general interest in crime control."

34. 440 U.S. 648 (1979). *See* subsection [A], *supra*.

35. 422 U.S. 873 (1975). *See* § 18.03[B][2], *supra*.

36. 496 U.S. 444 (1990); *contra, under the state constitution*, Sitz v. Department of State Police, 506 N.W.2d 209 (Mich. 1993) (a "reasonable basis" for the seizure is required); Ascher v.

guidelines for conducting sobriety checkpoints. In the only implementation of the state's procedures, 126 vehicles were stopped, and the drivers were briefly examined for signs of intoxication. On average, each detention took 25 seconds. Two drivers who appeared to be intoxicated were required to move out of the traffic flow, to another point where a second officer could check their licenses and conduct sobriety tests. One of these drivers was arrested. Another motorist, who attempted to break through the checkpoint, was also arrested.

The state courts ruled that this sobriety checkpoint was unconstitutional. In reaching this result, a lower court applied a three-pronged test set out in *Brown v. Texas*,[37] in which the Court invalidated a suspicionless seizure of a person on the street. The lower court held that, although the state's interest in curbing drunken driving was "grave and legitimate" (the first *Brown* prong[38]), the checkpoint program was ineffective and, therefore, did not significantly advance the public interest (the second prong). Also, the lower court determined that the overall intrusion on drivers' liberty (the third factor) was considerable: the objective intrusion (a 25-second delay) was minimal, but the subjective intrusion was substantial, because the checkpoint generated fear and surprise among motorists in much the same way that roving border patrols were condemned by the Supreme Court in *Brignoni-Ponce*.

The Supreme Court disagreed. Chief Justice Rehnquist, for the Court, held that the sobriety checkpoint did not violate the Fourth Amendment insofar as it pertained to the initial stop and associated preliminary questioning and observation of each motorist. The Court did not address the legitimacy of the detention of motorists for more extensive field sobriety tests, which it stated "may require satisfaction of an individualized suspicion standard."

The initial suspicionless seizures here, the Court determined, were reasonable. The Chief Justice stated that "[n]o one can seriously dispute the magnitude of the drunken driving problem or the States' interest in eradicating it." On the other side of the scale, the Court described the intrusion on motorists' security as "slight." Unlike the state courts that equated sobriety checkpoints to roving border patrols, thus requiring reasonable suspicion, the Court analogized the roadblock here to *suspicionless*, fixed interior border checkpoints set up to detect illegal aliens, a procedure previously approved

---

Commissioner of Public Safety, 519 N.W.2d 183 (Minn. 1994) (individualized reasonable suspicion is required); State v. Hunt, 924 A.2d 424 (N.H. 2007) (sobriety checkpoints must be more effective than less intrusive approaches, and its value must outweigh the intrusion) State v. Sims, 808 P.2d 141 (Utah Ct. App. 1991) (the police may not conduct suspicionless highway roadblocks unless and until the state legislature authorizes the practice).

37. 443 U.S. 47 (1979). In *Brown*, police officers in a patrol car observed *B* and *X* in an alley. The officers did not detain *X*, but they stopped *B* and requested identification because he "looked suspicious," and had not been seen in the area before. The question on appeal was "whether [*B*] was validly convicted for refusing to comply with a policeman's demand that he identify himself," pursuant to a state statute making it an offense for a person lawfully stopped to refuse to provide identification to the police on request. The Court held that *B* had not been lawfully seized (thus rendering the criminal statute inapplicable to *B*). Summarizing prior case law, Chief Justice Warren Burger described a three-pronged test for determining whether a brief seizure of a person is reasonable: "Consideration of the constitutionality of such seizures involves a weighing of [1] the gravity of the public concerns served by the seizure, [2] the degree to which the seizure advances the public interest, and [3] the severity of the interference with individual liberty." The Court stated that seizure of a person must be based on reasonable suspicion or "be carried out pursuant to a plan embodying explicit, neutral limitations on the conduct of individual officers."

38. The three-pronged test is set out in *id*.

by the Supreme Court in *United States v. Martinez-Fuerte*.[39] The *Sitz* Court saw "virtually no difference between the levels of intrusion on law-abiding motorists from the brief stops necessary to the effectuation of these two types of checkpoints. . . ."

Perhaps the most significant aspect of *Sitz* is that the majority discounted the state court's finding that the checkpoint here was an ineffective way to combat drunken driving and, therefore, did not satisfy the requirement in *Brown* that courts weigh "the degree to which the seizure advances the public interest." The Chief Justice stated, in critical language, that the *Brown* test "was not meant to transfer from politically accountable officials to the courts the decision as to which among reasonable alternative law enforcement techniques should be employed to deal with a serious public danger."

But didn't *Delaware v. Prouse* weigh the degree to which the seizure in *that* case advanced the public interest?[40] It did, but *Sitz* distinguished *Prouse* on the ground that the latter case involved a "complete absence of empirical data," whereas the state here provided data and expert testimony[41] regarding the effect of the checkpoints. This evidence satisfied the Court that a sobriety roadblock is "*among* reasonable alternative law enforcement techniques" that may be employed to combat drunken driving. Having overcome that hurdle, courts are required by *Sitz* to leave the matter of *comparative* efficacy to "politically accountable officials."

In dissent, Justice Stevens, joined by Justices Brennan and Marshall, asserted:

> The Court overvalues the law enforcement interest in using sobriety checkpoints, undervalues the citizen's interest in freedom from random, unannounced investigatory seizures, and mistakenly assumes that there is "virtually no difference" between a routine stop at a permanent, fixed checkpoint and a surprise stop at a sobriety checkpoint.

Justice Stevens stated that the element of surprise—and, thus, the subjective intrusion on the security of motorists—is the "most obvious distinction" between a sobriety roadblock and the suspicionless interior-border stops approved in *Martinez-Fuerte*. In the latter case, the checkpoint site was known to all drivers because of its permanent nature, whereas the procedures implemented in *Sitz* called for roving checkpoints. Furthermore, in *Martinez-Fuerte*, many of the stops occurred during the daytime; in contrast, sobriety checkpoints are usually set up at night, when fear is more easily generated.

The dissent also criticized the majority's treatment of the societal interest factor. Justice Stevens accused the majority of "tampering with the scales of justice" by "plac[ing] a heavy thumb on the law enforcement interest by looking only at gross receipts instead of net benefits." He stated that "there is absolutely no evidence" that the arrest rate for intoxication at the checkpoint "represents an increase over the number of arrests that would have been made by using the same law enforcement resources in conventional patrols."

---

39. 428 U.S. 543 (1976). *See* § 18.03[B][3], *supra*.

40. See § 18.04[A], *supra*.

41. An expert testified that checkpoints in other states had resulted in approximately a 1% arrest rate among persons stopped.

[2] Anti-Drug, Anti-Crime, Anti-Terrorism (and Still Other) Checkpoints

The police sometimes set up checkpoints or roadblocks for reasons other than to look for intoxicated drivers. For example, they have set up checkpoints for general criminal law investigations, such as to look for drugs in automobiles. On occasion, they create a roadblock to try to prevent the escape of a kidnapper and his victim, or a sniper from the scene of his crime. One can also foresee a checkpoint based on very specific or highly general information regarding a feared terrorist attack. All of these examples involve seizures of the vehicles and their passengers caught up in the process; and the police will almost certainly lack individualized suspicion as to any particular car occupant at the roadblock. Does the Supreme Court's approval of the sobriety checkpoint in *Michigan Department of State Police v. Sitz,*[42] discussed in the last subsection, mean that all of these checkpoints are constitutional?

The Court is struggling with this issue. To begin to understand the Court's approach(es) to the question, one must keep in mind an important point of this chapter, which is that the Supreme Court has sought to draw a Fourth Amendment distinction between searches and seizures conducted in criminal investigations and ones that are performed for non-criminal law purposes. This line, however, is hard to draw, as the *Sitz* sobriety-checkpoint case demonstrates: Although the purpose of such checkpoints is to enhance roadway safety, police officers are the agents for promoting that safety, *and they do so by stopping and arresting intoxicated drivers.* So, sobriety checkpoints also have a criminal law enforcement aspect to them.

The result in *Sitz* may have emboldened some police departments to see how far they could go with checkpoints. As it turns out, the "criminal investigation"/"non-criminal law purpose" distinction (and the difficulty in drawing it) came to the forefront in *City of Indianapolis v. Edmond,*[43] where the Court considered the constitutionality of a narcotics interdiction checkpoint. The City of Indianapolis conducted six roadblocks during a four-month period in order to discover illegal drugs. Pursuant to a written plan, more than 1,000 vehicles were stopped on the highway, mostly in the daytime, for two to three minutes each. Each driver was informed that he was being stopped at a drug checkpoint and was asked to produce a license and registration. A police officer also looked for signs of intoxication. Meanwhile, a narcotics-detection dog walked around the outside of each vehicle and conducted a "non-search" sniff for contraband. The "hit rate" of the program—arrests for drug and non-drug related offenses—was nine percent, of which more than half were for drug-related crimes.

Despite the success of the checkpoint and the vital societal interest in combating drug use, the Supreme Court ruled, 6–3, that the drug interdiction checkpoint violated the Fourth Amendment. It drew a line, on the one hand, between the border-stop[44] and sobriety-checkpoint cases—cases "designed primarily to serve purposes closely related to the problems of policing the border or the necessity of ensuring roadway safety"—and the case at hand, namely, a roadblock "whose primary purpose was to detect evidence of ordinary criminal wrongdoing." Notice a key word here: "primary."

---

42. 496 U.S. 444 (1990).
43. 531 U.S. 32 (2000).
44. *See* § 18.03, *supra.*

The City sought to bring their action under the border-stop and sobriety-checkpoint umbrella by arguing that the latter "checkpoints . . . had the same ultimate purpose of arresting those suspected of committing crimes." The *Edmond* Court, per Justice Sandra Day O'Connor, would have none of this. In an effort to draw some firmer lines, she wrote:

> If we were to rest the case at this high level of generality, there would be little check on the ability of the authorities to construct roadblocks for almost any conceivable law enforcement purpose. Without drawing the line at roadblocks designed primarily to serve the general interest in crime control, the Fourth Amendment would do little to prevent such intrusions from becoming a routine part of American life.

Although the social harm resulting from drugs is "of the first magnitude," O'Connor explained that the "gravity of the threat alone cannot be dispositive of questions concerning what means law enforcement officers may employ to pursue a given purpose. . . . We are particularly reluctant to recognize exceptions to the general rule of individualized suspicion where governmental authorities primarily pursue their general crime control ends." She stated: "[w]hen law enforcement authorities pursue primarily general crime control purposes at checkpoints . . . , stops can only be justified by some quantum of individualized suspicion." Notice, again: "primarily."

The seeming impact of *Edmond* is this: When the police seek to defend a checkpoint program that authorizes suspicionless seizures of individuals, courts will be required to determine the "primary purpose" of the police plan—is it, for example, to police the border, ensure roadway safety, or is it "just" to conduct non-specific crime control?—because that test seemingly will determine whether individualized suspicion is required.

But didn't the Court suggest in *Whren v. United States*[45] that courts are not supposed to inquire into the motivations of police officers? So, why would a court look into the police department's purpose for a checkpoint? *Edmond* explained that *Whren* stands for the principle that an inquiry into an *officer's* subjective motivations has no place in *probable cause* analysis; in contrast, "programmatic purposes"—not the motivations of the individual officers acting at the scene—"may be relevant to the validity of Fourth Amendment intrusions undertaken pursuant to a general scheme without individualized suspicion."[46]

Notice the difficulty *Edmond* presents: The officers asked to see the licenses and registration materials of motorists, a procedure potentially permitted under *Delaware v. Prouse*,[47] and they checked for intoxication, a procedure approved by the Court in *Sitz*. Therefore, what if the City had *not* identified the process as a "drug interdiction checkpoint," as it did, but had characterized it as a sobriety checkpoint during which the dog incidentally sniffed for drugs as well? Would *that* have been allowed? Post-*Edmond*, the Court has stated that "[i]n looking to the programmatic purpose, we consider all the available evidence in order to determine the relevant primary purpose."[48] Thus, the police cannot simply change the label on a checkpoint to escape the strictures of *Edmond*.

---

45. 517 U.S. 806 (1996). *See* § 8.02[F], *supra*.

46. In *Ashcroft v. Al-Kidd*, 563 U.S. 731, 736 (2011), the Court emphasized that this last element—"the absence of individualized suspicion"—was the critical component that made a subjective inquiry appropriate in the *Edmond* context, "not the absence of probable cause."

47. *See* § 18.04[A], *supra*.

48. Ferguson v. City of Charleston, 532 U.S. 67, 81 (2001).

But, realistically, how does a court distinguish the "primary" purpose of a program from a secondary one?

Assuming one can draw this distinction, *Edmond* expressly left open the issue of "whether the State may establish a checkpoint program with the primary purpose of checking licenses or driver sobriety and a secondary purpose of interdicting narcotics." If the Court eventually answers this question affirmatively, the exceedingly thin — and potentially formalistic — line between "primary" and "secondary" purposes will become critical to Fourth Amendment analysis and the long-term significance of *Edmond*.

In measuring *Edmond*'s broader significance, one should keep in mind that what made the suspicionless checkpoint impermissible was its "*general* crime control purpose." The Court stated in dictum:

> Of course, there are circumstances that may justify a law enforcement checkpoint where the primary purpose would otherwise, but for some emergency, relate to ordinary criminal control. For example, . . . the Fourth Amendment would almost certainly permit an appropriately tailored roadblock set up to thwart an imminent terrorist attack or to catch a dangerous criminal who is likely to flee by way of a particular route. . . . The exigencies created by these scenarios are far removed from the circumstances under which authorities might simply stop cars as a matter of course to see if there just happens to be a felon leaving the jurisdiction.[49]

In these scenarios — involving specific crimes already committed or about to be committed — the Court appears prepared to justify suspicionless seizures. However, if we are to take this dictum seriously, the checkpoints must be "appropriately tailored" and, for future crime, must involve *imminent* danger.

What about a roadblock, however, set up merely to obtain information from drivers about a previous crime, where there is no contemplation of finding the wrongdoer in the roadblock? Do such circumstances fall within *Edmond*'s "general crime control" rule requiring individualized suspicion?

This question was considered in *Illinois v. Lidster*,[50] in which a roadblock was put up to stop motorists and ask them for information regarding a fatal hit-and-run accident that had occurred *a week earlier*, at roughly the same hour and site as the checkpoint. The roadblock resulted in a traffic slow-down, a line of up to 15 cars in each lane, a few-minute delay for each driver, and approximately 10-to-15 seconds of conversation with a police officer.

The Court concluded that *Edmond* and, thus, an individualized suspicion requirement, does *not* apply in these circumstances. Writing for a unanimous Court, Justice Stephen Breyer stated that the *Edmond* Court's use of the language "general interest in crime control" was not intended to refer to cases such as the present one — a roadblock intended to obtain information about an earlier crime — because this context "is one in which, by definition, the concept of individualized suspicion has little role to play. Like certain other forms of police activity, say, crowd control or public safety, an information-seeking stop is not the kind of event that involves suspicion, or lack of suspicion, of the relevant individual." Also, Breyer said, information-seeking stops "are less likely to provoke anxiety or to prove intrusive. The stops are likely brief. The police are not likely to

---

49. *Edmond*, 531 U.S. at 44.
50. 540 U.S. 419 (2004).

ask questions designed to elicit self-incriminating information." He predicted that "an *Edmond*-type rule" requiring individualized suspicion was unneeded "to prevent an unreasonable proliferation of police checkpoints"; practical considerations (limited police resources and predicted community hostility) would adequately inhibit such proliferation.

In view of the *Lidster* Court's determination that an information-seeking roadblock does not *necessarily* require individualized suspicion, the Court applied the *Brown v. Texas* three-pronged test and determined that *this* checkpoint was reasonable: the public concern was "grave"; the roadblock "advanced this grave public concern to a significant degree" because it was set up near the location of the hit-and-run-accident at about the same hour of the day; and "[m]ost importantly, the stops interfered only minimally with liberty of the sort the Fourth Amendment seeks to protect."

§ 18.05 "Special Needs" Searches and Seizures[51]

[A] In General

An increasingly significant exception to the Fourth Amendment principle that searches and seizures are unreasonable if they are not authorized by a warrant and/or supported by probable cause is the so-called "special needs" (or "special governmental needs") doctrine. This exception applies when "special needs, beyond the normal need for law enforcement, make the warrant and[/or] probable-cause requirement[s] impracticable."[52] Although the early cases only dispensed with the warrant and/or probable cause provisions of the Fourth Amendment, more recent cases have authorized suspicionless searches.

Professor William Stuntz has observed that "little or no effort has been made to explain what these 'special needs' are; the term turns out to be no more than a label that indicates when a lax standard will apply."[53] Essentially, when the Court determines that "special needs" exist, it evaluates the governmental activity—the special need—by the general "reasonableness" balancing standard. Nearly always, the government interest "trumps" the requirements of a warrant and/or probable cause or even reasonable suspicion.[54]

Two initial points are worth making here. First, although the Supreme Court has often treated the administrative search, border search, and checkpoint cases separately from the "special need" cases, there is little or no reason for this distinction. Those cases involved specific governmental interests—special needs, if you will—beyond ordinary criminal investigations. Moreover, the process of determining the legitimacy of the governmental action is the same: application of the "reasonableness" balancing standard.

---

51. *See generally* Robert D. Dodson, *Ten Years of Randomized Jurisprudence: Amending the Special Needs Doctrine*, 51 S.C. L. Rev. 258 (2000); Gould & Stern, Note 1, *supra*; Gerald S. Reamey, *When "Special Needs" Meet Probable Cause: Denying the Devil Benefit of Law*, 19 Hastings Const. L.Q. 295 (1992); Stuntz, Note 1, *supra*; Sundby, Notes 1 and 29, *supra*.

52. Griffin v. Wisconsin, 483 U.S. 868, 872 (1987) (quoting New Jersey v. T.L.O., 469 U.S. 325, 351 (1985) (Blackmun, J., concurring in judgment)).

53. Stuntz, Note 1, *supra*, at 554.

54. Reamey, Note 50, *supra*, at 314.

Second, despite the shared justification and standard for these doctrines, the Supreme Court recently stated that the "special needs" exception does *not* apply when "the immediate objective" of the search is "to generate evidence for law enforcement purposes," even if the "ultimate goal" is to promote some value other than general crime control.[55] Most "special needs" cases have involved searches conducted by persons others than police officers, which has made it easier for the Court to conclude that a special need, beyond ordinary criminal law enforcement, justified the special rule. "Extensive entanglement of law enforcement" in the process, however, jeopardizes a "special needs" claim.

[B] Searches of Persons, Personal Property, and Premises

[1] Searches Directed at Public School Students[56]

New Jersey v. T.L.O.[57] gave birth to the "special needs" doctrine, although explicit enunciation of the principle is found in Justice Harry Blackmun's concurring opinion, rather than in Justice Byron White's opinion for the Court. In *T.L.O.*, two female students were caught smoking in a school lavatory, in violation of school rules. The students were brought to the vice principal. When one of them, *T*, denied that she had been smoking, the administrator demanded her purse, opened it, and observed a package of cigarettes. He removed the cigarettes, and in doing so discovered cigarette paper, which is often used to make marijuana cigarettes. Based on that observation, he conducted a full search of *T*'s purse, during which he found other evidence that implicated her in the sale of marijuana. The evidence was handed over to the police and used in a juvenile court proceeding against her.

The Supreme Court rejected the state's initial claim that the Fourth Amendment does not apply to the conduct of school officials,[58] and agreed that public school students retain a legitimate expectation of privacy in the private property they bring to school. Nonetheless, the Court determined that neither the warrant requirement nor the traditional doctrine of probable cause applies to public school searches. The Court disposed of the warrant requirement summarily. It stated that it is "unsuited to the school environment," as it would "unduly interfere with the maintenance of the swift and informal disciplinary procedures needed in the schools."

Regarding probable cause, Justice White observed that "[w]here a careful balancing of governmental and private interests suggests that the public interest is best served by a Fourth Amendment standard of reasonableness that stops short of probable cause, we have not hesitated to adopt such a standard." The Court found that this was such a case,

---

55. Ferguson v. City of Charleston, 532 U.S. 67, 83–84 (2001).

56. *See generally* Michael Pinard, *From the Classroom to the Courtroom: Reassessing Fourth Amendment Standards in Public School Searches Involving Law Enforcement Authorities*, 45 Ariz. L. Rev. 1067 (2003).

57. 469 U.S. 325 (1985).

58. The government's argument was based on the premise that school officials act *in loco parentis*, as mere agents of the parents, and, thus, are private parties whose actions fall outside the scope of the Fourth Amendment. The Court stated that this argument was "in tension with contemporary reality," and inconsistent with its prior rulings that school officials are subject to the commands of the Constitution.

and ruled that public school teachers and administrators may search students without a warrant if two conditions are met: (1) "there are reasonable grounds"—not "probable cause" in the criminal law context—"for suspecting that the search will turn up evidence that the student has violated or is violating either the law or the rules of the school"; and (2) once initiated, the search is "not excessively intrusive in light of the age and sex of the student and the nature of the infraction."

In his concurrence, Justice Blackmun tied the result to earlier cases in which the Court had abandoned the requirements of warrant and probable cause (such as *Terry v. Ohio* and the border-search cases) and argued that using a reasonableness balancing test instead of those requirements is permissible only "in those exceptional circumstances in which *special needs*, beyond the normal need for law enforcement, make the warrant and probable cause requirement impracticable."

Justices Brennan and Marshall dissented. They agreed with the majority that school officials should not be required to obtain warrants to conduct searches. However, as the search in this case was full-scale in nature, they "emphatically" rejected the majority's decision to "cast aside" the probable cause standard. They criticized the majority for "jettison[ing]" the latter standard, "the only standard that finds support in the text of the Fourth Amendment," and replacing it with the "Rohrschach [*sic*]-like 'balancing test.'"

Justice Stevens also dissented. In an opinion that the other two dissenters joined, he contended that a search by a school official should not be permitted at all if it is intended to "reveal evidence of . . . the most trivial school regulation." He complained that under the majority rule, "a search for curlers and sunglasses in order to enforce the school dress code is . . . just as important as a search for evidence of heroin addiction or violent gang activity." He would have limited warrantless public school searches to "uncover evidence that the student is violating the law or engaging in conduct that is seriously disruptive of school order, or the educational process."

The Court applied the *T.L.O.* standards in *Safford Unified School District #1 v. Redding*.[59] Unlike *T.L.O.*, which involved a search of a student's property (her purse), the Court in *Safford* confronted the issue of "whether a 13-year-old student's Fourth Amendment right was violated when she was subjected to a search of her bra and underpants"— what the Court characterized as a "strip search"—"by school officials acting on reasonable suspicion that she had brought forbidden prescription and over-the-counter drugs to school." The student was required to remove her clothes down to her underwear, and then pull out her bra and the elastic band on her underpants for a visual search. The search failed to turn up any pills.

Every member of the Court except Justice Thomas concluded that, on the facts of this case, the search violated the Fourth Amendment. The Court, per Justice Souter, stated that it violated the "rule of reasonableness as stated in *T.L.O.*," because the "the content of the suspicion failed to match the degree of intrusion." The principal who ordered the search knew "beforehand that the pills were prescription-strength ibuprofen and over-the-counter Naproxen, common pain relievers equivalent to two Advil, or one Aleve," and he "must have been aware of the nature and limited threat of the specific drugs he was searching for." As the Court put it, "[i]n sum, what was missing from the suspected facts . . . was any indication of danger to the students from the power of the drugs or

---

59. 557 U.S. 364 (2009).

their quantity, and any reason [specific to this student] to suppose that [she] was carrying pills in her underwear." The Court explicitly sought to emphasize that:

> the *T.L.O.* concern to limit a school search to reasonable scope requires the support of reasonable suspicion of danger or of resort to underwear for hiding evidence of wrongdoing before a search can reasonably make the quantum leap from outer clothes and backpacks to exposure of intimate parts. The meaning of such a search, and the degradation its subject may reasonably feel, place a search that intrusive in a category of its own demanding its own specific suspicions.

[2] Searches Directed at Public Employees

Another step in the development of the "special needs" doctrine came in *O'Connor v. Ortega*,[60] a case involving the reasonableness of a search conducted by a public employer of the office, including the desk and file cabinets, of an employee suspected of employment improprieties. Justice O'Connor, writing for a four-justice plurality, stated that the existence of Fourth Amendment protection for a public employee's business office should be assessed on a case-by-case basis—that some offices might be "so open to fellow employees or the public that no expectation of privacy is reasonable," and, thus, that the Fourth Amendment would not apply at all. But, on the facts here, the employee possessed a reasonable expectation of privacy. Consequently, the *O'Connor* plurality, adopting the "special needs" terminology from the concurring opinion in *T.L.O.*, approved the use of the "reasonableness" balancing test to determine the scope of an employee's Fourth Amendment rights in regard to searches and seizures conducted by a public employer.

The plurality concluded that "the realities of the workplace . . . strongly suggest that a warrant requirement would be unworkable." Regarding probable cause, the plurality was careful to note that it was only considering the issue in regard to "a noninvestigatory work-related intrusion" or "an investigatory search for evidence of suspected work-related employee misfeasance." In such circumstances, as with searches in the public school context, the employer's conduct is "judged by the standard of reasonableness," both at its inception and regarding the scope of the intrusion. For a search to be reasonable at its inception, there must exist "reasonable grounds for suspecting that the search will turn up evidence that the employee is guilty of work-related misconduct, or that the search is necessary for a noninvestigatory work-related purpose such as to retrieve a needed file." As for the scope of the search, the measures taken must be "reasonably related to the objectives of the search and not excessively intrusive in light of . . . the nature of the [misconduct]."

Justice Scalia concurred in the judgment. Except where an office is subject to "unrestricted public access," Scalia would hold that the offices of public employees are always covered by the Fourth Amendment. However, in Scalia's view, "government searches to retrieve work-related materials or to investigate violations of workplace rules—searches of the sort that are regarded as reasonable and normal in the private-employer context," are similarly reasonable and, therefore, do not violate the Fourth Amendment, when conducted in the public-employer context.[61]

---

60. 480 U.S. 709 (1987).

61. In *City of Ontario v. Quon*, 560 U.S. 746 (2010), the Court's most recent decision regarding a search directed at a public employee (here, a search of an employee's text messages), the justices

[3] Searches Directed at Probationers

The "special needs" doctrine reached majority opinion status in *Griffin v. Wisconsin.*[62] In *Griffin*, the Court approved a warrantless, non-exigent search by a probation officer (accompanied by the police) of the home of a probationer. The search, based on information provided by the police to the probation officer, was conducted pursuant to a Wisconsin administrative regulation that authorized such searches if there were "reasonable grounds" to believe that contraband would be discovered on the premises. In a 5–4 opinion, Justice Scalia announced that the warrantless search of the residence in conformity with the regulation was a reasonable response to a special governmental need.

Justice Scalia stated that a warrant requirement "would interfere to an appreciable degree with the probation system, setting up a magistrate rather than the probation officer as the judge of how close a supervision the probationer requires." Similarly, the Court believed that the concept of "probable cause" could properly be replaced (as in earlier "special needs" cases) by the "reasonable grounds" standard.[63]

---

treated *O'Connor* as dispositive without resolving the dispute between the plurality and Justice Scalia, stating that the search in *Quon* was reasonable under both tests.

62. 483 U.S. 868 (1987).

63. Even in the context of an ordinary criminal investigation by police officers—thus, outside the context of the "special needs" exception—the Supreme Court has held that probationers are entitled to fewer Fourth Amendment rights than non-probationers. In *United States v. Knights*, 534 U.S. 112 (2001), probationer *K* signed a probation order in which he agreed to submit himself, his property, and his home to searches at any time, with or without a warrant, and even in the absence of probable cause. Based on this condition, the police conducted a warrantless search of *K*'s apartment based on reasonable suspicion. The Court unanimously upheld the search. It refused to decide whether acceptance of the search condition itself constituted voluntary consent to the search. It concluded that the search here was reasonable without reaching the "consent" issue. The justices determined that *K*'s "status as a probationer subject to a search condition informs both sides of [the reasonableness] balance." From *K*'s perspective, probation is a form of punishment; a court granting probation, therefore, "may impose reasonable conditions that deprive the offender of some freedoms enjoyed by law-abiding citizens." Consequently, the probation condition in this case "significantly diminished [*K*]'s reasonable expectation of privacy." (The Court expressly did not decide whether the probation condition eliminated *all* reasonable expectations of privacy.) On the government's side of the scale, there is a significant societal interest in permitting broader police power: the hope that the probationer will successfully complete probation and be reintegrated into the community; and the concern, "quite justified, that he will be more likely to engage in criminal conduct than an ordinary member of the community." Based on these considerations, the Court ruled that the government did not need more than reasonable suspicion (and it follows, no warrant) to conduct a search of the probationer's home.

In *Samson v. California*, 547 U.S. 843 (2006), the Court went further than *Knights* in the context of a parolee. In order to be released on parole in California, a prisoner must agree to be subject to search by the police "at any time" and "with or without cause." *S* was searched by the police "based solely on [*S*'s] status as a parolee." The officer discovered methamphetamine in *S*'s pocket. Relying heavily on *Knights*, the Supreme Court, per Justice Thomas, upheld the search, holding that "a condition of release can so diminish or eliminate a released prisoner's reasonable expectation of privacy that a suspicionless search by a law enforcement officer" is reasonable under the Fourth Amendment. The Court concluded that "[t]he touchstone of the Fourth Amendment is reasonableness, not individualized suspicion." *Contra, applying the state constitution*, State v. Ochoa, 792 N.W.2d 260 (Iowa 2010) (a police officer, aware that *O* was a parolee, conducted a suspicionless search of *O*'s hotel room; held, that a parolee retains state search-and-seizure protection in a general criminal investigation; however, it reserved the issue of whether *Sampson* might apply in a "special needs" search by a parole officer, conducting ordinary monitoring of a parolee). For one parolee's (and law student's) view of *Samson*, see James M. Binnall, *They Released Me from My Cage . . . But They Still Keep Me Handcuffed: A Parolee's Reaction to Samson v. California*, 4 Ohio St. J. Crim. L. 541 (2007). See also United States v.

[C] Drug and Alcohol Testing

[1] Fourth Amendment Factors in Evaluating Testing

In specified circumstances, the Supreme Court has approved legally mandated drug and alcohol testing (by taking blood, urine, or breath samples) of some workers and of public school students, in the absence of a search warrant and even in the absence of individualized suspicion. Cases authorizing suspicionless testing are considered in subsection [2]; those prohibiting testing are covered in subsection [3].

Although the cases do not fit together perfectly, certain factors tend to support a finding that suspicionless alcohol or drug testing is constitutionally reasonable.

- Regardless of the ultimate goal of the testing, the immediate objective of the testing must *not* be to generate evidence for law enforcement purposes.

- Consistent with the administrative-search cases,[64] testing is more likely to be treated favorably if those being tested are working in a job already pervasively regulated by the government or, in non-employment contexts, have a reduced expectation of privacy.

- In the employment context, there should be a significant relationship between the employee's job responsibilities and the employer's concern about drug or alcohol use. In other circumstances, there should be a significant societal reason for identifying drug users or alcohol abusers.

- The case for testing is strengthened if there is empirical evidence of a substantial need for the random testing program in question. Specifically, random testing is much more likely to be approved if there is evidence that a system based on individualized suspicion is impracticable, and that the testing scheme devised will be reasonably effective in satisfying the governmental need motivating the testing.

- Testing is more likely to be upheld if the regulations authorizing it remove most, if not all, of the discretion of the government agency in determining who will be tested and under what circumstances the testing will occur.

- Scrupulous care must be taken to ensure that the dignity of persons being tested is respected in the specimen-collection process. This is particularly a matter of concern with urine collection.

[2] Approved Testing

[a] Public Employees

In the companion cases of *Skinner v. Railway Labor Executives' Association*[65] and *National Treasury Employees Union v. Von Raab*,[66] the Supreme Court upheld warrantless blood, breath, and urine testing of some public employees, conducted pursuant to administrative regulations, in the absence of individualized suspicion, in order to detect drug or alcohol usage. These cases nicely show how the factors set out immediately above come into play.

Tessier, 814 F.3d 432 (6th Cir. 2016) (police are permitted to search a probationer without any individualized suspicion as long as consenting to these searches was a condition of the probation order.)

64. *See* § 18.02, *supra*.
65. 489 U.S. 602 (1989).
66. 489 U.S. 656 (1989).

In *Skinner*, the Federal Railroad Administration (FRA) adopted regulations requiring railroad companies to conduct blood and urine tests for alcohol and drugs, of certain employees, such as train engineers, following major train accidents, and permitting them to administer breath or urine tests to employees who violate safety rules. The regulations were a response to detailed findings of the FRA, to the effect that drug or alcohol use by railroad employees was a causal factor in a significant number of accidents that had resulted in death or property damage, and that railroad companies were unable to detect on-the-job drug or alcohol use on the basis of visual observation.

In *Von Raab*, the United States Customs Service developed a drug-screening program to conduct urinalysis tests of employees seeking transfer or promotion to positions having a direct involvement in the Service's drug interdiction program or requiring the person to carry a firearm or handle classified materials.

As a beginning point, the Supreme Court ruled in *Skinner* that blood, breath, and urine tests intrude on Fourth Amendment interests. Blood tests, because they involve intrusions beneath the skin, constitute a search; the subsequent chemical testing of the blood to obtain "physiological data" invades an individual's privacy interests still further. In cursory fashion, the Court also held that a breath test "implicates . . . concerns about bodily integrity" similar to blood testing. Urine collection, "which may in some cases involve visual or aural monitoring of the act of urination," is a search. Moreover, a urine test "might also be characterized as a . . . seizure, since it may be viewed as a meaningful interference with the employee's possessory interest in his bodily fluids."

Although the testing constituted Fourth Amendment activity, the Supreme Court held that the tests in these cases fell within the "special needs" exception to the warrant and probable cause requirements of the Fourth Amendment. The *Skinner* Court disposed of the warrant requirement on three grounds. First, a warrant was not needed because the circumstances under which the testing was required or permitted, i.e., after serious train incidents or violations of safety rules, were specifically set out in the regulations authorizing the tests: "Indeed, in light of the standardized nature of the tests and the minimal discretion vested in those charged with administering the program, there [we]re virtually no facts for a neutral magistrate to evaluate."

Second, because evidence of the ingestion of alcohol and drugs is eliminated from the body quickly, imposing a warrant requirement would have "significantly hinder[ed], and in many cases frustrat[ed], the objectives of the testing program." Finally, the Court considered it unreasonable to impose "unwieldy warrant procedures" on the railroad companies, who are unfamiliar with the intricacies of the system.

The Court disposed of the probable cause requirement on the ground that the privacy interests implicated by the testing were minimal. It characterized as "not significant" the bodily intrusion occasioned by blood testing; breath testing was treated as less intrusive still, because it does not involve physical penetration of the skin.

The *Skinner* Court was more troubled by urine testing. It conceded that the excretory function "traditionally [is] shielded by great privacy." Nevertheless, the Court was satisfied that the employees' privacy needs were satisfied in this case, because the regulations did not require the employees to be observed while they urinated, and the urine was collected "in a medical environment" by non-employer personnel. Furthermore, and "more importantly" to the privacy issue, the Court found that the employees' expectations of privacy regarding the testing were "diminished by reason of their participation in an industry that is regulated pervasively to ensure safety."

Weighed against the employees' "minimal" privacy interests in this case was the government's "compelling" interest in random testing. The Court pointed to the conclusions of the FRA that impaired employees generally were able to escape visual detection. Furthermore, the Court concluded that the suspicionless testing in this case was an effective way to deter violations of safety regulations, because the employees were aware that testing would take place "upon the occurrence of a triggering event, the timing of which no employee [could] predict with certainty," e.g., a railroad accident.

The Court applied similar reasoning in *Von Raab* to justify the testing of Customs Service employees. It approved the regulations on various grounds, including the need to reduce the risk of bribe-taking, mishandling of weapons, use of drugs by employees with ready access to contraband, and "unsympathetic" enforcement of the narcotics laws by persons whose mission it would be to interdict narcotics.

Justice Antonin Scalia, who joined the majority in *Skinner*, and Justice Stevens, who concurred in *Skinner*, dissented in *Von Raab*. Justice Scalia stated their reason for dissenting: The majority in *Von Raab* failed to present "real evidence of a real problem that [would] be solved by urine testing of Customs Service employees." As he put it:

> What is absent in the Government's justifications — notably absent, revealingly absent, and as far as I am concerned dispositively absent — is the recitation of *even a single instance* in which any of the speculated horribles [of bribe-taking, poor aim, or unsympathetic law enforcement as the result of drug-usage] actually occurred.

The dissenters warned that "the impairment of individual liberties cannot be the means of making a point; that symbolism, even symbolism for so worthy a cause as the abolition of unlawful drugs, cannot validate an otherwise unreasonable search."

[b] Public School Students

The Supreme Court has authorized random drug testing of public school students in limited circumstances. In *Vernonia School District 47J v. Acton*,[67] the Supreme Court, 6–3, per Justice Scalia, upheld random urinalysis drug testing of students voluntarily participating in the petitioner school district's athletics programs. Pursuant to the policy of the Vernonia School District, all students wishing to play sports were required to sign a form consenting to urinalysis drug testing. Parental consent was also required.

Athletes were tested at the beginning of the season for their sport; and, once each week, 10 percent of the athletes were selected randomly for follow-up testing. An athlete undergoing testing was accompanied by an adult of the same sex into a restroom. Each boy selected would produce a sample at a urinal, while fully clothed, with his back to the monitor, who would stand about 12 to 15 feet behind. The monitor was permitted to watch while the sample was produced, and to listen for "normal sounds of urination." Girls produced their samples in an enclosed bathroom stall, where they could be heard but not observed. If a sample tested positive, a second test was required; if it also proved positive, the student had the option of participating in a six-week assistance program including weekly urinalysis, or suspension from athletics for a specified period.

---

67. 515 U.S. 646 (1995); *contra under the state constitution*, York v. Wahkiakum Sch. Dist. No. 200, 178 P.3d 995 (Wash. 2008) (stating that as Washington has not yet recognized a "special needs" warrant exception, school officials need reasonable and individualized suspicion in order to conduct searches of students, including drug testing of student athletes).

According to the trial court, Vernonia School District administered the testing after it observed a sharp increase in drug use by students, open discussion and glorification of the drug culture, and serious disciplinary problems. The trial court found that student athletes, "admired in their schools and in the community," were the leaders of the drug culture.

The Supreme Court approved the mass testings involved in this case, although they were conducted without warrants or individualized suspicion of wrongdoing. Citing *New Jersey v. T.L.O.*,[68] the majority stated that the warrant and probable cause requirements were impracticable in the public school context. In *T.L.O.*, however, the Court approved a search based on individualized suspicion of wrongdoing, whereas the testing conducted by Vernonia lacked this element. Justice Scalia stated, however, that there is no "irreducible" Fourth Amendment requirement of reasonable suspicion. Ultimately, the Court stated, the "measure of the constitutionality of a governmental search is 'reasonableness.'"

The Court balanced the competing interests. First, it considered the nature of the privacy interest upon which the search intruded: "Central . . . to the present case is the fact that the subjects of the [p]olicy are (1) children, who (2) have been committed to the temporary custody of the State as schoolmaster." As a result, school children have a lesser expectation of privacy than adults possess. Moreover, school athletes have further reduced expectations of privacy, because they must suit up and shower in public locker rooms, and must "voluntarily subject themselves to a degree of regulation even higher than that imposed on students generally," including the requirement of a preseason physical examination and adequate insurance coverage.

Regarding the character of the intrusion, the Court reiterated its comment in *Skinner* that collecting samples for urinalysis intrudes upon "an excretory function traditionally shielded by great privacy." The manner in which the production of the sample is monitored, therefore, is of critical importance. Here, the male students were fully clothed, and observed only from behind; the females had even greater privacy. As such, the conditions were nearly identical to those encountered by students in the restrooms on a regular basis. The Court also considered it significant that the information disclosed by the urine samples was limited: Vernonia only tested for drugs, and not for other medical conditions, such as epilepsy, pregnancy, or diabetes.

Finally, the Court considered the "nature and immediacy of the governmental concern at issue here, and the efficacy of this means for meeting it." The Court described the governmental interest in deterring drug use by schoolchildren as "important—indeed, perhaps compelling," and "at least as important" as the goals furthered by random drug testing in *Skinner* and *Von Raab*. Significantly, the Court was armed with the trial court finding that there was a serious drug problem in Vernonia, resulting in disruptions to the educational process, and requiring disciplinary actions of "epidemic proportions"; moreover, Justice Scalia wrote, "it must not be lost sight of that this program is directed more narrowly to drug use by school athletes, where the risk of immediate physical harm to the drug user or those with whom he is playing his sport is particularly high."

As to the efficacy of the means for addressing the drug problem, the Court stated that it is "self-evident that a drug problem largely fueled by the "role model" effect of athletes' drug use, and of particular danger to athletes, is effectively addressed by making sure that athletes do not use drugs." The Court rejected the claim that a less intrusive means

---

68. 469 U.S. 325 (1985). *See* § 18.05[B][1], *supra*.

existed, namely, drug testing of students suspected of drug use. The Court noted, first, that it has "repeatedly refused to declare that only the 'least intrusive' search practicable can be reasonable under the Fourth Amendment." It also noted difficulties with the alternative approach: parents willing to accept random drug testing might be unwilling "to accept accusatory drug testing . . . , which transforms the process into a badge of shame." Such a system might also result in arbitrary enforcement, and subsequent expensive litigation.

Vernonia School District was an expansion of the "special needs" doctrine by authorizing random suspicionless drug-testing outside the public employment sphere to which some commentators believed the doctrine would be limited. But, the Court did provide a warning, of sorts:

> We caution against the assumption that suspicionless drug testing will readily pass constitutional muster in other contexts. The most significant element in this case is the first we discussed: that the [p]olicy was undertaken in furtherance of the government's responsibilities, under a public school system, as guardian and tutor of children entrusted to its care.

Vernonia School District was not the Court's last public school drug testing case. In *Board of Education v. Earls*,[69] the Supreme Court, in a 5–4 decision, built on *Vernonia School District* and expanded the "special needs" doctrine within the confines of a public school. The policy in *Earls* required *all* middle and high school students who wished to participate in *any* "competitive" extra-curricular activity (e.g., choir, band, academic teams) to submit to drug testing. Furthermore, the documented extent of the drug problem was less: In *Vernonia* the drug problem was of "epidemic proportions," whereas in *Earls* there was simply *some* evidence of drug use in the district's schools. The Court majority concluded, however, that "the need to prevent and deter the substantial harm of childhood drug use provide[d] the necessary immediacy for a school drug testing policy." In combination with the Court's view that the invasion of students' privacy caused by the drug testing was "not significant," the general risk of harm from drug use led the Court majority to conclude that the drug testing policy was reasonable.

Given the absence of some of the justifications for suspicionless testing that were noted in *Vernonia School District* — the group being tested in that case faced an increased risk of sports-related injuries and were "leaders" of a "drug culture" of "epidemic proportions" — *Earls* could signal a willingness of the Court someday to approve suspicionless drug testing of *all* students in public schools. However, Justice Breyer, who provided the crucial fifth vote in *Earls*, noted in his concurrence that the school drug policy did not subject the entire school to testing and that, therefore, a "conscientious objector . . . can refuse testing while paying a price (nonparticipation) that is serious, but less severe than expulsion from school."

[3] Disapproved Testing

If observers — and lawmakers — interpreted the cases discussed in the preceding subsection as providing a green light from the Supreme Court to conduct *any* form of suspicionless drug testing desired, this "understanding" was false. *Skinner, Von Raab,*

---

69. 536 U.S. 822 (2002); *contra under the state constitution*, Theodore v. Delaware Valley School Dist., 836 A.2d 76 (Pa. 2003) (similar policy to *Earls* is invalid, unless the school district provides evidence of an existing drug or alcohol problem, and furnishes an explanation of its basis for believing the policy will address that need).

Vernonia School District, and *Earls* offer only a cautionary yellow light to such testing programs.

Indeed, one caution light illuminated by the dissenters in *Von Raab* has proved significant. As quoted above, they warned that "symbolism, even symbolism for so worthy a cause as the abolition of unlawful drugs, cannot validate an otherwise unreasonable search." In *Chandler v. Miller*,[70] that warning proved prophetic. The Supreme Court in *Chandler* ruled, 8–1, that Georgia's requirement that various candidates for state office pass a drug test did "not fit within the closely guarded category of constitutionally permissible suspicionless searches."

The Georgia statute required candidates for state office to submit to urinalysis drug tests within 30 days prior to qualifying for nomination or election. A candidate could not be placed on the ballot if the tests were positive for specified illegal drugs. Writing for the Court, Justice Ginsburg stated that the Fourth Amendment "shields society" from a urinalysis drug test that "diminishes personal privacy [solely] for a symbol's sake."

The problem with the Georgia testing regime was not its invasiveness. Justice Ginsburg stated that the procedure was "relatively noninvasive"—indeed, it was less so than the process approved in *Vernonia School District*—as the intended candidate could provide the requisite urine specimen in the privacy of his or her private physician's office. Instead, what was missing was proof of a "substantial" special need "sufficiently vital" to override the privacy interest of the candidates. Unlike *Vernonia*, in which evidence of a serious drug problem was proven, "[n]otably lacking in [the State of Georgia's] presentation [was] any indication of a concrete danger demanding departure from the Fourth Amendment's main rule" that individualized suspicion is required. The Court wrote that a "demonstrated problem of drug abuse, while not in all cases necessary to the validity of a testing regime, . . . would shore up an assertion of a special need for a suspicionless general search program." Here, the law was not passed in response to *any* fear or suspicion of drug use by state officials.

This was not the only failing of the testing program. The Court stated that, unlike the testing approved in *Skinner*, *Von Raab*, and *Vernonia*, the scheme here was "not well designed to identify candidates who violate antidrug laws. Nor [was] the scheme a credible means to deter illicit drug users from seeking election to state office." Because the test date was no secret and could be scheduled anytime within 30 days prior to the individual qualifying for a place on the ballot, a drug-taking candidate could "abstain for a pretest period sufficient to avoid detection."

Also, the State of Georgia failed to show why suspicionless testing was necessary. Unlike the circumstances in *Von Raab*, in which it was not feasible to subject employees to day-to-day scrutiny for drugs, "[c]andidates for public office . . . are subject to relentless scrutiny—by their peers, the public, and the press." Consequently, all that was left to the Georgia testing regime was "the image the State seeks to protect." "However well-meant," the Court said, "[t]he Fourth Amendment shields society against that state action."

The Supreme Court also sent a significant limiting message in *Ferguson v. City of Charleston*.[71] In *Ferguson*, the Supreme Court invalidated procedures devised to identify and nonconsensually test any maternity patient suspected of drug use (who, thereby, was jeopardizing the health of her unborn child) who came to the Charleston public hospital

---

70. 520 U.S. 305 (1997).
71. 532 U.S. 67 (2001).

operated by the Medical University of South Carolina. The procedures were formulated by a task force composed of representatives of the hospital, police, and local officials. According to the policy, if the results of a urine test proved incriminating, they were handed over to the police for prosecution of the mother. As the Court explained:

> [The procedures] provided that a patient should be tested for cocaine through a urine drug screen if she met one or more of nine criteria. It also stated that a chain of custody should be followed when obtaining and testing urine samples, presumably to make sure that the results could be used in subsequent criminal proceedings. The policy also provided for education and referral to a substance abuse clinic for patients who tested positive. Most important, it added the threat of law enforcement intervention that "provided the necessary "leverage" to make the policy effective." . . . That threat was, as respondents candidly acknowledge, essential to the program's success in getting women into treatment and keeping them there.

Despite the importance of the ultimate goal, and despite the fact that the program was limited to mothers who fit a medical drug-user profile, six members of the Court[72] ruled the warrantless testing program constitutionally unreasonable. "As an initial matter," the Court noted that "the invasion of privacy in this case [was] far more substantial" than in the earlier "special needs" drug testing cases, because the individuals being tested in the earlier cases knew precisely the purpose of the testing and "there were protections against the dissemination of the results to third parties." Here, the Court stated, the pregnant mothers had "[t]he reasonable expectation of privacy enjoyed by the typical patient undergoing diagnostic tests in a hospital . . . that the results of those tests will not be shared with nonmedical personnel"—such as the police—"without her consent."

But, this was not the most critical fault with the procedure. What distinguished this case from the earlier ones, "lies in the nature of the 'special need' asserted as justification for the warrantless searches." In the prior cases, the special need "advanced as a justification . . . was one divorced from the State's general interest in law enforcement." In such circumstances, the majority wrote, the Court "tolerated suspension of the Fourth Amendment's warrant and probable cause requirement in part because there was no law enforcement purpose behind the searches . . . and there was little, if any, entanglement with law enforcement."

In contrast, here the Court found that the policy's "central and indispensable feature . . . from its inception was the use of law enforcement to coerce patients into substance abuse treatment." Even though the policy's "ultimate purpose" was a beneficent one, "the immediate objective of the [testing] was to generate evidence for law enforcement purposes in order to reach that [beneficent] goal." In such circumstances, the Court announced, the "special needs" exception does not apply and, therefore, a valid search warrant is required.

How did the Court determine the "immediate objective" (or, for that matter, "relevant primary purpose") of the program? It stated that it would consider all the available evidence. Here, "an initial and continuing focus of the policy was on the arrest and prosecution of drug-abusing mothers." The Court was troubled by evidence that the document setting out the policies and procedures devoted attention to chain-of-custody

---

72. Justice Stevens delivered the opinion of the Court for himself and Justices O'Connor, Souter, Ginsburg, and Breyer. It is noteworthy that three of these justices no longer are on the Court. Justice Kennedy, the sixth vote, concurred in the judgment.

matters, to the range of possible criminal charges that could be brought, and to the procedures for notifying the police. Indeed, "Charleston prosecutors and police were extensively involved in the day-to-day administration of the policy."[73] Meanwhile, "[n]owhere . . . [did] the document discuss different courses of medical treatment for either mother or infant, aside from the treatment for the mother's addiction."

The dissenters, per Justice Scalia, sharply criticized the majority's analysis. First, they disputed the implication they drew from the majority opinion, namely, that the "medical rationale [of the testing] was merely a pretext; there was no special need." Justice Scalia pointed to the fact that the testing began "neither at police suggestion nor with police involvement." A few months after the testing began, however, a Medical Center nurse learned that the local prosecutor was arresting cocaine-taking pregnant mothers for child abuse. She informed her superiors, and the hospital's counsel contacted the prosecutor, resulting in the disputed policy. To the dissent, this history demonstrated that the original purpose of the testing was to provide health benefits, and that it would be "incredible" to believe that this was no longer the goal after formulation of the policy. Thus, the dissent reasoned, there was no basis for distinguishing the policy here from a situation in which a physician, in the course of ordinary medical procedures, comes across incriminating information that the physician is required by law to report to the police.

To the dissent, "the addition of a law-enforcement-related purpose to a legitimate medical purpose [should not] destroy [the] applicability of the "special-needs" doctrine." Moreover, the dissent argued, this limitation is inconsistent with *Griffin v. Wisconsin*,[74] in which the Court approved a "special needs" search by a probation officer who conducted the search with the police present, and based on information provided by the police.[75]

---

73. It is this aspect of the case that convinced Justice Kennedy to concur in the judgment. He rejected the majority's distinction between "ultimate goals" and "immediate purposes." However, "[n]one of our special needs precedents has sanctioned the routine inclusion of law enforcement, both in the design of the policy and in using arrests, either threatened or real, to implement the system designed for the special needs objectives."

74. 483 U.S. 868 (1987); *see* § 18.05[B][3], *supra*.

75. In response, the majority quoted language from *Griffin* that "[a]lthough a probation officer is not an impartial magistrate, neither is he the police officer who normally conducts searches against the ordinary citizen." The *Ferguson* Court also indicated that "*Griffin* is properly read as limited by the fact that probationers have a lesser expectation of privacy than the public at large."

Chapter 19

Fourth Amendment: Standing

§ 19.01 The Role of "Standing" in Fourth Amendment Law[1]

[A] In General

The Fourth Amendment guarantees "[t]he right of the people to be secure in their persons, houses, papers, and effects against unreasonable searches and seizures." Very generally speaking, this right is enforced by application of the exclusionary rule, which provides that evidence secured in violation of the Fourth Amendment may not be used in a criminal trial.[2]

It has long been the case, however, that with a few exceptions, a constitutional right may only be raised by one who has "standing" to assert the right. The Fourth Amendment is no exception to this rule. That is, a person who makes a motion to suppress evidence that the government intends to use against her at trial[3] must show that she was "a victim of a search or seizure . . . as distinguished from one who claims prejudice only through the use of evidence gathered as a consequence of a search or seizure directed at someone else."[4]

In short, Fourth Amendment rights are personal. They may not be vicariously asserted.[5] The fact that, for example, X's home was unconstitutionally searched, during which search evidence was seized that incriminates D, does not give D a right to have such evidence excluded at *her* trial — even though the same evidence would be inadmissible against X — unless D can show that *her* Fourth Amendment rights were violated by the search of X's home. In essence, D must show that *her* "person, house, papers, and/or effects" were implicated by the police conduct. This chapter explains under what circumstances a person is considered a "victim" of a search or seizure and, thus, has "standing" to challenge the police conduct.

---

1. *See generally* 6 Wayne R. LaFave, Search and Seizure § 11.3 (4th ed. 2004); Sherry F. Colb, *Standing Room Only: Why Fourth Amendment Exclusion and Standing Can No Longer Logically Co-exist*, 28 Cardozo L. Rev. 1663 (2007); Richard B. Kuhns, *The Concept of Personal Aggrievement in Fourth Amendment Standing Cases*, 65 Iowa L. Rev. 493 (1980); Lloyd L. Weinreb, *Your Place or Mine? Privacy of Presence under the Fourth Amendment*, 1999 Sup. Ct. Rev. 253.

2. *See* Chapter 20, *infra*.

3. A person aggrieved by a Fourth Amendment violation may make a pretrial motion to have the seized property returned to her as well as to exclude the evidence at her trial. *E.g.*, Fed. R. Crim. P. 41(g)-(h).

4. Jones v. United States, 362 U.S. 257, 261 (1960), *overruled on other grounds*, United States v. Salvucci, 448 U.S. 83 (1980).

5. Alderman v. United States, 394 U.S. 165, 174 (1969).

[B] Is "Standing" a Separate Concept?

Conceptually, "standing" is a threshold issue: A person seeking to have evidence excluded at her trial must first demonstrate that she has standing to contest the search and/or seizure. If she does not have standing, the court does not need to evaluate the police conduct—the defendant is, as it were, locked out of court in regard to the merits of the suppression issue. However, the Supreme Court stated in *Rakas v. Illinois:*[6]

> [T]he question necessarily arises whether it serves any useful analytical purpose to consider this principle [that Fourth Amendment rights may not be vicariously asserted] a matter of standing, distinct from the merits of a defendant's Fourth Amendment claim. . . . [T]he type of standing requirement discussed in [prior cases] . . . is more properly subsumed under substantive Fourth Amendment doctrine. . . . The inquiry under either approach is the same. But we think the better analysis forth-rightly focuses on the extent of a particular defendant's rights under the Fourth Amendment, rather than on any theoretically separate, but invariably intertwined concept of standing.

In other words, after *Rakas,* "standing," as such, is no longer the issue that the Supreme Court wants lower courts to resolve.[7] Instead, the Court prefers to ask a single question: Were *D*'s Fourth Amendment rights—as distinguished from someone else's—violated by the police action? As will be seen,[8] this usually means that a court asks, simply, whether the *defendant* had a legitimate expectation of privacy in the area searched by the police.

However, as Justice Harry Blackmun,[9] Professor Wayne LaFave,[10] and some lower courts[11] have pointed out, it is not analytically improper for a court to treat "standing" and the issue of whether a substantive Fourth Amendment violation has occurred, as distinct inquiries. Indeed, it is important to keep in mind that it is conceptually possible for a claimant to have standing to raise a Fourth Amendment challenge, but to lose on the merits, just as it is possible for one *not* to have standing, although a Fourth Amendment violation affecting *another* person has occurred. To lose sight of this distinction can sometimes invite confusion.

Consider the facts in *Minnesota v. Carter.*[12] In *Carter, X* and his two guests, *D1* and *D2*, conducted illegal activities in *X*'s ground-level apartment. A police officer, standing outside the residence, observed the parties' illegal conduct through a gap in the window shades covering *X*'s window. *D1* and *D2* sought to have evidence later seized by the police from their host's apartment suppressed at their trial on the ground that the police surveillance was unconstitutional.

Notice that under traditional "standing" analysis, the first issue in *Carter* would be whether *D1* and *D2* had standing to contest the police "snooping" at *X*'s apartment and then, if they did have standing, the second issue would be whether this "snooping"

---

6. 439 U.S. 128, 138–39 (1978) (footnote omitted).

7. Minnesota v. Carter, 525 U.S. 83, 87 (1998) (criticizing a state court for analyzing the facts of the case "under the rubric of 'standing' doctrine, an analysis which this Court expressly rejected 20 years ago in *Rakas*").

8. *See* § 19.04, *infra.*

9. Rawlings v. Kentucky, 448 U.S. 98, 112 (1980) (concurring opinion).

10. 6 LaFave, Note 1, *supra,* at 131.

11. *E.g.,* State v. Alston, 440 A.2d 1311, 1314 n.2 (N.J. 1981).

12. 525 U.S. 83 (1998).

constituted an unconstitutional warrantless "search" of *X*'s home. However, when these two questions are collapsed into one, as *Rakas* would have courts do, it is easy to confuse the issue of whether a "search" occurred (whether *someone's* reasonable expectation of privacy was violated) with the issue of whether *D1* and *D2*, in particular, were victimized.

Indeed, in *Carter*, three dissenting justices (Ginsburg, Stevens, and Souter) did not seem to notice the conceptual distinction. They defended the proposition that *D1* and *D2*, as invited guests in *X*'s apartment, had standing to challenge the police conduct (according to these justices *X*'s home, in a sense, was as much their home as *X*'s), but they never reached the second question, raised in the petition for certiorari—whether the surveillance violated the Fourth Amendment. Justice Breyer saw this problem. Although he agreed with the dissenters on the first issue ("standing"), he ultimately found no Fourth Amendment violation because, in his view, no "search" occurred. In the pre-*Rakas* world, it would have been clear to Justices Ginsburg, Stevens, and Souter that they had a second issue to resolve; because of the *Rakas* approach, they apparently failed to see it.

So, the lessons are these. First, a defendant must have standing to raise a Fourth Amendment challenge. Second, the previously distinct issues (does the movant have standing?; and if so, what should the result be on the merits of the motion?) have now collapsed into just one question: Were the *movant's* Fourth Amendment rights violated? Finally, unless lawyers are *very* careful, the *Rakas* Court's approach to "standing" can result in incomplete or incorrect analysis, so be careful.

§ 19.02 Rationale of the Standing Requirement

Professor Anthony Amsterdam once noted that there are two competing perspectives on the Fourth Amendment. One view, the "atomistic" perspective, is that the Fourth Amendment is "a collection of protections of atomistic spheres of interest of individual citizens." That is, the Fourth Amendment protects isolated individuals ("atoms"), in the sense that the amendment "safeguard[s] *my* person and *your* house and *her* papers and *his* effects against unreasonable searches and seizures."[13] The second view, the "regulatory" perspective, is that the Fourth Amendment functions "as a regulation of governmental conduct." In other words, the Amendment is intended to safeguard the collective "people"—as in "we, the people"—from governmental overreaching.

As Fourth Amendment jurisprudence has developed, the concept of standing—based as it is on the premise that a person may only raise a Fourth Amendment challenge if she *personally* was a victim of unreasonable police activity—is based on the atomistic philosophy. In contrast, the exclusionary rule is regulatory in nature, in that its purpose (as is developed in Chapter 20) is to deter police misconduct, in order to safeguard society as a whole. Understood this way, the standing requirement and the exclusionary rule act, at least in part, in opposition to each other:[14] Evidence seized in violation of the Fourth

---

13. Anthony G. Amsterdam, *Perspectives on the Fourth Amendment*, 58 Minn. L. Rev. 349, 367 (1974).

14. Colb, Note 1, *supra*, at 166 ("[T]he standing doctrine necessarily entails the demise of the Fourth Amendment exclusionary rule"; and arguing that a coherent approach to Fourth Amendment jurisprudence requires either the abolition of the exclusionary rule or the standing requirement).

Amendment is excluded at trial in order to deter police misconduct; but, the requirement of standing to raise a Fourth Amendment claim often undercuts this deterrence goal, as it limits the number of people ("atoms") who can bring the misconduct to the attention of the courts so that the exclusionary rule can be applied.

In this regard, consider *United States v. Payner*.[15] In *Payner*, Internal Revenue Service (IRS) agents launched an investigation into the financial activities of taxpayers living in the Bahamas. As part of "Operation Trade Winds," the IRS approved a plan in which a private investigator it hired surreptitiously entered a bank official's, *X*'s, apartment, removed his briefcase, and delivered it to an IRS agent who photographed the contents, after which the briefcase was returned to *X*'s apartment. The IRS intended to use the contents of the briefcase against *P*, a target of the IRS investigation. A district court found that the IRS "affirmatively counsel[ed] its agents that the Fourth Amendment standing limitation permits them to purposefully conduct an unconstitutional search and seizure of one individual in order to obtain evidence against third parties." Based on this record, *P* sought to have the evidence from *X*'s briefcase excluded from his (*P*'s) trial, but the standing requirement prevented him from successfully asserting this Fourth Amendment claim.

Payner points up the problem: Government agents purposely flouted Fourth Amendment values by securing evidence against *P* by invading the privacy of *X*, knowing that the target of their investigation would lack standing to object to the misconduct. From a regulatory perspective, this was an ideal case for application of the exclusionary rule. But, the atomistic standing requirement frustrated that effort; indeed, it functioned as an *incentive* to the government to act unlawfully.

As a policy matter, the Fourth Amendment standing requirement makes sense only if it is treated as a purposeful limitation on the effect of the exclusionary rule.[16] As examined in the next chapter, the exclusionary rule is a potentially expensive doctrine. That is, in the law's efforts to deter unreasonable searches and seizures by the police, courts suppress relevant and reliable evidence—the fruits of the police misconduct—at criminal trials. The consequence of this is that guilty people may be convicted less often than they would be if society were willing to use the wrongfully gathered evidence. Essentially, the standing requirement is the Supreme Court's declaration that the cost of the exclusionary rule can become too great to bear.

Even understood this way, the question remains how narrowly or broadly courts should define the concept of a "victim" in the context of the standing requirement, because this term is not self-defining. The Supreme Court has explained that, in determining where the standing line should be drawn, it must consider whether "the additional benefits of extending the exclusionary rule to other defendants [beyond the immediate victim] would justify further encroachment upon the public interest in prosecuting those accused of crime and having them acquitted or convicted on the basis of all the evidence which exposes the truth."[17] In turn, analysis of *this* matter should depend on the resolution of two empirical questions: how expensive *really* is the exclusionary rule?; and to what extent does the standing requirement *actually* undermine the purposes of the exclusionary rule?

---

15. 447 U.S. 727 (1980).
16. Kuhns, Note 1, *supra*, at 509–13.
17. Alderman v. United States, 394 U.S. 165, 175 (1969).

As discussed in the next chapter, the Supreme Court has become increasingly critical of the exclusionary rule. At the same time, it does not believe that a narrow interpretation of the standing requirement appreciably undermines any justifiable goals of the exclusionary rule. Therefore, it is more difficult today to raise a Fourth Amendment claim than it was decades ago, and even harder for a defendant to have evidence unconstitutionally seized excluded at her criminal trial.

§ 19.03 The Law of Standing: Pre-*Rakas v. Illinois*

[A] In General

The law of standing took a significant turn in 1978, when the Supreme Court decided *Rakas v. Illinois*.[18] The implications of *Rakas* are discussed in the next chapter section. However, to appreciate the significance of *Rakas*, it is helpful to understand the law preceding it.

Prior to *Rakas*, the Supreme Court handed down only 12 opinions dealing with the doctrine of standing.[19] However, based on the Court's few opinions and lower court jurisprudence, the following summary of pre-*Rakas* law is possible.

A defendant had standing to raise a Fourth Amendment claim if she: (1) owned or had a possessory interest in the premises searched;[20] (2) was legitimately on the premises at the time of the search;[21] (3) owned the property seized;[22] or (4) had lawful possession of the property seized, such as in the status of a bailee.[23] For awhile, it also appeared to some courts and observers that one could claim standing if she was a co-defendant or co-conspirator of a person who had Fourth Amendment standing. This so-called "derivative standing" doctrine, however, was rejected by the Supreme Court prior to *Rakas*.[24]

---

18. 439 U.S. 128 (1978).
19. Kuhns, Note 1, *supra*, at 514 & n.143.
20. *See* Brown v. United States, 411 U.S. 223, 229 (1973).
21. Jones v. United States, 362 U.S. 257 (1960).
22. *See* United States v. Jeffers, 342 U.S. 48 (1951).
23. 6 LaFave, Note 1, *supra*, at 226.
24. In *McDonald v. United States*, 335 U.S. 451 (1948), the Supreme Court reversed *M*'s conviction because evidence used against him had been seized in violation of the Fourth Amendment rights of *X*, his co-defendant. The Court reasoned that *X* had the right to have his property returned to him prior to trial as the result of the Fourth Amendment violation; therefore, the evidence would not have been in the government's custody to use against *M*. Although *McDonald* did not speak in terms of "standing," many lower courts interpreted the case to mean that a defendant had the right to raise a Fourth Amendment claim if the rights of any co-defendant or co-conspirator were violated. The doctrine of derivative standing, if it ever existed at the Supreme Court level, was overruled *sub silentio* in Wong Sun v. United States, 371 U.S. 471 (1963), when the Court held that evidence unconstitutionally seized from one defendant, James Toy, was admissible against another defendant, Wong Sun, because the unlawful police conduct relating to Toy invaded no Fourth Amendment right of Wong Sun. The Court made the point explicit in *Alderman v. United States*, 394 U.S. 165 (1969), when it stated that "[c]oconspirators and codefendants [are] . . . accorded no special standing." The Court concluded that the potential deterrent benefit of applying the exclusionary rule to co-defendants who did not otherwise have standing was outweighed by the exclusionary rule costs of such an approach.

For approximately two decades, even for two years after *Rakas*, the Supreme Court also recognized a doctrine called "automatic standing," which is considered immediately below.

[B] Automatic Standing[25]

The Supreme Court unanimously held in *Jones v. United States*[26] that a defendant did not have to prove standing to raise a Fourth Amendment claim if possession of the evidence seized was a necessary element of the crime for which the defendant was being prosecuted. For example, in *Jones*, federal agents seized narcotics belonging to *J* in a search of *X*'s apartment. *J* was prosecuted for possession of the narcotics. Under the automatic standing rule announced in the case, *J* was allowed to contest the legality of the search of *X*'s apartment: he did not have to prove that the narcotics belonged to him, which would have been the usual basis for securing standing in such circumstances.

The Court permitted automatic standing for two reasons. First, the Court expressed concern about the dilemma confronting a defendant charged with a crime of possession who wished to contest a search: To prove standing to raise a Fourth Amendment claim she might have to testify in a pretrial hearing that she owned or possessed the seized evidence, the very "facts the proof of which would tend, if indeed not be sufficient to convict" the defendant; and lower courts had held that such incriminating pretrial testimony could be used against the defendant at her trial. The automatic standing rule freed the defendant from that dilemma.

Second, the *Jones* Court believed that a prosecutor should not "have the advantage of contradictory positions," i.e., that *J* possessed the contraband in violation of the law, and yet that he lacked standing to contest the search because he did not have a possessory interest in the seized materials.

The Court abandoned the automatic standing rule in *United States v. Salvucci*.[27] In *Salvucci*, the Court observed that the self-incrimination dilemma described in *Jones* was eliminated by the Court in *Simmons v. United States*.[28] In *Simmons*, the Court held that the testimony of a defendant in support of a Fourth Amendment motion to suppress evidence may not be used against her at trial, over her objection, on the issue of guilt.[29]

Salvucci disposed of the remaining justification for the automatic standing rule—that prosecutors should not be permitted the advantage of contradictory claims—by stating that post-*Jones* "standing" decisions, in particular the Court's watershed opinion in *Rakas v. Illinois*,[30] demonstrate that there is nothing inherently self-contradictory about a prosecutor charging a defendant with possession of contraband and simultaneously maintaining that the defendant was not the victim of an unconstitutional search. This

---

25. 6 LaFave, Note 1, *supra*, at 11.3(g).

26. 362 U.S. 257 (1960), *overruled in* United States v. Salvucci, 448 U.S. 83 (1980).

27. 448 U.S. 83 (1980); *contra, under the state constitution*, Commonwealth v. Amendola, 550 N.E.2d 121 (Mass. 1990); State v. Sidebotham, 474 A.2d 1377 (N.H. 1984); State v. Wright, 596 A.2d 925 (Vt. 1991); State v. Simpson, 622 P.2d 1199 (Wash. 1980) (all retaining the automatic standing rule).

28. 390 U.S. 377 (1968).

29. *Salvucci* expressly reserved the question of whether the *Simmons* rule prevents the prosecutor from using the defendant's testimony at the suppression hearing to *impeach* her trial testimony.

30. 439 U.S. 128 (1978).

conclusion stems from the fact that, as discussed immediately below, standing to contest a search now requires proof that the person asserting the claim had a reasonable expectation of privacy in the area that was searched. It is possible, therefore, for a person to possess contraband and yet lack standing to object to the search that turned it up, if the contraband was seized from a place in which the defendant lacked a legitimate privacy expectation, such as another person's residence or vehicle.

§ 19.04 Standing to Contest a Search: *Rakas v. Illinois*

[A] The New Approach

Rakas v. Illinois[31] is the leading Supreme Court case in modern "standing" jurisprudence. It brought a new language and a different approach to the doctrine.

In *Rakas*, police officers stopped an automobile that purportedly met the description of the car used in a robbery that had transpired moments earlier. The four occupants, including its owner who had been driving, were ordered out of the car, after which the police searched the passenger compartment. Rifle shells were found in the locked glove compartment, and a sawed-off rifle was found under the front passenger seat.

R,[32] a passenger, moved to suppress the rifle and the shells found in the car, apparently on the ground that the police lacked adequate cause for the search. As the Court pointed out various times, *R* did not base his claim for standing on the ground that he had an ownership interest in the vehicle or in the property seized, which were grounds for standing prior to *Rakas*.[33] Instead, the key[34] standing claim was that *R* was "legitimately on the premises" at the time of the search, another basis for standing authorized by the Court in *Jones v. United States*.[35]

---

31. 439 U.S. 128 (1978); *contra, under the state constitution*, State v. Wood, 536 A.2d 902 (Vt. 1987) (to establish standing, a defendant need only assert a possessory, proprietary, or participatory interest in the item seized or the area to be searched).

32. Actually, there were two petitioners in the *Rakas* appeal. For purposes of clarity, they are subsumed under "*R*."

33. *See* § 19.03, *supra*.

34. *R* also claimed standing on the ground that he was the target of the search. Language in a few earlier cases hinted at the possibility of "target standing." *E.g.*, United States v. Jeffers, 342 U.S. 48, 52 (1951) (observing that the search and seizure in that case were "bound together by one sole purpose—to locate and seize the narcotics of [defendant]"); Jones v. United States, 362 U.S. 257, 261 (1960) (describing a person with standing as one who is "a victim of a search or seizure, *one against whom the search was directed*") (emphasis added). The Supreme Court rejected this basis of standing. (The dissenters in *Rakas* stated that "[f]or the most part," they agreed with the majority's rejection of target standing. 439 U.S. at 157 n.1.) The *Rakas* Court concluded that target standing is not required to obtain the beneficial deterrent effect of the exclusionary rule. According to Justice Rehnquist, the police will be deterred from improperly intruding on a non-target's privacy because *she* will have ample motivation to raise her own Fourth Amendment claim; and, where the non-target is *not* charged with a crime, the police will be deterred because she may recover damages in a civil action for violation of her privacy.

35. 362 U.S. 257 (1960).

By a 5–4 vote, the Court, per Justice Rehnquist, held that *R*'s motion to suppress the evidence on the basis of his status as a legitimate passenger in the car was properly denied by the trial court. In so holding, the Court announced a new way to look at the issue of standing. According to the majority, the question of standing should not be considered "distinct from the merits of a defendant's Fourth Amendment claim."[36] That is, beginning with this case, the issue of standing to contest a search collapses into the basic "*Katz*-ian"[37] matter of whether the defendant had a reasonable or legitimate expectation of privacy in the area searched. According to *Rakas*, the new test for standing to contest a search — or what the Court described as the "capacity to claim the protection of the Fourth Amendment" — is "whether the person who claims the protection of the Amendment has a legitimate expectation of privacy in the invaded place." The Court minimized the significance of this restatement of standing law. It stated that "[w]e can think of no decided cases of this Court that would have come out differently had we concluded, as we do now, that the . . . standing requirement . . . is more properly subsumed under substantive Fourth Amendment doctrine."

Justice Rehnquist explained that although the holding in *Jones* was correct,[38] the phrase used in that case — "legitimately on premises" — "creates too broad a gauge for measurement of Fourth Amendment rights." According to the *Jones* standard, the *Rakas* Court reasoned, a casual visitor to another person's home would have standing to contest a search of the basement that the visitor had never seen or been permitted to enter. Similarly "a casual visitor who walks into a house one minute before a search of the house commences and leaves one minute after the search ends would be able to contest the legality of the search." To the *Rakas* Court, neither outcome was sensible, as the first visitor had no legitimate expectation of privacy in the basement, and the second visitor had no expectation of privacy in the home at all.[39] Rehnquist pointed out, however, that "[t]his is not to say that such visitors could not contest the lawfulness of the seizure of evidence or the search if their own property were seized. . . ."[40]

On the facts of *Rakas*, the majority concluded that *R* failed to prove that he had any legitimate expectation of privacy in the areas searched, namely, in the locked glove compartment and the area under the front passenger seat. According to the Court, "[l]ike the trunk of an automobile, these are areas in which a passenger *qua* passenger simply

---

36. For further discussion of this point, *see* § 19.01[B], *supra*.

37. Katz v. United States, 389 U.S. 347 (1967).

38. The facts of *Jones* are considered in § 19.04[B][1][a], *infra*.

39. Rehnquist's first example seems correct to this extent: if *X* invites *G*, a guest, into her home, and gives *G* access only to one part of the home, *G* has no reason to object to a search of an entirely different part of the house. As a guest in the kitchen, *G* does not have a reasonable expectation of privacy if the area searched is the basement. But what if the police have to enter the kitchen, where *G* is sitting with *X*, in order to get to the basement to conduct the unlawful search? If *entry of the house* — as distinguished from the specific basement search — is also at issue, it is submitted that *G* *should* have standing to contest *that* aspect of the police conduct. In regard to Justice Rehnquist's second hypothetical, why shouldn't *G*, a casual visitor to *X*'s home, albeit present there for just a few minutes, have a legitimate expectation of privacy if the police break into the house in violation of the Fourth Amendment during precisely those few minutes *G* is present? If *G* is there permissively, it is submitted that her expectations of privacy should begin as soon as she enters the sanctuary of *X*'s "castle," and *G*'s expectations that the police won't break in are no less legitimate because it is a short visit.

40. The implication of this quote is that a person *could* claim standing on the basis of ownership of the property seized, a pre-*Rakas* basis for standing. *But see* § 19.04[B][4], *infra*.

would not normally have a legitimate expectation of privacy." Therefore, *R* could not successfully claim the protections of the Fourth Amendment.

Justice White, with whom Justices Brennan, Marshall, and Stevens joined, dissented. He warned that the Court had "declare[d] an 'open season' on automobiles." He interpreted the case to stand for the proposition that "a legitimate occupant of an automobile may not invoke the exclusionary rule and challenge a search of that vehicle unless he happens to own or have a possessory interest in it." The dissent argued that the holding in *Rakas* would undercut the purpose of the exclusionary rule, as it would serve as an invitation to the police to search any automobile containing more than one person, on the ground that any evidence unlawfully found in it would probably be admissible against at least one of the occupants.

The dissent objected to the Court's approach on two other grounds. First, it criticized the majority for rejecting *Jones*'s legitimately-on-the-premises rule, which was relatively easy to apply by police and courts, and substituting for it a non-bright-line test ("legitimate expectation of privacy in the invaded place"), which it predicted would present greater difficulties of application.[41]

Second, the dissent accused the Court of returning to pre-*Katz* property rights distinctions, even as it denied that it was doing so. As the dissent viewed the facts in *Rakas*, *R* was in a private place (an automobile) with the permission of the owner of that place, yet this did not entitle him under the majority's analysis to a legitimate expectation of privacy. "But," the dissent asked rhetorically, "if that is not sufficient, what would be?" Its answer was that "it is hard to imagine anything short of a property interest [in the car] that would satisfy the majority."

As a matter of privacy rights, Justice White believed that the majority's holding was not only contrary to precedent, "but also to the everyday expectations of privacy that we all share." He suggested that if the owner of the car in *Rakas* had invited *R* to be a passenger and had said, "I give you a temporary possessory interest in my vehicle so that you will share the right of privacy that the Supreme Court says that I own," then the majority "apparently" would have reached a different conclusion. "But," he said, "people seldom say such things, though they may mean their invitation to encompass them if only they had thought of the problem."

In view of the dissent's claims regarding the meaning of *Rakas*, and the majority's observation that "[i]t is not without significance that these statements of today's "holding" come from the dissenting opinion, and not from the Court's opinion,"[42] a closer look at the impact of *Rakas* is in order.

[B] The Impact of *Rakas*: A Closer Look

Nothing in *Rakas* suggests any change in the previous rule that a person with a possessory interest in premises searched by the police has standing to contest the search of

---

41. The majority replied that the *Jones* rule had only "superficial clarity" and concealed "underneath that thin veneer all of the problems of line drawing which must be faced in any conscientious effort to apply the Fourth Amendment."

42. *Rakas*, 439 U.S. at 149 n.17.

her own residence, even if she is absent at the time of the intrusion.[43] The analysis that follows considers more difficult issues.

[1] Search of Another Person's Residence

[a] When the Owner or Lessor is Absent

After *Rakas*, a person may not challenge a search of *another person*'s residence merely on the ground that he was "legitimately on the premises" at the time of the intrusion. Although this was a satisfactory basis in *Jones v. United States*,[44] it is now necessary to determine whether the guest had a reasonable expectation of privacy in the premises searched.

A non-resident defendant may have standing to contest a search if she was the sole occupant of the premises with the permission of the resident, and has some significant connections to the premises. For example, the defendant in *Jones* was alone in his friend's apartment when the search occurred. He had a key to the premises, which he used to admit himself to the apartment, had clothing in the closet, had slept there "maybe a night," and had "complete dominion and control" (*Rakas*'s words) over the apartment, except *vis a vis* the absent host. As *Rakas* analyzed *Jones*, the latter case stood "for the unremarkable proposition that a person can have a legally sufficient interest in a place other than his own home so that the Fourth Amendment protects him from unreasonable governmental intrusion into that place."

[b] When the Owner or Lessor is Present

As it turns out, a person may sometimes successfully challenge a search of another person's residence, *even when the resident is present*. This is evident from *Minnesota v. Olson*.[45] In *Olson*, the Supreme Court held, 7–2, that O, an overnight guest in his girlfriend's home, could challenge the police entry of the premises, notwithstanding the fact that O was never alone in the home, did not have a key, and lacked dominion and control over the premises.

Speaking for the Court, Justice Byron White (the author of the *Rakas* dissent) stated that "[w]e do not understand *Rakas* . . . to hold that an overnight guest can never have a legitimate expectation of privacy except when his host is away and he has a key. . . ." Instead, any overnight guest, even one who lacks "untrammeled power to admit and exclude" others because the host is present, can challenge a search of his host's home. According to Justice White, this holding "merely recognizes the everyday expectations of privacy that we all share." If a guest were required to have complete dominion and control in order to have standing, he pointed out, "an adult daughter living temporarily in the home of her parents would have no legitimate expectation of privacy because her right to admit or exclude would be subject to her parents' veto."

If an overnight guest may challenge a search, will a lesser connection to the premises suffice? The Supreme Court has provided insight into this question. In *Minnesota v. Carter*,[46] X, the lessee of a ground-level apartment, and *D1* and *D2*, his guests, sat bagging

---

43. 6 LaFave, Note 1, *supra*, at 131–32.
44. 362 U.S. 257 (1960).
45. 495 U.S. 91 (1990).
46. 525 U.S. 83 (1998); *contra applying the state constitution*, State v. Cuntapay, 85 P.3d 634 (Hawaii 2004) (short-term guests have a reasonable privacy expectation in their hosts' homes).

cocaine in *X*'s apartment. These activities were observed by a police officer who looked through a gap in a drawn window blind. *D1* and *D2* were out-of-town visitors who, as explained by the Court, "had come to the apartment for the sole purpose of packaging the cocaine. [They] had never been to the apartment before and were only in the apartment for approximately 2½ hours."

The Court held, 5–4, that the Fourth Amendment rights of *D1* and *D2* were *not* violated by the officer's surveillance of their activities. Whereas an overnight guest may claim the protections of the Fourth Amendment (*Olson*), "one who is merely present with the consent of the householder may not" (*Carter*). Chief Justice Rehnquist, writing for the majority, explained:

> If we regard the overnight guest in *Minnesota v. Olson* as typifying those who may claim the protection of the Fourth Amendment in the home of another, and one merely "legitimately on the premises" as typifying those who may not do so, the present case is obviously somewhere in between.

The Court then focused on three factors that, in its view, placed this case on the no-right-to-challenge side of the line:

> [T]he purely commercial nature of the transaction engaged in here, the relatively short period of time on the premises, and the lack of any previous connections between [*D1* and *D2*] and [*X*], all lead us to conclude that [their] situation is closer to that of one simply permitted on the premises.

This language, however, does not mean that only an overnight guest may challenge a search in another person's home. Although this *is* the view of Justices Scalia and Thomas—they joined the Rehnquist opinion but also separately concurred[47]—the separate opinions of Justice Kennedy (who, like Scalia and Thomas, joined the majority opinion), Justice Breyer (who concurred only in the judgment), and the three dissenters (Justices Ginsburg, Stevens, and Souter) suggest a broader standing rule, at least if Justices Sotomayor and Kagan, who have replaced Justices Souter and Stevens, agree with the dissent's position.

It may be worthwhile, first, to look at the dissent. The three dissenters, per Justice Ginsburg, would have announced a much broader "standing" rule than the majority: "[W]hen a homeowner or lessor personally invites a guest into her home to share in a common endeavor, whether it be for conversation, to engage in leisure activities, or for business purposes licit or illicit, that guest should share his host's shelter against unreasonable searches and seizures."[48] Their position in this regard was joined by Justice Breyer who, while concurring in the judgment against the defendants, stated that he agreed with

---

47. According to Justices Scalia and Thomas, the text of the Fourth Amendment, "which protects people in 'their' persons, houses, papers, and effects," and common law precedent support the view that the Fourth Amendment does not protect a person in *another*'s home. What about *Olson*? "We went to the absolute limit of what text and tradition permit . . . , when we protected a mere overnight guest against an unreasonable search of his hosts' apartment." In *Olson*, however, unlike in the present case, "it is plausible to regard a person's overnight lodging as at least his 'temporary' residence. . . ."

48. Justice Ginsburg observed, "[o]ur decisions indicate that people have a reasonable expectation of privacy in their homes in part because they have the prerogative to exclude others. The power to exclude implies the power to include. Our Fourth Amendment decisions should reflect these complementary prerogatives."

the dissent that *D1* and *D2* "can claim the Fourth Amendment protection."[49] Thus, there were four votes for the Ginsburg rule.

That brings us to Justice Kennedy, the swing vote. He explained that he joined the majority opinion because he believed that "its reasoning is consistent with my view that almost all social guests have a legitimate expectation of privacy, and hence protection against unreasonable searches, in their host's home." Why, then, did he join the opinion, since *D1* and *D2* were in *X*'s residence with the latter's consent? According to Kennedy:

> In this case, [*D1* and *D2*] have established nothing more than a fleeting and insubstantial connection with [*X*'s] home. For all that appears in the record, [they] used [*X*'s] house simply as a convenient processing station. . . . There is no suggestion that [*D1* and *D2*] engaged in confidential communications with [*X*] about their transaction. [They] had not been to [*X*'s] apartment before, and they left it even before their arrest.

Kennedy concluded that the defendants' Fourth Amendment rights were not violated because they had "established no meaningful tie or connection to the owner, the owner's home, or the owner's expectation of privacy."

Thus, it appears that Justice Kennedy would have ruled for the defendants if one, or certainly more, of the following factors were present: (1) they had been in the residence for non-commercial reasons; (2) they had spoken confidentially to *X* regarding their commercial (and illegal) activities; and/or (3) they had previous or more substantial current connections to the premises. Thus, his ruling against the defendants was narrow. When coupled with the dissenters' and Justice Breyer's position, there is reason to believe that on occasion a social, or even business, guest will be permitted to challenge a search in the host's residence, even if the guest does not stay overnight.

[2] Search of One's Own Automobile When Absent

A person retains a legitimate expectation of privacy in her own home even when she is temporarily absent from it. Does the same rule apply to the owner of an automobile who is not present when her vehicle is searched? Lower court case law is split. Most courts have held that when a car owner lends her vehicle to another, at least if the bailment is of short duration, the owner maintains a legitimate expectation of privacy in it and, therefore, can challenge a search of the car that takes place in her absence.[50]

A few courts have held that possession, and not ownership, of the car is the key; therefore, a nonpresent owner of an automobile lacks standing to contest the search of her vehicle.[51] More often, however, if a court is going to rule against the car owner, it is because she gave another person complete control of the car and its contents for an

---

49. Justice Breyer concurred, rather than dissenting, because he went on to conclude that, although *D1* and *D2* could claim the Fourth Amendment's protections, in his view the officer's observations (made from a public area outside the curtilage of the home) did not violate the Fourth Amendment. In short, *D1* and *D2* had standing, but lost on the merits.

50. *E.g.*, United States v. Dotson, 817 F.2d 1127, *modified*, 821 F.2d 1034 (5th Cir. 1987) (*D* had standing after he loaned his car to a friend for a brief time to get the car washed); State v. Bartlett, 999 P.2d 274 (Kan. 2000) (*B* loaned the car to another to take it to fill a water container).

51. *E.g.*, United States v. Dall, 608 F.2d 910, 915 (1st Cir. 1979).

extended period, especially if the vehicle will be driven a considerable distance away from the owner.[52]

[3] Search of Another Person's Automobile

The general rule after *Rakas* is easy to state, but difficult to apply: A person has standing to contest a search of an automobile in which she is an occupant, although she is not its owner, if she has a reasonable expectation of privacy in the area of the automobile searched. Despite the concerns of Justice White in the dissent in *Rakas* (that the majority "declare[d] 'open season' on automobiles"), a non-owner occupant *may* have standing in limited circumstances.

[a] When the Owner Is Absent

The most likely case for standing of an occupant of someone else's car is when the owner of the car is absent, and the person challenging the search has a possessory interest in the vehicle comparable to that of the occupant of the premises in *Jones*. For example, if car owner *X* lends her car to *D* for a week, *D* should be able to challenge a search of the vehicle if it is stopped while she is driving it in *X*'s absence. At the time of the search, *D* has exclusive dominion and control over the car and, thus, would have a legitimate expectation of privacy in it.

Under some circumstances, a non-owner might only have a legitimate expectation of privacy in certain portions of the vehicle. Standing is not necessarily an all-or-nothing proposition. It should be remembered that *Rakas* only suggested that *R* lacked a reasonable expectation of privacy *in the particular areas of the car searched*. Similarly, regarding the right of a guest in a house to contest a search, the Court distinguished between a search of the kitchen, where a hypothetical guest was invited to be, and the basement, to which the guest was not invited. Suppose, therefore, car owner *X* has two keys to the vehicle: an ignition key that also unlocks the doors to the automobile and the trunk, and a separate key to the glove compartment. If *X* loans the car to *D*, but does not furnish the latter key, it is likely that *D*—if she has no other access to the glove compartment— would not have standing to contest a search of it, although she could challenge a search of the remainder of the vehicle.

[b] When the Owner Is Present

May a "mere"[53] passenger in a vehicle containing the owner of the car have a reasonable expectation of privacy in the automobile (or, at least, in portions of it)? Before answering this question, it is important to clarify the issue at hand. The question is whether an occupant may challenge a *search* of the car in which the owner is present. A separate question arises if the occupant wishes to challenge the *forcible stop*—the initial *seizure* of the vehicle and herself—preceding the search. This latter question is considered in Section 19.05. Also, please note that we are concerned here with a search of the vehicle, and not a search of the occupant *herself*. Even if one lacks an expectation of privacy in

---

52. *E.g.*, State v. Abramoff, 338 N.W.2d 502 (Wis. 1983) (*A* permitted others to drive his car for a trip between Florida and Wisconsin).

53. Of course, a special relationship between the passenger and the car owner, such as by marriage, falls outside the "mere" passenger situation. In such circumstances, the spouse-passenger has standing to object, as lower courts have consistently held. 6 LaFave, Note 1, *supra*, at 214.

another person's home or car, she retains a legitimate expectation of privacy regarding her own person, even as she sits in another person's home or automobile.

What, then, about a *search* of an automobile driven by the owner, in which *D* is a mere passenger? May *D ever* have standing to challenge such a search? Some courts have answered this question negatively.[54] But is this result appropriate? For example, suppose that, in a week-long cross-country drive, *X*, the owner of a vehicle, gives *D* a car key, with the explicit understanding that *D* may place her belongings in the trunk any time she wishes. Does *X*'s presence in the car preclude a finding that *D* has a protectible privacy interest in the trunk?

Although the matter is disputable, *D* should have standing. Indeed, in view of the Court's holding in *Minnesota v. Olson*,[55] namely, that an overnight guest in a home may have a reasonable expectation of privacy in that dwelling even if the host is present at all times, it should be possible for *D* to challenge a search of at least some portions of a car in which she is a week-long guest. As the Court said in *Olson*, "hosts will more likely than not respect the privacy interests of their guests, who are entitled to a legitimate expectation of privacy despite the fact they have no legal interest in the premises and do not have the legal authority to determine who may or may not enter."

On the other hand, *Rakas* expressly left open the issue of "whether the same expectations of privacy are warranted in a car as would be justified in a dwelling house in analogous circumstances."[56] In view of the long line of cases that provide that we possess a lesser expectation of privacy in our automobile than in our home, it is conceivable that the reasoning of *Olson* will not transfer to an automobile.

[4] Contesting a Search Resulting in the Seizure of One's Own Property

The preceding discussion focused the question of whether a defendant may challenge a search of another person's residence or car in which the defendant was an occupant. But suppose that we add an additional factor: the property seized in the search belongs to the defendant. Assuming that the defendant does not otherwise have standing, may she now challenge the search because it resulted in the seizure of her own property?[57] Prior to *Rakas*, the answer was clear: A person had standing to contest a search if she claimed an ownership or possessory interest in the property seized during the search.[58]

Rakas did not expressly overrule this principle. Indeed, a fair reading of *Rakas* is that the Court left the old law undisturbed in this regard. The *Rakas* Court various times stated that *R*, a passenger in the car, had not claimed that either the rifle or ammunition seized in the search were his, the implication of this being that had either been his property, *R* would have had standing to object to the search. The Court also implied in *Rakas* that a casual visitor to a house, even one who lacks a reasonable expectation of privacy

---

54. *Id.* at 172.

55. 495 U.S. 91 (1990); *see also* Minnesota v. Carter, 525 U.S. 83 (1998) (in which five justices indicated support for the proposition that a *non*-overnight guest in a home will often have standing to challenge a search that occurs in his presence). *See* § 19.04[B][1][b], *supra*.

56. *Rakas*, 439 U.S. at 148.

57. Again, this must be distinguished from the question of whether the *seizure* of her property may be challenged, a matter considered in Section 19.05, *infra*.

58. *See* § 19.03, *supra*.

in it, could contest a search that culminated in the seizure of her own property on the premises.[59]

Nonetheless, any such implication in *Rakas* was rejected in *Rawlings v. Kentucky*.[60] *Rawlings* holds that a person may *not* successfully challenge a search of an area in which she has no reasonable expectation of privacy even though she has a possessory or ownership interest in the property seized during the search of that area.

In *Rawlings*, R placed a jar and vials containing controlled substances in X's purse shortly before the police entered a home in which R and X were guests in order to arrest the owner of the house. When the police arrived, they smelled marijuana and observed marijuana seeds, so two officers left to apply for a search warrant. The remaining officers informed the occupants that they could not leave pending the execution of the warrant unless they submitted to a body search. Shortly thereafter, after the warrant was obtained, the police ordered X to empty her purse.[61] When she did, the officers discovered the controlled substances. R, who was sitting next to X on a couch, admitted ownership of them.

The Court held that, in light of *Rakas*, R could not contest the search of X's purse simply on the basis that he had an ownership interest in the property seized. The Court, again per Justice Rehnquist, stated that *Rakas* rejected the view that "arcane" concepts of property law controlled the issue; therefore, the question that had to be considered was whether R had a reasonable expectation of privacy in X's purse, of which R's ownership of the drug vial was only one factor in that determination.

The Court held that R did not have a reasonable expectation of privacy in X's purse. Among the reasons given by the Court were: (1) at the time of the "sudden bailment" R had known X for only a few days; (2) R had never before sought or received access to X's purse; (3) R did not have a right to exclude others from the purse; (4) Y, a "longtime acquaintance and frequent companion" of X, had "free access" to her purse and, in fact, had rummaged through it for a hairbrush that morning; (5) the "precipitous nature of the transaction hardly supports a reasonable inference that [R] took normal precautions to maintain his privacy"; and (6) the record of the suppression hearing "contains a frank admission by [R] that he had no subjective expectation that [X's] purse would remain free from governmental intrusion."

Professor LaFave has written that "[n]o one of the several points made by Justice Rehnquist can withstand close scrutiny . . ."[62] There is no reason why a bailor—here, R—should not expect privacy in the area in which his goods are kept by the bailee. Indeed, the selection of a bailee is made in large part on the basis of the bailor's belief that his goods will be protected and his privacy in them respected. In any case, any expectation of privacy that would otherwise exist is not diminished merely because the bailor recently met the bailee (point 1) or was using that person for the first time (point 2).

Nor should it be fatal to the R-bailor's claim that he cannot exclude others from the bailee's "premises" (here, the purse) (point 3). The *Rawling*s Court's conclusion is inconsistent with the Court's later reasoning in *Minnesota v. Olson*[63] that the mere fact that

---

59. *See* the text accompanying Note 40, *supra*.
60. 448 U.S. 98 (1980).
61. The police incorrectly believed that the warrant authorized them to search the persons in the house.
62. 6 LaFave, Note 1, *supra*, at 171–72.
63. 495 U.S. 91 (1990). *See* § 19.04[B][1][b], *supra*.

a homeowner has the right to admit persons into a house in which she has a guest does not deprive the guest of a legitimate expectation of privacy in the premises. It should follow from this that *X*'s right to allow others to look in her purse, even over *R*'s objection, should not render *R*'s expectation of privacy in the purse illegitimate. As for *Y*'s access to the purse (point 4), this point should add very little. The right to privacy is not lost merely because it is shared, as long as it is not shared with the public at large.

The Court's fifth point, that *R* did not take reasonable precautions to protect his privacy, is also unpersuasive. *R* did not leave the jar and vials on a table; he put it in *X*'s purse. A person ordinarily has a reasonable expectation of privacy in a container as long as it is closed.[64] *X*'s purse was such a container.

Finally, as to the sixth point, the "frank admission" noted by the majority was a "[n]o, sir" answer to the question, "[d]id you feel that [*X*'s] purse would be free from the intrusion of the officers as you sat there?" As the question demonstrates, *R* was being asked whether he thought *X*'s purse would remain inviolate *after* the police had already entered the home and told the guests that they could not leave without submitting to a personal search. As Professor LaFave has cogently pointed out,[65] if *R*'s admission precludes a challenge to the search of *X*'s purse, it would also preclude *R* from challenging a search of his own person, a silly result.

§ 19.05 Standing to Contest
a Seizure: Post-*Rakas*

Nearly everything the Supreme Court has said about standing, both before and after its benchmark ruling in *Rakas v. Illinois*,[66] has concerned challenges to police searches, rather than to seizures. For example, in *Rakas*, *R* challenged the search of *X*'s car, in which property apparently not belonging to *R* was seized and used against him at his trial. In *Rawlings v. Kentucky*,[67] *R* challenged the search of *X*'s purse, in which drugs belonging to *R* were discovered and seized.

Although lower court case law is thin, apparently there is no doubt that a person may challenge a seizure of her own person, but lacks standing to challenge the seizure of someone else.[68] However, the former point is an important one. Suppose that the police, without probable cause or reasonable suspicion of any unlawful activity, stop a car on the highway in which *D* is a non-owner passenger. After the stop, they conduct a search of the car, during which they find illegal drugs belonging to *D* in the trunk. Based on *Rakas*, it is doubtful that *D* would have standing to challenge the trunk *search*, but she *would* have standing to challenge the forcible detention of the car, because *that* act constituted an unlawful *seizure* of her person.[69] As various courts have recognized, if a

---

64. *See* United States v. Ross, 456 U.S. 798, 822 (1982).

65. 6 LaFave, Note 1, *supra*, at 175.

66. 439 U.S. 128 (1978). *See* § 19.04[A], *supra*.

67. 448 U.S. 98 (1980). *See* § 19.04[B][3], *supra*.

68. 6 LaFave, Note 1, *supra*, at 129–30.

69. Brendlin v. California, 551 U.S. 249, 251 (2007) (holding that "[w]hen a police officer makes a traffic stop . . . a passenger is seized as well and so may challenge the constitutionality of the stop").

defendant successfully challenges the seizure of her person, the evidence found in the car may be excluded as a fruit of that unlawful conduct.[70]

Under what circumstances may a person challenge *seizure* of an *object*? For example, suppose that in *Rawlings* R had placed a sealed envelope containing drugs in *X*'s purse. Suppose further that when the police ordered *X* to empty her purse, they found the sealed envelope and, although they had no idea what was inside, seized it. Four days later, after a dog sniff of the envelope confirmed their hunch that it contained illegal drugs, assume they obtained a warrant to search the envelope. On these facts, R would not have standing to contest the *search* of *X*'s purse, but would he have standing to contest the four-day-long *seizure* of the envelope? If so, and assuming that this seizure was unlawful,[71] the subsequent search would be tainted.

If the Supreme Court is consistent, it should treat seizures as it does searches. That is, if the issue of standing to contest a *search* is subsumed under substantive Fourth Amendment doctrine, the same should occur here. If so, as a seizure of an object occurs "when there is some meaningful interference with an individual's possessory interest in that property,"[72] the issue of standing would be whether the seizure constituted a meaningful interference with the *defendant's* possessory interest in the property seized. In the hypothetical *Rawlings* scenario, R would have standing to contest the seizure of the envelope.

---

70. 6 LaFave, Note 1, *supra*, at 173 & n.231 (and cases cited therein).
71. *See* United States v. Place, 462 U.S. 696 (1983). *See* § 17.09, *supra*.
72. United States v. Jacobsen, 466 U.S. 109, 113 (1984). *See* § 7.02[A], *supra*.

Chapter 20

Fourth Amendment: Exclusionary Rule

§ 20.01 Historical Development of the Fourth Amendment Exclusionary Rule[1]

[A] Rights versus Remedies

The Fourth Amendment text describes "[t]he right of the people": "to be secure in [our] persons, houses, papers, and effects, against unreasonable searches and seizures." And we are told that "no Warrants shall issue, but upon probable cause, supported by Oath or affirmation, and particularly describing the place to be searched, and the persons or things to be seized."

Rights presumably come with remedies for their violation. What is the remedy for violation of our Fourth Amendment rights? The constitutional text does not answer this question. Ultimately, however, the Supreme Court concluded that an exclusionary rule is a non-exclusive remedy for such violations. *Very generally speaking*, evidence gathered in violation of the Fourth Amendment is inadmissible at the criminal trial of the victim of the unreasonable search or seizure. As will be seen later sections in this chapter,[2] however, the exclusionary rule is controversial and, consequently, the Court has gradually narrowed its scope.

[B] Federal Exclusionary Rule: *Weeks v. United States*

The Supreme Court adopted the Fourth Amendment exclusionary rule in 1914 in *Weeks v. United States*.[3] In *Weeks*, the Court held that in *federal* trials the Fourth Amendment bars the use of evidence unconstitutionally seized by federal law enforcement

---

1. *See generally* 1 Wayne R. LaFave, Search and Seizure § 1.1(a)-(e) (4th ed. 2004); Francis A. Allen, *Federalism and the Fourth Amendment: A Requiem for Wolf*, 1961 Sup. Ct. Rev. 1; Craig M. Bradley, *Mapp Goes Abroad*, 52 Case W. Res. L. Rev. 375 (2001); Dennis M. Dorin, *Marshaling Mapp: Justice Tom Clark's Role in Mapp v. Ohio's Extensions of the Exclusionary Rule to State Searches and Seizures*, 52 Case W. Res. L. Rev. 401 (2001); Potter Stewart, *The Road to Mapp v. Ohio and Beyond: The Origins, Development and Future of the Exclusionary Rule in Search-and-Seizure Cases*, 83 Colum. L. Rev. 1365 (1983).

2. *See especially* §§ 20.04–.07, *infra*.

3. 232 U.S. 383 (1914).

officers. Without such a rule, the Court subsequently explained, the Fourth Amendment would be reduced to a mere "form of words."[4]

[C] Exclusionary Rule for the States?

[1] Step 1: *Wolf v. Colorado*

When *Weeks v. United States* was decided, the Supreme Court had not yet held that the guarantees of the Fourth Amendment applied to the states pursuant to the Fourteenth Amendment Due Process Clause.[5] Therefore, the Court in *Weeks* had no reason to consider whether the exclusionary rule applied in *state* criminal trials.

In 1949, in *Wolf v. Colorado*,[6] the Supreme Court, per Justice Felix Frankfurter, offered a "good news/bad news" message to criminal defendants. First, it held that "security of one's privacy against arbitrary intrusion by the police — which is at the core of the Fourth Amendment — is basic to a free society." As a consequence of *Wolf*, therefore, states are now subject to the substantive provisions of the Fourth Amendment, albeit through the Fourteenth Amendment Due Process Clause.

On the other hand — the bad news for criminal defendants — the *Wolf* Court indicated that "the ways of enforcing such a basic right raise questions of a different order." According to *Wolf*, the exclusionary rule adopted in *Weeks* "was not derived from the explicit requirements of the Fourth Amendment. . . . The decision was a matter of judicial implication." The Court seemed to be hinting by this remark that the federal exclusionary rule of *Weeks* might not be constitutionally required. It stated that "a different question [than was raised in *Weeks*] would be presented if Congress . . . were to pass a statute purporting to negate the *Weeks* doctrine." In "default of that judgment," the Court indicated, it would "stoutly adhere" to *Weeks*.

Although the Court was unwilling to back down from its holding in *Weeks*, it refused to extend the exclusionary rule to the states. The Court concluded that the states were *not* compelled to exclude "logically relevant evidence" from their trials, even if that evidence was obtained unconstitutionally as a result of an unreasonable search or seizure.

[2] Step 2: *Rochin v. California* and Its Progeny

Although *Wolf v. Colorado*[7] held that evidence was not inadmissible in a state criminal trial merely because it was gathered in violation of the principles underlying the Fourth Amendment, the Court demonstrated in *Rochin v. California*[8] that it was prepared to require the adoption of an exclusionary rule in state trials, albeit by a different constitutional route.

In *Rochin*, police officers, acting without a search warrant and perhaps without probable cause, entered *R*'s home at night, forcibly opened his second-floor bedroom door, and found *R* and his wife on the bed. When *R* swallowed capsules that had been on a

---

4. Silverthorne Lumber Co. v. United States, 251 U.S. 385, 392 (1920).
5. *See* Chapter 3, *supra*, for an explanation of the relationship of the Fourteenth Amendment Due Process Clause to the Bill of Rights.
6. 338 U.S. 25 (1949), *overruled on other grounds*, Mapp v. Ohio, 367 U.S. 643 (1961).
7. 338 U.S. 25 (1949).
8. 342 U.S. 165 (1952).

night stand, three officers "jumped" on him and tried to extract them from his mouth. They failed, so they took *R*, handcuffed, to a hospital where they directed physicians to force an emetic solution through a tube into his stomach in order to cause him to expel the capsules, which he did. The capsules contained morphine. *R* was prosecuted for the possession of the morphine. *R* sought to have evidence of the capsules excluded from his criminal trial.

The Court, per Justice Frankfurter (the author of *Wolf*), held that the police conduct in this case — specifically, "[i]llegally breaking into the privacy of the petitioner, the struggle to open his mouth and remove what was there, the forcible extraction of his stomach's contents" — "shock[ed] the conscience." It said that the police conduct was "bound to offend even hardened sensibilities," and was "too close to the rack and the screw to permit."

The Court concluded that the Fourteenth Amendment Due Process Clause prohibits the use at trial of evidence, even of a reliable nature, secured in a manner that violates "certain decencies of civilized conduct." To hold otherwise, *Rochin* concluded, "would be to afford brutality the cloak of law. Nothing would be more calculated to discredit law and thereby to brutalize the temper of society."

Subsequently, the Court interpreted *Rochin* narrowly. In *Irvine v. California*,[9] the Court ruled, 5–4, over Justice Frankfurter's dissent, that the government was within its rights to introduce at trial statements that the police had obtained illegally by entering *I*'s home to install, and then later move, a hidden microphone. *Rochin* was distinguished on the ground that it, unlike the present case, involved "coercion, violence, or brutality to the person."

Rochin was again distinguished in *Breithaupt v Abram*.[10] In *Breithaupt*, the police took a blood sample from *B* while he was unconscious. Because the blood was extracted non-violently by a physician in a hospital, the Court concluded that the "sense of justice of which we spoke in *Rochin*" was not offended.

The Due Process Clause shock-the-conscience test of *Rochin* remains good law. However, in light of its narrow scope, and the Supreme Court's post-*Rochin* Fourth Amendment exclusionary rule jurisprudence that brings *that* constitutional right into play, the doctrine has only occasionally been invoked, generally to exclude real evidence secured in a violent manner.[11]

---

9. 347 U.S. 128 (1954).

10. 352 U.S. 432 (1957).

11. The Supreme Court has acknowledged that *Rochin* "today would be treated under the Fourth Amendment, albeit with the same result." County of Sacramento v. Lewis, 523 U.S. 833, 849 n.9 (1998). The doctrine still "point[s] the way" to courts, however, when they must identify the point at which abusive use of police power violates the Constitution. *Id.* at 847. Indeed, the principles of *Rochin* can come into play when there is no search or seizure, and where there is no evidence — tangible or intangible — to exclude from a criminal trial. For example, in *Chavez v. Martinez*, 538 U.S. 760 (2003), *M* was arrested following an altercation with the police in which he was shot several times, causing injuries that left him permanently blinded and paralyzed from the waist down. While *M* was being treated at the hospital in the aftermath of the shooting, the police obtained incriminating statements from *M*. There was evidence that they secured the statements by allowing *M*, who was screaming in pain and coming in and out of consciousness, to believe that medical treatment would be withheld until he answered their questions. Although *M* was not subsequently charged with any crime, and thus his statements were never used against him, the Supreme Court agreed that, on proper facts, a person may pursue a civil suit, pursuant to 42 U.S.C. § 1983, for violation of the Due Process Clause. The Court remanded the case to the Ninth Circuit,

[3] Step 3: *Mapp v. Ohio*

In *Mapp v. Ohio*,[12] officers who claimed they were conducting an investigation of a bombing sought to enter *M*'s house in order to find and question a suspect they believed was hiding there. When they demanded entrance, *M* telephoned her attorney and, on his advice, refused to admit them without a search warrant.

After keeping the house under surveillance for three hours, the officers returned to the house, apparently[13] still without a warrant. When *M* did not come to the door immediately, they forcibly entered, damaging the door in the process. Once inside, the officers displayed a piece of paper that they claimed was a search warrant. *M* grabbed it and "placed it in her bosom." A struggle ensued, in which *M*'s hand was twisted, after which the police removed the "warrant" from her clothing.

The officers forcibly moved *M* upstairs to her bedroom, where they searched her belongings. Later, the rest of the house, including her child's bedroom, the living room, the kitchen, and the basement were thoroughly searched. No suspect, nor any evidence regarding the bombing, was found. However, "obscene materials"[14] were discovered and seized. *M* was convicted for their possession.

Although the Fourth[15] Amendment aspects of the case were not briefed, argued, or discussed in the state courts, nor raised by *M*'s attorney,[16] the Supreme Court granted hearing in the case and used it as its vehicle to overrule *Wolf*.

Mapp held that the Fourth Amendment exclusionary rule applies in state criminal trials, just as it does in the federal system via *Weeks v. United States*.[17] Justice Tom Clark, for the Court, stated that "the exclusionary rule is an essential part of both the Fourth and Fourteenth Amendments." To hold otherwise, *Mapp* said, would be "to grant the right [to be free from unreasonable searches and seizures] but in reality to withhold its privilege and enjoyment."

---

which subsequently ruled that *M*'s suit could proceed against the police on due process grounds. Martinez v. City of Oxnard, 337 F.3d 1091 (9th Cir. 2003).

12. 367 U.S. 643 (1961); *see generally* Carolyn N. Long, *Mapp v. Ohio*: Guarding Against Unreasonable Searches and Seizures (2006); Thomas Y. Davies, *An Account of Mapp v. Ohio That Misses the Larger Exclusionary Rule Story*, 4 Ohio St. J. Crim. L. 619 (2007).

13. No warrant was produced by the prosecutor, nor was this failure ever explained.

14. The materials consisted of four books — *Affairs of a Troubadour, Little Darlings, London Stage Affairs*, and *Memories of a Hotel Man* — and a hand-drawn picture "of a very obscene nature." Stewart, Note 1, *supra*, at 1367.

15. Although the Fourteenth, and not the Fourth, Amendment applies in state prosecutions, *see* Chapter 3, *supra*, this Text ordinarily uses "Fourth Amendment" as shorthand for the fundamental rights in the Fourth Amendment that have been incorporated to the states through the Fourteenth Amendment.

16. *M*'s counsel raised two constitutional claims: (1) that the police conduct shocked the conscience, in violation of *Rochin v. California*; and (2) that the conviction for possession of obscene materials violated the First Amendment. An *amicus* brief included one paragraph calling on the Supreme Court to overrule *Wolf*. When *M*'s attorney was questioned about this in oral argument, he indicated that he had never heard of *Wolf*. Stewart, Note 1, *supra*, at 1367; *see also* Dorin, Note 1, *supra* (describing Justice Clark's role in *Mapp*).

17. 232 U.S. 383 (1914).

§ 20.02 Rationale of the Exclusionary Rule[18]

Mapp v. Ohio[19] provided two justifications for the exclusionary rule. First, the "purpose of the exclusionary rule 'is to deter—to compel respect for the constitutional guaranty in the only effectively available way—by removing the incentive to disregard it.'"[20] In essence, the reasoning is that if we assume that the threat of punishment deters many would-be wrongdoers from violating penal laws, we may also assume that police officers will be deterred from violating constitutional rights if they know that the government cannot take advantage of the fruits of their illegal conduct by use of the evidence at a criminal trial.[21]

A second justification for the exclusionary rule—one that has been described as "a more majestic conception"[22]—is "the imperative of judicial integrity."[23] This rationale was first identified by the Court (although not in "integrity" terms) in *Weeks v. United States.*[24] In *Weeks*, the Court stated that the judiciary is "charged at all times with support of the Constitution" and that "people . . . have a right to appeal [to the courts] for the maintenance of . . . fundamental rights." To permit prosecutors to use unconstitutionally seized evidence, *Weeks* reasoned, "would be to affirm by judicial decision a manifest neglect if not an open defiance of the prohibitions of the Constitution." In such circumstances, judges would be acting as "accomplices in the willful disobedience of a Constitution they are sworn to uphold."[25] In essence, judges "shouldn't soil their hands by allowing in unconstitutionally acquired evidence."[26]

After *Mapp* was decided, however, the Supreme Court began to de-emphasize the judicial integrity justification of the exclusionary rule to the point of extinction.[27] "[W]hile it is quite true," Justice Rehnquist once observed, "that courts are not to be participants in 'dirty business,' neither are they to be ethereal vestal virgins of another world."[28]

---

18. 1 LaFave, Note 1, *supra*, at § 1.1(f); Jerry E. Norton, *The Exclusionary Rule Reconsidered: Restoring the Status Quo Ante*, 33 Wake Forest L. Rev. 261 (1998); Scott E. Sundby & Lucy B. Ricca, *The Majestic and the Mundane: The Two Creation Stories of the Exclusionary Rule*, 43 Texas Tech L. Rev. 391 (2010).

19. 367 U.S. 643 (1961).

20. *Id.* at 656 (quoting Elkins v. United States, 364 U.S. 206, 217 (1960)).

21. On the question of whether the deterrence reasoning is valid, *see* § 20.04[C], *infra*.

22. Herring v. United States, 555 U.S. 135, 151 (2009) (Ginsburg, J., dissenting).

23. Mapp v. Ohio, 367 U.S. at 659 (quoting Elkins v. United States, 364 U.S. at 222).

24. 232 U.S. 383 (1914).

25. Elkins v. United States, 364 U.S. at 223.

26. McGuigan, *An Interview with Judge Robert H. Bork*, Jud. Notice, June, 1986, at 1, 6 (quoting Judge Bork, who rejected this argument).

27. For arguments in favor of the "judicial integrity" doctrine, *see* Fred Gilbert Bennett, *Judicial Integrity and Judicial Review: An Argument for Expanding the Scope of the Exclusionary Rule*, 20 UCLA L. Rev. 1129 (1973); Robert M. Bloom & David H. Fentin, *"A More Majestic Conception": The Importance of Judicial Integrity in Preserving the Exclusionary Rule*, 13 U. Pa. J. Const. L. 47 (2010); and Sundby & Ricca, Note 18, *supra*.

28. California v. Minjares, 443 U.S. 916, 924 (1979) (Rehnquist, J., dissenting); *see also* McGuigan, Note 26, *supra* (in which Judge Bork observed that "I have never been convinced by that [judicial integrity] argument because it seems the conscience of the court ought to be at least equally shaken by the idea of turning a criminal loose upon society.").

The Court now states that "the [exclusionary] rule's sole purpose, we have repeatedly held, is to deter future Fourth Amendment violations."[29]

The subordination of "judicial integrity" to "deterrence" in exclusionary rule jurisprudence has a pragmatic explanation. The concept of judicial integrity potentially functions as a moral imperative—"thou shalt not be an accessory to an illegal act"—and, as such, does not allow for cost-benefit analysis of the exclusionary rule, a process favored by most Supreme Court justices, particularly by those who believe that the rule's costs outweigh its benefits. Indeed, as the Court has pointed out,[30] if judicial integrity is taken seriously, evidence obtained unlawfully would need to be suppressed in *all* judicial proceedings, not merely (as is now the case) in criminal trials, and it would seemingly require abandonment of the "standing" requirement. These are consequences that the Court, even during the Warren Court era, was unprepared to accept.

§ 20.03 Is the Exclusionary Rule Constitutionally Required?[31]

Weeks v. United States[32] implicitly, and *Mapp v. Ohio*[33] explicitly, determined that the exclusionary rule is an essential component—"part and parcel" according to *Mapp*— of the Fourth (and Fourteenth) Amendments. That is, according to *Mapp*, the Fourth Amendment itself, albeit implicitly, not only safeguards people against unreasonable searches and seizures, but it guarantees that evidence obtained in violation of their Fourth Amendment rights will not be used against them in criminal trials. Indeed, even Justice Harlan, who dissented in *Mapp* because he did *not* believe that the exclusionary rule was constitutionally required, had no doubt that this was the holding of *Mapp.* As he observed:

> Essential to the majority's argument against *Wolf* [*v. Colorado*[34]] is the proposition that the [exclusionary] rule . . . derives not from the "supervisory power" of this Court over the federal judicial system, but from Constitutional requirement. This is so because no one, I suppose, would suggest that this Court possesses any general supervisory power over the state courts.

Despite Harlan's unassailable observations and the explicit reasoning of the *Mapp* majority, the Supreme Court implicitly overruled the constitutional reasoning, although not the holding, of *Mapp*—an exclusionary rule remains, but its constitutional

---

29. Davis v. United States, 564 U.S. 229, 236 (2011). This is an overstatement by the Court. Previously, it had stated that the judicial integrity rationale had only a "limited role [to play] . . . in the determination whether to apply the rule in a particular context." Stone v. Powell, 428 U.S. 465, 485 (1976); *see also* United States v. Janis, 428 U.S. 433, 446 (1976) ("deterrence is the 'prime purpose' of the rule, if not the sole one").

30. Stone v. Powell, 428 U.S. at 485.

31. *See generally* Thomas S. Schrock & Robert C. Welsh, *Up From Calandra: The Exclusionary Rule as a Constitutional Requirement*, 59 Minn. L. Rev. 251 (1974); Sundby & Ricca, Note 18, *supra.*

32. 232 U.S. 383 (1914). *See* § 20.01[B], *supra.*

33. 367 U.S. 643 (1961). *See* § 20.01[C][3], *supra.*

34. *See* § 20.01[C][1], *supra.*

pedigree has been lost—in *United States v. Calandra*.[35] In *Calandra*, Justice Lewis Powell, speaking for six members of the Court, described the exclusionary rule as "a judicially created remedy designed to safeguard Fourth Amendment rights generally through its deterrent effect, rather than a personal constitutional right of the party aggrieved." In other words, the exclusionary rule is no longer considered an essential component of the Fourth Amendment, but is merely a remedy devised by the justices to deter unconstitutional governmental misconduct. As the Court recently put it, "the exclusionary rule is not an individual right and applies only where it 'results in appreciable deterrence.' We have repeatedly rejected the argument that exclusion is a necessary consequence of a Fourth Amendment violation."[36]

What is the significance of the de-constitutionalization of the Fourth Amendment exclusionary rule? Justice William Brennan, dissenting in *Calandra*, expressed his concern this way: "I am left with the uneasy feeling that today's decision may signal that a majority of my colleagues have positioned themselves to . . . abandon altogether the exclusionary rule in search-and-seizure cases. . . ." Indeed, if the exclusionary rule is *not* constitutionally commanded by the Constitution—if it is merely a "prudential" rule devised by the Supreme Court—then what the Court "giveth" it can "taketh" away or, at a minimum, narrow dramatically.

In fact, since *Calandra* was decided, the Court *has* substantially narrowed the exclusionary rule's scope.[37] And, if the only basis for the exclusionary rule is an empirical claim that it deters official misconduct, then the justices have the authority to abolish the exclusionary rule if and when they determine it lacks sufficient deterrent bite to outweigh its costs (loss of reliable evidence at trial). The Supreme Court recently highlighted this possibility in *Hudson v. Michigan*, when it described application of the exclusionary rule as "forcing the public today to pay for the sins and inadequacies of a legal regime that existed almost half a century ago [at the time of *Mapp v. Ohio*]."[38]

The de-constitutionalization of the exclusionary rule also means that Congress seemingly has authority to abolish the rule, if it replaces it with remedial protections sufficient to meet some yet unclear constitutional minimum standard. And, state legislatures would have similar authority to replace the exclusionary rule with another, perhaps civil or administrative, remedy thought to possess sufficient bite to safeguard search-and-seizure rights.

---

35. 414 U.S. 338 (1974).

36. Herring v. United States, 555 U.S. 125, 141 (2009) (quoting United States v. Janis, 428 U.S. 433, 454 (1976)). More recently still, in Davis v. United States, 564 U.S. 229 (2011), the Court reiterated the view that exclusion is not a constitutional right. This opinion was delivered by Justice Alito for himself, Chief Justice Roberts, and Justices Scalia, Kennedy, Thomas, and Kagan. In *Herring, supra*, Justice Ginsburg, writing also for Justice Breyer and now-retired Justices Stevens and Souter, asserted that she shares a "more majestic conception" of the exclusionary rule—as an "essential" and "inseparable" "auxiliary" to the Fourth Amendment prohibition on unreasonable searches and seizures.

37. *See* §§ 20.05–.07, *infra*.

38. 547 U.S. 586, 597 (2006). For the view that the "bad old days" are not, in fact, behind us, see Jon B. Gould & Stephen D. Mastrofski, *Suspect Searches: Assessing Police Behavior Under the U.S. Constitution*, 3 Criminology & Pub. Pol'y 315 (2004) (concluding that there were Fourth Amendment violations in almost one-third of all observed police investigations).

§ 20.04 Exclusionary Rule: Should It Be Abolished?[39]

[A] Political and Historical Overview

Justice William Douglas predicted that *Mapp v. Ohio*[40] would end the "storm of constitutional controversy" evoked by *Wolf v. Colorado.*[41] It did nothing of the sort. Debate regarding *Mapp* and the exclusionary rule commenced almost as soon as the decision was announced, and it has not ceased. Indeed, with the rule's deconstitutionalization in *United States v. Calandra,*[42] the doctrine finds itself on thin ice that can crack at any time.

One scholar — and now liberal critic — of the exclusionary rule has observed that the rule "is one of the mainstays of liberal ideology. Among those who place themselves somewhere left of center, a stance against using unconstitutionally seized evidence is as *de rigueur* as being anti-death penalty or pro-choice."[43] In part, liberal support for the exclusionary rule is a response to the almost-immediate attack on the rule that arose from political conservatives, who rejected it even before its effects could be measured.

There is some irony in the development of this left/right dichotomy. One view of post-*Mapp* Fourth Amendment jurisprudence suggests that the controversial nature of the exclusionary rule induced the Supreme Court — even during the heyday of the Warren Court era, and certainly after — to narrow the scope of *substantive* Fourth Amendment doctrine. That is, to avoid the application of the exclusionary rule and consequent potential acquittal of factually guilty defendants, the Court has interpreted the substance of the Fourth Amendment narrowly, effectively making it more difficult for defendants to demonstrate that their rights were violated.[44] There is also reason to believe that many trial judges have chosen to accept questionable testimony by police officers regarding searches and seizures, in order to prevent the exclusion of otherwise reliable

---

39. *See generally* Guido Calabresi, *The Exclusionary Rule*, 26 Harv. J.L. & Pub. Pol'y 111 (2003); Gary S. Goodpaster, *An Essay on Ending the Exclusionary Rule*, 33 Hastings L.J. 1065 (1982); William C. Heffernan & Richard W. Lovely, *Evaluating the Fourth Amendment Exclusionary Rule: The Problem of Police Compliance with the Law*, 24 U. Mich. J.L. Reform 311 (1991); Yale Kamisar, *In Defense of the Search and Seizure Exclusionary Rule*, 26 Harv. J.L. & Pub. Pol'y 119 (2003); John Kaplan, *The Limits of the Exclusionary Rule*, 26 Stan. L. Rev. 1027 (1974); William J. Mertens & Silas Wasserstrom, *The Good Faith Exception to the Exclusionary Rule: Deregulating the Police and Derailing the Law*, 70 Geo. L.J. 365 (1981); Norton, Note 18, *supra*; Dallin H. Oaks, *Studying the Exclusionary Rule in Search and Seizure*, 37 U. Chi. L. Rev. 665 (1970); Myron W. Orfield, Jr., *Deterrence, Perjury, and the Heater Factor: An Exclusionary Rule in the Chicago Criminal Courts*, 63 U. Colo. L. Rev. 75 (1992); Richard A. Posner, *Rethinking the Fourth Amendment*, 1981 Sup. Ct. Rev. 49; Christopher Slobogin, *Why Liberals Should Chuck the Exclusionary Rule*, 1999 U. Ill. L. Rev. 363; Stewart, Note 1, *supra*; William J. Stuntz, *The Virtues and Vices of the Exclusionary Rule*, 20 Harv. J.L. & Pub. Pol'y 443 (1997).

40. 367 U.S. 643 (1961). *See* § 20.01[C][3], *supra*.

41. 338 U.S. 25 (1949). *See* § 20.01[C][1], *supra*.

42. 414 U.S. 338 (1974).

43. Slobogin, Note 39, *supra*, at 364.

44. Calabresi, Note 39, *supra*, at 112 ("The interesting paradox is this: liberals ought to hate the exclusionary rule because the exclusionary rule, in my experience [as a professor and federal judge], is most responsible for the deep decline in privacy rights in the United States.").

evidence of a defendant's guilt. Thus, it is possible that the "political right" has gained far more from the exclusionary rule than have the rule's defenders on the "political left," even as the "Right" seeks to undo the exclusionary rule and the "Left" reflexively defends it.

Some of the controversies surrounding the exclusionary rule are considered below.

[B] Is There Historical Foundation for the Exclusionary Rule?

What the critics say: Some critics attack the doctrine on historical grounds. Professor Akhil Amar argues that "[t]he modern Court has . . . distorted Fourth Amendment remedies."[45] He reasons that the Amendment's text "should remind us of background common law principles protecting these interests of personhood, property, and privacy— in a word, the law of tort." According to Amar, when a person, house, paper, or effect was "unreasonably trespassed upon" in pre-Revolutionary England and America, the remedy was a civil action against the trespasser. In Amar's view, therefore, tort remedies against constitutional wrongdoers were "clearly the ones presupposed by the Framers of the Fourth Amendment and counterpart state constitutional provisions."[46]

What defenders of the rule say: Justice Potter Stewart believes that "[t]he actual 'legislative history' of the fourth amendment reveals little" — one way or the other — "about the . . . origin and development of the exclusionary rule."[47] According to Stewart, neither the history of the Fourth Amendment's "immediate ancestors" in state constitutions, nor congressional debates over the text of the Fourth Amendment "shed . . . light on whether it was intended to require the exclusion of illegally obtained evidence."[48]

In any case, defenders of the exclusionary rule contend that history should not be determinative. "[T]he framers meant the Constitution to mean more than it says, and more than they could conceive."[49] That is, for advocates of "constitutional dynamism— the principle that interpretations of the Constitution will and should change over time to accommodate the needs of different historical ages" — the Framers' intentions, although important, are best formulated "at a level of abstraction that leaves room for changing particular applications."[50] We should ask ourselves what *values* the Framers held dear, and then determine what *means* of enforcing those values will best work in modern times. As there are strong non-historical reasons for an exclusionary rule in modern times, the rule should be supported.

---

45. Akhil Reed Amar, *Fourth Amendment First Principles*, 107 Harv. L. Rev. 757, 785 (1994).

46. *Id.* at 786.

47. Stewart, Note 1, *supra*, at 1371.

48. *Id.*

49. Telford Taylor, Two Studies in Constitutional Interpretation 43 (1969); *see* Tracey Maclin, *When the Cure for the Fourth Amendment is Worse than the Disease*, 68 S. Cal. L. Rev. 1, 46 (1994) ("If constitutional interpretation was simply a matter of identifying whether a particular historical practice was permitted in 1789 . . . , it would be better to appoint historians to the Court and leave the lawyers on the sidelines.").

50. Carol S. Steiker, *Second Thoughts About First Principles*, 107 Harv. L. Rev. 820, 825–26 (1994).

[C] Does the Exclusionary Rule Deter Constitutional Violations?

The exclusionary rule applies after a victim's Fourth Amendment rights have been violated, i.e., after an unreasonable search or seizure has already occurred. But "[t]he rule is calculated to prevent, not to repair."[51] That is, privacy lost as the result of police wrongdoing "cannot be restored. Reparation comes too late."[52] Therefore, in determining whether the exclusionary rule represents good policy, one critical question to ask is: Does the exclusionary rule serve the stated purpose of preventing unlawful searches and seizures in the first place?

What the critics say: Early empirical studies,[53] and even contemporary ones,[54] teach us that the exclusionary rule does not—and common sense suggests that it cannot—function as a meaningful deterrent. Most violations of the Fourth Amendment occur at its edges: an officer in good faith misunderstands a complex Fourth Amendment rule,[55] or interprets the facts regarding a search or seizure differently than a court does. These errors cannot be prevented; by definition, they are inadvertent. In any case, we would not want to deter good-faith police activity; all we can ask of the police is that they make reasonable, good-faith efforts to obey the Constitution.

In contrast, those who knowingly violate the Fourth Amendment theoretically *can* be deterred, but the exclusionary rule is too indirect and attenuated a form of punishment to do the job adequately.[56] For the exclusionary rule to be fully effective, the undesired conduct must always be detected, and the "punishing stimulus" of the exclusion of evidence must be given *immediately* after *every* incident of misconduct. But experience teaches us that most constitutionally questionable searches and seizures on the street are not litigated because the police do not make an arrest (they may act solely in order to establish authority, to obtain information, or to harass); when they do arrest, many harried defense lawyers plea bargain rather than litigate. Furthermore, suppression motions are often unsuccessful even when litigated. Bad faith officers believe, perhaps with reason, that by committing perjury they can avoid suppression of evidence.[57] Finally, suppression of evidence, if it occurs at all, happens long after the wrongful conduct has occurred and may not even be communicated to the offending officer.

---

51. Elkins v. United States, 364 U.S. 206, 217 (1960).

52. Linkletter v. Walker, 381 U.S. 618, 637 (1965).

53. *E.g.*, Ronald L. Akers & Lonn Lanza-Kaduce, *The Exclusionary Rule: Legal Doctrine and Social Research on Constitutional Norms*, 2 Sam Houston St. U. Crim. Just. Center Res. Bull. 1 (1986); Oaks, Note 39, *supra*; James E. Spiotto, *Search and Seizure: An Empirical Study of the Exclusionary Rule and its Alternatives*, 2 J. Legal Stud. 243 (1973).

54. *See* Note 38, *supra*.

55. *See* Heffernan & Lovely, Note 39, *supra*, at 332–45 (finding that even well-trained officers are mistaken about Fourth Amendment jurisprudence approximately 25 percent of the time).

56. Slobogin, Note 39, *supra*, at 374–77.

57. Police perjury "disturbingly [is] a well-documented aspect of criminal justice administration." Richard Van Duizend et al., The Search Warrant Process: Preconceptions, Perceptions, and Practices 108 (National Center for State Courts 1984); Orfield, Note 39, *supra*, at 82–83 (in a study of Cook County, Illinois, criminal courts, the author discovered "pervasive police perjury," including "systematic fabrications in case reports and affidavits for search warrants, creating artificial probable cause"). For general discussion of the problem of police perjury (or what has come to be called "testilying"), *see* Gabriel J. Chin & Scott C. Wells, *The "Blue Wall of Silence" as Evidence of Bias and Motive to Lie: A New Approach to Police Perjury*, 59 U. Pitt. L. Rev. 233 (1998); Christopher Slobogin, *Testilying: Police Perjury and What to Do About It*, 67 U. Colo. L. Rev. 1037 (1996).

Beyond these deterrence problems, bad-faith officers may find suppression of evidence, even if communicated to them, of marginal concern. Although officers doubtlessly want those whom they arrest to be convicted, the possibility that evidence may be excluded at trial does not negate other powerful motivations to act unlawfully; malicious officers obtain considerable satisfaction from the knowledge that they have imposed other hardships on a suspect, such as invasion of privacy, the expense and ordeal of a criminal prosecution, family disruption, and loss of employment.

Furthermore, the existence of the rule encourages bad behavior by actors in the criminal justice system. Police officers may be more likely to commit perjury in order to avoid the effects of the rule. Jurors (who are probably aware of the rule even though they are not explicitly told about it) may make inferences based on other evidence and assume (correctly or incorrectly) that the rule has excluded critical evidence in the trial, thus reducing its effectiveness as a deterrent.[58]

What defenders of the rule say: As with all arguments regarding deterrence, it is easier to prove that a penalty has *not* had a deterrent effect than that it is to show that it has succeeded. If Fourth Amendment violations occur today in perhaps one-third of all searches and seizures notwithstanding the exclusionary rule,[59] who is to say what the violation rate would be if there was *no* exclusionary rule—or, for that matter, if the rule was more strenuously enforced by the courts? As one commentator has stated, "there is virtually no likelihood that the Court is going to receive any 'relevant statistics' which objectively measure the 'practical efficacy' of the exclusionary rule."[60] For this reason, all arguments, pro or con, based on deterrence are "partly a matter of logic and psychology, [but] largely a matter of faith."[61]

Fair-minded critics of the exclusionary rule admit that "[n]o one actually knows how effective the exclusionary rule is as a deterrent."[62] Indeed, Professor Dallin Oaks, the author of the classic study most commonly cited by the rule's critics, candidly warned that his study "obviously fall[s] short of an empirical substantiation or refutation of the deterrent effect of the exclusionary rule."[63] His harshest comments about the exclusionary rule are found in the postscript to the study, in which he presented his self-described "polemic on the rule," one that "brushes past the uncertainties identified in the discussion of the data."[64]

In any case, to a considerable extent the criticisms of the exclusionary rule based on deterrence are misdirected. They seek to show that the rule does not deter specific police officers. But, systemic (or general) deterrence, not specific deterrence, is the primary goal of the exclusionary rule.[65] According to Justice Brennan, "the chief deterrent function of the rule is its tendency to promote institutional compliance with Fourth Amendment requirements on the part of law enforcement agencies generally."[66] The exclusionary

---

58. *See* Tonja Jacobi, *The Law and Economics of the Exclusionary Rule*, 87 Notre Dame L. Rev. 585 (2011).

59. *See* Note 38, *supra*.

60. Critique, *On the Limitations of Empirical Evaluations of the Exclusionary Rule: A Critique of the Spiotto Research and United States v. Calandra*, 69 Nw. U. L. Rev. 740, 763–64 (1974).

61. Roger B. Dworkin, *Fact Style Adjudication and the Fourth Amendment: The Limits of Lawyering*, 48 Ind. L.J. 329, 333 (1973).

62. Posner, Note 39, *supra*, at 54 (footnote deleted).

63. Oaks, Note 39, *supra*, at 709.

64. *Id.* at 755.

65. Mertens & Wasserstrom, Note 39, *supra*, at 394.

66. United States v. Leon, 468 U.S. 897, 953 (1984) (dissenting opinion).

rule is meant to deter unconstitutional police conduct by promoting professionalism within the ranks, specifically by creating an incentive for police departments to hire individuals sensitive to civil liberties, to better train officers in the proper use of force, to keep officers updated on constitutional law, and to develop internal guidelines that reduce the likelihood of unreasonable arrests and searches.

There is anecdotal evidence that *Mapp* had these effects in many police departments. Justice Stewart has observed that "[t]he world has changed . . . since the *Mapp* decision was announced."[67] Various observers of police practices have reported that *Mapp* promoted professionalism. For example, Oaks found that police adherence to constitutional doctrine increased after *Mapp* was decided, and that the rule "contributed to an increased awareness of constitutional requirements by the police";[68] more recent studies support this conclusion,[69] as do the observations of Justice Scalia, a critic of the exclusionary rule.[70]

Furthermore, search warrants were sought more often immediately after *Mapp* than before. Police departments and prosecutors that once paid no attention to the Fourth Amendment "at least . . . consider[ed] the parameters of an unconstitutional search and seizure."[71] And, flagrant cases of police misconduct—such as occurred in *Mapp*—appear to have diminished.[72] Defenders of the exclusionary rule worry that its abolition would cause police departments to return to the "bad old days."

Some defenders of the exclusionary rule attack the issue differently. They reason that deterrence criticisms of the sort summarized earlier are disingenuous. According to Professors Wasserstrom and Seidman, "it is difficult to believe that the exclusionary rule debate would have the same intensity if the rule's opponents believed that it should be replaced by a more effective deterrent."[73] They point out that most critics of the rule, besides arguing that the rule does not deter, also claim that the rule results in too many criminals being set free. Yet, "[t]his state of affairs would be made worse, not better, if fourth amendment violations were more effectively deterred." That is, if a remedy for Fourth Amendment violations does its job exceptionally well, there will be more, not fewer, cases of important evidence *not* coming to light, and guilty people avoiding conviction. Thus, these scholars reason, "[i]t seems likely . . . that the real source of the opponents' discontent is not with the rule's *ineffectiveness* but with its *effectiveness*."[74]

---

67. Stewart, Note 1, *supra*, at 1386.

68. Oaks, Note 39, *supra*, at 708.

69. *E.g.*, Orfield, Note 39 *supra*, at 80, 94 (in a study of Cook County, Illinois, criminal courts, the exclusionary rule had an "institutional deterrent effect," in that "police and prosecutorial institutions respond[ed] to the exclusionary rule by designing programs and procedures to ensure compliance with the Fourth Amendment.").

70. Scalia recently observed that one "development over the past half-century . . . is the increasing professionalism of police forces, including a new emphasis on internal police discipline." Hudson v. Michigan, 547 U.S. 586, 598 (2006). It isn't a coincidence that this development "over the past half-century" covers the time since *Mapp v. Ohio* recognized the exclusionary rule for state proceedings.

71. Kaplan, Note 39, *supra*, at 1034.

72. David Alan Sklansky, *Is the Exclusionary Rule Obsolete?*, 5 Ohio St. J. Crim. L. 567, 579 (2008) (contrasting pre-*Mapp* police departments—possessing "a culture of violence and secrecy"—with post-*Mapp* departments, describing the differences as "fundamental and far-reaching").

73. Silas J. Wasserstrom & Louis Michael Seidman, *The Fourth Amendment as Constitutional Theory*, 77 Geo. L.J. 19, 36–37 (1988).

74. *Id.* at 37.

[D] Is the Rule (Even If It Deters) Worth Its Cost?

[1] Should This Question Even Be Asked?[75]

Exclusionary rule critics provide a list of the alleged costs to society of the doctrine, the sum of which, they argue, is greater than the rule's possible deterrent benefits. Advocates of the exclusionary rule believe that the costs have been exaggerated, just as its deterrent benefits have supposedly been undervalued. A brief discussion of some of the alleged costs of the rule follows.

At the outset, however, it should be noted that cost-benefit calculations of the sort described here are not without critics. According to Justice Brennan, "the language of deterrence and of cost/benefit analysis . . . can have a narcotic effect. It creates an illusion of technical precision and ineluctability."[76] These critics maintain that it is nearly impossible to analyze objectively the costs and benefits of the exclusionary rule, because the process involves "measuring imponderables and comparing incommensurables."[77] For example, what is the precise "cost" of an unlawful invasion of privacy? How many such invasions outweigh the loss of the conviction of a guilty person?

Some defenders of the exclusionary rule have a "more majestic conception"[78] of the exclusionary rule and, therefore, contend that courts ought to focus more on the principled, rather than pragmatic, grounds for the exclusionary rule. Courts ought to focus on the need to preserve judicial integrity—to "avoid the taint of partnership in official lawlessness"[79]—by barring unconstitutionally seized evidence. The exclusionary rule, they argue, is most defensible not because it deters the police (which it may or may not do) but because it is fair; it puts the citizen and the government back in the procedural position they would have found themselves if the Constitution had not been violated.[80]

At the current time, however, non-consequentialist arguments of this sort carry no sway with the Supreme Court. Indeed, the Court recently stated that "the exclusionary rule has *never* been applied except where its deterrence benefits outweigh its substantial social costs."[81]

---

75. *See generally* Yale Kamisar, *Does (Did) (Should) the Exclusionary Rule Rest on a "Principled Basis" Rather than an "Empirical Proposition"?*, 16 Creighton L. Rev. 565 (1983); see also the cites in Note 27, *supra*.

76. United States v. Leon, 468 U.S. 897, 929 (1984) (dissenting opinion).

77. Yale Kamisar, *Gates, "Probable Cause," "Good Faith," and Beyond*, 69 Iowa L. Rev. 551, 613 (1984).

78. Herring v. United States, 555 U.S. 135, 151 (2009) (Ginsburg, J., joined by Stevens, Souter, and Breyer, JJ., dissenting).

79. United States v. Calandra, 414 U.S. 338, 357 (1974) (Brennan, J., joined by Douglas and Marshall, JJ, dissenting).

80. *Id.* (The rule "assur[es] the people—all potential victims of unlawful government conduct—that the government would not profit from its lawless behavior").

81. Hudson v. Michigan, 547 U.S. 586, 594 (2006) (internal quotations omitted) (emphasis added).

[2] The "Costs"

[a] The Rule Protects the Wrong People

What the critics say: The purpose of a criminal trial is to learn the truth regarding a defendant's innocence or guilt, to "sort[] the innocent from the guilty."[82] When a murderer's bloody knife is introduced at his trial, the truth is learned, the guilty person is convicted, and people are more secure in their persons, houses, papers, and effects.[83] The Fourth Amendment exclusionary rule, however, "deflects the truthfinding process"[84] by excluding reliable evidence, such as the murderer's bloody knife.

As a result of the suppression of the truth, the exclusionary rule "often frees the guilty."[85] Without the bloody knife, the murderer goes free, and people are *less* secure in their persons, houses, papers, and effects. And, while the guilty go free, innocent people receive no benefit from the rule, because an innocent person has nothing to be seized. The innocent person must turn instead to a civil remedy to obtain redress if his privacy is unconstitutionally invaded.

What defenders of the rule say: First, the preceding argument is misdirected. If the criminal justice system is an obstacle course, it is the Fourth Amendment itself and not the exclusionary rule that constructs the barriers that make it more difficult to convict the guilty.[86]

Second, the cost of guilty people going free is vastly overstated by the critics. A study by Professor Thomas Davies[87] — described by Professor Wayne LaFave as "the most careful and balanced assessment of all available empirical data"[88] — suggests that the "most striking feature of the data is the concentration of illegal searches in drug arrests . . . and the extremely small effects in arrests for other offenses, including violent crimes."[89] In short, if one considers the exclusionary rule critics' "favorite stalking horse"[90] — the murderer's bloody knife — there is little reason to worry about the exclusion doctrine. Although nonprosecutions or nonconvictions in the drug area due to illegal searches were significant in the period studied — 2.8 percent to 7.1 percent — Davies concluded that "available empirical evidence casts considerable doubt on both the alleged 'high costs' of the exclusionary rule and the purported prevalence of 'legal technicalities' as the cause of illegal searches."[91]

Other studies support Davies' conclusions. A 1979 survey by the General Accounting Office — a study of a period when the Fourth Amendment was more vigorously enforced than today — showed that Fourth Amendment problems explained only 0.4 percent of

---

82. Amar, Note 45, *supra*, at 759.

83. *Id.* at 793.

84. Stone v. Powell, 428 U.S. 465, 490 (1976).

85. *Id.*

86. Stewart, Note 1, *supra*, at 1393.

87. Thomas Y. Davies, *A Hard Look at What We Know (and Still Need to Learn) About the "Costs" of the Exclusionary Rule: The NIJ Study and Other Studies of "Lost" Arrests*, 1983 Am. B. Found. Res. J. 611.

88. Wayne R. LaFave, *"The Seductive Call of Expediency": United States v. Leon, Its Rationale and Ramifications*, 1984 U. Ill. L. Rev. 895, 904.

89. Davies, Note 87, *supra*, at 680.

90. Maclin, Note 49, *supra*, at 44.

91. Davies, Note 87, *supra*, at 688.

the total number of cases declined for federal prosecution.[92] Another study found that, in cases in which warrants had been issued in seven communities, evidence was found in more than 90 percent of the resulting searches, yet motions to suppress evidence seized during those successful searches were filed in only 30 percent of the prosecutions and were granted in just 12 percent of the cases, for an overall suppression rate of slightly less than five percent of the total number of warrant-related prosecutions.[93] Perhaps even more significantly, convictions were obtained in at least 70 percent of the cases in which suppression motions were granted. Overall, therefore, the exclusionary rule prevented conviction of criminal defendants in no more than 1.4% of the cases studied.

Third, it is inaccurate to state that innocent people do not benefit from an exclusionary rule. If the rule serves its deterrent purpose, the police will not enter homes, search cars, or otherwise intrude upon the privacy of persons about whom there is little objective evidence of guilt. There is no way to know, of course, how many innocent people have *not* been the victims of unreasonable searches and seizures because of *Mapp*. In any case, even if it *were* true that innocent persons do not derive benefits from the rule, this "does not suggest that the rule is not a necessary remedy, only that it is not a sufficient one."[94]

[b] The Rule Promotes Cynicism

What the critics say: The exclusionary rule promotes cynicism among members of the public and parties in the criminal justice system, including trial judges and even criminal defendants.

The exclusionary rule treats a criminal defendant as a "surrogate for the larger public interest in restraining the government. The criminal defendant is a kind of private attorney general."[95] But, the defendant is "the worst kind" of surrogate, because he is "self-serving." As a person in possession of criminal evidence, he is "often unrepresentative of the larger class of law-abiding citizens, and his interests regularly conflict with theirs."[96] No wonder, then, that a "solid majority of Americans rejects the idea that '[t]he criminal is to go free because the constable has blundered.' "[97] "The public is *revulsed* [sic]"[98] by the sight of guilty people going free because reliable evidence that could convict them is suppressed by judges on the basis of a "technicality."

This cynicism runs even deeper. Police officers lie in order to avoid suppression of evidence, and some trial judges wink at the dishonesty in order to avoid allowing guilty defendants to go free. Professor William Pizzi writes:

> Rather than contributing to police professionalism, a draconian exclusionary rule feeds into [an] "us versus them" mentality among police officers and encourages cynicism about the system and even the practice referred to by police

---

92. Comptroller General of the United States, Rep. No. GGD-79-45, Impact of the Exclusionary Rule on Federal Criminal Prosecutions 14 (1979).

93. Van Duizend et al., Note 57, *supra*, at 48–56.

94. Stewart, Note 1, *supra*, at 1396.

95. Amar, Note 45, *supra*, at 796.

96. *Id.*

97. Kaplan, Note 39, *supra*, at 1035 (quoting Justice Benjamin Cardozo in *People v. Defore*, 150 N.E. 585, 587 (N.Y. 1926)).

98. Statement of the Co-Chairman of the Attorney-General's Task Force on Violent Crime, *quoted in* N.Y. Times, Aug. 18, 1981, at 10, *as reported in* Wayne R. LaFave, *The Fourth Amendment in an Imperfect World: On Drawing "Bright Lines" and "Good Faith,"* 43 U. Pitt. L. Rev. 307, 336 (1982).

as "testilying". . . . When the crime is a serious one and the consequences of suppression would mean that the guilty person will go free, judges are tempted to credit testimony that they have good reason to believe has been embellished, to avoid suppression. . . . [¶] . . . [A] system with harsh rules becomes less honest all around as we struggle to avoid the harshness of the rules. . . . An attitude of cynicism starts to pervade courthouses as the criminal justice system comes to expect and tolerate dishonesty under oath.[99]

What defenders of the rule say: If the public is outraged by the exclusionary rule, it should not be. First, as noted above, fewer guilty people go free than is believed. Second, although the rule obstructs the truth by suppressing reliable evidence, responsibility for this should be placed at the door of the government, whose officers violated the Fourth Amendment. As Justice Harlan has explained, judges "do not release a criminal from jail because we like to do so, or because we think it is wise to do so, but only because the government has offended constitutional principle in the conduct of [the defendant's] case."[100] The public's outrage should be aimed, therefore, at those who fail to obey the Constitution's edicts — hardly "technicalities" — and at those who lie under oath and countenance lies at trial.

Moreover, abolishing the exclusionary rule will not prevent testilying. As one scholar suggested, "any remedial scheme that imposes a personal sanction on an officer is likely to encourage perjury."[101]

[c] The Rule Results in Disproportionate Punishment[102]

What the critics say: Even if the exclusionary rule should not be abandoned, the *Mapp* version of the doctrine goes too far because the "penalty" for violation of the Fourth Amendment is often disproportionate to the "crime" committed by the police. First, *Mapp* applies as much to the inadvertent mistake of a good-faith police officer as it does to the malicious conduct of a bad-faith actor. Although "[f]reeing either a tiger or a mouse in a schoolroom is an illegal act, . . . no rational person would suggest that these two acts should be punished in the same way."[103] Second, the rule does not distinguish between a trial for a serious crime and one for a minor offense. Therefore, a potentially dangerous offender may escape incarceration, even if the wrong committed by the officer was relatively trivial in nature. Evidence of a crime should be excluded, if at all, when "the reprehensibility of the officer's illegality is greater than the defendant's."[104]

What defenders of the rule say: The proportionality argument wrongly assumes that the exclusionary rule is intended as compensation for the victim of a Fourth Amendment violation. In fact, its purpose is to instill professionalism in police ranks, in order to prevent *future* violations. Just as punishment of a criminal is not calibrated to the facts of a particular case if we seek general deterrence, it is wrong to measure the effect of the exclusionary rule in an individual case.

---

99. William T. Pizzi, Trials Without Truth 38–39 (1999).

100. Desist v. United States, 394 U.S. 244, 258 (1969) (dissenting opinion).

101. Myron W. Orfield, Jr., Comment, *The Exclusionary Rule and Deterrence: An Empirical Study of Chicago Narcotics Officers*, 54 U. Chi. L. Rev. 1016, 1055 (1987); *see* Kamisar, Note 39, *supra*, at 130–31.

102. *See generally* Yale Kamisar, *"Comparative Reprehensibility" and the Fourth Amendment Exclusionary Rule*, 86 Mich. L. Rev. 1 (1987).

103. Bivens v. Six Unknown Named Agents, 403 U.S. 388, 419 (1971) (Burger, C.J. dissenting).

104. Kamisar, Note 102, *supra*, at 3 (articulating, but rejecting, the argument).

[E] Are There Better Remedies?[105]

What the critics say: Even if the exclusionary rule deters, and even if its benefits slightly outweigh its costs, there are other remedies that would provide greater net benefits. Furthermore, as long as the exclusionary rule is in place, courts and legislatures have no incentive to implement alternative remedies.

Some commentators believe that the primary remedy for a Fourth Amendment violation should be a civil action. Whether the proceeding is a common law tort action (e.g., battery or trespass) or a federal civil rights suit,[106] the jury would apply a tort concept of reasonableness, in order to determine whether the Fourth Amendment was violated. The defendants—the individual police officers and government agencies—would pay compensatory and punitive damages, when appropriate.[107] With the abolition of the exclusionary rule, a criminal trial could focus on determining the guilt or innocence of the defendant; at the same time, a plaintiff (whether guilty or innocent) could obtain redress for violation of his Fourth Amendment rights. And substantial money judgments would send a direct, more powerful, message than the exclusionary rule to police departments to train and supervise their officers.

Other police-accountability remedies, potentially in conjunction with actions for money damages, have been mentioned, including: criminal prosecutions of officers who maliciously violate the Fourth Amendment;[108] injunctive relief; implementation of police review boards with authority to discipline or fire officers for constitutional wrongdoing; and statutory procedures to decertify wrongdoing police officers, so that they cannot be re-employed by another department in the same jurisdiction.[109]

What defenders of the rule say: In a perfect world, a complete spectrum of civil and criminal remedies, such as those suggested by abolitionists, would be "superior to evidentiary exclusion as a system for deterring governmental misconduct."[110] Nonetheless, "[d]espite its many flaws, the exclusionary rule is . . . the best we can realistically do."[111]

The key word is "realistically." Criminal prosecutions of the police for Fourth Amendment violations are virtually unheard of. The reason is obvious: Prosecutors rarely want

---

105. David A. Harris, *How Accountability-Based Policing Can Reinforce—Or Replace—the Fourth Amendment Exclusionary Rule*, 7 Ohio St. J. Crim. L. 149 (2009); Kenneth W. Starr & Audrey L. Maness, *Reasonable Remedies and (or?) the Exclusionary Rule*, 43 Texas Tech. L. Rev. 373 (2010).

106. *E.g.*, 42 U.S.C. § 1983 (it is actionable for any person "under color of any statute, ordinance, regulation, custom, or usage, of any State" to subject any person "to the deprivation of any rights, privileges, or immunities secured by the Constitution"); 28 U.S.C. § 2680(h) (permitting a civil suit against federal officers for constitutional violations).

107. Contrary to the suggestion in the text, Professor Donald Dripps has proposed that the exclusionary rule be retained but that judges be authorized to enter *contingent* suppression orders when the police violate the Fourth Amendment; suppression of evidence could be avoided if the state pays damages in an amount determined by the judge. Donald Dripps, *The Case for the Contingent Exclusionary Rule*, 38 Am. Crim. L. Rev. 1 (2001). *But see* George C. Thomas III, *Judges Are Not Economists and Other Reasons to Be Skeptical of Contingent Suppression Orders: A Response to Professor Dripps*, 38 Am. Crim. L. Rev. 47 (2001).

108. *E.g.*, 18 U.S.C. § 242 (making it a federal crime for anyone acting under color of law to deprive a person of his constitutional rights).

109. Roger Goldman & Steven Puro, *Decertification of Police: An Alternative to Traditional Remedies for Police Misconduct*, 15 Hastings Const. L.Q. 45, 48 (1987).

110. Steiker, Note 50, *supra*, at 848.

111. *Id.*

to proceed against their natural allies, the police. Civil suits, too, are "relatively punch-less as punishing mechanisms."[112] This is, in part, because individual officers and the government itself are immune from civil liability in many circumstances.[113] Legislatures, therefore would have to fashion a system that permits greater opportunities for liability. It is unclear whether lawmakers, buffeted by political forces, would be prepared to make such changes: "The history of attempts to regulate police practices should make us extremely doubtful about reliance on legislatures to create effective remedial structures."[114]

Moreover, many defenders of the exclusionary rule doubt that "we [can] be confident that juries would award Fourth Amendment remedies sufficient to create litigation incentives and thus to promote adequate deterrence."[115] Jurors, fearful of crime, will hesitate to rule against the police. Jurors are apt to focus less on the police behavior, and more on their assessment of the plaintiff's character,[116] which in turn invites the jury to decide whether they "fear the robbers more than the cops."[117]

Policing the police is a good idea. However, "[c]ivilian review boards, commonly hailed as a panacea for police abuse and illegality, do not work in isolation and are often weak substitutes for effective control of police misconduct."[118]

§ 20.05 When the Exclusionary Rule Does Not Apply: In General

The Supreme Court has stated that, "[a]s with any remedial device, the application of the [exclusionary] rule [should be] restricted to those areas where its remedial objectives are thought most efficaciously served."[119] In other words, in determining whether the rule should be applied, the issue is whether the cost of its use is likely to outweigh the incremental deterrent benefit of extending the doctrine to the new situation.

As the Supreme Court has grown increasingly disenchanted with the exclusionary rule, it has placed a greater and greater burden on those who would invoke the rule to justify suppression of evidence. The Court now says that exclusion of evidence is "our last resort, not our first impulse."[120] In view of "the rule's 'costly toll' upon truth-seeking

---

112. Slobogin, Note 39, *supra*, at 385.
113. Sklansky, Note 72, *supra*, at 572 ("Chief among the barriers to suing the police . . . are the expanding doctrines of official immunity. . . ."; "[m]ore and more, these doctrines look like the Blob That Ate [Civil Rights] Section 1983").
114. Steiker, Note 50, *supra*, at 849.
115. *Id.*
116. Maclin, Note 49, *supra*, at 64.
117. Steiker, Note 50, *supra*, at 850.
118. Maclin, Note 72, *supra*, at 64–65; *see also* Debra Livingston, *The Unfulfilled Promise of Citizen Reviews*, 1 Ohio St. J. Crim. L. 653 (2004) (Judge Livingston, a former law professor and commissioner on New York City's Civilian Complaint Review Board, characterizes review boards as only a "mixed success"); Sklansky, Note 71, *supra*, at 572 (describing civil review boards as "more sympathetic to rank-and-file officers than the [police] unions feared and than most of the original backers of the idea expected").
119. United States v. Calandra, 414 U.S. 338, 348 (1974) (alteration in original).
120. Hudson v. Michigan, 547 U.S. 586, 591 (2006).

and law enforcement objectives," this "presents a high obstacle for those urging [its] application."[121]

The Supreme Court has gone about blunting the effect of the Fourth Amendment exclusionary rule in two ways: (1) holding that it does not apply at all in certain types of proceedings or when certain types of Fourth Amendment issues are raised; and (2) limiting its use, even when it is otherwise applicable, when the police officer's culpability is not sufficiently egregious. The first of these two approaches is considered in this section; the second is considered in the chapter section that follows.

As you will see, the cumulative effect of these various exceptions to the exclusionary rule is quite extensive. Some commentators have argued that there are now so many limits on the exclusionary rule that it is effectively dead, or at the very least it is only a matter of time before it is explicitly overruled or limited to the rarest of cases.[122]

[A] Non-Criminal Proceedings

[1] In General

The exclusionary rule applies in some quasi-criminal contexts, such as in proceedings in which property will be forfeited because of criminal wrongdoing.[123] On the other hand, the rule does not apply in ordinary civil suits, civil tax proceedings, or deportation hearings.[124]

[2] Habeas Corpus

Although the exclusionary rule generally applies in state criminal trials, a state's failure to apply it in a particular case usually may *not* be remedied in a federal habeas corpus civil proceeding brought to overturn a state criminal conviction. In *Stone v. Powell*,[125] the Supreme Court balanced "the utility of the exclusionary rule against the costs of extending it to collateral review of Fourth Amendment claims." It characterized the costs of the rule as "well known." As for the deterrent benefits of the rule, "[t]here is no reason to believe . . . that the overall educative effect of the exclusionary rule would be appreciably diminished if search-and-seizure claims could not be raised in federal habeas corpus review of state convictions." Therefore, the Court held that "where the State has provided an opportunity for full and fair litigation of a Fourth Amendment claim, the Constitution does not require that a state prisoner be granted federal habeas corpus relief on the ground that evidence obtained in an unconstitutional search or seizure was introduced at his trial."

---

121. Pennsylvania Bd. of Probation and Parole v. Scott, 524 U.S. 357, 364–365 (1998).

122. *See, e.g.,* Tracey Maclin, *No More Chipping Away: The Roberts Court Uses an Axe to Take Out the Fourth Amendment Exclusionary Rule*, 81 Miss. L. J. 1183, 1227 (2012) (arguing that the Supreme Court will soon take a case "involving a routine search and seizure violation and rule that the exclusionary rule does not apply unless there is proof of culpable or egregious police conduct.")

123. One 1958 Plymouth Sedan v. Pennsylvania, 380 U.S. 693 (1965).

124. United States v. Janis, 428 U.S. 433 (1976) (civil tax proceeding); I.N.S. v. Lopez-Mendoza, 468 U.S. 1032 (1984) (deportation hearing).

125. 428 U.S. 465 (1976).

The Supreme Court has not clarified what it meant by the phrase "an opportunity for a full and fair litigation of a Fourth Amendment claim." Under *Stone*, however, a habeas petitioner may not claim simply that a state court misapplied search-and-seizure doctrine. According to Professor Wayne LaFave, the effect of *Stone* is "there will be few occasions when a state prisoner will be able to obtain an adjudication of his Fourth Amendment claim in a federal habeas court."[126]

[B] Criminal Proceedings

[1] Non-Trial Proceedings

Evidence seized unconstitutionally may be introduced in grand jury proceedings without violation of the Fourth Amendment.[127] Apparently, such evidence may also constitutionally be used in preliminary hearings,[128] at bail proceedings,[129] in sentencing,[130] and at proceedings to revoke parole.[131]

[2] At a Criminal Trial

[a] Impeachment Exception[132]

As the result of a string of complicated and seemingly conflicting Supreme Court opinions, the rule now is that a prosecutor may introduce evidence obtained from a defendant in violation of his Fourth Amendment rights for the limited purpose of impeaching the defendant's: (1) direct testimony; or (2) answers to legitimate questions put to him during cross-examination. For example, if *D* testifies in a drug prosecution that he has never seen narcotics,[133] or denies in cross-examination that he previously possessed particular evidence of a crime,[134] the prosecutor may introduce testimony that contradicts these claims in order to impeach *D*'s credibility, even though the impeachment evidence was secured in violation of *D*'s Fourth Amendment rights.

The impeachment exception applies because the Supreme Court has determined that use of Fourth Amendment tainted evidence to impeach a defendant's false testimony significantly furthers the truth-seeking process by deterring perjury; at the same time, use of such evidence in this limited manner creates only a speculative possibility that the police will be encouraged to violate the Fourth Amendment.

---

126. 6 LaFave, Note 1, *supra*, at 490.

127. United States v. Calandra, 414 U.S. 338 (1974).

128. *See* Giordenello v. United States, 357 U.S. 480 (1958) (magistrates lack authority to adjudicate the admissibility of evidence); Fed. R. Crim. P. 5.1(e) ("At the preliminary hearing, the defendant . . . may not object to evidence on the ground that it was unlawfully acquired").

129. *E.g.*, 18 U.S.C. § 3142(f) ("The rules concerning admissibility of evidence in criminal trials do not apply to the presentation and consideration of information at the hearing.").

130. United States v. McCrory, 930 F.2d 63 (D.C. Cir. 1991) (evidence seized in violation of the Fourth Amendment may be considered by the judge in determining the defendant's appropriate sentence under the federal sentencing guidelines).

131. Pennsylvania Bd. of Probation and Parole v. Scott, 524 U.S. 357 (1998).

132. *See generally* 6 LaFave, Note 1, *supra*, at § 11.6(a); James L. Kainen, *The Impeachment Exception to the Exclusionary Rules: Policies, Principles, and Politics*, 44 Stan. L. Rev. 1301 (1992).

133. Walder v. United States, 347 U.S. 62 (1954).

134. United States v. Havens, 446 U.S. 620 (1980).

Notwithstanding the impeachment exception set out above, the Supreme Court held in *James v. Illinois*[135] that evidence obtained in violation of a defendant's Fourth Amendment rights may *not* be used to impeach all of the defendant's witnesses. In a 5–4 opinion, the Court stated that extension of the impeachment exception to all of the defendant's witnesses—and not simply to impeach the defendant himself—would not further the truth-seeking process to the same degree, because use of a statement in this manner might deter defendants from calling witnesses who would otherwise provide truthful and probative evidence, out of fear that the truthful witnesses might unexpectedly make a statement "in sufficient tension with the tainted evidence" to allow impeachment. The Court also thought that expansion of the exception to all defense witnesses would significantly weaken the exclusionary rule's deterrent effect, as it would greatly increase the number of times such evidence could be used during a trial.

[b] Knock-and-Announce Exception

In *Hudson v. Michigan*,[136] a decision that has been harshly attacked by exclusionary rule advocates,[137] the Supreme Court held that the exclusionary rule does not apply to the fruits of a search conducted pursuant to a valid warrant executed in violation of the constitutional knock-and-announce rule.[138]

In *Hudson*, police went to *H*'s home with a valid warrant authorizing a search for drugs and guns, both of which they found upon entering and searching *H*'s home. In executing the warrant, however, the police entered *H*'s home just three to five seconds after announcing their presence, which the state conceded amounted to a knock-and-announce violation. The question before the Supreme Court was whether the drugs and guns should be suppressed in *H*'s subsequent prosecution, i.e., "whether the exclusionary rule is appropriate for violations of the knock-and-announce requirement."[139]

Justice Scalia, writing for a 5–4 majority,[140] described application of the exclusionary rule as a "last resort" and offered a smorgasbord of reasons for finding the exclusionary rule inapplicable in the knock-and-announce context. First, exclusion was not warranted because the "illegal *manner* of entry was *not* a but-for cause of obtaining the evidence,"[141] i.e., the police presumably would have executed the valid warrant and found the guns

---

135. 493 U.S. 307 (1990).

136. 547 U.S. 586 (2006); see generally Albert W. Alschuler, *The Exclusionary Rule and Causation: Hudson v. Michigan and Its Ancestors*, 93 Iowa L. Rev. 1741 (2008); Sharon L. Davies & Anna B. Scanlon, *Katz in the Age of Hudson v. Michigan: Some Thoughts on "Suppression as a Last Resort,"* 41 U.C. Davis L. Rev. 1035 (2008); Eric A. Johnson, *Causal Relevance in the Law of Search and Seizure*, 88 B.U. L. Rev. 113 (2008); Sklansky, Note 72, *supra*; James J. Tomkovicz, *Hudson v. Michigan and the Future of Fourth Amendment Exclusion*, 93 Iowa L. Rev. 1819 (2008).

137. *E.g.*, 6 LaFave, Note 1, *supra*, at § 11.4 (Pocket Pt.) ("*Hudson* deserves a special niche in the Supreme Court's pantheon of Fourth Amendment jurisprudence, as one would be hard-pressed to find another case with so many bogus arguments piled atop one another.").

138. *Contra*, State v. Cable, 51 So.3d 434 (Fla. 2010) (holding that, notwithstanding *Hudson*, violations of the knock-and-announce rule in Florida require suppression of the evidence seized under the state's knock-and-announce statute; although the statute is silent as to the proper remedy for its violation, the court stated that the statute "would be undermined if the exclusionary rule did not apply to its violation").

139. *Hudson*, 547 U.S. at 592.

140. Timing can be everything in the law. As Professor David Sklansky points out, "*Hudson* was reargued [in the Supreme Court] after Justice Alito replaced [retired] Justice O'Connor, and there is some evidence that the initial vote had gone the other way." Sklansky, Note 72, *supra*, at 568 n.8.

141. *Hudson*, 547 U.S. at 593 (emphasis in original).

and drugs even in the absence of the violation. This is a controversial (some say incorrect) application of the so-called "independent source" doctrine. As this doctrine is considered later in this chapter,[142] this aspect of *Hudson* will be put aside for now.

Second, even if the constitutional violation was the but-for cause of the seizure of the evidence, it has long been the case that the connection between a Fourth Amendment violation and the evidence obtained as a result of it may become sufficiently causally attenuated so as to render the connection too remote to justify exclusion of the evidence.[143] The *Hudson* Court, however, developed a new "attenuated connection" doctrine:[144] the exclusionary rule applies only when "the interest protected by the constitutional guarantee that has been violated" would be served by suppression of the evidence. The Court identified the interests protected by the constitutional guarantee of the knock-and-announce requirement: (1) protection of "human life and limb" from the self-defensive actions of "surprised resident[s]," unaware of the identity of the officers forcibly entering their home; (2) protection of property from damage or destruction, which often results from forcible entry; and (3) protection of the privacy interests of residents, by giving occupants the "opportunity to prepare themselves" for police entry. Because these three interests do not include "the shielding of potential evidence from the government," the Court deemed exclusion an inappropriate remedy.

Third, and "[q]uite apart" from the first two arguments, the *Hudson* Court stated that the exclusionary rule "has never been applied" unless the resulting benefits in deterrence outweigh the rule's "substantial" social costs. Weighing the costs and benefits in the knock-and-announce context, the Court concluded that application of the exclusionary rule is unjustified.

On the cost side, the Court noted the "grave adverse consequence that exclusion of relevant incriminating evidence always entails 'viz., the risk of releasing dangerous criminals into society'." In addition, applying the exclusionary rule to knock-and-announce cases would cause "a constant flood" of litigation of a depth that courts had "never before" experienced with the exclusionary rule, because "[u]nlike the warrant or *Miranda* requirements, compliance with which is readily determined," knock-and-announce compliance "is difficult for the trial court to determine and even more difficult for an appellate court to review." Finally, on the cost side, the Court argued that, given the difficulty of determining when entry is permitted and the "massive" consequences of suppression, application of the exclusionary rule could cause the police to "refrain[] from timely entry after knocking and announcing" when they lawfully could do so, thereby risking violence against the police and destruction of evidence.

On the benefit side of the ledger, the Court questioned whether much or any deterrence is necessary in the knock-and-announce context, because the police have little incentive to violate the rule, and because the "right not to be intruded upon in one's nightclothes" is not of the greatest significance. Moreover, civil remedies and internal police discipline provide "substantial" deterrence—deterrence "incomparably greater" than that which existed "when *Mapp* [v. *Ohio*] was decided."[145]

---

142. *See* § 20.08[C], *infra*.

143. The attenuation doctrine, and *Hudson*'s significance in this regard, are discussed in greater depth in § 20.08[E], *infra*.

144. It was "created out of whole cloth." 6 LaFave, Note 1, *supra*, at § 11.4 (Pocket Pt.).

145. But, is this so? See Notes 110–118, *supra*, and the text thereto.

This latter aspect of the opinion is noteworthy. Notice that the *Hudson* majority defended its holding in part on the ground that other remedies—the same remedies potentially available for *all* Fourth Amendment violations—are sufficient to deter knock-and-announce violations. According to Scalia: "We cannot assume that exclusion . . . is necessary deterrence simply because we found that it was necessary deterrence in different contexts and long ago. This would be forcing the public today to pay for the sins and inadequacies of a legal regime that existed almost half a century ago."[146] As Justice Breyer, writing for the four dissenters, noted, this reasoning "is to argue that *Wolf* [*v. Colorado*, which held the exclusionary rule inapplicable to the states], not *Mapp* [*v. Ohio*, which overruled *Wolf*] is now the law."[147]

Each of the majority's proffered grounds for decision in *Hudson* singly and particularly in conjunction suggested to many legal observers the possibility of future additional categorical limitations on the exclusionary rule. Perhaps for this reason, Justice Kennedy, who was part of the 5–4 majority, found it necessary to write a concurrence, stating that "the continued operation of the exclusionary rule . . . is not in doubt," and that *Hudson* "determines only that in the specific context of the knock-and-announce requirement" application of the exclusionary rule is not justified.

§ 20.06 When the Exclusionary Rule Does Not Apply: The Police Culpability Factor

[A] Historical Overview

In *Mapp v. Ohio*,[148] the police egregiously violated the Fourth Amendment, but the rule of evidentiary exclusion announced in the case was not limited to egregious police misconduct: the rule applied to *all* violations of the Fourth Amendment, including inadvertent ones. However, over time, the Supreme Court grew increasingly hostile to the exclusionary rule, and the process of narrowing the rule—by limiting its applicability to cases in which police-culpability could be proven—began.

The police-culpability approach seriously began with *United States v. Leon*,[149] a case in which the police obtained a warrant later determined to be invalid. *Leon* is considered in the next subsection. Subsequently, the Supreme Court extended the culpability approach to *warrantless* searches and, while doing so, narrowed the scope of the exclusionary rule even further. This latter change, described in subsection [C], accelerated after John Roberts (who had previously worked on a memorandum for the Ronald Reagan White House "to amend or abolish the exclusionary rule"[150]) joined the Court as Chief Justice.

---

146. *Hudson*, 547 U.S. at 597.
147. *Id.* at 611.
148. 367 U.S. 643 (1961).
149. 468 U.S. 897 (1984).
150. Adam Liptak, *Justices Step Closer to Repeal of Evidence Ruling*, N.Y. Times, Jan. 31, 2009, at A1.

[B] The Culpability Approach in its Infancy: *United States v. Leon*[151]

[1] The "Good Faith" Rule

In *United States v. Leon*,[152] police officers executed a facially valid search warrant. Later, a district court held that, "while recognizing that the case was a close one," the warrant was invalid because it was not supported by probable cause.

In *Massachusetts v. Sheppard*,[153] a companion case to *Leon*, the police seized evidence related to a homicide pursuant to a warrant later declared invalid because of a technical error committed by the issuing magistrate. The error was that the magistrate signed a warrant form normally used to conduct searches for illegal drugs, but he forgot to cross out the language in the form that authorized the police to search for controlled substances. In turn, the executing officer did not look at the warrant after the magistrate signed it because he was assured by the judge that the offending language had been excised. As a consequence of the judge's error, the warrant did not satisfy the particularity requirement of the Fourth Amendment.

Under the exclusionary rule announced in *Mapp*, the evidence obtained in these cases would have been inadmissible at the defendants' criminal trials (except for impeachment purposes) because the warrants supporting the searches were invalid. Nonetheless, the Supreme Court permitted the evidence to be introduced at the trials.

According to *Leon*, as detailed below, evidence obtained pursuant to a search warrant later declared to be invalid may be introduced at a defendant's criminal trial in the prosecutor's case-in-chief, if a reasonably well-trained officer would have believed that the warrant was valid.

[2] "Good Faith": What Does This Mean?

Notwithstanding the "good faith" label often attached to the *Leon* rule, the test is not a subjective one: evidence is not admissible merely on a finding that the officer involved in the search honestly believed that the warrant he was executing was valid. *Leon* states that the inquiry into "good faith" is limited "to the objectively ascertainable question whether a reasonably well trained officer would have known the search was illegal despite the magistrate's authorization." The test, in short, is an objective one; if the officers in *Leon* (or companion case, *Sheppard*) had acted unreasonably — negligently — in

---

151. *See generally* Craig M. Bradley, *The "Good Faith Exception" Cases: Reasonable Exercises in Futility*, 60 Ind. L.J. 287 (1985); Donald Dripps, *Living With Leon*, 95 Yale L.J. 906 (1986); Steven Duke, *Making Leon Worse*, 95 Yale L.J. 1405 (1986); Andrew E. Taslitz, *The Expressive Fourth Amendment: Rethinking the Good Faith Exception to the Exclusionary Rule*, 76 Miss. L.J. 483 (2006).

152. 468 U.S. 897 (1984). The good-faith exception to the exclusionary rule announced in *Leon* was rejected by various states. *E.g.*, State v. Marsala, 579 A.2d 58 (Conn. 1990); Dorsey v. State, 761 A.2d 807 (Del. 2000); Harvey v. State, 469 S.E.2d 176 (Ga. 1996); State v. Guzman, 842 P.2d 660 (Idaho 1992); State v. Cline, 617 N.W.2d 277 (Iowa 2000); State v. Lacasella, 60 P.3d 975 (Mont. 2002); State v. Canelo, 653 A.2d 1097 (N.H. 1995); State v. Novembrino, 519 A.2d 820 (N.J. 1987); State v. Gutierrez, 863 P.2d 1052 (N.M. 1993); People v. Bigelow, 488 N.E.2d 451 (N.Y. 1985); State v. Carter, 370 S.E.2d 553 (N.C. 1988); Commonwealth v. Edmunds, 586 A.2d 887 (Pa. 1991); State v. McKnight, 352 S.E.2d 471 (S.C. 1987); State v. Oakes, 598 A.2d 119 (Vt. 1991).

153. 468 U.S. 981 (1984).

relying on the warrant issued by the magistrate, the evidence would seemingly have been inadmissible.[154]

Notice an odd possibility: Because the test is objective, does this mean that evidence obtained by a *bad-faith* officer—for example, one who believes the warrant he is executing is invalid, but he doesn't care—is admissible, as long as a "reasonably well trained officer" would have believed that the warrant was good? Professor LaFave has suggested that this need not be the case, based on the following example: Officer takes his warrant affidavit to Prosecutor for a judgment as to its sufficiency. Prosecutor informs Officer in no uncertain terms that the affidavit is insufficient to show probable cause. Officer ignores this appraisal and goes to a magistrate who (mistakenly) issues a warrant. According to LaFave, the likely state of mind of the "reasonably well trained officer" would take into account Officer's awareness that Prosecutor, a trained lawyer, believed there was insufficient basis for a warrant.[155] This conclusion follows from language in *Leon* that, in determining whether an officer's reliance on a warrant was objectively reasonable, "all of the circumstances—including whether the warrant application had previously been rejected by a different magistrate"—or, it may be assumed here, by a prosecutor—"may be considered."

[3] When "Good Faith" Does Not Exist

[a] In General

Leon noted four situations in which a reasonably well-trained officer would *not* rely on a warrant subsequently declared defective. First, the non-suppression rule of *Leon* would not apply if the magistrate who issued the warrant relied on information supplied by a police officer who knew that statements in the document were false or who recklessly disregarded the truth, in violation of the principles of *Franks v. Delaware*.[156]

Second, evidence is properly excluded if, in the language of *Leon*, the "issuing magistrate wholly abandoned his judicial role in the manner condemned in *Lo-Ji Sales, Inc. v. New York*."[157] In other words, *Leon* does not apply if the magistrate's behavior was so lacking in neutrality that a reasonable officer would have realized that the magistrate was not functioning in an impartial, judicial manner. Although *Leon* specified only the circumstances of *Lo-Ji Sales*, the exclusionary rule ought to apply to *any* situation in which the magistrate acts as an obvious rubber stamp for the police, for example, if he signs the warrant without reading it while in the presence of the officer who later claims reliance.[158]

Third, an officer may not rely "on a warrant based on an affidavit "so lacking in indicia of probable cause as to render official belief in its existence entirely unreasonable." The Court apparently means that an officer may not rely on a warrant issued by a magistrate based on a wholly conclusory—"bare bones"—affidavit, in gross violation of the totality-of-the-circumstances test of probable cause enunciated in *Illinois v. Gates*.[159] That

---

154. Herring v. United States, 555 U.S. 135, 142 (2009) "We (perhaps confusingly) called this objectively reasonable reliance 'good faith.'").

155. 1 LaFave, Note 1, *supra*, at 72.

156. 438 U.S. 154 (1978). *See* § 10.03[B], *supra*.

157. 442 U.S. 319 (1979) (magistrate accompanied police to an "adult bookstore" and selected the materials to be seized). *See generally* § 10.03[A], *supra*.

158. United States v. Decker, 956 F.2d 773 (8th Cir. 1992).

159. 462 U.S. 213 (1983). *See* § 8.05, *supra*.

is, an officer may ordinarily assume that a magistrate knows what he is doing when he makes a probable cause finding. Even if it turns out later, based on a higher court ruling, that the magistrate's probable cause judgment was faulty, the officer's reliance on the magistrate will protect the evidence from exclusion. Only if the magistrate's finding of probable cause is grossly off the mark will this exception to *Leon* apply and the evidence be excluded.

The fourth exception to *Leon*'s "good faith" non-suppression rule applies when an officer relies on a warrant "so facially deficient — i.e., in failing to particularize the place to be searched or the things to be seized — that the executing officers cannot reasonably presume it to be valid." For example, an officer may not reasonably rely on a warrant authorizing him to search "an apartment" of a multi-unit building, or to seize "all stolen goods" in a particularly described house. In these cases, the warrant is obviously deficient because it fails to satisfy the particularity requirement of the Fourth Amendment.[160]

[b] Improperly Executed Warrants

The Court in *Leon* warned in a footnote that the reasoning of the case "assumes, of course, that the officers properly executed the warrant and searched only those places and for those objects that it was reasonable to believe were covered by the warrant." In other words, the *Leon* "good faith" rule should not protect *unreasonably executed*, albeit facially valid, warrants.

For example, suppose that O, an officer, executes a warrant authorizing him to search D's bedroom for clothing related to a rape. If O, conducting the bedroom search, inspects files and seizes incriminating papers found in them, this latter search should not be protected by *Leon*, as it was not reasonable for O to rely on a warrant, which authorizes him only to search for clothing, to look through written materials.

[4] Why the Exception?: The Reasoning of *Leon*

Much of the Court's opinion in *Leon* stressed the costs of the exclusionary rule, and thus reads like a well-reasoned, but not out-of-the-ordinary, general criticism of the suppression rule. These aspects of *Leon* could be used to support the outright abolition of the exclusionary rule. Other features of *Leon* were directed to the narrower question before it, namely, whether the deterrent benefits of the exclusionary rule outweigh its costs in the context of an officer's reasonable reliance on a warrant that has been authorized by a neutral and detached magistrate.

Justice White, writing for the Court, provided a threefold justification for limiting the scope of the suppression rule to circumstances in which a warrant has been secured, albeit later determined to be defective:

> First, the exclusionary rule is designed to deter police misconduct rather than to punish the errors of judges and magistrates. Second, there exists no evidence

---

160. How, then, do we explain *Massachusetts v. Sheppard*, 468 U.S. 981 (1984), *Leon*'s companion case, in which the warrant was invalid on particularity grounds and yet the Court allowed the evidence to be introduced? In that case, the magistrate forgot to cross out irrelevant portions of the form, but he assured the officer seeking the warrant, who was also the one who executed it, that the corrections had been made. On these facts, reliance on the magistrate's assurances was deemed reasonable. *Sheppard* left open the question of "[w]hether an officer who is . . . [un]familiar with the warrant application or who has unalleviated concerns about the proper scope of the search would be justified in failing to notice a defect [in the warrant]."

suggesting that judges and magistrates are inclined to ignore or subvert the Fourth Amendment or that lawlessness among these actors requires application of the extreme sanction of exclusion. [¶] Third, and most important, we discern no basis, and are offered none, for believing that exclusion of evidence seized pursuant to a warrant will have a significant deterrent effect on the issuing judge or magistrate.[161]

On the third—"and most important"—point, the Court reasoned that "[m]any of the factors that indicate that the exclusionary rule cannot provide an effective . . . deterrent for individual offending law enforcement officers applies as well to judges or magistrates." As for systemic deterrence, the exclusionary rule "clearly" cannot have such an influence, since judges are not adjunct law enforcement officers and, therefore, "have no stake in the outcome of particular criminal prosecutions." Therefore, the threat of exclusion of evidence "cannot be expected significantly to deter them."

If the exclusionary rule will not deter judges and magistrates, the Court reasoned, the rule can only make sense if it will "alter the behavior of individual law enforcement officers or the policies of their department." The majority doubted that a change in the exclusionary rule of the sort announced in *Leon* would have a counter-deterrent effect on police officers. First, it treated as "speculative" the fear that the rule would result in "magistrate shopping," i.e., officers seeking out more lenient judges to issue warrants. In any case, "[i]f a magistrate serves merely as a 'rubber stamp' for the police or is unable to exercise mature judgment, closer supervision or removal provides a more effective remedy than the exclusionary rule."

Beyond this, Justice White stated, "even assuming that the rule effectively deters some police misconduct," exclusion of evidence "cannot be expected, and should not be applied, to deter objectively reasonable law enforcement activity." In such circumstances, exclusion of the evidence "will not further the ends of the exclusionary rule in any appreciable way; for it is painfully apparent that . . . the officer is acting as a reasonable officer would and should act in similar circumstances."

The holding in *Leon*, not surprisingly, proved controversial. Some critics maintained that, even if a cost-benefit analysis is appropriate in determining whether to retain the exclusionary rule (itself a controversial proposition[162]), the *Leon* majority's approach to the subject was skewed.[163] According to Justice Brennan in dissent in *Leon*, the Court created a "curious world where the 'costs' of excluding illegally obtained evidence loom to exaggerated heights and where the 'benefits' . . . are made to disappear with a mere wave of the hand." In particular, the Court included on the scale *all* of the supposed costs of the exclusionary rule—not simply those that might be avoided by the *Leon* rule—while it considered *only* those benefits of the exclusionary rule that arise in "objective good-faith" cases.

Also, the Court arguably understated the value of the exclusionary rule in inducing magistrates to act more carefully. Current data suggest that some magistrates provide little oversight of the warrant process.[164] Perhaps some judges *do* function as adjunct law

---

161. *Leon*, 468 U.S. 897, 916 (1984).

162. *See* § 20.04[D][1], *supra.*

163. *See* Yale Kamisar, *The Warren Court and Criminal Justice: A Quarter-Century Retrospective*, 31 Tulsa L.J. 1, 32 (1995) (accusing the post-Warren Court of doing its balancing "in an empirical fog," and of conducting cost-benefit analysis by giving "back the values and assumptions the Court fed into it").

164. *See* § 10.02, *supra.*

officers, albeit while "disguised" in judicial robes; if so, *Leon* invites these magistrates to protect the prosecution from exclusion of evidence.

[C] Warrantless Searches: Moving Beyond *Leon*

[1] Warrantless Searches Authorized by Statute

The "objective good-faith" rule announced in *United States v. Leon*[165] involved searches conducted with warrants — that is, to the situation in which a police officer reasonably relies on the validity of a warrant, and thus reasonably relies on the magistrate's determination of the constitutional validity of the authorized search.

It was just a small step from *Leon* to *Illinois v. Krull*.[166] *Krull* involved a warrantless administrative search of an automobile-wrecking yard conducted by a police detective. An Illinois statute authorized the search. Subsequent to the search, which resulted in the seizure of stolen items, the statute was declared unconstitutional because it permitted officers unbridled discretion in their warrantless searches.

The United States Supreme Court held, 5–4, that the "approach used in *Leon* is equally applicable to the present case." Justice Blackmun, who delivered the opinion, stated that:

> application of the exclusionary rule to suppress evidence obtained by an officer acting in objectively reasonable reliance on a statute would have as little deterrent effect on the officer's actions as would the exclusion of evidence when an officer acts in objectively reasonable reliance on a warrant. . . . To paraphrase the Court's comment in *Leon*: "Penalizing the officer for the [legislature's] error, rather than his own, cannot logically contribute to the deterrence of Fourth Amendment violations."

[2] Computer Databases

[a] Reliance on Court-Managed Databases

In *Arizona v. Evans*,[167] E was arrested during a routine traffic stop because the patrol car's computer reported that there was an outstanding misdemeanor warrant for *E*'s arrest. A subsequent warrantless search incident to the arrest revealed marijuana. As it turned out, the arrest warrant had previously been quashed, but *E*'s name had not been removed from the computer due to a clerical error by a court employee responsible for updating the records.

The Court held, 7–2, that the exclusionary rule did not require suppression of the marijuana. According to Chief Justice Rehnquist, *Leon*'s reasoning justified a "categorical exception to the exclusionary rule for clerical errors of court employees." The Court applied the three-pronged argument set out in *Leon*,[168] but restated it in terms of court employees, rather than magistrates. Then, applying the objective good-faith rule of *Leon*, the Court observed that "[t]here is no indication that the arresting officer was not acting objectively reasonably when he relied upon the police computer record." The Court expressly

---

165. 468 U.S. 897 (1984).
166. 480 U.S. 340 (1987).
167. 514 U.S. 1 (1995); *see generally* Wayne R. LaFave, *Computers, Urinals, and the Fourth Amendment: Confessions of a Patron Saint*, 94 Mich. L. Rev. 2553 (1996).
168. *See* the text to Note 160, *supra*.

declined to answer the question of whether "evidence should be suppressed if police personnel [rather than court employees] were responsible for the error."[169]

Computer errors of the sort involved in *Evans* are not uncommon.[170] This concern apparently stirred Justices O'Connor, Souter and Breyer to write a concurring opinion. Although they joined the majority opinion, these justices warned that it "would *not* be reasonable for the police to rely, say, on a recordkeeping system, their own or some other agency's, that has no mechanism to ensure its accuracy over time and that routinely leads to false arrests." Although the police "are entitled to enjoy the substantial advantage" of computer technology, they may not "rely on it blindly."

[b] Reliance on Police-Managed Databases

The gradual path the Court took from *Leon* to *Krull* to *Evans* took another, far more significant, step in 2009 in *Herring v. United States*,[171] another case involving a computer database error—but this database was one managed by a law enforcement agency, rather than a court. In *Herring*, sheriff officers in Coffee County, Alabama arrested *H* based on an active warrant listed in a neighboring county's sheriff-run database. In a warrantless search incident to the arrest, the officers discovered drugs and a gun. As it turned out, however, the computer had not been updated and the warrant had actually been recalled months earlier. As a result, the arrest was unlawful (the State of Alabama conceded this point) and, thus, the search incident to the *unlawful* arrest was also in violation of the Fourth Amendment. A federal court determined that the error by the neighboring county sheriff's department constituted negligence.

In *Herring*, therefore, the Court had to determine whether an error by law enforcement agents—not by the legislature (*Krull*), a judge (*Leon*) or a court clerk (*Evans*)—changed the outcome. It did not. The Supreme Court held, 5–4, that the exclusionary did not apply to these facts. Chief Justice Roberts delivered the Court's opinion, attempting to bring the facts of the case within prior case law:

> Our cases establish that . . . suppression is not an automatic consequence of a Fourth Amendment violation. Instead, the question turns on the culpability of the police and the potential of exclusion to deter wrongful police conduct. Here the error was the result of isolated negligence attenuated from the arrest. We hold that *in these circumstances* the jury should not be barred from considering all the evidence. (Emphasis added)

The Chief Justice stated that the exclusionary rule, which "is not an individual right," only applies if "appreciable" deterrence will result, the benefits of deterrence will outweigh the costs of suppression, and—in very important language—

---

169. *Evans*, 514 U.S. 16 n.5.

170. According to 1985 projections of the Federal Bureau of Investigation—when computer databases were far less common than today—as many as 12,000 invalid or inaccurate reports on suspects wanted for arrest were transmitted *daily* to federal, state, and local police agencies. David Burnham, *F.B.I. Says 12,000 Faulty Reports on Suspects Are Issued Each Day*, N.Y. Times, Aug. 25, 1985, at 1.

171. 555 U.S. 135 (2009); *see generally* Craig Bradley, *Is the Exclusionary Rule Dead?*, 102 J. Crim. L. & Criminology 1 (2012); Wayne R. LaFave, *The Smell of Herring: A Critique of the Supreme Court's Latest Assault on the Exclusionary Rule*, 99 J. Crim. L. & Criminology 757 (2009); Tracey Maclin & Jennifer Rader, *No More Chipping Away: The Roberts Court Uses an Axe to Take Out the Fourth Amendment Exclusionary Rule*, 81 Miss. L.J. 1183 (2012).

the police conduct . . . [is] sufficiently culpable that such deterrence is worth the price paid by the justice system. As laid out in our cases, the exclusionary rule serves to deter deliberate, reckless, or grossly negligent conduct, or in some circumstances recurring or systemic negligence. The error in this case does not rise to that level.[172]

The Chief Justice went on to discuss the "level" of database error that *would* justify suppression of evidence:

We do not suggest that all recordkeeping errors by the police are immune from the exclusionary rule. . . . If the police have been shown to be *reckless* in maintaining a warrant system, or to have *knowingly* made false entries to lay the groundwork for future false arrests, exclusion would certainly be justified. . . . The dissent also adverts to the possible unreliability of a number of databases not relevant to this case. In a case where *systemic* errors were demonstrated, it might be *reckless* for officers to rely on an unreliable warrant.[173]

In language concluding the opinion, the majority stated that "isolated police negligence"—as distinguished from "gross," "recurring," or "systemic" negligence—does not "automatically trigger[] suppression." The Chief Justice wrote:

In light of our repeated holdings that the deterrent effect of suppression must be substantial and outweigh any harm to the justice system [citing *Leon*], we conclude that when police mistakes are the result of negligence *such as that described here*, rather than systemic error or reckless disregard of constitutional requirements, any marginal deterrence does not "pay its way." (Emphasis added.)

Justice Ginsburg delivered a dissent joined by Justice Breyer and now-retired Justices Stevens and Souter. She advocated a "more majestic conception" of the exclusionary rule, one not tied exclusively to deterrence principles.[174] She also rejected the majority's deterrence analysis on its own terms. She reasoned that suppression of evidence would have had deterrent value: the "record reflects no routine practice of checking the database for accuracy. . . . Is it not altogether obvious that the [Sheriff's] Department could take further precautions to ensure the integrity of its database?" In view of the "paramount importance of accurate recordkeeping in law enforcement," the fact that "[e]lectronic databases form the nervous system of contemporary criminal justice operations," and the "grave concerns for individual liberty" at stake, the dissenters believed that the exclusionary rule should be enforced.

Herring has received sharp criticism from many legal commentators, both on grounds of precedent and policy.[175] However one feels about the exclusionary rule, *Herring* surely narrowed its scope further: *Leon*, *Krull*, and *Evans* involved law enforcement agents who reasonably relied on non-law enforcement agents (judges, legislators, court employees);

---

172. The *Herring* majority did not deny the dissenter's claim that "liability for negligence"—and, here, someone in the neighboring sheriff's department *did* act negligently—"creates an incentive to act with greater care." But, Chief Justice Roberts wrote, the degree of deterrence that would be gained by excluding the evidence "is not worth the cost." § 555 U.S. at 144, n.4.

173. *Id.* at 146 (emphasis added).

174. *See* Note 36, *supra*.

175. *E.g.*, LaFave, Note 171, *supra* at 758 ("*Herring* . . . I am chagrined to say, appears to deserve a category of its own, and not on the positive side of the scale."; its holding "is not simply wrong; it is wrong over and over again").

there was no police misconduct to deter in those cases. Here, for the first time, the Court announced that even when there *is* police non-gross, non-systemic negligence, at least of an "attenuated" nature, the exclusionary rule does not apply. It said this even as it admitted that exclusion of the evidence in this case would have incentivized greater police care.[176]

Herring also left the legal community unsure of its scope. Is the deterrence analysis in this case limited to computer databases? Beyond this, the Court described the negligence here as "attenuated," but what made it attenuated? Is it because the negligence was committed by a law enforcement agent in another county? What if the officer in *Herring* had received the information from his county's computer database? And, assuming this case is not limited to mismanaged computer databases, what if Officer X obtains information from a suspect by negligently violating the Fourth Amendment and then provides this information to partner Officer Y who, unaware of the violation, reasonably relies on it to conduct a warrantless search? Would the exclusionary rule apply?

Beyond this, what constitutes "recurrent," "systemic," and "gross" negligence, and how will the Court define "reckless"? And, to the extent that the exclusionary rule depends on the state of mind of the officer — that he is deliberately violating the Fourth Amendment or is consciously aware of the risk that he is doing so (a possible definition of "recklessness") — doesn't this run counter to the Supreme Court's usual approach in Fourth Amendment cases of applying "objective standards of conduct, rather than standards that depend upon the subjective state of mind of the officer"?[177]

These and other questions remain. But, not surprisingly, *Herring* did not prove to be the last word on the subject.

[3] Reliance on Binding Precedent

The Court applied the *Leon* objective good-faith exception in still another case — this time not involving computer databases — in *Davis v. United States.*[178] In the process, the Court not only confirmed that *Herring* was not limited to computer databases, but it apparently narrowed the exclusionary rule even further.

In *Davis*, D was a passenger in a car subjected to "a routine traffic stop" that led to D's arrest (for giving a false name to the police) and the driver's arrest for driving while intoxicated. D and the driver were handcuffed and placed in the back of patrol cars, at which point the police searched the car and found a gun in the pocket of D's coat. D was subsequently charged with possession of the gun, and when his motion to suppress the gun failed, he was convicted.

The proper disposition of D's suppression motion turned on the rules governing automobile searches incident to lawful arrest.[179] At the time of D's arrest, most jurisdictions understood Supreme Court precedent to authorize substantially contemporaneous searches of the passenger compartment of a car incident to the arrest of a recent occupant, even if the arrestee was no longer in the vehicle and was in police control. Indeed, the precedent in the federal circuit in which D was charged expressly approved

---

176. See Note 172, *supra*.
177. Horton v. California, 496 U.S. 128, 138 (1990).
178. 564 U.S. 229 (2011); *see generally* Bradley, Note 171, *supra*; Maclin & Rader, Note 171, *supra*.
179. *See* § 12.05, *supra*.

automobile searches in circumstances such as *D*'s. While *D*'s case was on appeal, however, the Supreme Court handed down its decision in *Arizona v. Gant*,[180] narrowing the automobile-search doctrine and making clear that searches in circumstances such as *D*'s violated the Fourth Amendment. Because *D*'s case was still on direct appeal, the *Gant* decision applied retroactively and meant that the search that discovered his gun violated the Fourth Amendment.

The Court stated the question in the case this way: "The question . . . is whether to apply the exclusionary rule when the police conduct a search in objectively reasonable reliance on binding judicial precedent."[181] So stated, and in view of the *Leon* line of cases, the answer to this question was a "no-brainer."[182] After all, the search was constitutional at the time of the police conduct. How could one justify exclusion here if there was no exclusion in *Leon*, *Krull*, or *Evans*, where there was also no police negligence, and no exclusion in *Herring*, where there *was* police negligence? The Court did not surprise.[183] It held, 7–2, in an opinion by Justice Alito, that the exclusionary rule does not apply in such circumstances.

Much of the opinion quoted language from the prior exclusionary rule-narrowing cases, particularly *Herring*: the sole purpose of the exclusionary rule is to deter future violations; because the police in this case were following governing precedent "to the letter," the Court concluded that "[a]bout all that exclusion would deter in this case is conscientious police work," and therefore the exclusionary rule should not apply. After conceding that "there was a time when our exclusionary-rule cases were not nearly so discriminating in their approach to the doctrine,"[184] Justice Alito returned to the police-culpability issues and stated that:

> [p]olice practices trigger the harsh sanction of exclusion only when they are deliberate enough to yield "meaningfu[l]" deterrence, and culpable enough to be "worth the price paid by the justice system." [Quoting *Herring*.] The conduct of the officers here was neither of these things. The officers who conducted the search did not violate Davis's Fourth Amendment rights deliberately, recklessly or with gross negligence. [Citing *Herring*.] Nor does this case involve any "recurring or systemic negligence" on the part of law enforcement. [Citing *Herring*.][185]

What is potentially significant in the Court's quotations from *Herring*—besides the fact that it applied *Herring* outside the database area—is that it did *not* note the fact that *Herring*, multiple times, described the negligence in that case as "attenuated." That word is missing from the Alito opinion. Thus, *Davis* can be interpreted as eliminating, *sub silentio*, that factor in exclusionary rule analysis. Now, it seems, all non-"recurring" and non-"systemic" negligence falls on the "no exclusion" side of the Fourth Amendment line.

---

180. 557 U.S. 519 (2009). *See* § 12.05[C], *supra*.

181. *Davis*, 564 U.S. at 239.

182. 1 LaFave, Note 1, *supra*, § 1.3, at 21 (Supp. 2011–2012).

183. One possible surprise: Justice Kagan, generally one of the more liberal members of the Court, signed on to the Alito opinion without comment.

184. *Davis*, 564 U.S. at 237

185. *Id*. at 240.

Justice Sotomayor concurred in the judgment. She emphasized that the police were relying on binding appellate precedent; to her this case "does not present the markedly different question whether the exclusionary rule applies when the law governing the constitutionality of a particular search is unsettled."[186] As the dissenters noted, however, the potential reach of the decision goes well beyond the relatively narrow circumstance of police reliance on binding appellate precedent. The police frequently engage in conduct in the belief that it complies with the Constitution but that, it turns out, "falls just outside the Fourth Amendment's bounds." Therefore, the dissent warned:

> if the Court means what it now says, if it would place determinative weight upon the culpability of an individual officer's conduct, and if it would apply the exclusionary rule only where a Fourth Amendment violation was "deliberate, reckless, or grossly negligent," then the "good faith" exception will swallow the exclusionary rule.

The future of the exclusionary rule in the wake of *Davis* is still unclear. The police officer in *Davis* was merely negligent; it appears from the dictum in the case that police conduct that represents "systemic negligence" or "gross negligence" would still trigger the exclusionary rule.[187]

§ 20.07 "Fruit of the Poisonous Tree" Doctrine

[A] Warning: *Hudson v. Michigan*

Before we start the final journey of this chapter, a warning is in order: *Hudson v. Michigan*.[188] *Hudson* has been cited various places in this chapter and was discussed in some depth earlier.[189] It is also considered in this chapter section. The reason for the warning, however, is this: Because of *Hudson*, fruit-of-the-poisonous-tree law, which previously was relatively straightforward (if, as always, complex), is no longer so. The law in this area is now, at a minimum, in flux, therefore less clear, and even more complicated than before; at worst, *Hudson* has rendered the law in this area inconsistent in certain regards.

Justice Breyer worried in oral argument in *Hudson* that the Supreme Court, by its ruling in this case, might "let a kind of computer virus loose in the Fourth Amendment. I don't know what the implications of that are."[190] The "virus," indeed, was set loose, and its implications uncertain. Critics of *Hudson* hope (some might say, fantasize) that *Hudson* will be "confined to its particular facts, if not promptly overruled."[191] Whether or not one considers *Hudson* so harshly, it is indisputable that it has changed the law under discussion in ways not yet fully known.

---

186. *Id.* at 250.

187. *See* Bradley, Note 171, *supra*, at 3.

188. 547 U.S. 586 (2006). For excellent scholarly sources for understanding this case, see the cites in Note 136, *supra*; *see also* Bradley, Note 171, *supra*; Maclin & Rader. Note 171, *supra*.

189. *See* § 20.05[B][2][b], *supra*. It may profitably be reviewed at this time.

190. http://www.supremecourtus.gov/oral_arguments/argument_transcripts/04-1360b.pdf (page 50).

191. *E.g.,* 1 LaFave, Note 1, *supra*, at § 1.8 (Supp. 2011–2012).

[B] Conceptual Overview

[1] General Principles

In general, when the Fourth Amendment exclusionary rule applies at all, it extends not only to the direct products of governmental illegality, but also to secondary evidence that is the "fruit of the poisonous tree."[192] For example, suppose that P, a police officer, on a sheer hunch, unconstitutionally searches D's house for evidence of D's suspected connection to a murder. During the search, the officer seizes a diary. The diary names a witness (W) to the murder, who agrees to testify against D at his trial.

The unconstitutional search of the house constitutes the initial illegality: It is the "poisonous tree." Under ordinary exclusionary rule principles, the diary is inadmissible at D's trial because it was the direct product of the unlawful search. However, is W's testimony admissible? The government learned about W from the diary that was searched as the result of the initial illegality; as such W's testimony—"secondary" or "derivative" evidence—is a fruit of the poisonous tree.

Assuming that the exclusionary rule is otherwise applicable, evidence that is a fruit of the poisonous tree—such as W's testimony in the hypothetical above—is ordinarily inadmissible. However, the fruit-of-the-poisonous-tree doctrine is subject to three qualifications: (1) the independent source doctrine; (2) the inevitable discovery rule; and (3) the attenuated connection principle. The first doctrine involves circumstances in which the evidence at issue is *not*, in fact, a fruit of the poisonous tree and, therefore, is not subject to exclusion on this ground. The remaining two doctrines serve as exceptions to the rule that a fruit of a poisonous tree must be excluded at the criminal trial.

[2] Identifying the Poisonous Tree

The fruit-of-the-poisonous-tree doctrine applies to constitutional provisions other than the Fourth Amendment, i.e., there are Fifth Amendment and Sixth Amendment poisonous trees, as well.[193] On the other hand, there is no or only a very limited *Miranda*[194] poisonous tree doctrine.[195] Therefore, it can be critical to identify the nature of the poisonous tree.

For example, suppose that D is arrested *without probable cause*, informed of his *Miranda* rights, voluntarily waives those rights, and confesses. The confession is not inadmissible under Fifth Amendment, Sixth Amendment, or *Miranda* principles. Nonetheless, the confession could be inadmissible as a fruit of a *Fourth Amendment* poisonous tree (the unlawful arrest).

On the other hand, suppose that D is *lawfully* arrested, *not* informed of his *Miranda* rights, and subjected to custodial interrogation, during which time he informs the police where he concealed a gun used in the crime. Here, as we will see, D's confession is inadmissible under *Miranda* principles. The gun is a fruit of that *Miranda* violation. Therefore, its admissibility is a matter of *Miranda* jurisprudence—which ordinarily

---

192. Nardone v. United States, 308 U.S. 338, 341 (1939).

193. *See* §§ 22.03[C][2][b] (Fifth/Fourteenth Amendment Due Process Clause, interrogations), 23.05[B][3][b][ii] (Fifth Amendment, interrogations), 25.07[D] (Sixth Amendment right to counsel, interrogations), and 26.02[A] (*id.*, eyewitness identification procedures), *infra*.

194. Miranda v. Arizona, 384 U.S. 436 (1966).

195. *See* § 24.12[B], *infra*.

permits fruits of *Miranda* violations to be introduced at trial—and not of Fourth Amendment law.

The lesson, again, to be grasped: Be clear as to the nature of the "poisonous tree," i.e., the constitutional violation that constitutes the initial illegality.

[C] Independent Source Doctrine[196]

The threshold issue in any fruit-of-the-poisonous-tree claim should be whether "the challenged evidence is in some sense the product of illegal governmental activity."[197] Evidence that is not causally linked to governmental illegality is admissible pursuant to the "independent source doctrine."[198] Such evidence, in essence, is a fruit of a *non*-poisonous tree. As the Supreme Court has explained:

> [T]he interest of society in deterring unlawful police conduct and the public interest in having juries receive all probative evidence of a crime are properly balanced by putting the police in the same, not a *worse* position that they would have been in if no police error or misconduct had occurred. . . . When the challenged evidence has an independent source, exclusion of such evidence would put the police in a worse position than they would have been in absent any error or violation.[199]

In its simplest application, the independent source doctrine applies if the challenged evidence is discovered for the *first* time during *lawful* police activity. For example, suppose that the police *lawfully* seize *D*'s diary in a criminal investigation. The diary identifies *W*, an eyewitness to *D*'s conduct. The police contact *W*, who agrees to testify against *D*. Later, the police search *D*'s premises again, but this time *unlawfully*. In the second search, the police discover *W*'s name in another document. Under the independent source doctrine, *D* may not successfully challenge *W*'s trial testimony as a fruit of the poisonous tree, because the police originally obtained *W*'s name in the first—lawful—search.

The independent source doctrine also applies, however, if evidence is initially discovered *unlawfully*, but is later obtained lawfully in a manner independent of the original discovery. This lesson is learned from the Court's controversial analysis in *Murray v. United States.*[200] In *Murray*, police officers unconstitutionally (they possessed probable cause for the search, but lacked a necessary search warrant) entered a warehouse and observed burlap-wrapped bales, which they suspected contained marijuana. The officers left the warehouse without seizing the bales. While they kept the area under surveillance, other officers obtained a warrant to search the building based on an untainted affidavit, i.e., an affidavit only containing information the police gathered *lawfully before* the unlawful entry. The officers, now armed with a warrant, returned and seized the bales.

---

196. *See generally* Craig M. Bradley, *Murray v. United States: The Bell Tolls for the Search Warrant Requirement*, 64 Ind. L.J. 907 (1989).

197. United States v. Crews, 445 U.S. 463, 471 (1980).

198. *See* Silverthorne Lumber Co. v. United States, 251 U.S. 385 (1920).

199. Nix v. Williams, 467 U.S. 431, 443 (1984).

200. 487 U.S. 533 (1988); *contra under the state constitution*, Commonwealth v. Melendez, 676 A.2d 226 (Pa. 1996) (application of the "independent source doctrine" is proper only if the "independent source" is independent of the police or investigative team that engaged in the initial unlawful conduct).

Justice Scalia, writing for a four-justice plurality, remanded the case to a lower court "for determination whether the warrant-authorized search of the warehouse was an independent source of the challenged evidence." As the Court analyzed the situation, however, the warranted search very possibly constituted an independent source because the warrant was supported by probable cause, which in turn was based on an affidavit that did not include anything learned by the police during the illegal entry. Under such circumstances, the evidence seized was a product of the second — lawful — warranted search, and *not* a product of the first — unlawful — warrantless search.

According to the plurality, there was one way that the second search could be a fruit of the original illegality, namely, "if the agents' decision to seek the warrant was prompted by what they had seen during the initial entry." That is, if the police would not have applied for the warrant *but for* the illegal search, then the second search *would* be a fruit of the illegality. On such hypothesized facts, the warrant would be a fruit of the unlawful entry — the warrant would be poisoned — because the first, unlawful search *motivated* the request for the warrant for the second search.

How does a court determine whether an officer's decision to apply for a warrant was prompted by an earlier unlawful search? Does *Murray* invite an officer to testify, perhaps falsely, that he would have sought a warrant even if he had not originally entered the premises illegally? Such an incentive is undesirable. As the Court has stated elsewhere, "evenhanded law enforcement is best achieved by the application of objective standards of conduct, rather than standards that depend upon the subjective state of mind of the officer."[201] Under *Murray*, a finding regarding the agent's state of mind — his motivation for seeking the warrant — is required. However, according to the plurality, an officer's assurance on the point — "I would have requested this warrant anyway" — is not dispositive: "Where the facts render those assurances implausible, the independent source doctrine will not apply."

Murray arguably also provides an incentive to police to conduct unlawful confirmatory searches. That is, the risk is that, because the warrant application process is inconvenient, officers may want to confirm their suspicions, even if they believe they have probable cause, before they apply for a warrant. If they unlawfully search and find nothing, they will have saved the time of applying for a warrant, and yet the individual's constitutional right to be free from an unreasonable search will have been violated.

Justice Scalia discounted this concern. He reasoned that if the police have probable cause before they search, as in *Murray*, they would be "foolish" to conduct a confirmatory warrantless search because, if they do find what they were looking for, they will later have to prove that all of the information in the subsequent warrant affidavit was obtained lawfully, and that they were not motivated to apply for the warrant by the fact of the confirmatory search, an "onerous" burden. And, of course, if they lacked probable cause before the confirmatory search, nothing learned during the search may be used to strengthen their case.

As controversial as *Murray* has proved to be, it pales in comparison to *Hudson v. Michigan*.[202] Whereas in *Murray* the police entered premises twice, the first time unlawfully and the second time lawfully, in *Hudson*, as discussed earlier in this chapter,[203] the police entered *H*'s home just once — unlawfully. Although they were armed with a valid

---

201. Horton v. California, 496 U.S. 128, 138 (1990).
202. 547 U.S. 586 (2006).
203. *See* § 20.05[B][2][b], *supra*.

warrant, they executed it unconstitutionally, in violation of the Fourth Amendment knock-and-announce requirement.

Justice Scalia, writing for the five-justice majority, upheld the admission of the seized evidence. The Court did so on various grounds, one of which was the surprising claim that the constitutional violation was *not* the but-for cause of the discovery and seizure of the contested evidence, i.e., that the independent source doctrine applied to the facts of the case:

> In this case, of course, the constitutional violation of an illegal *manner* of entry was *not* a but-for cause of obtaining the evidence. Whether that preliminary misstep had occurred *or not*, the police would have executed the warrant they had obtained, and would have discovered the [evidence] inside the house.[204]

As Professor Sharon Davies and Anna Scanlon explain this aspect of *Hudson*, "[t]his reasoning implied that if there was a 'but for' cause of the search and seizure of [H]'s home, the cause was the *warrant* that authorized the search, not the *entry* that immediately preceded it."[205] In broader terms, taken to its logical conclusion, "*Hudson* is a declaration that the exclusionary rule is inapplicable whenever a seemingly unitary search is divisible into multiple, independent Fourth Amendment events and evidence is causally linked to the event that satisfies the Fourth Amendment, not the separate event that violates its commands."[206]

The Court's brief causation analysis is subject to criticism. First, it "runs directly contrary to hundreds of decided fruit-of-the-poisonous-tree decisions in which courts have declined to adopt such a distorted version of the but-for test. . . ."[207] As Justice Breyer, writing for the *Hudson* dissenters, put it:

> [T]aking causation as it is commonly understood in the law, I do not see how [the majority's causation analysis] can be so. . . . Although the police might have entered [H]'s home lawfully, they did not in fact do so. Their unlawful behavior inseparably characterizes their actual entry; that entry was a necessary condition of their presence in [H]'s home; and their presence in [H]'s home was a necessary condition of their finding and seizing the evidence.[208]

---

204. *Hudson*, 547 U.S. at 592.

205. Davies & Scanlon, Note 136, *supra*, at 1059.

206. Tomkovicz, Note 136, *supra*, at 1857.

207. 6 LaFave, Note 1, *supra*, at §11.4 (Supp. 2011-2012). One case, *New York v. Harris*, 495 U.S. 14 (1990), however, arguably supports *Hudson*. In *Harris*, the police had probable cause to arrest *H*, but they violated the Fourth Amendment by arresting him in his home without an arrest warrant. The police transported *H* to the police station where they informed *H* of his *Miranda* rights. *H* waived his constitutional rights, and made a statement that the prosecutor sought to introduce at his trial. *Harris* held that this statement was admissible notwithstanding the initial illegal entry of the home, because *H* "was in legal custody [since there was probable cause] . . . and because the statement, while the product of an arrest and being in custody, *was not the fruit of the fact that the arrest was made in the house rather than someplace else.*" *Id.* at 20 (emphasis added). As the *Harris* Court also explained, "[b]ecause the officers had probable cause to arrest [H] for a crime, [H] was not unlawfully in custody when he was removed to the station house ... For Fourth Amendment purposes, the legal issue is the same as it would be had the police arrested [H] on his doorstep, illegally entered his home to search for evidence, and later interrogated [H] at the station house."*Harris* has been rejected pursuant to state constitutional law in various jurisdictions. State v. Geisler, 610 A.2d 1225 (Conn. 1992) (applying ordinary attenuated connection principles); State v. Mariano, 160 P.3d 1258 (Haw. App. 2007) (same); People v. Harris, 570 N.E.2d 1051 (N.Y. 1991) (same).

208. *Hudson*, 547 U.S. at 615.

In actuality, what the majority did was to confuse the independent source doctrine (in which there is no "but for" link between the violation and the evidence) with the inevitable discovery doctrine, which is considered in the next subsection. *That* doctrine applies when the constitutional violation *was* the cause of the seizure of the challenged evidence, but the court is satisfied that the evidence *would* have been seized lawfully anyway. Even a cursory reading of Justice Scalia's causation statement set out above[209] demonstrates that he blurred the distinction between these two doctrines.

[D] Inevitable Discovery Rule

The independent source doctrine, described immediately above, provides that evidence is admissible, despite police illegality, if the evidence seized was not causally linked to that illegality. Suppose, however, that the evidence in question *is* causally tied to earlier governmental illegality, but the prosecutor asserts that the police *would* have discovered the evidence lawfully despite the unconstitutional conduct. If this is the case, is the derivative evidence admissible?

The Supreme Court held in *Nix v. Williams*[210] that evidence linked to an earlier illegality *is* admissible in a criminal trial *if* the prosecutor proves by a preponderance of the evidence that the challenged evidence "ultimately or inevitably would have been discovered by lawful means." This is the so-called "inevitable discovery" (or "hypothetical independent source") rule. Although the violation in *Nix* involved the Sixth Amendment right to counsel, the fruit-of-the-poisonous-tree analysis applies in the same manner in Fourth Amendment cases.

In *Nix*, police officers, in violation of *D*'s Sixth Amendment right to counsel, deliberately elicited incriminating information from him as they transported him in their police vehicle, and induced him thereby to lead them to the body of the murder victim. At the time that *D* agreed to show the police where the body was buried, a search team, entirely independent of the activities going on in the police vehicle, were within a few miles of discovering the corpse; however, the search was temporarily called off after *D* agreed to cooperate.

The Court ruled that the evidence relating to the victim's body—a fruit of the unconstitutionally obtained statement by *D*—was admissible notwithstanding the Sixth Amendment illegality, on the basis of the inevitable discovery doctrine. The trial court found that the body would have been discovered "within a short time" in "essentially the same condition" as a result of the independent search.

Justices Brennan and Marshall dissented. They agreed that evidence that would ultimately be discovered lawfully should be admissible, but they would have required the prosecutor to prove such inevitability by the higher standard of "clear and convincing evidence." They reasoned that the inevitable discovery doctrine, although akin to the independent source doctrine, critically differs from it in that there is *not* an independent source of the evidence, only a hypothetically independent one. The higher burden of

---

209. See the text to Note 204, *supra*.

210. 467 U.S. 431 (1984); *contra under the state constitution*, Smith v. State, 948 P.2d 473 (Alaska 1997) (requiring proof by "clear and convincing" standard); State v. Garner, 417 S.E.2d 502 (N.C. 1992) (*id.*); Commonwealth v. O'Connor, 546 N.E.2d 336 (Mass. 1989) (applying a "certain as a practical matter" standard); State v. Winterstein, 220 P.3d 1226 (Wash. 2009) (rejecting *any* inevitable discovery doctrine).

proof is needed, the dissenters claimed, in order to confine the inevitable discovery rule to circumstances that closely resemble the independent source doctrine.

[E] Attenuated Connection Principle (The *Wong Sun* Rule)

[1] Overview

In *Nardone v. United States*[211] the Supreme Court held that evidence secured as the result of police illegality is admissible if the connection between the illegality and the challenged evidence has "become so attenuated as to dissipate the taint."

The Court explained the attenuated connection principle further in *Wong Sun v. United States*.[212] In *Wong Sun*, the Court stated that not all evidence "is 'fruit of the poisonous tree' simply because it would not have come to light but for the illegal actions of the police." Instead, the critical question is "whether, granting establishment of the primary illegality, the evidence to which instant objection is made has been come at by exploitation of that illegality or instead by means sufficiently distinguishable to be purged of the primary taint." Put differently, even if certain evidence *is* causally tied to an earlier illegality—even if the tree *is* poisoned—at some point the fruit from that tree is sufficiently untainted so as to be admissible in a criminal trial.

Before the Supreme Court's ruling in *Hudson v. Michigan*,[213] the attenuation doctrine worked in much the same way as the proximate causation concept in torts and substantive criminal law. That is, as with proximate cause, there is no bright-line test for determining whether or when derivative evidence is free of the original taint. Each case is determined on its own facts, and no single factor is always dispositive. Ultimately, the attenuated connection principle is tied to the perceived purposes and costs of the exclusionary rule: "the 'dissipation of the taint' concept . . . 'attempts to mark the point at which the detrimental consequences of illegal police action become so attenuated that the deterrent effect of the exclusionary rule no longer justifies its cost.'"[214]

However, the preceding, no-bright-line, description of attenuation law is now subject to a significant exception announced in *Hudson*. There seemingly *is* one bright-line situation, discussed immediately below, in which taint *always* is legally dissipated.

[2] Attenuation Factors: The "Protected Interest" Limitation

In *Hudson v. Michigan*,[215] the police possessed a valid warrant to enter *H*'s home but executed it unconstitutionally in violation of the knock-and-announce rule. The Court held that the exclusionary rule did not apply, in part on attenuation grounds. Justice Scalia explained:

> [E]ven if the illegal entry here could be characterized as a but-for cause of discovering what was inside, we have "never held that evidence is 'fruit of the

---

211. 308 U.S. 338 (1939).
212. 371 U.S. 471 (1963).
213. 547 U.S. 586 (2006).
214. United States v. Leon, 468 U.S. 897, 911 (1984) (quoting Brown v. Illinois, 422 U.S. 590, 609 (1975) (Powell, J., concurring)).
215. 547 U.S. 586 (2006).

poisonous tree' simply because 'it would not have come to light but for the illegal actions of the police.' " . . . Rather, but-for cause . . . can be too attenuated to justify exclusion. . . . [¶] Attenuation can occur, of course, when the causal connection is remote. . . . *Attenuation also occurs when, even given a direct causal connection, the interest protected by the constitutional guarantee that has been violated would not be served by the suppression of the evidence.*[216]

The *Hudson* majority reasoned that the interests served by the knock-and-announce rule—home-dweller privacy, protection of property, and suppression of violence[217]—are not served by the exclusion of the evidence that was the fruit of the violation: "The interests protected by the knock-and-announce requirement are quite different—and do not include the shielding of potential evidence from the government's eyes."[218] In short, on this "protected interests" ground alone, the connection between the illegality and the challenged evidence is considered sufficiently attenuated as to dissipate the original taint.

[3] Other Attenuation Factors

The "protected interest" limitation aside[219]—all of the remaining factors relating to attenuation are just that—factors to be weighed with one another. Those factors are set out below.

[a] Temporal Proximity

The shorter the time lapse between the initial illegality and the acquisition of the challenged evidence, the more likely a court will conclude that the evidence is tainted. For example, in *Wong Sun v. United States*,[220] the police obtained a statement from *T* in his bedroom immediately after his unlawful arrest. The Court suppressed this evidence because, critically, it "derive[d] so immediately from the unlawful entry."

[b] Intervening Events

[i] In General

The greater the number of factors that intervene between the initial illegality and the seizure of the challenged evidence, the more likely the evidence will be admitted as untainted. As the causal chain of events lengthens, the less likely it is that the police "foresaw

---

216. *Id.* at 593 (emphasis added).

217. *See* § 10.04[C], *supra.*

218. The "protected interest" concept arguably was applied once before in *New York v. Harris*, 495 U.S. 14 (1990), the facts of which are set out in Note 207, *supra.* In *Harris*, the Supreme Court justified the admission of *H*'s post-Miranda confession at the police station, after he was unconstitutionally arrested in his home (for lack of a warrant), in part on the following ground: "[S]uppressing the statement taken outside the house *would not serve the purpose of the rule that made [H]'s in-house arrest illegal.* The warrant requirement for an arrest in the home is imposed to protect the home." *Id.* at 20 (emphasis added). Once any incriminating evidence found in the home is excluded, *Harris* ruled, "the purpose of the rule [prohibiting warrantless entry into the house] has . . . been vindicated."

219. Of course, we don't know yet how the Court will apply this limitation beyond the knock-and-announce context, so we don't know yet how often this limitation can be put aside.

220. 371 U.S. 471 (1963).

the challenged evidence as a probable product of their illegality."[221] Consequently, the deterrent value of the exclusionary rule is reduced.

[ii] Intervening Act of Free Will

An intervening act of free will often removes the taint of an earlier illegality. For example, in *Wong Sun*, WS was released from jail after his unlawful arrest. Subsequently, he voluntarily returned to the police station and provided a written statement. The Court found that the voluntary nature of WS's conduct—returning to police headquarters and answering questions propounded to him—rendered his statement sufficiently free of taint to be admissible.

On the other hand, the Court has consistently held that *Miranda*[222] warnings "*alone and per se, cannot always make the act* [of confessing] *a product of free will to break, for Fourth Amendment purposes*, the causal connection between the illegality and the confession."[223] Therefore, if the police arrest a suspect on less than probable cause, read him the *Miranda* warnings, obtain a waiver, and thereafter secure a confession, the question of whether the subsequent statement was the product of the suspect's free will—and, thus, whether the taint of the initial illegality of the arrest has been sufficiently dissipated—must be determined on the totality of the circumstances. For example, in *Kaupp v. Texas*,[224] three uniformed and two plainclothes officers, concededly without probable cause, came to the family home of *K*, a 17-year old suspect, at 3:00 a.m., awakened him in his bedroom, and said, "we need to go and talk" about a murder. The police thereafter unlawfully took *K* into custody and transported him, handcuffed, to the police station. At the station they removed the handcuffs, advised *K* of his *Miranda* rights, and shortly thereafter obtained his admission to the murder. On these facts, the Supreme Court stated that, except for the *Miranda* warnings, everything else pointed against dissipation of the taint; therefore, it said, "[u]nless, on remand [to the lower court], the state can point to testimony undisclosed on the record . . . , and weighty enough to carry the state's burden despite the clear force of the evidence [of taint] shown here, the confession must be suppressed."

[iii] Valid Arrest Warrant

The Court has held that the presence of an arrest warrant for the defendant is a strong indicator that any subsequent search incident to the arrest will be valid, regardless of whether the police officer engaged in illegal activity prior to the discovery of the arrest warrant. In *Utah v. Strieff*,[225] a police officer stopped the defendant without reasonable suspicion—that is, he conducted an illegal *Terry* stop. During the stop he conducted a routine warrant check on the defendant and found that the defendant had a valid outstanding warrant for a traffic offense. The officer then arrested the defendant, searched him pursuant to that arrest, and recovered methamphetamine and drug paraphernalia. The Supreme Court upheld the search, holding that the officer's "arrest of Strieff thus

---

221. Comment, *Fruit of the Poisonous Tree—A Plea for Relevant Criteria*, 115 U. Pa. L. Rev. 1136, 1148–49 (1967).

222. Miranda v. Arizona, 384 U.S. 436 (1966).

223. Brown v. Illinois, 422 U.S. 590, 603 (1975) (emphasis added); *see also* Dunaway v. New York, 442 U.S. 200 (1979).

224. 538 U.S. 626 (2003) (per curiam).

225. 136 S. Ct. 2056 (2016).

was a ministerial act that was completely compelled by the pre-existing warrant. And once [the officer] was authorized to arrest Strieff, it was undisputedly lawful to search Strieff as an incident of his arrest to protect [the officer's] safety."[226]

The *Strieff* decision was seen as yet another heavy blow against the exclusionary rule, since the officer's initial stop had been so clearly illegal. Writing in dissent, Justice Sotomayor argued that the case would allow police to illegally stop anyone on the street, check for warrants, and then conduct a search if the person ended up having a warrant.[227] Since there are nearly eight million outstanding arrest warrants in this country, Justice Sotomayor argued that the case will legitimize (and provide an incentive for) indiscriminate police searches, a practice that will likely have a disproportionate impact on people of color.[228] The majority responded to the dissent's concerns by noting that such a "dragnet" approach would expose the police to civil liability, and would not trigger the attenuation doctrine because of the flagrancy of the violation (see subsection [c] below).[229]

[c] Flagrancy of the Violation

Derivative evidence is less likely to be free of taint if the initial illegality was deliberate rather than accidental.[230] Metaphorically, a flagrant violation results in greater poison, and thus takes longer to dissipate than a less culpable violation. It is justifiable to apply the exclusionary rule more extensively if the secondary evidence is causally linked to egregious police misconduct and, thus, to police behavior in greater need of deterrence.[231]

In *Utah v. Strieff*, the Court clarified that stopping a suspect without reasonable suspicion is not a "flagrant" violation as long as the officer has a "legitimate" suspicion—in *Strieff*, the suspicion was based on the fact that the suspect had just emerged from a house where drugs were being sold.[232] This contrasts with the "flagrantly" illegal conduct of a police officer on a "fishing expedition" who stops a suspect without any legitimate suspicion in the mere "hope that something would turn up."[233]

[d] Nature of the Derivative Evidence

According to the Supreme Court, some contested evidence *by its nature* is more susceptible to dissipation of taint than other evidence. In particular, verbal evidence is more likely to be deemed admissible than physical evidence.

---

226. *Id.* at 2063.

227. *Id.* at 2056 (Sotomayor, J., dissenting).

228. *Id.* at 2070 (Sotomayor, J., dissenting).

229. *Id.* at 2064.

230. *See* Brown v. Illinois, 422 U.S. 590, 604 (1975). In view of recent Supreme Court decisions primarily limiting the scope of the exclusionary rule to cases of deliberate, reckless, or grossly negligent violations of the Fourth Amendment (*Herring v. United States*, 555 U.S. 135 (2009), and *Davis v. United States*, 131 S. Ct. 2419 (2011), discussed in § 26.06[B][2]-[3], *supra*), "accidental" Fourth Amendment violations will not typically be excluded, irrespective of the attenuation doctrine.

231. *See* George C. Thomas III & Barry S. Pollack, *Balancing the Fourth Amendment Scales: The Bad-Faith Exception to Exclusionary Rule Limitations*, 45 Hastings L.J. 21 (1993) (arguing that bad-faith conduct in obtaining evidence not only requires a more extensive application of the exclusionary rule to secondary evidence, but also justifies use of the rule when it otherwise would not be available—e.g., when victims of bad-faith conduct lack standing and in civil proceedings brought by the government against the Fourth Amendment victim).

232. *Strieff*, 136 S. Ct. at 2063.

233. *Id.*

In *United States v. Ceccolini*,[234] the police unlawfully obtained the name of *X*, a witness to a crime, through an unlawful search. When contacted by the police, *X* offered to provide important testimony against *C*. *C* sought to exclude *X*'s testimony as a fruit of the unlawful search. The Court rejected the prosecutor's argument that the testimony of a witness should *never* "be excluded at trial no matter how close and proximate the connection between it and a violation of the Fourth Amendment." However, the Court also rejected language from *Wong Sun*, which stated that "the policies underlying the exclusionary rule [do not] invite any logical distinction between physical and verbal evidence."

Instead, the Court held that a witness' testimony is more likely than physical evidence to be free of taint. It offered two reasons in support of this proposition. First, witnesses often come forward of their own volition, whereas inanimate objects must be discovered by others. Therefore, there is a greater likelihood that the police will discover a witness by lawful means; consequently, the police have less incentive to violate the Constitution in order to obtain witness testimony.

This reasoning is debatable. Essentially, the majority's reasoning is that testimony will often be admissible under the independent-source or inevitable-discovery doctrines, because witnesses (unlike inanimate objects) can and often do come forward voluntarily. But *Ceccolini* suggests that even if a witness does *not* come forward in a particular case, the mere possibility that he *might* have done so renders the taint more attenuated. This reasoning, however, amounts to nothing more than, as the dissent put it, "judicial double counting" of the free-will factor.

The second reason for the Court's belief that the testimony of witnesses should more easily be purged of taint than physical evidence is that if this were not the case, relevant and material testimony of witnesses would be "permanently disabled." However, as the dissent in *Ceccolini* observed, physical evidence is also susceptible to permanent disability, and witness testimony is more apt to be unreliable than physical evidence. It is unclear, therefore, why a special rule should be devised to make it easier to introduce verbal testimony than physical evidence.

---

234. 435 U.S. 268 (1978).

Chapter 21

Interrogation Law: Overview

§ 21.01 Reflections on Modern Interrogation Law[1]

Police interrogation law has come a long way since the "stone age"[2] of American criminal procedure. Although the Supreme Court in 1884 adopted the common law rule of evidence that a suspect's statement to the police is inadmissible at trial if it was made involuntarily,[3] this rule did not become a part of constitutional law until 1897 in the federal courts,[4] and 1936 in the state courts.[5]

The second half of the twentieth century was a volatile and controversial period in interrogation law, and there is little reason to believe that the new century will bring an end to the controversies, particularly in light of recent studies that suggest that between 15 and 25 percent of DNA-exonerated innocent defendants confessed to crimes they did not commit as a result of police interrogation practices.[6] The law and various controversies surrounding the interrogation process are considered in detail in the next four chapters of the Text. As will be seen, some rulings, and broad language in various Supreme Court opinions, particularly in the 1960s, suggested to some contemporary legal observers that "the doctrines converging upon the institution of police interrogation are

---

1. *See generally* Richard A. Leo, Police Interrogation and American Justice (2008).
2. Yale Kamisar, *Kauper's "Judicial Examination of the Accused" Forty Years Later—Some Comments on a Remarkable Article*, 73 Mich. L. Rev. 15, 16 (1974).
3. Hopt v. Utah, 110 U.S. 574 (1884).
4. Bram v. United States, 168 U.S. 532 (1897).
5. Brown v. Mississippi, 297 U.S. 278 (1936).
6. Sam M. Kassin, *On the Psychology of Confessions: Does Innocent Put Innocents at Risk?*, 60 Am. Psychologist 215, 216 (2005); *see also* Welsh S. White, *What is an Involuntary Confession Now?*, 50 Rutgers L. Rev. 2001, 2005 (1998) ("Over the past few decades, standard interrogation techniques have apparently led to false confessions in a significant number of cases."); and Jan Hoffman, *Police Refine Methods So Potent, Even the Innocent Have Confessed*, New York Times, March 10, 1998, at A1 (although there is considerable dispute regarding the frequency of false confessions, their number "is shaking the confidence of both prosecutors and juries in the reliability of confessions"). Some false confessions appear highly reliable, thereby increasing the likelihood of improper conviction. For example, one recent study of false confessions (confessions of persons later proven with DNA evidence to be innocent) reported that police officers with some frequency intentionally or accidentally introduce important facts about the case into the interrogation. The suspect, perhaps because of youthfulness, mental disability, or simply the strain of a long interrogation, will ultimately confess, repeating the facts the officer told the suspect about the crime. The factually-detailed confession will appear to be reliable—after all, how would a person know how the crime was committed if she was innocent?—but only because the police fed the facts to the suspect who later repeated them back to the interrogators. *See* Brandon L. Garrett, *The Substance of False Confessions*, 62 Stan. L. Rev. 1051 (2010) (shedding light on the phenomenon of "confession contamination").

threatening to push on to their logical conclusion — *to the point where no questioning of suspects will be permitted.*"[7]

This prediction proved wildly wrong. It is clear, however, that interrogation law experienced significant changes during the Warren Court era, as the Supreme Court sought to "even the playing field" in the interrogation room — or, at least, to make it less one-sided — by setting limits on interrogation techniques, requiring the police to inform suspects of their constitutional rights relating to interrogations, and implementing procedures making it possible for suspects to have counsel present during questioning.

In large part, the trend toward expansion of the rights of criminal suspects in the interrogation room ended when the balance of power on the Supreme Court shifted,[8] as justices wedded to "due process model" values were replaced by advocates of the "crime control model" of criminal justice.[9] Although the leading Warren Court interrogation cases have not been overruled, they are mostly "battered and bruised."[10] The "new" Court has applied existing law narrowly, sometimes reinterpreted or overruled precedent, and announced various exceptions to earlier rules. The effect is an uneasy alliance of the old and the new — old law founded on considerable suspicion of the interrogation process, and new law that views confessions not only as good for the soul but as necessary in a crime-fighting society.

§ 21.02 Police Interrogation Techniques: Historically and at Present

In order to appreciate the reasons why the United States Supreme Court and, to a lesser extent, lower courts, became involved in setting limits on police interrogation procedures, it is necessary to put police practices in historical context.

Professor Richard Leo, after describing abuse suffered by a 1930 murder suspect at the hands of Cleveland, Ohio, police officers (it included repeatedly slapping the suspect in the face and forcing him to lie naked on a table while he was beaten with a rubber hose until he confessed), observed that "[b]y the standards of the time, there was nothing unusual about the manner in which the Cleveland detectives obtained [the] confession. . . ."[11] Indeed, according to Leo, "[w]hat had come to be known . . . as the 'third degree'" — the infliction of physical pain or mental suffering to extract information — was, by virtually all accounts, widely and systematically practiced"[12] during the nineteenth century through the early 1930s, to wring confessions from the guilty and, perhaps not rarely, from the innocent. As police interrogations were conducted incommunicado, this ensured not only that suspects were isolated (and, thus, more susceptible to the tactics used), but the violence conducted in interrogation rooms went largely unknown to the public.

---

7. Walter V. Schaefer, The Suspect and Society 9 (1967) (emphasis added).

8. *See* 1.04[E], *supra*.

9. *See* § 2.02, *supra*.

10. Yale Kamisar, *The Warren Court and Criminal Justice: A Quarter-Century Retrospective*, 31 Tulsa L.J. 1, 54 (1995).

11. Leo, Note 1, *supra*, at 43.

12. *Id.*

Change began to occur in the early 1930s with the publication of a blue-ribbon commission study, *Report on Lawlessness in Law Enforcement*, headed by then United States Attorney General George Wickersham.[13] The report exposed the third-degree interrogation techniques to a largely shocked public. As a result of public revulsion and increased judicial attention to the problem, police departments initiated reforms. Physical coercion declined as a consequence in the 1930s and 1940s.

By the 1960s, police interrogation techniques had become sophisticated. Sociologist Gary Marx observed, however, "[t]here is an interesting irony at work here: restrict police use of coercion, and the use of deception increases."[14] That is, with limitations placed on the use of violence to secure confessions, the police turned to psychological pressures and deceptions. Consistent with the social psychology literature of the time,[15] police manuals instructed officers on the proper arrangement of interrogation rooms,[16] on the characteristics of the ideal interrogator,[17] and on the most effective means to manipulate suspects to confess.

Modern police strategy has been described as possessing "many of the essential hallmarks of a confidence game."[18] According to one police officer, "interrogation [now] is *not* a matter of forcing suspects to confess but of 'conning' them. Really what we do is just bullshit them."[19] Contemporary interrogation tactics have also been characterized as, on occasion, "ingenious," but still "uncivilized, at best."[20]

Since the 1960s and largely continuing today, police officers attempt to foster anxiety in suspects, for example by stating (often falsely) that they have sufficient evidence to convict, and then using this disclosure to convince a suspect that it is hopeless to resist the officers' entreaties. Or, the police may follow the very different tactic of displaying false sympathy for the suspect, blaming the victim, and minimizing the moral significance of the charges against the arrestee, in order to secure the individual's confidence and convince her that the court and jury will show leniency if she confesses.[21]

In summary, police procedures have evolved from violent to sophisticated, from the "third degree" to the psychologically manipulative. These changes have been brought about as a result of public demands for change and by pressure exerted by the judiciary.

---

13. National Commission on Law Observance and Law Enforcement, Report on Lawlessness in Law Enforcement (1931).

14. Gary T. Marx, Undercover: Police Surveillance in America 47 (1988).

15. *See* Edwin D. Driver, *Confessions and the Social Psychology of Coercion*, 82 Harv. L. Rev. 42 (1968).

16. *E.g.*, they should give the suspect the "illusion that the environment . . . is withdrawing." Arthur S. Aubry & Rudolph R. Caputo, Criminal Interrogation 38 (1965).

17. *E.g.*, the interrogator should be male, tall, deep voiced, and dressed in a business suit.

18. Richard A. Leo, *Miranda's Revenge: Police Interrogation as a Confidence Game*, 30 Law & Soc. Rev. 259, 260–61 (1996).

19. Richard A. Leo, *From Coercion to Deception: The Changing Nature of Police Interrogation in America*, 18 Crime, Law & Soc. Change 35, 35 (1992) (quoting William Hart, *The Subtle Art of Persuasion*, Police Magazine (January, 1981) at 15–16) (emphasis added).

20. Akhil Reed Amar & Renée B. Lettow, *Fifth Amendment First Principles: The Self-Incrimination Clause*, 93 Mich. L. Rev. 857, 873–74 (1995) (summarizing the findings of David Simon, who observed a Baltimore homicide unit for a year, as reported in David Simon, Homicide: A Year on the Killings Streets (1991)).

21. Kassin, Note 6, *supra*, at 221 (summarizing the steps often taken by police as "isolation," "confrontation," and "minimization").

§ 21.03 Interrogation Law: Constitutional Issues

The interrogation materials covered in the next four chapters are organized based on three different constitutional provisions (the Fifth and Fourteenth Amendment Due Process Clauses; the Fifth Amendment privilege against compelled self-incrimination; and the Sixth Amendment right to counsel), and the special issues relating to the *Miranda v. Arizona*[22] decision. The interrogation issues to be considered in these chapters in part overlap among the three constitutional provisions. What follows are the basic constitutional issues relating to police interrogations.

[A] Was the Confession Obtained Involuntarily (or by Coercion)?

[1] Due Process Clause

The Fifth Amendment, which applies to conduct by agents of the federal government, provides that "[n]o person shall . . . be deprived of life, liberty, or property, without due process of law." The Fourteenth Amendment, which applies to state and local governments, has a similar Due Process Clause. As examined and clarified in the next chapter, a person is denied due process of law if an involuntary statement, i.e., a statement obtained as the result of undue police pressure, is used against her at a criminal trial. Thus, the primary Due Process Clause issue is: What constitutes an "involuntary" confession?

[2] Fifth Amendment Compulsory Self-Incrimination Clause

The Fifth Amendment provides that "[n]o person . . . shall be compelled in any criminal case to be a witness against himself." This right has come to be known, in shorthand, as the "privilege against self-incrimination" (or, even, "Fifth Amendment privilege"), but more accurately it is the "privilege against *compelled* self-incrimination." The Fifth Amendment privilege uncontroversially applies at federal criminal trials: A defendant may not be compelled to testify (to be a witness) against herself. The role of the Fifth Amendment privilege in the *pre*trial context, most particularly in the interrogation room, is more controversial and complicated.

In 1964, the Supreme Court held that the privilege against compelled self-incrimination is a fundamental right, applicable to the states pursuant to the Fourteenth Amendment Due Process Clause.[23] Consequently, the admissibility of a confession in a state criminal prosecution, as in a federal one, can now be tested by either self-incrimination or due process principles.

It should be observed that the text of the Fifth Amendment privilege uses the word "compelled," whereas Due Process Clause case law prohibits the admissibility of "involuntary" statements. Outside the police interrogation context, the two concepts—compulsion and involuntariness—are distinguishable and, therefore, are not properly

---

22. 384 U.S. 436 (1966).
23. Malloy v. Hogan, 378 U.S. 1 (1964).

equated.[24] However, in the police interrogation context, the concepts have been conflated by the Supreme Court: At this point in time, there is little evident difference in the case law between a confession that is barred at trial because it was "compelled" (Fifth Amendment privilege) and one that was secured "involuntarily" (Due Process Clause).

[B] Was the Confession Obtained in Violation of *Miranda v. Arizona*?

In *Miranda v. Arizona*,[25] the Supreme Court devised a set of warnings that the police must give a suspect in custody before they may interrogate her, in order to protect her privilege against compelled self-incrimination. The Court stated that in the absence of the procedural safeguards set out in the case, "no statement obtained from the defendant [during custodial interrogation] can truly be the product of his free choice."

The original understanding of *Miranda* was that a violation of the rules set out in that opinion constituted a violation of the Fifth Amendment privilege against compulsory self-incrimination. Thus, *Miranda* law constituted a new version of Fifth Amendment law. Subsequently, however, the Supreme Court characterized the *Miranda* safeguards as "prophylactic" in nature; it stated that the *Miranda* rules "serve" the Fifth Amendment, but "sweep more broadly than the Fifth Amendment itself."[26] In other words, one can violate the *Miranda* rules *without* violating the Fifth Amendment. Put still differently, not all statements obtained in violation of *Miranda* are "compelled."

In 2000, the Supreme Court, faced with a claim that the *Miranda* ruling was not constitutionally mandated at all, stated that *Miranda* is a "constitutional decision"[27] and "constitutional rule,"[28] which seemed to some to return *Miranda* law to its original interpretation. However, the Court has not disavowed any of its prior rulings that distinguish *Miranda* violations from traditional coercion/involuntariness claims. Consequently, although *Miranda* law is a branch of Fifth Amendment "privilege against compelled self-incrimination" law, it is essential for analytical purposes to treat *Miranda* jurisprudence separately from "pure" self-incrimination doctrine. Consequently, this Text provides a separate chapter on *Miranda* law.

[C] Was the Defendant Entitled to Counsel?

[1] Sixth Amendment Right to Counsel

Whether or not a statement was obtained by the police in a coercive manner (or "involuntarily"), the statement is inadmissible at trial if it was obtained in violation of the accused's Sixth Amendment right to counsel. This amendment provides in relevant part

---

24. For example, a threat to discharge a police officer if she refuses to testify at a hearing renders her statement *compelled* under the Fifth Amendment. Garrity v. New Jersey, 385 U.S. 493, 497 (1967). But such a statement is far from *involuntary* in the sense that the latter concept is used in the confession cases. Stephen J. Schulhofer, *Reconsidering Miranda*, 54 U. Chi. L. Rev. 435, 440–46 (1987).

25. 384 U.S. 436 (1966).

26. Oregon v. Elstad, 470 U.S. 298, 306 (1985).

27. Dickerson v. United States, 530 U.S. 428, 432, 438 (2000).

28. *Id.* at 437, 438, 441, 444.

that "[i]n all criminal prosecutions, the accused shall enjoy the right to . . . the Assistance of Counsel for his defence." This right applies to the states through the Fourteenth Amendment Due Process Clause.[29]

Generally speaking, the Sixth Amendment right to counsel is violated if the government deliberately elicits statements from a suspect in the absence of her counsel or valid waiver of the right. However, the Sixth Amendment right does not attach until adversary judicial criminal proceedings commence, such as when a suspect is arraigned or indicted. The complexities of the Sixth Amendment right-to-counsel provision are considered in Chapter 25.

[2] "*Miranda*" Right to Counsel

The Fifth Amendment does not expressly contain a right to counsel. However, as a result of the *Miranda* opinion, a suspect—even before adversary judicial criminal proceedings have commenced—is entitled to what may be best described as the "*Miranda* right to counsel." This right attaches when a suspect is subjected to custodial interrogation. The purpose of the *Miranda* right to counsel is narrower than the full-blooded Sixth Amendment version—the only purpose is to protect the suspect's privilege against compulsory self-incrimination.

It is necessary to treat the *Miranda* and Sixth Amendment versions of the right to counsel separately. They attach at different times, under different circumstances, for different reasons, and sometimes with different outcomes.[30]

§ 21.04 Interrogation Law: An Overview to the Policy Debate[31]

[A] Societal Ambivalence Regarding Confessions

Interrogation law is controversial. In large part this is because there is an "uneasy conflict of worthy interests [that] produces a curious ambivalence of attitudes toward the confession of crime by one taken into police custody."[32] This "uneasy conflict of worthy interests" is considered in detail in subsequent chapters, but readers should be sensitive to the debate at the outset.

[1] Why the Public Favors Confessions

On one level, the public likes the idea of wrongdoers confessing. People believe it is good for wrongdoers to admit their guilt. One who confesses and accepts responsibility

---

29. Gideon v. Wainwright, 372 U.S. 335 (1963).

30. *See* § 25.08, *infra*.

31. *See generally* Joseph P. Grano, Confessions, Truth, and the Law (1993); Yale Kamisar, Police Interrogation and Confessions (1980); Yale Kamisar, *Remembering the "Old World" of Criminal Procedure: A Reply to Professor Grano*, 23 U. Mich. J.L. Reform 537 (1990).

32. Arthur E. Sutherland, Jr., *Crime and Confession*, 79 Harv. L. Rev. 21, 22 (1965); *see also* Peter Brooks, Troubling Confessions 2 (2000) ("We want confessions, yet we are suspicious of them.").

for her actions has taken a significant step toward paying her debt to society. The admission of responsibility may also be the first step in the criminal's rehabilitation.[33]

From a law enforcement perspective, confession is good because a conviction may be impossible without it. Moreover, if a defendant confesses, this relieves the public of its fear that it may be prosecuting an innocent person. The public considers confessions reliable. As Justice Jackson observed, "[i]t probably is the normal instinct to deny and conceal any shameful or guilty act."[34] Therefore, when an accused person takes the "unnatural" step of admitting his guilt we assume that the admission is true. Why else would a person confess?

[2] Why the Public Is Concerned About Confessions

As much as society values confessions, it also worries about them. The answer to the question ending the last subsection — "Why would a person confess if she were not guilty?" — might be: "Because she was coerced to do so."[35] That is, it is precisely because the act of confession runs contrary to ordinary behavior (at least in the criminal law context) that we are suspicious it might be the result of police overreaching.

The public fears police overreaching for at least two reasons. First, if a confession is coerced, its reliability is called into serious question; the truth-seeking process of the criminal trial is jeopardized rather than advanced by its admission.[36]

Second, if the police are left to their own devices to obtain confessions from persons they believe are guilty, there is an enhanced risk that they will turn to inquisitorial techniques that not only create an undue risk of false confessions but also violate "the law's ethical or moral responsibility to treat criminal suspects and defendants in a manner consistent with their dignity as autonomous human beings."[37] As Supreme Court Justice Arthur Goldberg once observed: "We have learned the lesson of history . . . that a system of criminal law enforcement which comes to depend on the 'confession' will, in the long run, be less reliable and more subject to abuses than a system which depends on extrinsic evidence independently secured through skillful investigation."[38]

[B] Has the Law Gone Far Enough — or Too Far — in Controlling Confessions?

In view of society's conflicting attitudes regarding confessions, an overarching question in the interrogation law field is whether the Supreme Court has found the proper balance in placing restrictions on the police.

---

33. Brooks, Note 32, *supra*, at 2 ("Confession of wrongdoing is considered fundamental to morality because it constitutes a verbal act of self-recognition as wrongdoer and hence provides the basis of rehabilitation.").

34. Ashcraft v. Tennessee, 322 U.S. 143, 160 (1944) (dissenting opinion).

35. *See also* Note 6, *supra*.

36. On the problem of reliability in eliciting confessions, *see generally* Richard A. Leo, Peter J. Neufeld, Steven A. Drizin, and Andrew E. Taslitz, *Promoting Accuracy in the Use of Confession Evidence: An Argument for Pretrial Reliability Assessments to Prevent Wrongful Convictions*, 85 Temp. L. Rev. 759 (2013).

37. George E. Dix, *Federal Constitutional Confession Law: The 1986 and 1987 Supreme Court Terms*, 67 Tex. L. Rev. 231, 261 (1988).

38. Escobedo v. Illinois, 378 U.S. 478, 488–89 (1964).

People who are suspicious of police interrogations have argued that there should be as much justice "in the gatehouses" of American criminal procedure as in its "mansions."[39] That is, just as the defendant in the courtroom (the mansion) is provided many adversarial protections (not the least of which is a lawyer and a judge overseeing the process), the suspect in the police station (the gatehouse) needs comparable safeguards. Indeed, a criminal trial, with all of its adversarial protections, may prove meaningless if an accused person is left alone and helpless during the pretrial police investigatory period. Therefore, some people favor providing broad constitutional protections to the suspect in the interrogation room. To the argument that this will impede enforcement efforts, they contest the proposition that such protections undermine the truth-seeking function and further respond: "If the exercise of constitutional rights will thwart the effectiveness of a system of law enforcement, then there is something very wrong with that system."[40]

Other commentators believe, however, that "a civilized, decent society need not be embarrassed by police interrogation and confessions."[41] They argue that courts have created an "equality in the police station [that] thwarts rather than serves the goal of truth."[42] In particular, they claim it is unwise — even downright silly — to allow defense lawyers into the interrogation room, because their only purpose is to prevent their guilty clients from talking and, far more often than not, this means that the truth-seeking process is retarded.[43]

Critics of "pro-defendant" interrogation law contend that the Supreme Court has devised a system of criminal justice intended to "even the playing field" between the criminal suspect and the police. But, they ask, why would we want to do this? This "sporting view of justice"[44] is irrational. As long as police procedures do not create an undue risk of false confessions, the system *should* be unequal, because it is desirable to give the police the upper hand in the battle to convict the guilty. Justice Antonin Scalia has expressed this perspective as follows:

> [E]ven if I were to concede that an honest confession is a foolish mistake [by the suspect], I would welcome rather than reject it; a rule that foolish mistakes do not count would leave most offenders not only unconvicted but undetected. More fundamentally, however, it is wrong, and subtly corrosive of our criminal justice system, to regard an honest confession as a "mistake." ... We should ... rejoice at an honest confession, rather than pity the "poor fool" who has made it; and we should regret the attempted retraction of that good act, rather than seek to facilitate and encourage it.[45]

---

39. Yale Kamisar, *Equal Justice in the Gatehouses and Mansions of American Criminal Procedure*, reprinted in Yale Kamisar, Police Interrogation and Confessions 27 (1980).

40. Escobedo v. Illinois, 378 U.S. at 490.

41. Joseph D. Grano, Police Interrogation and Confessions: A Rebuttal to Misconceived Objections 1 (Occasional Papers from the Center for Research in Crime and Justice, New York University School of Law, No. 1, 1987).

42. *Id.* at 4.

43. William J. Stuntz, *Lawyers, Deception, and Evidence Gathering*, 79 Va. L. Rev. 1903, 1906, 1955 (1993) ("the earlier lawyers become part of the process, the greater the likelihood that their participation will be a relative benefit to the least deserving parties"; lawyers "retard evidence gathering by their opponents," yet "evidence gathering facilitates the separation of good claims or defenses from bad ones.").

44. Roscoe Pound, *The Causes of Popular Dissatisfaction with the Administration of Justice*, 40 Am. Law Rev. 729, 738 (1906).

45. Minnick v. Mississippi, 498 U.S. 146, 166–67 (1990) (dissenting opinion).

[C] Questions to Think About

In studying interrogation law, the key policy question to consider is the one raised in the last subsection: Has the law gone far enough—or too far—in protecting suspects in the interrogation process? But, there are a number of sub-issues and independent questions, some empirical in nature and others normative, that are worthy of consideration.

1. *To what extent were confessions obtained coercively before the Supreme Court became involved?* The answer to this question is the easiest one to answer: physical abuse was common before the Supreme Court sought to fix the system.

2. *Are there circumstances in which the government should be able to use coercion, even torture, to obtain information from suspects?* The authors of this Text did not consider asking this question in pre-2001 editions because they assumed that few people would consider coercion or torture justifiable. However, the question must now be asked: Do recent terrorist attacks and threats suggest that extreme techniques in securing information are sometimes (albeit, rarely) justifiable? Or, do the scandals surrounding the American-run prison of Abu Ghraib in Iraq and other examples of governmental mistreatment of terrorist suspects reinforce the traditional view that coercion is always wrong? In thinking about this issue, readers should distinguish two issues: (a) Is coercion ever justifiable?; and (b) Even if you answer "yes" to the first question, should statements or physical evidence obtained as a result of coercion be inadmissible in a criminal proceeding?

3. *Why does the law prohibit coerced confessions? Is it solely a function of seeking the truth or are there other concerns as well?* Just because a confession is coerced does not mean that it is false. After all, sometimes people are coerced to tell the truth. Coerced confessions, if coupled with independent corroborating evidence of guilt, presumably further the truth-seeking process at trial. To what extent, if at all, should our concern with police overreaching extend beyond the risk of false confessions?

4. *To what extent are modern police techniques, which generally eschew violence, but which involve psychological pressures and manipulations, acceptable?* This question ties in directly to the last question: Are confessions obtained in this more subtle manner reliable? And are we troubled by police use of psychological ploys to secure truthful incriminating statements?

5. *How important are confessions in the prosecution of crime?* Is police interrogation "an indispensable instrumentality of justice"?[46] To what extent are there other reliable (and even more reliable) methods to prove a person's guilt, such that a reduction in the number of confessions should not be a matter of legitimate concern?

6. *To what extent, in fact, has the Supreme Court made it more difficult for the police to obtain reliable confessions?* The empirical questions here are various. First, have the constitutional rules significantly reduced the number of confessions obtained by the police? If the answer is "no," is police efficiency undermined in other ways? On the other hand, if there has been a reduction in confessions attributable to the Court's decisions, does this mean that the truth-seeking process has been retarded, or are the police primarily "losing" the unreliable confessions that they used to obtain by coercion? Is it also possible that the stringent rules have provided an incentive for the police to seek more reliable methods to prove guilt?

---

46. Ashcraft v. Tennessee, 322 U.S. 143, 160 (1944) (dissenting opinion).

7. Regardless of the answers to the preceding questions, is the Supreme Court the proper institution to develop interrogation rules? This question has two components. First, has the Supreme Court gone beyond its legitimate constitutional authority to develop the confession rules? Second, even if the Court has not exceeded its authority, is the federal judiciary the best institution to develop the law, or should it defer more often to others, such as to state courts and legislatures?

Chapter 22

Interrogation Law: Due Process Clause

§ 22.01 Historical Development[1]

[A] Common Law

In early English common law, all statements of a suspect, even those obtained by torture, were admissible at trial. By the end of the eighteenth century, however, the rule had changed, and it was determined that "no credit" was to be given to "a confession forced from the mind by the flattery of hope, or by the torture of fear."[2] This rule was applied strictly against the government. Over the years, as interpreted by English courts, confessions gathered by brutality or threat of force were inadmissible at a defendant's criminal trial, but so too were statements induced by promises not to prosecute or to seek leniency in sentencing.

A crucial purpose of the English common law exclusionary rule was to remove from consideration by the factfinder any statement obtained in a manner likely to produce a false confession, which in turn might result in the conviction of an innocent person. With that goal in mind, English courts phrased the issue to be whether the defendant's statement was made voluntarily or involuntarily. Over time, the involuntariness of the confession procedure itself became the basis for its exclusion, "irrespective of any attempt to measure its influence to cause a false confession."[3]

American state and federal courts, including the Supreme Court, generally followed the English lead. In *Hopt v. Utah*,[4] for example, the Supreme Court adopted for the federal courts the common law rule of evidence regarding confessions. The Court stated in *Hopt* that a "confession, if freely and voluntarily made, is evidence of the most satisfactory character." However, it warned that a confession is inadmissible if it is obtained "because of a threat or promise by or in the presence of [one in authority], which, operating upon the fears or hopes of the accused . . . deprives him of that freedom of will or self-control essential to make his confession voluntary within the meaning of the law."

---

1. Yale Kamisar, *What is an "Involuntary" Confession? Some Comments on Inbau and Reid's Criminal Interrogation and Confessions*, 17 Rutgers L. Rev. 728 (1963); Welsh S. White, *What Is an Involuntary Confession Now?*, 50 Rutgers L. Rev. 2001 (1998).
2. Rex v. Warickshall, 1 Leach C.L. 263, 264, 168 Eng. Rep. 234, 235 (K.B. 1783).
3. 3 Wigmore on Evidence § 825, at 346 (Chadbourne Rev. 1970).
4. 110 U.S. 574 (1884).

[B] Constitutional Law

In 1897, the Supreme Court announced in *Bram v. United States*[5] that the Fifth Amendment privilege against compelled self-incrimination "was but a crystallization of the [common law] doctrine relative to confessions." As a consequence, *Bram* brought the common law rule under the umbrella of the Fifth Amendment: thereafter, compelled statements were inadmissible in *federal* criminal trials as a matter of constitutional law.

At the time of *Bram*, the Fifth Amendment privilege against compelled self-incrimination was not considered a fundamental right, so *Bram* did not apply to the states. State courts remained free to apply (or disregard, if they chose) the common law voluntariness requirement. There was no constitutional basis for excluding an involuntarily obtained confession in a *state* criminal trial until 1936. In that year, the Supreme Court, in *Brown v. Mississippi*,[6] for the first time invoked the Fourteenth Amendment Due Process Clause to invalidate a murder conviction obtained solely on the basis of confessions "shown to have been extorted by officers of the State by brutality and violence."

In *Brown*, three defendants, "all ignorant negroes" who denied involvement in a murder, were brutalized by sheriff's deputies, and in one case by a mob of white vigilantes with a deputy's participation. One suspect was hung by a rope to the limb of a tree twice and tied to a tree and whipped; two others were stripped, laid over chairs in the jail, and whipped with a leather strap so severely that their backs were "cut to pieces."

The *Brown* Court stated that "[i]t would be difficult to conceive of methods more revolting to the sense of justice than those taken to procure the confessions of these [defendants]." It compared the actions of the state officials—"[c]ompulsion by torture to extort a confession"—to use of "[t]he rack and torture chamber," and concluded that a conviction secured in this manner "was a clear denial of due process."

The facts in *Brown* were so shocking that the Supreme Court did not need to examine in any useful way what distinguishes a voluntary from an involuntary confession. Later cases, at least prior to the Court's watershed decision in *Miranda v. Arizona*,[7] suggested that a confession should be considered involuntary if the police interrogation methods were "repellant to civilized standards of decency or which, under the circumstances, [were] thought to apply a degree of pressure to an individual which unfairly impair[ed] his capacity to make a rational choice."[8]

The next chapter section looks at the voluntariness requirement in detail.

---

5. 168 U.S. 532 (1897).

6. 297 U.S. 278 (1936).

7. 384 U.S. 436 (1966).

8. *Id.* at 507 n.4 (Harlan, J., dissenting) (quoting Paul M. Bator & James Vorenberg, *Arrest, Detention, Interrogation and the Right to Counsel*, 66 Colum. L. Rev. 62, 73 (1966)); *see also* Lawrence Herman, *The Supreme Court and Restrictions on Police Interrogation*, 25 Ohio St. L.J. 449 (1964).

§ 22.02 Due Process Clause: The Voluntariness Requirement

[A] General Principles

[1] Rule

A statement obtained involuntarily from a suspect, by a law enforcement agent,[9] is inadmissible at the defendant's state criminal trial pursuant to the Fourteenth Amendment Due Process Clause.[10] As explained more fully in subsection [B], the voluntariness of a confession is determined based on the totality of the circumstances. There is no bright-line rule for drawing the voluntariness/involuntariness distinction.

Language can be found in some of the Supreme Court's interrogation-law cases that might suggest that the Due Process Clause is not violated, no matter how egregious the police conduct, if the statements obtained from a suspect are not used against him at his criminal trial.[11] That is, it seemed arguable until recently that the "involuntariness" Due Process Clause prohibition was exclusively a trial right. More recently, however, the Court ruled that police conduct resulting in an involuntary confession can, at least sometimes, violate due process even if the confession is not used at a criminal trial. In *Chavez v. Martinez*,[12] eight justices, in three separate opinions,[13] stated that a victim of police brutality *could* bring a civil action based on a claimed violation of the Due Process Clause, even though the statements were not used at the suspect's criminal trial (in fact, no charges were ever brought in the case).

[2] Rationale of the Voluntariness Requirement[14]

The Supreme Court has stated that a "complex of values"[15] underlie the voluntariness requirement of the Due Process Clause.[16] What are those values? First, and most

---

9. Regarding this requirement, *see* § 22.03[A], *infra*.

10. *E.g.*, Brown v. Mississippi, 297 U.S. 278 (1936); Spano v. New York, 360 U.S. 315 (1959).

11. *E.g.*, Leyra v. Denno, 347 U.S. 556, 558 (1954) ("[U]se in a state criminal trial of a defendant's confession obtained by coercion . . . is forbidden by the Fourteenth Amendment"); Mincey v. Arizona, 437 U.S. 385, 398 (1978) ("[A]ny criminal trial use of a defendant's involuntary statement is a denial of due process of law. . . .").

12. 538 U.S. 760 (2003).

13. The Court was deeply splintered when it came to the facts of the case before it. Three members of the Court (Chief Justice Rehnquist and Justices Scalia and Thomas) stated that police abuse could constitute a substantive due process violation, but they did not believe that the conduct alleged in the case before it violated the Constitution. Two more justices (Souter and Breyer) stated that brutality that "shocks the conscience" violates due process, but preferred to leave it to a lower court to determine whether this standard was violated here. Three more justices (Kennedy, Stevens, and Ginsburg) found such a violation in the current case. Justice O'Connor did not state her position on the issue.

14. *See generally* Kamisar, Note 1, *supra*; Welsh S. White, *False Confessions and the Constitution: Safeguards Against Untrustworthy Confessions*, 32 Harv. C.R.-C.L. L. Rev. 105 (1997); White, Note 1, *supra*.

15. Blackburn v. Alabama, 361 U.S. 199, 207 (1960).

16. In light of the Supreme Court's merger of Fifth Amendment self-incrimination jurisprudence (regarding what constitutes "compulsion" in the interrogation context) with the due process

obviously, there is a heightened risk of false confessions—and, thus, of convicting innocent persons—if the police are permitted at trial to use statements obtained from suspects through coercive means.[17]

But, even if there is independent evidence corroborating a confession that was obtained involuntarily—so the risk of convicting an innocent person is reduced—the Supreme Court has stated that "[t]he aim of the [voluntariness] requirement . . . is not to exclude presumptively false evidence, but to prevent fundamental unfairness in the use of evidence, whether true or false."[18] Thus, the Court has concluded that an involuntary statement should also be excluded at trial because, quite simply, the police should "obey the law while enforcing the law."[19]

A third and related reason for the voluntariness requirement is that use of statements that have been obtained through torture or other forms of egregious governmental conduct is "so offensive to a civilized system of justice that [it] must be condemned."[20]

Fourth, "ours is an accusatorial and not an inquisitorial system."[21] One principle of an accusatorial system is that "the mind, as the center of the self, may not be pressed by the government into an instrument of its own destruction."[22] Indeed, the use of coercion to obtain a confession "was the chief inequity, the crowning infamy of . . . the Inquisition. . . ."[23]

Fifth, values of human dignity, personal autonomy and mental freedom support the premise that a person should not be subjected to abusive governmental conduct, including that which results in an involuntary confession. Finally, of course, beyond the moral principles of protecting human dignity is the pragmatic, utilitarian justification: exclusion of a confession obtained involuntarily may deter police misconduct and reduce the likelihood of future abuses.[24]

"involuntariness" cases, *see* § 23.05[A][2], *infra*, much of the reasoning for Due Process Clause exclusion of involuntary confessions is commingled by courts with self-incrimination analysis.

17. Spano v. New York, 360 U.S. 315, 320 (1959) (expressing concern regarding the "inherent untrustworthiness" of coerced confessions). The risk that police interrogation techniques will result in false confessions and miscarriages of justice is not trivial. *See* § 21.01, *supra*, especially the text to Note 6. *See generally* Richard A. Leo, *False Confessions: Causes, Consequences, and Solutions*, in Wrongly Convicted: Perspectives on Failed Justice 36 (Saundra D. Westervelt & John A. Humphrey eds., 2001); Richard A. Leo & Richard J. Ofshe, *The Consequences of False Confessions: Deprivations of Liberty and Miscarriages of Justice in the Age of Psychological Interrogation*, 88 J. Crim. L. & Criminology 429 (1998).

18. Lisenba v. California, 314 U.S. 219, 236 (1941).

19. *Spano*, 360 U.S. at 320.

20. Miller v. Fenton, 474 U.S. 104, 109 (1985).

21. Rogers v. Richmond, 365 U.S. 534, 541 (1961).

22. H. Richard Uviller, *Evidence from the Mind of the Criminal Suspect: A Reconsideration of the Current Rules of Access and Restraint*, 87 Colum. L. Rev. 1137, 1146 (1987). This argument has special resonance when considering the Fifth Amendment privilege against compelled self-incrimination. *See* § 23.03[B], *infra*.

23. Brown v. Mississippi, 297 U.S. 278, 287 (1936) (quoting Fisher v. State, 110 So. 361, 365 (Miss. 1926)).

24. *See* Colorado v. Connelly, 479 U.S. 157, 165–66 (1986).

[B] The Voluntariness Requirement in Greater Detail[25]

[1] Critical Overview

In *Bram v. United States*,[26] the Supreme Court's first effort to define "involuntariness" in a constitutional context, the Court stated that a confession "must not be extracted by any sort of threat or violence, nor obtained by any direct or implied promises, however slight, nor by the exertion of any improper influence." The Court warned that because "the law cannot measure the force of the influence used, or decide upon its effect upon the mind of the prisoner," it would hold a confession inadmissible "if any degree of influence" was exerted.

This bright-line rule has not prevailed. The voluntariness of a confession is now assessed—whether a court applies the Due Process Clause or the Fifth Amendment privilege against compulsory self-incrimination[27]—from "the totality of all the surrounding circumstances—[considering] both the characteristics of the accused and the details of the interrogation."[28]

There are at least two problems with this standard. First, as with any rule that must be determined from the totality of the circumstances, the police receive less guidance than if they were required to obey a bright-line rule, and courts can become overwhelmed adjudicating highly fact-sensitive claims of coercion. Second, and perhaps more critically, the Supreme Court has wavered between what might be characterized as an empirical approach to the voluntariness question and a normative approach[29]—and when the Court has followed the latter approach, it has left unclear what the normative standard is.

To explain: The Supreme Court often applies—or, at least, purports to apply—the "overborne will" standard. Thus, it has described the issue of voluntariness this way:

> Is the confession the product of an essentially free and unconstrained choice by its maker? If it is, *if he has willed to confess*, it may be used against him. If it is not, *if his will has been overborne* and his capacity for self-determination critically impaired, the . . . confession [is inadmissible].[30]

The implication of this language is that voluntariness is an empirical issue. It is as if a court can look into the suspect's psyche or soul and determine whether he "freely chose" to confess or, instead, had his will overborne by the police. As the Court in *Bram* acknowledged, however, there is no practical way to measure the influence of a

---

25. *See generally* Mark A. Godsey, *Rethinking the Involuntary Confession Rule: Toward a Workable Test for Identifying Compelled Self-Incrimination*, 93 Cal. L. Rev. 465 (2005); Joseph D. Grano, *Voluntariness, Free Will, and the Law of Confessions*, 65 Va. L. Rev. 859 (1979); Catherine Hancock, *Due Process Before Miranda*, 70 Tul. L. Rev. 2195 (1996); Kamisar, Note 1, *supra*; White, Note 1, *supra*; and White, Note 14, *supra*.
26. 168 U.S. 532 (1897).
27. *See* § 23.05[A], *infra*.
28. Dickerson v. United States, 530 U.S. 428, 434 (2000) (quoting Schneckloth v. Bustamonte, 412 U.S. 218, 226 (1973)).
29. For discussion of how the Supreme Court has wavered between these two approaches, *see* Kamisar, Note 1, *supra* (pre-*Miranda* case law), and White, Note 1, *supra* (post-*Miranda* case law).
30. Culombe v. Connecticut, 367 U.S. 568, 602 (1961) (opinion of Frankfurter, J.) (emphasis added); *see also* Dickerson v. United States, 530 U.S. at 434 (quoting Schneckloth v. Bustamonte, 412 U.S. 218, 226 (1973)) (the due process cases "refined the test into an inquiry that examines "whether a defendant's will was overborne" by the circumstances surrounding the giving of a confession").

particular police practice on a particular suspect. Ultimately, the issue of coerced confessions, like the defense of duress in the substantive criminal law,[31] should be seen as presenting a normative question: How much, and what kind of, pressure placed on a person is morally permissible? Or, put another way, "how much mental freedom should be afforded the suspect?"[32]

Ultimately, a normative analysis is inevitable. On the one hand, all confessions, even those obtained by torture, are "free" in the sense that the speaker preferred confessing to the continuation of the suffering. Professor George Thomas has observed that ([i]f . . . 'voluntary' means only that one exercises choice between alternatives, then . . . '[a]ll conscious verbal utterances are and must be voluntary.' "[33] If that were the standard, all confessions would be admissible. On the other hand, nearly all confessions are "unfree" in the sense that they are the result of pressures on the individual's will, and surely few would disagree with the view that any police interrogation, no matter how benign, exerts significant pressures on the individual undergoing questioning. If "voluntary" meant the absence of any influence, or at least the absence of any *external* influence to confess (thus, allowing for the possibility of "the conscience-stricken urge to 'rid one's soul of a sense of guilt' "[34]), then (almost) no confessions would be admissible. So, the answer must be somewhere in between, and the issue must come down to this: How "free" is "free enough"?

The Supreme Court has conceded that voluntariness is "an amphibian"[35] notion. Although the determination of voluntariness requires a finding of the "crude historical facts"[36] regarding the acquisition of the suspect's confession, the ultimate issue is a legal one.[37] In resolving the legal issue, the Court's decisions inevitably "reflect a . . . recognition that the Constitution requires the sacrifice of neither security nor liberty."[38] That is, the Court has balanced society's perceived need for confessions against the importance of ensuring that the interrogation process does not undermine the "complex of values" supporting the Due Process Clause and Fifth Amendment privilege against self-incrimination.

The result of this balancing process, not surprisingly, has been a collection of Supreme Court cases expressing conflicting value judgments, and results that are not always easily explained (or explained away). As a practical matter, the totality-of-the-circumstances test makes "everything relevant but nothing determinative."[39] The typical involuntary-confession case is one "in which the court[] provide[s] a lengthy factual description followed by a conclusion . . . , without anything to connect the two."[40]

---

31. *See* Joshua Dressler, *Exegesis of the Law of Duress: Justifying the Excuse and Searching for Its Proper Limits*, 62 S. Cal. L. Rev. 1331 (1989).

32. White, Note 1, *supra*, at 2010.

33. George C. Thomas III, *Justice O'Connor's Pragmatic View of Coerced Self-Incrimination*, 13 Women's Rts. L. Rep. 117, 121 (1991) (quoting 2 John Henry Wigmore on Evidence § 824 n.1 (2d ed. 1923)).

34. *Id.* at 120 (quoting Ashcraft v. Tennessee, 322 U.S. 143, 161 (1944) (Jackson J., dissenting)).

35. Culombe v. Connecticut, 367 U.S. at 605.

36. *Id.* at 603.

37. Miller v. Fenton, 474 U.S. 104, 110 (1985).

38. Schneckloth v. Bustamonte, 412 U.S. 218, 225 (1973).

39. Joseph D. Grano, *Miranda v. Arizona and the Legal Mind: Formalism's Triumph Over Substance and Reason*, 24 Am. Crim. L. Rev. 243, 243 (1986).

40. Lloyd L. Weinreb, *Generalities of the Fourth Amendment*, 42 U. Chi. L. Rev. 47, 57 (1974).

[2] Some Reflections on the Use of Torture in the Post-9/11 World[41]

As discussed below, the closest the Supreme Court has come to a bright-line rule in the Due Process Clause interrogation cases is the assertion that actual or threatened use of violence to obtain a statement from a suspect violates the Constitution.

One may inquire at the outset: What constitutes "violence" or "torture"? Consider, for example, the procedures used by American military and civilian officers in Iraq's infamous Abu Ghraib prison during the American occupation of Iraq. The procedures included placement of hoods over the heads of suspects, sleep deprivation, use of strobe lights and loud music, the shackling of suspects "in awkward positions for long hours and manipulating levels of pain medication,"[42] in order to "soften up" detainees for later interrogation. Are these procedures, individually or collectively, "torture"?

Assuming that at least some of these techniques constitute torture—at least a few detainees were allegedly beaten to death in the prison,[43] so these cases would certainly satisfy the "violence" standard—does it follow that such methods should always be forbidden by the Constitution? The answer seemed obvious to virtually everyone in the twentieth century. However, in the post-September 11, 2001, era of actual, threatened, and feared acts of terrorism, some people have begun to question a no-torture rule.

If one reconsiders the "complex of values" that inhere in the Due Process Clause,[44] one finds that some of the reasons for condemning coercion lose their power if one imagines, for example, federal officers seeking information from a suspect regarding what they believe to be an imminent nuclear attack of an American city. If the rationale for the exclusionary rule, for example, is deterrence of governmental overreaching, it is unlikely that excluding at trial the fruits of the federal agent's coercive interrogation techniques (*e.g.*, confessions and tangible evidence) would deter an agent from using whatever methods he believes necessary to learn where the "ticking time bomb" is set to go off.

On the other hand, other Due Process Clause justifications for excluding statements obtained involuntarily remain cogent (e.g., torture often results in inaccurate information). And, separate from the admissibility-at-trial issue, deeply held moral principles of human dignity and mental freedom, as well as the anti-inquisitorial values of our legal system, quite arguably render torture, regardless of the reason for its implementation, morally objectionable.

Finally, even if torture could extract otherwise unavailable, truthful information from an individual that could prevent a massive attack, constitutional values and historical experience provide reasons to question whether government agents charged with

---

41. *See generally* Mary Strauss, *Torture*, 48 N.Y. L. Sch. L. Rev. 201 (2004).

42. Don Van Natta, Jr., *Interrogation Methods in Iraq Aren't All Found in Manual*, N.Y. Times, May 7, 2004, at A11; *see also* Neil A. Lewis, *Broad Use Cited of Harsh Tactics at Base in Cuba*, N.Y. Times, Oct. 17, 2004, at A1 (reporting that, according to one military official at Camp Delta, where many Guantanamo Bay detainees were held, one common procedure used was "making uncooperative prisoners strip to their underpants, having them sit in a chair while shackled hand and foot to a bolt in the floor, and forcing them to endure strobe lights and screamingly loud rock and rap music played through two close loudspeakers, while the air conditioning was turned up to maximum levels.").

43. James Risen & David Johnston, *Photos of Dead Show the Horrors of Abuse*, N.Y. Times, May 7, 2004, at A11.

44. *See* § 22.02[A][2], *supra*.

protecting lives, or even judges for that matter, can determine *when* such circumstances exist with sufficient accuracy. How many "mistaken" tortures would be too many?

Whether torture is ever right or always wrong, Professor Alan Dershowitz has written:

> I think that if we ever confront as actual case of imminent [domestic] mass terrorism that could be prevented by the infliction of torture we would use torture, (even lethal torture), and the public would favor its use. That is my empirical conclusion. It is either true or false, and time will probably tell.[45]

Based on his prediction that torture would be used, Dershowitz has asked: "[W]ould it be normatively better or worse to have such torture regulated by some kind of [judicial] warrant, with accountability, record-keeping, standards, and limitations"?[46] As he recognizes, the creation of such procedures would, at least to a limited extent, legitimate torture. In turn, it is possible this might result in more, not less, torture overall.[47]

The issues, therefore, are presented: Should the Due Process Clause serve as an absolute bar on the use of torture or violence as a means of securing information from individuals and, if so, why? And, if so, what constitutes prohibited torture or violence? Or, are there circumstances when the Constitution should allow government-conducted torture or violence? If so, what are those circumstances, and should there be judicial procedures to authorize the methods? Finally, if such methods are permitted, should the fruits of the torture nonetheless be excluded at any subsequent criminal trial, on the possible ground that "half a constitutional guarantee is better than none"?[48]

[3] "Voluntariness": Factors

[a] Actual or Threatened Use of Physical Force

A confession obtained by threatened or actual use of violence is inadmissible. The Court has consistently condemned such police practices as whipping[49] or slapping[50] a suspect in order to obtain a confession. "[O]ne truncheon blow on the head"[51] will render a statement inadmissible, as will express or credible implied threats of violence, such as holding a gun to a suspect's head.[52]

Confessions have also been invalidated when the police have "warned" a suspect that, unless he confesses, he may be the victim of mob violence[53] or deadly attacks from fellow

---

45. Alan M. Dershowitz, *The Torture Warrant: A Response to Professor Strauss*, 48 N.Y. L. Sch. L. Rev. 275, 277 (2004).

46. *Id.*

47. Strauss, Note 41, *supra*, at 275.

48. *See* Minnesota v. Dickerson, 508 U.S. 366, 382 (1985) (Scalia, J., concurring) (suggesting the possibility that police officers should be permitted to conduct *Terry v. Ohio* frisks for weapons when they fear for their safety, but that they should not be permitted to use any non-weapon evidence secured thereby at a later trial).

49. Brown v. Mississippi, 297 U.S. 278 (1936).

50. Haynes v. Washington, 373 U.S. 503 (1963).

51. Fikes v. Alabama, 352 U.S. 191, 198 (1957) (Frankfurter and Brennan, JJ., concurring) (assuming that it is "common ground" that a confession obtained in this manner violates due process).

52. Beecher v. Alabama, 389 U.S. 35 (1967).

53. Payne v. Arkansas, 356 U.S. 560 (1958) (*P* was told that there would be "30 or 40 people" arriving at the police station to do violence to him, but that if *P* told the truth, the police would prevent them from hurting him).

prisoners.[54] Confessions have also been suppressed in less extreme cases in which the police deprived a suspect of food, water, or sleep, for an extended period of time.[55]

Arguably, even a *lawful* threat to inflict pain should render a confession inadmissible in unusual circumstances. For example, in one Nebraska case,[56] a court invalidated an incriminating statement—an admission by a rape suspect, after initial denial, that he had had intercourse with the victim—secured after the interrogating officer warned the suspect that if he did not admit to the intercourse, he would have to submit to a penile swab for a semen sample. After the suspect asked for details, the officer described the procedure (which includes placing a Q-tip inside the penis) and, when asked by the suspect if the procedure was painful, confirmed that it would be. The court observed that "to render a defendant's statement involuntary, [the procedure] need not be of such nature or degree that would have resulted in recoil by Tomas de Torquemada of the Spanish Inquisition."

Why did making a lawful threat—to have medical personnel perform a legitimate medical procedure as part of a legitimate criminal investigation—render the statement involuntary? The court was not specific. It would seem that the confession was suppressed either because the trial court believed that this particular suspect's will was overborne by the description of the procedure or, perhaps, even if this were not the case, because the officer admitted in court that he raised the threat of the procedure in order to secure the confession ("it was an interrogation technique"). The former argument is based on an empirical overborne-will claim, and the latter is founded on a normative claim that police officers should not tell suspects that the only way they can avoid a painful medical procedure is by making an inculpatory statement.

[b] Psychological Pressures

"[C]oercion can be mental as well as physical, and . . . the blood of the accused is not the only hallmark of an unconstitutional inquisition."[57] Among the relevant factors in determining whether the psychological pressures are too great are: the length of custodial detention; the length of the interrogation itself; whether the questioning occurred during the daytime or at night; whether the interrogation was conducted incommunicado; and the personal characteristics of the suspect (e.g., age,[58] intelligence, level of education, psychological makeup, and prior experience with the police). Of course, if non-psychological factors are included—for example, food deprivation—a finding of involuntariness is enhanced. As before, a court may find a confession involuntary either because it believes that the individual's will was overborne—seemingly, the usual basis here—or because it considers the interrogation techniques morally unacceptable.

---

54. Arizona v. Fulminante, 499 U.S. 279 (1991) (*F*, a prison inmate, was physically threatened by fellow prisoners because of a rumor that he was suspected of an unsolved child murder; *X*, a paid government informant, offered to protect *F* from such violence in exchange for an admission about the crime).

55. Brooks v. Florida, 389 U.S. 413 (1967); Reck v. Pate, 367 U.S. 433 (1961).

56. State v. Phelps, 456 N.W.2d 290 (Neb. 1990).

57. Blackburn v. Alabama, 361 U.S. 199, 206 (1960).

58. *E.g.*, a factor weighing against voluntariness of an interrogation of a juvenile is the failure of the police to permit the youth's parents to be present during the interrogation. State v. Presha, 748 A.2d 1108 (N.J. 2000) (despite the "highly significant" factor that a 17-year-old youth was interrogated in the parents' absence, confession was voluntary; but announcing the rule that any interrogation of a juvenile under the age of 14 that is conducted in the absence of a parent or other adult representative is inadmissible as a matter of law).

In relatively early, pre-*Miranda*, cases, the Supreme Court took a fairly firm stand in this realm. It described nearly 36 hours of nonstop incommunicado interrogation as "*inherently* coercive."[59] And it suppressed a confession of a foreign-born suspect—who had limited education, no criminal record, and a history of emotional instability—that was obtained as the result of an eight-hour, middle-of-the-night interrogation capped off by police use of a long-time friend of the suspect to manipulate the suspect's emotions.[60] The Court expressly stated there that, "considering all the facts," the suspect's "will was overborne by official pressure, fatigue and sympathy falsely aroused."

[c] Promises of Leniency and Threats of Harsh Legal Treatment[61]

Bram v. United States,[62] a Fifth Amendment self-incrimination case, declared any confession "compelled" if it was "obtained by any direct or implied promises, however slight." The Supreme Court has since repudiated this statement for purposes of due process and, seemingly, Fifth Amendment self-incrimination, analysis.[63] Today, promises of leniency are only infrequently considered coercive.

Supreme Court cases in this area are relatively rare. Lower courts, however, have sometimes determined that a promise of leniency will render a confession involuntary. According to one survey, "lower courts have often held that a confession is involuntary if made in response to a promise that the result will be nonprosecution, the dropping of some charges, medical treatment, or a certain reduction in the punishment the defendant may receive."[64] Even here, however, courts are less inclined today to invalidate leniency-based confessions than in the past.[65] And, standing alone, courts will virtually never find involuntariness if the police merely promise to bring the defendant's cooperation to the prosecutor's attention, or promise that a prosecutor will *discuss* leniency in exchange for a confession.

What if the police, rather than promising a benefit in exchange for a confession, threaten especially harsh legal treatment if the suspect refuses to confess? Such threats *sometimes* invalidate a confession. For example, in *Rogers v. Richmond,*[66] the Supreme Court suppressed a confession as involuntary because it was secured in response to a wrongful police threat to take the suspect's wife into custody. In a less extreme circumstance, where a threat was of harsh, but not otherwise unlawful, legal treatment, one state court held that a confession is presumptively involuntary if an officer tells a suspect that "if you try and hide [the truth] from me you're really going to get hammered [by the prosecutor]."[67] Another state court held that the defendant's confession was involuntary when the interrogator told the defendant that he would likely not receive a fair trial because the defendant was an African-American and the jury would likely be prejudiced against him.[68]

---

59. Ashcraft v. Tennessee, 322 U.S. 143 (1944) (emphasis added).
60. Spano v. New York, 360 U.S. 315 (1959).
61. *See generally* Welsh S. White, *Confessions Induced by Broken Government Promises,* 43 Duke L.J. 947 (1994).
62. 168 U.S. 532 (1897).
63. Arizona v. Fulminante, 499 U.S. 279, 285 (1991).
64. 2 Wayne R. LaFave et al., Criminal Procedure §6.2(c) at 623–625 (3d. ed. 2007).
65. *Id.* at 625.
66. 365 U.S. 534 (1961).
67. Beavers v. State, 998 P.2d 1040, 1042 (Alaska 2000).
68. Bond v. State, 9 N.E.3d 134, 138 (Ind. 2014).

[d] Deception[69]

When the Supreme Court began to suppress confessions obtained by violence and torture, police departments turned to more sophisticated interrogation techniques, especially deception.[70] Among other strategies, a police officer may display false sympathy for the accused, falsely claim to have incriminating evidence proving the accused's guilt, or falsely assert that a co-defendant has implicated the accused in the crime. Sometimes, police officers concoct highly creative ways to "con" suspects into confessing.[71]

In *Miranda v. Arizona*,[72] the Court sharply criticized deceptive police practices.[73] Nonetheless, the high court's decisions in this area, especially in recent years, demonstrate that police deception is usually permissible. Indeed, although the case law in this area is hardly consistent, one safe generalization is that deception *alone*—lying to the suspect—will almost never invalidate a confession. Thus, if the police falsely inform a suspect that the case against her is strong because a co-conspirator has already confessed, this lie, although relevant as is every factor in the voluntariness analysis, will not by itself render the confession involuntary.[74]

In the early years of the Warren Court era, the Supreme Court took a stricter approach to deception. For example, it suppressed a confession because interrogating officers falsely claimed that the suspect's right to retain custody of her children was dependent on her cooperation with them.[75] It also held that the police violated due process when they masqueraded a police psychiatrist as a physician called in to treat the suspect's very painful sinus condition, during which "treatment" the "physician" interrogated him.[76] However, both of these cases included aggravating features: in the first case, the police also promised leniency; and the second ruse was especially troubling in light of the accused's physical pain at the time.

In contrast, the Court has more recently approved the technique of placing an undercover officer, masquerading as a burglar, in a jail cell where the "fellow inmate" could

---

69. *See generally* Margaret L. Paris, *Trust, Lies, and Interrogation*, 3 Va. J. Soc. Pol'y & L. 3 (1995); Christopher Slobogin, *Lying and Confessing*, 39 Texas Tech. L. Rev. 1275 (2007); Christopher Slobogin, *Deceit, Pretext, and Trickery: Investigative Lies By the Police*, 76 Or. L. Rev. 775 (1997); George C. Thomas III, *Regulating Police Deception During Interrogation*, 39 Texas Tech. L. Rev. 1293 (2007); Welsh S. White, *Police Trickery in Inducing Confessions*, 127 U. Pa. L. Rev. 581 (1979).

70. *See* § 21.02, *supra*.

71. Consider the following ruse by O, a New York homicide investigator. In an effort to obtain a confession from D, a murder suspect, O told D that "when a person is murdered the last thing a person sees is the person who killed them. And this image remains on the lens of their eyes after they die." O went on to say that modern technology made it possible to remove the eyes during autopsy and have them "developed" like film in a photo lab, and thereby identify the killer. Based on this deception, D confessed. Ron Rosenbaum, *Crack Murder: A Detective Story*, New York Times Mag., Feb. 15, 1987, at 24; or see the facts in *State v. Patton*, 826 A.2d 783 (N.J. Super. A.D. 2003) (in which the police made an audiotape in which an officer, impersonating an eyewitness to a murder supposedly being interviewed by the police, sprinkled in certain accurate information about the crime followed by a declaration that he saw P shoot the victim; P, after originally denying the crime, admitted to the offense once he heard the fraudulent audiotape).

72. 384 U.S. 436 (1966).

73. *See* § 24.04[C][1], *infra*.

74. Frazier v. Cupp, 394 U.S. 731, 739 (1969) ("The fact that the police misrepresented the statements that [the other party] had made is, while relevant, insufficient . . . to make this otherwise voluntary confession inadmissible.").

75. Lynumn v. Illinois, 372 U.S. 528 (1963).

76. Leyra v. Denno, 347 U.S. 556 (1954).

purposely elicit incriminating statements from the suspect.[77] Lower courts, as well, have permitted many forms of police deception, most especially telling a defendant that they possess incriminating evidence that they do not in fact possess.[78]

§ 22.03 Due Process Clause: Remedies for Violation of the Right

[A] Requirement of State Action (Official Overreaching)

According to *Colorado v. Connelly*, "[t]he most outrageous behavior by a private party seeking to secure evidence against a defendant does not make that evidence inadmissible under the Due Process Clause."[79] That is, in order to exclude a confession on due process grounds (or, presumably, to find a violation of the Due Process Clause in any civil action[80]), there must be a "link between coercive activity of the State, on the one hand, and a resulting confession by a defendant, on the other."[81]

In *Connelly, C*, a person suffering from chronic schizophrenia, in a psychotic state, and responding to "command hallucinations" (he heard "the voice of God" order him to confess or commit suicide), approached a police officer on the street and confessed to a murder. The perplexed officer ascertained that *C* was not drunk or on drugs, but was told by *C* that he had been a patient in several mental hospitals. After the officer informed *C* of his constitutional rights, *C* answered questions about the crime.

According to expert testimony, *C*'s mental condition at the time of his conversations with the police "interfered with [his] 'volitional abilities; that is, his ability to make free and rational choices'," including the decision whether to confess. *C*'s confession, motivated as it was by perceived orders from God, was as involuntary—and, potentially as untrustworthy—as a confession wrung from him by the police. Nonetheless, the Court concluded that the 'involuntary confession' jurisprudence is entirely consistent with the settled law requiring some sort of 'state action' to support a [Due Process Clause] violation."

The Court indicated that the potential unreliability of *C*'s confession was a matter that "the Constitution rightly leaves . . . to be resolved by state laws governing the admission of evidence." As Justice Stevens observed in his partial concurrence, "[t]he fact that the statements [made by *C*] were involuntary—just as the product of Lady Macbeth's

---

77. Illinois v. Perkins, 496 U.S. 292 (1990).

78. State v. Patton, 826 A.2d 783, 793 (N.J. Super. A.D. 2003) (citing cases). In *Patton*, however, the court held that the police crossed the constitutional line when they did more than falsely claim that they had incriminating evidence, but actually *created* such false evidence and showed it to the suspect. (*See* Note 71, *supra*, for the facts.)

79. 479 U.S. 157, 166 (1986); *contra, under the state constitution*, State v. Bowe, 881 P.2d 538 (Haw. 1994) (private action may be sufficient to render a confession inadmissible); State v. Rees, 748 A.2d 976 (Me. 2000) (same). For a fascinating account of *Connelly*, including a great deal of previously unpublished information about the case, see William T. Pizzi, *Colorado v. Connelly: What Really Happened*, 7 Ohio St. J. Crim. L. 277 (2009).

80. *See* § 22.02[A][1], *supra*.

81. *Connelly*, 479 U.S. at 165.

nightmare was involuntary—does not mean that their use for whatever evidentiary value they may have is fundamentally unfair or a denial of due process." Thus, just as unreliability of a suspect's confession is not a *necessary* condition for excluding a statement,[82] neither is it a *sufficient* basis.

The *Connelly* dissenters objected. They contended that "due process derives much of its meaning from a conception of fundamental fairness that emphasizes the right to make vital choices voluntarily." Although they conceded that police overreaching had been an element of every previous confession case, "it is also true that in every case [until now] the Court has made clear that ensuring that a confession is a product of free will is an independent concern."

[B] Standing to Raise an Involuntary Confession Claim

Suppose that the police coerce *X* to make a statement in which he incriminates *D*. Is this statement, gathered as a fruit of *X*'s coerced confession, inadmissible at *D*'s criminal trial, or is the direct victim of the coercion the only person with standing to seek suppression of the evidence?

The Supreme Court has not ruled directly on the standing question in the context of an involuntary or coerced statement, but there is virtually no doubt that standing is a requirement.[83] Abandonment of a standing requirement in interrogation cases, whether litigated on self-incrimination or due process grounds, would expand the applicability of the exclusionary rule, an unlikely outcome in view of the Supreme Court's expressed concern "that the exclusionary rule imposes a substantial cost on the societal interest in law enforcement."[84]

[C] Exclusionary Rule

[1] Constitutional Basis of the Exclusionary Rule

From a due process perspective, two constitutional wrongs exist: obtaining a confession by coercive police conduct; and using the statement at trial. As Professor Arnold Loewy has observed, using *Brown v. Mississippi*[85] as an example, the beating that Brown suffered was "clearly wrong in itself, regardless of whether any confession [was] used or even obtained."[86] Thus, if that torture had occurred today, Brown could have sued the police for violation of his constitutional rights.[87] Beyond this, the *Brown* opinion provided that "use of the confessions thus obtained as the basis for conviction and sentence was a clear denial of due process." In short, exclusion of a confession obtained involuntarily is

---

82. *See* the text accompanying Note 18, *supra*.

83. The issue of "standing" most commonly arises in the Fourth Amendment context. *See* Chapter 19, *supra*.

84. Colorado v. Connelly, 479 U.S. at 166 (quoting United States v. Janis, 428 U.S. 433, 448–49 (1976)).

85. 297 U.S. 278 (1936). *See* § 23.01[B][2], *supra*.

86. Arnold H. Loewy, *Police-Obtained Evidence and the Constitution: Distinguishing Unconstitutionally Obtained Evidence from Unconstitutionally Used Evidence*, 87 Mich. L. Rev. 907, 934 (1989).

87. *Accord* Chavez v. Martinez, 538 U.S. 760 (2003); *see* § 22.02[A][1], *supra*.

not simply a remedy for a constitutional violation (as is the case with Fourth Amendment violations); *the exclusionary rule is part of the right enforced by the Due Process Clause.*

[2] Scope of the Exclusionary Rule

[a] Impeachment

A confession obtained involuntarily is inadmissible at the defendant's criminal trial for *all* purposes. That is, a coerced confession may not be introduced in the prosecutor's case-in-chief to prove the defendant's guilt, *and* it is also inadmissible for impeachment purposes.[88] As such, this exclusionary rule is broader than the exclusionary rules relating to the Fourth Amendment, *Miranda*, and to at least certain aspects of the Sixth Amendment right to counsel.[89]

[b] Fruit-of-the-Poisonous-Tree Doctrine

If *D*'s confession is obtained involuntarily, the incriminating statement is inadmissible. May the government, however, introduce at trial other evidence—such as an instrumentality used in the offense—that would not have been obtained but for the information provided in the coerced statement? In short, is there a fruit-of-the-poisonous-tree doctrine[90] applicable to involuntary or coerced confessions?

At original common law, the basis for the exclusionary rule was the unreliability of the confession. Therefore, there was no reason to bar admission of a reliable, tangible fruit (e.g., a weapon found as a result of the suspect's involuntary statement) of a coerced confession. But the unreliability of a suspect's statement is now neither a necessary nor sufficient condition for its exclusion at trial. Consequently, the common law logic presumably no longer applies. Although the Supreme Court has not expressly resolved the fruit-of-the-poisonous-tree matter in the Due Process Clause context, it is generally assumed that the doctrine applies as least as forcefully as it does in Fourth and Sixth Amendment contexts.[91]

[3] Wrongful Admission of Statement at Trial

The Supreme Court ruled in *Arizona v. Fulminante*[92] that if a defendant's coerced confession is wrongfully introduced into evidence at trial over his objection,[93] and he is therefore convicted, the judgment of conviction must be reversed *unless* the government proves beyond a reasonable doubt that the erroneous admission of the confession did not affect the trial outcome. Until *Fulminante*, the consistent rule had been that the wrongful admission of a coerced confession required automatic reversal of the conviction, even if there was overwhelming independent evidence of the defendant's guilt.[94]

---

88. Mincey v. Arizona, 437 U.S. 385 (1978).

89. *See* §20.05[B][2][b], *supra* (Fourth Amendment); §24.12[A] (*Miranda*); and §25.07[C] (Sixth Amendment), *infra*.

90. *See generally* §20.08, *supra*.

91. 3 LaFave et al., Note 64, *supra*, at §9.5(a) at 467 (describing this position as "unquestionably correct").

92. 499 U.S. 279 (1991).

93. A defendant must make a timely pretrial motion to suppress a confession. *E.g.*, Fed. R. Crim. P. 12(b)(3)(C). Failure to do so constitutes a waiver of the claim. Fed. R. Crim. P. 12(e).

94. *E.g.*, Payne v. Arkansas, 356 U.S. 560 (1958). *See generally* 2 Joshua Dressler & Alan C. Michaels, Understanding Criminal Procedure chapter 16 (4th ed. 2006).

Chapter 23

Interrogation Law: Privilege against Compelled Self-Incrimination

§ 23.01 Fifth Amendment Self-Incrimination Clause: Overview

The Fifth Amendment to the United States Constitution provides that "[n]o person . . . shall be compelled in any criminal case to be a witness against himself. . . ." The privilege—often called, in shorthand, "the Fifth Amendment privilege" or "Fifth Amendment privilege against self-incrimination," but which is more accurately characterized as the "Fifth Amendment privilege against *compelled* self-incrimination"—applies to the states through the Fourteenth Amendment Due Process Clause.[1]

Generally speaking, the privilege may be asserted in any proceeding, civil or criminal, formal or informal, if the testimonial evidence that would be produced there might incriminate the speaker in a criminal proceeding.[2] Consequently, legal issues regarding the self-incrimination privilege arise throughout the legal process. As the title of this chapter suggests, however, the primary focus here will be on the role of the Fifth Amendment privilege in the police interrogation context. Other aspects of the Fifth Amendment provision are considered in the second volume of this treatise.

There is an enormous body of case law and scholarly literature in the field. According to one observer, "[t]he privilege against self-incrimination is much discussed but little understood."[3] It is "unlikely that anyone could argue persuasively that . . . the elements of fifth amendment law . . . fit neatly into an internally consistent, sensible whole."[4] Indeed, some consider the Fifth Amendment privilege "an unsolved riddle of vast proportions, a Gordian knot in the middle of our Bill of Rights."[5] It is "a mandate in search of a meaning."[6]

Because of the complexity and importance of the Fifth Amendment privilege against compelled self-incrimination in American law, and in order to more fully appreciate its role in shaping police interrogation procedures, this chapter touches on the history of, the policies underlying, and the general contours of, the privilege against compulsory self-incrimination before turning directly to interrogation law.

---

1. Malloy v. Hogan, 378 U.S. 1 (1964).
2. Lefkowitz v. Turley, 414 U.S. 70 (1973).
3. Robert B. McKay, *Self-Incrimination and the New Privacy*, 1967 Sup. Ct. Rev. 193, 193.
4. William J. Stuntz, *Self-Incrimination and Excuse*, 88 Colum. L. Rev. 1227, 1228 (1988).
5. Akhil Reed Amar & Renée B. Lettow, *Fifth Amendment First Principles: The Self-Incrimination Clause*, 93 Mich. L. Rev. 857, 857 (1995).
6. *Id.* at 922.

§ 23.02 The Origins of the Privilege against Self-Incrimination[7]

The origins of the Fifth Amendment Self-Incrimination Clause "lie in a tangled web of obscure historical events."[8] According to Wigmore, the roots of the Fifth Amendment privilege against self-incrimination lie in a twelfth-century power struggle between the Crown and the Church.[9] Leonard Levy, however, believes that this reading of history is too narrow, and that the privilege is also the result of political, constitutional, and human-rights debates that racked England during the sixteenth and seventeenth centuries.[10]

What seems fairly clear is that the concept of a right against self-incrimination had "become a significant feature of the common law [by] Coke's time,"[11] i.e., the early seventeenth century, as judges sought to limit inquisitorial interrogations conducted in the ecclesiastical courts, which investigated claims of heresy, and by the Court of Star Chamber. Under then-existing procedures, a person "could be plucked from the street,"[12] often on nothing more than a "fishing expedition[]" by an ecclesiastical court,[13] and administered an "oath *ex officio*," which required the individual to answer truthfully all questions put to him by the court, even before he was informed of the nature of any charges eventually leveled against him.

The oath *ex officio* was abolished in 1641. Gradually, according to traditional historical accounts, opposition to the oath turned into a general rejection of the perceived "unjust, unnatural, and immoral"[14] inquisitorial requirement that persons furnish evidence to convict themselves of crimes. Thus, Blackstone reported that, "at the common law, *nemo tenebatur prodere seipsum* [no man is bound to accuse himself]; and his fault was not to be wrung out of himself, but rather to be discovered by other means, and other men."[15]

This English opposition to compulsory self-accusation was imported to this country by colonists, who were ardent critics of the ecclesiastical oaths. Over time, the colonies enacted laws that prohibited the oath *ex officio*, as well as the use of torture to obtain confessions. By the time of the Revolution, according to Levy, the privilege was viewed by the Constitution's framers as "a self-evident truth."[16]

---

7. *See generally* Leonard W. Levy, The Origins of the Fifth Amendment (1968); Albert W. Alschuler, *A Peculiar Privilege in Historical Perspective: The Right to Remain Silent*, 94 Mich. L. Rev. 2625 (1996); Thomas Y. Davies, *Farther and Farther from the Original Fifth Amendment: The Recharacterization of the Right Against Self-Incrimination as a "Trial Right" in Chavez v. Martinez*, 70 Tenn. L. Rev. 987 (2003); John H. Langbein, *The Historical Origins of the Privilege Against Self-Incrimination at Common Law*, 92 Mich. L. Rev. 1047 (1994); Eben Moglen, *Taking the Fifth: Reconsidering the Origins of the Constitutional Privilege Against Self-Incrimination*, 92 Mich. L. Rev. 1086 (1994).

8. Laurence A. Benner, *Requiem for Miranda: The Rehnquist Court's Voluntariness Doctrine in Historical Perspective*, 67 Wash. U. L.Q. 59, 68 (1989).

9. 8 John H. Wigmore, Evidence § 2251, at 317 (McNaughton rev. 1961).

10. Levy, Note 7, *supra*, at 42; *see* Charles T. McCormick, McCormick on Evidence § 114 (Cleary rev. 1984) (stating that the privilege was, in part, the result of "important policies of individual freedom and dignity").

11. Davies, Note 7, *supra*, at 1001.

12. Amar & Lettow, Note 5, *supra*, at 896.

13. Davies, Note 7, *supra*, at 1001

14. Levy, Note 7, *supra*, at 330.

15. 4 William Blackstone, Commentaries on the Laws of England 293 (1769).

16. Levy, Note 7, *supra*, at 404, 430.

The preceding summary represents the traditional explanation of the origins of the Fifth Amendment privilege. A somewhat different historical account suggests that the Fifth Amendment privilege has less to do with the heroic battles for religious and human freedom of those earlier centuries than previously thought. According to a revisionist view, "the true origins of the common law privilege are to be found not in the high politics of the English revolutions, but in the rise of adversary criminal procedure at the end of the eighteenth century. The privilege against self-incrimination at common law was the work of defense counsel."[17]

According to *this* reading of history, the criminal procedure of the sixteenth and seventeenth centuries consisted of "a set of rules and practices whose purpose and effect were to oblige the accused to respond to the charges against him."[18] In this period, the "bedrock" principle was that a person accused of crime not only was not furnished a lawyer, but was *forbidden* to have one. Indeed, during this period, "[t]he essential purpose of the criminal trial was to afford the accused an opportunity to reply in person to the charges against him."[19] The view was that a defendant did not need counsel because, if he was innocent, "he will be as effective as any lawyer"[20] in explaining his case; and if he was guilty, "the very Speech, Gesture, and Countenance . . . may often help disclose the Truth. . . ."[21]

The bar on defense counsel was relaxed in 1696 in treason prosecutions. By the 1730s, defense counsel was permitted in ordinary criminal trials.[22] And with the advent of defense counsel, as John Langbein has put it, the criminal process shifted from an "accused speaks" trial to a "testing the prosecution" form of trial. According to this reading of history,

> [c]ounsel . . . turned a system directed at getting the defendant to attempt rebuttal of the adverse evidence into one in which the prosecutor was expected to prove his case, beyond a reasonable doubt, in the face of a learnedly uncooperative defense. This reversal of the nature of the criminal trial had as one of its consequences the creation of a right against coercive self-incrimination; it replaced a system in which . . . self-incrimination was the whole point.[23]

This historical interpretation adds to our understanding of the Fifth Amendment privilege. Nonetheless, one should not minimize the significance of the earlier battles for religious and human freedom because, as a result of them, "compulsory examination of the accused . . . acquired a bad name."[24] As a result of this English history, American courts, including the United States Supreme Court especially during the middle of the twentieth century, came to view the self-incrimination privilege as a highly valued right, if not a self-evident truth.

---

17. Langbein, Note 7, *supra*, at 1047.
18. *Id.* at 1049.
19. *Id.* at 1047.
20. *Id.* at 1053.
21. 2 William Hawkins, A Treatise of the Pleas of the Crown ch. 39, §2 (1721).
22. Langbein, Note 7, *supra*, at 1067–68.
23. Moglen, Note 7, *supra*, at 1088 (explaining Langbein's thesis).
24. Stephen J. Schulhofer, *Some Kind Words for the Privilege Against Self-Incrimination*, 26 Val. U. L. Rev. 311, 312 (1991).

§ 23.03 Is the Privilege a Good Idea? The Controversy[25]

[A] In General

Professor Stephen Schulhofer describes the Fifth Amendment Self-Incrimination Clause as "probably our most schizophrenic amendment."[26] On the one hand, the Supreme Court, particularly during the Warren Court era, "waxed eloquent"[27] about the privilege, stating that it "reflects many of our fundamental values and most noble aspirations,"[28] and that it "registers an important advance in the development of our liberty—"one of the great landmarks in man's struggle to make himself civilized."[29] Yet, the Supreme Court, per Justice Benjamin Cardozo, once observed that "[j]ustice . . . would not perish if the accused were subject to a duty to respond to orderly inquiry."[30]

Among scholars, too, the privilege has had its eloquent advocates,[31] but it has also been the object of withering criticism. Early on, Wigmore described it as a "mark of traditional sentimentality."[32] Jeremy Bentham sought to trivialize the privilege by claiming that it was based on "the old woman's reason" that "tis hard upon a man to be obliged to criminate himself."[33] Modern scholars, if anything, have been even more critical. One of them has concluded that "the leading . . . efforts to justify the privilege as more than a historical relic are uniformly unsatisfactory."[34] Professor Schulhofer, only exaggerating a bit, has stated that "[i]t is hard to find anyone these days who is willing to justify and defend the privilege against self-incrimination."[35]

In view of these disparate observations, the question must be asked: *Is the privilege against compelled self-incrimination defensible?* Some of the arguments pertaining to

---

25. *See generally* Erwin N. Griswold, The Fifth Amendment Today (1955); Stephanos Bibas, *The Right to Remain Silent Helps Only the Guilty*, 88 Iowa L. Rev. 421 (2003); David Dolinko, *Is There a Rationale for the Privilege Against Self-Incrimination?*, 33 UCLA L. Rev. 1063 (1986); Henry J. Friendly, *The Fifth Amendment Tomorrow: The Case for Constitutional Change*, 37 U. Cin. L. Rev. 671 (1968); Robert S. Gerstein, *The Demise of Boyd: Self-Incrimination and Private Papers in the Burger Court*, 27 UCLA L. Rev. 343 (1979); R. Kent Greenawalt, *Silence as a Moral and Constitutional Right*, 23 Wm. & Mary L. Rev. 15 (1981); Susan R. Klein, *Enduring Principles and Current Crises in Constitutional Criminal Procedure*, 24 Law & Soc. Inquiry 533 (1999); John T. McNaughton, *The Privilege Against Self-Incrimination: Its Constitutional Affectation, Raison d'Etre and Miscellaneous Implications*, 51 J. Crim. L., Criminology & Police Sci. 138 (1960); Schulhofer, Note 24, *supra*; Daniel J. Seidmann & Alex Stein, *The Right to Silence Helps the Innocent: A Game-Theoretic Analysis of the Fifth Amendment Privilege*, 114 Harv. L. Rev. 430 (2000); Stuntz, Note 4, *supra*; Peter W. Tague, *The Fifth Amendment: If An Aid to the Guilty Defendant, An Impediment to the Innocent One*, 78 Geo. L.J. 1 (1989).

26. Schulhofer, Note 24, *supra*, at 311.

27. Stephen A. Saltzburg, *The Required Records Doctrine: Its Lessons for the Privilege Against Self-Incrimination*, 53 U. Chi. L. Rev. 6, 6 (1986).

28. Murphy v. Waterfront Comm'n, 378 U.S. 52, 55 (1964).

29. Ullmann v. United States, 350 U.S. 422, 426 (1956) (quoting Griswold, Note 25, *supra*, at 7).

30. Palko v. Connecticut, 302 U.S. 319, 326 (1937).

31. *E.g.*, Levy, Note 7, *supra*; Gerstein, Note 25, *supra*; Greenawalt, Note 25, *supra*.

32. 8 John Wigmore, Note 9, *supra*, § 2251, at 317.

33. 7 Jeremy Bentham, Rationale of Judicial Evidence 452 (Bowring ed. 1843).

34. Dolinko, Note 25, *supra*, at 1064.

35. Schulhofer, Note 24, *supra*, at 311.

the privilege relate to its invocation at trial; other arguments apply with as much force in the pretrial, police interrogation context that is primary focus of this chapter. What follows is a taste of the arguments in defense of, and against, the Fifth Amendment privilege against compelled self-incrimination. However, it should be noted that even if the privilege is abstractly indefensible as some critics maintain, few people seriously suggest that it should now be abolished by constitutional amendment. As one writer has pointed out, "one does not, when he performs the surgery on one part of the body, do it without regard for the impact on other parts of the body."[36] Professor David Dolinko, a critic of the rule, has observed that "[a] rule whose existence lacks any principled justification may nevertheless come to serve important functions in the legal system as a whole, so that its repeal would do violence to the entire system."[37]

[B] The Modern Debate

[1] The "Cruel Trilemma" Thesis

What the defenders of the privilege say: The Fifth Amendment privilege "[a]t its core, . . . reflects our fierce unwillingness to subject those suspected of crime to the cruel trilemma of self-accusation, perjury or contempt."[38] That is, if there were no privilege against self-incrimination, a person could be forced (as he was in the ecclesiastical courts and the Star Chamber) to testify under oath and either admit the truth, which could result in punishment, lie under oath (and thus be subjected to punishment for perjury), or be held in contempt of court for failing to answer the questions (and thus be jailed on the latter charge).

Response: It is hardly self-evident that it is cruel to require a guilty person to admit her guilt or accept the consequences of her refusal to testify truthfully. In any case, this "cruelty" is far less so than many other "cruelties" the law uncontroversially allows. A person in a civil proceeding, for example, may be compelled to provide damaging answers to questions in discovery and on a witness stand, yet nobody considers this too cruel to permit. Perhaps more to the point, a parent may be compelled to testify at a criminal trial against her child, under penalty of contempt, even though her testimony will send a loved one to prison or even Death Row. To require "a mother . . . to testify against her son and send him to the gallows"[39] is surely an example of greater psychological cruelty than requiring a criminal defendant to testify at trial regarding her own alleged violation of a relatively minor offense.

Beyond this, to the extent that the Fifth Amendment privilege is justified on the grounds of the "cruel trilemma," it benefits only the guilty. The "innocent defendant faces no trilemma, no dilemma, in fact no problem at all."[40] She simply tells the truth.[41] Why should the Constitution provide a special privilege to the guilty?

---

36. McNaughton, Note 25, *supra*, at 153.
37. Dolinko, Note 25, *supra*, at 1064.
38. Pennsylvania v. Muniz, 496 U.S. 582, 596 (1990) (internal quotation marks omitted).
39. Amar & Lettow, Note 5, *supra*, at 890.
40. Schulhofer, Note 24, *supra*, at 318.
41. *But see* subsection [4], *infra*, for arguments against this claim.

[2] Compelled Self-Accusation as a Moral Wrong

What the defenders of the privilege say: The Fifth Amendment privilege is founded on deep moral principles supporting the right of persons to a "special zone of mental privacy,"[42] human dignity, and personal autonomy. "Self-incrimination is both self-harming and self-accusing. . . . [T]he sovereign intrudes on a narrow autonomous sphere when it encourages self-harming self-accusation."[43] Society rightly "hesitate[s] to say that someone has a moral duty to bring conviction and imprisonment upon himself."[44] Most especially, the "government impermissibly disrespects a person when it uses him as the means of his own destruction,"[45] when it "subordinates a person to the state [by using] . . . her private thoughts as the active means of her own destruction."[46]

Even if an admission of guilt is in the wrongdoer's best interests, the decision to admit culpability should be one's own: "[A]n individual ought to be autonomous in his efforts to come to terms in his own conscience with accusations of wrongdoing against him."[47] Our society properly has "respect for the inviolability of the human personality and of the right of each individual 'to a private enclave where he may lead a private life.' "[48]

Response: First, the privilege is morally counter-intuitive: "No parent would teach such a doctrine to his children; the lesson parents preach is that while a misdeed . . . will generally be forgiven, a failure to make a clean breast of it will not be."[49]

Second, civil litigants and witnesses, for example in divorce proceedings, may be required to testify to highly embarrassing—and damaging—facts and intensely personal aspects of their lives, yet the privilege does not apply in such circumstances. Third, the government can avoid the obstacles of the Fifth Amendment by giving immunity to a witness,[50] in which case she *can* be compelled to testify about matters that she considers to be part of her private enclave.

Finally, abolition of the privilege would not seriously threaten privacy. By the time of trial, the prosecutor is not interested in obtaining an "admission of wrongdoing, self-condemnation or personal feelings about the crime. What interests her are just the basic facts—where the defendant was, who he saw, what he did."[51] These are external facts, not deeply private matters.

---

42. Klein, Note 25, *supra*, at 552.

43. George C. Thomas, III, *An Assault on the Temple of Miranda*, 85 J. Crim. L. & Criminology 807, 815 (1995).

44. Greenawalt, Note 25, *supra*, at 36.

45. Amar & Lettow, Note 5, *supra*, at 892.

46. Klein, Note 25, *supra*, at 552 n.65 (summarizing an argument advanced in David Luban, Lawyers and Justice: An Ethical Study (1988)).

47. Gerstein, Note 25, *supra*, at 347.

48. Murphy v. Waterfront Comm'n 378 U.S. 52, 55 (1964) (quoting United States v. Grunewald, 233 F.2d 556, 581–82 (2d Cir. 1956)); *see also* Bram v. United States, 168 U.S. 532, 544 (1897) (the Fifth Amendment privilege embodies "principles of humanity and civil liberty, which had been secured in the mother country only after years of struggle"); Miranda v. Arizona, 384 U.S. 436, 460 (1966) ("[T]he constitutional foundation underlying the privilege [against compulsory self-incrimination] is the respect a government . . . must accord to the dignity and integrity of its citizens. . . . [It must] respect the inviolability of the human personality. . . .").

49. Friendly, Note 25, *supra*, at 680.

50. That is, a person is not permitted to assert the Fifth Amendment privilege at a grand jury or trial proceeding if she is provided formal immunity from use of her compelled testimony at a subsequent criminal trial. 2 Joshua Dressler & Alan C. Michaels, Understanding Criminal Procedure chapter 12 (4th ed. 2006).

51. Schulhofer, Note 24, *supra*, at 320.

[3] The Privilege as a Critical Component of the Adversary System

What the defenders of the privilege say: The Fifth Amendment privilege is defensible on systemic grounds. It functions as a core feature of our accusatorial system of justice, specifically, by preserving a fair balance between the state and the accused in the prosecution of crime, and by reducing the risk that inhumane methods to extract testimony from persons suspected of crime will be used by the government.[52]

The privilege became an essential part of the legal system once a society moves from an inquisitorial system, in which criminal defendants are barred from using lawyers and judges may compel the testimony of defendants, to an adversarial one that prefers that the truth be determined by allowing the parties in dispute, through their attorneys, to present their conflicting versions of the events to the decisionmaker. In such a system, the decision should be left to the defense to determine whether it is in the defendant's best interests to speak.

The privilege against self-incrimination is also founded on the view that, if it were not for the privilege, the government, through its agents, could too easily abuse the rights of individuals caught up in criminal investigations. Without the Fifth Amendment protections, we could regress to a time when governmental overreaching was commonplace. By application of the privilege, therefore, we promote a "sense of fair play which dictates 'a fair state-individual balance by requiring the government . . . in its contest with the individual to shoulder the entire load.'"[53]

Response: The anti-inquisitorial arguments for the privilege have little place in the American constitutional system. We do not have Star Chambers or heresy trials. Nor would abolition of the privilege result in inhumane treatment of suspects: If torture were used to obtain incriminating statements, the Due Process Clause would safeguard the victim. Once one ensures against such abuses, there is no basis — other than "slogans"[54] about the adversary system — to deny the government the right to compel testimony from the defendant.

Let's look beyond the slogans. To call for a "fair balance" is simply to state the conclusion. What *is* a *fair* balance? How much advantage is an *undue* advantage for the government? Why should the government shoulder the *entire* load? Is it that we want to "boost the odds for criminals just to keep the game interesting"?[55] If so, that makes no sense.

Finally, if we are going to take the proponents' arguments seriously, we need to go further. If the government must shoulder the *entire* load, we should never compel a suspect to participate in a lineup, to give handwriting exemplars, or furnish blood, because each of these acts may serve to convict her. Yet, as discussed elsewhere,[56] the Fifth Amendment privilege against compulsory self-incrimination does *not* prevent the government from compelling any of these acts, and few would advocate stripping the government of authority to obtain physical evidence from a suspect.

---

52. *Id.* at 317.

53. Murphy v. Waterfront Comm'n, 378 U.S. 52, 55 (1964) (quoting 8 Wigmore, Note 9, *supra*, § 2251, at 317).

54. Amar & Lettow, Note 5, *supra*, at 893.

55. *Id.*

56. *See* § 23.04[D][1], *infra.*

[4] Protection of the Innocent

What the defenders of the privilege say: The privilege against compulsory self-incrimination, although "sometimes a 'shelter to the guilty,' is often 'a protection to the innocent.'"[57] It protects the innocent in at least two ways, one that relates to interrogation procedures by the police, and the other that focuses on a defendant's right not to testify at trial.

First, as to police interrogation: Compelled testimony is inherently unreliable. Even innocent persons can be forced to utter incriminating words in order to avoid extreme pain to themselves or loved ones. It is true, as the critics point out, that the Due Process Clause can serve to bar brutal police conduct. But history tells us that the Due Process Clause, standing alone, only moderated police interrogation procedures. It was only with *Miranda v. Arizona*,[58] and the forceful application of the Fifth Amendment privilege, that there was significant improvement. Professor Schulhofer suggests the following thought experiment:

> What would happen if there was no right to silence, and if officers were told that it was permissible (and perhaps therefore their duty) to use all pressures short of actually breaking the suspect's will [and, thus, violating due process]? Realistically, there can be little doubt that more abuses would occur, even though the worst abuses would still be theoretically prohibited by other rules.[59]

Second, regarding the privilege at trial, it is wrong to believe that it is only the guilty who benefit from the Fifth Amendment privilege. Unfortunately, there is a genuine risk that an innocent person, if forced to testify at trial, will convict herself by a bad performance on the witness stand. In the real world, innocent persons do not always come across truthfully to a jury. Also, a person innocent of the crime charged—and, therefore, entitled to acquittal—might nonetheless have a prior criminal record, a fact the jury usually learns if, but only if, the defendant testifies.[60] Again, a thought experiment:

> Suppose that you are representing a criminal defendant who persuades you that he is innocent. Can you think of any reason why you might prefer that your innocent client not be called to the stand? . . . Of course you can. Every lawyer can. Your client might have a highly prejudicial prior record that will become admissible once he takes the stand. There are likely to be suspicious transactions or associations that your client will have to explain. But he may look sleazy. He may be inarticulate, nervous or easily intimidated. His vague memory on some of the details may leave him vulnerable to a clever cross-examination. Most ordinary citizens find that being a witness in any formal proceeding is stressful and confusing. The problems are bound to be heightened when the witness happens to be on trial for his life or his liberty.[61]

---

57. Murphy v. Waterfront Comm'n 378 U.S. 52, 55 (1964) (quoting Quinn v. United States, 349 U.S. 155, 162 (1955)).

58. 384 U.S. 436 (1966).

59. Schulhofer, Note 24, *supra*, at 326.

60. When a defendant testifies, she may usually be cross-examined at least to some degree about her prior criminal record—not to show her propensity to commit crimes, but rather to show that she is the kind of person not to be believed. The very realistic fear for defendants, however, including innocent ones, is that the jury will nonetheless use the information as "propensity" evidence.

61. Schulhofer, Note 24, *supra*, at 330.

Response: The protect-the-innocent arguments are unpersuasive. First, regarding coerced confessions, in most cases they serve only to corroborate other reliable evidence of the defendant's guilt. And, even without the Constitution, a state could choose to enforce a rule that coerced confessions are inadmissible at trial, but that the physical (and reliable) fruits of the coerced confession would be admissible.[62]

Second, innocent persons would rarely hurt themselves on the witness stand. The "truth is consistent with itself, and everyone who is speaking the truth can tell in the main a straight story."[63] Third, those concerned for the plight of the innocent should keep in mind that, thanks to the Fifth Amendment, an innocent person accused of a crime cannot successfully compel a guilty person to testify and admit the truth; meanwhile, "the guilty [can] wrap themselves in the self-incrimination clause and walk free."[64]

Finally, if the concern is for the innocent defendant who may come across poorly in front of a jury, the problem could be solved by allowing the defendant to refuse to testify at trial, but permitting the government to compel the defendant to talk to the government prior to trial and only admitting at trial the reliable fruits of the pretrial interrogation.[65]

§ 23.04 The Fifth Amendment Privilege: The Elements[66]

The Fifth Amendment to the United States Constitution provides that "[n]o person ... shall be compelled in any criminal case to be a witness against himself. ..." The protection of the clause is available only when four elements are met: (i) the "person" element, (ii) the compulsion element, (iii) the criminal case element, and (iv) the "witness against himself" element.[67] Each of these requirements is discussed in turn in this section. In addition, because the compulsion element presents an issue in almost every police interrogation, it is considered in greater detail in Section 23.05.

---

62. Amar & Lettow, Note 5, *supra*, at 895.

63. Henry T. Terry, *Constitutional Provisions Against Forcing Self-Incrimination*, 15 Yale L.J. 127, 127 (1906).

64. Akhil Reed Amar, The Constitution and Criminal Procedure: First Principles 48 (1997).

65. Amar & Lettow, Note 5, *supra*, at 895.

66. Ronald J. Allen & M. Kristin Mace, *The Self-Incrimination Clause Explained and Its Future Predicted*, 94 J. Crim. L. & Criminology 243 (2004).

67. To this list a fifth requirement must sometimes be added: the defendant must invoke the privilege at the time of the questioning. *See* Salinas v. Texas, 133 S. Ct. 2174 (2013). In *Salinas*, S had voluntarily accompanied the police to the station for questioning and, during a one-hour interview (without arrest or *Miranda* warnings), fell silent when asked whether the shells recovered at the scene of a murder would match S's shotgun. When this silence was used against S at his subsequent trial, S objected on Fifth Amendment grounds. In a plurality opinion, the Court held that S's Fifth Amendment claim should fail "because he did not expressly invoke the privilege against self-incrimination in response to the officer's question." *Id.* at 2178. The plurality and the dissent in *Salinas* both recognized that there are exceptions to this invocation requirement, and that interrogation involving *Miranda* warnings is one such exception (*Miranda* is fully explained in Chapter 24, *infra*), but the plurality found that express invocation *is* required in the context of voluntary, noncustodial police questioning.

[A] "No Person"

Because the Fifth Amendment begins with the words "no person," the Supreme Court has declared that artificial entities, such as corporations,[68] labor unions,[69] and partnerships,[70] may not assert the privilege against self-incrimination, although a sole proprietor may.[71] Furthermore, pursuant to the so-called "collective entity" doctrine, a custodian of an entity's records may not oppose a subpoena *duces tecum* (an order to a person in possession of specified documents, relevant to a proceeding, to produce them for possible use at trial) by invoking her personal privilege against self-incrimination in order to protect the entity.[72] In short, a collective-entity is not a "person," and cannot assert the privilege, whether the result is incrimination of the entity or actual individuals.

With that proviso, however, the Fifth Amendment generally applies to any (real) person. Therefore, any witness in a criminal trial — not only the criminal defendant — may invoke the personal privilege. Thus, as critics of the Fifth Amendment privilege like to point out, an innocent defendant cannot compel a person with guilty knowledge to testify and, "according to every court that considered the issue . . . [cannot] force [the w]itness to invoke the privilege before the jury."[73]

[B] "Shall Be *Compelled*"

The Fifth Amendment prohibits compelled self-incrimination, but it is not the case that any form of state-created pressure constitutes impermissible compulsion. Far from it, as the Supreme Court has observed:

> The criminal process, like the rest of the legal system, is replete with situations requiring "the making of difficult judgments" as to which course to follow. Although a defendant may have a right, even of constitutional dimensions, to follow whichever course he chooses, the Constitution does not by that token always forbid requiring him to choose.[74]

Put another way, "the government need not make the exercise of the Fifth Amendment privilege cost free."[75] Indeed, as Fifth Amendment jurisprudence has developed, "the Court has placed various kinds of compulsion along a continuum, producing a list of acceptable and unacceptable governmental actions."[76]

In the police interrogation field, use of physical force, psychological pressures, or deception can render a confession "compelled," although more must be said on this topic.[77] The required compulsion occurs, as well, if the holder of the privilege[78] is forced by

---

68. Hale v. Henkel, 201 U.S. 43 (1906).

69. United States v. White, 322 U.S. 694 (1944).

70. Bellis v. United States, 417 U.S. 85 (1974).

71. United States v. Doe, 465 U.S. 605 (1984).

72. Wilson v. United States, 221 U.S. 361 (1911).

73. Tague, Note 25, *supra*, at 5.

74. McGautha v. California, 402 U.S. 183, 213 (1971).

75. McKune v. Lile, 536 U.S. 24, 41 (2002).

76. Allen & Mace, Note 66, *supra*, at 252.

77. *See* § 23.05, *infra*.

78. Notice that the compulsion must be directed at the person who is asserting the privilege. *See* subsection [D][3], *infra*.

subpoena to testify at trial[79] or to produce incriminating documents. A witness's free choice is also foreclosed by a threat of discharge from state employment for refusal to testify.[80] Thus, a statement by a police officer in an internal police investigation of corruption, given after being warned that she would lose her job if she asserted her Fifth Amendment privilege, is "compelled" and may not be used against her at a subsequent criminal trial.[81] The Fifth Amendment is probably violated as well if a person provides testimonial evidence against herself as an alternative to submitting "to a test so painful, dangerous, or severe, or so violative of religious beliefs, that almost inevitably a person would prefer 'confession.'"[82]

On the other hand, some difficult choices are not considered constitutionally "compelled." For example, Fifth Amendment values are not violated if the government requires a driver stopped on suspicion of driving under the influence of alcohol to choose between submitting to a "painless" blood test, on the hand, and having her refusal used against her in a criminal trial and her driving privileges revoked for up to one year, on the other. The forced choice, while not "an easy or pleasant one," does not amount to Fifth Amendment compulsion.[83]

[C] "In Any Criminal Case"

The privilege against self-incrimination does not apply if the only concern of the person asserting the claim is that her statements will result in personal disgrace,[84] loss of employment,[85] or civil confinement.[86] Her claim must be that the evidence she is required to produce will incriminate her in a criminal proceeding in the United States.[87]

Although the language of the Fifth Amendment might suggest that the privilege against compulsory self-incrimination may only be asserted *during* a criminal case, the Court has interpreted the Fifth Amendment to mean that the privilege may be asserted in any "proceeding, civil or criminal, formal or informal, where the answers might incriminate him in future criminal proceedings."[88] As a consequence, a person may invoke the Fifth Amendment privilege, among other places, in grand jury proceedings, civil trials,

---

79. South Dakota v. Neville, 459 U.S. 553, 563 (1983) (the "classic Fifth Amendment violation" occurs in "telling a defendant at trial to testify"). As a result, the defendant in a criminal trial is *not* required to take the stand. Moreover, in order that there is no penalty for the exercise of the right, neither the prosecutor nor the judge may comment adversely on the defendant's silence.

80. *See generally*, Peter Westen, *Answer Self-Incriminating Questions or Be Fired*, 37 Am. J. Crim. L. 97 (2010).

81. Garrity v. New Jersey, 385 U.S. 493 (1967).

82. South Dakota v. Neville, 459 U.S. at 563.

83. *Id.; contra*, Opinion of Justices to Senate, 591 N.E.2d 1073, 1074, 1078 (Mass. 1992) (observing that state courts are divided on the wisdom of *Neville*, and holding that evidence of a driver's refusal to submit to a chemical test or analysis of her breath is inadmissible under the state constitution).

84. *See* Brown v. Walker, 161 U.S. 591 (1896)

85. Ullmann v. United States, 350 U.S. 422 (1956).

86. Allen v. Illinois, 478 U.S. 364 (1986).

87. This includes both federal and state proceedings. *See* Murphy v. Waterfront Comm'n, 378 U.S. 52 (1964). A person may *not*, however, invoke the Fifth Amendment privilege to answer legitimate questions propounded by federal or state law enforcement officers if the sole ground for refusal is that her testimony might be used against her in a criminal prosecution in a foreign country. United States v. Balsys, 524 U.S. 666 (1998); *see* Diane Marie Amann, *A Whipsaw Cuts Both Ways: The Privilege Against Self-Incrimination in an International Context*, 45 UCLA L. Rev. 1201 (1998).

88. Lefkowitz v. Turley, 414 U.S. 70, 77 (1973).

legislative and administrative hearings, and police stations, if the testimony she would give will be used against her in a domestic criminal trial.[89]

[D] "To Be a Witness Against Himself"

As described in this subsection, a person is not "a witness against himself" unless his compelled action is both testimonial and incriminating.[90]

[1] What Makes a Person a "Witness"

[a] "Testimonial or Communicative" Evidence: The Rule

"The word 'witness' in the constitutional text limits the relevant category of compelled incriminating communications to those that are 'testimonial' in character."[91] The Court stated this limitation in *Schmerber v. California*,[92] when it held that a person is not an involuntary "witness" against herself unless she is "compelled to testify . . . or otherwise provide the State with evidence of a testimonial or communicative nature." As the *Schmerber* Court explained, "[t]he distinction which has emerged, often expressed in different ways, is that the privilege is a bar against compelling 'communications' or 'testimony,' but that compulsion which makes a suspect or accused the source of 'real or physical evidence' does not violate it."[93] Thus, in *Schmerber*, the Court held that the Fifth Amendment privilege was not implicated—the defendant was not compelled to be a "witness" against himself—when the police ordered a physician to extract the defendant's blood, and the government used the results of a blood test to convict the defendant of driving his vehicle under the influence of alcohol.

In *Doe v. United States*,[94] the Supreme Court further explored the "testimony or communications" requirement. It stated that "in order to be testimonial, an accused's communication must itself, explicitly or implicitly, relate a factual assertion or disclose information." *Doe* explained that "the privilege is [intended] to spare the accused from having to reveal, directly or indirectly, his knowledge of facts relating him to the offense or from having to share his thoughts and beliefs with the Government."

According to *Doe*, this definition of "testimony"—and, thus, the meaning of the "witness" requirement in the Fifth Amendment—stems from the historical point that "the privilege was intended to prevent the use of legal compulsion to extract from the accused a sworn communication of facts which would incriminate him," as occurred in the ecclesiastical courts and the Star Chamber.

---

89. Please note: Although a person may properly *invoke* the *privilege* in non-criminal contexts, *violation* of the constitutional *right* against self-incrimination may only arise if the compelled incriminatory statements are used against the speaker in a criminal case.

90. *See* Fisher v. United States, 425 U.S. 391, 408 (1976).

91. United States v. Hubbell, 530 U.S. 27, 34 (2000).

92. 384 U.S. 757 (1966).

93. This testimonial/physical distinction is arguably outdated in light of modern neuroscience. Today, it would be possible for the police, among other things, to measure a suspect's "automatic emotional and physiological responses to stimuli such as a photograph of the [victim] . . . [and/or] elicit brain-based but interpretable responses to their questions. . . ." Nita A. Farahany, *Incriminating Thoughts*, 64 Stanford L. Rev. 351, 354 (2012) (suggesting a more nuanced approach to the issue in light of the "neuroscience revolution").

94. 487 U.S. 201 (1988).

The outer boundaries of the "testimony or communications" requirement remain uncertain. However, the Court stated in *Pennsylvania v. Muniz*[95] that, at its core, a person is compelled to be a "witness" against himself "at least whenever he must face the modern-day analog" of the "cruel trilemma" of self-accusation, perjury, or contempt that confronted sixteenth-century Star Chamber witnesses.

[b] Application of the Rule

Because "the protection of the privilege reaches an accused's communications, whatever form they might take,"[96] and "[t]he privilege applies to both verbal and nonverbal conduct,"[97] the line between privileged "testimony or communications," on the one hand, and unprotected "real or physical evidence, on the other, is not always easy to draw.

According to the Supreme Court, "[t]here are very few instances in which a verbal statement, either oral or written, will not convey information or assert facts."[98] Most obviously, trial testimony, oral confessions to the police, and statements expressed in personal documents,[99] satisfy the "testimony or communications" element. Indeed, in view of the history of the Self-Incrimination Clause, "[w]hatever else it may include, . . . the definition of 'testimonial' evidence . . . must encompass all responses to questions that, if asked of a sworn suspect during a criminal trial, could place the suspect in the 'cruel trilemma'."[100]

Nonetheless, not all uses of the human voice or written words are protected. For example, a person may lawfully be compelled at a lineup to utter the words expressed by the malefactor, if the purpose is to require the suspect "to use his voice as an identifying *physical* characteristic, not to speak his guilt."[101] Likewise, a person may be required to put words down on paper if the purpose of the demand is to exhibit the suspect's handwriting, another physical characteristic, for identification purposes.[102] In neither of these cases is the person compelled by the government to reveal her knowledge of facts relating to the offense or to share her thoughts or beliefs.[103]

Non-verbal conduct falls within the scope of the Fifth Amendment privilege if it "reflects the actor's communication of his thoughts to another,"[104] such as when a person nods or shakes her head. On the other hand, the actor does *not* communicate her thoughts to another, and therefore the privilege does *not* apply, when the government compels her

---

95. 496 U.S. 582 (1990).
96. Schmerber v. California, 384 U.S. 757, 763–64 (1966).
97. Pennsylvania v. Muniz, 496 U.S. at 595 n.9.
98. Doe v. United States, 487 U.S. at 213.
99. See Boyd v. United States, 116 U.S. 616 (1886).
100. Pennsylvania v. Muniz, 496 U.S. at 596–97.
101. United States v. Wade, 388 U.S. 218, 222–23 (1967) (emphasis added).
102. United States v. Dionisio, 410 U.S. 1 (1973); Gilbert v. California, 388 U.S. 263 (1967).
103. Another question arises when law enforcement seeks to obtain an order to force a suspect to reveal the password to a cell phone or a hard drive. In these cases, the government has already complied with the Fourth Amendment by obtaining a warrant to search the digital device, but they are unable to access the data because it is encrypted or password protected. Circuit courts are now attempting to determine whether these passwords are testimonial, and if so whether forcing the suspect to reveal the password violates her Fifth Amendment rights. *Compare* in RE Subpoena Duces Tecum Dated Mar. 25 2011, 870 F.3d 1335 (11th Cir. 2012) (holding that forced decryption was a testimonial act and that the forgone conclusion doctrine did not apply); *with* United States v. Apple MacPro Computer, 851 F.3d 238 (3rd Cir. 2017) (disagreeing with the 11th Circuit in dictum and implying that the forgone conclusion doctrine should apply).
104. Pennsylvania v. Muniz, 496 U.S. at 595 n.9.

to put on clothing to see if it fits,[105] to stand in a lineup,[106] to move her eyes or walk on a straight line as part of a sobriety test,[107] or (as noted above) to give blood after being arrested for driving under the influence of alcohol,[108] although in each of these cases the product of the compulsion might be incriminating.

[c] A Closer Look at the Rule: Pennsylvania v. Muniz

The difficulty in drawing the line between testimonial communications and real or physical evidence is apparent in the Court's treatment of the facts in *Pennsylvania v. Muniz*.[109] In *Muniz*, M, arrested for driving under the influence of alcohol, was compelled to give his name, address, height, weight, date of birth, current age, and the date of his sixth birthday, as part of a sobriety test. M's slurred answers to these questions were videotaped and introduced at his subsequent trial.

The Court, 8–1, held that M's compelled answers to the questions were not inadmissible merely because the slurred nature of his speech incriminated him. M's physical inability to clearly articulate words, due to his lack of muscular coordination in his tongue and mouth, was not a testimonial component of his responses to the questions asked. Instead, M's slurred words were physical evidence of his intoxication; he was not compelled "to share his thoughts and beliefs with the Government," or to relate a factual assertion.

On the other hand, the Court also held, 5–4, that M's answer "No, I don't," to the question, "Do you know what the date was of your sixth birthday?" *was* testimonial in nature and, therefore, implicated the Fifth Amendment. The majority was unpersuaded by the government's claim that the Fifth Amendment privilege did not apply because the police did not have an investigative interest in the actual date of M's sixth birthday, nor even in M's "assertion of belief that was communicated by his answer to the question." According to the government, the incriminating aspect of M's answer—that his mental state was confused—concerned the physiological function of M's brain, a matter "every bit as 'real or physical' as the physiological make up of his blood and the timbre of his voice." The majority reasoned, however, that even if the fact to be inferred from M's words related to the physical status of his brain, "[t]he correct question . . . [was] whether the incriminating inference of mental confusion [was] drawn from a testimonial act or from physical evidence." The majority concluded that M's answer to the sixth-birthday question was a testimonial act, i.e., his words—and not just his slurred response—supported the factual inference that his mental faculties were impaired, just as much as if he had said directly, "I cannot answer your question because I am intoxicated."

[2] Seriousness of the Threat of Incrimination

The Fifth Amendment "operates only where a witness is asked to incriminate himself—in other words, to give testimony which may possibly expose him to a *criminal charge*."[110] Thus, as noted above, the risk that compelled testimony might cause a person to lose her job or be used in a civil case is irrelevant for Fifth Amendment

---

105. Holt v. United States, 218 U.S. 245 (1910).
106. United States v. Wade, 388 U.S. 218 (1967).
107. Pennsylvania v. Muniz, 496 U.S. 582 (1990).
108. Schmerber v. California, 384 U.S. 757 (1966).
109. 496 U.S. 582 (1990).
110. Hale v. Henkel, 201 U.S. 43, 67 (1906) (emphasis added).

purposes. But, the privilege extends not only "to answers that would in themselves support a conviction . . . but likewise embraces those which would furnish a link in the chain of evidence needed to prosecute the claimant."[111]

How much risk of incrimination must there be? The risk of incrimination confronted by the claimant must be "substantial and 'real,' and not merely trifling or imaginary."[112] That standard is not very precise. Although the Court once has said that the privilege is to "be accorded liberal construction in favor of the right it was intended to secure,"[113] a recent article concluded that "there is no analytical dividing point that can explain why courts find no violation with an incrimination of x, but do find a violation with a quantity of $x + 1$."[114]

The "liberal construction" principle might explain *Ohio v. Reiner.*[115] In *Reiner*, the father of a two-month-old baby was charged with involuntary manslaughter after the infant died from abuse. The defendant's claim was that a babysitter had caused the fatal injuries. The Court held that the babysitter, who denied all culpability, could use her Fifth Amendment privilege to refuse to be a witness at the defendant's trial. The Court said that "we have never held . . . that the privilege is unavailable to those who claim innocence. . . . [W]e [have] recognized that truthful responses of an innocent witness, as well as those of a wrongdoer, may provide the government with incriminating evidence from the speaker's own mouth." The Court pointed to facts in the case—that the babysitter had spent considerable time with the victim in the weeks immediately preceding discovery of the child's injuries, and had been with the child "within the potential timeframe of the fatal trauma"—as providing the Fifth Amendment claimant with justification "to fear that answers to possible questions might tend to incriminate her."

In contrast, the Fifth Amendment privilege arguably was not accorded a liberal construction in *Hiibel v. Sixth Judicial District Court of Nevada.*[116] In *Hiibel*, a police officer, acting on reasonable suspicion sufficient to justify a brief on-the-street seizure, demanded identification from a suspect, *H*. When *H* repeatedly refused to give his name, he was arrested and subsequently convicted of "willfully . . . obstructing a police officer" on the basis of that refusal. By a 5–4 vote, the Court sustained *H*'s conviction against Fourth and Fifth Amendment challenges.[117] Regarding the Fifth Amendment, Justice Kennedy, writing for the Court, concluded that "disclosure of [*H*'s] name presented no reasonable danger of incrimination." According to Kennedy, "a name is likely to be so insignificant in the scheme of things as to be incriminating only in unusual circumstances." The Court acknowledged the possibility that a case might arise in which "furnishing identity at the time of a stop would . . . give[] the police a link in the chain of evidence needed to convict the individual of a separate offense," but left consideration of the application of the Fifth Amendment in such a case to a future date.

In dissent, Justice Stevens reiterated the Court's statement in *United States v. Hubbell*,[118] that Fifth Amendment "incrimination" includes "statements that lead to the discovery of incriminating evidence even though the statements themselves are not

111. Hoffman v. United States, 341 U.S. 479, 486 (1951).
112. Marchetti v. United States, 390 U.S. 39, 53 (1968).
113. Hoffman v. United States, 341 U.S. at 486.
114. Allen & Mace, Note 66, *supra*, at 258.
115. 532 U.S. 17 (2001) (per curiam).
116. 542 U.S. 177 (2004).
117. *See* § 9.04, *supra*, for consideration of the Fourth Amendment issues.
118. 530 U.S. 27 (2000).

incriminating." With this background, Justice Stevens found "quite wrong" the argument that the identity information would be incriminating only in "unusual circumstances." To the contrary, he contended, the Court held that the demand for identity passed muster as reasonable under the *Fourth* Amendment only *because* of the potential for incrimination, namely, that it might inform the police officer that *H* was wanted for another offense.

§ 23.05 Privilege against Self-Incrimination in the Police Interrogation Context[119]

[A] General Principles

[1] Original, Bright-Line Approach

In 1897, the Supreme Court in *Bram v. United States*[120] announced that the Fifth Amendment privilege against compelled self-incrimination "was but a crystallization of the [common law] doctrine relative to confessions." Thus, the common law involuntariness rule came under the umbrella of the Fifth Amendment. After *Bram*, compelled statements were inadmissible in *federal* criminal trials as a matter of constitutional law. *Bram*, moreover, announced a strict, virtual bright-line, definition of "involuntariness":

> [A] confession, in order to be admissible, must be free and voluntary: that is, must not be extracted by *any* sort of threats or violence, nor obtained by *any* direct or implied promises, *however slight*, nor by the exertion of *any* improper influence. . . . A confession can *never* be received in evidence where the prisoner has been *influenced* by *any* threat or promise.[121]

At the time of *Bram*, the Fifth Amendment privilege against compelled self-incrimination was not considered a fundamental right. Therefore, *Bram* did not apply to the states. In 1964, however, the Court ruled in *Malloy v. Hogan*[122] that the Fifth Amendment self-incrimination privilege is a fundamental right applicable to the states through the Fourteenth Amendment. Consequently, a defendant in a *state* trial may now assert the privilege, and not simply cite general due process principles, as a basis for excluding a coerced confession.

---

119. *See generally* Laurence A. Benner, *Requiem for Miranda: The Rehnquist Court's Voluntariness Doctrine in Historical Perspective*, 67 Wash. U. L.Q. 59 (1989); Mark A. Godsey, *Rethinking the Involuntary Confession Rule: Toward a Workable Test for Identifying Compelled Self-Incrimination*, 93 Cal. L. Rev. 465 (2005); Lawrence Herman, *The Unexplored Relationship Between the Privilege Against Compulsory Self-Incrimination and the Involuntary Confession Rule (pts 1 & 2)*, 53 Ohio St. L.J. 101, 497 (1992); Yale Kamisar, *What Is an "Involuntary" Confession? Some Comments on Inbau and Reid's Criminal Interrogation and Confessions*, 17 Rutgers L. Rev. 728 (1963).

120. 168 U.S. 532 (1897).

121. *Id.* at 542–43 (emphasis added).

122. 378 U.S. 1 (1964).

[2] Modern Totality-of-Circumstances Test: Two Constitutional Provisions (and Standards) Become One[123]

Notice the text of the Fifth Amendment: It prohibits *compelled* self-incrimination. The Due Process Clause, as interpreted by the Supreme Court, prohibits the admissibility of *involuntary* confessions. Are these two standards—"compulsion" and "involuntariness"—the same?

Initially, the federal self-incrimination cases and state due process decisions may have been traveling down different paths. As noted above, *Bram v. United States* announced a strict test for determining what constitutes compulsion in the interrogation process, and described it almost as a bright-line rule. In contrast, the early due process cases seemingly required proof that the suspect's will was broken by the police, a factor not required under *Bram*, and were (and continue to be) decided on a case-by-case totality-of-the-circumstances basis.

So, the standards were not identical. Consequently, once *Malloy v. Hogan* incorporated the privilege against compelled self-incrimination to the states, one might have expected state defendants contesting interrogation practices to assert the privilege against self-incrimination, rather than due process, on the ground that the strict *Bram* test offered stronger, and more certain, protection than the more flexible due process standard. One might have predicted the Due Process Clause standard to fall into disuse.

An historical quirk in the interrogation field, however, yielded a different story. During the nearly seven-decade period in which the Fifth Amendment privilege applied exclusively in the federal courts (from the time of *Bram* to *Malloy*), the Supreme Court decided fewer than a dozen cases dealing with coerced confessions in federal trials. Meanwhile, during the less than 30 years in which state confessions had to be resolved according to due process principles (from *Brown v. Mississippi*[124] to *Malloy*), the high court decided no fewer than t35 coerced-confession cases.[125] As a result of this disparity, the Court had many opportunities to focus on the Due Process Clause voluntariness standard; in contrast, the Fifth Amendment self-incrimination privilege cases were "low-visibility events."[126] Consequently, as one scholar reported, "*Bram* had little impact [on interrogation law] . . . and, as late as 1951, it was not clear whether the exclusion of involuntary confessions in *federal* cases was based on the Fifth Amendment's self-incrimination provision, the Fifth Amendment's due process provision, or the common law confession rule."[127]

We come, therefore, to an irony: The process of incorporating federal rights to the states tended to work in an opposite direction than one might have expected: state courts did not move to the originally more vigorous federal standard; federal courts moved toward the due process standard! Indeed, in *Arizona v. Fulminante*,[128] the Supreme Court observed that the Fifth Amendment self-incrimination bright-line rule of *Bram* "does

---

123. *See generally* Herman, Note 118, *supra*, at 502–511; Stephen J. Schulhofer, *Reconsidering Miranda*, 54 U. Chi. L. Rev. 435, 440–46 (1987).

124. 297 U.S. 278 (1936).

125. Charles Whitebread & Christopher Slobogin, Criminal Procedure: An Analysis of Cases and Concepts 401 (4th ed. 2000).

126. Hof v. State, 629 A.2d 1251, 1269 (Md. Ct. Spec. App. 1993).

127. Herman, Note 118, *supra*, at 500.

128. 499 U.S. 279 (1991).

not state the standard for determining the voluntariness of a confession."[129] And, in *Dickerson v. United States*,[130] in the Court's historical account of state and federal confession law, it stated that "we evaluate[] the admissibility of a suspect's confession under a [totality-of-circumstances] voluntariness test," which it stated had two constitutional bases, the Fifth Amendment privilege against compelled self-incrimination and the Due Process Clause. More recently still, the Court has characterized the two constitutional provisions as reflecting similar policies, and resulting in "parallel" and "unifying" tests.[131]

In short, in the interrogation field, there is no legal difference today between a "compelled" confession under the Fifth Amendment and an "involuntary" one in the due process framework.[132] *Bram* has given way to the totality-of-circumstances approach described in detail in Chapter 22.[133] Therefore, the principles set forth there should be incorporated by reference here.[134]

---

129. *See also* Colorado v. Connelly, 479 U.S. 157, 163 (1986) (noting that the "Court has retained [the] due process focus, even after holding, in [*Malloy*], that the Fifth Amendment privilege against compulsory self-incrimination applies to the States").

130. 530 U.S. 428 (2000).

131. Missouri v. Seibert, 542 U.S. 600, 607 (2004).

132. There remains a distinction outside the interrogation realm. See Chapter 21, Note 24, *supra*.

133. *See* § 22.02, *supra*.

134. There is one way in which federal and state interrogation rules differ, which should be noted. At the same time that federal courts were applying the totality-of-circumstances constitutional standard in interrogation cases—essentially rejecting the bright-line *Bram* rule—the Supreme Court developed a bright-line rule, which has come to be known as the *McNabb-Mallory* doctrine, applicable only in federal courts, that applies to a narrow category of confessions. By federal statute in the 1940s and 1950s, and by federal rule now, an arrestee must be brought before a magistrate (arraigned) "without unnecessary delay" following her arrest. Fed. R. Crim. P. 5(a)(1)(A). In *McNabb v. United States*, 318 U.S. 332 (1943), and *Mallory v. United States*, 354 U.S. 449 (1957), the Supreme Court used its supervisory power over the federal courts to rule that federal officers may not delay a defendant's appearance before a magistrate in order to interrogate her, i.e., such a delay is "unnecessary" within the meaning of the "prompt arraignment" rule. The Court's remedy for violation of the rule is to exclude from federal trials any statement obtained during the "unnecessary delay" period, *whether or not the confession was involuntary under traditional constitutional principles*. Because the *McNabb-Mallory* rule is not of constitutional origin, it does not apply to the states. Although the practical significance of the *McNabb-Mallory* rule in federal courts was limited by the Supreme Court's later ruling in *Miranda v. Arizona*, 384 U.S. 436 (1966), *Miranda* has not entirely supplanted *McNabb-Mallory*. A 1968 federal statute, 18 U.S.C. § 3501(c) provides that a confession, voluntarily given, "shall not be inadmissible solely because of delay in bringing such person before a magistrate judge . . . if such confession is . . . made . . . within six hours of [arrest]." In *Corley v. United States*, 556 U.S. 303 (2009), the Court held that Congress intended by this provision to limit, but not eliminate, *McNabb-Mallory*. Thus, even if *Miranda* warnings are given, and even if a confession is otherwise voluntary, if the incriminating statement comes more than six hours after arrest, "the exclusionary rule applies and courts have to see whether the delay [in bringing the arrestee before a magistrate] was unnecessary or unreasonable."

[B] Remedies for Violation of the Fifth Amendment Privilege

[1] Requirement of State Action

As explained elsewhere,[135] the Supreme Court in *Colorado v. Connelly*[136] held that "[o]ur 'involuntary confession' jurisprudence is entirely consistent with the settled law requiring some sort of 'state action' to support a claim of violation of the Due Process Clause of the Fourteenth Amendment." There is no doubt that this same principle—a requirement of official overreaching—applies to Fifth Amendment self-incrimination claims.

[2] Standing to Raise Claim

As with "involuntary confession" cases under the Due Process Clause,[137] there is no United States Supreme Court case dealing directly with the issue of standing to raise a Fifth Amendment privilege against self-incrimination claim in the interrogation context. However, there is no doubt that only the person coerced can seek a remedy for violation of the Fifth Amendment privilege. As the Court has noted in non-interrogation contexts, the Fifth Amendment privilege against compulsory self-incrimination is "intimate and personal,"[138] and the privilege "adheres basically to the person, not to information that may incriminate him."[139]

[3] Exclusionary Rule

[a] Constitutional Basis of the Exclusionary Rule

The Fifth Amendment provides that a person shall not be "compelled to be a witness against himself." As this language suggests, *use* at trial of a compelled statement violates the Fifth Amendment, for its admission effectively makes the defendant a "witness against himself." In short, exclusion of a coerced confession or admission of any other compelled statement—unlike exclusion of evidence obtained as a result of an unreasonable search or seizure under the Fourth Amendment—is not simply a remedy for violation of a constitutional right; *it is the core of the right itself.*

Suppose, however, a person is compelled—even tortured—to incriminate herself, but the government does not use any of the compelled statements, or fruits of those statements, in a criminal proceeding. Is the Fifth Amendment privilege violated in these circumstances? Can a person so victimized bring a federal suit for violation of her constitutional rights? As discussed elsewhere,[140] the Supreme Court held in *Chavez v. Martinez*[141] that a civil suit based on a *Due Process Clause* claim *may* be brought in such circumstances. However, the Court in *Chavez* held that a similar action may *not* be brought based on a Fifth Amendment self-incrimination claim.

---

135. *See* § 22.03[A], *supra.*
136. 479 U.S. 157 (1986).
137. *See* § 22.03[B], *supra.*
138. Couch v. United States, 409 U.S. 322, 327 (1973).
139. *Id.* at 328.
140. *See* § 22.02[A][1], *supra.*
141. 538 U.S. 760 (2003).

Four justices (Justice Thomas, joined by Chief Justice Rehnquist and Justices O'Connor and Scalia) in *Chavez* indicated that "[a]lthough our cases have permitted the Fifth Amendment's self-incrimination privilege to be asserted in noncriminal cases, . . . that does not alter our conclusion that a violation of the constitutional *right* against self-incrimination occurs only if one has been compelled to be a witness against himself in a criminal case." Essentially, as the plurality explained prior case law, the "privilege" to assert a self-incrimination claim outside a criminal case is in the nature of a prophylactic rule intended "to preserve[] the core Fifth Amendment right from invasion by the use of that compelled testimony in a subsequent criminal case."

Although this is only a statement of a Court plurality, Justices Souter and Breyer agreed with the plurality to a significant degree, stating that the text of the Fifth Amendment "focuses on courtroom use of a criminal defendant's compelled, self-incriminating testimony, and the core of the guarantee against compelled self-incrimination is the exclusion of such evidence."[142] They recognized a role for the courts to protect the core right outside the criminal trial context, but were unwilling to go far enough outside "the core" to recognize a civil action against the police for questioning in violation of the privilege against self-incrimination.[143]

[b] Scope of the Exclusionary Rule

[i] Impeachment

As with the Due Process Clause,[144] a statement obtained in violation of the Fifth Amendment privilege against compelled self-incrimination is inadmissible at the defendant's trial for *all* purposes. That is, the statement is not admissible in the prosecutor's case-in-chief as substantive evidence of the defendant's guilt, nor may it be used to impeach the defendant.[145]

[ii] Fruit-of-the-Poisonous-Tree Doctrine

As with the Due Process Clause,[146] the Supreme Court has not had direct occasion to decide whether, *in the police interrogation context*, the exclusionary rule requires suppression of reliable fruits of a statement obtained in violation of the Fifth Amendment. There is little doubt that this is the rule, however. First, the Court held in *Counselman v. Hitchcock* that the Fifth Amendment privilege prevents the government from using compelled grand jury testimony to obtain "knowledge of . . . sources of information which may supply other means of convicting" a defendant.[147] As Professor Yale Kamisar has observed, "ever since the 110-year-old case of *Counselman* . . . was decided, it has been

---

142. *Id.* at 777 (concurring in the judgment).

143. A related question arises in deciding what constitutes a "trial" for the purposes of the Fifth Amendment; i.e., does the use of compelled statements in pretrial hearings constitute a Fifth Amendment violation? This question is currently the basis of a circuit split, with the Third, Fourth, and Fifth circuits holding that the Fifth Amendment only applies during a criminal trial, while the Second, Seventh, and Tenth circuits have held that using compelled statements in certain pretrial hearings can constitute a Fifth Amendment violation. Compare Renda v. King, 347 F.3d 550, 552 (3d. Cir. 2003) with Higazy v. Templeton, 505 F.3d 161, 171, 173 (2d Cir. 2007).

144. *See* § 22.03[C][3][a], *supra.*

145. See New Jersey v. Portash, 440 U.S. 450 (1979) (prohibiting the use at trial, for impeachment purposes, of *P*'s compelled grand jury testimony).

146. *See* § 22.03[C][3][b], *supra.*

147. 142 U.S. 547, 586 (1892).

plain that the privilege prohibits the derivative use, as well as the direct use, of compelled utterances."[148] There is no reason to believe that a different rule applies to statements compelled by the police, rather than by the grand jury.

And the Court *has* applied the poisonous-tree principle in a police interrogation context, albeit outside the Fifth Amendment. In *Harrison v. United States*,[149] a prosecutor improperly introduced at trial three confessions that the police obtained from *H* in violation of the *McNabb-Mallory* rule.[150] As a result, *H* changed his trial strategy, and testified in his own behalf. Ultimately, *H*'s conviction was overturned because of the *McNabb-Mallory* violations. At *H*'s second trial, at which the confessions were properly excluded, the prosecutor sought to introduce *H*'s testimony from the first trial. The *Harrison* Court held, however, that this testimony was inadmissible because the prosecutor had not adequately proved that it "was obtained 'by means sufficiently distinguishable' from the underlying illegality 'to be purged of the primary taint.'" Since the "poisonous tree" in *Harrison* was a *non*-constitutional supervisory-authority rule, it follows that a violation of the Constitution itself similarly requires implementation of the poisonous-tree doctrine.

Finally, it is worth observing that a plurality of the Court—including its most conservative members—recently recognized a Fifth Amendment fruit-of-the-poisonous-tree doctrine in dictum. In *Chavez v. Martinez*,[151] Justice Thomas, writing for the Chief Justice and Justices O'Connor and Scalia, observed that "our cases provide that those subjected to coercive police interrogations have an *automatic* protection from the use of their involuntary statements (*or evidence derived from their statements*) in any subsequent criminal trial."[152] Of course, the Fifth Amendment version of the fruit-of-the-poisonous-tree doctrine is subject to the same general limiting principles as its counterparts in the Fourth and Sixth Amendments—the independent-source, inevitable-discovery, and dissipation-of-taint doctrines.[153]

---

148. Yale Kamisar, *A Look Back on a Half-Century of Teaching, Writing and Speaking About Criminal Law and Criminal Procedure*, 2 Ohio St. J. Crim. L. 69, 83 (2004).

149. 392 U.S. 219 (1968).

150. The *McNabb-Mallory* rule is discussed in Note 133, *supra*.

151. 538 U.S. 760 (2003)

152. *Id.* at 769 (latter emphasis added). Not all commentators agree that the fruit-of-the-poisonous-tree doctrine *should* apply to tangible evidence. Amar and Lettow, for example, make the following textual argument: The Fifth Amendment prohibits a defendant from being a "witness" against herself; tangible evidence is not a "witness" (as it does not testify); therefore, "[p]hysical evidence . . . can be introduced at trial whatever its source—even if that source is a compelled pretrial utterance." Amar & Lettow, Note 5, *supra*, at 900. For the contrary view, *see* Yale Kamisar, *On the Fruits of Miranda Violations, Coerced Confessions, and Compelled Testimony*, 93 Mich. L. Rev. 929 (1995).

153. *See generally* §20.08, *supra*.

Chapter 24

Interrogation Law:
Miranda v. Arizona

§ 24.01 *Miranda*: A Brief Overview and Some Reflections[1]

Miranda v. Arizona[2] is one of the most famous Supreme Court decisions in American history. Thanks to the media and police shows on television, nearly every American and many citizens of other countries have heard of *Miranda*. According to one study of lawyers, it is the most memorable criminal case in Supreme Court jurisprudence, and the third most notable overall.[3]

Fame and acceptance, however, are two different concepts. The *Miranda* opinion itself mustered only five votes, and proved to be immediately controversial in many circles. According to one observer, the opinion "must rank as the most bitterly criticized, most contentious, and most diversely analyzed criminal procedure decision by the Warren Court."[4] The decision originally "evoked much anger and spread much sorrow"[5] among police officers and legislators, many of whom believed that the decision would impede law enforcement efforts to obtain confessions of guilt. As a result of these early criticisms of *Miranda*, Congress in 1968—just two years after the decision was handed down—sought to "overrule" the holding by legislation.[6] In more recent years, however, matters have been turned on their head: Most large city police administrators do not want *Miranda* overruled,[7] while some pro-defense scholars have come to criticize

---

1. *See generally* Commentary Symposium, *Miranda at Forty*, 5 Ohio St. J. Crim. L. 161–203 (2007) (articles reflecting on the past, present, and future of *Miranda* and police interrogations); George C. Thomas III & Richard A Leo, *The Effects of Miranda v. Arizona: "Embedded" in Our National Culture?*, 29 Crime and Justice: A Review of Research 203 (2002). *See also* Yale Kamisar, *The Rise, Decline, and Fall (?) of Miranda*, 87 Wash. L. Rev. 965 (2012). This article, written by the so-called "father of *Miranda*," will prove useful at *every* stage of your study of *Miranda*. *See also* Frederick Schauer, *The* Miranda *Warning*, 88 Wash. L. Rev. 155 (2013) (responding to Professor Kamisar's article).

2. 384 U.S. 436 (1966).

3. Jethro K. Lieberman, Milestones! 200 Years of American Law: Milestones in Our Legal History vi–vii (1976).

4. Henry J. Abraham, Freedom and the Court 125 (4th ed. 1982).

5. Yale Kamisar, *A Dissent From the Miranda Dissents: Some Comments on the "New" Fifth Amendment and the Old "Voluntariness" Test*, 65 Mich. L. Rev. 59, 59 (1966).

6. 18 U.S.C.A. § 3501. *See* § 24.06[A], *infra*.

7. Marvin Zalman & Brad W. Smith, *The Attitudes of Police Executives Toward Miranda and Interrogation Policies*, 97 J. Crim. L. & Criminology 873, 904–905 (2007). However, discipline of officers who violate *Miranda* rules is uncommon. *Id.* at 923.

Miranda for not going far enough to protect suspects from improper police interrogation procedures.[8]

Miranda's influence has stretched well beyond the police interrogation room. The decision, the values underlying it, and the public's perception of it were factors in the refusal of the United States Senate to confirm Abe Fortas, a member of the *Miranda* majority, as Chief Justice of the Supreme Court, and *Miranda* may have helped elect Richard Nixon to the presidency.[9]

Miranda—the legal doctrine—is alive,[10] but in deeply weakened condition. One former member of the Court, years ago, described the case as "twisting slowly in the wind."[11] As demonstrated in this chapter, the *Miranda* of 1966 is not the *Miranda* of the twenty-first century. Professor Yale Kamisar has observed that, with the departure of Earl Warren and other members of his Court, "almost all Court watchers expected the [Supreme] Court to treat *Miranda* unkindly. They did not have to wait very long."[12] In most regards, *Miranda* has been narrowly interpreted, waiver of "*Miranda* rights" have been made easier for the prosecution to prove, and exceptions to the doctrine have been created, so that much of the case's potential impact for good or ill has been diminished.[13]

§ 24.02 *Miranda*: Placing the Case in Historical Context

In a sense, the *Miranda* case tries to do two things at once: regulate police conduct during interrogations, and determine which statements made by defendants are presumptively compelled and therefore inadmissible under the Constitution's Self-Incrimination Clause.[14] Thus, as you read through the history and policy behind this landmark decision, keep in mind that these two goals may sometimes lead courts in different directions, creating tension and even inconsistency in the doctrine.

Before *Miranda*, the police typically interrogated suspects in private. Defense lawyers were excluded from the interrogation room. The incommunicado nature of the process facilitated police brutality, which was not uncommon well into the twentieth century. By mid-century, as the result of public opposition to violent police practices and a judicial

---

8. *E.g.*, Irene Merker Rosenberg & Yale L. Rosenberg, *A Modest Proposal for the Abolition of Custodial Confessions*, 68 N.C. L. Rev. 69, 73 (1989); Paul Marcus, *A Return to the "Bright Line Rule" of Miranda*, 35 Wm. & Mary L. Rev. 93, 109–10 (1993).

9. A major campaign position of Nixon, the candidate, was that he would fill Court vacancies with justices opposed to *Miranda*. *See generally* Liva Baker, Miranda: Crime, Law and Politics (1983).

10. That is more than can be said for Ernesto Miranda. He was killed in a barroom brawl 10 years after the case bearing his name was decided. His suspected killer was given *Miranda* warnings. *Id.* at 408–09.

11. Arthur J. Goldberg, *Escobedo and Miranda Revisited*, 18 Akron L. Rev. 177, 182 (1984). One recent scholar has described what the Court has done to the case as "stealth overruling." Barry Friedman, *The Wages of Stealth Overruling (With Particular Attention to Miranda v. Arizona)*, 99 Geo. L.J. 1 (2010).

12. Yale Kamisar, *The Warren Court and Criminal Justice: A Quarter-Century Retrospective*, 31 Tulsa L.J. 1, 13 (1995).

13. *See generally* Alfredo Garcia, *Regression to the Mean: How* Miranda *Has Become a Tragicomical Farce*, 25 St. Thomas L. Rev. 293 (2013).

14. *See* Michael J. Z. Mannheimer, *The Two* Mirandas, 43 N. Ky. L. Rev. 317 (2016).

crackdown on the use of torture to obtain confessions, police departments shifted from physical force to psychological ploys to secure confessions from unwilling suspects.

The new procedures troubled some observers, who believed that they differed only in degree from those used in totalitarian societies.[15] The authors of the police manuals, however, defended the new tactics on the ground that "[o]f necessity, criminal interrogators must deal with criminal offenders on a somewhat lower moral plane than that upon which ethical law-abiding citizens are expected to conduct their every day affairs."[16]

The move from force to psychological pressures did not satisfy a majority of the Supreme Court, which viewed confessions "darkly as the product of police coercion."[17] The Court came to believe that encounters in the interrogation room should be more evenly balanced between suspects and the police. The justices' ultimate goal was to "protect those suspects who were the most vulnerable in police interrogations—minorities and the poor—by informing them of their rights and empowering them against coercive tactics."[18]

Moreover, by the early 1960s the Court had become thoroughly dissatisfied with the imprecise "voluntariness" test[19] used by courts to evaluate the police interrogation techniques suggested in the police manuals. Based upon 30 years of struggle with the doctrine—with a test in which "[a]lmost everything was relevant, but almost nothing was decisive"[20]—the Court concluded that the totality-of-circumstance voluntariness test resulted in "intolerable uncertainty,"[21] and that a bright-line rule was needed.

Interrogation law took a dramatic turn in 1964. First, the Court held that the Fifth Amendment privilege against compulsory self-incrimination is a fundamental right applicable to the states through the Fourteenth Amendment.[22] Second, in *Massiah v. United States*,[23] the Court turned its sights toward the Sixth Amendment, and held that the government may not deliberately elicit statements from a person under indictment in the absence of counsel. Shortly thereafter, in *Escobedo v. Illinois*,[24] it extended the right to counsel to a pre-indictment interrogation.

Massiah, and especially *Escobedo*, generated confusion and controversy among observers.[25] The next year, the Court held a conference to consider which of 101"*Escobedo* cases" it would use to clarify the latter Sixth Amendment right-to-counsel decision.[26] It chose four appeals now treated collectively as *Miranda v. Arizona*. Instead of clarifying *Escobedo*, however, the Court used *Miranda* to shift focus from the Sixth Amendment right to counsel to the Fifth Amendment privilege against compulsory self-incrimination.

---

15. David L. Sterling, *Police Interrogation and the Psychology of Confession*, 14 J. Pub. L. 25, 37 (1965) ("[I]f the American police manuals are examined, there is a striking similarity between their recommendations and Russian and Chinese interrogation techniques.").

16. Fred E. Inbau & John E. Reid, Criminal Interrogation and Confessions 208 (1962).

17. Gerald M. Caplan, *Questioning Miranda*, 38 Vand. L. Rev. 1417, 1425 (1985).

18. Charles D. Weisselberg, *Saving Miranda*, 84 Cornell L. Rev. 109, 125 (1998).

19. *See* §§ 22.02, 23.05[A], *supra*.

20. Yale Kamisar, *Gates, "Probable Cause," "Good Faith," and Beyond*, 69 Iowa L. Rev. 551, 570 (1984).

21. Joseph D. Grano, *Voluntariness, Free Will, and the Law of Confessions*, 65 Va. L. Rev. 859, 863 (1979).

22. Malloy v. Hogan, 378 U.S. 1 (1964).

23. 377 U.S. 201 (1964). *See* § 25.01, *infra*.

24. 378 U.S. 478 (1964). *See* § 24.03, *infra*.

25. Geoffrey R. Stone, *The Miranda Doctrine in the Burger Court*, 1977 Sup. Ct. Rev. 99, 103.

26. Weisselberg, Note 18, *supra*, at 117–18.

§ 24.03 The Road to *Miranda:*
Escobedo v. Illinois

The road to *Miranda* runs through *Escobedo v. Illinois.*[27] In *Escobedo, E*, under arrest for murder, was taken into custody late in the evening and interrogated at the police station. During the questioning, he was handcuffed and kept standing.

At various times during the interrogation, *E* asked to consult with his privately retained lawyer, but his requests were refused on the false ground that his lawyer "didn't want to see" him. The truth was that shortly after the questioning began, *E*'s counsel arrived at the station, but he was not permitted to talk to his client because, as one officer candidly put it, "they hadn't completed questioning."

Later in the night, the police suggested to *E* that he confront *X*, an accomplice who (according to the police) had implicated *E* as the triggerman. *E* agreed to talk to *X* in their presence. During the encounter, *E* made statements to *X* that, for the first time, indicated his familiarity with the crime. Later, *E* made additional statements to the police implicating himself as an accomplice. At no time was *E* informed by the police of his privilege against self-incrimination.

E sought to exclude his statements on the basis that they were coerced in violation of the Due Process Clause, but the trial court found that they were voluntarily given. *E* was convicted. On appeal, the Supreme Court held that the confession was inadmissible because it was obtained in violation of *E*'s Sixth Amendment right to counsel.

Escobedo was path-breaking. Never before had the Court held that the Sixth Amendment right to counsel applied to one against whom criminal proceedings had not yet formally commenced, such as by indictment. Speaking for the Court, Justice Arthur Goldberg stated that the fact that *E* had not been indicted when the statements were obtained was irrelevant because, "[w]hen [*E*] requested, and was denied, an opportunity to consult with his lawyer, the investigation had ceased to be a general investigation . . ." By that time, the investigation had "focused" on *E*; for all practical purposes he had become the accused.

The Court observed that *E*, who purportedly had no prior criminal record, undoubtedly was unaware that his admissions of complicity were legally as damaging as an admission that he had fired the fatal shot. Therefore, he needed the "guiding hand of counsel" to advise him "in this delicate situation." According to *Escobedo*, it "would exalt form over substance to make the right to counsel . . . depend on whether at the time of the interrogation, the authorities had secured a formal indictment."

Despite broad language in the opinion, the Court's holding was narrow. It held only that a suspect's Sixth Amendment right to counsel is violated when, "as here": (1) the investigation focuses on him; (2) he is in custody; (3) the police interrogate him; (4) he requests and is denied an opportunity to consult with his lawyer; and (5) the police have not informed him of his privilege against self-incrimination.

Escobedo was controversial. Some criticized it for "opening the door" of the interrogation room to defense attorneys, while others criticized it for not going far enough in

---

27. 378 U.S. 478 (1964). Also on that road are two pre-*Escobedo* cases: *McNabb v. United States*, 318 U.S. 332 (1943) and *Mallory v. United States*, 354 U.S. 449 (1957).

that direction. Critics of the latter variety pointed out that under *Escobedo* a person who does not request an attorney is not protected. Effectively, this excludes indigents who are too timid or uninformed to ask for counsel during interrogation.

Escobedo's long-term impact as a Sixth Amendment case was soon undermined. The Court "in retrospect" concluded that the underlying rationale of the case was "not to vindicate the constitutional right to counsel as such, but, like *Miranda*, 'to guarantee full effectuation of the privilege against self-incrimination. . . .'"[28] In short, *Escobedo*, although nominally a right-to-counsel case, became a self-incrimination opinion after-the-fact.

The Supreme Court has limited the holding of *Escobedo* to its own facts.[29] Consequently, it is the only opinion of the Court to depart from the general rule that the Sixth Amendment right to counsel attaches only with commencement of formal adversarial criminal proceedings.[30]

Escobedo's long-term significance is not in its holding, but rather in the majority's expressed attitudes regarding interrogations and confessions, which formed the basis for *Miranda*.[31] *Escobedo* provides a classic Fifth Amendment privilege-against-self-incrimination defense of the accusatorial system of criminal justice,[32] which is founded on the view that the government should shoulder the entire load of proving a defendant's guilt, and that confessions—at least, uncounseled ones—are disfavored, if not disallowed. As one scholar recognized, "*Escobedo* launched such a broad attack on the government's reliance on confessions that it threatened (or promised) to eliminate virtually all police interrogation of suspects."[33]

The essence of the Court's reasoning was that *E*, as a suspect in custody on whom the police investigation had focused, needed the guiding hand of a lawyer in his encounter with the police. But, of course, had he been given that right, *E*'s lawyer almost certainly would have advised him not to talk. The Court's reaction to that point was, simply, that this demonstrated why custodial interrogation is a critical stage in the criminal justice process. "The right to counsel would indeed be hollow," *Escobedo* intoned, "if it began at a period when few confessions were obtained." Quoting Wigmore, Justice Goldberg observed that "any system of administration which permits the prosecution to trust habitually to compulsory self-disclosure as a source of proof must itself suffer morally thereby." It was with this attitude toward confessions that the Warren Court turned to *Miranda v. Arizona*.

---

28. Kirby v. Illinois, 406 U.S. 682, 689 (1972) (quoting Johnson v. New Jersey, 384 U.S. 719, 729 (1966)).

29. Johnson v. New Jersey, 384 U.S. 719 (1966).

30. *See* § 25.03, *infra*.

31. *See* Joseph D. Grano, *Selling the Idea to Tell the Truth: The Professional Interrogator and Modern Confessions Law*, 84 Mich. L. Rev. 662, 666 (1986).

32. *See* § 23.03[B][3], *supra*.

33. Kamisar, Note 12, *supra*, at 9; *see* Grano, Note 31, *supra*, at 666 ("[I]f one takes *Escobedo*'s reasoning seriously, all police interrogation should be prohibited until the defendant has had an opportunity to consult with a lawyer.").

§ 24.04 *Miranda*: The Case

[A] The Facts

Miranda v. Arizona involved four cases consolidated for appeal. In view of the *per se* holding of *Miranda*, the facts relating to the police investigations received little attention by the Court. Although the prosecutions involved police practices in four jurisdictions, there were significant common facts: (1) each of the suspects had been taken into custody (in three, by arrest; in one, before formal arrest); (2) they were questioned in an interrogation room; (3) the questioning occurred in a police-dominated environment in which each suspect was alone with the questioners; and (4) the suspects were never informed of their privilege against compelled self-incrimination.

[B] The Holding

What follows is a summary of the key points made in *Miranda*. As noted earlier, however, the post-*Miranda* Supreme Court has reshaped the law. This is the starting point.

[1] What Rights Does a Suspect Have in the Interrogation Room?

[a] Self-Incrimination

A suspect has a constitutional right not to be compelled to make incriminating statements in the police interrogation process. To enforce this right, *Miranda* holds that any statement, whether exculpatory or inculpatory, obtained as the result of custodial interrogation may not be used against the suspect in a criminal trial unless the prosecutor proves that the police provided procedural safeguards effective to secure the suspect's privilege against compulsory self-incrimination.

"Custodial interrogation" — the triggering mechanism of *Miranda* — is defined as "questioning initiated by law enforcement officers after a person has been taken into custody or otherwise deprived of his freedom of action in any significant way." The Court said that "[t]his is what we meant in *Escobedo* [*v. Illinois*] when we spoke of an investigation which had focused on an accused."[34]

[b] Right to Counsel

Miranda observed that "[t]he circumstances surrounding in-custody interrogation can operate very quickly to overbear the will of one merely made aware of his privilege" against compulsory self-incrimination. Therefore, the Court held that an in-custody suspect also has a right to consult counsel prior to questioning and to have counsel present during interrogation.[35]

---

34. *Escobedo* is considered in § 24.03, *supra*. This "was surely one of the least honest sentences in the opinion." Marcus, Note 8, *supra*, at 114. The *Miranda* Court's definition of "custody" is *not* what was meant by "focus" in *Escobedo*. In *Escobedo*, *both* focus and custody were required. As explained later, *Miranda* rejected the "focus" requirement described in *Escobedo*. See § 24.07[B][1], *infra*.

35. In an intriguing footnote in *Berkemer v. McCarty*, 468 U.S. 420, 434 n.21 (1984), the Court declined to answer the question "whether an indigent suspect has a right, under the Fifth

Under *Miranda*, the primary purpose of defense counsel during custodial interrogation is to assure that the suspect's ability to choose whether to speak or to remain silent is unfettered. The lawyer's presence in the interrogation room also serves "significant subsidiary functions": his presence reduces the likelihood that the police will act coercively; he can more effectively reconstruct events and, thus, better prepare a claim of coercion, if necessary, at a subsequent hearing or trial; and he can ensure that any statement given by his client is reported accurately at trial.[36]

The right to counsel discussed in *Miranda* may be described as the Fifth Amendment, or *Miranda*, right to counsel. It should not be confused with the Sixth Amendment right to counsel, discussed in the next chapter, which differs in certain respects.

[2] Procedural Safeguards: The "*Miranda* Warnings"

According to *Miranda*, Congress and the states are free to develop procedural safeguards for protecting a suspect's Fifth Amendment rights during custodial interrogation. However, unless they are "fully as effective" as those described in the opinion, the following warnings must be provided by the police prior to custodial questioning.

First, the police must "in clear and unequivocal terms" indicate that the suspect has a right to remain silent.

Second, the consequence of foregoing the preceding right must be explained to the suspect. Specifically, the first statement "must be accompanied by the explanation that anything said can and will be used against the individual in court."

Third, a suspect held for interrogation must "clearly" be informed that "he has the right to consult with a lawyer and to have the lawyer with him during interrogation."

Amendment, to have an attorney appointed to advise him regarding his responses to custodial interrogation when the alleged offense about which he is being questioned is sufficiently minor that he would not have a right, under the Sixth Amendment, to the assistance of appointed counsel at trial." As explained in § 28.03[B][4], *infra*, an indigent does not have a constitutional right to appointed counsel at trial of a misdemeanor offense for which he will not be incarcerated if convicted.

36. There is increasing belief that, in light of these subsidiary functions of the right to counsel, all custodial police interrogations should be videotaped. The Alaska Supreme Court, for example, has held that, an "unexcused failure to electronically record a custodial interrogation conducted in a place of detention violates a suspect's right to due process, under the Alaska Constitution, and . . . any statement thus obtained is generally inadmissible." Stephan v. State, 711 P.2d 1156, 1158 (Alaska 1985). The Minnesota Supreme Court has held that a "substantial" violation of its rule — requiring the recording of all custodial interrogations, including the reading of the *Miranda* rights and any waivers thereof — requires suppression of any statements made. State v. Scales, 518 N.W.2d 587 (Minn. 1994). Massachusetts has ruled that, although an otherwise valid unrecorded interrogation conducted in police custody or in a place of detention is admissible at trial, the defendant is entitled to an instruction that jurors evaluate the unrecorded statement with "particular caution." Commonwealth v. DiGiambattista, 813 N.E.2d 516 (Mass. 2004). And, as of 2008, North Carolina by statute requires all custodial interrogations in homicide cases to be electronically recorded (audio or video) from the time *Miranda* warnings are given until interrogation is completed. N.C. Gen. Stat. § 15A-211 (2007). At least 12 police departments, on their own, now record interrogations, at least in their most serious felony cases, Stephanie Simon, *Smile and Say Fess Up*, Los Angeles Times, Apr. 8, 2004, at A1; and three-fifths of large city police administrators favor videotaping. Zalman & Smith, Note 7, *supra*, at 920–922. One critic of *Miranda* has argued that videotaping should *replace* the right to counsel during custodial interrogation. Paul G. Cassell, *The Paths Not Taken: The Supreme Court's Failures in Dickerson*, 99 Mich. L. Rev. 898 (2001); *but see* Stephen J. Schulhofer, *Miranda, Dickerson and the Puzzling Persistence of Fifth Amendment Exceptionalism*, 99 Mich. L. Rev. 941 (2001) (unless videotaping supplements *Miranda* rather than substituting for it, it will make matters worse).

Fourth, because the financial ability of the suspect has no relation to the scope of the right to counsel or its importance, the police must inform him that "if he is indigent a lawyer will be appointed to represent him."

[3] Waiver of a Suspect's "*Miranda* Rights"

[a] In General

A suspect may waive his privilege against self-incrimination and his *Miranda* right to counsel before or during interrogation. However, according to *Miranda*, a "heavy burden" rests on the prosecutor to demonstrate that the defendant "voluntarily, knowingly, and intelligently"[37] waived his rights.

[b] Voluntariness of the Waiver

The *Miranda* Court stated that the mere "fact of lengthy interrogation or incommunicado incarceration before a statement is made is strong evidence" of involuntary relinquishment of the Fifth Amendment privilege. Furthermore, evidence that the suspect was "threatened, tricked, or cajoled into a waiver will . . . show that [he] did not voluntarily waive his privilege."

[c] Intelligence of the Waiver

A waiver is not "knowing and intelligent" unless the *Miranda* warnings are given. The Court stated that because the rights at stake are fundamental, it "will not pause to inquire in individual cases whether the defendant was aware of his rights without a warning being given"; and "[n]o amount of circumstantial evidence that the person may have been aware of [his] right[s] will suffice to stand in its stead."

[4] Enforcing the Rights

[a] Privilege Against Self-Incrimination

After the warnings are given, an "express statement" by a suspect that he is willing to make a statement, and that he does not want an attorney present, "followed closely by a statement could constitute a waiver." A waiver of the privilege against self-incrimination "will not be presumed simply from the silence of the accused after warnings are given."

If the suspect "indicates in any manner, at any time prior to or during questioning, that he wishes to remain silent, the interrogation must cease." The Court stated that any statement obtained after the suspect invokes his privilege "cannot be other than the product of compulsion, subtle or otherwise." However, if a person asserts his privilege in his attorney's presence, the Court stated that "there may be some circumstances in which further questioning would be permissible," particularly "[i]n the absence of evidence of overbearing."

[b] Right to Counsel

As with a suspect's right to remain silent, once warnings are given, an express statement by a suspect that he is willing to be interrogated without counsel, "followed closely by a statement could constitute a waiver."

---

37. *See* Johnson v. Zerbst, 304 U.S. 458 (1938).

If a suspect at any time prior to or during the questioning states that he wants to consult with an attorney, "the interrogation must cease until an attorney is present." When the lawyer is furnished, "the individual must have an opportunity to confer with the attorney and to have him present during any subsequent questioning."

[C] Reasoning of the Court

[1] Custodial Interrogation As "Compulsion"

The Court was critical of police interrogation techniques, as evidenced by the police manuals available at the time and quoted extensively in the opinion. According to police procedures, the "guilt of the subject is to be posited as a fact." The manuals train officers to give a suspect the psychological impression that a confession would be nothing more than an "elaboration" of the obvious, the subject's guilt. When "appeals and tricks" fail, the officers "must rely on an oppressive atmosphere of dogged persistence."

Other ploys recommended in the manuals, and described by the Court, include the technique of the police interrogator offering excuses for the suspect's conduct in order to gain his confidence and elicit an admission of guilt, use of a "Mutt and Jeff" act in which a friendly police officer fends off a hostile officer to protect the subject, and outright trickery. In the latter category, the manuals at the time of *Miranda* advised police departments to use lineups in which fictitious witnesses identify the suspect, in order to convince him that there is no value in remaining silent.

Based on such police practices, the Court concluded that custodial interrogation "exacts a heavy toll on individual liberty and trades on the weakness of individuals." Suspects are "thrust into an unfamiliar atmosphere and run through menacing police interrogation procedures." They are "surrounded by antagonistic forces," kept "incommunicado" in a "police-dominated atmosphere," and "deprived of every psychological advantage."

As the preceding language might suggest, the most common reading of *Miranda* in 1966 was that the case stands for the proposition that "compulsion *inheres* in custodial interrogation to such an extent that *any* confession, in *any* case of custodial interrogation, is compelled."[38] That is, in the absence of procedural safeguards (i.e., the "*Miranda* warnings" or their equivalent) custodial interrogation necessarily *will*—not simply *can*—result in unconstitutional compulsion.[39] In short, the Court appeared to replace the totality-of-circumstances "voluntariness" test with a bright-line, *per se* definition of "compulsion" in the custodial interrogation context.

Further support for this reading of *Miranda* is evident from the Court's observations that custodial interrogation "carries its own badge of intimidation," and that persons "subjected to the techniques of persuasion described above cannot be otherwise than under compulsion to speak." The Court also stated that in the absence of warnings or their equivalent, which are "employed to dispel the compulsion inherent in custodial

---

38. Lawrence Herman, *The Supreme Court, the Attorney General, and the Good Old Days of Police Interrogation*, 48 Ohio St. L.J. 733, 735 (1987).

39. Stephen J. Schulhofer, *Reconsidering Miranda*, 54 U. Chi. L. Rev. 435, 447 (1987).

surroundings, no statements obtained from the defendant can truly be the product of his free choice."[40]

[2] The Limited Importance of Confessions in Law Enforcement

As one scholar has observed, "*Miranda* . . . represents a preference for Fifth Amendment values over the interests of law enforcement officers in obtaining incriminating statements."[41] The *Miranda* Court stated that it was "not unmindful of the burdens which law enforcement officials must bear, often under trying circumstances," to obtain evidence to convict the guilty. It was not persuaded, however, by the "recurrent argument . . . that society's need for interrogation outweighs the privilege."

Although the justices conceded that "confessions may play an important role in some convictions," it considered the cases at hand "graphic examples of the overstatement of the 'need' for confessions." The Court noted that in each case before it, the police had considerable incriminating evidence against the suspects that was obtained through standard non-interrogation investigatory practices.

[3] Fifth Amendment Values and the Importance of the Adversarial System

In perhaps the most important explanatory language of the opinion—and certainly the most stirring—the Supreme Court described the Fifth Amendment privilege against compelled self-incrimination as a "noble principle," based on the "individual's substantive right, a 'right to a private enclave where he may lead a private life. That right is the hallmark of our democracy.'"—Chief Justice Earl Warren characterized the privilege as "the essential mainstay of our adversary system." According to *Miranda*, the principles underlying it add up "to one overriding thought":

> [The respect a government . . . must accord to the dignity and integrity of its citizens. To maintain a "fair state-individual balance," to require the government "to shoulder the entire load," . . . to respect the inviolability of the human personality, our accusatory system of criminal justice demands that the government seeking to punish an individual produce the evidence against him by its own independent labors, rather than by the cruel, simple expedient of compelling it from his own mouth.[42]

Consequently, *Miranda* suggested, it "is not for the authorities to decide" when a suspect should speak; rather, it is the fundamental right of the individual, with such assistance as he may wish to obtain from an attorney, to decide whether and when to talk to the police. When an attorney recommends to his client that he remain silent, he "is merely carrying out what he is sworn to do under his oath—to protect to the extent of his ability the rights of his client." As such, the defense attorney in the interrogation room "plays a vital role in the administration of criminal justice under our Constitution."

---

40. Not all of the language in *Miranda* supports the thesis that custodial interrogation is inherently coercive. For example, the opinion states that "we might not find the defendants' statements [in these cases] to have been involuntary in traditional terms. . . . [However,] [t]he *potentiality* for compulsion is forcefully apparent . . ." 384 U.S. at 457 (emphasis added).

41. Weisselberg, Note 18, *supra*, at 121.

42. *Miranda*, 384 U.S. at 460. For fuller discussion of the history of, the policies supporting, and the general contours of, the privilege against compulsory self-incrimination, *see* Chapter 23, *supra*.

§ 24.05 Criticisms of *Miranda*[43]

Although it did not seem so to critics at the time, *Miranda* constituted a compromise, of sorts.[44] Although it apparently created a bright-line, *per se* rule of "involuntariness" to supplant the more flexible totality-of-circumstances standard, it did *not* eliminate uncounseled custodial interrogations, as some observers wanted. What follows is a brief survey of some of the criticisms of *Miranda* from "both directions," as well as arguments in its favor.

[A] "*Miranda* Did Not Go Far Enough"

What the critics say: The Court did not take the logic of *Escobedo*[45] and *Miranda* to its logical conclusion, which is to prohibit custodial confessions altogether,[46] permit questioning but only in the presence of a lawyer,[47] or, at a very minimum, prohibit interrogation until the suspect has consulted with counsel.[48]

If one takes seriously the principle stated in *Miranda* that the government must "shoulder the entire load" in an accusatorial system of justice, and that it must "respect the inviolability of the human personality," it follows from this that the government should not be permitted to establish guilt by use of admissions obtained in the "inherently coercive" environment described by the Supreme Court. Even if this is too extreme a position, the Court acted inconsistently in stating that custodial interrogations are inherently coercive, yet allowing suspects to "voluntarily" waive their rights in the same coercive environment. At a minimum, therefore, a lawyer needs to be present or consulted before a waiver can truly be effective.

What the defenders say: Defenders of *Miranda* do not necessarily disagree with the preceding criticisms, but they suggest that "these [critics] do not seem to appreciate the fact that in 1966 the Court was barely able to go as far as it did—that at the time it was probably not possible to persuade a majority of the Court to go one inch further. . . ."[49]

---

43. For criticisms of *Miranda, see generally* Caplan, Note 17, *supra*; Joseph D. Grano, *Miranda's Constitutional Difficulties: A Reply to Professor Schulhofer*, 55 U. Chi. L. Rev. 174 (1988); Joseph D. Grano, *Miranda v. Arizona and the Legal Mind: Formalism's Triumph over Substance and Reason*, 24 Am. Crim. L. Rev. 243 (1986); Grano, Note 31, *supra*; Office of Legal Policy, U.S. Dept. of Justice, Report to the Attorney General on the Law of Pre-Trial Interrogation (1986). For a defense of *Miranda* and/or criticisms of it on the ground that it did not go far enough in limiting confessions, *see generally* Kamisar, Notes 5 and 12, *supra*; Charles J. Ogletree, *Are Confessions Really Good for the Soul?: A Proposal to Mirandize Miranda*, 100 Harv. L. Rev. 1826 (1987); Rosenberg & Rosenberg, Note 8, *supra*; Stephen J. Schulhofer, *Bashing Miranda Is Unjustified—And Harmful*, 20 Harv. J. Law & Pub. Pol'y 347 (1997); Schulhofer, Note 39, *supra*; Welsh S. White, *Miranda's Failure to Restrain Pernicious Interrogation Practices*, 99 Mich. L. Rev. 1211 (2001); Welsh S. White, *Defending Miranda: A Reply to Professor Caplan*, 39 Vand. L. Rev. 1 (1986).
44. Kamisar, Note 12, *supra*, at 11.
45. Escobedo v. Illinois, 378 U.S. 478 (1964). *See* § 24.03, *supra*.
46. Rosenberg & Rosenberg, Note 8, *supra*.
47. Otis H. Stephens, Jr., The Supreme Court and Confessions of Guilt 205 (1973).
48. Ogletree, Note 43, *supra*, at 1830.
49. Kamisar, Note 12, *supra*, at 12.

[B] "*Miranda* Went Too Far"

[1] "*Miranda* Lacks Historical and Textual Support"[50]

What the critics say: The holding of *Miranda* has "no significant support in the history of the privilege or in the language of the Fifth Amendment."[51] Professor Albert Alschuler has stated that "neither the English nor the American version of the privilege afforded suspects and defendants a right to refuse to respond to incriminating questions."[52] In England, the privilege against compulsory self-incrimination applied only to *judicial* interrogations. Wigmore, too, concludes that the American privilege against compulsory self-incrimination does not apply to police interrogations.[53] Moreover, the most sensible reading of the text of the Fifth Amendment — "No person . . . shall be compelled to be a *witness* against himself" — is that the privilege was intended only to prevent the compulsion of oral testimony by the defendant at his criminal trial.

What the defenders say: The preceding criticism is not really directed at *Miranda*, but at the pre-*Miranda* proposition that the Fifth Amendment requires exclusion of statements secured by police coercion. Wigmore's historical view of the Fifth Amendment has been questioned by some legal historians.[54] Beyond this, it is wrong to tie the Fifth Amendment privilege to an historical period in which investigatory and trial procedures differed so markedly from present-day processes. Divining the framers' intent is always a murky enterprise, but it is odd to think that they would have intended to allow modern-day police coercion while they barred judicial compulsion.[55] Even the Office of Legal Policy in the Department of Justice, which called in 1986 for the Supreme Court to overrule *Miranda*, conceded that the applicability of the Fifth Amendment to custodial police interrogations is consistent with a historical understanding of the privilege.[56]

[2] "The Rule Is Unnecessary and Irrational"

What the critics say: The per se rule of *Miranda* is unnecessary. The "Due Process Clauses [of the Fifth and Fourteenth Amendments] provide an adequate tool for coping with confessions."[57] The due process totality-of-the-circumstances voluntariness test is workable, effective, sophisticated, and sensitive. The claim that it provides inadequate guidance to the police is a "great exaggeration."[58] Supreme Court case law makes clear that if the police engage in certain types of conduct (e.g., physical abuse of any kind, prolonged detention, food or sleep deprivation), they place resulting convictions at risk.

---

50. *See generally* Albert W. Alschuler, *A Peculiar Privilege in Historical Perspective: The Right to Remain Silent*, 94 Mich. L. Rev. 2625 (1996); Eben Moglen, *Taking the Fifth: Reconsidering the Origins of the Constitutional Privilege Against Self-Incrimination*, 92 Mich. L. Rev. 1086 (1994).

51. *Miranda*, 384 U.S. at 526 (White, J., dissenting).

52. Alschuler, Note 50, *supra*, at 2631.

53. 3 John H. Wigmore, Evidence 401 (Chadbourn rev. 1970).

54. *E.g.*, Lawrence Herman, *The Unexplored Relationship Between the Privilege Against Compulsory Self-Incrimination and the Involuntary Confession Rule (Part I)*, 53 Ohio St. L.J. 101 (1992).

55. Kamisar, Note 5, *supra*, at 73–74.

56. Office of Legal Policy, Note 43, *supra*, at 42.

57. *Miranda*, 384 U.S. at 505 (Harlan, J., dissenting).

58. Caplan, Note 15, *supra*, at 1432.

In contrast, the *Miranda* rule is formalistic.[59] The premise that *every* custodial interrogation is coercive is counter-intuitive and empirically false. If a suspect in custody blurts out a confession, it is admissible despite the compulsion inherent in custody. Meanwhile, a single question—"Did you commit the crime?"—asked of the suspect in the absence of warnings and waiver supposedly renders the process coercive. "Common sense informs us to the contrary."[60] It cannot be the case that *any* question of *any* person— regardless of the subject's internal fortitude, and regardless of the nature of the custodial interrogation—overbears the will.

What the defenders say: Only a person with "an extravagant faith" in the voluntariness test "could fail to see that the safeguards provided by [it] . . . were largely 'illusory.' "[61] Even a critic of *Miranda* has conceded that the old test resulted in "intolerable uncertainty."[62] As with other bright-line rules, *Miranda* sends a clearer message to the police than the totality-of-the-circumstances test could ever send.

Moreover, criticism of the per se nature of the rule is historically misguided: *Miranda* merely returned the law to the point at which it began.[63] In *Bram v. United States*,[64] the Supreme Court applied a similar definition of Fifth Amendment "compulsion." Although the *Bram* Court used the term "involuntary" in its analysis, it did not mean by this that the suspect's will had to be overborne in the due process sense for there to be a constitutional violation. Quite the contrary: Only later did the Court begin to use the term "involuntariness" interchangeably with "compulsion."[65]

In self-incrimination analysis, the amount of pressure required to invalidate a confession should be less than is required in the due process context, and should not be balanced against law enforcement interests, because the Fifth Amendment is linked to the anti-inquisitorial values of the Fifth Amendment's framers. The critical question should be, as in *Miranda*, whether the pressure was "imposed for the *purpose* of discouraging the silence of a criminal suspect."[66]

[3] "*Miranda* is Anti-Confession and Pro-Fox Hunt"

What the critics say: The "obvious underpinning of [*Miranda*] . . . is a deep-seated distrust of all confessions." The "not so subtle overtone of the opinion [is] . . . that it is inherently wrong for the police to gather evidence from the accused himself."[67] Whatever else the Court may say, "the thrust of the new rules is to negate all pressures, to reinforce the nervous or ignorant suspect, and ultimately to discourage any confession at all."[68]

The *Miranda* majority opinion seeks a pure adversary system, but the American system of justice is and should be one mixed with non-adversarial procedures. *Miranda*

---

59. *See* Grano, *Legal Mind*, Note 43, *supra*, at 246.
60. *Miranda*, 384 U.S. at 534 (White, J., dissenting).
61. Kamisar, Note 5, *supra*, at 62.
62. Grano, Note 21, *supra*, at 863.
63. *See* Schulhofer, Note 39, *supra*, at 440–46.
64. 168 U.S. 532 (1897). *See* § 23.05[A][1], *supra*.
65. *See* § 23.05[A][2], *supra*.
66. Schulhofer, Note 39, *supra*, at 445.
67. *Miranda*, 384 U.S. at 537, 538 (White J., dissenting).
68. *Id.* at 505 (Harlan, J., dissenting).

ignores the fact that, according to Justice White, "[t]he most basic function of any government is to provide for the security of the individual and of his property." Respect for the inviolability of the suspect is not all that is valued by the Constitution: "[T]he human personality of others in the society must also be preserved."[69]

Miranda treats criminal suspects as if they were underdogs, in need of lawyers to match wits with the police and to protect them against the pressures generated by custodial interrogation.[70] *Miranda* places the suspect on an even playing field with the police,[71] and thereby gives an underdog suspect a sporting chance to be acquitted, even when he is factually guilty.

This "sporting theory of justice,"[72] however, is senseless. Bentham contemptuously labeled this impulse to give the guilty a chance to avoid punishment as the "fox hunter's reason," that is, "[t]he fox is to have a fair chance for his life: he must have . . . leave to run a certain length of way, for the express purpose of giving him a chance for escape."[73] Nobody who believes in the basic legitimacy of a society, however, should "endorse the view that a guilty suspect, like a fox during a hunt, must be given a sporting chance to escape conviction and punishment."[74] We should want guilty people to confess, and not make it easier for them to remain silent.[75]

What the defenders say: The critics' real objection is not with *Miranda*, but with the Fifth Amendment and the accusatorial system of justice that underlies it. It is the Constitution, not the Supreme Court, that prohibits compelled self-incrimination. It is the Fifth Amendment, not *Miranda*, that values a system of justice in which the government must prove guilt by its independent labors.

Miranda is not based on a "fox hunt" or "sporting" approach to justice. It is based on the premise that it is "unseemly" for the police "systematically to . . . take advantage of the psychological vulnerabilities of a citizen."[76] The weak—which is what a suspect is when dealing alone with the police while in custody—should not be exploited by agents of the government. Values of human autonomy and dignity require no less than what *Miranda* safeguards.[77]

---

69. *Id.* at 537, 539 (White, J., dissenting).

70. *See* Caplan, Note 15, *supra*, at 1441.

71. It may do more: "[I]t gives the suspect too great an advantage. If the police are too formidable for the average offender, a lawyer will be too formidable for the average investigator." *Id.* at 1443.

72. Roscoe Pound, *The Causes of Popular Dissatisfaction with the Administration of Justice*, 29 A.B.A. Re. 395 (1906) (*reprinted in* 35 F.R.D. 273, 281 (1964)).

73. 5 Jeremy Bentham, Rationale of Judicial Evidence 238–39 (1827).

74. Grano, Note 29, *supra*, at 677.

75. *See* Rosenberg & Rosenberg, Note 8, *supra*, at 70–71 (reproducing portions of the comic strip "Amazing Spider-Man," in which Peter Parker, the web-slinger's alter ego, expresses dismay at the release of the evil bad-guy "just because of a technicality"—the absence of *Miranda* warnings; Parker says "[w]e're treating justice like a game! The crook is 'safe at first' because the cop dropped the ball! That's insanity.").

76. Stephen J. Schulhofer, *Confessions and the Court*, 79 Mich. L. Rev. 865, 872 (1981).

77. *See* R. Kent Greenawalt, *Silence as a Moral and Constitutional Right*, 23 Wm. & Mary L. Rev. 15, 40–41 (1981).

[4] "*Miranda* Is Injurious to Law Enforcement"[78]

What the critics say: Police questioning of suspects "is an indispensable instrumentality of justice."[79] "[W]e cannot read an undiscriminating hostility to mere interrogation into the Constitution without unduly fettering the States in protecting society from the criminal."[80] The logical implication of *Miranda* is that once a suspect is informed of his privilege against compulsory self-incrimination and of his right to talk to a lawyer before any interrogation occurs, he *will* talk to his lawyer, and any lawyer worth his salt will tell his client to remain silent. *Miranda's* effect, therefore, is to make it more difficult for the police to obtain critical confessions. As a consequence, more guilty people will escape justice.

Miranda has taken its toll. Researchers in Pittsburgh found that, before *Miranda*, 48.5% of suspects confessed their offenses; immediately after, the rate dropped to 32.3%, and a somewhat later sample produced an even lower figure of 27.1 percent.[81] "Before and shortly after" figures obtained in other communities (New York County, Philadelphia, New Haven, Washington, D.C., Kansas City, Chicago, and Los Angeles) suggest that *Miranda* results in a lost *confession* in about one out of every six criminal cases in this country, and in a lost *conviction* in 3.8% of all serious criminal cases.[82]

Miranda continues to hamper the police. Figures from a more recent study in Salt Lake City suggest that the police were successful in obtaining confessions in only one-third of the cases surveyed, compared to a 55% to 60% rate before *Miranda*.[83] According to Professor Paul Cassell, the various *Miranda* studies conducted at various times in various jurisdictions demonstrate that *Miranda* has resulted in dismissal of charges in approximately 28,000 violent felony cases yearly.[84]

What the defenders say: The practical effect of *Miranda* has been "substantial benefits and vanishingly small social costs."[85] Indeed, many early critics of *Miranda* now concede that the decision has not handcuffed the police.[86]

---

78. *See generally* Paul G. Cassell, *Miranda's Social Costs: An Empirical Reassessment*, 90 Nw. U. L. Rev. 387 (1996); Paul G. Cassell, *All Benefits, No Costs: The Grand Illusion of Miranda's Defenders*, 90 Nw. U. L. Rev. 1084 (1996); Paul G. Cassell & Bret S. Hayman, *Police Interrogation in the 1990s: An Empirical Study of the Effects of Miranda*, 43 UCLA L. Rev. 839 (1996); Richard A. Leo, *The Impact of Miranda Revisited*, 86 J. Crim. L. & Criminology 621 (1996); Richard A. Leo, *Inside the Interrogation Room*, 86 J. Crim. L. & Criminology 266 (1996); Stephen J. Schulhofer, *Miranda's Practical Effect: Substantial Benefits and Vanishingly Small Social Costs*, 90 Nw. U. L. Rev. 500 (1996); George C. Thomas III, *Is Miranda a Real-World Failure? A Plea for More (and Better) Empirical Evidence*, 43 UCLA L. Rev. 821 (1996); George C. Thomas III, *Plain Talk About the Miranda Empirical Debate: A "Steady-State" Theory of Confessions*, 43 UCLA L. Rev. 933 (1996).

79. Ashcraft v. Tennessee, 322 U.S. 143, 160 (1944) (Jackson, J., dissenting).

80. *Id.*

81. Richard H. Seeburger & R. Stanton Wettick, Jr., *Miranda in Pittsburgh—A Statistical Study*, 29 U. Pitt. L. Rev. 1 (1967).

82. Cassell, *Empirical Reassessment*, Note 78, *supra*, at 417, 438.

83. Cassell & Hayman, Note 78, *supra*, at 871.

84. Cassell, *Empirical Reassessment*, Note 78, *supra*, at 440.

85. Schulhofer, Note 78, *supra*.

86. *See* Schulhofer, Note 39, *supra*, at 456; George C. Thomas III, *Stories About Miranda*, 102 Mich. L. Rev. 1959, 1999 (2004) ("My study is the latest piece of evidence that *Miranda* has not changed very much about police interrogation. Perhaps history will record the *Miranda* revolution as a mere blip on the screen in centuries of evolving [interrogation] law. . . .").

The studies reported above are flawed on various complicated empirical grounds.[87] Nonetheless, critics of *Miranda* "devote[] considerable effort to milking them for empirical conclusions."[88] Even if we had rigorous empirical calculations of lost confessions, which we do not, there would be reasons "to be skeptical of evidence of a *Miranda* effect: (1) the possibility of independent long-term trends; (2) the likelihood of competing causal events; and (3) the instability in the confession rates."[89]

Probably "[t]he only reliable evidence of a statistically significant reduction in confessions is the . . . study in Pittsburgh."[90] Yet, even in that city the Chief of Police told the researchers that *Miranda* had been good for his department, as it "provided an opportunity to professionalize the police."[91] As for the Salt Lake City 3.8% lost-conviction figure, closer scrutiny by Professor Stephen Schulhofer suggests that the figure is based on "inconsistent and highly partisan procedures" that, when removed, results in a finding of, *at most*, a lost-conviction figure of "a mere seventy-eight one-hundredths of one percent [0.78%] for the immediate post-*Miranda* period, and most likely even less today. For all practical purposes, *Miranda*'s empirically detectable harm to law enforcement shrinks virtually to zero."[92] It follows, therefore, that the Cassell calculation of dismissed cases is grossly overinflated.[93]

One reason why *Miranda* has had so little impact on the confession rate is that, as one critic of *Miranda* has conceded, "[a]ll the studies suggest that suspects frequently waive their [*Miranda*] rights."[94] Police almost always read suspects the warnings, the suspects predictably[95] and commonly[96] waive their rights, and the interrogations proceed. As a result, *Miranda* "liberate[s] the police,"[97] because the warnings reduce the likelihood that a court will find that the interrogation process was coercive under traditional voluntariness principles.[98]

---

87. For a thorough critique of the methodologies in the *Miranda* studies, *see especially* Schulhofer, Note 76, *supra*; and Thomas, *Plain Talk*, Note 76, *supra*.

88. Schulhofer, Note 78, *supra*, at 505.

89. Thomas, *Plain Talk*, Note 78, *supra*, at 937 (crediting Schulhofer, Note 76, *supra*, for identifying these reasons).

90. Thomas, *Real-World Failure*, Note 78, *supra*, at 830; *see* White, *Defending Miranda*, Note 43, *supra*, at 18–19.

91. Yale Kamisar, *Landmark Ruling's Had No Detrimental Effect*, Boston Globe, Feb. 1, 1987, at A27, *as quoted in* Schulhofer, Note 39, *supra*, at 458 n.59.

92. Schulhofer, Note 78, *supra*, at 502.

93. Schulhofer, *id.* at 546, warns, as well, against citing absolute numbers of dismissed cases that are mere extrapolations based on inherently soft figures and assumptions. Thus, the specific figure Cassell quoted of lost felony cases—or, indeed, *any* specific figure—necessarily tells a misleading story, because it gives a false impression of precision.

94. Caplan, Note 17, *supra*, at 1466.

95. As previously noted, *Miranda* is a compromise. The Court did not take its own reasoning to its logical conclusion, namely, to prohibit suspects from waiving their constitutional right to silence in the coercive environment of the interrogation room until suspects consult with counsel.

96. In the Salt Lake City study, *Miranda* waivers were obtained in 83.7% of the cases. Cassell & Hayman, Note 78, *supra*, at 860.

97. Schulhofer, Note 39, *supra*, at 454.

98. Berkemer v. McCarty, 468 U.S. 420, 433 n.20 (1984) ("[C]ases in which a defendant can make a colorable argument that a self-incriminating statement was 'compelled' despite the fact that the law enforcement authorities adhered to the dictates of *Miranda* are rare.").

§ 24.06 Is *Miranda* a Constitutionally Based Decision?

[A] Act 1: Congress and *Miranda*

In 1968, Congress passed the Omnibus Crime Control and Safe Streets Act. It provided in pertinent part:

§ 3501

Admissibility of confessions

(a)

In any criminal prosecution brought by the United States or by the District of Columbia, a confession . . . shall be admissible in evidence if it is voluntarily given. Before such confession is received in evidence, the trial judge shall, out of the presence of the jury, determine any issue as to voluntariness. If the trial judge determines that the confession was voluntarily made it shall be admitted in evidence. . . .

(b)

The trial judge in determining the issue of voluntariness shall take into consideration all the circumstances surrounding the giving of the confession, including (1) the time elapsing between arrest and arraignment of the defendant making the confession, if it was made after arrest and before arraignment, (2) whether such defendant knew the nature of the offense for which he was charged or of which he was suspected at the time of making the confession, (3) whether or not such defendant was advised or knew that he was not required to make any statement and that any such statement could be used against him, (4) whether or not such defendant had been advised prior to questioning of his right to the assistance of counsel; and (5) whether or not such defendant was without the assistance of counsel when questioned and when giving such confession.

The presence or absence of any of the above-mentioned factors to be taken into consideration by the judge need not be conclusive on the issue of voluntariness of the confession.

As the Supreme Court later observed in *Dickerson v. United States*,[99] "[g]iven § 3501's express designation of voluntariness as the touchstone of admissibility, its omission of any warning requirement, and the instruction for trial courts to consider a nonexclusive list of factors relevant to the circumstances of a confession, . . . [it is evident] Congress intended by its enactment to overrule *Miranda*."

But, Congress cannot overrule a constitutional right. Therefore, Section 3501's legitimacy—or, put another way, *Miranda*'s continued vitality—was placed in issue with enactment of this legislation. For approximately three decades, however, Section 3501 remained dormant: Federal law enforcement officers continued to give *Miranda* warnings as a matter of course, and federal prosecutors did not claim that Section 3501 undid *Miranda*.

---

99. 530 U.S. 428, 436 (2000).

[B] Act 2: *Miranda* as a "Prophylactic Rule"

The constitutional underpinnings of *Miranda* were seemingly cut out from under it by the Supreme Court in *Michigan v. Tucker*.[100] In *Tucker, T* was not fully informed of his constitutional rights as mandated by *Miranda*. Consequently, *T*'s statement obtained by the police was excluded at his trial. At issue, however, was whether the fruit of the confession—the testimony of a witness whose name came to light in *T*'s *Miranda*-less statement—was also inadmissible, as a "fruit of the poisonous tree."

In order to resolve the fruit issue, the Court, per then-Associate Justice William Rehnquist, asked a foundational question: "[W]hether the police conduct complained of directly infringed upon [*T*'s] right against compulsory self-incrimination or whether it instead violated only the prophylactic rules developed to protect that right." The Court's answer was that "[c]ertainly no one could contend that the interrogation faced by [*T*] bore any resemblance to the historical practices at which the right against compulsory self-incrimination was aimed," namely, the "ecclesiastical inquisitions and Star Chamber proceedings occurring several centuries ago." Therefore, "the police conduct here did not deprive [*T*] of his privilege against compulsory self-incrimination as such, but rather failed to make available to him the full measure of procedural safeguards associated with that right since *Miranda*."

What did the Court mean by speaking of *Miranda* as "only" a "prophylactic" rule? Essentially, what lawyers and scholars typically took from *Tucker* was this: The failure of police to provide proper warnings to a suspect prior to custodial interrogation does not *in itself* render a confession involuntary in violation of the Fifth Amendment; rather, the omission of full warnings only violates judicially created procedural safeguards intended to prevent an *actual* violation of the Constitution. As the Court subsequently put it explicitly in *Oregon v. Elstad*,[101] "[t]he *Miranda* exclusionary rule . . . serves the Fifth Amendment and *sweeps more broadly than the Fifth Amendment itself. It may be triggered even in the absence of a Fifth Amendment violation.*"

The *Tucker* Court's interpretation of *Miranda* was criticized as "an outright rejection of *Miranda*'s core premises,"[102] and inconsistent with language in *Miranda* and various pre-*Tucker* explanations of the case.[103] Although the Court in *Miranda* stated that Congress could devise alternative means to prevent involuntary confessions, it also indicated that in the absence of the warnings or remedies at least as effective, *any* custodial interrogation was *inherently coercive* and, therefore it would seem, in violation of the Fifth Amendment prohibition on compelled self-incrimination.

There is more, however, to the characterization of *Miranda* warnings as "prophylactic": If *Miranda* did not announce a constitutional rule, Congress presumably possessed the authority in Section 3501 to reject *Miranda* and return the law to its pre-*Miranda* position. Moreover, because the Supreme Court, absent a *constitutional* violation, lacks supervisory authority over state judicial proceedings,[104] *Tucker* called into question the federal judiciary's authority to require states to follow *Miranda*'s dictates.

---

100. 417 U.S. 433 (1974).

101. 470 U.S. 298, 306 (1985) (emphasis added).

102. Stone, Note 25, *supra*, at 118.

103. *E.g.*, Orozco v. Texas, 394 U.S. 324, 326 (1969) ("[T]he use of these admissions obtained in the absence of the required warnings was a *flat violation of the Self-Incrimination Clause of the Fifth Amendment. . . .*") (emphasis added).

104. Smith v. Phillips, 455 U.S. 209, 221 (1982).

[C] Act 3: *Miranda* is (Sort of) Re-Constitutionalized

[1] Dickerson v. United States[105]

In *Dickerson v. United States, D* moved to suppress statements he made to FBI agents during custodial interrogation in the absence of *Miranda* warnings. The trial court granted his motion, but the United States Court of Appeals for the Fourth Circuit reversed on the ground that Section 3501 superseded *Miranda*; applying that statute, the Fourth Circuit concluded that *D*'s statements were voluntarily made. The Supreme Court granted a hearing in *Dickerson* to decide, at last, whether Section 3501 was constitutional.

Writing for a seven-member majority, Chief Justice Rehnquist—the author of the *Tucker* opinion that seemed to deconstitutionalize *Miranda*—stated that *Miranda* was "a constitutional decision" and, as he also put it, that *Miranda* has "constitutional origin," "constitutional underpinnings," and a "constitutional basis." Therefore, the majority held, *Miranda* could *not* be overruled by an Act of Congress.[106] Moreover, the Court declined to overrule *Miranda* itself.

The Supreme Court found support for the constitutional basis of *Miranda* in the language of *Miranda* itself, and in various post-*Miranda* cases. The Chief Justice conceded "that there is language in some of our opinions"—*Michigan v. Tucker* and *Oregon v. Elstad* would be examples—"that supports the view" that *Miranda* is not constitutionally based. But, Rehnquist parsed the language of the *Miranda* opinion to show that it was "replete with statements indicating that the majority thought it was announcing a constitutional rule." This observation is correct—that is why the Chief Justice's opinion in *Tucker* was criticized for rejecting *Miranda*'s core premises.

The Chief Justice also found support for the proposition that *Miranda* has constitutional underpinnings from the *Miranda* Court's "invitation for legislative action to protect the constitutional right against coerced self-incrimination." Rehnquist stated that the *Miranda* decision, by inviting congressional action, intended to avoid creating a "constitutional straightjacket," but that "a review of our opinion . . . clarifies that this disclaimer was intended to indicate that the Constitution does not require police to administer the particular *Miranda* warnings, not that the Constitution does not require a procedure that is effective in securing Fifth Amendment rights."

There was a more basic reason why the Court affirmed *Miranda* as a constitutional rule: "[F]irst and foremost of the factors on the other side—that *Miranda* is a constitutional decision" is that both *Miranda* and two of its companion cases applied the rule to

---

105. 530 U.S. 428 (2000); *see generally* Symposium, *Miranda After Dickerson: The Future of Confession Law*, 99 Mich. L. Rev. 879-1247 (2001); Evan H. Caminker, *Miranda and Some Puzzles of "Prophylactic" Rules*, 70 U. Cin. L. Rev. 1 (2002); Donald A. Dripps, *Constitutional Theory for Criminal Procedure: Dickerson, Miranda, and the Continuing Quest for Broad-but-Shallow*, 43 Wm. & Mary L. Rev. 1 (2001); Yale Kamisar, *Miranda Thirty-Five Years Later: A Close Look at the Majority and Dissenting Opinions in Dickerson*, 33 Ariz. St. L.J. 387 (2001); Daniel M. Katz, *Institutional Rules, Strategic Behavior, and the Legacy of Chief Justice William Rehnquist: Setting the Record Straight on Dickerson v. United States*, 22 J. Law & Politics 303 (2006).

106. Dickerson's confession, therefore, had to be excluded. However, as frequently occurs in such circumstances, the suppression did not result in a lost conviction for the government. Dickerson was convicted of robbery in a retrial, even without the statement. *Man Sentenced in Case That Upheld Miranda*, New York Times, Jan. 6, 2001, at A9.

proceedings in state courts. . . ." That is, since the Supreme Court lacks non-constitutional supervisory authority over state proceedings, and since the high court enforced the rule it announced in *Miranda* in state cases, this means that *Miranda must* be a constitutional decision!

Justice Scalia (writing also for Justice Thomas) described the latter argument as "a classic example of begging the question." To him, the issue was not whether the Court once (or even now) considered *Miranda* a constitutional decision, but rather whether the dictates of *Miranda, in fact*, are constitutionally based. If they are not, Scalia wrote, "our continued application of the *Miranda* code to the States despite our consistent statements that running afoul of its dictates does not necessarily—or even usually—result in an actual constitutional violation, represents not the source of *Miranda*'s salvation but rather evidence of its ultimate illegitimacy."

The majority had no direct answer to Justice Scalia's illegitimacy point. Indeed, the majority in *Dickerson*, while refusing to overrule *Miranda*, provided no ringing endorsement of the case or the rule announced in it. The Chief Justice stated that "[w]hether or not we would agree with *Miranda*'s reasoning and its resulting rule, were we addressing the issue in the first instance, the principles of *stare decisis* weigh heavily against overruling it now." The majority stated that while "'*stare decisis* is not an inexorable command,'" the doctrine should be followed absent some special justification. Here, there "is [no] such justification for overruling *Miranda*. *Miranda* has become embedded in routine police practice to the point where the warnings have become part of our national culture."

[2] *Dickerson*'s Significance

Dickerson seemingly ensures the life of *Miranda*, if only because of the doctrine of *stare decisis*. But observers of *Dickerson* were interested in the case for another reason. As is developed below, the Court has created exceptions to the *Miranda* rules, justifying them on the ground that *Miranda* announced a mere prophylactic rule, rather than a constitutional violation. If *Dickerson*, however, re-constitutionalizes *Miranda*, the pre-*Dickerson* cases that narrowed the *Miranda* doctrine are called into question as well.

There is less, however, to *Dickerson* than it might seem at first glance. Yes, it invalidated Congress' effort to overrule *Miranda*. Yes, *Miranda* remains in force in state criminal proceedings. However, *Dickerson* did not, in any meaningful way, put *Miranda* law back where it stood in 1966 when the Court announced its opinion, In this regard, consider language found in *Chavez v. Martinez*.[107] In *Chavez*, M was arrested following an altercation with the police in which M was shot several times, causing injuries that left him permanently blinded and paralyzed from the waist down. The police questioned M, without giving *Miranda* warnings, while M was receiving treatment at the hospital in the immediate aftermath of the shooting. M was never charged with a crime, so his *Miranda*-less statements were never used against him in a criminal trial. M, however, brought suit under 42 U.S.C. § 1983 claiming that the interrogating officer violated his Fifth Amendment constitutional rights, in part by violating *Miranda*.

The Supreme Court rejected M's Fifth Amendment claim. Although there was no majority opinion on this issue, six justices concluded that the violation of *Miranda* could not amount to an actionable violation of M's rights under the Self-Incrimination Clause

---

107. 538 U.S. 760 (2003); *see generally* Thomas Y. Davies, *Farther and Farther from the Original Fifth Amendment: The Recharacterization of the Right Against Self-Incrimination as a "Trial Right" in Chavez v. Martinez*, 70 Tenn. L. Rev. 987 (2003); Marcy Strauss, *Torture*, 48 N.Y.L. Sch. L. Rev. 201 (2004).

because his statements were never used in a criminal proceeding. In other words, obtaining a statement in violation of *Miranda* is not, by itself, an actionable constitutional violation. The constitutional violation is not complete until a compelled incriminating statement is used at trial.[108]

Language in the opinion, however, is more revealing than the holding itself. Justice Thomas, writing for himself, the Chief Justice, and Justices Scalia and O'Connor, explained: "In the Fifth Amendment context, we have created prophylactic rules designed to safeguard the core constitutional right protected by the Self-Incrimination Clause." He cited *Michigan v. Tucker* and *Oregon v. Elstad*—the *Miranda* cases that seemingly undermined its constitutional pedigree, and yet the same cases which one might have assumed were themselves undermined by *Dickerson*—in support of the "prophylactic" versus "core constitutional right" distinction. Thus, whatever *Dickerson* means when it characterizes *Miranda* as a "constitutional rule," it seemingly remains the case that violation of *Miranda* itself does not trigger a "core" constitutional violation. And, as will be seen later in this chapter,[109] the pre-*Dickerson* rules that narrowed *Miranda*'s scope have not been overruled. In short, *Dickerson*'s impact on *Miranda*, other than not overruling it, has been minimal.

§ 24.07 Meaning of *Miranda*: "Custody"[110]

[A] General Principles

Miranda warnings prior to questioning are required "only where there has been such a restriction on a person's freedom as to render him 'in custody.'"[111] According to *Miranda*, "custody" arises when a person is "taken into custody or otherwise deprived of his freedom of action in any significant way." As the Court has subsequently explained that statement, a person is "in custody" for purposes of receiving *Miranda* warnings if "there is a 'formal arrest or restraint on freedom of movement' of the degree associated with a formal arrest."[112]

In determining whether a person is in custody, "a court must examine all of the circumstances surrounding the interrogation."[113] Ironically, therefore, although *Miranda* was intended to serve as a bright-line alternative to the totality-of-the-circumstances voluntariness standard, there is no bright line (formal arrests aside) for determining whether "custody" exists and, therefore, whether *Miranda* potentially applies.

One matter that is *not* a factor in determining whether a subject is in custody is an "officer's subjective and undisclosed view concerning whether the person being

---

108. *See* 23.05[B][3][a], *supra*.

109. *See* §§ 24.11–24.12, *infra*. In particular, *see* § 24.12[B][3], and discussion of *United States v. Patane*, 542 U.S. 630 (2004).

110. *See generally* Daniel Yeager, *Rethinking Custodial Interrogation*, 28 Am. Crim. L. Rev. 1 (1990).

111. Oregon v. Mathiason, 429 U.S. 492, 495 (1977).

112. California v. Beheler, 463 U.S. 1121, 1125 (1983) (quoting Oregon v. Mathiason, 429 U.S. at 495)).

113. Stansbury v. California, 511 U.S. 318, 322 (1994); *see also* Howes v. Fields, 132 S. Ct. 1181, 1189 (2012) ("the determination of custody should focus on all of the features of the interrogation").

interrogated is a suspect."[114] Indeed, according to the Court, "the initial determination of custody depends on the objective circumstances of the interrogation, not on the subjective views harbored by *either the interrogating officers or the person being questioned.*"[115] Put simply, "the only relevant inquiry is how a reasonable man in the suspect's position would have understood his situation."[116]

For example, in *Berkemer v. McCarty,*[117] *O*, a police officer, observed *M* driving erratically on a highway. *O* forced *M* to pull over and get out of his car. When *M* complied, *O* observed that *M* had difficulty standing. At that moment, *O* *subjectively* determined that *M* would be charged with a driving offense and taken to jail — *M* was not free to leave and would soon be formally arrested. Without informing *M* of his *Miranda* rights, *O* asked *M* whether he had been using intoxicants.

The Supreme Court held that *M*'s answer to *O*'s question was admissible, because *M* was not in custody for purposes of *Miranda*. *O*'s unarticulated plan to arrest *M* had no bearing on the issue. The correct issue was what a reasonable person in *M*'s shoes would have understood to be his situation. The Court concluded that at the time of the brief questioning, a reasonable driver in *M*'s shoes would *not* have believed that he was under arrest or in "the functional equivalent of formal arrest." The relevant inquiry in all cases is, simply, "how a reasonable person in the position of the individual being questioned would gauge the breadth of his or her 'freedom of action.'"[118]

As the preceding discussion suggests, there are "two discrete inquiries" in custody analysis: (1) "what were the circumstances surrounding the interrogation"; and (2) "given those circumstances, would a reasonable person have felt he or she was not at liberty to terminate the interrogation and leave."[119] In the *Miranda* context, this latter inquiry requires more than that the interrogated party would reasonably believe he has been temporarily detained, but, as noted above, that the restraint constitutes a formal arrest or a restriction on his movement comparable to a formal arrest.

---

114. Stansbury v. California, 511 U.S. at 319.

115. *Id.* at 323 (emphasis added).

116. Berkemer v. McCarty, 468 U.S. 420, 442 (1984). What if the suspect is not a "man" but a youth? Is that relevant to the issue of custody? In *J.D.B. v. North Carolina*, 564 U.S. 261 (2011), the Court concluded, 5–4, that because "children will often feel bound to submit to police questioning when an adult in the same circumstance would feel free to leave," a child's age is a part of the "objective circumstances" to be considered in making the custody determination. In other words, "so long as the child's age was known to the officer at the time of police questioning, or would have been objectively apparent to a reasonable officer," then the question becomes how a reasonable person of the child's age in the suspect's position would have understood his situation. The majority offered two responses to the dissenting judges' worry that this result might turn the objective test into a subjective one in which many of the suspect's personal characteristics must be considered. First, the Court contended that a child's age is a special case because it has an "objectively discernable relationship to a reasonable person's understanding of his freedom of action." Second, the Court argued that considering age does not involve "a determination of how youth 'subjectively affects the mindset' of any particular child," so that accounting for age does not require looking into the mind of the particular child, as would, for example, "consideration of whether a particular suspect is 'unusually meek or compliant.'"

117. 468 U.S. 420 (1984).

118. Stansbury v. California, 511 U.S. 318, 325 (1994) (quoting Berkemer v. McCarty, 468 U.S. at 440).

119. Thompson v. Keohane, 516 U.S. 99, 112 (1995).

More recently, in *Howes v. Fields*,[120] the Court summarized "custody" analysis this way:

> [T]he initial step is to ascertain whether, in light of "the objective circumstances of the interrogation," a "reasonable person [would] have felt he or she was not at liberty to terminate the interrogation and leave." And, in order to determine how a suspect would have "gauge[d] his 'freedom of movement,'" courts must examine "all of the circumstances surrounding the interrogation." Relevant factors include the location of the questioning, its duration, statements made during the interview, the presence or absence of physical restraints during the questioning, and the release of the interviewee at the end of the questioning.
>
> Determining whether an individual's freedom of movement was curtailed, however, is simply the first step in the analysis, not the last. Not all restraints on freedom of movement amount to custody for purposes of *Miranda*. We have "decline[d] to accord talismanic power" to the freedom-of-movement inquiry, and have instead asked the additional question whether the relevant environment presents the same inherently coercive pressures as the type of station house questioning at issue in *Miranda*.

[B] Commonly Asked "Custody" Questions

[1] Does "Focus" Equal "Custody"?

The *Miranda* opinion suggested that "custody" and "focus" (as the latter term was used in *Escobedo v. Illinois*[121]) were synonyms.[122] In fact, however, as the Court has since conceded, "focus" can exist in the absence of "custody," in which case *Miranda* warnings are not required.

A good example of this is *Beckwith v. United States*:[123] IRS agents questioned *B* at his home. At the time of his questioning, *B* was the focus of a criminal tax investigation. Nonetheless, because *B* was not in custody during the interrogation—a reasonable person in *B*'s situation would have believed that he was free to leave or to ask the agents to go—*Miranda* warnings were not required.

[2] Does *Miranda* Apply Outside the Police Station?

Miranda warnings are required prior to custodial interrogation, even if the interrogation occurs outside the police station. According to the Court, the question is whether "the relevant environment presents the same inherently coercive pressures as the type of station house questioning at issue in *Miranda*."[124]

A person theoretically may be in custody in his own home. In *Orozco v. Texas*,[125] for example, the Court held that *O* was in custody when four police officers entered his bedroom and questioned him there at 4:00 a.m. One of the officers testified that *O* was

---

120. 132 S. Ct. 1181, 1189–90 (2012) (citations omitted).
121. 378 U.S. 478 (1964). *See* § 24.03, *supra*.
122. *See* the text accompanying Note 34, *supra*.
123. 425 U.S. 341 (1976).
124. Howes v. Field, 132 S. Ct. at 1190.
125. 394 U.S. 324 (1969).

under arrest at the time of the questioning, although *O* had not been informed of this fact. Presumably, however, in light of the timing of the interrogation, the pointed nature of the questions, and the fact that four armed officers were present, a reasonable person in *O*'s situation would have understood that he was in custody. Therefore, *Miranda* warnings were required.

On the other hand, as *California v. Beheler* teaches,[126] a person is not necessarily in custody in an interrogation room. In *Beheler*, *B* voluntarily agreed to accompany police to the station house, in order to be questioned about a homicide that he had reported to them. At the police station, he answered questions that the police did not preface with *Miranda* warnings. The questioning took 30 minutes, after which he was permitted to leave. Five days later, *B* was arrested in connection with the homicide. The Court held that the *Miranda*-less statements *B* made were admissible: Although the interrogation occurred in a police station, *B* was not in custody.

A person may also be in custody in prison, of course, but it does not follow that an inmate is *always* "in custody" in the *Miranda* sense of that term in a prison environment. In *Howes v. Fields*,[127] the Supreme Court's most thorough discussion of *Miranda* "custody" law in the context of a prison, the Court reiterated that there is no categorical rule for determining "custody," even in prison. Therefore, if a prison inmate, as in *Fields*, is taken from his cell and moved to a different portion of the facility for questioning (in this case, questioning for between five and seven hours), in private, "about events in the outside world" (here, alleged sexual abuse of a boy many years earlier), this is "not necessarily enough to create a custodial situation for *Miranda* purposes." On the facts of this case, the Court determined, by a 6–3 vote, that the inmate was not in *Miranda* "custody."

Certain factors favored a finding of custody: the interrogators were armed; one of the questioners "[u]sed a very sharp tone"; and the interrogation was long and conducted late at night. These factors, however supposedly were offset by others, including: the inmate was not restrained or threatened; the room was well-lit, an "average-sized conference room" and "not uncomfortable"; he was offered food and water; the conference door was sometimes open; and "most important," he was told at the start of the interrogation and reminded again later, that he could leave and return to his cell whenever he wanted.

[3] Does *Miranda* Apply to Minor Offenses?

In *Berkemer v. McCarty*,[128] *M* was arrested for driving his car under the influence of alcohol, a misdemeanor offense. He was transported to the jail, where he was questioned without *Miranda* warnings. The government argued that *Miranda* warnings should not be required prior to questioning for minor traffic offenses. With such offenses, it argued, "the police have no reason to subject . . . a suspect to the sort of interrogation that most troubled the Court in *Miranda*." Also, enforcement of minor traffic offenses "would be more expeditious and effective" without the warnings.

The Court refused to carve out the suggested exception. The Court reaffirmed that *Miranda* warnings are required prior to custodial interrogation for *any* criminal offense. According to Justice Thurgood Marshall, "[o]ne of the principal advantages of the

---

126. 463 U.S. 1121 (1983).
127. 132 S. Ct. 1181 (2012).
128. 468 U.S. 420 (1984).

[*Miranda*] doctrine . . . is the clarity of that rule," which would be undermined by the proposed exception. Justice Marshall pointed out that the police are often unaware whether the person arrested has committed a felony or a misdemeanor; therefore, if a felony/misdemeanor exception were recognized, an arresting officer would not always know whether *Miranda* warnings were required. There is also the possibility that questioning about one offense, a misdemeanor, might move imperceptibly into questioning about another, more serious, crime. The Court also discounted the assumption that police abuses never occur during interrogations for offenses denominated by the state as minor.

[4] Does *Miranda* Apply to a "*Terry* Stop"?

Miranda warnings, as originally explained, are required if a person is deprived of his freedom of action "in any significant way." The key word is "significant." One might have thought that whenever a person is "seized" in a Fourth Amendment sense, he is in "custody" for purposes of *Miranda*. However, that is not the case: A person is *not* in custody for purposes of *Miranda* if he has only been seized in a *Terry v. Ohio*[129] sense of that term.

Thus, in *Berkemer v. McCarty*,[130] the Supreme Court held that a motorist, subjected to roadside questioning during a routine traffic stop, was not in custody. As the Court saw it, traffic stops are brief, occur in public, and usually involve only one or two officers. Consequently, the motorist does not feel "completely at the mercy of the police." "Custody" does not take place in the absence of objective, coercive conditions at the scene that would cause a reasonable person to believe that he is more than temporarily detained, but rather is in a situation that may "fairly be characterized as the functional equivalent of formal arrest."

[5] Are *Miranda* Warnings Required in All "Coercive Environments"?

As the preceding analysis of "custody" law might suggest, there is no inevitable correlation between "custody" and a "coercive environment." In a significant sense, therefore, the law of "custody" has been cut off from the conceptual underpinnings of *Miranda*.

For example, in *Oregon v. Mathiason*,[131] M was a parolee suspected of a burglary. At the request of the police, M agreed to come to the police station, where he was questioned in the absence of *Miranda* warnings, in an office with the door closed. A reviewing court found that the questioning took place in a coercive environment. Moreover, the police used a technique noted and criticized in *Miranda*—they falsely told M that they had evidence implicating him in the crime.

The Supreme Court held that, on these facts, *Miranda* warnings were *not* required because M was not in custody during the interview: prior to questioning he was told he was not under arrest; and he left the station after the questioning. According to *Mathiason*, "[s]uch a non-custodial situation is not converted to one in which *Miranda* applies simply because a reviewing court concludes that . . . the questioning took place in a 'coercive environment.'" In dissent, Justice Marshall complained that "surely formalities

---

129. 392 U.S. 1 (1968); *see* § 17.02, *supra*.
130. 468 U.S. 420 (1984).
131. 429 U.S. 492 (1977).

alone cannot control." Justice Stevens, also in dissent, called the majority's reasoning "formalistic." In this case, however, form trumped substance.

The converse is also the case. Suppose that the police formally arrest *D* in his home for a very minor offense. Without giving *Miranda* warnings, the police ask a single question, "Did you do it?" Because *D* is in custody, his incriminating answer is inadmissible under *Miranda*. Yet the environment in which the one question was asked—in *D*'s home, perhaps in the presence of family members; a minor offense; and no threats or tricks— is far less coercive than the conditions that confronted the suspect in *Mathiason*.

§ 24.08 Meaning of *Miranda*: "Interrogation"[132]

[A] In General

[1] Rule

In *Rhode Island v. Innis*,[133] *I* was arrested for a murder in which the weapon used in the crime had not yet been discovered. *I* was placed in a police car with three officers. En route to the police station, one of the officers remarked to a colleague that a school for handicapped children was in the vicinity, and that "God forbid one of [the children] might find a weapon with shells and they might hurt themselves." After the officer added that "it would be too bad if a little girl would pick up the gun, maybe kill herself," *I* interrupted and offered to show the police where he had abandoned the weapon.

These events occurred after *Miranda* warnings had been given. However, *I* had previously asked to see a lawyer, and in such circumstances the police are required to cease interrogation until the suspect talks to his attorney.[134] The precise issue in the case, therefore, was whether the handicapped-children statement by the officer constituted "interrogation," so as to violate the "cease interrogation" rule.

According to *Innis*, for purposes of *Miranda*, "interrogation" refers not only to "express questioning," but also to its "functional equivalent." The "functional equivalent" of express questioning is "any words or actions on the part of the police (other than those normally attendant to arrest and custody) that the police should know are reasonably likely to elicit an incriminating response from the suspect."

[2] A Closer Look at the Rule

According to *Innis*, the "functional equivalent" form of interrogation "focuses primarily upon the perceptions of the suspect, rather than the intent of the police." In other words, the officer's subjective intent to elicit an incriminating response by his words or actions is not the key. Instead, the *Innis* test is primarily objective: *Should* the officer have realized that his actions or words were *reasonably likely* to result in an incriminating

---

132. *See generally* Jesse C. Stewart, *The Untold Story of Rhode Island v. Innis: Justice Potter Stewart and the Development of Modern Self-Incrimination Doctrine*, 97 Va. L. Rev. 431 (2011); Welsh S. White, *Interrogation Without Questions: Rhode Island v. Innis and United States v. Henry*, 78 Mich. L. Rev. 1209 (1980); Yeager, Note 110, *supra*.

133. 446 U.S. 291 (1980).

134. *See* § 24.10[B][3][a], *infra*.

response from the suspect? In criminal *mens rea* terms, an "interrogation" occurs if an officer was negligent in failing to foresee that his words or actions were likely to result in an incriminating response from the suspect.

Although the mental state of the police officer is not the focus of the *Innis* test, it may be relevant in determining whether an interrogation has occurred. The Court warned that "any knowledge the police may have had concerning the susceptibility of a defendant to a particular form of persuasion might be an important factor in determining whether the police should have known that their words or actions were reasonably likely to elicit an incriminating response."

Brewer v. Williams,[135] a Sixth Amendment case,[136] provides an example of what the Court probably had in mind in *Innis*. In *Williams*, the police subjected W, a person whom they knew to be a highly religious man and a recent escapee from a mental hospital, to a "Christian burial speech." The speech was designed to convince W to tell the officers where the body of a young rape-homicide victim had been hidden, so that her parents could give her a "Christian burial." Although W did not respond immediately, he eventually made incriminating remarks and led them to the body.

The Court in *Williams* did not evaluate the police conduct in light of *Miranda*. However, under the definition of "interrogation" developed in *Innis*, and in light of the officers' knowledge of W's mental instability and his susceptibility to religious pleas, it seems very likely that a court would have concluded that a reasonable police officer would or should have realized that the Christian burial speech was likely to elicit an incriminating response — that is, that the speech was a functional equivalent of interrogation.

In *Innis*, however, the majority concluded that the handicapped-children statement did *not* amount to the functional equivalent of "interrogation." The Court noted that the police conversation here was brief (it was not "a lengthy harangue in the presence of the suspect"); the comments were not especially "evocative"; and there was no evidence that the officers knew that I was "peculiarly susceptible to an appeal to conscience"[137] or that he was disoriented or upset when the remarks were made.[138]

[B] When Is an Interrogation Not a *Miranda* "Interrogation"?

The "interrogation" standard examined above is subject to two limitations. First, *Miranda* warnings are not required, *even in response to direct questioning or its functional*

---

135. 430 U.S. 387 (1977).

136. *Innis* states that the definition of "interrogation" for *Miranda* purposes is *not* informed by the Court's Sixth Amendment right-to-counsel jurisprudence. Under the latter provision, the government may not "deliberately elicit" an incriminating response from a person formally charged with a crime in the absence of the accused's lawyer. Thus, the latter test is explicitly subjective. *See* § 25.05, *infra*.

137. This conclusion is dubious. As Justice Marshall pointed out in dissent, an appeal to a suspect's conscience is a classic interrogation technique recommended in the police manuals criticized in *Miranda*. An officer's call-to-conscience will often succeed where a direct, accusatorial question may not.

138. The state of mind of a police officer may be relevant in "interrogation" analysis for a second reason, notwithstanding the objective nature of the *Innis* test. In a footnote, the Court stated (without further explaining) that the officer's intent "may well have a bearing on whether the police should have known that their words or actions were reasonably likely to evoke an incriminating response."

equivalent, if the person interrogated does not know that the questioner is a law enforcement officer. In short, custodial interrogation by an undercover officer is not the type of "interrogation" that triggers a requirement of *Miranda* warnings.[139]

Second, *Miranda* warnings are intended to protect a custodial suspect's Fifth Amendment privilege against compulsory self-incrimination. However, the Fifth Amendment does *not* protect a person from being compelled to produce "real or physical evidence," as distinguished from evidence of a "testimonial or communicative" nature.[140] Thus, the Fifth Amendment is *not* violated if a person is ordered, for example, to produce a blood sample or voice exemplar, even though the results may incriminate him.

It follows from this that *Miranda*—a case intended to protect a person's Fifth Amendment rights—only applies if the police interrogation implicates the "testimonial or communicative" component of the Fifth Amendment. For example, suppose that *O* arrests *D* for drunk driving. Without providing *Miranda* warnings, *O* conducts a sobriety test in which *D*'s responses to direct questions (e.g., "what is your name?"; "how old are you?"; "who is the President of the United States?") are videotaped. *D*'s answers to these direct questions—interrogation—are not rendered inadmissible by *Miranda* merely because the slurred nature of his answers, if shown to the jury in the videotape, will incriminate him. As the Court has explained, "[r]equiring a suspect to reveal the physical manner in which he articulates words, like requiring him to reveal the physical properties of the sound produced by his voice . . . does not, without more, compel him to provide a 'testimonial' response for purposes of the privilege."[141]

In contrast, the Fifth Amendment (and, therefore, *Miranda*) *is* implicated if the *content* of *D*'s answers—e.g., if *D* answers the questions incorrectly—suggests that his mental state is confused. In such circumstances, the inference of *D*'s intoxication is drawn from a testimonial act (his answers) and not from physical evidence (slurred speech).[142]

§ 24.09 Adequacy of *Miranda* Warnings

The Supreme Court announced in *California v. Prysock*[143] that no "talismanic incantation" of the *Miranda* warnings is required, as long as the officer's explanation of the suspect's constitutional rights is a "fully effective equivalent" of the *Miranda* warnings. Thus, although a benefit of *Miranda* is its supposed bright-line nature, and the *Miranda* warnings themselves are easily stated, the Court has approved a case-by-case factual inquiry when officers "ad lib" or a police department develops a different version of the warnings.

Although this rule is not in direct conflict with *Miranda*, the Court's application of it in *Duckworth v. Eagan*[144] arguably "dealt *Miranda* a heavy blow."[145] In *Duckworth*, the police read *D* a set of warnings that included the following remarks:

---

139. Illinois v. Perkins, 496 U.S. 292 (1990). *See* § 24.11[B], *infra*, for further explanation.

140. Schmerber v. California, 384 U.S. 757 (1966). This important distinction is explained in detail, and may best be reviewed at this time, at § 23.04[D], *supra*.

141. Pennsylvania v. Muniz, 496 U.S. 582, 592 (1990).

142. *Id.* at 593.

143. 453 U.S. 355 (1981).

144. 492 U.S. 195 (1989).

145. Yale Kamisar, *Duckworth v. Eagan: A Little-Noticed Miranda Case That May Cause Much Mischief*, 25 Crim. L. Bull. 550, 552 (1989).

Anything you say can be used against you in court. You have a right to talk to a lawyer for advice before we ask you any questions, and to have him with you during questioning. You have this right to the advice and presence of a lawyer even if you cannot afford to hire one. *We have no way of giving you a lawyer, but one will be appointed for you, if you wish, if and when you go to court. . . .*

In view of the second italicized remark, a federal court concluded that the warnings were defective because *D*, an indigent, could reasonably have interpreted the words to mean that a lawyer would not be available to him until formal charges were brought, even if the questioning proceeded immediately.

The Supreme Court declared the warnings adequate.[146] According to Chief Justice Rehnquist, "[t]he inquiry is simply whether the warnings reasonably 'conve[y] to [a suspect] his rights as required by *Miranda*.'"[147] He stated that, in view of the first italicized sentence above, the warnings made sufficiently clear that questioning would not occur until *D* had a lawyer or waived the right. The warnings "touched all of the bases required by *Miranda*," and the officer's additional comment was accurate in terms of state law and under *Miranda*.[148] Professor Yale Kamisar has observed, however, that "if [*D*] were a smart, sophisticated fellow, he might have dissected the . . . police warning the way [the Court] did. . . . But the *Miranda* warnings weren't designed for smart, sophisticated people."[149]

§ 24.10 Waiver of *Miranda* Rights

[A] In General

[1] Overview

Most suspects in custody waive their constitutional rights after receiving *Miranda* warnings.[150] And, as the Supreme Court has acknowledged, "giving the warnings and getting a waiver has generally produced a virtual ticket of admissibility"[151]: that is, if

---

146. *Duckworth* demonstrates that divergence from the *Miranda* warnings will not always render the warnings inadequate. However, on the other side of the coin, it is important to note that the Supreme Court—or, at least a plurality of the Court—has stated that even faithful quotation of the *Miranda* warnings will not be adequate in certain circumstances: "[I]t would be absurd to think that mere recitation of the litany suffices to satisfy *Miranda* in every conceivable circumstance." Missouri v. Seibert, 542 U.S. 600, 611 (2004) (plurality opinion of Souter). *Seibert*—a case in which the plurality determined that *Miranda* warnings, without further elaboration, could actually mislead, rather than edify, the suspect—is explained in detail in § 24.12[B][4], *infra*.

147. *Duckworth*, 492 U.S. at 203 (alteration in original) (quoting California v. Prysock, 453 U.S. 355, 361 (1981)); see also Florida v. Powell, 559 U.S. 50 (2010) (holding, 7–2, that as long as the police "clearly inform" suspects of their legal rights, divergence from the specific *Miranda* warnings is not violative of *Miranda v. Arizona*).

148. That is, *Miranda* does not require the presence of a "stationhouse lawyer." Waiver issues aside, *Miranda* only requires that the police not interrogate a suspect until counsel can be obtained.

149. Kamisar, Note 145, *supra*, at 554.

150. *See* Notes 94–98 and accompanying text, *supra*; for discussion of the techniques used by police to secure waivers, *see* Richard A. Leo & Welsh S. White, *Adapting to Miranda: Modern Interrogators' Strategies for Dealing with the Obstacles Posed by Miranda*, 84 Minn. L. Rev. 397, 431–450 (1999).

151. Missouri v. Seibert, 542 U.S. 600, 609 (2004) (plurality opinion).

Miranda warnings are given and the suspect validly waives his *Miranda* rights, a defendant's claim that his incriminating statements were obtained involuntarily in violation of the Due Process Clause or the Self-Incrimination Clause will almost never be successful.[152] Therefore, *Miranda* waiver jurisprudence is of great practical significance. And, as discussion in this chapter section should demonstrate, the post-*Miranda* Court has made it easier for a prosecutor to prove the existence of a valid *Miranda* waiver than, perhaps, the *Miranda* Court itself had in mind.

The general principles relating to waiver are considered in this subsection. Special issues arise if, before or during interrogation, a custodial suspect asserts his Fifth Amendment privilege against self-incrimination, or if he requests assistance of counsel. The law in *this* regard in considered in subsection [B].

[2] Types of Waiver: Express versus Implied

The *Miranda* opinion stated that a prosecutor must overcome a "heavy burden" to demonstrate a valid waiver of a custodial suspect's *Miranda* rights. Because of this "heavy burden," "a valid waiver will not be presumed simply from the silence of the accused after warnings are given or simply from the fact that a confession was in fact actually obtained." An express waiver, followed "closely" by a statement, "could" constitute a valid waiver. The implication from this seemed to be that the *Miranda* Court intended for waivers to be express, rather than implied.

Nonetheless, the Court held in *North Carolina v. Butler* that "an explicit statement of waiver is not invariably necessary to support a finding that the defendant waived the right to remain silent or the right to counsel guaranteed by the *Miranda* case."[153] According to *Butler*, although the burden of proof is on the government to prove that the suspect validly waived his *Miranda* rights, "in at least some cases waiver can be clearly inferred from the actions and words of the person interrogated" after *Miranda* warnings are given.

For example, in *Butler*, B was read his *Miranda* warnings. He acknowledged that he understood his rights, but he refused to sign a written waiver form. B verbally waived his right to silence ("I will talk to you but I am not signing any form"), but he did not say anything regarding his right to counsel. The Court held that no *per se* "express waiver" requirement should apply. Instead, the issue of whether a person has waived his right should be determined on "the particular facts and circumstances surrounding that case, including the background, experience, and conduct of the accused."[154]

Indeed, in *Berghuis v. Thompkins*,[155] discussed in detail in subsection [5] below, the Court expanded on the circumstances in which an implied waiver can be found, and did so to a degree one would never have anticipated from *Miranda*'s language about "heavy burdens" and waivers *not* being presumed. The Court virtually turned waiver law on its head: it now says that "[w]here the prosecution shows that a *Miranda* warning was given and that it was understood by the accused, an accused's uncoerced statement establishes an implied waiver of the right to remain silent."[156]

---

152. *See* Note 98, *supra*.
153. 441 U.S. 369, 375–76 (1979).
154. *Id.* at 374–75 (quoting Johnson v. Zerbst, 304 U.S. 458, 464 (1938)).
155. 560 U.S. 370 (2010).
156. *Id.* at 384.

[3] Elements of a Valid Waiver

[a] Generally

Miranda provides that a "defendant may waive effectuation of [his] rights, provided that the waiver is made voluntarily, knowingly and intelligently." By this statement, the Court effectively adopted the waiver standard first announced in *Johnson v. Zerbst*,[157] which declared that a constitutional right may not be waived unless there is "an intentional relinquishment or abandonment of a known right or privilege."

In *Miranda*, the Court stated that a suspect's waiver is not valid unless the prosecutor overcomes an unspecified "heavy burden" of proof that the waiver was voluntary, knowing, and intelligent. In *Colorado v. Connelly*,[158] the Court held that this "heavy burden" is met if the prosecutor proves, from the totality of the circumstances, the validity of the waiver by a preponderance of the evidence.

[b] Voluntariness of the Waiver

A waiver must be voluntary, i.e., "the product of a free and deliberate choice rather than intimidation, coercion, or deception."[159] In determining voluntariness, the Court has stated that "[t]here is obviously no reason to require more in the way of a 'voluntariness' inquiry in the *Miranda* waiver context than in the Fourteenth Amendment confession context."[160]

As with rights located in the Due Process Clause, a waiver of *Miranda* rights is not involuntary if the "moral and psychological pressures to confess emanat[e] from sources other than official coercion."[161] For example, a suspect's waiver of his *Miranda* rights is valid if he was "coerced" to do so by his belief that God commanded him either to confess or commit suicide.[162] Furthermore, the Court has held that the internal psychological pressures that arise from having a "guilty secret" do not invalidate a subsequent decision to confess.[163] In summary, due process "voluntariness" jurisprudence[164] applies to the voluntariness prong of *Miranda* waiver law, and may be incorporated by reference here.

This result presents an historical irony. *Miranda* was intended as a bright-line alternative to the much-criticized, totality-of-the-circumstances "voluntariness" standard that preceded it. Yet, through the vehicle of *Miranda* waiver law, "voluntariness" jurisprudence has returned.

---

157. 304 U.S. 458 (1938); *see* Edwards v. Arizona, 451 U.S. 477, 482 (1981) (acknowledging that *Zerbst* is the applicable test).
158. 479 U.S. 157 (1986).
159. Moran v. Burbine, 475 U.S. 412, 421 (1986).
160. Colorado v. Connelly, 479 U.S. 157, 169–70 (1986).
161. Oregon v. Elstad, 470 U.S. 298, 305 (1985).
162. Colorado v. Connelly, 479 U.S. 157 (1986).
163. Oregon v. Elstad, 470 U.S. 298 (1985).
164. *See* § 22.02, *supra*.

[c] Knowing and Intelligent Waiver[165]

To be valid, a "waiver must have been made with a full awareness of both the nature of the right being abandoned and the consequences of the decision to abandon it."[166]

The Court has not always enforced this rule strictly. Consider *Oregon v. Elstad*:[167] E confessed to a crime during brief police questioning in E's home. Due to an oversight, *Miranda* warnings had not been given, so E's statements in his home were inadmissible at trial. Later, at the police station, the police read E the *Miranda* warnings, after which E waived his rights and provided more incriminating statements. E argued that his post-*Miranda* statements should be excluded, in part[168] on the ground that he wrongly believed that "the cat was out of the bag." That is, E did not realize when he made the second statement that his earlier incriminating statements were inadmissible; therefore, he wrongly believed that he had nothing to lose in confessing a second time, and thus (according to E) his waiver was not knowingly and intelligently made.

The Court disagreed. It stated that "a suspect who has once responded to unwarned yet uncoercive questioning is not thereby disabled from waiving his rights and confessing after he has been given the requisite *Miranda* warnings." But, what about E's claim that he didn't know that the cat was *not* out of the bag? Shouldn't the police have supplemented the *Miranda* warnings with a statement that his earlier admissions were inadmissible? No, according to the *Elstad* Court: A requirement of an additional, clarificatory warning in such circumstances was "neither practicable nor constitutionally necessary." The Court explained that it "has never embraced the theory that a defendant's ignorance of the full consequences of his decisions vitiates their voluntariness."[169] It is *not* the case that "the *sine qua non* for a knowing and voluntary waiver of the right to remain silent is a full and complete appreciation of all of the consequences flowing from the nature and quality of the evidence in the case."[170]

---

165. *See generally* Morgan Cloud et al., *Words Without Meaning: The Constitution, Confessions, and Mentally Retarded Suspects*, 69 U. Chi. L. Rev. 495 (2002); Robert P. Mosteller, *Police Deception Before Miranda Warnings: The Case for Per Se Prohibition of an Entirely Unjustified Practice at the Most Critical Moment*, 39 Texas Tech L. Rev. 1239 (2007).

166. Moran v. Burbine, 475 U.S. 412, 421 (1986).

167. 470 U.S. 298 (1985).

168. *See also* § 24.12[B][3], *infra*.

169. In *Colorado v. Spring*, 479 U.S. 564 (1987), the Court rejected the same "ignorance-of-the-full-consequences-of-his-decision" argument in a different *Miranda* context. S was arrested for interstate transportation of stolen firearms; S was read the *Miranda* warnings and waived his rights; based on prior information that linked him to a murder, the after-waiver interrogation quickly turned from the firearms charge to the uncharged murder. S ultimately confessed to the murder. The Court held that S's waiver was knowing and intelligent although he did not know he was going to be questioned about the murder when he gave up his rights: he knew what his rights were, including the right to cut off questioning at any time; and he knew that *any* statement he made could be used against him.

170. *See generally* Andrew Guthrie Ferguson, *The Dialogue Approach to* Miranda *Warnings and Waiver*, 49 Am. Crim. L. Rev. 1437 (2012) (arguing for an adoption of a "dialogue approach" to ensure that the waiver is knowing and voluntary by requiring suspects to restate their rights in their own words before interrogation can begin).

[4] *Moran v. Burbine*: Waiver in the Post-*Miranda* Era (Part 1)

Moran v. Burbine[171] is a case that deserves special attention. It is important not only for what it says about *Miranda* waiver law, but also for what it demonstrates about the distance the Court has traveled since the days of *Escobedo v. Illinois*[172] and *Miranda*.

In *Burbine*, B was arrested for a murder. As a result of B's sister's efforts, an attorney called the police station in the evening and informed a detective that she would act as B's counsel in the event that the police intended to interrogate him. The officer assured the lawyer that B would not be interrogated that night, In fact, however, less than an hour later, the police conducted the first of a series of interviews with B regarding the homicide. Prior to each session, B was informed of his *Miranda* rights, and he signed written forms waiving his right to counsel. At no time, however, was B informed that his sister had retained counsel for him, nor was he aware of his counsel's telephone conversation with the police.

In an opinion written by Justice Sandra Day O'Connor, the Court held, 6–3, that the police followed acceptable *Miranda* procedures, and that the record supported the state court finding that B's waiver of his *Miranda* rights, his right to counsel in particular, was voluntary, knowing, and intelligent.

The Court granted that the police conduct was "objectionable as a matter of ethics." It "share[d] [B's] distaste for the deliberate misleading of an officer of the court." However, "even deliberate deception of an attorney could not possibly affect a suspect's decision to waive his *Miranda* rights." That is, unlike *Escobedo*, in which the police falsely told the *suspect* that his attorney did not want to see him, the deception here was directed at the *attorney*. Therefore, the police misconduct, unknown to B, could not have affected the voluntariness of his waiver.

The Court concluded, as well, that the undisclosed information did not deprive B of the "knowledge essential to his ability to understand the nature of his rights and the consequences of abandoning them." Once the prosecutor shows that a suspect was fully informed of his *Miranda* rights and that he was not coerced to waive them, "the analysis is complete and the waiver is valid as a matter of law."

In essence, *Burbine* teaches that, although a suspect must be informed of his right to assistance of counsel, he is not constitutionally entitled to know that his counsel wishes to see him. As Justice O'Connor wrote, the information withheld by the police "would have been useful to [B]; perhaps even it might have affected his decision to confess." "But," she wrote, "we have never read the Constitution to require that the police supply

---

171. 475 U.S. 412 (1986); *contra, under the state constitution*, Bryan v. State, 571 A.2d 170 (Del. 1990) (waiver is invalid if police intentionally or negligently fail to inform a suspect during custodial interrogation that his lawyer wants to confer); People v. McCauley, 645 N.E.2d 923 (Ill. 1994) (due process is violated if police interfere with an attorney-client relationship by preventing a custodial suspect, under interrogation, from receiving the immediately available assistance of his own attorney); Commonwealth v. Mavredakis, 725 N.E.2d 169 (Mass. 2000) (information regarding the immediate availability of an identified attorney who is actually able to provide assistance has a bearing on the suspect's ability to knowingly and intelligently waive his constitutional rights); People v. Bender, 551 N.W.2d 71 (Mich. 1996) (plurality opinion) (suspect has a right to know that his lawyer wishes to see him, whether the request comes in person, over telephone, or by way of messenger); State v. Reed, 627 A.2d 630 (N.J. 1993) (waiver is invalid if the police refuse to inform the suspect before or during interrogation that an attorney wishes to confer with him).

172. 378 U.S. 478 (1964). *See* § 24.03, *supra*.

a suspect with a flow of information to help him calibrate his self-interest in deciding whether to speak or stand by his rights." The Court lacked "the authority to mandate a code of behavior for state officials wholly unconnected to any federal right or privilege."

The justices who decided *Escobedo* and *Miranda* would probably have disallowed the confession in *Burbine*. The Warren Court distrusted confessions, was critical of police deception, and was inclined to set up an even "playing field" in the interrogation room. To the *Escobedo-Miranda* Court, defense lawyers play a critical and positive role in the adversary system by neutralizing some of the coercive influences in the interrogation process and by assisting the suspect in deciding whether to invoke his constitutional rights.

The Supreme Court that decided *Burbine* was a Court of a different philosophical cast. Whereas the Warren Court viewed suspects as underdogs in need of assistance, the *Burbine* justices and most members of the current Court are critical of the "fox hunt" theory of justice,[173] and are disinclined to apply *Miranda* more broadly than necessary. Consequently, the officers' efforts to keep defense counsel away from her client was permitted on the ground that any rule to the contrary would be "wholly unconnected to any federal right or privilege."

[5] *Berghuis v. Thompkins:* Waiver in the Post-*Miranda* Era (Part 2)

In *Berghuis v. Thompkins,*[174] the Supreme Court's journey of easing the process of finding *Miranda* waivers reached its apogee. In *Thompkins, T* was interrogated by two police detectives for approximately three hours while seated in a hard chair in a room measuring about eight feet by 10 feet. At the start of the interrogation, Detective *H* gave *T* a form that included a version of the *Miranda* warnings and noted that "[y]ou have the right to decide at any time before or during questioning to use your right to remain silent. . . ." At *H*'s request, *T* read the final warning out loud. *H* then read the rest of the form to *T* and asked *T* to sign the form "to demonstrate that he understood his rights." *T* refused. The interrogation then proceeded. *T* did not say he wanted to remain silent, or that he did not want to talk to the police, or that he wanted a lawyer. In fact, he barely said anything, remaining largely silent during the three hours of questioning, except for "a few limited verbal responses, . . . such as 'yeah,' 'no,' or 'I don't know.' After about two hours and 45 minutes, *H* asked *T* if he believed in God; *T* said yes (as his eyes 'welled up with tears).'" *H* asked if *T* prayed to God; *T* said yes. *H* asked whether *T* prayed to God "to forgive you for shooting that boy down?" *T* "answered 'Yes' and looked away." This exchange was introduced at *T*'s trial for first-degree murder, and *T* was convicted and sentenced to life without parole.

In a 5–4 decision written by Justice Kennedy, the Court concluded that *T*'s statements were properly admitted on an implied waiver theory. While noting the language in the *Miranda* opinion indicating "that waivers are difficult to establish absent an explicit written waiver or a formal, express oral statement," the Court stated that the "course of decisions since *Miranda*" and the use of the warnings "in the whole course

---

173. *See* § 24.05[B][3], *supra.*

174. 560 U.S. 370 (2010); *contra under the state constitution,* Commonwealth v. Clarke, 960 N.E.2d 306 (Mass. 2011) (criticizing *Thompkins* for "turning *Miranda* upside down," holding that the state constitution does not require a suspect to employ "the utmost clarity" when invoking his right to silence).

of law enforcement, demonstrate[] that waivers can be established" without the "formal or express statements of waiver that would be expected" in other contexts.

So what does it take to establish waiver? Not much. "The main purpose of *Miranda*" the Court explained, "is to ensure that an accused is advised of and understands the right to remain silent and the right to counsel." So the prosecution must show that the accused was given the *Miranda* warnings and that they were understood. Here, the provision of the written warnings and the demonstration, by reading aloud, that *T* could read and understand English "was more than enough evidence . . . to conclude that [*T*] understood his *Miranda* rights." Therefore, the "knowing" requirement for waiver was met. Since the warning said he could assert his rights "at any time," the fact that hours of questioning passed between the warnings and the statement was, the Court concluded, beside the point. As for the voluntariness requirement, "there [was] no evidence that [*T*'s] statement was coerced," so this requirement was met as well. Three hours of interrogation seated in a straight-backed chair was not "inherently coercive," and *T* was not "threatened or injured." Finally, *T*'s answer "yes" that he prayed to God for forgiveness was "a 'course of conduct indicating' waiver" of the right to remain silent.

The Court concluded with a neat summary of its current rule for waiver in this context: "A suspect who has received and understood the *Miranda* warnings, and has not invoked his *Miranda* rights, waives the right to remain silent by making an uncoerced statement to the police." Thus, without repudiating the statement in *Miranda* that "a valid waiver will not be presumed simply . . . from the fact that a confession was in fact eventually obtained," the Court has made clear that in most circumstances the confession will, in fact, constitute a waiver.

[B] Waiver Law: If a Suspect Invokes His Rights

[1] Overview

Subsection [A] described what the government must show in order to convince a court that a suspect validly waived his constitutional rights after receiving *Miranda* warnings.

The present subsection considers a related question: What procedures must the police follow if a defendant invokes his Fifth Amendment right to remain silent and/or if he requests assistance of counsel? Under what circumstances may the police obtain a valid waiver after the custodial suspect invokes one or both of these rights? As will be seen, the rules differ depending on which right is asserted. The police must follow stricter rules when a suspect asks to consult with a lawyer.

Before turning to the invocation issue, it is important to recognize the distinction between the question of whether a defendant has *waived* his rights (discussed in subsection [A]) and the question whether a defendant has *invoked* his rights (discussed below). The Court recently stated that "if a suspect receives adequate *Miranda* warnings, understands them, and has an opportunity to invoke the rights," the interrogation can continue until the suspect invokes one of the rights, even if the suspect has not yet waived the rights.[175] In other words, "after giving a *Miranda* warning, police may interrogate a suspect who has neither invoked nor waived his or her *Miranda* rights."[176] Because an

---

175. Thompkins, 560 U.S. at 387 (2010).
176. *Id.* at 388.

eventual statement will be presumed to constitute an implicit waiver (as discussed in subsection [A]), the separate question of whether the rights were invoked prior to the statement has particular importance.

[2] Right to Remain Silent

The *Miranda* opinion states that, once warnings are given, if the suspect "indicates in any manner, at any time prior to or during questioning, that he wishes to remain silent, the interrogation must cease."

Recently, however, the Court has backed away from the "indicates in any manner" standard for invoking the right to remain silent. Following a precedent regarding invocation of the *Miranda* right to counsel,[177] the Court held in *Berghuis v. Thompkins*[178] that "an accused who wants to invoke his or her right to remain silent . . . [must] do so unambiguously." An ambiguous or equivocal assertion will not invoke the custodial suspect's right to silence nor, critically, will simply remaining silent invoke the right.[179] If the right is invoked, however, for example by stating "I don't want to talk to you," then *Miranda*'s requirement that interrogation must cease comes into play.

That cessation, however, is not permanent. In *Michigan v. Mosley*,[180] the Court held that the "interrogation must cease" language from *Miranda* does not mean that the police may never resume interrogation after a suspect asserts his right to silence, but neither does it mean that they need only cease questioning momentarily. Instead, the Court ruled, the suspect's right to cut off questioning is satisfied if the police "scrupulously honor" his right to silence after he asserts the privilege.

In *Mosley*, M was arrested and read his *Miranda* rights. M invoked his Fifth Amendment privilege. The police ceased interrogation and placed M in a jail cell. Two hours later, a different officer, who wanted to interrogate M about a different crime (one for which M was not in custody), went to the cell and re-read the *Miranda* warnings. M signed a waiver form and answered questions. The Court held that on these facts—the police ceased interrogation immediately upon request; two hours had elapsed; a different officer conducted the subsequent questioning, in a different location, for a different crime; and *Miranda* warnings were restated before the new questioning occurred—the police "scrupulously honored" the suspect's Fifth Amendment rights.

[3] Right to Counsel

[a] The Edwards v. Arizona Rule

In *Edwards v. Arizona*,[181] the police read E his *Miranda* warnings. Although E originally agreed to talk, he later told the police, "I want an attorney before making a deal." Interrogation ceased, and E was taken to a jail cell. The next morning, two officers came

---

177. This precedent, *Davis v. United States*, 512 U.S. 452 (1994), is discussed at (24.10[B][3][b][i], *infra*.

178. 560 U.S. 370, 381 (2010).

179. Note that some states will give legal weight to ambiguous invocations of the right to remain silent. *See, e.g.,* State v. Aguirre, 301 Kan. 950 (2015) (defendant's statement: "This is—I guess where I, I'm going to take my rights" was sufficient to invoke *Miranda*.)

180. 423 U.S. 96 (1975).

181. 451 U.S. 477 (1981).

to the cell to resume questioning. When *E* said that he did not want to talk, the jail guard said "he had" to talk. The officers re-informed *E* of his *Miranda* rights, and *E* agreed to answer questions.

The *Edwards* Court held that when a suspect invokes his right under *Miranda* to consult with an attorney prior to interrogation, the suspect "is not subject to further interrogation by the authorities until counsel has been made available to him, unless the accused himself initiates further communication, exchanges, or conversations with the police." The purpose of the bright-line *Edwards* rule — a stricter rule than the *Mosley* rule relating to the invocation of the right to silence — is "to prevent police from badgering a defendant into waiving his previously asserted *Miranda* rights."[182] To the extent *Miranda* is a prophylactic rule,[183] and the *Edwards* rule is intended to enforce *Miranda*, it constitutes a "second layer of protection"[184] i.e., a double prophylaxis.

The *Edwards* bright-line rule, when it applies, is strict. First, it bars police-initiated interrogation, even regarding offenses unrelated to the subject of the original interrogation.[185] Second, as the Court announced in *Minnick v. Mississippi*,[186] once a suspect in custody invokes his *Miranda* right to counsel, the police must not only permit the suspect to consult with an attorney prior to questioning, but they may not re-initiate questioning *unless counsel is present*. In short, according to *Edwards-Minnick*, once a person in custody requests counsel, it is as if a protective shield surrounds him. However, this shield is removed if the *defendant* initiates "further communication, exchanges, or conversations with the police," and the police obtain a valid waiver.

What constitutes "further communication, exchanges, or conversations with the police," so as to justify police re-interrogation of a suspect after a valid waiver? Is it enough, for example, for the suspect to ask a police officer for food and water? In *Oregon v. Bradshaw*,[187] a four-justice plurality ruled that communications, exchanges or conversations are "initiated" for purposes of the *Edwards* rule by any comment or inquiry that can "be fairly said to represent a desire . . . to open up a . . . generalized discussion relating directly or indirectly to the investigation." In contrast, comments or inquiries "relating to routine incidents of the custodial relationship," such as a request for water or to use a telephone, fall outside the scope of this definition.

The Court has interpreted "related to investigation" broadly. Thus, in *Bradshaw*, the plurality determined that *B* "initiated" communications when he asked the police, "Well, what is going to happen to me now?" Although this statement apparently was intended only to find out where the police were going to take him at that time, the question was indirectly related to the general investigation. Therefore, the plurality held that the police did not act improperly by resuming their interrogation after they secured a valid waiver.

---

182. Michigan v. Harvey, 494 U.S. 344, 350 (1990).

183. *See* § 24.06[B], *supra*.

184. Michigan v. Harvey, 494 U.S. at 350.

185. Arizona v. Roberson, 486 U.S. 675 (1988); *see also* McNeil v. Wisconsin, 501 U.S. 171, 177 (1991) ("The *Edwards* rule . . . is *not* offense specific: Once a suspect invokes the *Miranda* right to counsel for interrogation regarding one offense, he may not be reapproached regarding *any* offense unless counsel is present.").

186. 498 U.S. 146 (1990).

187. 462 U.S. 1039 (1983).

[b] When the Edwards Rule Does Not Apply

[i] Ambiguous Request for Counsel

The Supreme Court held in *Davis v. United States*[188] that the *Edwards* rule does not apply unless a suspect unambiguously asserts his right to counsel. In *Davis,* D initially waived his *Miranda* rights and was interrogated. Ninety minutes into the questioning, D said, "Maybe I should talk to a lawyer." The interrogators attempted to clarify D's wishes; D responded by saying, "No, I'm not asking for a lawyer. . . . I don't want a lawyer," after which the interrogation resumed.

The Supreme Court, 5–4, per Justice O'Connor, held that if a suspect ambiguously or equivocally asserts his *Miranda* right to counsel, as D did, the police may ignore the remark and continue the interrogation. They do not even have to do what the police did here, namely, seek to clarify D's wishes, although Justice O'Connor conceded that such clarification "will often be good police practice."

The inquiry here is an objective one: If the suspect's reference to a lawyer "is ambiguous or equivocal in that a reasonable officer in light of the circumstances would have understood only that the suspect *might* be invoking the right to counsel," the interrogator may ignore the reference and proceed with the questioning.

O'Connor conceded that the rule announced in *Davis* "might disadvantage some suspects who—because of fear, intimidation, lack of linguistic skills, or a variety of other reasons—will not clearly articulate their right to counsel although they actually want to have a lawyer present." Nonetheless, the justices adopted the rule in the interest of "clarity and ease of application." She did not explain why a rule requiring the police to cease interrogation altogether, or to obtain clarification of the suspect's wishes, would be less clear or difficult to apply than the announced rule.

The *Davis* rule will have a disproportionate impact on disadvantaged members of society. As Professor Yale Kamisar has written, "[s]ociolinguistic research indicates that certain discrete segments of the population, such as women and a number of minority racial and ethnic groups, are far more likely than other groups to avoid strong, assertive means of expression and to use indirect and hedged speech."[189] Moreover, even among persons who do not usually use indirect modes of expression, the *Davis* rule will greatly undercut *Edwards,* because suspects undergoing custodial interrogation are "situationally powerless" and, therefore, apt often to "adopt a hedging speech register."[190]

---

188. 512 U.S. 452 (1994); *contra, under the state constitution,* State v. Hoey, 881 P.2d 504 (Haw. 1994) (when a suspect ambiguously or equivocally requests counsel during custodial interrogation, the police must cease all questioning or seek non-substantive clarification of the suspect's request); State v. Risk, 598 N.W.2d 642 (Minn. 1999) (same).

189. Kamisar, Note 12, *supra,* at 18.

190. *Id.* Regarding the tendency of powerless persons to talk indirectly when dealing with those in power, Kamisar has also said this:

> In *Fiddler on the Roof,* you will recall, Tevye the dairyman didn't come right out and say: "Lord, make me a rich man today" or "Lord, I want to be a wealthy man right now, before the sun sets." No, he was rather tentative. He sort of beat around the bush. At the outset he asks: "So what would have been so terrible if I had a small fortune?" At the end he asks: "Would it spoil some vast, eternal plan if I were a rich man?"

Yale Kamisar, Police Interrogation and Confessions 5 (Prepared Remarks at the U.S. Law Week's Sixteenth Annual Constitutional Law Conference, Sept. 9, 1994).

[ii] Request for Counsel for Non-*Miranda* Purposes

Not all unambiguous requests for counsel trigger the *Edwards* rule. In *McNeil v. Wisconsin*,[191] the Court stated that *Edwards* only applies if a suspect in custody expresses "his wish for the particular sort of lawyerly assistance that is the subject of *Miranda*. . . . It requires, at a minimum, some statement that can reasonably be construed to be an expression of a desire for the assistance of an attorney *in dealing with custodial interrogation by the police.*"

What is the Court getting at? It is essential here to distinguish between a request for counsel *under the Sixth Amendment*, a right which only comes into play after formal adversary proceedings have commenced regarding a specific offense,[192] and a request for a lawyer under *Miranda*. As *McNeil* explained, the right to counsel *under the Sixth Amendment*

> is to "protec[t] the unaided layman at critical confrontations" with his "expert adversary," the government, *after* "the adverse positions of government and defendant have solidified" with respect to a particular alleged crime. . . . The purpose of the *Miranda-Edwards* guarantee, on the other hand—and hence the purpose of invoking it—is to protect a quite different interest: the suspect's "desire to deal with the police only through counsel". . . . To invoke the Sixth Amendment interest is, as a matter of *fact, not* to invoke the *Miranda-Edwards* interest.

In *McNeil*, M was arrested pursuant to a warrant charging him with armed robbery. M asserted his request for counsel during a bail hearing—a judicial proceeding—on the robbery charge. Thereafter, the police visited M at his jail cell, where he was re-advised of his *Miranda* rights. M signed a waiver form and answered questions regarding offenses for which he was a suspect, but for which he had not yet been formally charged.

The Court held that the *Miranda-Edwards* no-interrogation rule did not apply in these circumstances. By requesting a lawyer at the bail hearing, M was invoking his *Sixth Amendment* right to counsel regarding the robbery charge. His statement could not "reasonably be construed to be an expression of a desire for the assistance of an attorney *in dealing with custodial interrogation by the police*" on the other offenses, for which he had not yet been charged.

[iii] Release from Custody

Once a custodial suspect invokes his right to counsel, and the *Edwards* rule comes into play, is the suspect shielded from police interrogation *forever*, unless he initiates the conversation himself?

In *Maryland v. Shatzer*,[193] a police officer questioned S in a Maryland prison, where he was incarcerated on a prior conviction, about a yet-unprosecuted allegation that he had sexually abused his son. S unambiguously invoked his *Miranda* right to counsel, which was honored. S was released back into the general prison population, and the investigation was closed. Approximately three years later, however, another officer sought to question S, who was still incarcerated, about the same abuse charge. During this interrogation, S waived his *Miranda* rights.

---

191. 501 U.S. 171 (1991).
192. *See* § 25.04, *infra*.
193. 559 U.S. 98 (2010).

A literal reading of *Edwards* might suggest that because *S* invoked his right to counsel and did not, himself, subsequently initiate conversations about the abuse investigation with law enforcement agents, the protective shield surrounding *S* continued, even when the officer came back to the prison to question *S* three years after his original assertion of the right to counsel.

The Supreme Court, per Justice Scalia, ruled, however, that the *Edwards* bright-line rule does not apply after a break in *Miranda* custody lasting more than two weeks between the first and subsequent attempt at interrogation. The Court explained that the fundamental purpose of *Edwards* is to preserve the integrity of a suspect's decision to communicate with the police only through counsel, and to prevent badgering of the suspect into waiving his *Miranda* right to counsel. Once a person has been released from custody and "returned to his normal life for some time," there is little basis for concern that a suspect's change of heart—and willingness to answer questions without counsel—has been coerced. The Court concluded that two weeks out of custody was sufficient time; at that point the *Edwards* rule no longer applies. And, in this case, the Court held that, for purposes of the *Edwards* rule, *S*'s release back into the general prison population—*S*'s "normal life"—constituted a break in *Miranda* custody, even though he remained in custody in a non-*Miranda* context!

[iv] Anticipatory Request for Counsel

In *McNeil v. Wisconsin*,[194] the Supreme Court expressed doubt that the *Miranda* right to counsel can be invoked anticipatorily. The Court stated that "[m]ost rights must be asserted when the government seeks to take the actions they protect against." Therefore, without deciding the issue, the Court hinted that an assertion of the *Miranda-Edwards* right to consult with counsel might not be effective if it is "asserted initially outside the context of custodial interrogation," such as at a judicial proceeding, or in a communication sent to the police before an impending arrest.

§ 24.11 Custodial Interrogation: When *Miranda* Warnings Are Not Required

[A] Public-Safety Exception[195]

In *New York v. Quarles*,[196] the Supreme Court recognized a "public safety" exception to *Miranda*. In *Quarles*, a woman informed two officers shortly after midnight that she had been raped, that her assailant was armed, and that he had fled into a nearby all-night grocery store with a weapon. One of the officers entered the store and spotted a man, *Q*, fitting the description of the assailant.

---

194. 501 U.S. 171 (1991).

195. *See generally* Susan R. Klein, *Miranda's Exceptions in a Post-Dickerson World*, 91 J. Crim. L. & Criminology 567 (2001); George C. Thomas III, *Separated at Birth But Siblings Nonetheless: Miranda and the Due Process Notice Cases*, 99 Mich. L. Rev. 1081 (2001); Joanna Wright, *Mirandizing Terrorists? An Empirical Analysis of the Public Safety Exception*, 111 Colum. L. Rev. 1296 (2011) (reviewing all 588 state and federal cases decided before October 4, 2010 that discussed the application of the "public safety" exception to admit or exclude un-Mirandized statements).

196. 467 U.S. 649 (1984).

Q fled to the rear of the store, with the officer in pursuit. The officer, now accompanied by three other officers, took *Q* into custody and handcuffed him. When the officer discovered that *Q* had an empty shoulder holster, he asked *Q* (without issuing *Miranda* warnings) where the gun was. *Q* nodded in the direction of some empty cartons and said "the gun is over there." The officers retrieved the weapon.

The lower courts suppressed *Q*'s statement about the gun. However, the Supreme Court reversed on the ground that the custodial interrogation occurred in a situation posing a threat to the public safety and, therefore, fit within this newly recognized exception to *Miranda*. Speaking for the majority, Justice Rehnquist stated that the police "were confronted with the immediate necessity" of finding the weapon. As long as the gun's whereabouts were unknown, it posed a "danger to the public safety: An accomplice might make use of it, a customer or employee might later come upon it."

The Court has not clarified the boundaries of the public-safety exception, leaving it to lower courts instead to reach conflicting fact-sensitive outcomes,[197] except to state in *Quarles* that there must be an "objectively reasonable need to protect the police or the public from [an] immediate danger"; there must exist an "exigency requiring immediate action by the officers beyond the normal need expeditiously to solve a serious crime." Moreover, the questions asked by the police in such circumstances must be "reasonably prompted by a concern for the public safety."

In *Quarles*, the Court considered it irrelevant that there was no evidence that the interrogating officer was motivated by a concern for public safety when he asked about the gun. Justice Rehnquist stated that the exception "should not be made to depend on *post hoc* findings at a suppression hearing concerning the subjective motivation of the ... officer." Indeed, the Court admitted that in emergency circumstances most officers act for a "host of different, instinctive, and largely unverifiable motives ... [including] the desire to obtain incriminating evidence from the suspect."

The Court conceded that recognition of the public-safety exception reduces the "desirable clarity" of *Miranda*. But, "[t]he exception will not be difficult for police officers to apply because in each case it will be circumscribed by the exigency which justifies it." The Court expressed confidence that the police "can and will distinguish almost instinctively between questions necessary to secure their own safety or the safety of the public and questions designed solely to elicit testimonial evidence from a suspect." According to the majority, the newly recognized exception, "far from complicating the thought processes and the on-the-scene judgments of police officers, will simply free them to follow their legitimate instincts when confronting situations presenting a danger to the public safety."[198]

The holding in *Quarles* is dubious on its facts. Where was the exigency? The events occurred in the middle of the night in a nearly deserted market. There were no customers in the store, and the clerks were at the checkout station. At the time of the interrogation, *Q* was handcuffed and surrounded by four officers. Despite the Court's concern that the gun might get into the hands of an accomplice, the police had no reason to believe that

---

197. *See* Wright, Note 195, *supra*, for a review of the lower court case law.

198. More than once, the Court described the police questioning in such circumstances as "instinctual" or "instinctive." This might suggest the possibility that the public-safety exception should be limited to brief questioning (in the present case, the Court observed that the officer asked only one question, directly related to the gun), but lower courts have not always drawn this conclusion.

any existed. By cordoning off the area, the gun could easily have been found without questioning Q.

Whatever the merits of a public safety exception, *Quarles* is a hard to justify in light of *Miranda*. *Quarles* characterized the *Miranda* warnings as prophylactic and non-constitutional in nature. In light of this, it balanced the costs and benefits of *Miranda* warnings and concluded that the benefits to the suspect of *Miranda* warnings were out-weighed by the goal of protecting the public from the missing gun.

In contrast, the *Miranda* Court believed it was rendering a constitutional decision, and there is little in the *Miranda* opinion to suggest that the holding in that case was founded on any cost-benefit calculation. Indeed, the Court spoke in ringing terms about the "respect a government . . . must accord to the dignity and integrity of its citizens," and of the requirement that the government "shoulder the entire load" and "respect the inviolability of the human personality."

In light of the Court's announcement in *Dickerson v. United States*[199] that *Miranda* is, indeed, a constitutionally based decision, has *Quarles* been undermined? Apparently not. The *Dickerson* Court stated that *Quarles* and other cases limiting the scope of *Miranda* simply

> illustrate the principle . . . that no constitutional rule is immutable. No court laying down a general rule can possibly foresee the various circumstances in which counsel will seek to apply it, and the sort of modifications represented by these cases are as much a normal part of constitutional law as the original decision."[200]

And, post-*Dickerson*, five members of the Court reiterated, albeit in dicta, that *Quarles* remains good law.[201]

[B] Covert Custodial Interrogation

Illinois v. Perkins[202] provides that "*Miranda* warnings are not required when the suspect is unaware that he is speaking to a law enforcement officer and gives a voluntary statement."

In *Perkins*, the police obtained information that P, a jail inmate, had made statements to another prisoner that implicated P in a murder then under investigation. The police placed X, an undercover police agent, in P's cellblock, and instructed him to engage P in "casual conversation and report anything he said about the . . . murder." As part of the ruse, X directed a conversation to the subject of murder, and asked P whether he had ever killed anybody. In response, P admitted that he had, and then proceeded to provide details of the crime.

The Court held that P's statements to X, although the result of interrogation while in custody, and in the absence of *Miranda* warnings, were admissible at P's trial. It reasoned that "[c]onversations between suspects and undercover agents do not implicate the concerns underlying *Miranda*." In essence, for purposes of *Miranda* warnings, "custodial

---

199. 530 U.S. 428 (2000); *see* § 24.06[C], *supra*.

200. *Id.* at 441.

201. United States v. Patane, 542 U.S. 630 (2004) (opinion of Thomas, J., joined by Rehnquist, C.J., and Scalia, J.; and opinion of Kennedy, J., joined by O'Connor, J.).

202. 496 U.S. 292 (1990).

interrogation" involves only express questioning or its functional equivalent[203] by a *known* law enforcement agent.

As *Perkins* explains, the *Miranda* rule was founded on the premise that the interplay between police custody and police interrogation triggers the need to provide protections against coercion. Coercion, however, is determined from the suspect's perspective; therefore, the requisite coercion is lacking when a custodial suspect encounters a person whom he believes is a cellmate rather than a law enforcement officer. The Court observed that " 'when the agent carries neither badge nor gun and wears not "police blue" but the same prison gray' as the suspect, there is no '*interplay* between police interrogation and police custody.' "[204]

[C] Routine-Booking-Questions Exception

In *Pennsylvania v. Muniz*,[205] a four-justice plurality announced a " 'routine booking question' exception which exempts from *Miranda*'s coverage questions to secure the 'biographical data necessary to complete booking or pretrial services.' "

In *Muniz*, M was arrested for driving his car under the influence of alcohol. At the police station, an officer asked M questions regarding his name, address, weight, eye color, date of birth, and age, as part of a "routine practice for receiving persons suspected of driving while intoxicated." These questions and his answers were videotaped with his knowledge, but before M was informed of his *Miranda* rights. The plurality held that these questions did not need to be preceded by *Miranda* warnings: the questions were routine, requested for record-keeping purposes only, and "reasonably related to the police's administrative concerns." The plurality warned, however, that the mere fact that a question is asked during the booking process does not necessarily immunize it. It stated that "[w]ithout obtaining a waiver of the suspect's *Miranda* rights, the police may not ask questions, even during booking, that are designed to elicit incriminating admissions."[206]

§ 24.12 Scope of the *Miranda* Exclusionary Rule[207]

[A] Impeachment Exception

The Supreme Court ruled in *Harris v. New York*[208] that a prosecutor may use a statement obtained in violation of *Miranda* to impeach a defendant who testifies at trial inconsistently with the custodial statement.

---

203. *See* § 24.08[A][1], *supra*.

204. *Perkins*, 496 U.S. at 297 (quoting Yale Kamisar, *Brewer v. Williams, Massiah, and Miranda: What Is Interrogation? When Does It Matter?*, 67 Geo. L.J. 1, 67, 63 (1978)).

205. 496 U.S. 582 (1990).

206. For a discussion of how courts are split on defining what is a "booking question," *see* George C. Thomas III, *Lost in the Fog of* Miranda, 64 Hast. L. J. 1501 (2013).

207. *See generally* Klein, Note 195, *supra*; Thomas, Note 195, *supra*.

208. 401 U.S. 222 (1971); *contra, under the state constitution*, State v. Batts, 195 P.3d 144 (Alaska Ct. App. 2008) (state constitution forbids the use of statements obtained in violation of *Miranda*

Speaking for the Court, Chief Justice Warren Burger conceded that "[s]ome comments in the *Miranda* opinion can indeed be read as indicating a bar to use of an uncounseled statement for any purpose. . . ." However, the Chief Justice characterized such language as dictum and, therefore, not controlling. Instead, Burger stated, the "shield provided by *Miranda* cannot be perverted into a license to use perjury by way of a defense, free from the risk of confrontation with prior inconsistent utterances." Once any witness, including the defendant, agrees to take the stand he must testify truthfully. If he does not, the prosecutor is entitled to use "the traditional truth-testing devices of the adversary process," including the use of prior statements to impeach the speaker's credibility. According to the Chief Justice, "[a]ssuming that the exclusionary rule has a deterrent effect on proscribed police conduct, sufficient deterrence flows when the evidence in question is made unavailable to the prosecution in its case in chief."

Harris is noteworthy. Outside the *Miranda* context, the Supreme Court has held that an incriminating statement made under compulsion in violation of the Fifth Amendment cannot be used for *any* purpose, including impeachment.[209] Therefore, although the *Harris* Court did not characterize *Miranda* as a prophylactic rule—that description did not come for three more years—the seeds of *Miranda*'s de-constitutionalization (or, at least, reduced constitutional stature) were planted in *Harris*.

[B] Fruit-of-the-Poisonous-Tree Doctrine[210]

[1] In General

Consider this simple scenario. The police interrogate *D*, who is in custody, about the murder of a missing child. The police fail to issue *Miranda* warnings. *D* makes various incriminating remarks, which the police wish to introduce at trial. Based on *Miranda*, of course, absent an exception (e.g., the public-safety exception), *D*'s incriminating statements are inadmissible in the prosecutor's case-in-chief.

That much is simple. However, what if the police use *D*'s statement to obtain something more? Maybe they convince *D* later to talk some more or even repeat his earlier inadmissible statements, but this time after *Miranda* warnings are given. *D*, convinced he has already "spilled the beans," might waive his rights and talk. Or, the police might use *D*'s statement to more usefully pursue a new investigation, which leads them to a third person who will testify against *D* at trial. Or, *D*'s statements may lead the police to the weapon used in the murder or to the child's body. In each of these cases, this additional evidence—*D*'s further statements, the third person's trial testimony, or the tangible evidence discovered—constitutes a fruit of the initial *Miranda* violation.

As discussed elsewhere in this text, the exclusionary rules relating to the Fourth Amendment, Due Process Clause, Self-Incrimination Clause, and Sixth Amendment right to counsel, apparently extend not only to the direct products of governmental

---

to impeach the defendant's testimony if the violation was either intentional or egregious); State v. Santiago, 492 P.2d 657 (Haw. 1972) (disallowing use of all *Miranda* violations for impeachment purposes); Commonwealth v. Triplett, 341 A.2d 62 (Pa. 1975) (same).

209. See § 23.05[B][3][b][i], *supra*.

210. Yale Kamisar, *Another Look at Patane and Seibert: The 2004 Miranda "Poisoned Fruit" Cases*, 2 Ohio St. J. Crim. L. 97 (2004); Yale Kamisar, *On the "Fruits" of Miranda Violations, Coerced Confessions, and Compelled Testimony*, 93 Mich. L. Rev. 929 (1995).

illegality, but also to secondary evidence that is the "fruit of the poisonous tree."[211] Does this same principle apply, however, when the "tree" containing the "fruit" is a *Miranda* violation? As was developed earlier,[212] the Supreme Court has come to treat "prophylactic" *Miranda* violations differently from "core" or "pure" Fifth Amendment self-incrimination violations, and it is here—in regard to the fruit-of-the-poisonous-tree doctrine—that this critical distinction developed.

As examined below, the *Miranda* rule supports no, or—depending on how one wishes to conceptualize one critical case—only a limited and (probably) rarely applicable fruit-of-the-poisonous-tree doctrine.

[2] A Tentative Start: *Michigan v. Tucker*

In *Michigan v. Tucker*,[213] the police arrested *T* for rape, and interrogated him. His questioning occurred before *Miranda v. Arizona* was decided, but the police nonetheless informed *T* that any statements he made might be used against him. They also asked him if he wanted an attorney, but they failed to inform him that one would be furnished free of charge if he could not afford counsel. Thus, the police provided *T* more notice of his rights than was constitutionally required at the time. However, *T*'s trial took place after the *Miranda* decision was announced and, pursuant to then-applicable retroactivity principles,[214] the *Miranda* rules applied to *T*'s interrogation. As a consequence, *T*'s statement obtained in violation of *Miranda* was ruled inadmissible at his trial. In *T*'s inadmissible statement, however, the police obtained the name of a witness, *X*, who was later called as a prosecution witness at *T*'s trial. *Tucker* raised the question of whether *X*'s testimony was inadmissible on the basis of the fruit-of-the-poisonous-tree doctrine.

Justice Rehnquist, writing for the Court, observed that the Fifth Amendment privilege against compulsory self-incrimination "was developed by painful opposition to a course of ecclesiastical inquisitions and Star Chamber proceedings occurring several centuries ago."[215] He went on to state that "[w]here there has been genuine compulsion of testimony, the [Fifth Amendment] right has been given broad scope." But, he said,

> [a] comparison of the facts in this case with the historical circumstances underlying the privilege . . . strongly indicates that the police conduct here did not deprive [*T*] of his privilege against compulsory self-incrimination as such, but rather failed to make available to him the full measure of procedural safeguards associated with that right since *Miranda*.

Thus, it is in *Tucker* that Justice Rehnquist stated for the first time that the *Miranda* warnings are "not themselves rights protected by the Constitution but [are] instead measures to insure that the right against compulsory self-incrimination [is] protected." According to the Court, the only harm that occurred in this case was that the police departed "from the prophylactic standards . . . laid down" in *Miranda*.

Having seemingly de-constitutionalized *Miranda*, the *Tucker* Court distinguished *Wong Sun v. United States*,[216] the Fourth Amendment fruit-of-the-poisonous tree case,

---

211. *See generally* §§ 20.08[B][1] (Fourth Amendment), 22.03[C][3][b] (Due Process Clause), 23.05[B][3][b][ii] (Self-Incrimination Clause), *supra*, and § 25.07[D], *infra* (Sixth Amendment).

212. *See* § 24.06, *supra*.

213. 417 U.S. 433 (1974).

214. Johnson v. New Jersey, 384 U.S. 719 (1966).

215. *See* § 23.02, *supra*, for greater details.

216. 371 U.S. 471 (1963).

on the ground that *Wong Sun* involved the admissibility of a fruit of a *constitutional* violation, whereas *X*'s testimony in the present case was only a fruit of a violation of a prophylactic rule (*Miranda*). Consequently, the Court concluded that it was not compelled by precedent to apply *Wong Sun* in the *Miranda* context.

As a matter of principle rather than precedent, the Court concluded that *X*'s testimony should be admissible. Although the justices were urged to announce a broad, no-fruit-of-the-poisonous-tree ruling for all cases, Justice Rehnquist stated that "we . . . place our holding on a narrower ground." He focused on the fact that the interrogation here occurred before *Miranda* was decided: The "deterrent purpose of the exclusionary rule necessarily assumes that the police have engaged in willful, or at the very least negligent, conduct"; here, however, "the official action was pursued in complete good faith." Therefore, the "deterrence rationale loses much of its force."

The Court went further, however, providing clues regarding how it might look at the issue in a genuine post-*Miranda* context. It stated that, beyond the matter of deterrence, the Fifth Amendment exclusionary rule protects the courts from relying on potentially untrustworthy (compelled) testimony. In contrast, here, the fruit—*X*'s testimony—was reliable, because *X* provided his statements voluntarily, and he was subject to cross-examination by *T* at trial. "There is plainly no reason to believe that [*X*'s] testimony is untrustworthy."

Tucker, then, was a technically narrow decision. But, its potential implications were enormous: *Miranda* was no longer a Fifth Amendment rule; it was a prophylactic rule. A statement obtained in violation of *Miranda* was not necessarily a "compelled" statement. And, the potential implication of *Tucker* was that the fruit-of-the-poisonous-tree doctrine need not apply as a remedy when dealing with violations of a mere prophylactic rule.

[3] Expanding on *Tucker: Oregon v. Elstad* and *United States v. Patane*

In *Oregon v. Elstad*,[217] the police went to the home of *E*, a youth, to question him about a recent burglary. An officer briefly questioned *E* in the living room, without informing *E* of his *Miranda* rights. During that conversation, *E* admitted to presence at the scene of the crime. *E* was then transported to the police station where he was read the *Miranda* warnings for the first time. *E* waived his rights and made a second, even more damaging, statement.

The government later conceded that *E* was in custody in the living room when he made his first statement. This was hardly obvious from the facts. Indeed, the Supreme Court observed that "[u]nfortunately, the task of defining 'custody' is a slippery one, and"—quoting *Michigan v. Tucker*—"policemen investigating serious crimes [cannot realistically be expected to] make no errors whatsoever.'" Nonetheless, because *E* was deemed to be in custody in his home, his statement there was inadmissible under *Miranda*. The issue on appeal, however, was whether the *second* confession, obtained after *Miranda* warnings and waiver, was also inadmissible, in part because it was a fruit of

---

217. 470 U.S. 298 (1985); *contra under the state constitution*, Commonwealth v. Smith, 593 N.E.2d 1288 (Mass. 1992) (*S*'s second custodial statement, although obtained noncoercively, is inadmissible as a fruit of an earlier confession obtained in violation of *Miranda*); State v. Smith, 834 S.W.2d 915 (Tenn. 1992) (same).

the earlier *Miranda* violation. That is, *E* would not have made incriminating statements in the police station if he had not let the "cat out of the bag" during the first, improper interrogation.[218]

The Supreme Court, per Justice Sandra Day O'Connor, rejected the fruit-of-the-poisonous-tree argument. Justice O'Connor stated that *E*'s contention that "his confession was tainted [by the *Miranda* violation] . . . and must be excluded as 'fruit of the poisonous tree' assumes the existence of a constitutional violation." According to the Court, the *Miranda* exclusionary rule "serves the Fifth Amendment and sweeps more broadly than the Fifth Amendment itself. It may be triggered in the absence of a Fifth Amendment violation." As a consequence, "in the individual case, *Miranda*'s preventive medicine provides a remedy even to the defendant who has suffered no identifiable constitutional harm."

Justice O'Connor pointed out that it refused in *Michigan v. Tucker* to extend "the *Wong Sun* fruits doctrine to suppress the testimony of a witness for the prosecution whose identity was discovered as the result of a statement taken from the accused without benefit of full *Miranda* warnings." And, she went on, the reasoning of *Tucker* "applies with equal force when the alleged 'fruit' of a noncoercive *Miranda* violation is neither a witness *nor an article of evidence* but [as in this case] the accused's own voluntary testimony."[219] It stated that in the absence of compulsion (and, thus, a pure Fifth Amendment violation) "or improper tactics,"[220] the "twin rationales" of the *Miranda* exclusionary rule—trustworthiness and deterrence—did not call for the exclusion of *E*'s testimony, although it was a fruit of the original violation.

It should be observed that *Tucker* and *Elstad* involved the admissibility of volitional statements by human beings—a witness's testimony (*Tucker*) and a statement by the suspect (*Elstad*). But, could there be a fruit doctrine if the fruit is physical evidence, such as a gun? The italicized dictum in the *Elstad* quotation in the immediately preceding paragraph ("nor an article of evidence") suggested, however, that the Court would not likely draw such a distinction.

And, as it turns out, in *United States v. Patane*,[221] the Supreme Court held, 5–4, that the failure to give a suspect the needed *Miranda* warnings does not require suppression

---

218. *E* also argued that the second statement should be excluded because his waiver was not "knowingly and voluntarily" granted. He claimed that he did not realize that his first statement was inadmissible and that, therefore, "the cat was *not* out of the bag," so that his decision to waive his rights was based on a significant misunderstanding. In regard to *this* argument, *see* § 24.10[A] [3][c], *supra*.

219. *Elstad*, 470 U.S. at 308 (emphasis added).

220. Why wasn't violation of *Miranda* itself an "improper tactic"? Could the answer be that the police here, as in *Tucker*, acted in apparent good faith, i.e., the violation of *Miranda* was inadvertent and not an "improper *tactic*"? Could (or should) it be that a purposeful violation of *Miranda* constitutes an "improper tactic" that *would* justify exclusion of a fruit of such a violation? *See* § 24.12[B] [4], *infra*.

221. 542 U.S. 630 (2004), *contra, under the state constitution,* Commonwealth v. Martin, 827 N.E.2d 198 (Mass. 2005) (holding that physical fruits of a *Miranda* violation are presumptively excludable at trial); State v. Farris, 849 N.E.2d 985 (Ohio 2006) (physical evidence discovered as a result of statements obtained in violation of *Miranda* is inadmissible); State v. Peterson, 923 A.2d 585 (Tenn. 2007) (same); State v. Knapp, 700 N.W.2d 899 (Wis. 2005) (physical evidence obtained as the direct result of an intentional *Miranda* violation is subject to the fruit-of-the-poisonous-tree doctrine).

of physical fruits (here, a firearm) of the suspect's "unwarned but voluntary statements."[222] Thus, *Elstad*'s dictum is now a holding.

Patane is noteworthy because it is a post-*Dickerson*[223] decision: It was decided after the Supreme Court described *Miranda* as a "constitutional decision." This latter characterization did not change the *Patane* Court's ultimate conclusion that *Miranda* does not, at least in ordinary circumstances, contain a fruit-of-the-poisonous-tree doctrine.

In *Patane*, however, the slim 5–4 holding contained its own division among the majority. Justice Thomas, joined by Chief Justice Rehnquist and Justice Scalia, delivered an opinion that treated *Dickerson* almost as if it did not exist.[224] Justice Thomas, in pre-*Dickerson* language, characterized the *Miranda* rule as a "prophylactic employed to protect against violations of the Self-Incrimination Clause." And, citing *Elstad*, it stated that prophylactic rules, including *Miranda*, "necessarily sweep beyond the actual protections of the Self-Incrimination Clause."

There is more. *Miranda* has reached, perhaps, its lowest point in stature with these three justices. Justice Thomas stated that "[t]he *Miranda* rule is not a code of police conduct, and police do not violate the Constitution (or even the *Miranda* rule, for that matter) by mere failures to warn." Why does failure to give the *Miranda* warnings not even violate *Miranda*? These justices seized on their position in *Chavez v. Martinez*,[225] namely, that the Fifth Amendment Self-Incrimination Clause "primarily focuses on the criminal trial." That is, these justices believe that there is no violation of the Fifth Amendment unless and until a compelled statement is used at trial—so it follows for them that there is no violation of the *Miranda* prophylactic rule merely from failing to give warnings. The violation of the prophylactic rule does not occur unless and until a statement obtained without warnings is used at trial.

Justices Kennedy and O'Connor wrote separately. They took a less drastic position about *Miranda*. They viewed *Elstad* and other cases limiting *Miranda*'s exclusionary rule scope as "based in large part on our recognition that the concerns underlying the *Miranda v. Arizona* . . . rule must be accommodated to other objectives of the criminal justice system." They expressly stated that *Dickerson* "did not undermine these precedents." They refused to join the plurality opinion because they found "it unnecessary to decide whether the detective's failure to give [P] the full *Miranda* warnings should be characterized as a violation of the *Miranda* rule itself, or whether there is '[any]thing to deter' so long as the unwarned statements are not later introduced at trial."

Justice Souter, joined by Justices Stevens and Ginsburg, sought to distinguish this case from *Elstad*. *Elstad* held that admission of a post-warning statement by the defendant is not necessarily barred because of an earlier failure to give *Miranda* warnings to the suspect: "[T]hat rule obviously does not apply to physical evidence seized once and for all." They did not explain, however, why the rule should be different, particularly in view of the fact that physical evidence is reliable, normally more so than even voluntary statements.

---

222. Notice the word "voluntary" in the Court's statement. A statement obtained in violation of the "core" Fifth Amendment privilege against compelled self-incrimination (or the Due Process Clause "voluntariness" requirement), as distinguished from a violation of the *Miranda* warnings, triggers fruit-of-the-poisonous-tree principles.

223. Dickerson v. United States, 530 U.S. 428 (2000). *See* § 24.06[C][1], *supra*.

224. Thomas and Scalia, of course, dissented in *Dickerson*. But, the Chief Justice, who joined this *Patane* opinion, was the author of *Dickerson*!

225. 538 U.S. 760 (2003). *See* § 23.05[B][3][a].

What apparently troubled the *Patane* dissenters is that they viewed the decision "as an unjustifiable invitation to law enforcement officers to flout *Miranda* when there may be physical evidence to be gained." In short, *Elstad* and *Patane* provide a powerful incentive to the police to purposely fail to give *Miranda* warnings—so-called "questioning outside *Miranda*"—if they believe it may lead to now-admissible fruits of the *Miranda* violation.

[4] When a "Fruit" May be Inadmissible: *Missouri v. Seibert*

Some police departments and prosecutors treated *Oregon v. Elstad*, discussed above, as an opportunity to ignore *Miranda* and admit the fruits. Some police departments even instructed their officers to "question outside *Miranda*" and then use the inadmissible statements to find critical tangible evidence or secure third-party testimony.[226] Another more specific "police protocol," as explained by the Supreme Court in *Missouri v. Seibert*,[227] "calls for giving no warnings of the rights to silence and counsel until interrogation has produced a confession. . . . [T]he interrogating officer follows it with *Miranda* warnings and then leads the suspect to cover the same ground a second time." It is this latter procedure—specifically, the admissibility of the repeated statements after the police officer's "midstream recitation of warnings"—that was at issue in *Seibert*.

In *Seibert*, S was arrested, taken to the police station, and questioned for 30 to 40 minutes by O without receiving *Miranda* warnings, at which point S made incriminating statements. Following a 20-minute "coffee and cigarette break," S was then given *Miranda* warnings, waived her rights, and submitted to questioning by the same officer. In part by confronting S with her prewarning incriminating statements, O obtained the incriminating statement from S again. At the suppression hearing, O explained that, in accordance with his training, he purposely withheld the *Miranda* warnings until he secured the first statement, which he then purposely convinced S to repeat after warnings were given.

The Court, by a 5–4 vote, held that the second statement was inadmissible. Why? The case might easily have been handled as a fruit-of-the-poisonous-tree case by distinguishing *Tucker* and *Elstad*, which involved inadvertent violations of *Miranda*, and by pointing to the limiting language in *Elstad* that warned that the fruit-of-the-poisonous-tree doctrine might apply if the police either coerced a statement or used "improper tactics." In fact, however, the Court resolved *Seibert* less straightforwardly. Indeed, the Court was so splintered as to the rationale for the result that *Seibert* leaves the future direction of police practices uncertain.

Writing for a four-justice plurality, Justice Souter framed the question this way: Whether the *Miranda* warnings here could "effectively advise the suspect that he had a real choice about giving an admissible statement at that juncture." In concluding that in this case the warnings were ineffective, Justice Souter cited a number of factors distinguishing these circumstances from those in *Elstad*: "the completeness and detail of the questions and answers in the first round of interrogation, the overlapping content of the two statements, the timing and setting of the first and the second [interrogation], the continuity of police personnel, and the degree to which the interrogator's questions

---

226. *See* Weisselberg, Note 18, *supra*; *see also* Steven D. Clymer, *Are Police Free to Disregard Miranda?*, 112 Yale L.J. 447 (2002). According to one study, however, most large city police administrators claim to oppose this practice. Zalman & Smith, Note 7, *supra*, at 912–918.

227. 542 U.S. 600 (2004).

treated the second round as continuous with the first." According to Justice Souter, it would "ordinarily be unrealistic" to find the *Miranda* warnings effective for a second, integrated interrogation.[228]

Explained this way, the plurality did not say that it was recognizing an exception to the *Tucker-Elstad-Patane* line of cases, which seemed to deny the existence of any fruit-of-the-poisonous-tree doctrine in ordinary *Miranda* cases. Instead, the Court essentially reasoned that *Miranda* warnings, when given as part of the "question-first" practice involved here, do not effectively apprise a suspect of his or her constitutional rights, thus preventing an informed waiver of rights.

Justice Breyer, who joined the plurality opinion, *did* see the case in "fruit" terms. He concurred separately to note his view that, when faced with this "two-stage interrogation" technique, courts should exclude the warned statement if it was the "fruit" of the unwarned statement, unless the failure to give warnings occurred in "good faith."[229] He believed examination of the circumstances the plurality used to measure the "effectiveness" of the warnings—such as a lapse in time or changes in location and interrogator—would amount to the same thing as asking whether the second statement was the "fruit" of the first.

Justice Kennedy, who provided the crucial fifth vote suppressing *S's* statement, placed great weight on the point that it was "a deliberate violation of *Miranda*." He stated that "*Elstad* reflects a balanced and pragmatic approach to enforcement of the *Miranda* warnings." But, in his view, "[t]his case presents different considerations." For Justice Kennedy, "postwarning statements should continue to be governed by the principles of *Elstad* unless the deliberate two-step strategy [involved in *Seibert*] was employed." If the strategy *is* deliberate—if the purpose of the police is "to obscure both the practical and legal significance of the admonition when finally given"—then the postwarning statements should be excluded, "unless curative measures are taken before the postwarning statement is made."

Justice Kennedy suggested that "curative measures" might include "a substantial break in time and circumstances" or "an additional warning that explains the likely inadmissibility of the prewarning custodial statement." On their face, these "curative measures" seem to provide an easier path to admissibility than the multiple factors the plurality described for measuring the effectiveness of the warnings for a second, integrated interrogation. And, neither the plurality opinion nor Kennedy intimated that *Seibert* would apply outside the specific context of the "police protocol" used here. Only Justice Breyer, in his concurrence, suggested a broader good faith/bad faith "fruit" approach.

Justice O'Connor, writing for the four dissenters, argued that the intent of the police officer ought to be irrelevant, and that any "two-step interrogation" can be handled, as it was in *Elstad*, simply by examining the voluntariness of the second statement. She would have sent the case back to the state court for consideration of whether *S's* postwarning

---

228. Justice Souter stated that because the officer's intent will "rarely" be admitted as candidly as it was here, "the focus is on facts apart from the intent."

229. Indeed, Justice Breyer would go further than the facts in *Seibert*. In *United States v. Patane*, 542 U.S. 630 (2004), discussed above in §24.12[B][3], Justice Breyer dissented from the admission of the weapon discovered as a fruit of an earlier *Miranda*-less statement, by stating that "I would extend to this context the 'fruit of the poisonous tree' approach, which I believe the Court has come close to adopting in *Seibert*." He went on to suggest that under his approach "courts [should] exclude physical evidence derived from unwarned questioning unless the failure to provide *Miranda* warnings was in good faith."

statement was voluntary, though she noted—perhaps hinting at the outcome she would prefer in the lower court—that O's use of the prewarning statement in the postwarning interrogation provided a basis for questioning its voluntariness.

The splintered decision leaves the net effect of *Seibert* uncertain. Justice Kennedy's opinion—the narrowest of the five justices voting to exclude the statement and, therefore, arguably the controlling opinion—leaves police departments some potentially easy ways to avoid the strictures of *Seibert*, depending upon how strictly his "curative measures" are interpreted.[230] And, *Seibert* did not address the issue of whether police will be able to use *physical evidence* obtained as a result of intentional *Miranda* violations.[231]

---

230. A majority of big city police administrators reportedly assert they agree with the outcome—the exclusion of the evidence—in *Seibert*. Zalman & Smith, Note 7, *supra*, at 912–918.

231. Justice Breyer's position is known, however. *See* Note 229, *supra*.

Chapter 25

Interrogation Law: Sixth Amendment Right to Counsel

The Sixth Amendment guarantees that "[i]n all criminal prosecutions, the accused shall enjoy the right . . . to have the Assistance of Counsel for his defence." This right is fundamental and applies to the states through the Fourteenth Amendment Due Process Clause.[1]

§ 25.01 *Massiah v. United States*[2]

[A] Historical Overview

When the Supreme Court announced its holding in *Massiah v. United States*,[3] it took "a giant step in a wholly new direction"[4] in police interrogation law. *Massiah* brought the Sixth Amendment guarantee of the assistance of counsel "out of the courtroom, . . . [and] into new precincts."[5] The Court held for the first time that the Constitution is violated when government agents, in the absence of defense counsel, deliberately elicit incriminating information from a person against whom adversary judicial criminal proceedings have commenced.

Miranda v. Arizona,[6] decided two years after *Massiah*, temporarily eclipsed the latter case. *Massiah* moved out from behind *Miranda*'s shadows in 1977, however, when the Court applied the Sixth Amendment in exceptionally controversial circumstances in

---

1. Gideon v. Wainwright, 372 U.S. 335 (1963). This chapter focuses exclusively on the Sixth Amendment right to counsel in the context of police interrogations. For discussion of the right to counsel in other procedural contexts, *see* § 26.02 (eyewitness identification procedures) and Chapter 28 (trial and on appeal), *infra*.

2. *See generally* Arnold N. Enker & Sheldon H. Elsen, *Counsel for the Suspect: Massiah v. United States and Escobedo v. Illinois*, 49 Minn. L. Rev. 47 (1964); Martin R. Gardner, *The Right to be Free from Uncounseled Interrogation: A Sixth Amendment Doctrine in Search of a Rationale*, 63 Baylor L. Rev. 80 (2011); Michael J. Howe, Note, *Tomorrow's Massiah: Towards a "Prosecution Specific" Understanding of the Sixth Amendment Right to Counsel*, 104 Colum. L. Rev. 134 (2004); Yale Kamisar, *Brewer v. Williams, Massiah, and Miranda: What is "Interrogation"? When Does it Matter?*, 67 Geo. L.J. 1 (1978); James J. Tomkovicz, *An Adversary System Defense of the Right to Counsel Against Informants: Truth, Fair Play, and the Massiah Doctrine*, 22 U.C. Davis L. Rev. 1 (1988); H. Richard Uviller, *Evidence From the Mind of the Criminal Suspect: A Reconsideration of the Current Rules of Access and Restraint*, 87 Colum. L. Rev. 1137 (1987).

3. 377 U.S. 201 (1964).

4. Uviller, Note 2, *supra*, at 1155.

5. *Id.* at 1159.

6. 384 U.S. 436 (1966).

Brewer v. Williams.[7] Indeed, after *Williams, Massiah* "had the audacity to expand"[8] in an era of rare criminal defense successes in the Supreme Court. Although expansion of *Massiah* has ended — indeed, in recent years the Court has cut back on its potential reach[9] — it remains the leading case in the field.

[B] *Massiah*: The Opinion

The federal government indicted *M* for violating federal narcotics laws. *M* retained a lawyer, pleaded not guilty, and was released from custody on bail. In the meantime, *C*, who was charged in the same indictment, agreed to cooperate with the government in its continuing investigation of *M*. *C* permitted federal agents to install a listening device in his car so that they could listen while *M* (unaware of *C*'s new informant status) had lengthy conversations with him. During the intercepted conversations, which occurred in the absence of *M*'s counsel, *M* made incriminating statements that were introduced at his trial over his objection.

M argued that admission at trial of the statements he made in *C*'s car violated various constitutional rights, including his Sixth Amendment right to counsel. The Supreme Court, per Justice Stewart, agreed with *M*'s right-to-counsel claim.

The majority opinion in *Massiah* was short and the holding narrow. According to Justice Stewart, the Sixth Amendment was violated "when there was used against [*M*] at his trial evidence of his own incriminating words, which federal agents had deliberately elicited from him after he had been indicted and in the absence of his counsel."

Justice Stewart reasoned that the Sixth Amendment applied in *M*'s circumstances because the period after a suspect is formally charged with an offense and before trial is "the most critical period of the proceedings." It is during this time that "consultation, thoroughgoing investigation and preparation [are] vitally important."[10] Therefore, to deny an accused counsel during this period would deny her "effective representation by counsel at the only stage when legal aid and advice would help." Most especially, for the right of counsel to be effective, the Court observed that it had to apply to the surreptitious conduct that occurred here: *M* was "more seriously imposed upon" than in a traditional encounter, because he was unaware that he was "under interrogation by a government agent."

The Solicitor General in *Massiah* argued "strenuously . . . that the federal law enforcement agents had the right, if not indeed the duty, to continue their investigation of [*M*] and his alleged criminal associates even though [*M*] had been indicted." Indeed, the government had reason to believe that *M* was part of a large, well-organized drug ring. The Court accepted "and, at least for present purposes, completely approve[d] all that this argument implies." It agreed that it was "entirely proper" for the agents to continue their post-indictment investigation of *M*. It stressed that "[a]ll that we hold is that the defendant's own incriminating statements, obtained by federal agents under the circumstances

---

7. 430 U.S. 387 (1977).

8. Tomkovicz, Note 2, *supra*, at 5.

9. *See* §§ 25.01[C], 25.04, and 25.06, *infra*.

10. Notice that this description of the role of counsel in the Sixth Amendment context is broader than the *Miranda* right to counsel, the primary purpose of which is simply to assure that the suspect's Fifth Amendment right to be free from compelled self-incrimination is not violated. *See* (24.04[B][1][b], *supra*.

here disclosed, could not constitutionally be used by the prosecution as evidence against *him* at his trial."[11]

[C] Making Sense of *Massiah*: The Sixth Amendment Role of Counsel[12]

The practical effect of the *Massiah* rule is that, in the instance of surreptitious deliberate elicitation of incriminating statements made after adversary criminal proceedings have commenced against an accused, "the government either [must] reveal its presence [to the accused] and afford the opportunity to consult with counsel,"—and, thus effectively undermine the undercover investigation—"or . . . suffer [at her trial] the exclusion of the product of its adversarial encounter with the accused."[13]

Can such a rule be defended? In his dissent, Justice Byron White criticized the majority because it barred the use by the government of "relevant, reliable, and highly probative evidence" obtained in a non-coercive environment. As a result of this case, he said, "the Constitution furnishes an important measure of protection against faithless compatriots and guarantees sporting treatment for sporting peddlers of narcotics." Justice White predicted that the effect of the *Massiah* rule would be that fewer confessed criminals would come forward to assist the government in its criminal investigations. Subsequently, Justice Rehnquist stated that *Massiah*'s "doctrinal underpinnings . . . have been largely left unexplained, and the result . . . is difficult to reconcile with the traditional notions of the role of an attorney."[14] Even a supporter of *Massiah* conceded that "[t]he original . . . opinion provides a good example of . . . analytical shallowness."[15]

Indeed, one must ask: How *was* M's Sixth Amendment right to counsel violated in C's automobile? His lawyer was not barred from the car during the conversations. Furthermore, in light of the surreptitious nature of the police activity, it likely would not have served any meaningful purpose if M's lawyer coincidentally *had* been present. The only way that he could have used his expertise to protect M would have been to tell him not to talk to C on the general principle that their legal interests might eventually conflict, but she could have given M this advice *before* the encounter in the car.[16]

---

11. *Massiah*, 377 U.S. at 207 (emphasis in the original).

12. *See generally* Martin R. Gardner, *The Sixth Amendment Right to Counsel and Its Underlying Values: Defining the Scope of Privacy Protection*, 90 J. Crim. L. & Criminology 397 (2000); Howe, Note 2, *supra*; William J. Stuntz, *Lawyers, Deception, and Evidence Gathering*, 79 Va. L. Rev. 1903 (1993); Uviller, Note 2, *supra*.

13. Tomkovicz, Note 2, *supra*, at 91.

14. United States v. Henry, 447 U.S. 264, 290 (1980) (Rehnquist, J., dissenting).

15. Tomkovicz, Note 2, *supra*, at 22.

16. In fact, M's lawyer's presence in C's car could have represented a more serious risk to M's Sixth Amendment rights than his absence, because the government would have been able to overhear any lawyer-client confidences. In *Weatherford v. Bursey*, 429 U.S. 545 (1977), B and W, an undercover agent, participated in the vandalization of private property. In order to protect W's undercover status, W also was charged with the offense. Prior to trial, B invited W to sit in while he discussed trial strategy with his attorney. At no time, however, did W pass on any of the lawyer-client conversations to the government. The Court held that under these limited circumstances— there was "no tainted evidence in this case, no communication of defense strategy to the prosecution, and no purposeful intrusion by [W]"—no Sixth Amendment violation resulted.

According to two scholars, "[t]he real problem facing the Court in *Massiah* was not one of the right to counsel but rather the permissible extent of governmental deceit inherent in undercover work and the use of informers."[17] In other words, the problem in *Massiah* arguably was not the absence of counsel but rather the government's surreptitious interrogation of *M* through an apparent friend and ally. If this observation is accurate, *Massiah* should have rested its holding on the Fourth Amendment or on general due process grounds. However, if the Court *had* applied Fourth Amendment or due process reasoning to declare the statements inadmissible, this outcome would have been inconsistent with existing and subsequent constitutional doctrine in those fields.[18]

Therefore, is there a way to find a *Sixth Amendment* interest implicated in *Massiah*? The answer depends on what the Constitution means by the words "assistance of counsel." In other words, what is the pretrial role of a defense attorney, and how could that role have been filled by *M*'s attorney in *Massiah*?

One scholar has helpfully identified three roles a lawyer might play in the pretrial phase of a criminal prosecution.[19] First, she can provide assistance in those encounters with the government in which her innocent client's "weakness, ignorance, or inertia"[20] threatens to result in an unjust conviction. The importance of this role of defense counsel is uncontroversial, but certainly there was no substantial reason to fear that an innocent person would make incriminating statements in the relatively non-coercive environment of *C*'s automobile.

Second, a lawyer can provide "preventive assistance." The concern here is that an accused—whether factually innocent or not—"alone and friendless, faces the immense forces of the state arrayed against [her]."[21] This purpose of counsel is not simply to reduce the risk that the government's "immense forces" will crush an innocent person (that concern is satisfied by the first role of counsel), but primarily to devise a criminal justice system for *all* accused persons, *even those who might be guilty*, that is more balanced.

This preventive-assistance concept is controversial. Critics characterize it as the "fox hunt" or "sporting" view of justice, i.e., making the process "fair" so that the "fox" has a sporting chance of winning,[22] which was what Justice White had in mind in his *Massiah* dissent when he criticized the majority for "guarantee[ing] sporting treatment for sporting peddlers of narcotics." However, even if this defense role is justifiable, there seemingly was no practical way for counsel in *Massiah* to assist *M* in the "fox hunt" occurring in *C*'s car, because neither *M* nor his counsel realized that the "game" was underway.

The third role of counsel is to provide "adversarial assistance." The premise here is that once the government commits itself to a prosecution—once the investigation turns "into a hardened adversarial alignment"[23]—a form of "closure," or limitation on access

---

17. Enker & Elsen, Note 2, *supra*, at 57.

18. Only two years after *Massiah*, *Hoffa v. United States*, 385 U.S. 293 (1966), reaffirmed the Fourth Amendment principle that one who talks to another person assumes the risk that the listener will betray her. *See* § 6.05[B], *supra. Hoffa* also rejected the claim that the use of secret government informers is a per se violation of the Due Process Clause.

19. Uviller, Note 2, *supra*, at 1168–83.

20. *Id.* at 1169.

21. *Id.* at 1173.

22. *See especially* § 24.05[B][3], *supra.*

23. Uviller, Note 2, *supra*, at 1176.

to the accused, should result. The reasoning is that once the adversarial system begins, the lawyer serves as the "guardian of the fortress."[24] Therefore, she should be "the essential medium through which the demands and commitments of the sovereign are communicated to the citizen."[25] According to this view, once adversarial proceedings have commenced, the prosecutor and the police "have an affirmative obligation not to act in a manner that circumvents and thereby dilutes the protection afforded by the right to counsel."[26] In particular, it is no longer appropriate for agents of the government knowingly to enter the fortress in order to obtain verbal evidence from the accused in the absence of counsel or a valid waiver of the right.

Massiah's holding certainly is justifiable if one accepts this last understanding of the role of counsel. The government violated the closure concept: it deliberately elicited incriminating information from *M* after he was indicted and in his counsel's absence; and, in view of the surreptitious approach used to obtain the evidence, *M* had no meaningful way to waive his right to counsel. It must be observed, however, that the *Massiah* Court never offered this justification for the rule it announced, nor did the Court expressly recognize any broad principle of closure.

For a time, the post-*Massiah* Court seemed to be moving in the direction of the adversarial-assistance closure approach. Thus, in *Maine v. Moulton*, it stated that the Sixth Amendment "guarantees the accused . . . the right to rely on counsel as a 'medium' between him and the State."[27] But, more recently, in *Texas v. Cobb*, the Court rejected a broad closure doctrine, stating that "there is no 'background principle' of our Sixth Amendment jurisprudence establishing that there may be no contact between a defendant and police without counsel present."[28] This language suggests that the government, through its agents, are not always barred from contacting a counseled defendant in order to seek a waiver of her right to counsel.

So, what *is* the purpose of the Sixth Amendment right to counsel in the pretrial interrogation context? In *Kansas v. Ventris*,[29] the Court stated that, although the "core [Sixth Amendment] right to counsel is . . . a trial right, ensuring that the prosecution's case is subjected to 'the crucible of meaningful adversarial testing,'"[30] the right also "covers pretrial interrogations to ensure that police manipulation does not render counsel entirely impotent—depriving the defendant of 'effective representation by counsel at the only stage when legal aid and advice would help him.'"[31]

This statement perhaps supports the "preventive assistance" role of the lawyer: An accused person, innocent or not, is entitled to a lawyer prior to trial in order to keep the government from "manipulating" her into convicting herself before trial. Without this pretrial right to counsel, the "core" right—to a lawyer at trial—would be rendered meaningless.

---

24. *Id.* at 1161.
25. Maine v. Moulton, 474 U.S. 159, 170 n.7 (1985) (quoting Brewer v. Williams, 430 U.S. 387, 415 (1977) (Stevens, J., concurring)).
26. *Id.* at 171.
27. *Id.* at 176.
28. 532 U.S. 162, 171 n.2 (2001).
29. 556 U.S. 586 (2009).
30. *Id.* at 591 (quoting United States v. Cronic, 466 U.S. 648, 656 (1984)).
31. *Id* (quoting *Massiah*).

§ 25.02 The Sixth Amendment (*Massiah*) Right to Counsel: Summary

The Sixth Amendment right to counsel has evolved since the Court announced its cautious holding in *Massiah v. United States*.[32] The right to counsel now applies not only to the conduct of federal agents, as in *Massiah*, but also in state prosecutions, through the Fourteenth Amendment Due Process Clause.[33] Although the Court in *Massiah* treated the surreptitious nature of the police conduct in that case as an aggravating circumstance, it is now clear that the Sixth Amendment applies as well to non-surreptitious efforts to elicit incriminating statements.

The Supreme Court's interpretation of the Sixth Amendment right to counsel, although not yet as complicated as the rules relating to *Miranda v. Arizona*,[34] requires an understanding of various principles summarized here, and considered in detail in the chapter sections that follow.

First, "[t]he Sixth Amendment right to counsel is personal to the defendant. . . ."[35] This means, obviously, that the right belongs to the accused person and not to her lawyer. More significantly, this demonstrates that, although the Supreme Court has never had occasion to so rule, there is no serious doubt that a Sixth Amendment right-to-counsel claim may only be raised in a criminal trial by the person whose counsel right was infringed, i.e., only *she* has standing to challenge the government's conduct. This assumption is well supported by the Court's language in *Massiah*, in which it stated that the Sixth Amendment is violated when the accused's own incriminating statement is "used by the prosecution as evidence against *him*"—the Court's own emphasis—"at his trial."

Second, the Sixth Amendment right to counsel only applies if adversary judicial criminal proceedings have commenced against the accused.[36] According to the Court, "the possibility that [an] encounter [between the government and an individual] may have important consequences at trial, standing alone, is insufficient to trigger the Sixth Amendment right to counsel."[37]

Third, the right to counsel announced in *Massiah* is not violated by the mere fact that government agents—police officers or prosecutors—have contact with a person accused of a crime in the absence of counsel. It is only when the agent "deliberately elicits" incriminating statements from the accused that the Sixth Amendment is potentially violated.

Fourth, as the Supreme Court has expressed it, the Sixth Amendment right to counsel is "specific to the offense."[38] There is much more to be said on the subject,[39] but the

---

32. 377 U.S. 201 (1964). *See* § 25.01, *supra*.

33. *See* Brewer v. Williams, 430 U.S. 387 (1977).

34. 384 U.S. 436 (1966). *See* Chapter 24, *supra*.

35. Texas v. Cobb, 532 U.S. 162, 171 n.2 (2001).

36. There is one marginal exception to this statement. In *Escobedo v. Illinois*, 378 U.S. 478 (1964), the Court applied the Sixth Amendment to a post-arrest custodial interrogation that occurred prior to initiation of adversary judicial criminal proceedings. However, the Court later reinterpreted *Escobedo* as a Fifth Amendment self-incrimination case. The holding of *Escobedo* is now limited to its facts. *See* § 24.03, *supra*.

37. Moran v. Burbine, 475 U.S. 412, 432 (1986).

38. Texas v. Cobb, 532 U.S. at 171 n.2.

39. *See* § 25.04, *infra*.

crime-specific nature of the Sixth Amendment means that law enforcement agents do *not* violate the Sixth Amendment, even if formal adversary proceedings have commenced against a person regarding Crime X, if the police deliberately elicit incriminating statements from the accused regarding Crime Y, for which formal proceedings have *not* yet been initiated.

Fifth, the right to counsel "may be waived by a defendant, so long as relinquishment of the right is voluntary, knowing, and intelligent."[40]

Sixth, generally speaking, a violation of the Sixth Amendment right to counsel requires exclusion of the improperly obtained statement of the accused, and its fruits, at the defendant's trial *in the prosecutor's case-in-chief.* The exclusionary rule does *not* apply, however, to the use of the unconstitutionally obtained statement to impeach the defendant's inconsistent testimony at trial.

As will be evident in the discussion that follows, in some regards Sixth Amendment jurisprudence provides a person accused of a crime with different protections in the police interrogation context than are obtained through *Miranda v. Arizona.* The key differences between the Sixth Amendment and *Miranda* rights to counsel are summarized in Section 25.08.

§ 25.03 Procedural Initiation of the Right to Counsel: Adversary Judicial Proceedings

In *Brewer v. Williams*,[41] the Court stated:

> Whatever else it may mean, the right to counsel granted by the Sixth and Fourteenth Amendments means at least that a person is entitled to the help of a lawyer at or after the time that judicial proceedings have been initiated against him — "whether by way of formal charge, preliminary hearing, indictment, information, or arraignment."[42]

Such proceedings include "the first appearance before a judicial officer at which a defendant is told of the formal accusation against him and restrictions are imposed on his liberty."[43]

Despite the non-limiting language in the preceding indented quotation — "whatever else it may mean" and "the right . . . means at least" — the Court, with one very narrow exception,[44] has shut the door on the possibility that the Sixth Amendment right-to-counsel provision might apply *before* judicial proceedings begin.

This threshold requirement is justified on the basis of the language of the Sixth Amendment itself, which provides that "in all criminal *prosecutions* . . . the *accused*

---

40. Montejo v. Louisiana, 556 U.S. 778, 786 (2009). *See* § 25.06, *infra.*
41. 430 U.S. 387 (1977).
42. *Id.* at 398 (quoting Kirby v. Illinois, 406 U.S. 682, 689 (1972)).
43. Rothgery v. Gillespie County, 554 U.S. 191, 194 (2008). This rule applies whether or not a prosecutor is present at, or even aware of, the proceeding. *Id.* at 194–195.
44. *See* Note 36, *supra.*

[is entitled] to have the assistance of Counsel for his *defence*." The Supreme Court has stated that it is when the "government . . . use[s] the judicial machinery to signal a commitment to prosecute"[45] that the "suspect" becomes the "accused." It is at this point, and not before, that the individual is "faced with the prosecutorial forces of organized society, and immersed in the intricacies of substantive and procedural criminal law."[46] It is at this time, therefore, that the "accused" needs to prepare a "defense."

This interpretation of the Sixth Amendment has been disputed. Some have argued that the arrest—an earlier procedural stage—should be understood as the commencement of the prosecution.[47] More recently, however, Justice Clarence Thomas has argued in the other procedural direction. His reading of Blackstone suggests to him that the term "criminal prosecution" at the time of the framing of the Sixth Amendment referred to "instituting a criminal suit" (Blackstone's language) "by filing a formal charging document—an indictment, presentment, or information—upon which the defendant was to be tried in a court with power to punish the alleged offense."[48] If this reading of the Sixth Amendment were accepted by a majority of the Supreme Court,[49] it would notably mean that a person does *not* have a Sixth Amendment right to counsel at her initial arraignment before a magistrate (typically, before an indictment or other formal document is prepared) when she first learns the charges against her.[50]

It should be noted, as well, that although the Sixth Amendment right to counsel *attaches* when "the government use[s] the judicial machinery to signal a commitment to prosecute," this does not necessarily mean that the Sixth Amendment is violated if a person is not furnished counsel at the precise moment of the right's attachment. The Supreme Court in *Rothgery v. Gillespie County*[51] stated only that, at the moment of attachment, there exists a "state obligation to appoint counsel [for an indigent defendant] within a reasonable time once a request for assistance is made,"[52] and the Court has only found counsel required prior to trial during a "critical stage."[53]

---

45. Rothgery v. Gillespie County, 554 U.S. at 211.

46. Kirby v. Illinois, 406 U.S. 682, 689 (1972).

47. Professor Richard Uviller has pointed out that "[n]either semantics nor reason obstructs the designation of an arrest as the point of accusation in the constitutional sense." Uviller, Note 2, *supra*, at 1167. Indeed, according to the text of the Sixth Amendment, the "accused" in all "criminal prosecutions" is entitled to a speedy trial, yet *this* right has been interpreted to attach at the time of arrest or the filing of an indictment or information, whichever comes first. United States v. Marion, 404 U.S. 307 (1971).

48. Rothgery v. Gillespie County, 554 U.S. at 221 (dissenting opinion).

49. Although no other member of the Court signed on to Justice Thomas's dissent, Chief Justice Roberts and Justice Scalia, in a concurring opinion in *Rothgery*, characterized Justice Thomas's historical analysis as "compelling." However, in their view, "[a] sufficient case [had] not been made for revisiting [prior] precedents." *Id.* at 213.

50. For an explanation of these pretrial stages, *see* § 1.03[C], *supra*.

51. 554 U.S. 191 (2008).

52. *Id.* at 198. In a concurring opinion in *Rothgery*, Justice Alito, with whom Chief Justice Roberts and Justice Scalia joined, stated that "I interpret the Sixth Amendment to require the appointment of counsel only after the defendant's prosecution has begun, and then only as necessary to guarantee the defendant effective assistance at trial." *Id.* at 217.

53. See § 28.02, *infra*.

§ 25.04 "Offense-Specific" Nature of the Right to Counsel[54]

The Sixth Amendment right to counsel is offense-specific. That is, in determining whether the Sixth Amendment applies to a particular effort by the government to deliberately elicit incriminating statements from an accused, the issue is not simply whether formal judicial proceedings have commenced against the accused for *some* crime, but rather whether such proceedings have commenced in regard to the *specific offense* at issue.

This was not always the case. Or, at least, the Supreme Court did not speak of the offense-specific nature of the Sixth Amendment in its early post-*Massiah* cases. For, example, in *Brewer v. Williams*,[55] W, a suspect in the abduction and murder of a young girl, was arraigned on the abduction charge, and thereafter (in the absence of counsel) was subjected to conduct tantamount to interrogation that resulted in incriminating statements relating to the child's death. Although at this point formal proceedings had not yet commenced in regard to the child's murder, the Supreme Court reversed W's murder conviction on Sixth Amendment grounds.

In 1991, in *McNeil v. Wisconsin*,[56] however, the Supreme Court expressly characterized the Sixth Amendment as offense-specific. In *McNeil*, the police questioned M, formally charged with armed robbery, in regard to a series of crimes for which M had not yet been arrested, much less formally charged. The Court held that, in view of the offense-specific nature of the right, the Sixth Amendment had not attached to the latter crimes at the time of interrogation, although it applied to the armed robbery.

The *McNeil* "offense-specific" concept was clarified—and the potential scope of the Sixth Amendment right to counsel seemingly narrowed—in *Texas v. Cobb*.[57] In *Cobb*, C confessed to the burglary of a home, but denied knowledge of a mother and her infant daughter missing from the home and later discovered dead. The government indicted C for the burglary, but later questioned him in the absence of counsel, and secured confessions regarding the murder victims. The Court held that the Sixth Amendment right to counsel did not extend to the unindicted offenses (here, the murders) simply because they were "factually related" to an offense (here, burglary) that had been charged. It would follow, therefore, that in *Brewer v. Williams* the Sixth Amendment did *not* in fact attach to the uncharged crime of murder, although that offense was inextricably intertwined with the abduction charge for which W had been arraigned. The Court's holding in *Williams*, therefore, was incorrect in light of *Cobb*.[58]

---

54. *See generally* Howe, Note 2, *supra*.

55. 430 U.S. 387 (1977).

56. 501 U.S. 171, 175 (1991).

57. 532 U.S. 162 (2001); *contra under the state constitution*, Jewell v. State, 957 N.E.2d 625 (Ind. 2011) (a police officer may not question a suspect about an uncharged offense that is "inextricably intertwined" with a charged offense for which the accused has counsel).

58. The *Cobb* Court explained that "[t]he Court's opinion [in *Brewer v. Williams*] ... simply did not address the significance of the fact that the suspect had been arraigned only on the abduction charge, nor did the parties in any way argue this question." In view of *Cobb*, W's conviction for murder should not have been overturned.

The *Cobb* Court did state, however, that the term "offense" is "not necessarily limited to the four corners of a charging instrument." Instead, the Court announced that the meaning of the term "offense" in the Sixth Amendment right-to-counsel context is the same as in the Fifth Amendment Double Jeopardy Clause, which prohibits a person from being prosecuted twice for the "same offense" ("nor shall any person be subject to the same *offense* to be twice put in jeopardy of life or limb").[59]

Cobb imported the so-called *Blockburger*[60] double jeopardy rule to the Sixth Amendment. According to *Blockburger*, "where the same act or transaction constitutes a violation of two distinct statutory provisions, the test to be applied to determine whether there are two offenses or only one, is whether each provision requires proof of a fact which the other does not." Thus, if Crime 1 requires proof of elements A, B, and C, and Crime 2 contains elements A, B, and D, these are distinct offenses because each crime, as defined, requires proof of an element that the other does not (Crime 1 requires proof of element C, which Crime 2 does not; Crime 2 requires proof of element D, which Crime 1 does not). However, suppose that Crime 1 requires proof of elements A, B, and C, and Crime 2 requires proof of elements A and B. These two statutory provisions (for example, "assault with a deadly weapon" and simple "assault") would constitute the same "offense" for purposes of double jeopardy law and, now, Sixth Amendment right-to-counsel law.

Consider, as well, the following example. Suppose that *D* is indicted for assault of *V*, who subsequently dies from the attack. (Assume assault is defined as "intentional application of unlawful force upon another.") Before *V*'s death, however, the police obtain a statement from *D* that is violative of her Sixth Amendment *Massiah* rights. Upon *V*'s death, the government secures a superseding indictment of *D* for murder. May the prosecution now use *V*'s statement against *D*, on the ground that it was obtained before *D* was indicted for the murder? Probably not. This is because, under *Blockburger*, assault (as defined above) and intent-to-kill murder seemingly are the "same offense." This is because "assault" as defined in the text consists of the elements: (a) intent; and (b) unlawful force upon another; intent-to-kill murder essentially involves: (a) intent; (b) unlawful force upon another; and (c) death. "Assault" is thus a lesser-included offense of the murder.[61] Therefore, indictment for one statutory violation would serve to trigger the Sixth Amendment in regard to both statutes.

However, as one commentator has observed, "[g]iven the abundance of overlapping and related statutory offenses, a single criminal transaction can be characterized—and prosecuted—as a number of offenses, all just different enough from one another to satisfy the *Blockburger* test."[62] Indeed, as the dissenters in *Cobb* warned, police officials now have freedom, for example, to "ask the individual charged with robbery about, say, the assault of the cashier not yet charged, or about any other uncharged offense (unless

---

59. *See generally* 2 Joshua Dressler & Alan C. Michaels, Understanding Criminal Procedure chapter 14 (4th ed. 2006).

60. Blockburger v. United States, 284 U.S. 299 (1932).

61. Of course, the words "unlawful force" are not found in the ordinary definition of murder, but it is an implicit aspect of the concept of killing another person. However, even this fairly straightforward example demonstrates, as Justice Breyer observed in his dissent in *Cobb*, that "the simple-sounding *Blockburger* test has proved extraordinarily difficult to administer in practice. Judges, lawyers, and law professors often disagree about how to apply it." Indeed, one can imagine a murder based on an omission, in which "unlawful force" by the defendant is *not* involved!

62. Howe, Note 2, *supra*, at 149–150.

under *Blockburger*'s definition it counts as the 'same crime'), *all without notifying counsel,*" or requiring the police to seek waiver of the Sixth Amendment right.[63]

There is an additional probable effect of *Cobb*, although the Supreme Court has not yet been called on to confirm this point. According to the "dual sovereignty doctrine" of the Double Jeopardy Clause, criminal statutes in separate "sovereigns" (i.e., different jurisdictions) are deemed "different offenses" for purposes of prosecution, *even if they have identical elements* and would constitute the "same offense" under *Blockburger*. Thus, a person may be prosecuted for the same conduct in a federal and state court,[64] or in two different states,[65] assuming both have jurisdiction over some aspect of the conduct. Therefore, the Supreme Court could import *this* double jeopardy doctrine to the Sixth Amendment, as some lower courts have already done.[66] Thus, for example, the fact that a person has been indicted for arson in a state proceeding—triggering the Sixth Amendment—would not preclude federal agents, investigating the same conduct under a federal arson statute, from questioning the federally *un*indicted suspect free of Sixth Amendment restrictions.[67]

§ 25.05 Requirement of "Deliberate Elicitation"[68]

[A] "Deliberate Elicitation" versus "Interrogation"

Although *Massiah v. United States*[69] prohibits "deliberate elicitation"—those were the words in its holding—Justice Potter Stewart stated in the opinion that the accused in that case was "under interrogation" by *C*, a covert agent. The use of the word "interrogation" in the opinion was misleading as there was no evidence presented that *C* ever questioned *M*, the accused; instead, they had "lengthy conversations."

The Court confused matters further in *Brewer v. Williams*.[70] In *Williams*, *W* was arrested and arraigned for the abduction of a child believed to have been killed. While being transported in a police car from one part of the state to another, a police officer subjected *W* to what has come to be known as "the Christian burial speech." In the speech, the officer prefaced his comments to *W* by saying, "I want to give you something to think about. . . ." He concluded his remarks by indicating, "I do not want you to answer me. I

---

63. Even though the Sixth Amendment would not apply to the uncharged assault of the cashier in the hypothetical set out in the text, the *Cobb* majority suggested that it is fair to assume that an individual charged with robbery will be informed of her *Miranda* rights and, therefore, retain the ability to refuse any and all police questioning in a custodial interrogation context (since *Miranda* is *not* offense-specific). Moreover, a person in such circumstances is likely to have met with her counsel on the charged offense, and thus she has the opportunity to receive her lawyer's advice whether to invoke her right to silence in regard to uncharged offenses.

64. United States v. Lanza, 260 U.S. 377 (1922).

65. Heath v. Alabama, 474 U.S. 82 (1985).

66. *E.g.*, United States v. Avants, 278 F.3d 510 (5th Cir. 2002); United States v. Coker, 433 F.3d 39 (1st Cir. 2005).

67. *Coker*, 433 F. 3d 39.

68. *See generally* Kamisar, Note 2, *supra*; Welsh S. White, *Interrogation Without Questions: Rhode Island v. Innis and United States v. Henry*, 78 Mich. L. Rev. 1209 (1980).

69. 377 U.S. 201 (1964).

70. 430 U.S. 387 (1977).

don't want to discuss it any further. Just think about it. . . ." In between, the officer, playing on *W*'s religious beliefs and psychological vulnerability as an escaped mental patient, expressed concern regarding the possibility that the little girl's body, which had not been discovered, would soon be buried under the Iowa winter's snow, thus depriving her parents of a chance to give the victim "a Christian burial." Sometime later in the police car, *W* made incriminating statements and agreed to show the police where he had buried the victim.

At no time during the "speech" did the officer question *W.* Nonetheless, the Court described "the clear rule of *Massiah*" to be that, once judicial criminal proceedings commence, the accused "has a right to legal representation when the government interrogates him." It also stated that "no such constitutional protection would have come into play if there had been no interrogation." And, it described the burial speech as "tantamount to interrogation." Yet, in language reminiscent of *Massiah*, the Court remarked that the officer "deliberately and designedly set out to elicit information . . . just as surely as—and perhaps more effectively than—if he had formally interrogated him."

This language in *Williams* suggested the possibility that the terms "deliberate elicitation" and "interrogation" were constitutional synonyms. If they were, the Court's *Miranda* jurisprudence relating to "custodial interrogation" might have applied in the Sixth Amendment context, and vice-versa. However, in *Rhode Island v. Innis*,[71] the first Supreme Court case to define "interrogation" under *Miranda*, the Court indicated that it was erroneous to suggest "that the definition of 'interrogation' under *Miranda* is informed by this Court's [Sixth Amendment] decision[s]. . . . The definitions of 'interrogation' under the Fifth and Sixth Amendments, *if indeed the term 'interrogation' is even apt in the Sixth Amendment context*, are not necessarily interchangeable. . . ."[72] And, more recently in *Fellers v. United States*,[73] the Court again observed that "we have expressly distinguished [the Sixth Amendment "deliberate elicitation"] standard from the Fifth Amendment custodial-interrogation standard."

The meaning of "deliberate elicitation" in the Sixth Amendment context is described more fully below. However, in view of the Court's warnings in *Innis* and *Fellers*, it is important to treat separately the Sixth Amendment (triggered by "deliberate elicitation") and Fifth Amendment ("custodial interrogation") versions of the right to counsel.

[B] What Does "Deliberate" Mean?

[1] "Deliberate" as "Purposeful"

"Deliberate elicitation" uncontroversially occurs when a government agent purposely elicits an incriminating statement from the accused, i.e., when it is her conscious object to obtain a statement from the defendant. For example, purposeful (and, therefore, deliberate) elicitation occurs when an officer formally interrogates the accused person. Or, as in *Massiah*, it occurs when an undercover agent engages the accused in a conversation in order to obtain incriminating comments. Or, as in *Brewer v. Williams*, the Sixth Amendment is triggered when an officer makes statements designed to play on the conscience of the accused in order to induce incriminating remarks.

---

71. 446 U.S. 291 (1980).
72. *Id.* at 300 n. 4 (emphasis added)
73. 540 U.S. 519 (2004).

Massiah's "deliberate elicitation" differs from the *Miranda-Innis* concept of "interrogation"[74] in that the former test centers on the subjective motivation of the officer, whereas the latter standard focuses on the suspect and is based on an objective finding that the process will likely result in incriminating information. Thus, there can be a *Miranda* "interrogation" based on negligent action by an officer, whereas the *Massiah* "deliberate elicitation" standard requires a higher standard of "culpability" by the officer.

[2] "Deliberate" As Meaning Something Less Than "Purposeful"?

Although the Supreme Court regularly states that the Sixth Amendment triggering standard is "deliberate elicitation,"[75] the Court has sometimes muddled the law by seemingly expanding on the meaning of the term beyond its apparent contours. In *United States v. Henry*,[76] for example, the FBI placed *I*, a paid informant, in a jail cell with *H* after the latter had been indicted. An FBI agent told *I* "to be alert to any statement" made by *H*, "but not to initiate any conversation with or question" him. However, *I* "engaged in conversation" with *H* various times, during which *H* made statements that the government sought to introduce at his trial.

In an opinion written by Chief Justice Warren Burger, the Court held that the government "deliberately elicited" the statements "within the meaning of *Massiah*." In reaching this conclusion, it focused on three facts: (1) *I* was paid on a contingent-fee basis, and thus had an incentive to obtain information from *H*; (2) *I* pretended to be a fellow inmate, which made it possible for him to engage in conversations with *H* without arousing suspicion; and (3) *H* was in custody, which "bring[s] into play subtle influences that . . . make [an inmate] particularly susceptible to the ploys of undercover Government agents."

Based on these facts, the Court concluded that the government "must have known" that *I*'s proximity to *H* "likely would lead" to the incriminating statements. And, in critical language of the opinion, the Court stated that "[b]y intentionally creating a situation likely to induce [*H*] to make incriminating statements without the assistance of counsel, the Government violated [*H*'s] Sixth Amendment right to counsel." This conclusion followed, it said, regardless of whether *I* or *H* raised the subject of the accused's criminal activities, and whether or not *I* questioned *H* about the crime or merely "engaged in general conversation about it."

A careful reading of the language of *Henry* raises questions about the meaning of the term "deliberate elicitation." If *Massiah* and *Williams* involved "purposeful" elicitation, *Henry* involved proof of no more than "knowledge" by the FBI agent that *I* would attempt to secure incriminating information. In fact, in view of the Court's statement that the government "must have known" that *I*'s conduct "likely" would result in information, the agent's state of mind might more accurately be described as "reckless,"[77] and not "purposeful." This conclusion is also consistent with the Court's statement that the government "intentionally" created a situation "likely to induce" the statements. That is,

---

74. *See* § 24.08, *supra*.

75. Fellers v. United States, 540 U.S. 519, 524 (2004) ("We have consistently applied the deliberate-elicitation standard in . . . Sixth Amendment cases. . . .").

76. 447 U.S. 264 (1980).

77. *E.g.*, Model Penal Code § 2.02(2)(c) ("A person acts recklessly . . . when he consciously disregards a substantial and unjustifiable risk [that incriminating statements] will result from his conduct").

the "intent" here relates not to the elicitation but to the creation of the circumstances in which the elicitation was likely to occur.

This broad, and seemingly improper, interpretation of "deliberate elicitation" was reinforced in *Maine v. Moulton*,[78] a case remarkably similar factually to *Massiah*. In *Moulton*, *M* and *C*[79] were indicted for theft and were released from custody pending trial. Unbeknownst to *M*, *C* agreed to cooperate with the prosecution and to testify against *M*.

C informed the police that *M* had suggested to him that a witness in the case ought to be killed. In order to obtain information regarding this proposed crime, the police received permission from *C* to install a recording device on his telephone. Thereafter, *M* telephoned *C* three times, during which conversations he commented on the pending theft charges.

In the last conversation, *M* asked *C* to meet with him to plan their defense in the theft case. *C* agreed and went to the meeting with a transmitter hidden on his body. During the conference, some of the discussion centered on *M*'s thoughts, by now discarded, about "eliminating" the witness, but most of the conversation "encouraged" by *C* involved the pending charges for which the Sixth Amendment applied. Specifically, *C* professed a bad memory and repeatedly asked *M* to "remind him" about the details of the theft. As a consequence, *M* made various incriminating statements about the crime.

The government sought to introduce statements made by *M* on the telephone as well as during his meeting with *C*. It argued that *Massiah* and *Henry* were distinguishable on the ground that, in those cases, the police set up the encounters with the defendants, whereas here it was *M* who initiated the telephone calls and meeting.[80]

The Supreme Court, per Justice William Brennan, disagreed. It stated that the Sixth Amendment right to counsel does not depend on the identity of the instigating party. Rather, the Sixth Amendment "guarantees the accused . . . the right to rely on counsel as a 'medium' between him and the State. . . . [T]his guarantee includes the State's affirmative obligation not to act in a manner that circumvents the protections accorded the accused by invoking this right."[81]

The Court agreed that the Sixth Amendment is not violated if the government obtains incriminating information from the accused "by luck or happenstance." But, it warned, "knowing exploitation by the State of an opportunity to confront the accused without counsel being present is as much a breach of the State's obligation . . . as is the intentional creation of such an opportunity."

Based, then, on the language of existing case law, "deliberate elicitation" for purposes of Sixth Amendment law occurs when the government through its overt or covert agent: (1) acts with the purpose of eliciting incriminating information from the accused regarding the pending charges, without regard to the likelihood that the elicitation will be successful (*Massiah*, *Williams*); (2) purposely sets up an encounter in which incriminating information is likely to be elicited (*Henry*); or (3) exploits an encounter set up by

---

78. 474 U.S. 159 (1985).

79. The last name of the surreptitious agent in *Moulton*—Colson—was the same as in *Massiah*, although the two Colsons were apparently unrelated. *Id.* at 172 n.8.

80. The government also argued that the statements were admissible because they were obtained during a legitimate investigation of the proposed murder, for which the Sixth Amendment clearly did *not* apply. This issue is considered at § 25.07[B], *infra*.

81. Maine v. Moulton, 474 U.S. at 176.

the accused with the agent of the government that it knows is likely to result in incriminating information (*Moulton*).

This being said, the essential Sixth Amendment language—the triggering activity—remains "deliberate elicitation." Although the Court has not expressly recanted the language quoted above in *Henry* and *Moulton*, it seems quite plausible that the currently constituted Supreme Court, which is less enamored of the *Massiah* right to counsel, will not apply the broad language found in those cases, and will only find "deliberate elicitation" when there is evidence of purposeful elicitation.[82]

[C] What Is "Elicitation"?

Massiah did not state that the government is barred from putting one of its agents in close proximity to an accused person, outside the presence of defense counsel. It only prohibited "deliberate elicitation" of incriminating statements. What, however, constitutes "elicitation"?

Massiah, Henry, and *Moulton* involved conversations by an informant with the accused.[83] *Brewer v. Williams* involved a speech given to the accused by a police officer.[84] In each of these cases, the Court ruled that the governmental conduct constituted "deliberate elicitation" of the ensuing incriminating remarks. Are there more subtle ways, however, for the government to elicit incriminating statements from an accused?

For example, is it permissible for the police to put *I*, an informant, in the accused's jail cell and instruct her as follows: "Pretend you are deaf and unable to communicate verbally. *D* is a blabbermouth, so just report anything that *D* says to you or others in your presence." If the agent follows these instruction—if she is a mere passive listener or "listening post"—is the Sixth Amendment violated, on the theory that the government "must have known" that "blabbermouth *D*" would talk?

The Court's answer came in *Kuhlmann v. Wilson.*[85] In the case, *I*, an informant, was placed in a jail cell with instructions to "keep his ears open," to avoid asking *W* any questions, and to report to the police any statements made by *W*. The trial court found that *I* followed these instructions. Subsequently, the prosecutor sought to introduce statements made by *W* to *I* in the jail.

The Supreme Court held that the Sixth Amendment is not violated by the placement of a police agent in a jail cell with a person against whom formal charges have been brought, as long as the government does not conduct "investigatory techniques that are the equivalent of direct police interrogation." According to *Wilson*, in order to prove a violation of the Sixth Amendment, "the defendant must demonstrate that the police and their informant took some action, beyond mere listening, that was designed deliberately to elicit incriminating remarks." As there was no evidence in the case of such affirmative conduct, the Sixth Amendment was not breached. *Wilson* is distinguishable from *Henry*,

---

82. It is worth observing that, in *Fellers v. United States*, 540 U.S. 519, 524 (2004), the Court quoted only the "deliberate elicitation" language, and not the broader text, of *United States v. Henry*, when it observed that "[w]e have consistently applied the deliberate-elicitation standard" in Sixth Amendment right-to-counsel cases.

83. The facts of *Massiah* are set out in §25.01[B], *supra*; for the facts in *Henry* and *Moulton, see* §25.05[B][2], *supra*.

84. *See* §25.05[A], *supra*, for the facts.

85. 477 U.S. 436 (1986).

because the informant in the latter case "stimulated" conversations with the accused, and from *Moulton*, where the informant asked the defendant questions to "refresh his memory."[86]

§ 25.06 Waiver of the Right to Counsel

[A] General Principles

There is no way for a person to waive her right to be free from police-initiated "interrogation" that she does not know is occurring.[87] Therefore, the issue of waiver does not come into play in the context of "secret interrogations," i.e., when an undercover agent deliberately elicits incriminating statements from an accused, as occurred in *Massiah v. United States*,[88] *United States v. Henry*,[89] and *Maine v. Moulton*.[90]

In all other circumstances, statements deliberately elicited by the government from an individual, in the absence of counsel, after formal adversary proceedings have commenced, are inadmissible in the prosecution's case-in-chief,[91] absent proof of a voluntary, knowing, and intelligent relinquishment of the Sixth Amendment right to counsel.[92] Difficulties arise, however, in determining what the police must do to obtain such a valid waiver, as the following materials suggest.

[B] The Court's First Waiver Case: *Brewer v. Williams*

In *Brewer v. Williams*,[93] W was arrested and arraigned in Davenport, Iowa, for the abduction of a young girl, believed to be dead, that occurred in Des Moines. W received *Miranda* warnings shortly after he was arrested, and twice more later. At his arraignment in Davenport, W spoke briefly to an attorney, who advised him to remain silent until he saw his Des Moines lawyer. W also spoke by telephone to his Des Moines counsel, who gave him the same advice. The police agreed not to question W while they transported him to Des Moines.

---

86. The facts in *Brewer v. Williams* suggest some lurking issues undeveloped by the Court in that case: W did not immediately respond to the "Christian burial speech" given in the police vehicle (*see* the text following Note 70, *supra*). Although the exact timing is unstated, seemingly some considerable time passed before W decided to speak about the whereabouts of the victim. Thus, the first question: Did the officer's deliberate conduct in fact *elicit* W's statements or were they a free will act of a conscience-stricken man that coincidentally followed the speech? Or, perhaps the burial speech triggered W's conscience, which in turn caused him to speak, but then the issue lurking in the "elicitation" area is the extent to which the concept of proximate causation—here, the accused's own reasons for "coming clean"—should inform the analysis.

87. United States v. Henry, 447 U.S. 264, 273 (1980).

88. 377 U.S. 201 (1964). *See* § 25.01, *supra*.

89. 447 U.S. 264 (1980). *See* § 25.05[B][2], *supra*.

90. 474 U.S. 159 (1985). *See* § 25.05[B][2], *supra*.

91. As for statements used for impeachment purposes, *see* § 25.07[C], *infra*.

92. Michigan v. Harvey, 494 U.S. 344, 348–49 (1990) (applying the test first announced in Johnson v. Zerbst, 304 U.S. 458 (1938)).

93. 430 U.S. 387 (1977).

On the trip, W told the officers in the car that he would talk to them about the crime after he arrived at his destination and spoke to his attorney. Nonetheless, an officer deliberately sought to elicit incriminating information from W by giving a so-called "Christian burial speech."[94] Later during the ride, presumably as the result of the officer's remarks,[95] W made incriminating statements and led the police to the body of the victim.[96]

The Supreme Court, per Justice Potter Stewart, held that W's incriminating statements to the police during the trip were obtained in violation of the Sixth Amendment. Adversary judicial proceedings had commenced against W, so his Sixth Amendment right to counsel had attached. The statements made were the result of deliberate elicitation (the Christian burial speech). And, although W could have waived his right to counsel, a valid waiver was not secured in this case.

Why was there no valid waiver here? The waiver had to be "knowing and intelligent," as well as voluntary. Wasn't it? W had been read his *Miranda* rights three times, so he knew that he had a right to assistance of counsel, and the Court agreed that he appeared to understand the warnings. Furthermore, the Court assumed that W's disclosures were voluntarily made, so there was no basis for contending that he was coerced to waive his right to counsel and talk.

The Court's simple answer to the question— "Why was there no valid waiver?"—was that there *had been no waiver at all*, valid or otherwise. The Court said that "waiver requires not merely comprehension but relinquishment, and [W's] consistent reliance upon the advice of counsel in dealing with the authorities refutes any suggestion that he waived that right." That is, W not only talked to his lawyers in both cities before he entered the police vehicle, but he told the officers in the car that he would tell them the whole story *after* he consulted with his Des Moines counsel.

However, W might have changed his mind after he heard the Christian burial speech. Does the Court's holding in *Williams* suggest, as Chief Justice Burger feared in dissent, that the Court "conclusively presumes a suspect is legally incompetent to change his mind and tell the truth until an attorney is present"?

The majority opinion did not go that far. It criticized the officers because, despite W's "express and implicit assertions of his right to counsel," the police sought to elicit incriminating statements without "prefac[ing] this effort by telling [W] that he had a right to the presence of a lawyer, and made no effort at all to ascertain whether [W] wished to relinquish that right." It would seem from this language that Justice Stewart meant that, once an accused asserts her right to counsel, a valid waiver *is* possible, but only if the officer reinforms the suspect of her right to counsel and secures an express waiver.

Concurring Justice Lewis Powell offered a different solution: A waiver could be obtained if the prosecutor proved that "police officers refrained from coercion and interrogation ... and that [W] freely on his own initiative ... confessed the crime." In short, under this approach, once an accused indicates a desire to talk to counsel, as

---

94. *See* § 25.05[A], *supra.*

95. *But see* Note 86, *supra.*

96. For a fascinating account of the facts regarding the crime, the Christian burial speech, and defense counsel's trial strategy, much of which is not evident in the Supreme Court opinion, *see* Phillip E. Johnson, *The Return of the "Christian Burial Speech" Case*, 32 Emory L.J. 349 (1983); Yale Kamisar, *Brewer v. Williams—A Hard Look at a Discomfiting Record*, 66 Geo. L.J. 209 (1977); *see also* Thomas N. McInnis, The Christian Burial Case (2001).

occurred here, police-initiated conversation about the crime should cease. As discussed immediately below, Justice Powell's "solution" prevailed, but only for a time.

[C] Seeking Waiver

At one time, in Sixth Amendment jurisprudence, the Supreme Court devised a specific rule to deal with those circumstances in which an accused person — one against whom formal adversary proceedings have commenced as to a specific crime — unambiguously requests the assistance of counsel. This rule has since been abolished, but it is useful to see how the law has evolved.

In *Michigan v. Jackson*,[97] the Court held that once the Sixth Amendment right to counsel attaches and the accused thereafter requests assistance of counsel, the government may no longer deliberately elicit information from her until she has consulted with her counsel, unless *she* initiates further communications, exchanges, or conversations with the government. In effect, the Court applied the protections announced in *Edwards v. Arizona*,[98] a *Miranda* waiver case, to the Sixth Amendment.

The facts of *Jackson* are significant to understanding the rule announced in that case — and the reason for its eventual demise. In *Jackson*, J was arraigned for murder. At the arraignment, the judge informed J of his right, as an indigent, to the appointment of counsel. J invoked the right. A notice of appointment of counsel was promptly mailed to a law firm. Before the firm received the notice, however, the police contacted J, read him his *Miranda* rights, and (after a valid *Miranda* waiver) questioned him. Although J asked several times about his lawyer, he never expressly asserted his right to counsel (Sixth Amendment or otherwise) during their questioning, and he answered their questions. The Supreme Court, per Justice John Stevens, held that the waiver was invalid because the police initiated the conversation — or "private interview," as Stevens has since described it[99] — after J had requested counsel at the arraignment.

Justice Stevens justified application of the Fifth Amendment *Edwards* rule in the Sixth Amendment context by stating that the "reasons for prohibiting the interrogation of an uncounseled prisoner who has asked for the help of a lawyer are even stronger after he has been formally charged with an offense than before." Once formal charges are brought — "and a person who had previously been just a 'suspect' has become an 'accused'" — a defendant is entitled "to rely on counsel as a 'medium' between him and the State."[100] In these circumstances, the Court concluded in *Jackson*, "the reasoning of . . . [*Edwards*] applies with even greater force. . . ."

Over time, however, *Jackson*'s vitality was undermined. Notwithstanding *Jackson*'s emphasis on the Sixth Amendment aspects of the case — and, indeed, the purported greater justification for the rule in the latter context — the Supreme Court subsequently stated that *Jackson*'s holding, although "based on the Sixth Amendment, . . . [has] its roots . . . in [the] Court's decisions in *Miranda* . . . , and succeeding cases."[101] And, just as *Edwards*

---

97. 475 U.S. 625 (1986).

98. 451 U.S. 477 (1981). *See* § 24.10[B][3][a], *supra*.

99. Michigan v. Harvey, 494 U.S. 344, 355 (1990) (dissenting opinion); Patterson v. Illinois, 487 U.S. 285, 302 (1988) (dissenting opinion).

100. Michigan v. Jackson, 475 U.S. at 632 (quoting Maine v. Moulton, 474 U.S. 159, 176 (1985)).

101. Michigan v. Harvey, 494 U.S. 344, 349–50 (1990); *see also* Texas v. Cobb, 532 U.S. 162, 175 (2001) (*Jackson* "was a wholesale importation of the *Edwards* rule into the Sixth Amendment")

is a prophylactic rule designed to enforce the *Miranda* doctrine, the Court began to characterize *Jackson* as a mere prophylactic rule, albeit one attached to the Sixth Amendment.[102] Then, in *Texas v. Cobb*,[103] Justice Kennedy (writing also for Justices Scalia and Thomas) characterized the "underlying theory" of *Jackson*—a case in which, it will be remembered, the accused had merely told a judge that, as an indigent, he wanted a lawyer to represent him—as "questionable." At a minimum, Kennedy suggested, "[e]ven if *Jackson* is to remain good law, its protections should apply only where a suspect has made a clear and unambiguous assertion of the right not to speak outside the presence of counsel, the same clear election required under *Edwards*."[104] And, *Cobb* further stated that "there is no 'background principle' of our Sixth Amendment jurisprudence establishing that there may be no contact between a defendant and police without counsel present."[105]

In 2009, the other shoe finally dropped. In *Montejo v. Louisiana*,[106] the Court, by a 5–4 vote, overruled *Jackson*. Over the strenuous dissent of Justice Stevens, *Jackson*'s author, the Court, per Justice Scalia, emphasized that *Jackson* had imported *Edwards*, a prophylactic rule from *Miranda* jurisprudence, in order (like *Edwards*) to prevent police badgering of suspects. But, Justice Scalia stated, as this protection from badgering is already guaranteed by *Edwards*, the *Jackson* prophylactic rule provides little additional protection.[107] And, the Court explained, "[w]hen [it] creates a prophylactic rule in order to protect a constitutional right, the relevant 'reasoning' is the weighing of the rule's benefits against its costs."[108] As the majority analyzed it, the *Jackson* rule's "marginal benefits" (beyond what *Miranda-Edwards* already provides) are "dwarfed by its substantial costs (viz., hindering 'society's compelling interest in finding, convicting, and punishing those who violate the law')."[109]

So, where does this leave the law after *Montejo*? From a *Sixth Amendment* perspective, government agents are no longer barred from approaching an accused in order to seek waiver of her Sixth Amendment right to counsel. This is true even if the accused has informed a magistrate of her desire for an attorney. If the accused is in custody at the time and, therefore, properly informed of her *Miranda* rights, she may either assert her *Miranda* right to counsel (in which case the *Edwards* rule applies, and interrogation must cease on that ground) or she may voluntarily and knowingly waive her *Miranda* rights. And, crucially, the Supreme Court held in *Patterson v. Illinois*[110] that an accused's valid waiver of her *Miranda* right to counsel serves, as well, as a valid waiver of her Sixth Amendment right to counsel.

(concurring opinion of Kennedy, J.).

102. Michigan v. Harvey, 494 U.S. 344 (1990).

103. 532 U.S. 162 (2001).

104. *Id.* at 176.

105. *Id.* at 171 n.2 (2001).

106. 556 U.S. 778 (2009). *Contra under state constitution*, State v. Bevel, 745 S.E.2d 257 (W.Va. 2013) (retaining the rule of *Michigan v. Jackson* under the state constitution).

107. The Court acknowledged that *Edwards* only applies when *Miranda* applies, namely, when the suspect is in custody, whereas the Sixth Amendment right to counsel also applies when an accused is not in custody. Therefore, to that extent, *Jackson*'s overruling denies to some persons the bright-line benefits of that case. Justice Scalia stated that such "uncovered situations are the *least* likely to pose a risk of coerced waivers. When a defendant is not in custody, he is in control, and need only shut his door or walk away to avoid police badgering." *Montejo*, 556 U.S. at 795.

108. *Id.* at 793.

109. *Id.* (quoting Moran v. Burbine, 475 U.S. 412, 426 (1986)).

110. 487 U.S. 285 (1988). *See* § 25.06[D][2], immediately *infra*, for more details.

What if the accused already has a lawyer and a police officer (or prosecutor) confronts the accused and seeks to interrogate her while the lawyer is absent? The Court acknowledged in this situation that the American Bar Association's *Model Rule 4.2 of Professional Conduct* mandates that a lawyer not communicate "about the subject of [a] representation with a party the lawyer knows to be represented by another lawyer in the matter, unless the lawyer has the consent of the other lawyer or is authorized to do so by law or a court order." Nonetheless, Justice Scalia wrote, "the Constitution does not codify the ABA's Model Rules, and does not make investigating police officers lawyers."[111] *Montejo* teaches that "[t]he defendant may waive the right [to counsel] whether or not [s]he is already represented by counsel; the decision to waive need not itself be counseled."

[D] Elements of a Valid Waiver

[1] "Voluntary"

The Supreme Court has not been called upon yet to determine what constitutes a voluntary waiver of the Sixth Amendment right to counsel in the post-*Montejo* context, but it will almost certainly look to its *Miranda* jurisprudence, which in turn is based on general due process concepts of voluntariness.[112]

[2] "Knowing and Intelligent"

The Sixth Amendment requirement that a waiver be "knowing and intelligent" is similar to the waiver rule with *Miranda* rights. According to *Patterson v. Illinois*,[113] at least when the accused is aware (as *P* was in *Patterson*) that formal proceedings have commenced against her,[114]

> [a]s a general matter, . . . an accused who is admonished with the warnings prescribed by . . . *Miranda*, . . . has been sufficiently apprised of the nature of his Sixth Amendment rights, and of the consequences of abandoning those rights, so that his waiver on this basis will be considered a knowing and intelligent one.[115]

According to *Patterson*, *Miranda* warnings convey "the sum and substance" of the Sixth Amendment right to counsel. The warnings inform the accused that she has the right to have a lawyer appointed prior to questioning and to have counsel present during questioning. The warnings also inform her of the "ultimate adverse consequence" of foregoing the right to counsel, namely that any statement she makes can be used against

---

111. *Montejo*, 556 U.S. at 790. Presumably, however, a *prosecutor*, as distinguished from a police officer, who approached a counseled defendant would be subject to ethical constraints, but even if she violated an ethical canon, the Constitution would not be violated and, consequently, any statement received by the prosecutor would not be barred from use at trial.

112. *See* §§ 24.10[A][3][b] (*Miranda*), and 22.02 (due process), *supra*.

113. 487 U.S. 285 (1988).

114. The Court stated that "we do not address the question whether or not an accused must be told that he has been indicted before a postindictment Sixth Amendment waiver will be valid." *Id.* at 296 n.8.

115. *Contra, under the state constitution*, State v. Sanchez, 609 A.2d 400 (N.J. 1992) (the "perfunctory recitation" of *Miranda* warnings does not provide sufficient information to the accused to make a knowing and intelligent waiver of the Sixth Amendment right to counsel).

her. And, the warnings tell her what a lawyer can do for her, "namely, advise [the accused] to refrain from making any such statements."

Justice Stevens, with whom Justices Brennan and Marshall joined, dissented. They argued that the defense lawyer's role after adversary proceedings have begun is more multi-dimensional than the majority suggested. To the dissenters, therefore, *Miranda* warnings inadequately inform an accused of the implication of giving up the Sixth Amendment right to counsel, as distinguished from the *Miranda* right to counsel. For example, the dissent argued, *Miranda* warnings do not convey the fact "that a lawyer might examine the indictment for legal sufficiency before submitting . . . her client to interrogation or that a lawyer is likely to be more skillful in negotiating a plea bargain and that such negotiations may be most fruitful if initiated prior to any interrogation."

§ 25.07 Scope of the Sixth Amendment Exclusionary Rule[116]

As already noted,[117] it is presumed that a person must have personal standing to raise a Sixth Amendment right-to-counsel claim. The following discussion, therefore, assumes that a defendant has the requisite standing.

[A] Right or Remedy?

It is sometimes necessary to distinguish between a constitutional *right* and the *remedy* for violation of the right. Thus, with the Fourth Amendment, the exclusionary rule is now treated as a judicially created remedy for a violation of the constitutional right to be free from unreasonable searches and seizures; it is not a constitutional right of its own.[118] As such—as a judicially created remedy—the Supreme Court may narrow the Fourth Amendment exclusionary rule, or even permit its abolition if a suitable alternative remedy is recognized. With the Due Process Clause and the Self-Incrimination Clause, however, exclusion at trial of the involuntarily obtained, or compelled, testimony is either *a* core, or *the* core, constitutional right itself.[119] *These* exclusionary rules cannot be judicially abolished.

What about the Sixth Amendment right to counsel? For a long time what the Court had to say on the subject was inconsistent. In *Massiah v. United States*,[120] Justice Stewart stated that the accused, "was denied the basic protections of that [Sixth Amendment] guarantee when there was used against him at his trial evidence of his own incriminating words." The implication here is that the Sixth Amendment right to counsel is violated when the uncounseled statement is used at trial, and perhaps not before. In contrast, in

---

116. *See generally* Gardner, Note 2, *supra*; Arnold H. Loewy, *Police-Obtained Evidence and the Constitution: Distinguishing Unconstitutionally Obtained Evidence from Unconstitutionally Used Evidence*, 87 Mich. L. Rev. 907 (1989); James J. Tomkovicz, *The Massiah Right to Exclusion: Constitutional Premises and Doctrinal Implications*, 67 N.C. L. Rev. 751 (1989).

117. *See* § 25.02, *supra*.

118. *See* § 20.03, *supra*.

119. *See* §§ 22.03[C][2] (due process), 23.05[B][3][a] (self-incrimination), *supra*.

120. 377 U.S. 201 (1964).

Maine v Moulton,[121] the justices stated that "[t]he Sixth Amendment protects the right of the accused not to be confronted by an agent of the State. . . . This right [is] violated as soon as the State's agent engage[s] [D] in conversation about the charges pending against him." According to this reading, therefore, the Sixth Amendment is violated at the moment of deliberate elicitation.

In *Kansas v. Ventris*,[122] the Supreme Court, per Justice Scalia, resolved the issue:

> [W]e conclude that the *Massiah* right is a right to be free of uncounseled interrogation, and is infringed at the time of the interrogation. That, we think, is when the "Assistance of Counsel" is denied. [¶] . . . A defendant is not denied counsel merely because the prosecution has been permitted to introduce evidence of guilt—even evidence so overwhelming that the attorney's job of gaining an acquittal is rendered impossible. In such circumstances the accused continues to enjoy the assistance of counsel; the assistance is simply not worth much. The assistance of counsel has been denied, however, at the prior critical stage which produced the inculpatory evidence. . . . It is *that* deprivation which demands a remedy.[123]

One implication of this analysis is that a person whose Sixth Amendment right to counsel is violated pretrial may sue the government for violation of her constitutional rights, whether or not the uncounseled statement is ever used at her trial. Another implication—one that cuts *against* the defendant—is seen in subsection [C] below.

[B] When the Police Investigate "Sixth Amendment" and "Non-Sixth Amendment" Offenses

The Sixth Amendment is offense-specific. Therefore, as previously explained in detail,[124] from a Sixth Amendment perspective the police may interrogate *D*, who is under indictment for Offense 1, regarding any or all uncharged separate offenses of which they suspect *D*. And statements made by *D* regarding a formally *uncharged* offense—call it Offense 2—is admissible against her in any subsequent prosecution for *that* offense.

Suppose, however, in *D*'s interrogation, she provides the police with incriminating statements regarding *both* indicted Offense 1 *and* uncharged Offense 2. May the government say that they were only seeking information about Offense 2, which they had a right to do, and therefore should be permitted to use the "inadvertent" statement they obtained from *D* regarding Offense 1? Or, suppose the government concedes (or the court finds) that their interrogation had dual purposes, improperly to obtain information on Offense 1 *and* properly to secure statements about Offense 2?

The Court observed in *Maine v. Moulton*:[125]

> To allow the admission of evidence obtained from the accused in violation of his Sixth Amendment rights whenever the police assert an alternative, legitimate reason for their surveillance invites abuse by law enforcement personnel

---

121. 474 U.S. 159 (1985).
122. 556 U.S. 586 (2009).
123. *Id*. at 592.
124. *See* § 25.04, *supra*.
125. 474 U.S. 159, 180 (1985).

in the form of fabricated investigations and risks the evisceration of the Sixth Amendment right recognized in *Massiah*. On the other hand, to exclude evidence pertaining to charges as to which the Sixth Amendment right to counsel had not attached at the time the evidence was obtained, simply because other charges were pending at that time, would unnecessarily frustrate the public's interest in the investigation of criminal activities.

The *Moulton* Court took the "more realistic view of police investigations" that "dual purposes may exist whenever police have more than one reason to investigate someone." Therefore, in such circumstances, *Moulton* provides that "incriminating statements pertaining to pending charges are inadmissible at the trial of those charges, notwithstanding the fact that the police were also investigating other crimes if, in obtaining this evidence, the State violated the Sixth Amendment by knowingly circumventing the accused's right to the assistance of counsel."[126] At the same time, incriminating statements regarding a crime for which the Sixth Amendment has *not* attached are *admissible*, even though the latter evidence might be considered a fruit of a constitutional violation.

[C] Use of Evidence for Impeachment Purposes

May a statement obtained from the accused in violation of the Sixth Amendment, although inadmissible at her trial in the prosecutor's case-in-chief, be introduced for impeachment purposes, if she testifies in a manner inconsistent with the excluded statement?[127]

The Supreme Court held in *Kansas v. Ventris*[128] that a statement obtained from a defendant in violation of her Sixth Amendment right to counsel is, nonetheless, admissible to impeach her inconsistent testimony at trial. Quoting the language and reasoning of its Fourth Amendment case law in this regard, the Court stated that "[i]t is one thing to say that the Government cannot make an affirmative use of evidence unlawfully obtained. It is quite another to say that the defendant can . . . provide himself with a shield against the contradiction of his untruths."[129]

The Court balanced the costs and benefits of applying the exclusionary rule in this context. On the one side are the truth-testing benefits of the adversary process, which would be frustrated if the statement could not be used to impeach the defendant's alleged "untruths" at trial. On the other side of the equation is the deterrent value of the exclusionary rule. As to this the *Ventris* Court stated that there would be "little appreciable deterrence" in excluding the statement for impeachment purposes. It reasoned that

---

126. What constitutes a *knowing* circumvention of the accused's right to counsel? The Court has not answered this question in this context. For example, what if the police only question *D* about Offense 2 and are genuinely surprised when *D*'s answer includes statements relevant to Offense 1? Seemingly, this is not a *knowing* circumvention of *D*'s right to counsel and, therefore, it would follow that the police might be able to use the statement against *D*. On the other hand, the Supreme Court might prefer to avoid the near-impossible effort of divining an interrogator's knowledge or purpose and conclude that there is a knowing circumvention if an interrogator is aware that her questioning might lead to statements about Offense 1.

127. For the answer to this question in the context of the Fourth Amendment, *see* § 20.05[B][2] [b], *supra*; regarding *Miranda* violations, *see* § 24.12[A], *supra*; regarding the Due Process Clause, *see* §§ 22.03[C][2][a]; and *see* § 23.05[B][3][b][I] for discussion of the privilege against self-incrimination.

128. 556 U.S. 586 (2009).

129. *Id.* at 593 (quoting Walder v. United States, 347 U.S. 62, 65 (1954)).

a police officer's incentive to obey the Sixth Amendment is her knowledge that statements obtained unconstitutionally will be inadmissible in the prosecutor's case-in-chief; "the *ex ante* probability that evidence gained in violation of *Massiah* would be of use for impeachment is exceedingly small."

[D] Fruit-of-the-Poisonous-Tree Doctrine

The fruit-of-the-poisonous-tree doctrine[130] applies to violations of the Sixth Amendment right to counsel, which means that the limitations on the rule— the independent source doctrine, the inevitable discovery rule, and the attenuated connection principle— also apply, although the Supreme Court has only infrequently considered the basic doctrine or its limitations in the Sixth Amendment context.

The inevitable discovery rule was expressly recognized in the Sixth Amendment context in *Nix v. Williams*,[131] a follow-up case to *Brewer v. Williams*.[132] In *Williams II*, the issue was whether the body of the victim found by the police as the result of their use of the Christian burial speech was inadmissible as a fruit of the initial Sixth Amendment violation. The Court held that the victim's body could be used in *W*'s trial because the prosecutor proved by a preponderance of the evidence "that the information [including forensic tests on the body] ultimately or inevitably would have been discovered by lawful means." The Court found no reason in this case to treat the inevitable discovery doctrine differently in the Sixth Amendment context than it would have done had there been a Fourth Amendment violation instead.

§ 25.08 Right-to-Counsel Summary: Sixth Amendment versus *Miranda*

How does the Sixth Amendment right to counsel differ from the *Miranda* right to counsel? Supreme Court winds have blown hot and cold in regard to this question. It has observed that "the policies underlying the two constitutional protections are quite distinct,"[133] and it has had occasion to warn that *Miranda* jurisprudence is not always informed by the Court's Sixth Amendment case law.[134] Indeed, the Supreme Court once conceded[135] that many courts and commentators had the impression that the Sixth Amendment version of the right to counsel is stronger, i.e., that it is a more difficult right to relinquish, than its *Miranda* cousin.

Particularly in recent years, however, the Court has denied the latter assertion. It has stated that it "never suggested that one right is 'superior' or 'greater' than the other,"[136] and it has sometimes merged its discussion of the two rights, as if the role of defense counsel were precisely the same, before and after the prosecution commences.

---

130. *See generally* § 20.08, *supra*.
131. 467 U.S. 431 (1984).
132. 430 U.S. 387 (1977). *See* § 25.05[A], *supra*.
133. Rhode Island v. Innis, 446 U.S. 291, 300 n.4 (1980).
134. *Id.*
135. Patterson v. Illinois, 487 U.S. 285, 297 (1988).
136. *Id.*

Nonetheless, some differences exist between the two rights. In some circumstances, the *Miranda* right to counsel may apply when the Sixth Amendment does not, and vice-versa. The following is a checklist of key areas in which the Court has recognized differences between the Sixth Amendment and *Miranda* rights to counsel.

1. Regarding when the right attaches:

First, the Sixth Amendment right applies only after adversary judicial criminal proceedings have been initiated against the accused; the *Miranda* right to counsel is not so limited, so it may attach earlier.

Second, it follows from the first point, that once the Sixth Amendment right to counsel is triggered (by formal adversarial proceedings), this right applies whether or not the accused is in custody, whereas the *Miranda* right applies to *custodial* interrogation. Therefore, the Sixth Amendment right can apply in situations where *Miranda* does not apply.

Third, the Sixth Amendment right is offense-specific (it only applies to the offense(s) for which criminal proceedings have commenced), whereas the *Miranda* right to counsel applies to all offenses, once custodial interrogation commences. Therefore, *Miranda* potentially applies to more offenses than does the Sixth Amendment.

Fourth, *Miranda* applies when the custodial suspect is "interrogated," whereas the Sixth Amendment prohibits "deliberate elicitation." The terms are not always equivalent. The *Miranda* version of interrogation focuses on the suspect, and the test is an objective one based on a finding of negligence by the officer; the Sixth Amendment right focuses on the intentions of the officer, and requires proof of deliberate misconduct, although the requisite "deliberate elicitation" has been found under circumstances approaching recklessness.

Fifth, the Sixth Amendment applies to deliberate elicitation by undercover agents. In contrast, *Miranda* does not apply to interrogation by undercover agents.

2. Regarding waiver of the right:

Under *Miranda*, the police must cease interrogation of a custodial suspect who requests a lawyer until the lawyer is present (and a waiver is obtained at that time), unless the suspect herself initiates communications with the police about the crime. No such rule now exists in regard to the Sixth Amendment.

3. Regarding the exclusionary rule:

Fruit-of-the poisonous-tree principles apply to Sixth Amendment violations. The doctrine does not exist or is far more limited in the *Miranda* context.

Chapter 26

Eyewitness Identification Procedures

§ 26.01 Eyewitness Identification: The Problem and Potential Safeguards[1]

[A] The Problem

[1] Overview of the Problem

Eyewitness misidentification of suspects has long been recognized as one of the most serious problems in the administration of justice. In 1967, in *United States v. Wade*,[2] the Supreme Court warned that "[t]he vagaries of eyewitness identification are well known," and "the annals of criminal law . . . rife with instances of mistaken identifications." And, in the Court's most recent pronouncement on eyewitness identification procedures,[3] the justices cited a brief of the petitioner, which in turn "cit[ed] studies showing that eyewitness misidentifications are the leading cause of wrongful convictions." The Court reiterated that "[w]e do not doubt . . . the fallibility of eyewitness identifications."

There are ample studies to support the Court's observations. A survey in 1932 reported that among 65 cases in which innocent persons were convicted, 29 of the improper verdicts were attributed to improper eyewitness identification.[4] Another study of wrongful convictions in the late 1980s estimated that eyewitness misidentifications accounted for 52 percent of the cases surveyed.[5]

Two more recent studies demonstrate that misidentifications remain a serious and common problem. A 2005 survey of all reported exonerations of convicted defendants between 1989 and 2003 (totaling 340) concluded that "[t]he most common cause of

---

1. *See generally* Elizabeth Loftus, Eyewitness Testimony (1979); Brandon L. Garrett, *Judging Innocence*, 108 Colum. L. Rev. 55 (2008); Felice J. Levine & June Louin Tapp, *The Psychology of Criminal Identification: The Gap from Wade to Kirby*, 121 U. Pa. L. Rev. 1079 (1973); Steve Penrod & Brian Cutler, *Witness Confidence and Witness Accuracy: Assessing Their Forensic Relation*, 1 Psychol. Pub. Pol'y, and L. 817 (1995); Sandra Guerra Thompson, *Judicial Blindness to Eyewitness Misidentification*, 93 Marquette L. Rev. 639 (2009); Gary L. Wells, *Police Lineups: Data, Theory, and Policy*, 7 Psychol. Pub. Pol'y & L. 791 (2001); Gary L. Wells & Eric P. Seelau, *Eyewitness Identification: Psychological Research and Legal Policy on Lineups*, 1 Psychol. Pub. Pol'y, & L. 765 (1995); Fredric D. Woocher, Note, *Did Your Eyes Deceive You? Expert Psychological Testimony on the Unreliability of Eyewitness Identification*, 29 Stan. L. Rev. 969 (1977).

2. 388 U.S. 218, 228 (1967).

3. Perry v. New Hampshire, 132 S. Ct. 716, 728 (2012).

4. Edwin M. Borchard, Convicting the Innocent 3–5 (1932).

5. Arye Rattner, *Convicted but Innocent: Wrongful Conviction and the Criminal Justice System*, 12 Law & Hum. Behav. 283, 289 (1988).

wrongful convictions is eyewitness misidentification"; 64 percent of the wrongful convictions involved an eyewitness misidentification, including 90 percent of the rape cases.[6] And in a 2008 study of the first 200 persons exonerated by post-conviction DNA testing in the United States, all of whom had been convicted of either rape or murder, 79 percent were convicted with incorrect eyewitness testimony.[7]

Despite the severity of the problem, the Supreme Court has expended relatively little time devising constitutional safeguards against false convictions based on misidentification. Ironically, the Court has adopted far more rigorous rules, resulting in the exclusion of far more reliable evidence, in the search-and-seizure and police interrogation areas than it has in the identification field, where attention is needed.

[2] Details of the Problem

Some eyewitness misidentifications result from the intentional use of suggestive techniques by police officers, such as by displaying a suspect in a lineup with persons who do not look like him or fit the witness's description of the criminal.[8]

Most misidentifications, however, are attributable to conditions beyond the control of the police, namely, the "inherent unreliability of human perception and memory and . . . human susceptibility to unintentional, and often quite subtle, suggestive influences."[9] As two observers have summarized the research data, "people quite often do not see or hear things which are presented clearly to their senses, see or hear things which are not there, do not remember things which have happened to them, and remember things which did not happen."[10]

A person can simultaneously perceive only a limited number of stimuli from his environment, even if his attention level is high.[11] As a consequence, it is difficult for a witness to observe concurrently the height, weight, age, and other features of a suspect at the time of a crime. Reliability is further reduced because the encounter between the witness or victim and the criminal is often brief, in poorly lit conditions, and in highly stressful circumstances. There is also substantial evidence of unreliability in cross-racial

---

6. *See* Samuel R. Gross et al., *Exonerations in the United States 1989 through 2003*, 95 J. Crim. L. & Criminology 523, 542 (2005).

7. Garrett, Note 1, *supra*, at 60.

8. *E.g.*, Ludovic Kennedy, The Airman and the Carpenter 176–77 (1985) (describing a lineup in which *D*, a suspect in the kidnapping and murder of the Lindbergh baby, was identified; the police told *X*, an eyewitness to certain critical events, prior to the lineup that "we've got the right man," "[t]here isn't a man in this room who isn't convinced he is the man," and "don't say anything until I ask you if he is the man"; then, *D*, a short man, was placed "between two beefy, 6-foot [uniformed] New York policemen" for identification).

9. Woocher, Note 1, *supra*, at 970; *see also* Perry v. New Hampshire, 132 S. Ct. 716, 727 (2012), in which Justice Ginsburg, writing for eight members of the Court observed:

> [M]any . . . factors [beyond purposeful suggestive acts by the police] bear on "the likelihood of misidentification"—for example, the passage of time between exposure to and identification of the defendant, whether the witness was under stress when he first encountered the suspect, how much time the witness had to observe the suspect, how far the witness was from the suspect, whether the suspect carried a weapon, and the race of the suspect and the witness.

10. Levine & Tapp, Note 1, *supra*, at 1087–88.

11. *See id.* at 1096–97.

identification cases, i.e., in which a person of one racial group seeks to identify a perpetrator of a crime who is a member of a different racial group.[12]

Another serious problem is that people tend to see what they expect to see. A hunter looking for deer may identify the silhouette of a human being as a deer, even though a non-hunter nearby, observing the same moving figure, will realize it is a human being.[13] This phenomenon is aggravated by stereotyping and prejudice: "[I]n particularly complex or ambiguous situations, individuals will necessarily structure events to make them understandable, and in cases of ambiguity may be guided more by past experiences, needs, and expectations than by the stimuli themselves."[14] In such circumstances, a person may unconsciously "see" a person who fits the viewer's expectation of a criminal.[15]

Beyond the difficulties that arise from the original observation, human memory decays over time. Worse still, "memory . . . is an active, constructive process,"[16] that is, a person tends to fill in memory gaps with new "information." People have a psychological need to reduce uncertainty and to render consistent what is not; therefore, witnesses often unconsciously fill in memory holes with details that are inaccurate.

The police identification process itself can aggravate the situation. By its nature, a lineup "is a multiple-choice recognition test"[17] in which the eyewitness-participant often believes (or is led to believe) that there is no "none of the above" option. The effect of this is that the witness picks the "most correct answer," i.e., the person who most resembles his memory of the culprit.[18] Thus, in one study,[19] after a staged crime, eyewitnesses were asked to select the offender from a lineup in which the "wrongdoer" was absent. When the witnesses were warned that the culprit might not be in the lineup, misidentifications occurred in 33 percent of the cases; without the warning, the error rate was 78 percent.[20]

Witnesses are also subject to socio-psychological pressures that can render identifications untrustworthy. For example, a subtle comment or action by a police officer (the authority figure), such as a change in voice intonation or even the hint of a smile, may inadvertently suggest the "right" choice in a lineup.[21]

Small-group pressures also influence the process. If witnesses are in each other's presence during the identification process,[22] there is a significant risk that once a person is

---

12. *See generally* Sherri Lynn Johnson, *Cross-Racial Identification Errors in Criminal Cases*, 69 Cornell L. Rev. 934 (1984); *Special Theme: The Other-Race Effect and Contemporary Criminal Justice: Eyewitness Identification and Jury Decision Making*, 7 Psychol. Pub. Pol'y & L. 3–200 (2001); *see also* State v. Allen, 255 P.3d 784, 787 (Wash. App. 2011) (describing a cross-racial identification as an "especially problematic identification," and citing studies in support of this proposition).

13. Loftus, Note 1, *supra*, at 36–37.

14. Levine & Tapp, Note 1, *supra*, at 1108.

15. *Id.*

16. Woocher, Note 1, *supra*, at 983.

17. *Id.* at 986.

18. Loftus, Note 1, *supra* at 144.

19. R.S. Malpass & P.G. Devine, *Eyewitness Identification: Lineup Instructions and the Absence of the Offender*, 66 J. Applied Psychol. 482 (1981).

20. *See also* Siegfried L. Sporer, *Eyewitness Identification Accuracy, Confidence, and Decision Times in Simultaneous and Sequential Lineups*, 78 J. Applied Psychol. 22 (1993) (misidentifications occurred 39 percent of the time when eyewitnesses looked at photographs of suspects one at a time; the error rate rose to 72 percent when they were shown the same pictures together and, therefore, believed that they should pick the person who most looked like the culprit).

21. Woocher, Note 1, *supra*, at 988.

22. *E.g.*, Gilbert v. California, 388 U.S. 263 (1967) (*G* was identified in an auditorium containing about 100 witnesses).

identified as the perpetrator by some witnesses, others will feel an unconscious pressure to select the same individual. In turn, group uniformity in identification strengthens the resolve of each witness to stand by his identification.[23] Once the identification is made, a witness ordinarily substitutes in his mind the accused's image as it appeared at the lineup for the prior image of the criminal at the time of the offense.

Finally, all of these problems with identifications are aggravated by the fact that juries place a high value on eyewitness testimony. Witnesses who make eyewitness identifications are believed by jurors approximately 80 percent of the time, regardless of the accuracy of the identifications.[24] According to social scientists, "[j]urors appear to overestimate the accuracy of identifications . . . , do not distinguish accurate from inaccurate eyewitnesses, and are generally insensitive to factors that influence eyewitness identification accuracy."[25]

Consider one study[26] in which three sets of jurors in a mock robbery trial were presented the same evidence, with one exception. With the first set of jurors, there were no eyewitnesses. In the second version, one eyewitness was presented who identified the defendant, although the defense lawyer argued that the witness was mistaken. In the third case, the defense was able to show that the eyewitness had only 20/400 vision and was not wearing his glasses on the day of the crime. With the first jury (no eyewitness), only 18 percent of the jurors convicted the defendant; in the second case, 72 percent voted to convict; in the third case, the conviction rate only dropped to 68 percent, despite the highly doubtful nature of the eyewitness identification.

[B] Non-Constitutional Reform Measures

Social scientists have suggested ways to reduce, although not eliminate, the risk of misidentification. Gary Wells and Eric Seelau[27] have urged police departments to follow four rules in conducting lineups and photographic displays: (1) eyewitnesses should be informed by the police that the offender may not be in the lineup or photographic array; (2) the suspect should not stand out in the display; (3) in order to avoid conscious or unconscious prompting, identifications should be conducted by someone unaware of the identity of the suspect; and (4) if a witness identifies someone, he should be asked how certain he is of his choice before other information "contaminates" his judgment. The United States Department of Justice has published a training manual for police that incorporates some of their recommendations,[28] and some local police departments have begun using these materials.

Other reform efforts are underway. New Jersey is leading the way. In 2001, New Jersey became the first state in the nation to stop using traditional lineups. Under new guidelines, individuals are to be presented to witnesses one at a time (sequentially) through

---

23. Woocher, Note 1, *supra*, at 988–89.

24. Gary L. Wells, *Effects of Expert Psychological Advice on Human Performance in Judging the Validity of Eyewitness Testimony*, 4 Law & Hum. Behav. 275, 278 (1980).

25. Penrod & Cutler, Note 1, *supra*, at 822, 819–22 (summarizing studies).

26. Elizabeth F. Loftus, *The Incredible Eyewitness*, Psychol. Today, Dec. 1974, at 117–18 (as reported in Cindy J. O'Hagan, Note, *When Seeing is Not Believing: The Case for Eyewitness Expert Testimony*, 81 Geo. L.J. 741, 749–50 (1993)).

27. Wells and Seelau, Note 1, *supra*.

28. Nat'l Inst. of Justice, U.S. Dep't of Justice, *Eyewitness Evidence: A Trainer's Manual for Law Enforcement* (2003).

one-way mirrors. Eyewitnesses may no longer browse through photographs of suspects in "mug shot" books; the pictures are displayed sequentially. If a witness wants a second look, he is required to view all of the photographs a second time, and ordinarily the officer showing the photographs does not know who the suspect may be.[29] The Supreme Court of New Jersey, exercising its rule-making authority, has also ruled that, as a condition of the admissibility at trial of any out-of-court identification, the police must make a written record detailing the identification procedure, including the site where the identification occurred and the dialogue between the witness and police interlocutor. If the identification procedure occurs in a station house, where tape recorders may be available, "electronic recordation is advisable, although not mandated."[30] Furthermore, at the trial stage, the burden of proof regarding the reliability of eyewitness testimony shifts to the prosecutor if the defendant introduces any evidence of suggestiveness.[31]

The Connecticut Supreme Court has invoked its supervisory power to require police officers conducting identification procedures to inform eyewitnesses that the perpetrator of the crime may not be present. If such a warning is not provided, evidence of the eyewitness's identification of the defendant must be accompanied by a jury instruction stating that "psychological studies have shown" that failure to provide such a warning "increases the likelihood that the witness will select one of the individuals in the procedure, even when the perpetrator is not present," and that "such behavior on the part of the procedure administrator tends to increase the probability of misidentification."[32]

As well, an increasing number of appellate courts have ruled that trial courts have discretion to admit expert testimony on the general unreliability of eyewitness identifications, or on the risks inherent in the identification techniques used in the particular case.[33] And, the Supreme Court has favorably observed that "[e]yewitness-specific jury instructions . . . warn the jury to take care in appraising identification evidence."[34] Some

---

29. Gina Kolata & Iver Peterson, *New Way to Insure Eyewitnesses Can ID The Right Bad Guy*, N.Y. Times, July 21, 2001, at A1.

30. State v. Delgado, 902 A.2d 888 (N.J. 2006).

31. State v. Henderson, 27 A.3d 872 (N.J. 2011).

32. State v. Ledbetter, 881 A.2d 290 (Conn. 2005); *see also* State v. Dubose, 699 N.W.2d 582 (Wis. 2005) (deploring the use of "showups," in which a suspect is displayed one-on-one to the eyewitness, and recommending that "procedures similar to those proposed by the Wisconsin Innocence Project [be adopted by police] to help make showup identifications as non-suggestive as possible"; those recommendations include: showups not be conducted in locations, such as police stations or squad cars, or in a manner (e.g., handcuffed) that implies the suspect's guilt; a warning similar to that set out in *Ledbetter, supra*, should be given to the eyewitness; and the suspect should be shown to the witness only once). *See also* Commonwealth v. Crayton, 21 N.E.3d 157 (Mass. 2014) (abrogating prior law and holding that, where a trial witness has not participated before trial in an identification procedure, an in-court identification is deemed unnecessarily suggestive and, therefore, inadmissible unless there is good reason for its admission).

33. *E.g.*, State v. DuBray, 77 P.3d 247 (Mont. 2003) (holding that a trial court may not exclude expert testimony "when no substantial corroborating evidence exists" to support an eyewitness identification); State v. Copeland, 226 S.W.3d 287 (Tenn. 2007) (overruling itself because "times have changed," judges now have discretion to permit introduction of expert testimony on the issue of the reliability of eyewitness identifications); State v. Guilbert, 49 A.3d 705 (Conn. 2012) (departing from prior Connecticut Supreme Court decisions that "disfavored" eyewitness testimony on the grounds that "mistaken eyewitness identification is by far the leading cause of wrongful convictions.")

34. Perry v. New Hampshire, 132 S. Ct. 716, 728–29 (2012); *e.g.*, State v. Cabagbag, 277 P.3d 1027 (Hawaii 2012) (a trial court is required to grant a defendant's request to give a cautionary instruction on the unreliability of eyewitness testimony); State v. Cromedy, 727 A.2d 457 (N.J. 1999) (in a case in which a defendant's guilt is based almost exclusively on cross-racial identification by an

scholars have also called for courts to tighten up their evidentiary standards of reliability in determining whether to admit eyewitness identification, and hold that unreliable evidence is inadmissible under the rules of evidence.[35]

A few federal constitutional safeguards exist. They are discussed below.

§ 26.02 Corporeal Identification Procedures: Right to Counsel[36]

[A] Rule

Pursuant to the so-called *Wade-Kirby*[37] doctrine discussed below, a person has a Sixth Amendment constitutional right to counsel at any "corporeal identification procedure"[38] conducted after, but not before, he has been indicted or other formal adversary judicial criminal proceedings have commenced against him.[39] For shorthand, this rule may be described as providing an accused a constitutional right to counsel at all "post-indictment" lineups.

Unless counsel is present at the post-indictment lineup, or the lawyer's presence is waived by the accused,[40] the prosecutor may not present evidence at trial of the results of the pretrial post-indictment identification procedure. That is, if *W* identifies *D* at a post-indictment lineup at which *D* was denied assistance of counsel, neither *W* nor anyone else may testify at trial regarding the results of the lineup.

Furthermore, if the accused is denied counsel at the lineup, the prosecutor is prohibited from obtaining an *in*-court identification of the accused by the witness, unless the prosecutor proves by clear and convincing evidence that the in-court identification is not a fruit of the tainted out-of-court procedure.[41] Among the factors that a trial court may consider in determining whether the prosecutor has met his burden of proof in this regard are those listed as examples by the Supreme Court:

> [The trial court may consider] the prior opportunity [of the witness] to observe the alleged criminal act, the existence of any discrepancy between any pre-lineup description and the defendant's actual description, any identification prior to lineup of another person, the identification by picture of the defendant prior to

---

eyewitness, the accused is entitled as a matter of law to a jury instruction on the pitfalls of such identifications).

35. *See, e.g.,* Sandra Guerra Thompson, Daubert *Gatekeeping for Eyewitness Identifications*, 65 SMU L. Rev. 593 (2012).

36. Joseph D. Grano, *Kirby, Biggers and Ash: Do Any Constitutional Safeguards Remain Against the Danger of Convicting the Innocent?*, 72 Mich. L. Rev. 719 (1974).

37. United States v. Wade, 388 U.S. 218 (1967); Kirby v. Illinois, 406 U.S. 682 (1972).

38. A "corporeal" identification procedure is one in which a suspect is physically presented to an eyewitness for identification. Typically, this is done by displaying the suspect in a lineup or by bringing him to the victim or eyewitness for a one-on-one confrontation.

39. For a definition of "adversary judicial criminal proceedings," *see* § 25.03, *supra*.

40. The waiver is valid if he voluntarily, knowingly, and intelligent relinquishes his right to counsel. *See* Johnson v. Zerbst, 304 U.S. 458 (1938).

41. *Wade*, 388 U.S. at 241.

the lineup, failure to identify the defendant on a prior occasion, and the lapse of time between the alleged act and the lineup identification.[42]

[B] How the Rule Developed

[1] The Start: *United States v. Wade*

The Supreme Court first considered the applicability of the Sixth Amendment to eyewitness identifications in *United States v. Wade*,[43] a case involving a post-indictment lineup. Quoting from *Powell v. Alabama*,[44] a case relating to the right to counsel *at trial*, the *Wade* Court, per Justice William Brennan, stated that a person is entitled to the "guiding hand of counsel" at all critical stages of a criminal proceeding. Justice Brennan defined a "critical stage" as "any stage of the prosecution, formal or informal, in court or out, where counsel's absence might derogate from the accused's right to a fair trial." The Court determined that absent legislative or police reform of eyewitness identification procedures, the pretrial exhibition of a suspect to a witness for identification purposes is a critical stage of the prosecution because the process is "peculiarly riddled with innumerable dangers and variable factors which might seriously, even crucially, derogate from a fair trial."

The Court expressed concern regarding the inherent unreliability of eyewitness identifications and the fact that it is seldom possible for defense counsel, if he is absent when the identification occurs, to reconstruct the procedure in order to demonstrate at trial why the witness's identification should be discounted. Justice Brennan pointed out that the identity of the other persons in a lineup may not be known or divulged to defense counsel, and it is unlikely that either the eyewitness or the defendant will be sufficiently alert to the potential deficiencies of the process to be able to testify to any suggestive features of the lineup. As a result, counsel cannot conduct effective cross-examination of the eyewitness at trial. In passing, the Court also noted that "presence of counsel [at the lineup] itself can often avert prejudice and assure a meaningful confrontation at trial."

Justice White dissented from the Court's right-to-counsel holding. He criticized the majority for its "pervasive distrust of all official investigations," and its "treacherous and unsupported assumptions" that lineups are unreliable and that police misconduct is undiscoverable if counsel is not present. He accused the majority of basing its rule on the premise that "improper police procedures are so widespread that a broad prophylactic rule must be laid down." He also worried that the introduction of lawyers into the lineup process would hamper law enforcement. His remarks in this regard are considered in subsection [C] below.

[2] Turning Away from *Wade: Kirby v. Illinois*

In *Kirby v. Illinois*,[45] the police brought a robbery eyewitness to the police station where he identified *K*, who was sitting at a table with a police officer. This identification procedure occurred six weeks before *K* was indicted for the robbery. Speaking for the Court, Justice Potter Stewart refused to apply—or, as he put it, to "extend"—the *Wade*[46]

---

42. *Id.*
43. 388 U.S. 218 (1967).
44. 287 U.S. 45 (1932).
45. 406 U.S. 682 (1972).
46. United States v. Wade, 388 U.S. 218 (1967).

right-to-counsel rule to this one-on-one *pre*-indictment confrontation. He stated that the Sixth Amendment right to counsel does not apply to police conduct that occurs prior to the initiation of formal judicial proceedings. As most lineups occur before formal charges are brought, the practical effect of *Kirby* is to render the *Wade* right-to-counsel rule largely ineffectual.

Today, in view of a long line of Sixth Amendment cases in other contexts,[47] *Kirby's* formalistic line-drawing is not surprising, but it was at the time. Although *Wade* involved a post-indictment lineup, Justice Brennan stated in *Wade* that courts must "scrutinize *any* pretrial confrontation of the accused to determine whether the presence of his counsel is necessary to preserve the defendant's basic right to a fair trial. . . ."[48] The implication of this statement is that the right to counsel could apply in pre-indictment circumstances, and this was the interpretation of *Wade* by many pre-*Kirby* commentators and lower courts.[49] Indeed, Justice White, dissenting in *Wade*, believed that the rule applied to pre-indictment lineups.[50] Because he believed that *Kirby* was controlled by *Wade*, Justice White dissented as well in *Kirby*.

From a policy perspective, the line drawn in *Kirby* is unjustifiable. The risks inherent in lineups and other identification procedures are as substantial before formal charges are brought as they are after. If defense counsel is needed at a post-indictment lineup, he is also needed at a pre-indictment identification procedure. This policy argument, however, has given way to a constitutional textual argument: The Sixth Amendment applies to the "accused"—a term suggesting formal charges have been brought—in "all criminal *prosecutions.*"

[C] The Role of Counsel in the Identification Process

In his dissent in *Wade*, Justice White expressed concern that introduction of defense lawyers into the identification process would undermine the state's legitimate interest in conducting prompt and efficient investigations and would even make the process less trustworthy.

Justice White's prediction was based on the assumption that defense lawyers would play an active role at lineups. He expected the process to become adversarial. Attorneys would "hover over witnesses and begin their cross-examination then," menacing truthful factfinding as thoroughly as the Court fears the police now do." Furthermore, because the role of defense counsel in the adversary system is to represent one's client faithfully, Justice White expected that lawyers would now advise their clients how to behave at lineups, e.g., not to move or talk when requested, or even to recommend that they not appear in them. He predicted that defense lawyers would "suggest rules for the lineup[s] and . . . manage and produce [them] as best [they] can."

Justice White's reading of the majority opinion in *Wade* is overblown. The role of the defense attorney at the lineup, at least as it is described in the majority opinion, is less

---

47. *See* § 25.03, *supra*.

48. *Wade*, 388 U.S. at 227.

49. Joseph D. Grano, *A Legal Response to the Inherent Dangers of Eyewitness Identification Testimony* in Eyewitness Testimony: Psychological Perspectives (Gary L. Wells & Elizabeth F. Loftus eds., 1984), at 321.

50. In *Wade*, Justice White warned that the counsel rule announced in that case "applies . . . regardless of when the identification occurs, . . . and whether before or after indictment or information."

active than White assumes. Primarily, counsel is present so that he can later reconstruct the events and cross-examine the eyewitness at trial. He is an observer of the events, not a catalyst for change.

It is true that the majority in *Wade did* state, without explaining, that the "presence of counsel [at the corporeal identification procedure] itself can often avert prejudice." That probably means only that if a lawyer is present, the police have an additional incentive to make sure that the procedure is non-suggestive. Although there is nothing in *Wade* that suggests that a lawyer cannot make suggestions to the police to improve the procedure, there is also nothing in it that suggests that counsel has a right to be heard on such matters, much less that a lawyer's suggestions must be taken.

Intriguing questions remain. First, if the role of counsel is primarily one of observation, could a police department eliminate the constitutional need for post-indictment counsel by videotaping the lineup process?[51] Second, if Justice White's reading of *Wade* is correct—if defense counsel *may* actively participate in the lineup process—*should* he try to improve the quality of a lineup? If the lawyer succeeds in making the lineup more reliable, this may backfire, as he would have less basis for criticizing the identification at trial if his client is identified during the procedure. Yet, if counsel says nothing, does the defense effectively waive its right to object later to the process?

§ 26.03 Non-Corporeal Identification Procedures: Right to Counsel[52]

In *United States v. Ash*,[53] the Supreme Court held that, notwithstanding *United States v. Wade*,[54] a person against whom adversary judicial proceedings have been initiated is *not* entitled to assistance of counsel when the police display one or more photographs, including one of the accused, to an eyewitness to see if he can identify the culprit. According to *Ash*, such a non-corporeal display, although it occurs after indictment, is not a critical stage of the prosecution.

The Court explained in *Ash* that the primary purpose of the Sixth Amendment right to counsel is to provide counsel at trial, when the defendant is "confronted with both the intricacies of the law and advocacy of the public prosecutor." The right was extended to certain pretrial stages, *Ash* reasoned, once the criminal justice system became more intricate. In the case of post-indictment lineups, counsel was required because "the lineup offered opportunities for prosecuting authorities to take advantage of the accused. . . . Counsel present at [the] lineup would be able to remove disabilities of the accused in precisely the same fashion that counsel compensated for the disabilities of the layman at trial."[55]

Based on this reasoning, the *Ash* Court concluded that a photographic display is not a critical stage of the prosecution. According to the majority, "[s]ince the accused himself is not present at the time of the . . . display, and asserts no right to be present, . . . no

---

51. One court has so held. State v. Jones, 849 So. 2d 438 (Fla. App. 2003).
52. *See generally* Grano, Note 36, *supra.*
53. 413 U.S. 300 (1973).
54. 388 U.S. 218 (1967). *See* § 27.02[B][1], *supra.*
55. *Ash*, 413 U.S. at 312.

possibility arises that the accused might be misled by his lack of familiarity with the law or overpowered by his professional adversary."

The Court also rejected the assertion that the lawyer's presence at a photographic display is necessary to protect the accused's trial rights. It concluded that the risks inherent in this type of procedure are not "so pernicious" that special safeguards are required. Furthermore, because of the tangible nature of photographs, an absent defense attorney can adequately reconstruct the display in order to determine if it was suggestive.

Ash is a questionable decision. Photographic displays, like corporeal identification procedures, are inherently unreliable.[56] And, as the dissenters in *Ash* pointed out, unless counsel or his representative is present, there is no way to know if "inflection, facial expressions, physical motions, and myriad other almost imperceptible means of communication . . . intentionally or unintentionally . . . compromise[d] the witness' objectivity."

§ 26.04 Identification Procedures: Due Process of Law[57]

The Due Process Clause requires the exclusion at trial of evidence of a pretrial identification of the defendant if, based on the totality of the circumstances, the police procedure used to obtain the identification was: (1) unnecessarily suggestive; and (2) conducive to mistaken identification.[58] This rule applies regardless of whether the identification was corporeal or non-corporeal, occurred before or after formal charges were initiated, and whether or not counsel was present.

Moreover, in *Perry v. New Hampshire*,[59] the Supreme Court made explicit what was implicit in the previous eyewitness-identification cases, namely, that the Due Process Clause is *not* violated by an identification procedure, *no matter how suggestive or conducive to misidentification*, unless the "identification [is] infected by improper police influence."[60] The Court, per Justice Ginsburg, stated that "[w]hen no improper law

---

56. See § 26.01[B], *supra*.

57. *See generally* Timothy P. O—Toole & Giovanni Shay, *Manson v. Brathwaite Revisited: Towards a New Rule of Decision for Due Process Challenges to Eyewitness Identification Procedures*, 41 Val. U. L. Rev. 109 (2006); Charles A. Pulaski, *Neil v. Biggers: The Supreme Court Dismantles the Wade Trilogy's Due Process Protection*, 26 Stan. L. Rev. 1097 (1974).

58. Stovall v. Denno, 388 U.S. 293 (1967); Neil v. Biggers, 409 U.S. 188 (1972). Recently, the Supreme Court "[s]ynthesizing previous decisions," described "the approach appropriately used to determine whether the Due Process Clause requires suppression of an eyewitness identification tainted by police arrangement": first, "due process concerns arise only when law enforcement officers use an identification procedure that is both suggestive and unnecessary"; and, second, "[e]ven when the police use such a procedure . . . suppression of the resulting identification is not the inevitable consequence." Instead, the Due Process Clause "requires courts to assess . . . whether [the] improper police conduct created a 'substantial likelihood of misidentification.'" Perry v. New Hampshire, 132 S. Ct. 716, 724 (2012).

59. 132 S. Ct. 716 (2012).

60. For example, in *Perry*, the police received a call at night from a citizen reporting that an African-American male was breaking into automobiles in an apartment parking lot. An officer who arrived discovered *P*, an African-American. between two parked cars holding a car stereo in his hands and a metal bat on the ground. Another officer went to the apartment building to talk to

enforcement activity is involved," evidence of the eyewitness's identification of the defendant is admissible; the defendant may then turn to nonconstitutional methods to demonstrate its unreliability, including "vigorous cross-examination" and "jury instructions on both the fallibility of eyewitness identification and the requirement that guilt be proved beyond a reasonable doubt."[61]

Looking, then, to the two-pronged Due Process Clause test, a defendant must first show, as a threshold matter, that the police procedure was unnecessarily suggestive. For example, in *Stovall v. Denno*,[62] S, an African-American male, was taken to the hospital the day after V, an eyewitness to the stabbing murder of her husband and also a stabbing victim, had undergone life-saving surgery. S was handcuffed to one of five white police officers. V identified S as the assailant.

The Court agreed that the procedure used was highly suggestive. It noted that the "practice of showing suspects singly to persons for the purpose of identification, and not as part of a lineup has been widely condemned." Nonetheless, due process was not offended, the Court explained, because the procedure used here was "imperative"—it was *necessarily*, not *unnecessarily*, suggestive—in that the police were unsure that V would survive the surgery to allow a later lineup. The Court did not explain why the police could not have conducted an in-hospital lineup or, at least, have included black non-suspects in the identification procedure.

However, even if an identification procedure *is* unnecessarily suggestive, due process is not necessarily violated. As the Court explained in *Manson v. Brathwaite*,[63] "reliability is the linchpin in determining the admissibility of identification testimony." Therefore, the ultimate issue to be determined is the likelihood that a misidentification has occurred as the result of the unnecessarily suggestive process. The relevant factors in determining reliability include:

> the opportunity of the witness to view the criminal at the time of the crime, the witness' degree of attention, the accuracy of the witness' prior description of the criminal, the level of certainty demonstrated by the witness at the confrontation, and the length of time between the crime and confrontation.[64]

If the *out*-of-court identification offends due process under the preceding analysis, it is barred at trial. In such circumstances, as well, no *in*-court identification by the

---

an eyewitness. When he asked for a more specific description of the suspect, the witness "pointed to her kitchen window and said the person she saw . . . was [now] standing in the parking lot [visible through the window, across the street] next to the police officer." There were reasons to be concerned about this identification, as noted by the trial court: (1) the parking lot was dark; (2) the suspect was standing next to a police officer; (3) the suspect was the only African-American male in the vicinity; and (4) the witness was later unable to pick P out of a photographic array. The trial court held that, despite these concerns, the Due Process Clause was not violated because the police did not arrange the suggestive identification procedure.

61. *Perry*, 132 S. Ct. at 721. Justice Ginsburg wrote that "[o]ur unwillingness to enlarge the domain of due process . . . rests, in large part, on our recognition that the jury, not the judge, traditionally determines the reliability of evidence." *Id.* at 728.

62. 388 U.S. 293 (1967).

63. 432 U.S. 98, 114 (1977); *contra, under the state constitution,* Commonwealth v. Johnson, 650 N.E.2d 1257 (Mass. 1995) (requiring per se exclusion of unnecessarily suggestive identifications, regardless of the reliability of the identification process); People v. Adams, 423 N.E.2d 379 (N.Y. 1981) (same).

64. Neil v. Biggers, 409 U.S. 188, 199–200 (1972).

witness is permitted unless the government proves that the out-of-court procedure did not create "a very substantial likelihood of *irreparable* misidentification."[65] In practice, however, trial courts rarely find that a police identification procedure offends due process, so *both* the pretrial and in-court identifications are allowed.

---

65. Simmons v. United States, 390 U.S. 377, 384 (1968) (emphasis added).

Chapter 27

Entrapment

§ 27.01 Entrapment: In General[1]

Entrapment is a criminal law defense. That is, like defenses such as insanity, duress, and self-defense, entrapment is pleaded by the defendant, and if the claim is adequately proved, she is acquitted. In short, a finding of entrapment does more than result in exclusion of evidence at trial—it bars the successful prosecution of the defendant.

Entrapment is not a constitutional doctrine. A police officer who entraps a citizen does not, by that fact alone, violate the Constitution. As a consequence, no jurisdiction is required to recognize the defense, although all of the states and the federal courts currently allow the claim;[2] and the definition of the defense and the procedural rules relating to it can and do vary by jurisdiction.

In general, there are two divergent approaches to the defense, frequently termed the "subjective" and "objective" tests of entrapment. Although the definition of entrapment depends on which test is used, both versions usually require proof that: (1) the defendant was induced to commit the crime by a government agent (typically, an undercover police officer); (2) the defendant or, at least, a hypothetical, average person, would not have committed the offense but for the inducement; and (3) the government agent acted as she did in order to obtain evidence to prosecute the defendant.

---

1. *See generally* Ronald J. Allen et al., *Clarifying Entrapment*, 89 J. Crim. L. & Criminology 407 (1999); Jonathan C. Carlson, *The Act Requirement and the Foundations of the Entrapment Defense*, 73 Va. L. Rev. 1011 (1987); Joseph A. Colquitt, *Rethinking Entrapment*, 41 Am. Crim. L. Rev. 1389 (2004); Anthony M. Dillof, *Unraveling Unlawful Entrapment*, 94 J. Crim. L. & Criminology 827 (2004); Paul Marcus, *The Development of Entrapment Law*, 33 Wayne L. Rev. 5 (1986); Roger Park, *The Entrapment Controversy*, 60 Minn. L. Rev. 163 (1976); Louis Michael Seidman, *The Supreme Court, Entrapment, and Our Criminal Justice Dilemma*, 1981 Sup. Ct. Rev. 111; Dru Stevenson, *Entrapment by Numbers*, 16 U. Fla. J.L. & Pub. Policy 1 (2005); Jessica A. Roth, *The Anomaly of Entrapment*, 91 Wash. U. L. Rev. 979 (2014).

2. Carlson, Note 1, *supra*, at 1013. Recent data indicate that entrapment cases are concentrated in a small number of states (California, Florida, Michigan, Ohio, Tennessee, Texas, Virginia, and Washington), and are declining overall throughout the country, having peaked in the 1980s and early 1990s. Stevenson, Note 1, *supra*, at 2, 16.

§ 27.02 Entrapment: The Subjective Test

[A] Rule

[1] In General

The Supreme Court recognized a federal court defense of entrapment for the first time in 1932 in *Sorrells v. United States*,[3] when Chief Justice Charles Evans Hughes, speaking for five members of the Court, allowed an entrapment defense based on what has come to be termed the "subjective" test of entrapment. The Court reaffirmed its support for the subjective version of the defense in *Sherman v. United States*[4] and *United States v. Russell*.[5]

As the Court has explained the subjective test, "[a]rtifice and stratagem may be employed to catch" criminals,[6] but a "different question is presented when the criminal design originates with the officials of the Government, and they implant in the mind of an innocent person the disposition to commit the alleged offense and induce its commission in order that they may prosecute."[7] In short, the Supreme Court distinguishes between the trap set for the "unwary criminal" (which is permitted) and for the "unwary innocent" (which is not).[8] Under the subjective test, entrapment is proved if a government agent induces an "innocent" person—a person *not* predisposed to commit the type of offense charged—to violate the law, so that she can be prosecuted.

[2] Proving Predisposition[9]

In the typical "subjective entrapment" prosecution, the critical issue is whether the defendant was predisposed to commit the offense charged. If she was not predisposed and yet committed the offense after contact with government agents, this is a matter of concern to the courts. As the Supreme Court explained in *Jacobson v. United States*,[10] "[w]hen the Government's quest for convictions leads to the apprehension of an otherwise law-abiding citizen who, if left to his own devices, likely would have never run afoul of the law, the courts should intervene."

Notwithstanding the preceding language in *Jacobson* and similar statements in other opinions, it is not the case that only an *entirely* law-abiding person can prevail with a claim of entrapment, although such a person provides the most attractive case.[11] It is

---

3. 287 U.S. 435 (1932).

4. 356 U.S. 369 (1958).

5. 411 U.S. 423 (1973).

6. *Sorrells*, 287 U.S. at 441.

7. *Sherman*, 356 U.S. at 372 (quoting *Sorrells*, 287 U.S. at 442).

8. *Id.* at 372–73.

9. *See generally* Damon D. Camp, *Out of the Quagmire After Jacobson v. United States: Towards a More Balanced Entrapment Standard*, 83 J. Crim. L. & Criminology 1055 (1993); Paul Marcus, *Presenting, Back From the [Almost] Dead, the Entrapment Defense*, 47 Fla. L. Rev. 205 (1996); Paul Marcus, *Proving Entrapment Under the Predisposition Test*, 14 Am. J. Crim. L. 53 (1987).

10. 503 U.S. 540 (1992).

11. In *Jacobson*, *id.*, the Court gratuitously described the defendant as "a 56-year-old veteran-turned-farmer, who supported his elderly father in Nebraska." Presumably this description was included to make the reader more sympathetic to the defendant, a purchaser of child pornography, whose conviction the Supreme Court reversed.

enough that the defendant was not predisposed to commit the type of offense for which she was prosecuted at the time the government first approached her. A life-long pickpocket, for example, is predisposed to commit minor larcenous acts, but is not by that fact alone disposed to commit, for example, drug offenses or murder. As to these latter offenses, she is a "non-predisposed" individual.

Predisposition may be proved at trial in various ways. First, the facts of the incident itself may demonstrate the defendant's "ready complaisance"[12] to commit the crime. For example, the prosecutor may point to the defendant's quick willingness to commit the offense, her ready knowledge of how to commit the crime, or her comments leading up to the offense that demonstrate her propensity to commit the crime.

Second, predisposition may be proved by reference to the defendant's character in the community prior to the time the government approached her. This is done by the prosecutor introducing evidence, in most other circumstances inadmissible at trial, of the defendant's bad reputation in the community and/or her prior criminal record, including arrests and convictions for related offenses.[13]

An example of predisposition is seen in *United States v. Russell*.[14] In *Russell*, an undercover federal agent met *R*, who was illegally manufacturing amphetamines, and stated that he represented an organization interested in controlling the manufacture and distribution of the drugs in the Pacific Northwest. The agent offered to supply *R* with a difficult-to-obtain chemical that was necessary in the production of the drug. *R* readily agreed to the arrangement. The Court held that entrapment was not proved, in view of *R*'s predisposition to commit drug offenses of the sort for which he was prosecuted.

Examples of non-predisposed persons are the defendants in *Sorrells v. United States*,[15] *Sherman v. United States*,[16] and *Jacobson v. United States*.[17] In *Sorrells*, *S* was prosecuted for violation of the National Prohibition Act after he sold a one-half gallon jug of whiskey to a government agent who posed as a tourist. *S* sold him the liquor, but only after three entreaties by the agent, who had befriended him by claiming to be a former member of the World War I military division in which *S* had served. The Court stated that *S* "had no previous disposition to commit [the criminal act] but was an industrious, law-abiding citizen . . . lured [by the agent] . . . to its commission by repeated and persistent solicitation . . ."

In *Sherman*, a government informer met *S* at a doctor's office where both men were being treated for narcotics addiction. After befriending *S*, the informer asked him if he knew of a good source of narcotics, and pleaded with *S* to supply him with the drugs. *S* turned him down various times before ultimately obtaining narcotics for the informer, based on the informer's "presumed suffering." The Court concluded that *S* was entrapped as a matter of law. It rejected the government's argument that *S* "evinced a 'ready complaisance' to accede" to the informant's request. Although *S* had previously

---

12. Sherman v. United States, 356 U.S. 369, 375 (1958) (internal quotation marks omitted).

13. On the other hand, there is some support for the proposition that a defendant is entitled to introduce evidence of prior *good* acts or conduct, including evidence of her *lack* of a criminal or arrest record, to *support* an entrapment claim. *E.g.*, United States v. Thomas, 134 F.3d 975 (9th Cir. 1998); Sykes v. State, 739 So. 2d 641 (Fla. App. 1999).

14. 411 U.S. 423 (1973).

15. 287 U.S. 435 (1932).

16. 356 U.S. 369 (1958).

17. 503 U.S. 540 (1992).

been convicted of drug-related offenses—thus, at one time he *was* disposed to commit drug crimes—the Court considered him to be non-predisposed at the time the government agent approached him for the first time: no evidence was presented that he was still in the drug trade; no narcotics were found in a search of his apartment; he did not seek profit from the sales; and his initial hesitancy to sell the drugs did not appear to be "the natural wariness of the criminal."

In *Jacobson*, the pertinent facts were these: In February, 1984, *J* ordered by mail and received two magazines (*Bare Boys I* and *Bare Boys II*) that contained photographs of nude pre-teen and teenage boys. Receipt of these magazines, which did not depict the youths in sexual activity, was lawful under then-existing federal and state law. A few months later, Congress passed the Child Protection Act of 1984, which prohibited the receipt by mail of sexually explicit depictions of children, such as those found in the *Bare Boys* magazines. Thereafter, various federal agencies began sophisticated operations intended to arrest violators of the new law.

J's name came to the government's attention after it obtained the mailing list from the bookstore that sold him the previously lawful *Bare Boys* magazines. Beginning in January, 1985, government agents sent mail to *J* through five fictitious organizations, such as the "American Hedonist Society." Some of the mailings promoted sexual freedom, expressed opposition to censorship, and called for statutory reform of the laws relating to sexually explicit materials. Two pieces of correspondence included "sexual attitude" surveys purporting to measure the recipient's enjoyment of various sexual materials. *J* responded to the surveys, indicating that he had a moderate level of interest in "pre-teen sex" and "preteen sex-homosexual" materials, but that he was opposed to pedophilia.

The government also sent *J*, again through a fictitious organization, a bogus list of "pen pals" with similar interests in sexual materials. When *J* failed to initiate correspondence with persons from the list, a government pen-pal wrote him instead. *J* answered twice before discontinuing the correspondence. In one letter he stated that he enjoyed "male-male items," although at no time did he mention child pornography.

In March 1987, *26 months after the government first targeted J*, a fictitious organization mailed *J* a brochure advertising photographs of young boys engaged in sex. *J* placed an order that was not filled, but shortly thereafter, he ordered another magazine from a second government-sponsored catalogue. *J* was arrested upon receipt of the magazine. In a subsequent search of *J*'s home, the government found the *Bare Boys* magazines purchased in 1984 and the materials sent to him from the government, but they discovered nothing else that suggested that *J* purchased or collected child pornography.

J asserted entrapment at trial. When asked why he purchased the illegal materials, he explained that "[w]ell, the statement was made [in the government correspondence] of all the trouble and the hysteria over pornography and I wanted to see what the material was." The jury rejected *J*'s entrapment claim.

The Supreme Court, 5–4, reversed *J*'s conviction. It ruled that as a matter of law the government failed to prove beyond a reasonable doubt that *J* was predisposed to purchase child pornography prior to being contacted by government agents. Consequently, although *J* "had become predisposed to break the law by May, 1987 [the date of purchase], . . . the Government did not prove that this predisposition was independent and not the product of the attention that the Government had directed at [*J*] since . . . 1985." In other words, *J was* predisposed to commit the offense when the government offered to sell him the magazines, but he was *not* so predisposed until after the government had "softened him up" for more than two years. As one writer has put it, the government did not prove "pre-predisposition."[18]

The Court considered the *lawful* purchase of the *Bare Boys* magazines as "scant if any proof of [J]'s predisposition to commit an illegal act. . . ." These purchases indicated "a predisposition to view sexually oriented photographs that are responsive to [J's] sexual tastes; but evidence that merely indicates a generic inclination to act within a broad range, not all of which is criminal, is of little probative value in establishing predisposition." As Justice White explained, "[e]vidence of predisposition to do what once was lawful is not, by itself, sufficient to show predisposition to do what is now illegal, for there is a common understanding that most people obey the law even when they disapprove of it."

Jacobson is a close case. Apparently, if the government had sold J child pornography as soon as it contacted him, a jury could properly have convicted him of the crime. Indeed, if the post-arrest search of J's house had turned up a stash of child pornography purchased from non-government sources over the years, J's conviction—even despite the government's entreaties—would probably not have been overturned.

What should the government have done differently? The Court hinted at an answer. It quoted favorably from the Attorney General Guidelines on FBI Undercover Operations, first announced in 1980, which provides that inducements should not be offered by federal officers unless "there is a reasonable indication . . . that the subject is engaging, has engaged, or is likely to engage in illegal activity of a similar type"—something like a "reasonable suspicion" standard relating to the individual being induced—or that "the opportunity for illegal activity has been structured so that there is reason for believing that persons drawn to the opportunity . . . are predisposed to engage in the contemplated illegal activity." The latter investigatory approach is one in which law enforcement agents devise a ruse that should only attract predisposed individuals, much like placing honey out so that the bees will come swarming.[19]

[B] Rationale of the Rule

The Supreme Court has justified the acquittal of persons induced to commit crimes by the government on the ground of legislative intent: "Congress could not have intended criminal punishment for a defendant who has committed all the elements of a proscribed offense, but was induced to commit them by the government."[20]

According to the Supreme Court, convictions in circumstances such as those set out in *Sorrells, Sherman,* and *Jacobson* can stand only if a court rests its interpretation of the applicable criminal statute "entirely upon the letter of the statute."[21] However, such a "[l]iteral interpretation of statutes at the expense of the reason of the law" results in "absurd consequences or flagrant injustice."[22] By passing specific criminal statutes, the Supreme Court has reasoned, Congress did not intend for the government to "use its resources

---

18. Camp, Note 9, *supra*, at 1083.
19. *E.g.*, People v. Watson, 990 P.2d 1031 (Cal. 2000) (in a sting operation to catch car thieves, the police left a vehicle in a parking lot, unlocked and with the keys in the ignition; held: no entrapment).
20. United States v. Russell, 411 U.S. 423, 435 (1973).
21. Sorrells v. United States, 287 U.S. 435, 446 (1932).
22. *Id.*

to increase the criminal population by inducing people to commit crimes who other-wise would not do so."[23]

[C] Procedural Features of the Rule

In "subjective entrapment" jurisdictions, the issue of whether the defendant was en-trapped is a question of fact, which is raised by the defendant at trial and resolved by the trier of fact, ordinarily the jury. The defendant is entitled to a jury instruction on the defense if she presents some evidence that government agents induced her to commit the offense. As this is a fairly easy standard to satisfy, the defense of entrapment typi-cally goes to the jury. Assuming that it does, the government must disprove entrapment beyond a reasonable doubt in the federal courts and in some states.

As with any other defense, a trial judge may refuse to submit the issue of entrapment to the jury, and may acquit the defendant, if there are no factual issues in dispute and entrap-ment exists as a matter of law, i.e., no reasonable juror could conclude that the defendant was *not* entrapped. However, if the defense goes to the jury, and the jury rejects it, the de-fendant can appeal, though a review of federal appellate decisions support the conclusion that the defense is "easy to raise and supremely difficult to establish as a matter of law."[24]

If the jury accepts the defense and acquits, double jeopardy forbids appellate review. And because an acquittal is non-appealable, jury nullification is possible when jurors finds the police techniques used against the defendant are especially outrageous.

§ 27.03 Entrapment: The Objective Test

[A] Rule

For more than three quarters of a century, the so-called "objective" version of the en-trapment defense has been defended by a minority of justices of the Supreme Court, and a majority of scholars who have written on the subject.[25] In *Sorrells v. United States*,[26] Justice Owen Roberts, speaking also for Justices Louis Brandeis and Harlan Stone, fa-vored an objective test. In *Sherman v. United States*,[27] Justice Felix Frankfurter wrote a four-justice concurrence in favor of the test. In *United States v. Russell*,[28] the objective test was favored again by four justices.

Whereas the subjective test primarily centers on the defendant—whether she was pre-disposed to commit the crime—the objective standard focuses more on police conduct. According to Justice Frankfurter in *Sherman*, entrapment occurs when the "the police conduct . . . falls below standards, to which common feelings respond, for the proper use of governmental power." As he explained the objective approach:

---

23. United States v. Hollingsworth, 9 F.3d 593, 598 (7th Cir. 1993) (opinion of Posner, J.), *aff'd en banc*, 27 F.3d 1196 (7th Cir. 1994).

24. Park, Note 1, *supra*, at 178 (footnote omitted). Although Professor Park's survey of the case law is quite dated, review of more recent appellate decisions does not suggest a different conclusion.

25. Regarding the attitudes of scholars, see Stevenson, Note 1, *supra*, at 2 (and cites therein).

26. 287 U.S. 435 (1932).

27. 356 U.S. 369 (1958).

28. 411 U.S. 423 (1973).

[The police] should act in such a manner as is likely to induce to the commission of crime only these persons [ready and willing to commit further crime should the occasion arise] and not others who would normally avoid crime and through self-struggle resist ordinary temptations. This test . . . [focuses on] the likelihood, objectively considered, that [the police conduct] would entrap only those ready and willing to commit crime.[29]

In evaluating police conduct according to the objective test, a court must consider how the police inducements would affect an individual. However, unlike the subjective test that focuses on the impact of police conduct on a specific person—the defendant—the question here is "whether, under the circumstances, the governmental activity would induce a hypothetical person not ready and willing to commit the crime to engage in criminal activity."[30]

The hypothetical person against whom the police conduct is measured apparently includes some of the characteristics of the actual defendant. For example, in *Sherman*, *S* was a drug addict in rehabilitation who distributed drugs to a government agent as a favor, and only after multiple pleas. The concurring justices believed that *S* was objectively entrapped as a matter of law. This view is hard to justify if the test is understood to be whether the police conduct would have caused an average law-abiding non-addict to supply illegal drugs. The justices' position is plausible, however, if the "hypothetical person" is described with *S*'s characteristics, as an addict seeking cure.[31]

[B] Rationale of the Rule

The objective standard is justified on grounds of judicial integrity and deterrence. The theme of judicial integrity was first expressed in the entrapment context by Justice Roberts in *Sorrells v. United States*,[32] when he stated that courts were obligated to enforce the defense in order to protect "the purity of its own temple."

Advocates of the objective standard argue, as well, that the acquittal of criminal defendants will deter egregious forms of police misconduct. For example, Justice Potter Stewart condemned the police conduct in *United States v. Russell*[33] on the ground that it was "precisely the type of governmental conduct that the entrapment defense is meant to prevent." Similarly, the drafters of the Model Penal Code justified their adoption of an objective standard of entrapment on the ground that "the attempt to deter wrongful conduct on the part of the government . . . provides the justification for the defense. . . ."[34]

[C] Procedural Features of the Rule

Many advocates of the objective test contend that the "objective entrapment" defense should be submitted to a judge rather than to the jury. They reason that courts, not

---

29. *Sherman*, 356 U.S. at 384.

30. People v. Jamieson, 461 N.W.2d 884, 891 (Mich. 1990); *see also* United States v. Russell, 411 U.S. 423, 434 (1973) (the question is whether the police conduct "might have seduced a hypothetical individual who was not . . . predisposed" to commit the crime).

31. Park, Note 1, *supra*, at 174.

32. 287 U.S. 435 (1932).

33. 411 U.S. 423 (1973). The facts of *Russell* are set out in the text following Note 14, *supra*.

34. American Law Institute, Model Penal Code and Commentaries, Comment to § 2.13, at 406–07 (1985).

jurors, should protect "the temple's purity," and that only through judicial opinions can appropriate police standards be developed. This is the approach followed by the Model Penal Code[35] and various states.[36] At least one state court has adopted a hybrid approach: A defendant must be acquitted on the ground of entrapment "if a jury finds as a matter of fact that police conduct created a substantial risk that an ordinary person not predisposed to commit a particular crime would have been caused to commit that crime, or if the trial court rules as a matter of law that police conduct exceeded the standards of proper investigation."[37]

Most states that apply the objective standard follow the lead of the Model Penal Code, which allocates the burden of proof to the defendant in entrapment cases. The Model Penal Code requires that the defendant prove entrapment by a preponderance of the evidence.

§ 27.04 Entrapment: The Debate

[A] Overview

Controversy swirls around the defense of entrapment. Most of it relates to the question of whether the subjective or the objective standard is preferable. Although most courts follow the Supreme Court's lead and apply the subjective test, scholars overwhelmingly favor the objective version.[38] The underlying issue in the debate is whether, on the one hand, the entrapped defendant should be excused because he is "innocent" (as subjectivists maintain) or should be exculpated, despite his guilt for the offense, because of the wrongdoing of the police (as objectivists argue).

Most of the entrapment debate is of a negative nature. That is, advocates of each standard generally point to the weaknesses in the opposing position rather than providing support for their own version of the defense. Many of the criticisms on both sides are powerful, so much so that one scholar has observed that "no member of the [Supreme] Court—and none of the numerous commentators on its work—has advanced a defense of the doctrine that is satisfactory."[39]

[B] Criticisms of the Subjective Test

[1] "The Legislative Intent Rationale is Fictional"

"[I]t is painfully obvious," according to one observer, that the rationale of the subjective test, namely that Congress did not intend for its statutes to be enforced by tempting innocent persons into violations, is "wholly fictional."[40] There is nothing in legislative history to suggest that Congress intended, on the one hand, for juries to acquit nondisposed

---

35. Model Penal Code § 2.13(2).

36. 2 Paul H. Robinson, Criminal Law Defenses § 209(c)(2) (1984).

37. State v. Vallejos, 945 P.2d 957, 961 (N.M. 1997).

38. Seidman, Note 1, *supra*, at 115 n.13.

39. *Id.* at 112.

40. *Id.* at 129–30; *see also* Sherman v. United States, 356 U.S. 369, 379 (1958) (Frankfurter J., dissenting) (the legislative intent theory is "sheer fiction").

persons who violate its laws as the result of police inducements, while, on the other hand, convicting predisposed persons subjected to the same blandishments.

The Supreme Court in *United States v. Russell*[41] virtually conceded the fictional nature of the legislative intent argument when it stated that criticism of the rationale was "not devoid of appeal." Nonetheless, it reaffirmed the subjective standard on the basis of *stare decisis*, the fact that the arguments raised against the objective test were "at least equally cogent," and because Congress, if the legislative intent rationale is unacceptable to it, can "address itself to the question and adopt any substantive definition of the defense that it may find desirable." This is hardly a spirited defense of the theoretical underpinnings of the subjective test.

[2] "The Subjective Test Acquits Culpable Persons"

The subjective test conflicts with existing substantive criminal law concepts. An entrapped person knowingly violates the law, and she does so under circumstances that would *not* constitute compulsion if the inducing party were another private person rather than a police officer. That is, in the non-entrapment context, the criminal law does not excuse persons who commit crimes because of tempting offers or who accede to minor threats.[42] The reason for this rule is that people who are tempted by others to commit crimes, or who are victims of minor threats, have sufficient free choice to be held accountable for their actions. One who responds to similar temptations or threats at the hands of the government is no less culpable—she has no less free will—than a victim of private temptation.[43]

Critics of the subjective test suggest that the real reason why we acquit the entrapped defendant, even as we convict another person who gives in to similar non-governmental inducements, is that non-coercive pressures are unacceptable if, but only if, it is the government that plays an ignoble part in producing them. In other words, the heart of the entrapment claim really is that, in certain circumstances, we want to punish the government more for *its* conduct than we want to punish the entrapped party for *hers*. But, *that* is the essence of the *objective* standard, not the *subjective* test!

[3] "The Subjective Test Is Unfair"

Because the subjective test focuses on the criminal disposition of the defendant, the standard is unfair. It permits the prosecution to introduce evidence of the defendant's bad character in the form of rumors, reputation evidence, and criminal history. Yet evidence of this sort ordinarily is inadmissible at trial because it is only of slight probative value and is apt to be prejudicial to the rights of the defendant.[44] Even an advocate of the subjective test has conceded that courts have, "[d]espite the lack of any pressing need, . . . permitted otherwise inadmissible evidence to be introduced. . . . Some of it has been shockingly unreliable."[45]

---

41. 411 U.S. 423 (1973).

42. Joshua Dressler, Understanding Criminal Law § 23.01 (6th ed. 2012).

43. American Law Institute, Model Penal Code and Commentaries, Comment to § 2.13, at 406 (1985).

44. Evidence of prior convictions apparently has a powerful impact on jurors in "subjective entrapment" trials. *See* Eugene Borgida & Roger C. Park, *The Entrapment Defense*, 12 Law & Hum. Behav. 19 (1988) (simulated-jury study).

45. Park, Note 1, *supra*, at 248.

[C] Criticisms of the Objective Test

[1] "The Test Leads to Inappropriate Results"

Because the objective standard focuses on the conduct of the police, critics of this test argue that it can lead to inappropriate results. A hardened criminal can avoid conviction if the police behave improperly. This result is not only dangerous to society but anomalous: When the police violate the Fourth Amendment or another constitutional provision, evidence obtained as the result of the illegal police conduct is excluded, but the prosecution of the defendant may proceed. In the case of entrapment, however, police conduct of which we do not approve, *but which is not unconstitutional*,[46] prevents society from bringing the defendant to justice.

[2] "The Test's Stated Rationales are Indefensible"

Critics maintain that the "purity of the temple" argument based on judicial integrity is unpersuasive. Society does not want judges to protect their temples' purity by releasing criminals to the streets. Opponents of the objective standard agree with Justice William Rehnquist who, in responding to similar "judicial integrity" claims in the Fourth Amendment context, observed that "while it is quite true that courts are not to be participants in 'dirty business,' neither are they to be ethereal vestal virgins of another world."[47]

The deterrence argument also fails, critics contend.[48] First, advocates of the objective standard fail to explain why courts should deter police conduct that is not unconstitutional or otherwise illegal. Second, the hypothetical-person test is too ambiguous to provide useful guidance to the police. Moreover, a general verdict of acquittal does not inform law enforcement agencies at what point the entrapment line is crossed.

Third, by its own standards, the objective test does not focus entirely on police conduct. Only conduct that *would cause the average person* to violate the law constitutes entrapment, a principle that seriously undercuts the deterrence goal. For example, suppose that undercover officers nab prostitutes by standing in alleys exposing their penises, or catch thieves by urinating in streets with $20 bills visibly hanging from their coat pockets.[49] Under the objective test, the police have not entrapped their "victims"—and, thus, will not be deterred—because ordinary people do not commit prostitution or theft when induced by such obnoxious conduct.

§ 27.05 Entrapment: Due Process[50]

In jurisdictions that apply the subjective standard of entrapment, no government inducements or threats, *no matter how egregious*, constitute entrapment if the "victim" of

---

46. *See* § 27.01, *supra*.

47. California v. Minjares, 443 U.S. 916, 924 (1979) (dissenting).

48. *See* Seidman, Note 1, *supra*, at 136–46; Park, Note 1, *supra*, at 225–39.

49. These police actions are not fanciful. See R.T. Rybak, *Officer Nabs Prostitute Suspect with 'Unbecoming' Technique*, Minneapolis Trib., Aug. 30, 1980, at 3A.

50. *See generally* Tim A. Thomas, Annotation, *What Conduct of Federal Law Enforcement Authorities in Inducing or Co-Operating in Criminal Offense Raises Due Process Defense Distinct from Entrapment*, 97 A.L.R. Fed. 273 (1990).

the police conduct was predisposed to commit the type of offense charged. But, could it be that, at some point, entrapment-like conduct, if outrageous enough, violates the Constitution and, therefore, serves as an alternative basis to bar prosecution even of a predisposed individual? As far as Supreme Court case law is concerned, the answer to the question is "perhaps." A survey of lower court opinions suggests that the answer is "theoretically yes, but virtually never."

In *United States v. Russell*,[51] R was convicted of the illegal manufacture of amphetamines after federal undercover agents furnished him with a difficult-to-obtain legal chemical necessary in the production of the narcotics. Because R was predisposed to commit the crime, an entrapment defense did not successfully lie. R argued, however, that the police violated the Due Process Clause by supplying him with the chemical and by becoming "enmeshed in the criminal activity."

In an opinion for five justices, Justice Rehnquist stated that "[w]hile we may some day be presented with a situation in which the conduct of law enforcement agents is so outrageous that due process principles would absolutely bar the government from invoking judicial processes to obtain a conviction . . . the instant case is distinctly not of that breed." Due process was not violated here, the majority concluded, because the chemical that the government furnished was lawful, harmless in itself, and not unobtainable elsewhere. As such, the government was not unduly enmeshed in the criminal activity.

Three years later, in *Hampton v. United States*,[52] some members of the Court rethought their position. In *Hampton*, an undercover agent arranged for H to sell heroin to another undercover agent. In short, the government was involved in "[t]he beginning and the end of [the] crime." Justice Rehnquist, this time speaking only for himself, Chief Justice Burger, and Justice White, backed off from his earlier due process remarks in *Russell*. He conceded that the government played a much more significant role in the crime in the present case. Nonetheless, Justice Rehnquist stated that the Due Process Clause "comes into play only when the Government activity in question violates some protected right of the *defendant*," which does not occur, he reasoned, if the police act in concert with a defendant to commit a crime. If the police acted illegally here, "the remedy lies, not in freeing the equally culpable defendant, but in prosecuting the police under the applicable provisions of state or federal law."

Despite the plurality's comments, a majority of the *Hampton* Court expressed the view that due process violations are possible, assuming the right facts. Justices Powell and Blackmun, while concurring in the judgment in *Hampton* (in their view, this narcotics transaction did not state a due process violation), noted that they were "unwilling to join the plurality in concluding that, no matter what the circumstances, . . . due process principles . . . could [not] support a bar to conviction." The three dissenters—Justices Brennan, Stewart, and Marshall—agreed with these remarks. Justice Stevens, who joined the Court after oral arguments were heard in the case, did not participate.

Thus, after *Hampton*, at least five members of the Court were prepared to find that the government could become sufficiently enmeshed in a crime or otherwise act so outrageously that the Due Process Clause would bar a prosecution. However, as all of the justices who participated in *Hampton* have left the Court, it is uncertain whether the new Court would support a due process claim.

---

51. 411 U.S. 423 (1973).
52. 425 U.S. 484 (1976).

Defendants have raised the due process "outrageousness" claim in many federal cases involving prosecutions of crimes, such as manufacture of narcotics, prison escape, mail fraud, and illegal sale or possession of firearms.[53] Although one federal circuit has held that, in the absence of binding precedent, it will not recognize a due process defense,[54] nearly every other federal circuit, and many state courts, have assumed that such a defense may lie.[55] However, a due process violation has been found to exist in only a few cases.[56]

---

53. *See especially* Thomas, Note 50, *supra.*

54. United States v. Tucker, 28 F.3d 1420 (6th Cir. 1994).

55. State v. Lively, 921 P.2d 1035, 1044–1045 (Wash. 1996).

56. *E.g.*, United States v. Twigg, 588 F.2d 373 (3d Cir. 1978) (due process violation: an informant suggested to *T* that he set up a "speed" laboratory, and the government supplied equipment, raw materials, and expertise at no cost, and even rented a farm for the production of illegal amphetamines); State v. Lively, 921 P.2d 1035 (Wash. 1996) (a government agent took advantage of *L*, a 21-year-old vulnerable single mother who attended Alcoholics Anonymous and Narcotics Anonymous meetings, by befriending her and beginning a sexual relationship in order to involve her in police-sponsored drug activities); *see* United States v. Cuervelo, 949 F.2d 559 (2d Cir. 1991) (in an international drug importation case, *C* was entitled to a hearing on her allegations of "outrageous governmental conduct," based on her claim that an undercover agent "sexually entrapped" her; dismissal of prosecution would be appropriate if she showed that the "government consciously set out to use sex as a weapon in its investigatory arsenal, or acquiesced in such conduct for its purposes upon learning that such a relationship existed," that the agent initiated the sexual relationship or allowed it to continue in order to further the investigation, and that the relationship was "entwined" with the criminal events).

Chapter 28

The Right to Counsel: At Trial and on Appeal

§ 28.01 Overview: The Importance of Defense Lawyers in the Adversary System

Defense lawyers occupy a unique role in the criminal justice system. Lionized by some, demonized by others, they are frequently the most important actors in a criminal case. Because a defense lawyer necessarily sometimes protects the guilty, he may seem to some to be "a nettlesome obstacle to the pursuit of wrongdoers."[1] During the adjudication phase of a criminal case, however, there is little dispute that the role of defense counsel is of critical importance — in the words of the Supreme Court, defense lawyers "are necessities, not luxuries."[2]

At every stage, the adjudication process is calibrated (whether successfully or not) both to reduce the risk of wrongful convictions of innocents and to assure due process for all. Yet that statutory and constitutional calibration — be it regarding discovery, plea bargaining, the trial itself or most any other stage — is conducted with the assumption that the defendant will have a competent attorney representing his interests. Because of this assumption of competent counsel in the adjudication process, it is no exaggeration to state that the very legitimacy of the American criminal justice system depends on the participation of competent and ethical defense lawyers who diligently represent their clients' best interests.

§ 28.02 When the Right to Counsel Applies[3]

The Sixth Amendment right to counsel applies only after the commencement of adversarial judicial proceedings; the Court has concluded that this commencement starts the "criminal prosecution" for right-to-counsel purposes.[4]

---

1. Moran v. Burbine, 475 U.S. 412, 468 (1986) (Stevens, J., dissenting). Indeed, some people believe that he has no proper role to play during certain police-citizen encounters, such as during interrogations and at lineups. *See* §§ 25.01[C] (police interrogations), § 26.02[C] (lineups), *supra*.

2. Gideon v. Wainwright, 372 U.S. 335, 344 (1963). This is *not* to say that the presence of defense counsel, even highly competent defense counsel, can *guarantee* that a trial will be fair and reliable. *See generally* Alexandra Natapoff, *Gideon Skepticism*, 70 Wash. & Lee L. Rev. 1049 (2013) (warning against such an assumption).

3. *See generally* Pamela R. Metzger, *Beyond the Bright Line: A Contemporary Right-to-Counsel Doctrine*, 97 Nw. U. L. Rev. 1635 (2003).

4. This issue is discussed more fully in § 25.03, *supra*.

Once the right-to-counsel has attached, it applies not only at the trial itself but also at any "critical stage" of the prosecution.[5] Importantly, however, whether the right to counsel has "attached," and whether a particular pretrial event constitutes a "critical stage," are distinct questions. The right to counsel attaches "when the government has used the judicial machinery to signal a commitment to prosecute," but immediate appointment of counsel is not required in the absence of a finding that the post-attachment stage is a "critical" one.[6]

The Court has used different phrases to describe what constitutes a critical stage. Its definitions include "those pretrial procedures that would impair defense on the merits if the accused is required to proceed without counsel"[7] and "any stage of the prosecution, formal or informal, in court or out, where counsel's absence might derogate from the accused's right to a fair trial."[8] Most recently, the Court summarized its "critical stage" definition from previous cases as those "proceedings between an individual and agents of the State . . . that amount to 'trial-like confrontations,' at which counsel would help the accused 'in coping with legal problems or . . . meeting his adversary.' "[9]

Applying this test, the Court has found that pretrial interrogation,[10] a pretrial lineup,[11] a preliminary hearing,[12] an arraignment at which rights may be lost (for example, the ability to plead not guilty by reason of insanity),[13] and a pretrial psychiatric exam[14] all constitute "critical stages," requiring the presence of counsel. The Court has also held that the right to counsel "extends to the consideration of plea offers that lapse or are rejected,"[15] as well as to guilty pleas.[16] The Sixth Amendment right to counsel also applies at sentencing proceedings.[17]

On the other hand, when the police display photographs, including those of the defendant, to witnesses for identification purposes,[18] or take a handwriting exemplar from the defendant,[19] this is not a "critical stage," so the Sixth Amendment right to counsel does not apply.

---

5. *See* Coleman v. Alabama, 399 U.S. 1 (1970); United States. v. Ash, 413 U.S. 300, 321 (1973) (Stewart, J. concurring).

6. *See* Rothgery v. Gillespie County, 554 U.S. 191, 211–212 (2008).

7. Gerstein v. Pugh, 420 U.S. 103, 122 (1975).

8. United States v. Wade, 388 U.S. 218, 226 (1967). *See* §27.02, *supra* (discussing *Wade* and its progeny).

9. Rothgery v. Gillespie County, 554 U.S. at 212 n.16.

10. Massiah v. United States, 377 U.S. 201 (1964). *See* §25.01, 25.02, *supra* (discussing *Massiah* rule).

11. *Wade*, 388 U.S. 218.

12. Coleman v. Alabama, 399 U.S. 1 (1970).

13. Hamilton v. Alabama, 368 U.S. 52 (1961).

14. Estelle v. Smith, 451 U.S. 454, 469–71 (1981).

15. Missouri v. Frye, 132 S. Ct. 1399 (2012).

16. Padilla v. Kentucky, 559 U.S. 431 (2010).

17. Mempa v. Rhay, 389 U.S. 128 (1967).

18. United States. v. Ash, 413 U.S. 300, 321 (1973). *See* §27.03, *supra* (discussing *Ash*).

19. Gilbert v. California, 388 U.S. 263, 266–67 (1967).

§ 28.03 The Right to Counsel: At Trial[20]

[A] The Right to Employ Counsel

It has always been clear that, at a minimum, the Sixth Amendment entitles an accused in a federal prosecution to employ a lawyer to assist in his defense at trial.[21] Moreover, since 1963, the right to counsel has been deemed a fundamental right of criminal justice;[22] therefore, an accused in a state prosecution has a similar Fourteenth Amendment right to retain an attorney to represent him during trial.

[B] Indigents: The Right to Appointed Counsel[23]

[1] Overview

Justice Hugo Black, speaking for the Supreme Court, wrote in 1956 that "[t]here can be no equal justice where the kind of trial a man gets depends on the amount of money he has."[24] If the "amount of money" an accused has cannot pay for a lawyer, he has little chance for "equal justice" without outside help. Moreover, given the historic correlation between race and poverty, "failure to provide adequate assistance of counsel to accused indigents draws a line not only between rich and poor, but also between white and

---

20. *See generally* American Bar Association, ABA Standards for Criminal Justice: Prosecution and Defense Function 117–248 (3d ed. 1993);William M. Beaney, The Right to Counsel in American Courts (1955); Barbara Allen Babcock, *The Duty to Defend*, 114 Yale L. J. 1489 (2005); Dennis E. Curtis & Judith Resnick, *Colloquium: What Does It Mean to Practice Law "In the Interests of Justice" in the Twenty-First Century?: Grieving Criminal Defense Lawyers*, 70 Fordham L. Rev. 1615 (2002); Anne Bowen Poulin, *Strengthening the Criminal Defendant's Right to Counsel*, 28 Cardozo L. Rev. 1213 (2006); Abbe Smith, *Defending Defending: The Case for Unmitigated Zeal on Behalf of People Who Do Terrible Things*, 28 Hofstra L. Rev. 925 (2000); Gerald F. Uelmen, *2001: A Train Ride: A Guided Tour of the Sixth Amendment Right to Counsel*, 58 Law & Contemp. Probs. 13 (1995). For a thoughtful dialogue on the role of defense counsel in representing "not just the damned but the damnable," *see* Michael E. Tigar, *Defending*, 74 Tex. L. Rev. 101 (1995), and a response by Monroe H. Freedman, *The Lawyer's Moral Obligation of Justification*, 74 Tex. L. Rev. 111 (1995).

21. Scott v. Illinois, 440 U.S. 367, 370 (1979); Chandler v. Fretag, 348 U.S. 3, 10 (1954) (holding that "a defendant must be given a reasonable opportunity to employ and consult with counsel").

22. Gideon v. Wainwright, 372 U.S. 335 (1963).

23. *See generally* Deborah L. Rhode, Access to Justice 122–32 (2004); Mary Sue Backus and Paul Marcus, *The Right to Counsel in Criminal Cases, A National Crisis*, 57 Hastings L. J. 1031 (2006); Stephen B. Bright, *Neither Equal Nor Just: The Rationing and Denial of Legal Services to the Poor When Life and Liberty Are at Stake*, 1997 Ann. Surv. Am. L. 783; Committee to Review the Criminal Justice Act, Report of the Committee to Review the Criminal Justice Act, *reprinted in* 52 Crim. L. Rep. (BNA) 2265 (1993); Adam M. Gershowitz, *Raise the Proof: A Default Rule for Indigent Defense*, 40 Conn. L. Rev. 85 (2007); Lawrence C. Marshall, Gideon's *Paradox*, 73 Fordham L. Rev. 955 (2004); National Right to Counsel Committee, *Justice Denied: America's Continuing Neglect of Our Constitutional Right to Counsel* (2009) (available at: www.constitutionproject.org); Stephen J. Schulhofer & David D. Friedman, *Rethinking Indigent Defense: Promoting Effective Representation Through Consumer Sovereignty and Freedom of Choice for All Criminal Defendants*, 31 Am. Crim. L. Rev. 73 (1993); Robert L. Spangenberg & Marea L. Beeman, *Indigent Defense Systems in the United States*, 58 Law & Contemp. Probs. 31 (1995).

24. Griffin v. Illinois, 351 U.S. 12, 19 (1956).

black."[25] The Supreme Court reacted gradually, but ultimately broadly, to the problem of representation for indigents in criminal cases.

In 1938, the Supreme Court announced in *Johnson v. Zerbst*[26] that the "Sixth Amendment withholds from federal courts, in all criminal proceedings, the power and authority to deprive an accused of his life or liberty unless he has or waives the assistance of counsel." From that point, therefore, indigents prosecuted in federal court had the right to have counsel appointed for them at government expense. For 25 years after *Zerbst*, however, the Court did not require the states (as distinguished from the federal government) to appoint counsel for indigents. Following a twisting path described below, the Court eventually mandated appointment of counsel in state prosecutions in its 1963 landmark decision in *Gideon v. Wainwright*.[27] Until *Gideon*, legal representation of indigents in state courts was sporadic and often ineffective.[28] Now it is mandatory, though very serious problems with provision of adequate indigent defense persist.[29]

[2] The Road to *Gideon*

[a] *Powell v. Alabama*

In *Powell v. Alabama*,[30] nine teenage black youths (ages 12 to 19) were prosecuted for the alleged rape of two white girls in an Alabama community that, due to the race of the parties, was "explosive with rage and vengeance."[31] The youths, residents of another state, and described by the Court as "ignorant and illiterate," were indicted, arraigned, and brought to trial less than two weeks after the capital offenses supposedly occurred.

As Supreme Court Justice George Sutherland explained, until the day of trial, "no lawyer had been named or definitely designated to represent the defendants." Instead, as the trial judge explained, he had "appointed all the members of the bar for the purpose of arraigning the defendants and then of course anticipated . . . [them to] continue to help the defendants if no counsel appeared." On the day of trial, two lawyers, one of whom was from out of state and unfamiliar with local law, offered to represent the youths. Once appointed, however, the lawyers were denied a continuance to adequately prepare

25. Charles J. Ogletree Jr., *An Essay on the New Public Defender for the 21st Century*, 58 Law & Contemp. Probs. 83 (1995).

26. 304 U.S. 458 (1938).

27. 372 U.S. 335 (1963).

28. *See generally* Beaney, Note 20, *supra*; Bertram F. Willcox & Edward J. Bloustein, *Account of a Field Study in a Rural Area of the Representation of Indigents Accused of Crime*, 59 Colum. L. Rev. 551 (1959).

29. *See, e.g.*, American Bar Association Standing Committee on Legal Aid and Indigent Defendants, Gideon's Broken Promise: America's Continuing Quest for Equal Justice (2004) (detailing problems with indigent defense systems and characterizing indigent defense as "in a state of crisis"), Backus & Marcus, Note 23, *supra* (same); National Right to Counsel Committee, Note 21, *supra* (same). On the other hand, pre-2000 evidence suggests that indigents provided with counsel and individuals with private counsel were convicted at about the same rate and, putting state drug prosecutions to one side, received about the same sentences. *See* Caroline Wolf Harlow, U.S. Dep't of Justice, Bureau of Justice Statistics, Defense Counsel in Criminal Cases (2000).

30. 287 U.S. 45 (1932).

31. Willcox & Bloustein, Note 28, *supra*, at 551. The case, which has come to be known as the "Scottsboro Case" (the site of the trial), has been the subject of voluminous scholarly research. *E.g.*, Dan T. Carter, Scottsboro: A Tragedy of the American South (1969); James E. Goodman, Stories of Scottsboro (1994); Claudia Johnson, *The Secret Courts of Men's Hearts: Code and Law in Harper Lee's To Kill a Mockingbird*, 19 Stud. Am. Fiction 129 (1991) (suggesting a relationship between the Scottsboro Case and the fictional Mockingbird trial).

their defense. Eight of the defendants were convicted and sentenced to death in the three one-day trials that followed.

The Court overturned the convictions. It treated the youths as constructively unrepresented by counsel at trial, given the manner in which their lawyers had not been allowed time to prepare. In oft-quoted language, Justice Sutherland expansively described the need for assistance of counsel:

> The right to be heard would be, in many cases, of little avail if it did not comprehend the right to be heard by counsel. Even the intelligent and educated layman has small and sometimes no skill in the science of law. . . . He is unfamiliar with the rules of evidence. Left without the aid of counsel he may be put on trial without a proper charge, and convicted upon incompetent evidence, or evidence irrelevant to the issue or otherwise inadmissible. He lacks both the skill and knowledge adequately to prepare his defense, even though he had a perfect one. He requires the guiding hand of counsel at every step in the proceedings against him. Without it, though he be not guilty, he faces the danger of conviction because he does not know how to establish his innocence.[32]

The Court's holding, however, was much narrower than that broad language might suggest and focused on the special circumstances of the case:

> All that it is necessary now to decide, as we do decide, is that *in a capital case*, where the defendant is unable to employ counsel, and is *incapable adequately of making his own defense* because of ignorance, feeble mindedness, illiteracy, or the like, it is the duty of the court, whether requested or not, to assign counsel for him as a necessary requisite of due process of law; and that duty is not discharged by an assignment at such a time or under such circumstances as to preclude the giving of effective aid in the preparation and trial of the case.[33]

[b] Johnson v. Zerbst

Powell involved a state prosecution. The Court's next significant step in providing counsel to indigents came at the federal level. In *Johnson v. Zerbst*,[34] as previously noted, the Court held that "[t]he Sixth Amendment withholds from federal courts, in all criminal proceedings, the power and authority to deprive an accused of his life or liberty unless he has or waives the assistance of counsel."

Quoting Justice Sutherland's above-noted passage about the importance of counsel, which the *Powell* Court used to explain why the Scottsboro defendants had been denied due process, the *Zerbst* Court used the same concerns to conclude that "the wise policy of the Sixth Amendment" is "a realistic recognition of the obvious truth that the average defendant does not have the professional legal skill to protect himself," especially because "the prosecution is presented by experienced and learned counsel."

[c] Betts v. Brady

In *Betts v. Brady*,[35] the Court was invited to announce that the federal *per se* constitutional right to appointed counsel it had found in the Sixth Amendment applied to the

---

32. *Powell*, 287 U.S. at 68–69.
33. *Id.* at 71 (emphasis added).
34. 304 U.S. 458 (1938).
35. 316 U.S. 455 (1942).

states as a matter of Fourteenth Amendment due process. It did not take the step. In *Betts*, B, an indigent, was indicted for robbery in state court. He requested, but was denied, the assistance of counsel at trial. B was convicted and sentenced to prison. B appealed his conviction on the ground that he was entitled to free assistance of counsel at trial.

The Supreme Court rejected the principle that "due process of law demands that in every criminal case, whatever the circumstances, a State must furnish counsel to an indigent defendant." Based on its reading of state constitutional history and contemporary state practices, the Court concluded that the right to counsel was not essential to a fair trial in light of the "common understanding of those who have lived under the Anglo-American system of law."

Instead, the Court looked to the individual circumstances of the case, as it had *Powell v. Alabama*.[36] This time, however, the Court concluded that no special circumstances existed in B's case to justify the appointment of counsel. In contrast to the *Powell* defendants, B was prosecuted for a non-capital crime, and the case presented only the "simple issue" of whether B's alibi claim should be believed. The Court concluded that B, "not helpless, . . . a man forty-three years old, [and] of ordinary intelligence," could handle his defense adequately by himself.

[3] *Gideon v. Wainwright*

Gideon v. Wainwright[37] overruled *Betts v. Brady*.[38] *Gideon* brought the protections of the Sixth Amendment right to counsel to the states, through the Fourteenth Amendment Due Process Clause. This incorporation of the Sixth Amendment right to counsel means that counsel must be appointed for indigents in state criminal cases, as they have been in federal cases since *Johnson v. Zerbst*,[39] without case-by-case examination of the circumstances.

In *Gideon*, G was prosecuted for the felony of breaking and entering a poolroom. G requested, but was denied, the assistance of counsel. According to the Court, he conducted his own defense "about as well as could be expected from a layman." Nonetheless, the jury convicted him, and he was sentenced to five years' imprisonment.

The Supreme Court, per Justice Hugo Black, overturned the conviction.[40] According to Justice Black, *Betts* had "made an abrupt break with [the Court's] own well-considered precedents," especially that of *Powell v. Alabama*,[41] from which the Court once again quoted Justice Sutherland's expansive passage about the importance of counsel. An "obvious truth," the Court found, is that "in our adversary system of criminal justice, any

---

36. 287 U.S. 45 (1932).

37. 372 U.S. 335 (1963). *See generally* Anthony Lewis, Gideon's Trumpet (1964); Jerold H. Israel, *Gideon v. Wainwright: The "Art" of Overruling*, 1963 Sup. Ct. Rev. 211; Yale Kamisar, *Betts v. Brady Twenty Years Later: The Right to Counsel and Due Process Values*, 61 Mich. L. Rev. 219 (1962); Yale Kamisar, *The Right to Counsel and the Fourteenth Amendment: A Dialogue on "The Most Pervasive Right" of an Accused*, 30 U. Chi. L. Rev. 1 (1962).

38. 316 U.S. 455 (1942).

39. 304 U.S. 458 (1938). *See* § 28.03[B][2][b], *supra*.

40. If a defendant is actually (as in *Gideon*) or constructively (as in *Powell v. Alabama*) denied his constitutional right to the assistance of counsel at trial, any resulting conviction must be reversed, i.e., the error is *never* harmless. *See* Strickland v. Washington, 466 U.S. 668, 692 (1984). Harmless-error doctrine is discussed in 2 Joshua Dressler & Alan C. Michaels, Understanding Criminal Procedure § 16.04 (4th ed. 2006).

41. 287 U.S. 45 (1932). *See* § 28.03[B][2][a], *supra*.

person haled into court, who is too poor to hire a lawyer, cannot be assured a fair trial unless counsel is provided for him." Justice Black further observed:

> Governments . . . quite properly spend vast sums of money to establish machinery to try defendants accused of crime. Lawyers to prosecute are everywhere deemed essential to protect the public's interest in an orderly society. Similarly, there are few defendants charged with crime, few indeed, who fail to hire the best lawyers they can get to prepare and present their defenses. [The implication of this is] . . . that lawyers in criminal courts are necessities, not luxuries. The right of one charged with crime to counsel may not be deemed fundamental . . . in some countries, but it is in ours.

By holding that the Constitution mandated universal representation, the *Gideon* Court sought to realize the "noble ideal" of "assur[ing] fair trials before impartial tribunals in which every defendant stands equal before the law."[42]

Justice Harlan, concurring in the judgment, agreed that *Betts* should be overruled, but considered it "entitled to a more respectful burial" than the Court gave it. According to Justice Harlan, *Betts's* application of the right to appointed counsel to the states in "special circumstances" was not "an abrupt break" from precedent, but rather an extension of *Powell v. Alabama*[43] beyond the context of capital trials. Nonetheless, Justice Harlan concluded, "[t]he Court has come to recognize . . . that the mere existence of a serious criminal charge constituted in itself special circumstances requiring the services of counsel at trial," so that imposition of the mandatory rule on the states was justified.

Following the Court's decision, *G* was retried, but now with the assistance of counsel. The jury returned a not-guilty verdict in one hour.[44]

[4] Post-*Gideon* Law: The Misdemeanor Cases

[a] *Argersinger v. Hamlin*

Gideon v. Wainwright[45] held that an indigent has a constitutional right to assistance of counsel at trial. *Gideon*, however, involved a felony offense. In *Argersinger v. Hamlin*,[46] the Supreme Court considered the applicability of *Gideon* to misdemeanor trials. In *Argersinger*, *A*, an indigent, was charged with carrying a concealed weapon, a misdemeanor for which the maximum penalty was imprisonment for six months, a $1,000 fine, or both. *A* requested, but was denied, the appointment of counsel. Consequently, *A* represented himself. He was convicted, and sentenced to 90 days in jail.

The state supreme court upheld the trial court's decision not to appoint counsel. It followed the line drawn by the United States Supreme Court in its Sixth Amendment trial-by-jury jurisprudence. In that field, the Supreme Court has held that the right to trial by jury applies only to "non-petty" offenses, which in the trial-by-jury context normally means offenses punishable by imprisonment in excess of six months.[47] The

---

42. *Gideon*, 372 U.S. at 344.
43. 287 U.S. 45.
44. *See* Lewis, Note 37, *supra*, at 226–37.
45. 372 U.S. 335 (1963).
46. 407 U.S. 25 (1972); *see generally* Lawrence Herman, The Right to Counsel in Misdemeanor Court (1974); Steven Duke, *The Right to Appointed Counsel: Argersinger and Beyond*, 12 Am. Crim. L. Rev. 601 (1975).
47. *See* 2 Dressler & Michaels, Note 40, *supra*, at § 10.02.

state court reasoned that the same rule should apply to the right to counsel, since it derives from the Sixth Amendment as well. Because *A*'s trial involved a "petty" offense (the maximum potential incarceration for the offense was imprisonment for six months), the state court concluded that *A* was not entitled to appointed counsel.

The Supreme Court, per Justice Douglas, overturned the conviction. Although both rights come from the Sixth Amendment, which by its language applies to "all criminal prosecutions," the Court concluded that the right to counsel "has a different genealogy" than the trial-by-jury right: "While there is historical support for limiting the . . . trial by jury [right] to 'serious criminal cases,' there is no such support for a similar limitation on the right to assistance of counsel. . . ."

The Court reasoned that the rationale of its cases mandating the provision of counsel by the states—*Gideon* and *Powell v. Alabama*[48]—"has relevance to any criminal trial, where an accused is deprived of his liberty." It warned that misdemeanor and petty offenses may implicate legal and constitutional issues as complex as those that arise in prosecutions for serious offenses. The Court also expressed concern that, in view of the high volume of misdemeanor cases and the prevalence of guilty pleas, defendants were becoming victims of "assembly-line justice." Therefore, the Court concluded that "even in prosecutions for offenses less serious than felonies, a fair trial may require the presence of a lawyer."

Although the reasoning of *Argersinger* could apply to all misdemeanor cases, the Court's holding was limited: "absent a knowing and intelligent waiver, no person may be imprisoned for any offense, whether classified as petty, misdemeanor, or felony, unless he was represented by counsel at his trial." In other words, an indigent is entitled to the appointment of counsel if he actually, not merely potentially, will be jailed (even for one day) if he is convicted. Importantly, this means that a judge who wishes to preserve the possibility of a jail term as part of a sentence *must* appoint counsel for an indigent defendant at the outset of the formal prosecution.

Justice Lewis Powell, with whom Justice William Rehnquist joined, concurred in the result. He described the imprisonment/no-imprisonment line drawn by the majority as "illogical" and "without discernible support" in the Constitution. Justice Powell argued that not all misdemeanor cases are complex and noted that the line between the difficult and simple ones is not drawn on the basis of whether a defendant is sentenced to imprisonment. Although he agreed that the right to a lawyer "does not mysteriously evaporate" when an indigent is charged with a misdemeanor, he would have directed trial courts to consider on a case-by-case basis whether appointment of counsel was necessary to assure a fair trial in misdemeanor cases, whatever punishment might be involved, much as they had been required to do for felonies under *Betts v. Brady*.[49]

The concurring justices also criticized the majority for being "disquietingly barren of details" as to how the new rule would be implemented. Under *Argersinger*, the trial judge is faced with an "awkward dilemma." He must decide before trial—before evidence is introduced—whether to appoint counsel. If he does not appoint counsel, he cannot jail a convicted defendant, no matter how justifiable such punishment might turn out to be. If the judge wishes to retain his option to incarcerate the defendant, he must provide counsel, incurring what the concurrence worried would be very substantial unnecessary

48. 287 U.S. 45 (1932). *See* § 28.03[B][2][a], *supra.*
49. 316 U.S. 455 (1942), *overruled by Gideon. See* § 28.03[B][2][c], *supra.*

costs. The concurrence predicted that the effect of the Court's decision would be to over-burden local courts, exacerbate delays, and increase court congestion.

[b] Scott v. Illinois

In *Scott v. Illinois*,[50] S, an indigent, was charged with theft, a misdemeanor that car-ried a potential penalty of one-year imprisonment, a $500 fine, or both. Denied the as-sistance of counsel, S was convicted and fined $50. On appeal, S argued that although he was not imprisoned he should have been provided counsel at his trial.

S's contention was plausible. First, the Court's reasoning in *Argersinger v. Hamlin*[51] — counsel is required because of the potential complexity of misdemeanor cases and the risk of assembly-line justice — applies with equal force in non-jail cases. Second, a bright-line rule — either that a lawyer is required in all petty-offense prosecutions or, at least, whenever imprisonment is authorized — would have resolved the "awkward dilemma" noted by the concurring justices in *Argersinger*.

Third, and perhaps most significantly, the crime for which S was prosecuted, although denominated a misdemeanor, was not a petty offense. Because the potential penalty was one year imprisonment, S was entitled to a trial by jury.[52] The *Argersinger* Court had indi-cated that the right-to-counsel extended *beyond* the limits of the jury-trial right,[53] so S's demand for counsel appeared plausible.

Nonetheless, by the slimmest of margins, the Supreme Court left the counsel/no-counsel line where it had been drawn in *Argersinger*. Justice Rehnquist, writing for a five-justice majority, spoke of the Sixth Amendment in far less expansive terms than the Court had in *Gideon*. He stated that "[t]here is considerable doubt that the Sixth Amend-ment itself, as originally drafted by the Framers of the Bill of Rights, contemplated any guarantee other than the right of an accused in a criminal prosecution in a federal court to employ a lawyer to assist in his defense." After review of the relevant case law, the ma-jority stated that "constitutional line drawing becomes more difficult as the reach of the Constitution is extended further, and as efforts are made to transpose lines from one area of Sixth Amendment jurisprudence to another."

Although the "intentions of the *Argersinger* Court [were] not unmistakably clear," the *Scott* majority concluded that *Argersinger* "did . . . delimit the constitutional right to ap-pointed counsel" to those cases resulting in *actual* imprisonment. And, even considering the matter anew, the Court concluded that the actual imprisonment line drawn in *Argersinger* "is eminently sound and warrants adoption . . . as the line defining the con-stitutional right to appointment of counsel." In short, *Scott* held that the Constitution requires "only that no indigent criminal defendant be sentenced to a term of impris-onment unless the State has afforded him the right to assistance of appointed counsel in his defense." Although *Scott* thus established the federal constitutional floor for

---

50. 440 U.S. 367 (1979); *see generally* Lawrence Herman & Charles A. Thompson, *Scott v. Illi-nois and the Right to Counsel: A Decision in Search of a Doctrine?*, 17 Am. Crim. L. Rev. 71 (1979).

51. 407 U.S. 25 (1972).

52. *See* 2 Dressler & Michaels, Note 40, *supra*, at § 10.02[A].

53. *Argersinger*, 407 U.S. at 30 ("While there is historical support for limiting the 'deep com-mitment' to trial by jury to 'serious criminal cases,' there is no such support for a similar limitation on the right to assistance of counsel . . .").

appointment of counsel in misdemeanor cases, a strong majority of states provide counsel in misdemeanor cases more frequently than the Sixth Amendment requires.[54]

Justice Powell, who wrote the concurrence in *Argersinger*, provided the crucial fifth vote for the majority opinion in *Scott*. In a separate concurrence he explained that he did so for *stare decisis* reasons, but that he continued to believe the *Argersinger/Scott* bright-line rule was both too generous and too strict in providing counsel and that he hoped that "in due time" the Court "will recognize that a more flexible rule is consistent with due process and will better serve the cause of justice."

[c] *Alabama v. Shelton*

With the rule clear that the right-to-counsel in misdemeanor cases applies when, but only when, the defendant is "sentenced to a term of imprisonment," the next question became what sentences fall into this category. In *Alabama v. Shelton*,[55] S, an indigent, was charged with third-degree assault, a misdemeanor that carried a potential penalty of one-year imprisonment and a $2,000 fine. S was not offered the assistance of counsel at state expense and was convicted following a jury trial at which S represented himself. The court sentenced S to 30 days in jail but immediately suspended that sentence and placed S on a two-year term of unsupervised probation, conditioned on the payment of some fines. On S's appeal, the Alabama Supreme Court affirmed the conviction and the fines but set aside the suspended sentence, concluding that the suspended sentence was a "term of imprisonment" under *Argersinger* and *Scott*.

The United States Supreme Court agreed, holding that when an indigent is not afforded counsel, "a suspended sentence that may 'end up in the actual deprivation of a person's liberty' may not be imposed." Although a suspended sentence does not make incarceration immediate or inevitable, the Court found such delay and contingency irrelevant. The key factor, in the Court's view, was that the incarceration—whenever it occurred—would be for the uncounseled conviction.

Justice Scalia, writing for the four dissenting justices, argued that the mere imposition of a suspended sentence did not deprive S of liberty and therefore did not activate S's Sixth Amendment right. In the dissenters' view, "[i]n the future, *if and when* the [state] seeks to imprison . . . on the previously suspended sentence, we can ask whether the procedural safeguards attending the imposition of that sentence comply with the Constitution." According to this argument, the Court's holding that S was denied his Sixth Amendment right upon imposition of a suspended sentence was premature, both because S might never be imprisoned and because, if the state decided to seek imprisonment, it might provide adequate procedures at that later time that would satisfy the Sixth Amendment.

The majority responded, however, that it made little sense to assess "the constitutionality of imposing a suspended sentence while simultaneously walling off the procedures that will precede its activation." Looking at the parole revocation procedures established

---

54. *See* B. Mitchell Simpson III, *A Fair Trial: Are Indigents Charged with Misdemeanors Entitled to Court Appointed Counsel?*, 5 Roger Williams Univ. L. Rev. 417 (2000) (noting that 35 states and the District of Columbia have expanded the right to counsel in misdemeanor cases beyond minimal federal requirements, including 20 states that provide counsel for any misdemeanor *punishable* by a jail sentence).

55. 535 U.S. 654 (2002).

by Alabama law, the majority saw no way in which they could render S's imprisonment constitutional.

[d] Two More Cases: Nichols and Gagnon

The result in *Shelton* may be contrasted with that in two other post-*Argersinger* cases: *Gagnon v. Scarpelli*[56] and *Nichols v. United States.*[57] In *Gagnon, S* was given a suspended sentence and a term of probation for a *counseled felony* conviction. The question for the Court was whether S was entitled to appointment of counsel at a probation revocation hearing, which could result in the "activation" of his suspended sentence and S being sent to jail. Justice Powell, who unsuccessfully urged a "flexible" case-by-case approach in *Argersinger* and *Scott*, won a majority of the Court to that view in *Gagnon*, and wrote for the Court that whether due process and fundamental fairness required appointment of counsel at revocation hearings would be left to the "sound discretion" of the local authorities to be resolved in accordance with the circumstances of the particular case. Because the probation revocation proceeding, unlike trial and sentencing,[58] was not a part of the "criminal prosecution," the Sixth Amendment right-to-counsel provision did not apply.[59]

In *Nichols*, the Court held that a valid *uncounseled misdemeanor* conviction (a conviction valid despite the absence of counsel, because the defendant did not receive a jail sentence) may be used as the basis for enhancing punishment of the defendant after a subsequent, *counseled* conviction.[60] N had pleaded guilty to a federal drug offense. Pursuant to sentencing guidelines, N received enhanced punishment of approximately two years because of his criminal record, which included a prior uncounseled misdemeanor conviction for which he had previously been fined, but not incarcerated. The Court upheld the additional punishment on the ground that the enhancement contained in the sentencing guidelines constituted punishment for the counseled drug offense and did "not change the penalty [no jail] imposed for the earlier conviction."[61]

The dissenters would not have allowed the uncounseled conviction to enhance the subsequent sentence because, in their view, it departed from the "animating principle" of the Court's jurisprudence in this area: "to ensure that no indigent is deprived of his liberty as a result of a proceeding in which he lacked the guiding hand of counsel."

---

56. 411 U.S. 778 (1973).

57. 511 U.S. 738 (1994).

58. *See* Mempa v. Rhay, 389 U.S. 128 (1967) (holding that Sixth Amendment right to counsel applies at sentencing).

59. *See also* Turner v. Rogers, 131 S. Ct. 2507 (2011) ("analyzing under the Due Process Clause a claim of a right to counsel in the context of a civil contempt proceeding for failure to pay child support that resulted in 12 months" imprisonment and concluding that an indigent is "not automatically" entitled to counsel in that context).

60. *See also* United States v. Bryant, 136 S. Ct. 1954 (2016). *B* had been convicted of misdemeanors and sentenced to imprisonment for less than one year in multiple tribal-court proceedings. Although *B* was indigent and was not appointed counsel, there was no constitutional violation for the simple reason that the Sixth Amendment does not apply in tribal-court proceedings. In *Bryant*, these tribal court convictions were used as the predicate crimes for a federal charge against *B* of committing domestic assault with two previous convictions. The Court held that this use of *B*'s uncounseled misdemeanor convictions did not violate the Sixth Amendment because those convictions were valid when obtained in tribal court.

61. *Contra under state constitution*, State v. Kelly, 999 So. 2d 1029 (Fla. 2008); State v. Sinagoga, 918 P.2d 228, 239–41 (Haw. Ct. App. 1996).

[5] Implementing the Right to Appointed Counsel

Appointed counsel play a very large role in the contemporary criminal justice system. In 1986, lawyers were appointed to represent indigents in 4.4 million state cases.[62] In 1994, the national figure reportedly skyrocketed to approximately 8 million.[63] In 1999, in the 100 most populous counties alone, 4.2 million state prosecutions were handled by indigent criminal defense programs.[64]

Indeed, appointed counsel is the dominant means of representation for criminal defendants. In 1989, approximately 80 percent of the nation's jail inmates reported that they had court-appointed lawyers representing them for the offenses for which they were charged.[65] In 1996, court-appointed attorneys represented 82 percent of state defendants in the 75 largest counties, and in 1998, two-thirds of federal defendants were represented by court-appointed counsel.[66]

Notwithstanding its mandate of publicly financed representation for indigents, the Supreme Court has never dictated what particular institutional form such representation must take or how it should be funded.[67] In the absence of a Supreme Court directive, states and counties[68] have utilized three basic systems to provide representation to

---

62. Bureau of Justice Statistics, U.S. Dep't of Justice, Criminal Defense for the Poor, 1986 1 (1988).

63. Andrew Blum, *Defense of Indigents: Crisis Spurs Lawsuits*, Nat'l L.J., May 15, 1995, at A1, A26 (quoting Robert Spangenberg).

64. Carol J. DeFrances & Marika F.X. Litras, U.S. Dep't of Justice, Bureau of Justice Statistics, Indigent Defense Services in Large Counties, 1999 1 (2000). An estimated $1.2 billion was expended on these programs. *Id.*

65. Steven K. Smith & Carol J. DeFrances, U.S. Dep't of Justice, Bureau of Justice Statistics, Indigent Defense 1 (1996).

66. Harlow, Note 29, *supra*, at 1.

67. Based on 1988 and 1990 data, less than one penny of every government dollar was spent on judicial and legal services, which includes appropriations for courts, prosecutors, and public defense counsel. *See* Bureau of Justice Statistics, U.S. Dep't of Justice, Justice Expenditure and Employment, 1988 1 (1990); Bureau of Justice Statistics, U.S. Dep't of Justice, Justice Expenditure and Employment, 1990 1 (1992). Typically, indigent criminal defense programs have received less funding than prosecutorial offices. For example, in 2005, state and local governments spent approximately $3.5 billion on indigent criminal defense, *see* The Spangenberg Group, *State and County Expenditures for Indigent Defense Services in Fiscal Year 2005* 35 (2006), compared to nearly $4.9 billion spent on prosecutor's offices in 2005. U.S. Dep't of Justice, Bureau of Justice Statistics Bulletin, *Prosecutors in State Courts, 2005* 4 (2006). Some commentators estimate a much larger overall disparity between prosecution and defense resources. *See* Backus and Marcus, Note 23, *supra*, at 1045 n.60. Litigation premised on inadequate funding of indigent defense has been widespread and sometimes successful. *See, e.g.*, New York County Lawyers' Ass'n v. New York, 763 N.Y.S.2d 397 (Sup. Ct. 2003) (imposing injunctive relief more than doubling hourly rates for assigned counsel, leading to the first statutory increase in more than 15 years); *see generally* National Right to Counsel Committee, Note 23, *supra*, at 103–46 (providing overview of cases, litigation strategies, and results). *See also* Darryl K. Brown, *Rationing Criminal Defense Entitlements: An Argument from Institutional Design*, 104 Colum. L. Rev. 801 (2004) (arguing that underfunding of indigent defense is a permanent condition and that indigent defense resources should be rationed to protect claims of factual innocence).

68. In somewhat more than half the states, indigent defense is funded almost entirely at the state level, but 18 states (including six of the seven most populous) place the funding burden primarily on counties, often resulting in funding inequities. *See* National Right to Counsel Committee, Note 23, *supra*, 53–55, though the trend is toward state-level funding. *Id.* at 55.

indigent defendants: public-defender programs, assigned-lawyer programs, and contract-attorney representation.[69]

A public-defender system is an organization of lawyers designated by a jurisdiction to provide representation to indigents in criminal cases.[70] The attorneys who work in a public defender office are full-time salaried government employees working together under a single head defender who has responsibility for indigent representation in a particular jurisdiction — just as prosecutors are typically salaried government employees working under a single district attorney for a jurisdiction. Virtually all states have at least a minority of counties with such defender programs.[71]

Many counties have an assigned-counsel program. Under this approach, often inexperienced or underemployed private practitioners are placed on a list to provide representation to poor defendants on a case-by-case basis. They are paid by the hour (usually well below ordinary rates for attorneys in the community) or receive a flat fee per case.[72] One recent study found that, in the federal system, public defenders achieved substantially lower conviction rates and sentence lengths than assigned-counsel achieved for similarly situated defendants.[73]

A contract-attorney program is one in which a jurisdiction enters into an agreement with private attorneys, law firms, or bar associations to represent indigents in the community.[74] Attorneys in such a system often maintain a substantial private practice apart from their contract work. They are paid either on a fixed-price basis (they agree to accept an undetermined number of cases for a determined flat fee) or on a fixed-fee-per-case basis.[75] Frequently, the fees are so low that quality representation, particularly in capital cases,[76] is difficult to obtain.[77]

---

69. *See generally* The Spangenberg Group, Note 67, *supra* (providing a state-by-state accounting of the methods of providing indigent defense); Harlow, Note 29, *supra*; Robert L. Spangenberg & Patricia A. Smith, American Bar Association, An Introduction to Indigent Defense Systems (1986); Floyd Feeney & Patrick G. Jackson, *Public Defenders, Assigned Counsel, Retained Counsel: Does the Type of Criminal Defense Counsel Matter?*, 22 Rutgers L.J. 361 (1991); Shulhofer & Friedman, Note 23, *supra*, at 83–96; Spangenberg & Beeman, Note 23, *supra*, at 32–44.

70. Spangenberg & Beeman, Note 21, *supra*, at 36.

71. *See* State and County Expenditures for Indigent Defense Services in Fiscal Year 2005, Note 67, *supra*.

72. *See* Spangenberg & Beeman, Note 23, *supra*, at 32–34.

73. *See* Radha Iyengar, *An Analysis of the Performance of Federal Indigent Defense Counsel*, National Bureau of Economic Research, Working Paper 13187 (2007).

74. Schulhofer & Friedman, Note 23, *supra*, at 89.

75. Spangenberg & Beeman, Note 23, *supra*, at 34.

76. *See, e.g.,* State v. Young, 172 P.3d 138 (N.M. 2007) (staying a death penalty prosecution on the ground that $165,000 compensation for two defense attorneys in an extremely complex capital case was so inadequate as to trigger a presumption that no lawyer could provide effective assistance); *see generally* Douglas W. Vick, *Poorhouse Justice: Underfunded Indigent Defense Services and Arbitrary Death Sentences*, 43 Buff. L. Rev. 329, 377–97 (1995); *see also* § 28.08[A], *infra*.

77. *See generally* sources cited in Note 29, *supra*. According to 2007 figures prepared by The Spangenberg Group, most states only pay court-appointed counsel $40 to $70 per hour for non-capital cases. Furthermore, many states have an overall per case compensation cap, though most states allow judges to waive those caps in "extraordinary circumstances." Outside of the capital context, these compensation caps ranged from Virginia's $445 per non-capital felony charge with punishment of less than 20 years (Virginia pays $90 an hour, so counsel apparently stops getting paid after five hours' work [though the fee is now waivable up to $600!]), to Vermont's $25,000 for a crime punishable by life imprisonment, with most caps in the $3,000 range. *See* The Spangenberg Group, *Rates of Compensation for Court-Appointed Counsel in Non-Capital Felonies at Trial: A State-by-State Overview* (2007). Supreme Court Justice Harry Blackmun described the rate of

Today, most large counties employ some combination of these programs. In 1999, 314 criminal defense programs were identified in the 100 most populated counties. About 40 percent of the programs were of the assigned-counsel variety; 39 percent were public-defender programs; and 21 percent were contract-attorney programs.[78] The use of contract systems has grown dramatically over the past 25 years, however, frequently replacing assigned counsel programs, both as a result of an increase in the percentage of criminal cases that involve indigent defendants and as a result of cost-cutting efforts.[79]

§ 28.04 The Right to Counsel: On Appeal

[A] Inapplicability of the Sixth Amendment

By its language, the Sixth Amendment does not apply to criminal appeals. The amendment entitles a person to the assistance of counsel "for his *defence*" in "criminal *prosecutions.*" By the time the trial and sentencing are completed, the "prosecution" has ended. On appeal, it is the defendant/appellant who seeks to upset the status quo, and it is the prosecutor who seeks to "defend" the conviction.

Despite the inapplicability of the Sixth Amendment to criminal appeals, appellate procedures are subject to the standards of the Fourteenth Amendment Equal Protection and Due Process Clauses. In *Griffin v. Illinois*,[80] the Supreme Court held that a state that requires a defendant to furnish a trial transcript to the appellate court as a condition of hearing his appeal must provide the transcript at state expense for indigents. Justice Black,

---

compensation in death-penalty cases as "perversely low." McFarland v. Scott, 512 U.S. 1256, 1256 (1994) (Blackmun, J., dissenting from denial of certiorari). In one infamous Texas capital case, the state paid defense counsel $11.84 per hour. *See* Stephen B. Bright, *Counsel for the Poor: The Death Sentence Not for the Worst Crime but for the Worst Lawyer*, 103 Yale L.J. 1835, 1838–39 (1994). Although these rates have increased in some states in recent years—14 states raised their capital case compensation rates between 2003 and 2007, but only two of them were among the top 10 states in size of death row (North Carolina, 7th, and Georgia, 9th), *see* The Spangenberg Group, *Rate of Compensation for Court-Appointed Counsel in Capital Cases at Trial: A State-by-State Overview* (2007)—they remain very low. Reported hourly compensation rates for capital cases, which require far more experienced and expert counsel than ordinary felony cases, typically fell in a range between $60 and $100 an hour, ranging from a low of $50 per hour (Maryland) to a high of $150 (certain California counties). *Id.* Compensation caps are less common in the capital context, but when imposed typically range from $15,000 to $30,000. Incredibly, Mississippi has a maximum of $2,000 plus $25 per hour for expenses, though reportedly Mississippi judges do not "strictly follow" the maximum. *Id.* Compare those figures with the total payments for capital cases in Los Angeles, which (without a cap) in 2002 typically ranged from $60,000 to $200,000 per attorney. *See* The Spangenberg Group, American Bar Association, *Rates of Compensation for Court-Appointed Counsel in Capital Cases at Trial, 2002* (2003). Florida's statutory cap on payments in capital cases of $3,500 was declared unconstitutional by the Florida Supreme Court 20 years ago. *See* White v. Bd. of County Commissioners, 537 So. 2d 1376, 1379 (Fla. 1989) (holding cap unconstitutional to the extent that it curtails the court's inherent power to secure effective, experienced counsel for the representation of indigent defendants in capital cases). The cap in Florida now stands at $15,000.

78. DeFrances & Litras, Note 64, *supra*, at 4.

79. *See* The Spangenberg Group, U.S. Dep't of Justice, Contracting for Indigent Defense Services, A Special Report 3 (2000). For example, Oklahoma largely switched from a court-appointed system to a contract-attorney system, with the result that the average cost per case for the year 2000 was a mere $183. *See id.* at 7.

80. 351 U.S. 12 (1956).

writing for a four-justice plurality, applied both due process and equal protection standards to reach this conclusion. He wrote:

> [A] State can no more discriminate on account of poverty than on account of religion, race, or color. Plainly the ability to pay costs in advance bears no rational relationship to a defendant's guilt or innocence. . . . [¶] There can be no equal justice where the kind of trial a man gets depends on the amount of money he has. Destitute defendants must be afforded as adequate appellate review as defendants who have money enough to buy transcripts.[81]

The *Griffin* equality principle has been applied in various contexts to ensure that indigent defendants at trial and on appeal obtain meaningful access to procedures available to nonindigents.[82] It serves as the point of departure for consideration of an indigent's right to assistance of counsel on appeal.

[B] First Appeal (as of Right)

[1] In General

The Court has frequently repeated the dictum that a convicted defendant has no constitutional right to appeal his conviction.[83] Nonetheless, every state permits a convicted person at least one appeal as of right following a conviction after trial. Thereafter, courts have discretion not to hear appeals of criminal convictions.

In *Douglas v. California*,[84] the Supreme Court, per Justice Douglas, held that the Fourteenth Amendment requires a state to provide counsel for an indigent on his first statutory appeal of right. In doing so, the Court invalidated a California rule that permitted appellate courts, on the request of an indigent for the assistance of appellate counsel, to look at the trial record to determine whether the defendant would be benefitted by appointment of counsel.

The Court stated that although states do not have to provide absolute equality to the rich and the poor in their procedures, "where the merits of the one and only appeal an indigent has as of right are decided without benefit of counsel, we think an unconstitutional line has been drawn between rich and poor." Without distinguishing between due process and equal protection principles, the justices concluded that it is impermissible to require an indigent appellant to "run this gantlet of a preliminary showing of merit," if persons wealthy enough to hire a lawyer do not have to face the same obstacle.

As Justice Douglas explained, the discrimination in the case was not between "possibly good and obviously bad cases," but between people rich enough to hire lawyers and

---

81. *Id.* at 17–18, 19.

82. *E.g.*, Ake v. Oklahoma, 470 U.S. 68 (1985) (due process requires that the state provide access to a psychiatrist to an indigent defendant who makes a preliminary showing that his sanity will be an issue at trial); Mayer v. Chicago, 404 U.S. 189 (1971) (*Griffin* rule applies to payment of transcripts in appeals of misdemeanor convictions); Draper v. Washington, 372 U.S. 487 (1963) (a state rule providing for a free transcript only if the defendant can convince the trial judge that the appeal is non-frivolous violates the Fourteenth Amendment); Burns v. Ohio, 360 U.S. 252 (1959) (a state rule that requires indigent defendants to pay a fee before filing a notice of appeal violates *Griffin*); *see also* M.L.B. v. S.L.J., 519 U.S. 102 (1996) (*Griffin* rule is extended to an appeal of a ruling terminating a mother's parental rights, a "quasi-criminal" case).

83. *See, e.g.*, McKane v. Durston, 153 U.S. 684 (1894); Jones v. Barnes, 463 U.S. 745 (1983).

84. 372 U.S. 353 (1963).

those who were not. In this case, the Court said, "[t]here is lacking that equality demanded by the Fourteenth Amendment . . . The indigent . . . has only the right to a meaningless ritual, while the rich man has a meaningful appeal."

[2] Special Problem: Frivolous Appeals

A defendant does not have a constitutional right to demand that his attorney act unethically by prosecuting a frivolous appeal, i.e., an appeal that includes no arguable claims for reversal of the conviction.[85] In other words, he does not have a constitutional right to require his attorney to file a brief making spurious arguments. Instead, an attorney appointed to represent an indigent on direct appeal may request that the appellate court allow him to withdraw from the case. On the other hand, the Supreme Court determined in *Anders v. California*[86] that "in order to protect indigent defendants" constitutional right to appellate counsel, courts must safeguard against the risk of granting such requests in cases where the appeal is not actually frivolous."[87]

For decades, the general understanding of *Anders* was that a state appellate procedure was constitutionally infirm unless the appointed appellate counsel, in seeking to withdraw, filed a brief referring to anything in the record that arguably supported the appeal, including citations to case or statutory authority supporting the attorney's conclusion that the appeal was frivolous. The appellate court was also required, it seemed from *Anders*, to permit the appellant to file his own brief, raising any additional points he chose. The appellate court would then determine either that the case was "wholly frivolous" (and rule against the appellant on the merits) or determine that the appeal was not wholly frivolous, in which case new counsel would be appointed to represent the appellant and file a full brief.

In *Smith v. Robbins*,[88] however, the Court concluded that appellate procedures as strong as those described in *Anders* (noted above) are not obligatory. States "are free to adopt different procedures, so long as those procedures adequately safeguard a defendant's right to appellate counsel." Moreover, according to *Smith*, a state's procedure is adequate "so long as it reasonably ensures that an indigent's appeal will be resolved in a way that is related to the merit of that appeal."

In *Smith*, the Court upheld a new California appellate procedure that provided fewer protections than those enunciated in *Anders*. In California, if appellate counsel determines that an appeal would be frivolous, he must file a brief with the court summarizing the procedural and factual history of the case, and attest that he has reviewed the record, explained the case to his client, provided the client with a copy of his brief, and informed the client of the latter's right to file a supplemental brief. The appellate court must then conduct its own review of the record. If it determines that there are no arguable issues, it affirms the conviction; if it finds arguable claims, it orders briefing on those issues.

The procedure approved in *Smith*, while sufficient to "reasonably assure" an outcome that is "related to the merits," is far less rigorous than that demanded in *Anders*. Among other matters, it does not require appellate counsel to set out any possible arguable claims. As the dissenters in *Smith* complained, the appellate counsel who seeks to withdraw is

---

85. McCoy v. Court of Appeals of Wisconsin, Dist. 1, 486 U.S. 429, 436 (1988).
86. 386 U.S. 738 (1967).
87. Smith v. Robbins, 528 U.S. 259, 264 (2000) (explaining *Anders*).
88. 528 U.S. 259 (2000).

not required "to show affirmatively . . . that he has made the committed search for [arguable] issues . . . that go[es] to the heart of appellate representation in our adversary system."[89] Instead, the approved system leaves it to the appellate court to search the record for arguable issues. This process does not assure that the adversarial system will be at play on appeal, because the appellate court will not be looking at the record with an adversary's eye for finding plausible claims, as is expected of a partisan defense lawyer.

[C] Subsequent (Discretionary) Appeals

In *Ross v. Moffitt*,[90] the Supreme Court held that the Fourteenth Amendment does not require the appointment of counsel to assist indigent appellants in discretionary state appeals and in applications for review in the United States Supreme Court. Since *Ross* was decided, the Court has extended the no-right-to-counsel principle, as well, to state *habeas corpus* proceedings.[91]

In *Ross*, the Court discussed separately the issues of due process (which "emphasizes fairness between the State and the individual dealing with the State") and equal protection (which "emphasizes disparity in treatment by a State between classes of individuals whose situations are arguably indistinguishable"), although there was little difference in the ultimate analysis.

In its due process discussion, the Court focused on the difference between trials and appeals: whereas states cannot dispense with trials, they do not have to permit appeals. Therefore, when appeals are permitted, it "does not automatically mean that a State then acts unfairly by refusing to provide counsel to indigent defendants at every stage of the way." According to *Ross*, the Due Process Clause requires only that indigents not be singled out "and denied meaningful access [to appellate courts] . . . because of their poverty."

In the Court's equal protection discussion, it gave lip service to the *Griffin* equality principle,[92] but it quoted language in both *Griffin* and *Douglas v. California*[93] that indicated that absolute equality between the rich and poor is not constitutionally required. According to *Ross*, the Equal Protection Clause does not require a state "to duplicate the legal arsenal that may be privately retained by a criminal defendant." All that the constitutional provision demands, the Court said, is that the indigent have "an adequate opportunity to present his claims fairly in the context of the . . . appellate process."

The Court conceded that "a skilled lawyer, particularly one trained in the somewhat arcane art of preparing petitions for discretionary review, would . . . prove helpful to any litigant able to employ" the lawyer. Nonetheless, it concluded that indigents on discretionary appeals have an "adequate opportunity" to present their claims (or, in due process

---

89. *Id.* at 297 (Souter, J., dissenting).

90. 417 U.S. 600 (1974).

91. Pennsylvania v. Finley, 481 U.S. 551 (1987); Murray v. Giarratano, 492 U.S. 1 (1989) (plurality opinion) (death penalty appeal). *But see* Eric M. Freedman, *Giarratano is a Scarecrow: The Right to Counsel in State Capital Postconviction Proceedings*, 91 Cornell L. Rev. 1079 (2006) (noting that Alabama is now the only "active" death penalty state that does not provide counsel to indigent Death Row inmates before they file their state habeas petitions and arguing that this and other developments have undercut *Giarratano* to the point that it should be overruled).

92. *See* § 28.04[A], *supra*.

93. 372 U.S. 353 (1963).

terms, they have "meaningful access" to appellate review) without the assistance of counsel.

In support of this view, the Court pointed out that, with discretionary appeals that follow an appeal as of right, the appellate court will have various documents to consider: a transcript or other record of the trial proceedings; a brief on the appellant's behalf filed by his attorney during the first (*Douglas*) appeal of right; often an opinion of the lower court disposing of the case; and any submission by the indigent himself. The Supreme Court concluded that with these materials the appellate court has "an adequate basis for its decision to grant or deny review."

The Court was also "fortified in this conclusion" by the fact that the purpose of the discretionary review under state law for which counsel was not provided was *not* to determine whether the defendant was properly convicted. Rather, the discretionary review was to see if the case involved issues of "significant public interest" or "of major significance to the jurisprudence of the State." The Supreme Court reasoned that, given that the issues would have already been organized "in a lawyerlike fashion" in a brief for the appeal as of right, the court engaging in discretionary review would be able to determine whether the case met the standard for such review, even if the appellant did not have further assistance of counsel.

[D] First (Discretionary) Appeal After a Guilty Plea

Most jurisdictions provide the first appeal as of right even if the defendant has pleaded guilty,[94] and, in these circumstances, *Douglas v. California*[95] plainly mandates that the state provide counsel for an indigent appellant. At least one state, however, amended its state constitution to provide that an appeal from a guilty plea is discretionary (requiring leave of the appellate court) rather than as of right. The state subsequently decided not to provide counsel for most indigents who sought leave to appeal their plea-based convictions.

This circumstance falls in between the *Douglas* requirement (counsel must be provided for first appeals *as of right*) and the rule of *Ross v. Moffitt*,[96] (the Constitution does not require appointment of counsel for *subsequent* discretionary appeals). Like *Douglas* it involves a first appeal, not a subsequent one, but, like *Ross*, it involves a discretionary appeal, not an appeal as of right. In *Halbert v. Michigan*,[97] the Court, by a vote of 6–3, chose the *Douglas* side of the line, holding that the Constitution mandates appointment of counsel for indigents in this situation. The Court offered two reasons for its

---

94. A defendant may raise a number of claims on appeal following a guilty plea, including, for example:

> constitutional defects that are irrelevant to his factual guilt, double jeopardy claims requiring no further factual record, jurisdictional defects, challenges to the sufficiency of the evidence at the preliminary examination, preserved entrapment claims, mental competency claims, factual basis claims, claims that the state had no right to proceed in the first place, including claims that a defendant was charged under an inapplicable statute, and claims of ineffective assistance of counsel.

Halbert v. Michigan, 545 U.S. 605, 612–22 (2005) (quoting People v. Bulger, 614 N.W.2d 103, 133–34 (Mich. 2000) (Cavanagh, J., dissenting)).

95. 372 U.S. 353 (1963). *See* § 28.04[B][1], *supra.*

96. 417 U.S. 600 (1974). *See* § 28.04[C], *supra.*

97. 545 U.S. 605 (2005).

conclusion, once again noting that the issue was both a matter of due process and equal protection, but not expressly distinguishing the two in its analysis.

First, the Court noted, the appellate court deciding whether or not to grant leave to appeal makes its determination on the basis of the merits of the indigent's claims, as opposed to the high court tribunals in *Ross*, which exercise their discretionary power to hear appeals based on the general importance of the question presented. As a result, the appellate tribunal in *Halbert*, unlike those in *Ross*, had to make some assessment of the merits of the indigent's claims—a circumstance the Court decided was relevant to the constitutional need for counsel.

Second, the Court concluded that, without counsel, indigents are "disarmed in their endeavor to gain first-tier review." The Court pointed to the opinion in *Ross*, which noted that indigents seeking *subsequent* discretionary review have already had the benefit of an appellate counsel's review of the trial court record and a brief reflecting the legal arguments that might be made on the basis of that record. Here, in contrast, "[a] first-tier review applicant, forced to act pro se, will face a record unreviewed by appellate counsel, and will be equipped with no attorney's brief prepared for, or reasoned opinion by, a court of review." The Court further noted that "[n]avigating the appellate process without a lawyer's assistance is a perilous endeavor for a layperson, and well beyond the competence of individuals [like the indigent in this case] who have little education, learning disabilities, and mental impairments." Therefore, the Court concluded, appointment of counsel is necessary to assure that the "entitlement to seek leave to appeal . . . [is not] more formal than real."

§ 28.05 The Right of Self-Representation[98]

[A] The Defense: Who is In Charge?[99]

The Supreme Court has stated that, even though represented by counsel, an "accused has the ultimate authority to make certain fundamental decisions regarding the case, as to whether to plead guilty, waive a jury, testify in his or her own behalf, or take an appeal."[100] In addition, for those decisions regarding "basic trial rights," counsel "must both consult with the defendant and obtain consent to the recommended course of action."[101]

Yet the Court has also stated that "the lawyer has . . . full authority to manage the conduct of the trial"[102] and "has authority to manage most aspects of the defense without obtaining his client's approval."[103] Thus, although the defendant must be "consult[ed]" regarding "important decisions" and issues of "overarching defense strategy," control of

---

98. *See generally* John F. Decker, *The Sixth Amendment Right to Shoot Oneself in the Foot: An Assessment of the Guarantee of Self-Representation Twenty Years After Faretta*, 6 Seton Hall Const. L.J. 483 (1996).

99. *See generally* Anne Bowen Poulin, *Strengthening the Criminal Defendant's Right to Counsel*, 28 Cardozo L. Rev. 1213, 1235–46 (2006).

100. Jones v. Barnes, 463 U.S. 745, 751 (1983).

101. Florida v. Nixon, 543 U.S. 175, 187 (2004).

102. Taylor v. Illinois, 484 U.S. 400, 418 (1988).

103. Florida v. Nixon, 543 U.S. at 187.

much of the defense lies with counsel. Indeed, as one scholar has summarized, "courts hold that counsel controls all but a few decisions," including "all tactical decisions" and "all but a few decisions at trial."[104]

As a result, the only way for a defendant to ensure control of his own defense is to act as his own attorney. As discussed in the next subsection, the Court has held that the Sixth Amendment does give him that right.

[B] *Faretta v. California*

[1] Recognition of the Right

In *Faretta v. California*,[105] the Supreme Court, per Justice Potter Stewart, held that a defendant has a constitutional right voluntarily and knowingly to waive his right to the assistance of counsel and to represent himself at trial. In essence, the Sixth Amendment right-to-counsel provision includes two rights: expressly, the right of a criminal defendant to the assistance of counsel; and, by implication, an independent right of self-representation that follows from waiver of the first right.

In *Faretta*, *F*, charged with theft, requested permission to represent himself at trial. The judge originally agreed to the request, but later changed his mind when *F* failed adequately to answer various questions intended to determine his knowledge of applicable procedural and evidentiary law. Represented at his trial by a public defender, *F* was convicted.

The Supreme Court reversed the conviction. It concluded that *F* had a constitutional right to represent himself. According to Justice Stewart, the Sixth Amendment "does not provide merely that a defense shall be made for the accused; it grants to the accused personally the right to make his defense." According to *Faretta*, the personal nature of the right is evident from the fact that it is the defendant—not counsel—who must be informed of the nature of the charges, who has the right to confront accusers, and who must be accorded compulsory process for obtaining witnesses. According to the Court, "[t]he right to defend is given directly to the accused; for it is he who suffers the consequences if the defense fails."

The Court also found support for the right of self-representation in the language and historical roots of the Sixth Amendment. Textually, the amendment provides that a defendant is entitled to the "assistance" of counsel. The lawyer is the assistant; the defendant is the master. Historically, the English common rule provided that no criminal defendant "can have counsel forced upon him against his will."[106] And, according to the majority, "[i]n the American colonies the insistence upon a right of self-representation was, if anything, more fervent than in England."

---

104. Poulin, Note 99, *supra*, at 1235. When the defendant expressly disagrees with counsel on a tactical trial decision, lower courts are divided as to whether the lawyer may override or must abide by his client's wishes, *see id.*, at 1241–46, and the Supreme Court has not clearly addressed the subject. The Court has held in the appellate context that a defendant does not have "a constitutional right to compel appointed counsel to press nonfrivolous points requested by the client, if counsel, as a matter of professional judgment decides not to present those points." *Jones*, 463 U.S. at 751.

105. 422 U.S. 806 (1975).

106. *Id.* at 826 (quoting R. v. Woodward [1944] K.B. 118, 119).

Justice Blackmun, joined by Chief Justice Burger and Justice Rehnquist, dissented. They argued that the fact that Sixth Amendment rights are personal does not "guarantee[] any particular procedural method of asserting those rights." The dissent also questioned the Court's historical analysis. In view of the fact that the framers "expressly constitutionalized the right to assistance of counsel but remained conspicuously silent on any right of self-representation," the dissenters believed that "it is at least equally plausible to conclude that the Amendment's silence . . . indicates that the Framers simply did not have the subject in mind when they drafted the language."

The dissenters were also troubled with the majority's holding as a policy matter. In the dissent's view, the Sixth Amendment does not require "the States to subordinate the solemn business of conducting a criminal prosecution to the whimsical—albeit voluntary—caprice of every accused who wishes to use his trial as a vehicle for personal or political self-gratification." The dissenters worried that allowing defendants the right to proceed without counsel "will cause procedural confusion without advancing any significant strategic interest of the defendant."

[2] Reflections on *Faretta*[107]

Justice Stewart conceded in *Faretta* that "[t]here can be no blinking the fact that the right of an accused to conduct his own defense seems to cut against the grain of this Court's [prior right-to-counsel] decisions." Indeed, ironically, the justices forming the majority in *Faretta*—an opinion that says, in essence, that defendants have the right to forego the "necessities, not luxuries"[108] of the assistance of counsel—are those who argued most strenuously for the expansion of the right to counsel. Meanwhile, it was the dissenters—members of the Court not generally sympathetic to such extensions—who were called on to point out that "representation by counsel is essential to ensure a fair trial."

The essence of *Faretta* is that a defendant has a protectible right of autonomy. As it is the defendant, not the lawyer, who will suffer the consequences of a conviction, it is the accused's personal right to decide whether counsel is a benefit or a detriment. As Justice Stewart explained, "whatever else may be said of those who wrote the Bill of Rights, surely there can be no doubt that they understood the inestimable worth of free choice." Even if the defendant's freely-willed decision is "ultimately to his own detriment, [the] choice must be honored out of 'that respect for the individual which is the lifeblood of the law.'"[109]

In dissent, Justice Blackmun quoted the proverb that "one who is his own lawyer has a fool for a client." He needled the majority by stating that the Court "now bestows a *constitutional* right on one to make a fool of himself." Justice Stewart's answer to the dissenters was that "[p]ersonal liberties are not rooted in the law of averages." As he pointed out, "it is not inconceivable that in some rare instances, the defendant might in fact present his case more effectively by conducting his own defense."

---

107. *See generally* Martin Sabelli & Stacey Leyton, *Train Wrecks and Freeway Crashes: An Argument for Fairness and Against Self-Representation in the Criminal Justice System*, 91 J. Crim. L. & Criminology 161 (2000); Robert E. Toone, *The Incoherence of Defendant Autonomy*, 83 N.C. L. Rev. 621 (2005).

108. Gideon v. Wainwright, 372 U.S. 335, 344 (1963).

109. *Faretta*, 422 U.S. at 834 (quoting Illinois v. Allen, 397 U.S. 337, 350–51 (1970) (Brennan, J., concurring)).

Justice Stewart's last observation is correct, of course. Indeed, a recent empirical study found, in a limited sample, that "*pro se* felony defendants in state courts are convicted at rates equivalent to or lower than the conviction rates of represented felony defendants," though this may be as much an indictment of the quality of appointed counsel as an endorsement of the quality of pro se representation.[110] However, it is also true, as Justice Stewart conceded, that "in most criminal prosecutions defendants could better defend with counsel's guidance than by their own unskilled efforts." And, as important as the right of autonomy may be, it is not the *only* value at stake in criminal trials. The majority opinion runs counter to "the established principle that the interest of the State in a criminal prosecution 'is not that it shall win a case, but that justice shall be done.'"[111] Moreover, "courts have an independent interest in ensuring that . . . legal proceedings appear fair to all who observe them."[112] *Faretta* quite arguably threatens these interests.

One other point has been made in favor of *Faretta*: Forcing counsel on a defendant not only impinges on the defendant's autonomy, but also, in the case of indigent defendants, means that the defendant is being represented by someone chosen and paid for by the government. In other words, the person who is supposed to protect the accused is, on some level, the employee of the accuser. With this fact in mind, Justice Scalia wrote in defense of *Faretta*, "I have no doubt that the Framers of our Constitution . . . would not have found acceptable the compulsory assignment of counsel *by the Government* to plead a criminal defendant's case."[113]

[3] Current Status of *Faretta*

There can be little doubt that the *Faretta* rule is unpopular with most trial judges and many prosecutors for very practical reasons. First, with a layperson (and frequently a poorly educated one at that) conducting the defense, trials are inevitably slowed down and complicated by a defendant's failures to understand or follow normal procedures; and the burden grows on both the judge and the prosecutor to ensure that reversible error is avoided. For this reason, trial courts will frequently appoint standby counsel to assist the *pro se* defendant.[114] Second, once the defendant asserts a preference to proceed *pro se*, the trial court must steer between the Scylla and Charybdis of erroneously denying the defendant the right to proceed *pro se*[115] and erroneously concluding that the defendant has effectively waived his right to counsel,[116] since either error results in automatic reversal. Nor is *Faretta* terribly popular with defense attorneys. In the words of one defender-turned-law-professor, the attorney is left "feeling as though one is being required to stand by and watch as a client steps in front of an oncoming bus."[117]

---

110. Erica J. Hashimoto, *Defending the Right of Self-Representation: An Empirical Look at the Pro Se Felony Defendant*, 85 N.C. L. Rev. 423 (2007).

111. *Faretta*, 422 U.S. at 849 (Blackmun, J., dissenting) (quoting Berger v. United States, 295 U.S. 78, 88 (1935)).

112. Wheat v. United States, 486 U.S. 153, 160 (1988).

113. Martinez v. Court of Appeal of California, 528 U.S. 152, 165 (2000) (Scalia, J., concurring) (emphasis in original).

114. *See* § 28.05[C][5], *infra*.

115. *See* § 28.05[C][7], *infra*.

116. *See* § 28.05[C][2], *infra*.

117. Hashimoto, Note 110, *supra*, 434 n.46 (2007).

The post-*Faretta* Supreme Court, while occasionally criticizing the case, has settled, for the time being at least, with retaining *Faretta* but narrowing its scope. The first shot at *Faretta* came in *Martinez v. Court of Appeal of California*,[118] in which the Court held that there is no comparable constitutional right of self-representation on appeal.[119] Justice Stevens, whose opinion for the Court was joined by all but one justice, evinced only lukewarm support for some of *Faretta*'s reasoning, particularly the historical evidence set out in the latter case. Indeed, the *Martinez* opinion included some arguably gratuitous swipes at *Faretta*. The Court noted, for example, that "no one . . . attempts to argue that as a rule *pro se* representation is wise, desirable or efficient," and that "[s]ome critics argue that the right to proceed *pro se* at trial in certain cases is akin to allowing the defendant to waive his right to a fair trial." Even with regard to the autonomy point, the Court noted that "[t]he requirement of representation by trained counsel implies no disrespect for the individual," because it tends to benefit him. Concurring Justice Breyer, too, noted "that judges closer to the firing line have sometimes expressed dismay about the practical consequences of [*Faretta*]."[120]

The majority's tepid support for *Faretta* motivated Justice Kennedy, in concurrence, to write that "[t]o resolve this case [of self-representation on appeal] it is unnecessary to cast doubt upon the rationale of *Faretta v. California*." And concurring Justice Scalia stated more directly that he does "not share the apparent skepticism of [the majority] opinion concerning the judgment of the Court . . . in *Faretta v. California*."

Eight years later, in *Indiana v. Edwards*,[121] the Court expressly declined an invitation to overrule *Faretta*, but it did make it harder for mentally ill defendants to assert the right of self-representation. In *Edwards*, discussed in detail below,[122] the Court authorized states to find mentally ill defendants *competent* to stand trial but *incompetent* to represent themselves at trial. The Court stated that "instances in which the trial's fairness is in doubt [as a result of self-representation] may well be concentrated in the 20 percent or so of self-representation cases where the mental competence of the defendant is also at issue."[123] Therefore, the Court opined, the freedom its *Edwards* decision provides trial courts to deny self-representation in such cases "may well alleviate those fair trial concerns." Because *Edwards* was a 7–2 decision, authored by Justice Breyer, a *Faretta* skeptic, *Faretta*'s core holding seems safe for now.

---

118. 528 U.S. 152 (2000); *contra under the state constitution*, State v. Rafay, 222 P.3d 86 (Wash. 2009).

119. The Sixth Amendment does not apply to criminal appeals, *see* §28.04[A], *supra*, so if a right of self-representation on appeal existed it would have to have been found in general principles of due process. The Court stated that neither the holding of *Faretta* nor its reasoning compels a state to recognize a constitutional right of self-representation on direct appeal from a criminal conviction. Although the Court conceded that *Faretta*'s concern for an individual's right of autonomy would seem to support a right of *appellate* self-representation, it determined that such a right is not a necessary component of a fair appellate procedure, nor are there meaningful historical roots of such a right.

120. *Martinez*, 528 U.S. at 164 (Breyer, J., concurring) (also *quoting* United States v. Farhad, 190 F.3d 1097, 1107 (9th Cir. 1999) (stating that the right of self-representation "frequently . . . conflicts squarely and inherently with the right to a fair trial").

121. 554 U.S. 164 (2008).

122. *See* §28.05[C][1], *infra*.

123. 554 U.S. at 178.

[C] Procedural Issues

[1] Competence

The Court recently narrowed *Faretta*'s scope by expanding the government's ability to declare a defendant incompetent—mentally unfit—to represent himself. The Court's initial statement regarding *Faretta* competence came in *Godinez v. Moran*.[124] In *Godinez* the Court held that the Constitution requires only the same standard of competence to waive counsel and plead guilty as is required for a defendant to be brought to trial. That standard is "whether the defendant has 'sufficient present ability to consult with his lawyer with a reasonable degree of rational understanding' and has 'a rational as well as factual understanding of the proceedings against him.'"[125] So, under *Godinez*, a unitary standard appeared to govern both mental competence to be tried and mental competence to represent oneself. In *Indiana v. Edwards*,[126] however, the Court established that this is not necessarily the case.

In *Edwards*, E, who suffered from schizophrenia, faced attempted murder and other charges arising from an incident in which he tried to steal a pair of shoes from a department store and, when he was discovered, fired a gun at a security officer and hit a bystander. Because of his mental illness, E was initially held incompetent to stand trial and was committed to a state hospital. About five years later, E, while still suffering from schizophrenia, had recovered to the point that the trial court concluded he was competent to stand trial. Under *Godinez*, this meant that E would have been competent to waive counsel and plead guilty, but that was not what E wanted to do. Instead, E wished to proceed to trial representing himself. The trial court found him *incompetent* to do so. E was represented at his trial by appointed counsel and convicted of attempted murder.

The *Edwards* Court held that the Constitution allowed the state to "insist[] that the defendant proceed to trial with counsel" and thereby potentially to deny E the right to represent himself. The Court distinguished *Godinez* on the grounds that the defendant in that case had not wished to represent himself *at a trial* and that the state had acquiesced in the defendant's waiver of counsel. The *Edwards* Court further reasoned that mental illness that might not prevent a defendant from helping his lawyer could nonetheless render him "unable to carry out the basic tasks needed to present his own defense without the help of counsel." Moreover, the Court added, the spectacle of a defendant who lacks such capacity representing himself at trial will not advance the dignity interest that underlies the *Faretta* right and would risk eliminating both the appearance and the reality of a fair trial.

Edwards's holding—that "the Constitution permits States to insist upon representation by counsel for those competent enough to stand trial . . . but who still suffer from severe mental illness to the point where they are not competent to conduct trial proceedings themselves"—is highly significant because it opens up the possibility of granting

---

124. 509 U.S. 389 (1993).

125. *Id.* at 396 (quoting Dusky v. United States, 362 U.S. 402, 402 (1960)). *See also* 2 Dressler & Michaels, Note 38, *supra*, at § 9.02[A].

126. 554 U.S. 164 (2008); *see generally* Christopher Slobogin, *Mental Illness and Self-Representation: Faretta, Godinez and Edwards*, 7 Ohio St. J. Crim. L. 391 (2009).

the *Faretta* right to many fewer defendants.[127] Yet, like many such decisions, it raises a host of further questions.

First, what level of mental incompetence is needed to deny the right to self-representation? As the dissenters complained, the Court expressly refused to provide any answer or even expressly to determine whether *E* was properly denied the right to represent himself. Definition of that standard will have to await future cases. Another question is whether, when a state *may* deny self-representation at trial, the Court will conclude that it *must* deny self-representation, and whether *Edwards'* distinction from *Godinez* will extend to the guilty plea context. *Godinez* held that a state may *allow* a minimally competent defendant to plead guilty *pro se*, but *Edwards* throws open the possibility that a state could refuse such permission, absent a showing of greater competence. Finally, on a practical level, the question arises whether trial courts will take *Edwards* as an invitation to circumscribe *Faretta* by frequently finding defendants incompetent to represent themselves, and/or whether trial courts will be more inclined to find defendants competent to stand trial, knowing that they may do so without simultaneously risking the ordeal of a trial with a *pro se* defendant.

[2] Making the Choice of Self-Representation

The right of self-representation is independent of the right to the assistance of counsel. Therefore, the question arises: Must the accused be informed of both rights and then waive one of them? Although a defendant must be informed of his right to trial counsel,[128] lower courts have held that he does not need to be informed of his right of self-representation unless he clearly indicates that he is considering the option.[129]

Because self-representation is an independent right, a defendant who expresses the desire to represent himself must be permitted to do so as long as he is mentally competent to give up the right to counsel.[130] However, since it is also a waiver of the right to counsel, the choice must be knowing and voluntary.[131] Specifically, the Court stated in *Faretta* that a defendant "should be made aware of the dangers and disadvantages of self-representation, so that the record will establish that 'he knows what he is doing and his choice is made with eyes open.'"[132] The bottom line, according to a recent sampling of state and federal data, is that between 0.3% and 0.5% of felony defendants end up representing themselves at the time their case is resolved.[133]

[3] Timeliness of the Request

A defendant must assert his right of self-representation in timely fashion. In *Faretta*, the Court noted that *F*'s request was made "well before" the trial began. The implication

---

127. The Court speculated that perhaps 20 percent of defendants seeking to represent themselves might be affected by the decision. *See id.* at 178.

128. *E.g.*, Fed. R. Crim. P. 5(d).

129. Wayne R. LaFave et al., Criminal Procedure § 11.5(b) (5th ed. 2009).

130. Regarding competence, *see* § 28.05[C][1], *supra*.

131. Johnson v. Zerbst, 304 U.S. 458 (1938).

132. *Faretta*, 422 U.S. at 835 (quoting Adams v. United States ex. rel. McCann, 317 U.S. 269, 279 (1942)); for one example of a jury instruction that explains the pitfalls of self-representation, *see* United States v. Hayes, 231 F.3d 1132, 1138–39 (9th Cir. 2000).

133. Hashimoto, Note 110, *supra*, at 447.

is that a defendant must not only make the request before commencement of the trial, but he must make it sufficiently early that his request does not unduly delay orderly processes.

[4] Hybrid Representation[134]

Courts have uniformly held that a defendant is not entitled to so-called "hybrid" representation.[135] That is, a person does not have an automatic right to assert both of his Sixth Amendment rights, i.e., the right to the assistance of counsel *and* to represent himself at trial. Trial courts permit hybrid representation only as a "matter of grace."[136]

[5] Standby Counsel[137]

The Supreme Court stated in *Faretta* that a trial court may, even over the objection of the defendant, appoint standby counsel in self-representation cases. According to *Faretta*, the purpose of standby counsel is limited: to assist the defendant if and when he seeks help, and to take over the case if self-representation must be terminated during trial.

In an apparent reigning in of *Faretta*, the Supreme Court in *McKaskle v. Wiggins*[138] upheld a conviction in which standby counsel provided unsolicited, and at times even unwanted, assistance. In *Wiggins*, the Court stated that the right of self-representation "exists to affirm the dignity and autonomy of the accused and to allow the presentation of what may, at least occasionally, be the accused's best possible defense." Therefore, in evaluating whether a defendant's self-representation rights have been vindicated, "the primary focus must be on whether the defendant had a fair chance to present his case in his own way."

According to *Wiggins*, the right of self-representation is not violated unless standby counsel substantially interferes with "significant tactical decisions" of the defendant, "control[s] the questioning of witnesses," speaks in defendant's place against his wishes "on . . . matter[s] of importance," or in some other way "destroy[s] the jury's perception that the defendant is representing" himself.

In *Wiggins*, the Court concluded that standby counsel did not violate W's right of self-representation, although the lawyer intervened without W's permission, and sometimes over his vocal objection, more than 50 times during the three-day trial. In part, the Court refused to disapprove of counsel's actions because some of the intrusions occurred outside the presence of the jury, and therefore did not destroy its perception that W was representing himself, and also because W wavered during the trial, sometimes vehemently objecting to standby counsel's participation but other times inviting it.

[6] Legal Significance of Poor Self-Representation

As explained in Section 28.08, a defendant has a constitutional right to effective assistance of counsel. However, one who chooses self-representation "cannot thereafter

---

134. *See generally* Joseph A. Colquitt, *Hybrid Representation: Standing the Two-Sided Coin on Its Edge*, 38 Wake Forest L. Rev. 55 (2003).

135. LaFave et al., Note 129, *supra*, at § 11.5(g).

136. State v. Melson, 638 S.W.2d 342, 359 (Tenn. 1982).

137. *See generally* Anne Bowen Poulin, *The Role of Standby Counsel in Criminal Cases: In the Twilight Zone of the Criminal Justice System*, 75 N.Y.U. L. Rev. 676 (2000).

138. 465 U.S. 168 (1984).

complain that the quality of his own defense amounted to a denial of 'effective assistance of counsel.' "[139] In essence, a person who validly waives his right to counsel assumes the risk that, indeed, he had a "fool for a client."

[7] Legal Effect of an Erroneous Denial of the Right

If a court wrongfully refuses to permit a defendant to represent himself at trial, or if the right is violated by standby counsel, any subsequent conviction must be reversed. The Supreme Court has reasoned that because the right of self-representation serves to affirm a defendant's personal autonomy and, indeed, is "a right that when exercised usually increases the likelihood of a trial outcome unfavorable to the defendant, its denial is not amenable to 'harmless error' analysis. The right is either respected or denied; its deprivation cannot [ever] be harmless."[140]

§ 28.06 The Right to Representation by One's Preferred Attorney[141]

[A] In General

The Sixth Amendment comprehends the right of a nonindigent defendant "to select and be represented by one's preferred attorney."[142] Indeed, the Court has described the right to select counsel of choice as the "root meaning"[143] of the Sixth Amendment's counsel provision. The provision "commands . . . that the accused be defended by the counsel he believes to be best."[144]

This right of a defendant to be represented by the attorney of his choice is, however, subject to significant limitations that, taken together, constitute a substantial litany. First, and perhaps most important, the Court has stated that "the right to counsel of choice does not extend to defendants who require counsel to be appointed for them;"[145] in short, the Sixth Amendment does not grant indigents a right to choose their appointed counsel.

Second, although defense counsel "should seek to establish a relationship of trust and confidence with the accused,"[146] the Supreme Court has declared that a defendant has no Sixth Amendment right to a "meaningful attorney-client relationship."[147] Third, a

---

139. *Faretta*, 422 U.S. at 835 n.46; *McKaskle*, 465 U.S. at 177 n.8.

140. *McKaskle*, 465 U.S. at 177 n.8. For discussion of "harmless error" law generally, *see* 2 Dressler & Michaels, Note 40, *supra*, at § 16.04.

141. *See generally* Feeney & Jackson, Note 69, *supra*; Bruce A. Green, *"Through a Glass, Darkly": How the Court Sees Motions to Disqualify Criminal Defense Lawyers*, 89 Colum. L. Rev. 1201 (1989); Schulhofer & Friedman, Note 21, *supra*; Peter W. Tague, *An Indigent's Right to the Attorney of His Choice*, 27 Stan. L. Rev. 73 (1974).

142. Wheat v. United States, 486 U.S. 153, 159 (1988).

143. United States v. Gonzalez-Lopez, 548 U.S. 140, 147–48 (2006).

144. *Id.* at 146.

145. *Id.* at 151.

146. ABA Standards for Criminal Justice, Note 20, *supra*, 4-3.1.

147. Morris v. Slappy, 461 U.S. 1 (1983).

defendant is not permitted to be represented by a non-attorney, except himself.[148] Fourth, a defendant is not entitled to be represented by an attorney who has a conflict of interest, even if the defendant is willing to accept the risks inherent in such representation.[149]

Fifth, a defendant "may not insist on representation by an attorney he cannot afford."[150] This limitation is of particular significance in view of the enactment of statutes that permit the government to seize assets, including money that would pay for an attorney, that allegedly were obtained illegally. This issue is discussed in the next subsection. Finally, the Court has "recognized a trial court's wide latitude in balancing the right to counsel of choice against the needs of fairness, . . . the demands of its calendar," and the need to ensure that trials are conducted "within the ethical standards of the profession."[151]

Notwithstanding these limitations, however, when the right to counsel of choice is improperly denied, the Sixth Amendment violation means that a resulting conviction is subject to automatic reversal without any showing of prejudice or other form of harmless-error analysis.[152]

[B] Special Problem: Seizing Lawyers' Fees

Certain statutes allow the government to seize a defendant's assets prior to trial if the assets were related to illegal activity[153] or in order to ensure the defendant will have the necessary funds to pay fines or restitution if convicted of the crime.[154] Defendants have challenged these seizures under the Sixth Amendment, arguing that if their assets are frozen, they will not be able to hire lawyers to defend themselves. In a series of cases, the Supreme Court has set out a clear dividing line: the government may legally seize any assets that are "tainted;" such as contraband, property obtained as a result of the crime, or property that is somehow traceable to the crime.[155] However, the government may not seize "untainted" assets that are not connected to criminal activity, because that would undermine the defendant's "Sixth Amendment right to be represented by a . . . qualified attorney whom that defendant can afford to hire."[156]

In two cases, *Caplin & Drysdale v. United States*[157] and *United States v. Monsanto*,[158] the Supreme Court held that the right to counsel is not violated if a court, pursuant to statute,[159] grants an *ex parte* motion by the government to freeze the defendant's assets, including assets that would be used to pay for legal representation, on the ground that they were obtained as a result of illegal drug activities. Nor is the Sixth Amendment

---

148. *See Wheat*, 486 U.S. at 159.

149. *See* § 28.09, *infra*.

150. *Wheat*, 486 U.S. at 159.

151. *Gonzalez-Lopez*, 548 U.S. at 152.

152. *Id.* For discussion of "harmless error" law generally, *see* 2 Dressler & Michaels, Note 40, *supra*, at § 16.04.

153. *See, e.g.,* 21 U.S.C. § 853 (2005).

154. *See, e.g.,* § 1345(a)(2).

155. Caplin & Drysdale v. United States, 491 U.S 617 (1989); United States v. Monsanto, 491 U.S. 600 (1989).

156. Luis v. United States, 136 S. Ct. 1083, 1089 (2016) (plurality opinion).

157. 491 U.S. 617 (1989).

158. 491 U.S. 600 (1989).

159. 21 U.S.C. § 853 (2005).

violated by an order that any monies paid to defense counsel be recaptured if the client is convicted of such drug activities.

The Court reasoned that forfeiture statutes of the sort involved in these two cases do not impinge on a defendant's constitutional right to counsel of choice because they do not prevent the defendant from hiring any attorney whom he can afford or who is willing to represent him without assurances that he will have adequate funds. Furthermore, even if such statutes prevent him from hiring an attorney, the right to the attorney of one's choice encompasses only the right to spend one's own money to hire a lawyer, not the right to spend another's. Justice White colorfully described the opposite conclusion as changing the rule to read "'crime doesn't pay, except for attorney's fees.'"

Justice Blackmun, joined by Justices Brennan, Marshall, and Stevens, dissented in the cases. They argued "that it is unseemly and unjust for the Government to beggar those it prosecutes in order to disable their defense at trial."[160] Perhaps the most intriguing feature of the dissent is its strenuous argument that a defendant wealthy enough to hire an attorney is ordinarily better served than one who must accept appointed counsel. The implication of the comments (if accepted as true) is that, despite the Supreme Court's efforts in the middle of the twentieth century to assure that the kind of trial a person gets does not depend on the amount of money he has,[161] this is exactly what happens.

The dissenters focused on four factors. First, to be an effective advocate, an attorney needs his client's trust. Trust is fostered when a defendant can choose his own attorney. It is undermined, the dissenters stated, "[w]hen the Government insists upon the right to choose the defendant's counsel" for him. As two scholars have put it:

> Most citizens would consider it shockingly unethical for an attorney representing one side in a lawsuit to be selected or paid, even indirectly, by the opposing party. Yet such principles are violated routinely in this country on a massive scale. In criminal cases, the great majority of defense attorneys are paid directly or indirectly by the prosecuting party, the state.[162]

Second, the right to hire private counsel "serves to assure some modicum of equality between the government and those it chooses to prosecute." The government expends considerable resources to prosecute persons accused of crime, "[b]ut when the Government provides for appointed counsel, there is no guarantee that levels of compensation and staffing will be even average."[163]

Third, according to the dissent, the "socialization" of criminal-defense representation too easily excludes "the maverick and risk taker, [whose approach] might not fit into the structured environment of a public defender's office, or that might displease a judge whose preference for nonconfrontational styles of advocacy might influence the judge's appointment decisions."[164]

---

160. *Caplin & Drysdale*, 491 U.S. at 635.

161. *Griffin v. Illinois*, 351 U.S. 12, 19 (1956).

162. Schulhofer & Friedman, Note 23, *supra*, at 74 (footnote omitted).

163. For example, in 1990, public expenditures on the defense of indigents was only 31 percent of that spent on their prosecution. *See* Sourcebook of Criminal Justice Statistics § 1993, tbl.1.2 (U.S. Dept. of Justice 1994).

164. *Caplin & Drysdale, Chartered*, 491 U.S. at 647.

Finally, private attorneys can more easily specialize in complex areas of the criminal law than can public defenders, who need a broader—but necessarily thinner—range of skills.[165]

In contrast, the Court has held that the seizure of *untainted* assets violates the defendant's Sixth Amendment rights. In *Luis v. United States*,[166] L was charged with obtaining more than $45 million in a health care fraud scheme. The government sought a pretrial order to seize not just the $45 million that were the proceeds of the crime, but also L's remaining $2 million in assets, which were unrelated to the crime. The government argued that it was important to seize the assets in order to preserve them to pay for the restitution and fines that L would have to pay if convicted. L argued that he had a Sixth Amendment right to use his untainted assets to pay for his attorney.

In a four-Justice plurality decision,[167] the Court sided with L and distinguished *Caplin & Drysdale* and *Monsanto*. First, the Court noted that the tainted assets in the previous cases had never legally been the property of the defendant; they always belonged to the victims of the crime. In contrast, the $2 million of untainted assets in *Luis* were legally the property of the defendant; thus, the government had far less authority to freeze those assets. Second, the Court pointed out that, in many cases, the tainted assets (which may legally be seized) could be used to pay restitution and fines. And finally, the Court was concerned that allowing the government to seize untainted assets would "unleash a principle of constitutional law that would have no obvious stopping place."[168] Congress could create ever broader pretrial asset seizure laws, thus rendering a large percentage of criminal defendants indigent and forcing them to use "publicly paid counsel, including overworked and underpaid public defenders."[169]

Writing for a two-Justice dissent, Justice Kennedy argued that the plurality decision would reward criminals "who hurry to spend, conceal or launder stolen property"[170] and ultimately harm victims who would be left without restitution. Justice Kennedy would have broadly interpreted *Caplin & Drysdale* and *Monsanto* to mean that a defendant has no Sixth Amendment rights in any assets that are forfeitable to the government under law. Justice Kagan echoed this concern in her own dissent, noting that the plurality's decision draws an "irrational" line between "[t]he thief who immediately dissipates his ill-gotten gains and thereby preserves his other assets" and the thief "who spends those two pots of money in reverse order."[171]

§ 28.07 Interference with the Right to Counsel

The right to counsel includes the right "that there . . . be no restrictions upon the function of counsel in defending a criminal prosecution in accord with the traditions of the

---

165. Perhaps worse, indigents in most counties are not represented by public defenders, but receive representation from private, often relatively inexperienced, attorneys who are paid on a low hourly or flat-fee basis. *See* § 28.03[B][5], *supra*.

166. 136 S. Ct. 1083 (2016).

167. Justice Thomas added a fifth vote to the holding with his concurrence.

168. *Id.* at 1086.

169. *Id.*

170. *Id.* at 1103 (Kennedy, J., dissenting).

171. *Id.* at 1113 (Kagan, J., dissenting).

adversary [system] . . . that has been constitutionalized in the Sixth and Fourteenth Amendments."[172] This means, among other things, that the government may not ordinarily: (1) restrict defense counsel's decision on whether, and when in the course of the presentation of the defendant's case, the accused will testify;[173] (2) prevent counsel from eliciting testimony from his client through direct examination;[174] or (3) deny counsel the opportunity to make a summation to the jury.[175]

The Constitution is also violated if a trial judge prohibits a defendant from consulting with his attorney during an overnight recess, even if the recess is called while the defendant is on the witness stand and is about to be cross-examined by the prosecutor.[176] However, the Supreme Court explained in *Perry v. Leeke*[177] that because "cross-examination often depends for its effectiveness on the ability of counsel to punch holes in a witness' testimony at just the right time, in just the right way," a judge may prohibit consultation between the defendant and his counsel during a brief same-day recess, while the accused is testifying, in order to further the truth-seeking function of the trial.

Direct interference by the government with the defendant's right to the assistance of counsel ordinarily requires automatic reversal of any resulting conviction.[178]

§ 28.08 Effective Assistance of Counsel: General Principles[179]

[A] Nature of the Issue

The fact "[t]hat a person who happens to be a lawyer is present at trial alongside the accused . . . is not enough to satisfy" the Sixth Amendment.[180] If the Sixth Amendment "is to serve its purpose, defendants cannot be left to the mercies of incompetent

---

172. Herring v. New York, 422 U.S. 853, 857 (1975).

173. Brooks v. Tennessee, 406 U.S. 605 (1972) (applying the Fifth Amendment self-incrimination and due process clauses).

174. Ferguson v. Georgia, 365 U.S. 570 (1961).

175. Herring, 422 U.S. 853.

176. Geders v. United States, 425 U.S. 80 (1976).

177. 488 U.S. 272, 282 (1989).

178. *E.g., Geders*, 425 U.S. at 91–92 (reversing conviction without expressly determining whether prejudice occurred).

179. *See generally* Lisa J. McIntyre, The Public Defender: The Practice of Law in the Shadows of Repute (1987); Donald A. Dripps, *Ineffective Assistance of Counsel: The Case for an Ex Ante Parity Standard*, 88 J. Crim. L. & Criminology 242 (1997); Bruce A. Green, *Lethal Fiction: The Meaning of "Counsel" in the Sixth Amendment*, 78 Iowa L. Rev. 433 (1993); Michael McConville & Chester L. Mirsky, *Criminal Defense of the Poor in New York City*, 15 N.Y.U. Rev. L. & Soc. Change 581 (1986–87); Mirsky, Note 19, *supra*; Amy R. Murphy, Note, *The Constitutional Failure of the Strickland Standard in Capital Cases Under the Eighth Amendment*, 63 Law & Contemp. Probs. 179 (2000); Victoria Nourse, *Gideon's Muted Trumpet*, 58 Md. L. Rev. 1417 (1999); Eve Brensike Primus, *Structural Reform in Criminal Defense: Relocating Ineffective Assistance of Counsel Claims*, 92 Cornell L. Rev. 679 (2007); George C. Thomas III, *History's Lesson for the Right to Counsel*, 2004 U. Ill. L. Rev. 543 (2004); David Wasserman, *The Appellate Defender as Monitor, Watchdog, and Gadfly* (Occasional Paper 7, The Center for Research in Crime and Justice, N.Y.U. School of Law, 1989); Willcox & Bloustein, Note 28, *supra*.

180. Strickland v. Washington, 466 U.S. 668, 685 (1984).

counsel."[181] The Constitution requires lawyers, whether retained or appointed, to provide effective assistance to their clients at trial and on the first appeal of right.[182]

Under widely accepted professional standards, effective representation entails various duties, including the following. First, "[t]he professional judgment of a lawyer should be exercised, within the bounds of the law, solely for the benefit of his or her client and free of any compromising influences and loyalties."[183] Second, a defense lawyer should interview his client early on in their relationship, keep his client informed of important developments in the case, and consult with his client on important decisions.[184] Third, and perhaps most fundamentally, counsel has a duty to "conduct a prompt investigation of the circumstances of the case and explore all avenues leading to facts relevant to the merits of the case and the penalty in the event of conviction,"[185] after which he must bring to bear (the legal knowledge, skill, thoroughness and preparation reasonably necessary for the representation."[186]

Issues regarding the effectiveness of counsel are especially acute in the representation of indigents, who must rely on often-harried lawyers in understaffed and underfinanced public defender offices, or who are represented, sometimes with less than complete vigor, by private attorneys through contract or judicial appointment.[187] For example, one study reported that private attorneys assigned to represent indigents frequently failed to perform such basic tasks as interviewing their clients, investigating the facts underlying the charges, and filing written motions to suppress evidence or to discover evidence from the prosecutor.[188] One commentator has suggested that death sentences are meted out in capital cases "not for the worst crime[s] but for the worst lawyer[s],"[189] and the "worst

---

181. McMann v. Richardson, 397 U.S. 759, 771 (1970). An interesting 2012 study of criminal case outcomes in Philadelphia demonstrated that public defenders were more effective than court-appointed private attorneys. On average, defendants with public defenders were 19 percent less likely to be convicted in murder cases, and their sentences were 24 percent lower than those who had court-appointed counsel. Although this does not mean that court-appointed counsel are ineffective, it does raise "important questions about the adequacy and fairness of the criminal justice system." James M. Anderson & Paul Heaton, *How Much Difference Does the Lawyer Make? The Effect of Defense Counsel on Murder Case Outcomes*, 122 Yale L.J. 154 (2012).

182. Due process, rather than the Sixth Amendment, entitles a convicted defendant to effective assistance of counsel on his first appeal of right. Evitts v. Lucey, 469 U.S. 387 (1985). On subsequent, discretionary appeals, for which there is no constitutional right to the assistance of counsel, *see* § 28.04[C], *supra*, there is also no constitutional right to effective assistance. *Evitts*, 469 U.S. at 396 n.7.

183. ABA Standards for Criminal Justice, Note 20, *supra*, Commentary to Standard 4-3.5, at 162.

184. *Id.* at 4-3.2, 4-3.8, and 4-5.2.

185. *Id.* at 4-4.1.

186. American Bar Association, Model Rules of Professional Conduct, Rule 1.1 (2004).

187. *See generally* § 28.03[B][5], *supra*.

188. McConville & Mirsky, Note 179, *supra*, at 746–74. According to the study of New York County during the mid-1980s, lawyers assigned to represent indigents interviewed their clients in only 26 percent of homicide cases and 18 percent of all other felonies; they conducted investigations in 27 percent of homicide cases and 12 percent of other felony cases; and they filed written motions in only a quarter of the homicide cases, and in 20 percent of other cases. A *New York Times* study of New York City records and court cases in the year 2000 found that "almost no part of the indigent defense system functioned as it was intended": most lawyers appointed to represent indigents failed to hire private investigators to look for witnesses or evidence, did not seek experts to rebut expert prosecutorial evidence, and did not go to the scene of the crime to conduct their own investigation. Most of the appointed lawyers did not make even a single visit to the jail to discuss the case with their clients. Jane Fritsch and David Rohde, *Lawyers Often Fail New York's Poor*, N.Y. Times, April 8, 2001, at A1.

189. Bright, Note 77, *supra*.

lawyers" are usually those representing indigents. A major reason for the poor quality of representation by private counsel is the inadequate compensation provided to such attorneys.[190]

[B] "Ineffective Assistance": The *Strickland* Test

[1] Overview

The Supreme Court's seminal decision defining the constitutional test for "ineffective assistance of counsel" under the Sixth Amendment came in *Strickland v. Washington*.[191] Prior to *Strickland*, many lower courts had already determined that a sufficiently poor performance by a defense attorney could mean that the defendant's Sixth Amendment right to counsel was not satisfied. As the Court had previously stated, "the right to counsel is the right to effective assistance of counsel."[192] Lower courts, however, had constructed a variety of tests for deciding when defense counsel's performance failed to satisfy the Sixth Amendment. These standards ranged from "the forgiving 'farce-and-mockery' standard,"[193] to a variety of tests of "reasonable competence."[194] Lower courts also disagreed about whether a defendant had to demonstrate that he was prejudiced by his attorney's poor performance, and, if so, to what degree.[195]

In *Strickland*, the Court, in an 8–1 decision authored by Justice O'Connor, set out to resolve these issues. The opinion began its analysis by noting that in assessing claims of "actual ineffectiveness," the purpose of the Sixth Amendment right to counsel — "to ensure a fair trial" — must be the guide. Therefore, the Court stated, "[t]he benchmark for judging any claim of ineffectiveness must be whether counsel's conduct so undermined the proper functioning of the adversarial process that the trial cannot be relied on as having produced a just result."

The Court then provided a two-pronged test for making that judgment. First, to establish a Sixth Amendment claim of ineffective assistance of counsel, a criminal defendant must show that counsel's performance was deficient — that it fell below "an objective standard of reasonableness." Second, a defendant must *also* show prejudice from the deficient performance — that absent the deficient performance there was "a reasonable probability" that the result of the proceeding would have been different.[196] The defendant

---

190. For state cases, *see* Note 77, *supra*. In the federal system, there are statutory caps on compensation set out in 18 U.S.C. 3006A(d)(2) (2008) (as of January 1, 2010, $9,700 for representation of a felony defendant before and during trial; lesser amounts are set for misdemeanor ($2,800) and appellate ($6,900) representation, *see* http://www.uscourts.gov/AppointmentOfCounsel.aspx).

191. 466 U.S. 668 (1984). Under federal law and in the majority of states, an ineffective assistance of counsel claim, which often requires factual development beyond the trial record, can be brought through a collateral attack on the conviction and need not (and often may not) be raised on direct appeal. *See* Massaro v. United States, 538 U.S. 500 (2003). *See also*, Primus, Note 179, *supra* (arguing that — because of the length of time direct appeals typically take — providing appellate counsel with a means to raise ineffective assistance of counsel in the trial court *prior* to adjudication of the appeal would more effectively enforce the right to effective assistance).

192. McMann v. Richardson, 397 U.S. 759, 771 n.14 (1970).

193. Strickland v. Washington, 466 U.S. at 713 (Marshall, J., dissenting) (*citing* State v. Pacheco, 588 P.2d 830, 833 (Ariz. 1978)).

194. *See Strickland* at 713–14.

195. *Id.* at 714.

196. In certain limited circumstances, such prejudice will be presumed. *See* § 28.08[B][3][a], *infra*.

must establish both elements; a court may reject an ineffective assistance claim on the basis of either prong, without considering the other.[197] This test applies both to criminal trials and to sentencing proceedings,[198] and to retained counsel as well as appointed counsel.[199]

In her opinion, Justice O'Connor urged that, notwithstanding its articulation of the two-pronged test, lower courts "should keep in mind that the[se] principles . . . do not establish mechanical rules" and that "[i]n every case the court should be concerned with whether, despite the strong presumption of reliability, the result of the particular proceeding is unreliable because of a breakdown in the adversarial process that our system counts on to produce just results." Notwithstanding this admonition, post-*Strickland* courts assessing ineffective assistance of counsel claims usually hew closely to the two-pronged test.

Ineffective-assistance-of-counsel claims are as easy to make as they are difficult to win. Thus, it is a claim that is frequently made but does not often succeed.[200] Many academics have concluded that the hurdles a defendant must clear to demonstrate ineffective assistance have proven too high in practice and that *Strickland* should be viewed as a failure.[201]

The *Strickland* two-pronged test is considered in detail in the next subsections. Two specific issues—a lawyer with a conflict of interest and the role of ethical rules regarding representation—receive separate treatment.[202]

[2] The First Prong: Deficiency of Representation

[a] The Standard

A defendant must prove that his counsel's performance was constitutionally deficient, which means that the "errors [were] so serious that counsel was not functioning as the 'counsel' guaranteed . . . by the Sixth Amendment."[203] The test for this judgment is whether "counsel's representation fell below an objective standard of reasonableness."[204]

In establishing the "objective-standard-of-reasonableness" test for ineffectiveness, the Court expressly rejected a checklist (or, indeed, any enumeration) of specific actions an "objectively reasonable" defense attorney would take. According to the Court, "[n]o particular set of detailed rules for counsel's conduct can satisfactorily take account of the variety of circumstances faced by defense counsel or the range of legitimate decisions regarding how best to represent a criminal defendant."

---

197. *Strickland*, 466 U.S. at 697.

198. *See* Alan C. Michaels, *Trial Rights at Sentencing*, 81 N. Car. L. Rev. 1771, 1791–94 (2003). This test also provides the framework for evaluating a claim of ineffectiveness based on an attorney's failure to file a notice of appeal. Roe v. Flores-Ortega, 528 U.S. 470 (2000).

199. Cuyler v. Sullivan, 446 U.S. 335, 342–45 (1980).

200. *See* Joshua Dressler & George C. Thomas III, Criminal Procedure: Principles, Policies and Perspectives 1025 (West 5th ed., 2012) (calculating that through 2001 about 1,200 of some 37,000 reported *Strickland* claims—roughly three percent—were successful).

201. *See, e.g.,* Donald A. Dripps, *Ineffective Litigation of Ineffective Assistance Claims: Some Uncomfortable Reflections on Massaro v. United States*, 42 Brandeis L.J. 793 (2004); Richard Klein, *The Constitutionalization of Ineffective Assistance of Counsel*, 58 Md. L. Rev. 1433 (1999); Thomas, Note 179, *supra*.

202. *See* § 28.09–28.10, *infra*.

203. *Strickland*, 466 U.S. at 687.

204. *Id.* at 688.

Justice Marshall's dissent charged that, by failing to articulate standards of "reasonable" performance, the Court "abdicated its . . . responsibility to interpret the Constitution," and left a standard that "is so malleable that, in practice, it will either have no grip at all or will yield excessive variation."

In practice, it has not proven easy for defendants to show that counsel's conduct fell below the objective standard of reasonableness. According to *Strickland*, a convicted defendant must identify with precision the acts or omissions that he claims were constitutionally unreasonable. Furthermore, the court evaluating an ineffectiveness claim must consider the issue from the lawyer's perspective at the time of the act or omission, rather than "second-guess" counsel's performance with the "distorting effects of hindsight." The court's scrutiny "must be highly deferential," and it "must indulge a strong presumption that counsel's conduct falls within the wide range of reasonable professional assistance."

A critical issue in many ineffective-assistance-of-counsel claims is whether the alleged deficiency of counsel's performance can be characterized as a "strategic choice."[205] Strategic decisions by a defense lawyer are "virtually unchallengeable" if they were made after thorough investigation of the law and facts relevant to the case.[206] Strategic choices made after "less than complete investigation are reasonable precisely to the extent that reasonable professional judgments support the limitations on investigation." As seen below, a claim of deficiency will often turn on whether a lawyer's lack of effort to investigate or to perform other tasks can be characterized as a matter of strategic choice rather than the result of inexcusable lack of attentiveness.

[b] Deficiency: Supreme Court Case Law

While determination of ineffectiveness under *Strickland* is very much a fact-based, case-by-case inquiry, some sense of the issue can be gleaned from the Supreme Court cases on the question.

[i] Failure to Perform Ordinary Tasks — Held Not Unreasonable

A counsel's failure to conduct ordinary tasks in defending his client does not automatically constitute Sixth Amendment "deficient" representation, far from it. The

---

205. Remarkably, one lower court found that counsel napping during trial may have been a "strategic move" to gain jury sympathy for the client (co-counsel remained awake). *See* McFarland v. Texas, 928 S.W.2d 482, 505 n.20 (Tex. Crim. App. 1996). More frequently, however, lower courts seem to hold that if a defense lawyer *frequently* falls asleep during trial or during significant pretrial hearings, this constitutes objectively unreasonable performance. For example, in one Second Circuit case, the court found a violation based on undisputed evidence that the defense counsel "was unconscious for numerous extended periods of time during which the defendant's interests were at stake." Tippins v. Walker, 77 F.3d 682, 685 (2d Cir. 1996). And in a Texas criminal case, the Fifth Circuit concluded that the conduct of a defense lawyer who fell asleep five to 10 times during the trial for as long as 10 minutes, and during which time the prosecutor was questioning witnesses or presenting evidence, constituted ineffective assistance. *See* Burdine v. Johnson, 262 F.3d 336 (5th Cir. 2001) (en banc). *See also* Ross v. Kemp, 393 S.E.2d 244 (Ga. 1990), and Harrison v. Zant, No. 88-V-1460 (reported in Paul Marcotte, *Snoozing, Unprepared Lawyer Cited*, 77 A.B.A. J., Feb. 1991, at 14) (death sentences were overturned due to the inadequacy of an 83-year-old counsel's representation, upon proof that he slept a "good deal" during the proceedings).

206. *Strickland*, 466 U.S. at 690. *See, e.g.*, Florida v. Nixon, 543 U.S. 175 (2004) (holding that the decision to concede guilt at trial in a capital murder case was a reasonable strategic choice); Bell v. Cone, 535 U.S. 685, 701–02 (2002) (per curiam) (concluding that the decision to forgo making a closing statement may be reasonable).

difficulties confronting a convicted defendant are evident from *Strickland* itself. Over his lawyer's objection, *W* pleaded guilty to three counts of capital murder. *W* told the judge that he had no significant prior criminal record, that he had acted under extreme stress due to economic problems in his family, but that he accepted responsibility for the crimes. The judge stated that he had "a great deal of respect" for persons who admit their responsibility, but that he was not prejudging the sentencing issue.

W's objection to his lawyer's conduct related to counsel's post-plea preparation for, and conduct at, the capital sentencing hearing. *W* alleged various omissions on his lawyer's part, including counsel's failures to request a psychiatric report, to investigate and present character witnesses at the hearing, to seek a presentence investigation report, and to present "meaningful arguments" for leniency to the sentencing judge.

The Court found each of these claims unpersuasive. It was satisfied that counsel, after talking to his client and *W*'s wife and mother, made "a strategic decision" to argue that *W*'s emotional stress mitigated his blameworthiness for the murders and to rely on his client's acceptance of responsibility for the crimes. Counsel's decision not to request a psychiatric report was justified because "his conversations with his client gave no indication that [*W*] had psychological problems." And, the Court found, counsel did not request a presentence report because he learned from his investigation that *W* had a somewhat more serious criminal history than *W* had disclosed to the judge. The Court stated that "[a]lthough counsel understandably felt hopeless about [*W*'s] prospects, . . . nothing in the record indicates . . . that counsel's sense of hopelessness distorted his professional judgment." The Court concluded that the lawyer's behavior "was well within the range of professionally reasonable judgments."

The Court demonstrated even greater deference to defense counsel's judgment in *Burger v. Kemp*.[207] In *Burger*, *B*'s counsel offered no mitigating evidence whatsoever during two capital sentencing hearings, although he could have presented evidence that his client, a minor at the time of the crime, had no adult criminal record, had an I.Q. of only 82, and "had an exceptionally unhappy and unstable childhood," all factors that were potential grounds for a decision by the sentencer not to impose the death penalty on a person convicted of murder.

B's lawyer was aware of some, but not all, of his client's background. Prior to the hearing, he had talked to *B*'s mother several times, to an out-of-state lawyer who had served as his client's "Big Brother" and who had offered to come to the hearing to testify, and to a psychiatrist who had conducted a pretrial examination of his client. Counsel had also reviewed various psychologists' reports based on meetings with *B* before the crime was committed.

The Supreme Court held, over the sharp dissent of four justices, that the lawyer's conduct was not deficient. It conceded that counsel "could well have made a more thorough investigation than he did." However, the Court stated that counsel's decision not to conduct an "all-out investigation" into his client's background was supported by reasonable professional judgment, in that his interviews and studies of the reports indicated that "an explanation of [*B*'s] history would not have minimized the risk of the death penalty."

A dismal chance of success can also supply a sufficient tactical reason for counsel not to act. In *Knowles v. Mirzayance*,[208] *M* initially pleaded both not guilty and not guilty by reason of insanity. Under the governing state procedure, *M* would be tried in a

---

207. 483 U.S. 776 (1987).
208. 556 U.S. 111 (2009).

bifurcated proceeding that addressed guilt in phase one and insanity in phase two, before the same jury. In phase one, *M*'s counsel offered evidence that *M* was insane to show he lacked the "premeditation and deliberation" the state required for the first-degree murder charge. When the insanity evidence apparently failed to convince the jury during the guilt phase (*M* was convicted of first-degree murder), *M*'s counsel advised *M* to withdraw his insanity plea, and *M* did so before phase two commenced. *M* subsequently argued that the advice to withdraw the insanity plea constituted ineffective assistance, and lower courts agreed on the ground that *M* had "nothing to lose" by attempting the plea and "nothing to gain" by dropping it. In unanimously rejecting *M*'s claim, the Supreme Court concluded that, having carefully and reasonably determined that the insanity defense was almost certain to lose, *M*'s counsel could decide to recommend dropping the claim; doing so did not show deficient performance. In the Court's view, the claim's weakness, though not so great as to make the claim frivolous, provided reason enough to drop it. The Court did not require demonstration that something either would be or might be lost by bringing the claim.

[ii] Failure to Perform Ordinary Tasks—Held Unreasonable

Notwithstanding the difficulty of showing that counsel's failure to perform ordinary tasks falls below an objective standard of reasonableness, the Court has reached that conclusion on several occasions. However, the Court's more rigorous application of the *Strickland* test, described immediately below, occurred before the retirement of Justice Sandra Day O'Connor. Her place on the Court is now occupied by Justice Alito.[209]

In *Williams v. Taylor*,[210] the deficient attorney failed to discover or failed to offer mitigating evidence at the defendant's capital sentencing hearing. For example, counsel failed to prepare for the hearing until a week beforehand, failed to uncover extensive records graphically setting out the defendant's "nightmarish" childhood, and failed to introduce available evidence of the client's borderline mental retardation, as well as his exemplary behavior in prison, which included the defendant's assistance in cracking a prison drug ring and returning a guard's missing wallet. The Court concluded that these failures were not the result of tactical decisions; instead, the omissions demonstrated that counsel did not fulfill his ethical obligation to conduct a thorough investigation of his client's background, and thus fell below an objective standard of reasonableness.

Similarly, in *Wiggins v. Smith*,[211] the Court held, 7–2, that counsel's decision not to go beyond the presentence investigation report and records from the city Department of Social Services in investigating the defendant's background in preparation for defendant's capital sentencing hearing, was not an exercise of "reasonable professional judgment" in light of "prevailing professional norms," and that the state court's contrary conclusion was objectively unreasonable.

Perhaps most interesting is the Court's examination of the performance of counsel at a capital sentencing hearing in *Rompilla v. Beard*.[212] The result in *Rompilla* is a remarkable counterpoint to *Strickland* and *Burger v. Kemp*,[213] when one considers the number of appropriate things the defendant's attorneys here *did* do. In *Rompilla*, defense

---

209. *Cf.* Schriro v. Landrigan, 550 U.S. 465 (2007) (rejecting claim of ineffective assistance for failure to investigate in a 5–4 decision, with Justice Alito in the majority).

210. 529 U.S. 362 (2000).

211. 539 U.S. 510 (2003).

212. 545 U.S. 374 (2005).

213. 483 U.S. 776 (1987), described in subsection [i], *supra*.

counsel did not "ignore[] their obligation to find mitigating evidence," and they interviewed their client, *R*, several members of his family, and three mental health experts in a largely unsuccessful effort to find mitigating evidence. Counsel failed, however, to examine a publicly available court file regarding *R*'s prior conviction. The Supreme Court concluded, 5–4, that because the state had given notice of its intention to introduce the fact of that prior conviction and to read from the trial transcript in that case at *R*'s capital sentencing proceeding, counsel was "deficient in failing to examine the court file" and that the state court's opposite conclusion was objectively unreasonable.

The dissent argued that counsel's decision not to review "the full prior conviction case file" was a "sound strategic calculation" given their limited resources, and that the majority decision effectively imposed "a rigid requirement to review all documents [regarding] any prior conviction that the prosecution might rely on at trial." These contentions did not prevail. However, Justice O'Connor, who provided the crucial fifth vote for the majority opinion, also wrote a separate concurrence rejecting the view that the Court was imposing any such "rigid requirement" and reiterating that counsel's performance is to be judged on a case-by-case basis.[214]

[iii] Ignorance of Relevant Law

Deficient representation linked to a counsel's ignorance of applicable law is a somewhat less daunting claim to prove than that a lawyer acted with undue vigor. For example, in *Kimmelman v. Morrison*,[215] defense counsel failed to file a timely motion to suppress evidence obtained in violation of the Fourth Amendment. The lawyer did not make the motion because he was unaware of the search that resulted in the seizure of highly incriminating evidence; his lack of knowledge of the search was the result of his failure to request discovery, which in turn was based on his mistaken belief that the

---

214. In its 2009–10 term, the Roberts Court exhibited an intense interest in ineffective-assistance-of-counsel claims in the death penalty context, deciding five cases, and ruling twice for petitioners under sentence of death (Porter v. McCollum, 558 U.S. 30 (2009) (per curiam); Jefferson v. Upton, 560 U.S. 284 (2010) (per curiam)), and three times for the state (Bobby v. Van Hook, 558 U.S. 4 (2009) (per curiam); Wong v. Belmontes, 558 U.S. 15 (2009) (per curiam); Wood v. Allen, 558 U.S. 290 (2009)). These cases arose in different procedural contexts, which meant different standards of review were invoked, and the decisions were highly fact-specific, making generalizations particularly difficult. Nonetheless, this heightened activity is somewhat remarkable by previous standards and several aspects are worthy of note. First, as the citations above indicate, four of the five decisions were per curiam opinions written on the basis of the petitions for certiorari without full briefing or oral argument, and each of them changed the result of the lower court. This suggests that the Supreme Court considers the correct outcome in such cases in this particular area so important that it is willing to engage in error correction—in both directions—even when the governing legal principles are well-settled. Second, the Court's willingness to find ineffective assistance of counsel in at least some cases has continued after Justice O'Connor's retirement. Indeed, in one unanimous per curiam opinion, *Porter v. McCollum*, in which the Court found deficient attorney performance, the Court relied in part on *Rompilla v. Beard*, the high-water mark for the Court's willingness to find deficient performance. Third, claims of failure to investigate have the most success at the Supreme Court level. That was the core of the claim in the three cases discussed in this chapter subsection, and was the core of the claim in the two cases the defendant won in the 2009–2010 term. *See also* Hinton v. Alabama, 134 S. Ct. 1081 (2014) (per curiam) (finding inadequate performance in a death penalty case and describing the attorney's "failure to perform basic research" on "a point of law that is fundamental to his case . . . a quintessential example of unreasonable performance"). *But see* Maryland v. Kulbicki, 136 S. Ct. 2 (2015) (per curiam) (summarily reversing a lower court finding of ineffective assistance that had been based on failure to uncover a report that could possibly have been used to undermine expert testimony).

215. 477 U.S. 365 (1986).

prosecutor was required on his own initiative to turn over to the defense all of the incriminating evidence in his possession.

The Court reversed the conviction, holding that, although counsel's representation of his client at trial was "creditable," his failure to conduct the pretrial discovery in this case, which would have put him on notice of the incriminating evidence that might have been suppressed, was contrary to prevailing professional norms. The deficiency prong of *Strickland* was satisfied because counsel's actions were not the result of a well (or even questionably) crafted trial strategy, but were based on his legally mistaken understanding of the law of discovery.

Similarly, in *Lockhart v. Fretwell*,[216] F was sentenced to death for a robbery-murder. One of the aggravating factors that the jury found at the sentencing phase was that the murder was committed for pecuniary gain. The evidence in this regard duplicated facts already proved at the guilt phase (that F had committed a robbery) and, therefore, was inadmissible at the capital sentencing phase according to case law at the time of the trial. F's attorney failed to object to introduction of this evidence, apparently because he was unaware of the relevant law. This failure by the attorney constituted deficient representation under the first prong of *Strickland*.

[3] The Second Prong: Prejudice

[a] The Standard

The *Strickland* Court concluded that because the right to counsel is "to ensure that a defendant has the assistance necessary to justify reliance on the outcome of the proceeding," deficiencies in counsel's performance do not constitute constitutionally ineffective assistance of counsel unless that performance is "prejudicial to the defense."[217]

According to *Strickland*, in particular limited circumstances, such prejudice may be presumed: (i) when the defendant is actually[218] or constructively[219] denied counsel; (ii) when the state unconstitutionally interferes with counsel's assistance;[220] or (iii) in the case of certain conflicts of interest.[221] In the first two circumstances, *Strickland* said, prejudice "is so likely that case-by-case inquiry into prejudice is not worth the cost. . . . Moreover, such circumstances involve impairments of the Sixth Amendment right that are easy to identify and, for that reason and also because the prosecution is directly responsible, easy for the government to prevent." In the third case, "it is difficult to measure the precise effect on the defense of representation corrupted by conflicting interests." In all other claims of actual ineffectiveness, however, the defendant must affirmatively prove prejudice.

To determine prejudice, the Court adapted the test for prejudice it had developed in judging the materiality of exculpatory information the prosecution fails to disclose to the defense.[222] In the ineffective assistance context, to prove prejudice, "[t]he defendant

---

216. 506 U.S. 364 (1993).
217. *Strickland*, 466 U.S. at 691–92.
218. *E.g.*, Gideon v. Wainwright, 372 U.S. 335 (1963). *See* § 28.03[B][3], *supra*.
219. *E.g.*, Powell v. Alabama, 287 U.S. 45 (1932). *See* § 28.03[B][2][a], *supra*.
220. *See* § 28.07, *supra*.
221. *See* § 28.09, *infra*. The "presumption of prejudice" in qualifying conflict-of-interest cases is a limited one, under which the defendant must still show that the conflict "adversely affected his attorney's performance." *Strickland*, 466 U.S. at 692.
222. *See* 2 Dressler & Michaels, Note 40, *supra*, at § 7.02.

must show that there is a reasonable probability that, but for counsel's unprofessional errors, the result of the proceeding would have been different." A "reasonable probability is a probability sufficient to undermine confidence in the outcome."[223] "Reasonable probability" is an imprecise term. Clearly, however, it *does* require that the defendant prove more than that the error "had some conceivable effect on the outcome of the proceeding," but *does not* require that he show that it is more likely than not that counsel's deficient conduct changed the outcome.

Justice Marshall, dissenting in *Strickland*, objected to the Court's imposition of a prejudice prong in cases of deficient attorney performance on both pragmatic and principled grounds. As to the former, Justice Marshall argued that reviewing courts would not be able to tell from the "cold record" of a convicted defendant's trial what a skilled attorney might have been able to do with the case, particularly because "evidence of injury to the defendant may be missing from the record precisely because of the incompetence of defense counsel."[224]

As to the latter, Justice Marshall charged that the majority assumed that "the only purpose of effective assistance of counsel is to ensure that innocent people will not be convicted," when in fact, he argued, it also serves to ensure convictions are only obtained through fundamentally fair procedures. Justice Marshall succinctly captured his difference with the majority on this point: "The majority contends that the Sixth Amendment is not violated when a manifestly guilty defendant is convicted after a trial in which he was represented by a manifestly ineffective attorney. I cannot agree."

[b] Prejudice: Supreme Court Case Law

The Court's opinion in *Strickland* made clear that courts were welcome to consider the prejudice question before deciding whether counsel's alleged deficiency fell below an objective standard of reasonableness, if doing so would make disposition of the case easier. Lower courts faced with *Strickland* claims have frequently accepted that invitation, so that it may be that a majority of ineffective-assistance claims are resolved on this ground, without any determination of the first prong. To an even greater degree than determinations of deficient performance, decisions on prejudice are fact specific. Nonetheless, a brief overview of some Supreme Court cases deciding the prejudice question may be instructive.

In *Strickland* itself, the Court found the "lack of merit of [the defendant's prejudice] claim . . . even more stark" than the lack of merit of his claim under the performance prong. The alleged deficiency in performance was counsel's failure to offer a variety of evidence at defendant's capital sentencing hearing.[225] The Court gave this evidence the back of its hand: At most it would have showed that numerous people thought defendant was a good person, but would "barely have altered the sentencing profile presented to the sentencing judge." "Given the overwhelming aggravating factors," the Court

---

223. When a defendant challenges a conviction, this means that absent the error "the factfinder would have had a reasonable doubt respecting guilt." *Strickland*, 466 U.S. at 695. When a defendant challenges a death sentence, it means that absent the error the sentencer would have concluded that death was not warranted. *Id.* In the case of a prison sentence, it means a reasonable probability that the error caused an increase of any amount in actual jail time. *See* Glover v. United States, 531 U.S. 198, 203 (2001).

224. *Strickland*, 466 U.S. at 710 (Marshall, J., dissenting).

225. *See* § 28.08[B][2], *supra*.

summarily concluded, "there is no reasonable probability that the omitted evidence would have changed the conclusion. . . ."[226]

In several recent cases, however, the Court has found that counsel's deficient performance did prejudice the defendant under the *Strickland* test.[227] In most of these cases, the Court concluded that constitutionally adequate performance by defense counsel would have led to the introduction of additional evidence at a capital sentencing hearing and created a reasonable probability that the defendant would not have been sentenced to death. *Rompilla v. Beard*, a 5–4 decision, is perhaps the most notable of these cases. Indeed, according to one commentator, application of the *Strickland* standard with the vigor shown in *Rompilla* would assure victory in the post-conviction appeals in so many capital cases that it "might come close to abolishing the death penalty in many states."[228] A more recent case in this line, *Schriro v. Landrigan*,[229] suggests that Justice Alito's appointment replacing Justice O'Connor may leave *Rompilla* as the Court's high-water mark for tending to find prejudice in ineffective assistance cases. However, the most recent ineffective assistance case, *Buck v. Davis*, found prejudice when the defense attorney introduced racially charged evidence that the jury should never have heard

In *Rompilla*, the performance of *R*'s attorneys did not meet an objective standard of reasonableness because they failed to examine an available court file on one of *R*'s prior convictions after receiving notice that the prosecution intended to introduce the fact of the conviction and some of the trial transcript at *R*'s capital sentencing hearing. Had counsel examined that file, "they would have found a range of mitigation leads that no other source opened up." According to the Court, "[w]ith this information, counsel would have become skeptical of the impression given by the five family members and would unquestionably have gone further to build a mitigation case." This further investigation, in turn, would have led "to a mitigation case that bears no relation to the few naked pleas for mercy actually put before the jury."

The dissenters argued that the Court could find the prejudice standard satisfied only through a "remarkable leap." The dissent noted that "[t]he range of leads to which the Court refers is in fact a handful of notations within a single 10-page document"—called an Initial Transfer Petition—that apparently was prepared to facilitate *R*'s prison assignment, *after* his earlier case had ended in conviction. According to the dissent, "nothing in the record indicates that [*R*'s] trial attorneys would have discovered the transfer petition, or the clues contained in it, if they had reviewed the old file." If defense counsel had reviewed the file for the purpose that led to their deficient performance under *Strickland*'s first prong, the dissenters argued, "they almost surely would have attributed no significance to the transfer petition following only a cursory review." Thus, according to the dissent, "[p]rejudice could only be demonstrated if the deficiency in counsel's performance were to be described not as the failure to perform a purposive review of the file,

---

226. More recently, in cases on habeas corpus review of a state conviction, the Court has reinstated state convictions after lower federal courts had concluded that the states had not applied the "reasonable probability" standard following findings of deficient performance. *See* Holland v. Jackson, 542 U.S. 649 (2004); Woodford v. Visciotti, 537 U.S. 19 (2002) (per curiam). In these cases, however, the Court reached its conclusion on the ground that the state court *did* apply the right standard, without determining whether the conclusion of no prejudice was actually correct.

227. *See* Rompilla v. Beard, 545 U.S. 374 (2005); Wiggins v. Smith, 539 U.S. 510 (2003); Williams v. Taylor, 529 U.S. 362 (2000); Buch v. Davis, 137 S.Ct. 759 (2017). *See* § 28.08[B][2][b][ii], *supra*.

228. Albert W. Alschuler, *Celebrating Great Lawyering*, 4 Ohio St. J. Crim. L. 223, 225 (2006).

229. 550 U.S. 465 (2007).

but instead as the failure to accord intense scrutiny to every single page of every single document in that file, regardless of the purpose motivating the review."

In *Rompilla*, Justice O'Connor joined the four more liberal justice to create a majority, but she announced her retirement from the Court less than two weeks later. In the Court's next significant ineffective assistance case, *Schriro v. Landrigan*,[230] the eight justices who remained on the Court from *Rompilla* voted the same way as they had in that earlier case: four for the defendant and four for the state.[231] Unlike Justice O'Connor, however, Justice Alito did not find merit in the ineffective assistance claim.

In *Landrigan*, L was attempting to overturn his death sentence on ineffective assistance of counsel grounds, specifically counsel's failure to conduct further investigation into mitigating circumstances, though L himself had prevented his counsel from calling certain witnesses in mitigation and interfered with counsel's proffer of the mitigating evidence of which counsel was aware. In rejecting L's effort to obtain an evidentiary hearing regarding his claim, a five-justice majority of the Court upheld a lower court's finding that certain mitigating evidence — evidence that L argued his counsel would have discovered with competent investigation and should have used — was not sufficient to demonstrate prejudice, given L's resistance at sentencing to the proffering of mitigating evidence. To be sure, *Landrigan*, with its element of the defendant's interference in counsel's work, is distinguishable from *Rompilla*. Nonetheless, the lineup of the justices may prove telling.

In *Buck*, B had been convicted of capital murder and the trial moved to the sentencing phase to determine whether the defendant should be sentenced to death or to life in prison. Under Texas law, B would be sentenced to death if the jury determined (1) a probability that the defendant would commit criminal acts of violence that would constitute a continuing threat to society, and (2) there were not sufficient mitigating circumstances to warrant a sentence of life imprisonment. The sentencing phase of the trial focused almost exclusively on the first question, in which the prosecutor focused on the brutality of B's crime (he killed his ex-girlfriend and her friend, while the ex-girlfriend's children stood by and begged for their mother's life); his lack of remorse (he was "happy" and "upbeat" and "smiling and laughing" in the police cruiser after his arrest) and his previous acts of violence (another former girlfriend testified that he routinely hit her and twice pointed a gun at her). The defense called two psychologists as expert witnesses, who testified that in their opinion the defendant would not pose a danger to others in the prison system. One of those witnesses, however, had written a report in which he considered seven factors in determining whether B would pose a danger of future violence. The fourth factor stated: "Race. Black. Increased probability. There is an over-representation of Blacks among the violent offenders." The expert witness testified that this factor was "known to predict future dangerousness," though he concluded that on balance B was unlikely to pose a danger to others. On cross-examination the prosecutor also asked a question about that factor.

B later brought an ineffective assistance of counsel claim. Lower courts agreed that his attorney's performance was deficient because it would tend to support any racial prejudice held by the jury, but they found insufficient evidence of prejudice. They concluded that the introduction of the racial evidence was "de minimis" (mentioned only

---

230. *Id.*
231. Justice Souter, who has since been replaced on the Court by Sonia Sotomayor, voted for the defendant in both *Rompilla* and *Landrigan*.

twice during a lengthy sentencing phase) and the legitimate evidence offered to prove future dangerousness was overwhelming.

The Supreme Court overturned the lower court findings and found that even those two brief statements linking race to violence were sufficient to meet the *Strickland* standard of prejudice because there was a "reasonable probability that the omitted evidence would have changed the conclusion." Even though there were only two references linking race to violence, that type of argument is so prejudicial that its impact on the jury "cannot be measured simply by how much air time it received at trial or how many pages it occupies in the record. Some toxins can be deadly in small doses." This supposed link plays into some of the deepest racial prejudices from our country's history, and the fact that the evidence came from a scientific expert, supposedly with "statistical proof" to back it up, increased its potential effect on the jury.

The *Buck* decision was 6–2, with only Justices Thomas and Alito dissenting. However, this does not necessarily represent a turning point for the prejudice prong of the Strickland standard. More likely, it merely reflects a view that statements of racial prejudice are uniquely powerful in their ability to unduly affect a jury's decision.

[c] *Prejudice: Special Problems*

[i] The Factually Guilty Defendant

Strickland stated that a defendant is not prejudiced unless his counsel's deficiencies rendered the trial unreliable. Does this mean that a factually guilty defendant cannot be prejudiced by ineffective representation? Put another way, suppose that a convicted defendant's claim, without conceding guilt, comes down to this: "If my lawyer had provided competent representation, he would have been able to get me off by getting the (overwhelming) evidence of my guilt excluded at trial, but he failed in this regard." Has the defendant been "prejudiced"? The short answer to this question appears to be "yes, the defendant has been prejudiced," but some justices have clearly thought the answer should be "no," and the Court does not have a holding squarely resolving the issue.

In *Kimmelman v. Morrison*,[232] M's lawyer failed to raise a Fourth Amendment claim that arguably would have resulted in the exclusion of reliable, but unconstitutionally seized, evidence of M's guilt. As explained above,[233] counsel's error constituted deficient representation (the first prong of *Strickland*).

Rather than determine whether counsel's deficient conduct prejudiced his client, the *Kimmelman* Court remanded the case to a lower court to conduct a hearing on the matter. In doing so, however, the Court stated that to win his Sixth Amendment claim, M would have to prove that it was reasonably probable that he would have won his Fourth Amendment claim if it had been properly made and, further, that in the absence of the incriminating evidence, "there is a reasonable probability that the [the factfinder] would have had a reasonable doubt as to [M's] guilt." Application of this standard would mean that a person who may have *factually* committed an offense *can* prove prejudice, if he can demonstrate that there is a reasonable probability that, but for counsel's errors, his guilt would not have been proven on the basis of *legally* admissible evidence. The Court in *Kimmelman* also stated (in rejecting an argument that a *Strickland* claim based on failure to seek exclusion of illegally seized evidence was not subject to federal habeas corpus

---

232. 477 U.S. 365 (1986).
233. *See* the text following Note 215, *supra*.

review) that "we decline to hold . . . that the guarantee of effective assistance of counsel belongs solely to the innocent."

Justice Powell, joined by Chief Justice Burger and Justice Rehnquist, concurred in the judgment, but disagreed with the preceding analysis. Justice Powell argued that the alleged prejudice suffered by *M* was "the absence of a windfall." The fact that *M*'s lawyer failed to make a motion that arguably would have resulted in the exclusion of reliable incriminating evidence did not affect "the fundamental fairness of the trial. . . . [O]ur reasoning in *Strickland* strongly suggests that such harm does not amount to prejudicial ineffective assistance of counsel under the Sixth Amendment." In Justice Powell's view, notwithstanding the language of the Court's opinion, the definition of "prejudice" in this context was neither an issue presented to the Court nor necessary to its holding, and therefore not resolved by the Court's decision.

In contrast to *Kimmelman*, consider *Lockhart v. Fretwell*,[234] in which *F* was sentenced to death because his attorney, apparently out of ignorance, failed to object to the introduction of evidence that, under then-applicable case law, was inadmissible at *F*'s sentencing hearing. This failure to object satisfied the first prong of *Strickland*—it fell below an objective standard of reasonableness. The Supreme Court held, however, that this deficiency did not prejudice *F* because the lower court case law that rendered the evidence inadmissible was effectively overruled by Supreme Court case law decided *after F's* sentencing hearing, but *before* his Sixth Amendment ineffective-assistance claim was raised. According to the Court, prejudice does not result if the lawyer's error "does not deprive the defendant of any substantive or procedural right to which the law entitles him." Although case law supported *F* at the time of the sentencing proceeding, that law proved to be erroneous. Therefore, to grant *F*'s *Strickland* claim would be to grant him a "windfall" (the same word used by the *concurring* justices in *Kimmelman*).

Notice the effect of the holding in *Lockhart*: *F* would have received a more favorable verdict—he would not have been sentenced to death—had his lawyer provided reasonable representation at the time of the sentencing proceeding, because the law as understood at that time favored *F*'s interests. Notwithstanding this, *F* suffered no legally cognizable "prejudice."

Kimmelman is distinguishable from *Lockhart* in a key regard: the *law* under which the defendant in *Kimmelman* was convicted, *both at the time of trial and at the time that the Sixth Amendment claim was litigated*, entitled him to a ruling that (based on reasonable probabilities) might have resulted in a more favorable verdict. In *Lockhart*, the law favored the defendant only at the time of counsel's error. Indeed, since the subsequent change in the law was not the result of legislative rethinking, but rather of Supreme Court jurisprudence that essentially demonstrated that the prior case law on which *F*'s counsel could have relied was wrong, in some sense the "true" law was never in the defendant's favor.

Thus a finding of prejudice would have been a "windfall" for the defendant in *Lockhart* in a way that it would not have been for the defendant in *Kimmelman*. Absent the errors of counsel *and* absent erroneous applications of law, only the latter defendant might have achieved a different result. And, indeed, the Court has subsequently rejected the view that *Lockhart* "modified or in some way supplanted the rule set down in *Strickland*," explaining that *Lockhart* was based on the unusual fact that the defendant attempted to claim prejudice on the basis of a consideration—incorrect case law,

---

234. 506 U.S. 364 (1993). *See* § 28.08[B][2][b][iii], *supra*.

corrected prior to his Sixth Amendment appeal—that ought not to have informed the prejudice inquiry.[235]

[ii] The Sleeping Lawyer

As noted above,[236] although in most cases a defendant must demonstrate prejudice, prejudice is presumed if the defendant is actually or constructively denied counsel. Where a lawyer's sleeping during proceedings is found to satisfy the first prong of the *Strickland* test, lower courts have concluded that, while "episodes of inattention or slumber are perfectly amenable to analysis under the *Strickland* prejudice test,"[237] at some point a sleeping lawyer becomes equivalent to no counsel at all. In such circumstances—where "counsel was repeatedly unconscious at trial for periods of time in which defendant's interests were at stake"—prejudice should be presumed.[238]

[iii] Racially Tainted Evidence

The Supreme Court has held that a defendant is prejudiced when his attorney admits an expert's opinion that the defendant's race was a relevant factor in determining whether the defendant deserved the death penalty. In *Buck v. Davis*[239], B had been convicted of capital murder and the trial moved to the sentencing phase to determine whether the defendant should be sentenced to death or to life in prison. Under Texas law, one of the questions the jury needed to determine was whether there was a likelihood that B would commit violent criminal acts in the future. The prosecutor focused on the brutality of B's crime (he killed his ex-girlfriend and her friend, while the ex-girlfriend's children stood by and begged for their mother's life); his lack of remorse (he was "happy" and "upbeat" and "smiling and laughing" in the police cruiser after his arrest) and his previous acts of violence (another former girlfriend testified that he routinely hit her and twice pointed a gun at her). The defense called two psychologists as expert witnesses, who testified that in their opinion the defendant would not pose a danger to others in the prison system. One of those witnesses, however, mentioned that there were many factors that went into his analysis, and one of those factors was the race of the defendant. Based on his interpretation of the statistical studies, the expert stated that the fact that B was black increased his chances of being dangerous in the future.

B later brought an ineffective assistance of counsel claim. Lower courts all agreed that his attorney's performance satisfied the first prong of the *Strickland* test. However, they concluded that the second prong was not met because the introduction of the racial evidence was "de minimis" (mentioned only twice during a lengthy sentencing phase) and the legitimate evidence offered to prove future dangerousness was overwhelming.

The Supreme Court overturned the lower court findings and found that even those two brief statements linking race to violence were sufficient to meet the *Strickland* standard of prejudice, holding that there was a reasonable probability that the omitted evidence would have changed the conclusion. Even though there were only two references linking race to violence, that type of argument is so prejudicial that its impact on the

---

235. Williams v. Taylor, 529 U.S. 362, 391 (2000).
236. *See* § 28.08[B][3][a], *supra*.
237. Tippins v. Walker, 77 F.3d 682, 686 (2d Cir. 1996).
238. *Id.* at 687. *Accord*, Burdine v. Johnson, 262 F.3d 336 (5th Cir. 2001) (en banc) (holding that prejudice should be presumed when there is credible evidence that a defense lawyer has repeatedly slept during the trial).
239. 137 S.Ct. 759 (2017).

jury "cannot be measured simply by how much air time it received at trial or how many pages it occupies in the record. Some toxins can be deadly in small doses."[240] This supposed link plays into some of the deepest racial prejudices from our country's history, and the fact that the evidence came from a scientific expert, supposedly with "statistical proof" to back it up, increased its potential effect on the jury.

The *Buck* decision was 6–2, with only Justices Thomas and Alito dissenting. However, this does not necessarily represent a turning point for the prejudice prong of the *Strickland* standard. More likely, it merely reflects a view that statements of racial prejudice are uniquely powerful in their ability to unduly affect a jury's decision.

§ 28.09 Effective Assistance of Counsel: Conflicts of Interest[241]

[A] Nature of the Issue

A defendant is entitled to the undivided loyalty of his attorney. However, when one attorney or law firm (including a public defender's office)[242] represents multiple clients, particularly co-defendants, there is the possibility that the interests of the clients will clash, and that the attorney (or firm) will be unable to represent all of the clients effectively. For this reason, joint representation is generally considered unethical if representation of one client will materially limit a counsel's ability to represent another client.[243]

A breach of ethical standards, however, does not constitute a per se violation of the Sixth Amendment. The subsections that follow relate to the constitutional right to conflict-free legal representation and its relation to the standards of *Strickland v. Washington*.[244]

[B] Pretrial Procedures to Avoid Conflicts

The Supreme Court ruled in *Holloway v. Arkansas*[245] that when an attorney representing co-defendants makes a timely pretrial motion for appointment of separate counsel,

---

240. *Id.* at 777.

241. *See generally* John Stewart Geer, *Representation of Multiple Criminal Defendants: Conflicts of Interest and the Professional Responsibilities of the Defense Attorney*, 62 Minn. L. Rev. 119 (1978); Green, Note 141, *supra*; Nancy J. Moore, *Conflicts of Interest in the Simultaneous Representation of Multiple Clients: A Proposed Solution to the Current Confusion and Controversy*, 61 Tex. L. Rev. 211 (1982); Peter W. Tague, *Multiple Representation and Conflicts of Interest in Criminal Cases*, 67 Geo. L.J. 1075 (1979).

242. Although the Supreme Court has acknowledged that "[t]here is certainly much substance to [the] argument that the appointment of two partners to represent coindictees . . . creates a possible conflict of interest," it has only assumed, but not decided, that law partners should be treated as if they were one attorney for purposes of conflict-of-interest analysis. Burger v. Kemp, 483 U.S. 776, 783 (1987). Most public defenders have strong policies against representing co-defendants and many have outright bans. *See* Gary T. Lowenthal, *Joint Representation in Criminal Cases: A Critical Appraisal*, 64 Va. L. Rev. 939, 950 (1978).

243. Model Rules, Note 186, *supra*, Rule 1.7(a)-(b).

244. 422 U.S. 668 (1984). *See* § 28.09[B], *supra*.

245. 435 U.S. 475 (1978).

based on his assertion of a potential conflict of interest, a trial judge is required either to grant the motion or "to take adequate steps to ascertain whether the risk [is] too remote to warrant separate counsel." If defense counsel is forced to represent co-defendants over his timely objection, reversal of any subsequent conviction is automatic, unless the trial court has determined that there is no conflict.[246]

According to *Holloway*, joint representation is constitutionally suspect. Because a defense lawyer is in a better position than a court to know prior to trial whether a conflict exists or may develop—he is more familiar with the facts of the case, and he may become aware of a conflict as the result of confidential communications with a client—the Supreme Court generally favors the granting of motions for separate counsel. However, to protect the authority of the trial court and to avoid the possibility of abuse by unscrupulous attorneys, the Court stated in *Holloway* that it does not "preclude a trial court from exploring the adequacy of the basis of defense counsel's representations," as long as it can do so without requiring counsel to disclose confidential communications.

The Sixth Amendment does not require a trial court *on its own motion* to inquire into joint-representation arrangements. The Court "may assume [absent a motion] either that multiple representation entails no conflict or that the lawyer and his clients knowingly accept such risk of conflict as may exist."[247]

[C] Post-Trial Proof of a Conflict

The *Holloway* rule of automatic reversal does not apply if the allegation of a conflict of interest is not raised until after trial.[248] Nonetheless, a post-trial allegation of conflict of interest can sometimes lead to a reversal without a showing of "a reasonable probability that the outcome would have been different," which is the prejudice standard applied in ordinary ineffective-assistance-of-counsel cases.[249]

In *Cuyler v. Sullivan*,[250] the Court established that a defendant who raised no objection at trial could establish a violation of the Sixth Amendment by showing: (i) that he suffered from an *actual* conflict of interest and (ii) that the conflict adversely affected his lawyer's performance. This requirement of demonstrating "adverse effect" is more strenuous than the automatic reversal of *Holloway*, but less strenuous than the "reasonable probability" test of *Strickland*.

Possibly foreshadowing a narrowing of the application of *Sullivan*'s exception to *Strickland*, however, the Supreme Court recently noted that, although the Courts of Appeals

---

246. Mickens v. Taylor, 535 U.S. 162, 168 (2002).

247. Cuyler v. Sullivan, 446 U.S. 335, 347 (1980). The Federal Rules of Criminal Procedure are more demanding than this constitutional rule, limiting the latter's importance in federal cases. The federal rules provide that when persons jointly charged with an offense are represented by the same attorney or by different attorneys from the same law firm, "the court must promptly inquire about the propriety of joint representation and must personally advise each defendant of the right to the effective assistance of counsel, including separate representation." Fed. R. Crim. P. 44(c)(2). Unless there is good cause to believe that no conflict is likely to arise, the trial court must "take appropriate measures to protect each defendant's right to counsel." *Id.*

248. *See Mickens*, 535 U.S. 162 (holding that defendant was not entitled to automatic reversal when counsel failed to raise conflict of interest prior to trial, even though trial court had reason to be aware of conflict and failed to inquire).

249. *See* § 28.08[B][3], *supra.*

250. 446 U.S. 335 (1980).

have applied the *Sullivan* standard to many kinds of attorney conflicts, *Sullivan* itself referred to an attorney who "*actively represented* conflicting interests."[251] Thus, the Court continued, "[w]hether *Sullivan* should be extended to [other conflict-of-interest] cases remains, as far as the jurisprudence of this Court is concerned, an open question."

[D] Waiver of the Right to Conflict-Free Representation[252]

Although representation of co-defendants by a single attorney or law firm often leads to a conflict of interest, co-defendants may nonetheless wish to be represented by the same attorney or law firm. For example, by pooling their resources, co-defendants may be able to afford an attorney whose services would otherwise be unavailable to them, or the defendants may commit themselves in advance to a united sink-or-swim strategy that reduces or eliminates the risk of conflict.

Nonetheless, the Supreme Court ruled in *Wheat v. United States*[253] that a trial court has the authority to disqualify defense counsel over his client's objection if it concludes that there is a serious possibility that a conflict of interest exists. Put somewhat differently, a defendant does not have unlimited authority to waive his right to conflict-free representation in order to be represented by the attorney of his choice.

In *Wheat*, W was indicted for participation in an alleged drug conspiracy. I, an attorney, represented G and B, co-conspirators of W. Prior to W's trial, I secured G's acquittal on some of the conspiracy charges and helped him to negotiate a guilty plea on lesser charges. I also assisted B to negotiate a guilty plea. A few days prior to his own trial, W sought to substitute I for his own attorney.

The prosecutor objected to the substitution. He raised two possible conflicts of interest. First, the trial court had not yet accepted G's guilty plea; if the plea were rejected, and if G ultimately had to go to trial, the prosecutor warned that he might need to call W as a witness at G's trial. In such circumstances, I would be faced with a conflict, because he could not effectively cross-examine W without disclosing confidences. Second, the prosecutor indicated that he was likely to call B as a witness at W's trial, which would again result in a conflict. Based on these representations, the trial court refused to grant W's request to substitute I as his counsel. In doing so, the trial judge conceded that "[w]ere I in [W's] position, I'm sure I would want [I] representing me, too. He did a fantastic job in . . . [G's] trial."

The Supreme Court, 5–4, upheld the trial court's decision. It stated that although the right to "be represented by one's preferred attorney is comprehended by the Sixth Amendment, the essential aim of the Amendment is to guarantee an effective advocate for each criminal defendant. . . ." Furthermore, it said, courts "have an independent interest in ensuring that criminal trials are conducted within the ethical standards of the profession and that legal proceedings appear fair to all who observe them."[254]

---

251. *Mickens*, 535 U.S. at 175 (2002) (quoting *Sullivan*, 446 U.S. at 350) (emphasis added in *Mickens*).

252. *See generally* Pamela S. Karlan, *Discrete and Relational Criminal Representation: The Changing Vision of the Right to Counsel*, 105 Harv. L. Rev. 670, 687–97 (1992).

253. 486 U.S. 153 (1988).

254. Note that the latter argument was minimized by the Court in *Faretta v. California*, 422 U.S. 806 (1975), *see* §28.05, *supra*, when it held that defendants have a constitutional right of

The majority stated that when a court finds an actual conflict of interest, "there can be no doubt that it may decline a proffer of waiver, and insist that defendants be separately represented." Furthermore, it held that, as in the present case, trial courts "must be allowed substantial latitude" to refuse waivers of conflict of interest "where a [serious] potential for conflict exists which may or may not burgeon into an actual conflict as the trial progresses."

The Court conceded that prosecutors might manufacture conflicts in order to prevent a defendant from being represented by a particularly able attorney. However, it stated that "trial courts are undoubtedly aware of this possibility, and must take it into consideration along with all of the other factors which inform this sort of a decision."

§ 28.10 Effective Assistance: The Role of Ethical Canons[255]

Violation of an ethical canon by a defense lawyer does not constitute a per se violation of the Sixth Amendment. The lesson of *Strickland v. Washington*[256] is that "[p]revailing norms of practice as reflected in American Bar Association standards and the like . . . are guides to determining what is reasonable [representation], but they are only guides."

But, what if a defendant argues that his lawyer provided ineffective assistance, and the basis of his claim is that counsel *obeyed* ethical canons? Put another way, is a lawyer immunized from a Sixth Amendment "verdict" of inadequate representation if he acts in conformity with recognized ethical rules? The issue arose in *Nix v. Whiteside*.[257]

In *Whiteside*, *W* was prosecuted for stabbing *L* to death. In conversations with *R* (his lawyer), *W* claimed that he killed *L* in self-defense because he believed that *L* was pulling a gun out from under a bed. No weapon was found on or around *L*, and witnesses observed no gun. Furthermore, *W* admitted to *R* that he had not actually seen the weapon. *R* explained that this was not fatal to *W*'s self-defense claim, as long as he reasonably believed that the victim was armed. A week before trial, however, *W* told *R* for the first time that he saw something metallic at the time of the incident. He explained: "There was a gun. If I don't say I saw a gun, I'm dead."

R explained to *W* that such testimony would constitute perjury. He warned his client that if he persisted in his wish to testify in this manner, it was *R*'s duty to advise the court of *W*'s plan, that he "probably would be allowed to attempt to impeach that particular testimony," and that he would seek to withdraw from the case. *R*'s warnings apparently worked: although *W* testified at trial, he did not make the false claim.

---

self-representation, even though (as the dissenters there argued) assertion of this right will often result in a "lawyer" having a fool for a client. In *Faretta*, the defendant's right of autonomy trumped society's interest in ensuring a fair and reliable trial; in *Wheat*, the latter interest won out.

255. *See generally* Brent R. Appel, *The Limited Impact of Nix v. Whiteside on Attorney-Client Relations*, 136 U. Pa. L. Rev. 1913 (1988); Curtis & Resnick, Note 20, *supra*; Monroe H. Freedman, *Client Confidences and Client Perjury: Some Unanswered Questions*, 136 U. Pa. L. Rev. 1939 (1988); A. Kenneth Pye, *The Role of Counsel in the Suppression of Truth*, 1978 Duke L.J. 921.

256. 466 U.S. 668, 688 (1984). *See generally* § 28.08, *supra*.

257. 475 U.S. 157 (1986).

Whiteside involves a comparatively easy perjury scenario. First, *R* had good reason to believe, based on *W*'s prior admissions, that *W*'s testimony would be perjurious. The case does not raise the question of whether *R*'s forceful actions would have been constitutionally justified if he had merely suspected perjury. Second, *R* knew of the planned perjury before trial; the case does not raise the issue of "what a lawyer must, should, or may do after his client has given [surprise] testimony that the lawyer does not believe."[258] Third, *W* testified truthfully. The case does not dispose of the problem of whether a lawyer acts properly if he convinces his client not to testify at all.

The Court unanimously agreed that *W* failed to make out a case of ineffective representation by *R*. Chief Justice Warren Burger, for five justices, held that neither prong of the *Strickland* ineffective-representation test was proved in the case. The four concurring justices relied solely on the prejudice prong of *Strickland*.

Regarding the first ("deficiency of representation") prong, the Chief Justice ruled that the lawyer's conduct "fell within the wide range of professional responses to threatened client perjury acceptable under the Sixth Amendment." He stated that the ethical and constitutional duty of a lawyer to be loyal to his client "is limited to legitimate, lawful conduct compatible with the very nature of a trial as a search for truth." The majority emphasized that *R*'s conduct in the case was ethically appropriate. Although a breach of an ethical canon does not by itself make out a violation of the Sixth Amendment, Chief Justice Burger stated that where "there has been no breach of any recognized professional duty, it follows that there can be no deprivation of the right to assistance of counsel under the *Strickland* standard."

Second, the Court unanimously held that *as a matter of law*, *R*'s conduct here — preventing a client from committing perjury — could not establish the prejudice required for relief under *Strickland*. As the benchmark of the inquiry under *Strickland* is the fairness of the adversary proceeding, *W* "ha[d] no valid claim that confidence in the result of his trial ha[d] been diminished by his desisting from the contemplated perjury."

---

258. *Id.* at 191 (Stevens J., concurring).

Table of Cases

Index

[References are to sections]